A Programmer's Guide to
Java® SE 8
Oracle Certified Associate (OCA)

A Programmer's Guide to

Java® SE 8

Oracle Certified Associate (OCA)

A Comprehensive Primer

Khalid A. Mughal

Rolf W. Rasmussen

Pearson

Original edition, entitled *Programmer's Guide to Java SE 8 Oracle Certified Associate (OCA), A*, 1st Edition, by Mughal, Khalid A; Rasmussen, Rolf W., Published by Published by Pearson Education, Inc, publishing as Addison-Wesley Professional, Copyright © 2017 by Pearson Education, Inc.

Indian edition

ISBN: 978-93-325-7937-8

First Impression, 2017
Third Impression, 2019
Fourth Impression, 2023

This edition is manufactured in India and is authorized for sale only in India, Bangladesh, Bhutan, Pakistan, Nepal, Sri Lanka and the Maldives. Circulation of this edition outside of these territories is UNAUTHORIZED.

Published by Pearson India Education Services Pvt. Ltd, CIN: U72200TN2005PTC057128.

Head Office: 1st Floor, Berger Tower, Plot No. C-001A/2, Sector 16B, Noida – 201 301, Uttar Pradesh, India.
Registered Office: Featherlite, 'The Address' 5th Floor, Survey No 203/10B, 200 Ft MMRD Road, Zamin Pallavaram, Chennai - 600044
Website: in.pearson.com, Email: companysecretary.india@pearson.com

Printed in India at Saurabh Printers Pvt. Ltd.

To the loving memory of my mother, Zubaida Begum,
and my father, Mohammed Azim
—K.A.M.

For Olivia E. Rasmussen and
Louise J. Dahlmo
—R.W.R.

Contents Overview

Contents

Figures

Tables

Examples

Foreword

Java is now over twenty years old and the current release, JDK 8, despite its name, is really the eleventh significant release of the platform. Whilst staying true to the original ideas of the platform, there have been numerous developments adding a variety of features to the language syntax as well as a huge number of APIs to the core class libraries. This has enabled developers to become substantially more productive and has helped to eliminate a variety of common situations that can easily result in bugs.

Java has continued to grow in popularity, which is in large part attributable to the continued evolution of the platform, which keeps it fresh and addresses things that developers want. According to some sources, there are more than nine million Java programmers across the globe and this number looks set to continue to grow as most universities use Java as a primary teaching language.

With so many Java programmers available to employers, how do they ensure that candidates have the necessary skills to develop high-quality, reliable code? The answer is certification: a standardized test of a developer's knowledge about the wide variety of features and techniques required to use Java efficiently and effectively. Originally introduced by Sun Microsystems, the certification process and exam has been updated to match the features of each release of Java. Oracle has continued this since acquiring Sun in 2010.

Taking and passing the exams is not a simple task. To ensure that developers meet a high standard of knowledge about Java, the candidate must demonstrate the ability to understand a wide variety of programming techniques, a clear grasp of the Java syntax, and a comprehensive knowledge of the standard class library APIs. With the release of JDK 8, not only do Java developers need to understand the details of imperative and object-oriented programming, they now need to have a grasp of functional programming so they can effectively use the key new features: lambda expressions and the Streams API.

Which is why, ultimately, you need this book to help you prepare for the exam. The authors have done a great job of presenting the material you need to know to pass the exam in an approachable and easy-to-grasp way. The book starts with the fundamental concepts and language syntax and works its way through what you need to know about object-oriented programming before addressing more complex topics like generic types. The latter part of the book addresses the most recent changes in JDK 8, that of lambda expressions, the Streams API, and the new Date and Time API.

Having worked with Java almost since it was first released, both at Sun Microsystems and then at Oracle Corporation, I think you will find this book an invaluable guide to help you pass the Oracle Certified Associate Exam for Java SE 8. I wish you the best of luck!

—Simon Ritter
Deputy CTO, Azul Systems

Preface

Writing This Book

Dear Reader, what you hold in your hand is the result of a meticulous high-tech operation that took many months and required inspecting many parts, removing certain parts, retrofitting some old parts, and adding many new parts to our previous book on an earlier Java programmer certification exam, until we were completely satisfied with the result. After you have read the book and passed the exam, we hope that you will appreciate the TLC (tender loving care) that has gone into this operation. This is how it all came about.

Learning the names of Java certifications and the required exams is the first item on the agenda. This book provides coverage for the exam to earn *Oracle Certified Associate (OCA), Java SE 8 Programmer Certification* (also know as OCAJP8). The exam required for this certification has the name *Java SE 8 Programmer I Exam* (*Exam number 1Z0-808*). It is the first of two exams required to obtain *Oracle Certified Professional (OCP), Java SE 8 Programmer Certification* (also known as OCPJP8). The second exam required for this professional certification has the name *Java SE 8 Programmer II Exam* (*Exam number 1Z0-809*). To reiterate, this book covers only the topics for the *Java SE 8 Programmer I Exam* that is required to obtain OCAJP8 certification.

A book on the new Java SE 8 certification was a long time coming. The mantle of Java had been passed on to Oracle and Java 7 had hit the newsstand. We started out to write a book to cover the topics for the two exams required to earn the *Oracle Certified Professional, Java SE 7 Programmer Certification*. Soon after the release of Java 8, Oracle announced the certification for Java SE 8. We decided to switch to the new version. It was not a difficult decision to make. Java 8 marks a watershed when the language went from being a pure object-oriented language to one that also incorporates features of functional-style programming. As the saying goes, Java 8 changed the whole ballgame. Java passed its twentieth birthday in 2015. Java 8, released a year earlier, represented a significant milestone in its history. There was little reason to dwell on earlier versions.

The next decision concerned whether it would be best to provide coverage for the two Java SE 8 Programmer Certification exams in one or two books. Pragmatic reasons dictated two books. It would take far too long to complete a book that covered both exams, mainly because the second exam was largely revamped and would require a lot of new material. We decided to complete the book for the first exam. Once that decision was made, our draft manuscript went back on the operating table.

Our approach to writing this book has not changed from the one we employed for our previous books, mainly because it has proved successful. No stones were left unturned to create this book, as we explain here.

The most noticeable changes in the exam for OCAJP8 are the inclusion of the core classes in the new Date and Time API and the writing of predicates using lambda expressions. The emphasis remains on analyzing code scenarios, rather than individual language constructs. The exam continues to require actual experience with the language, not just mere recitation of facts. We still claim that proficiency in the language is the key to success.

Since the exam emphasizes the core features of Java, this book provides in-depth coverage of topics related to those features. As in our earlier books, supplementary topics are also included to aid in mastering the exam topics.

This book is no different from our previous books in one other important aspect: It is a one-stop guide, providing a mixture of theory and practice that enables readers to prepare for the exam. It can be used to learn Java and to prepare for the exam. After the exam is passed, it can also come in handy as a language guide.

Apart from including coverage of the new topics, our discussions of numerous topics from the previous exam were extensively revised. All elements found in our previous books (e.g., sections, examples, figures, tables, review questions, mock exam questions) were closely scrutinized. New examples, figures, tables, and review questions were specifically created for the new topics as well as for the revised ones. We continue to use UML (Unified Modeling Language) extensively to illustrate concepts and language constructs, and all numbered examples continue to be complete Java programs ready for experimenting.

Feedback from readers regarding our previous books was invaluable in shaping this book. Every question, suggestion, and comment received was deliberated upon. We are grateful for every single email we have received over the years; that input proved invaluable in improving this book.

Dear Reader, we wish you all the best should you decide to go down the path of Java certification. May your loops terminate and your exceptions get caught!

About This Book

This book provides extensive coverage of the core features of the Java programming language and its core application programming interface (API), with particular emphasis on its syntax and usage. The book is primarily intended for professionals who want to prepare for the *Java SE 8 Programmer I* exam, but it is readily accessible to any programmer who wants to master the language. For both purposes, it provides in-depth coverage of essential features of the language and its core API.

The demand for well-trained and highly skilled Java programmers remains unabated. Oracle offers many Java certifications that professionals can take to validate their skills (see `http://education.oracle.com`). The certification provides members of the IT industry with a standard to use when hiring such professionals, and it allows professionals to turn their Java skills into credentials that are important for career advancement.

The book provides extensive coverage of all the objectives defined by Oracle for the *Java SE 8 Programmer I* exam. The exam objectives are selective, however, and do not include many of the essential features of Java. This book covers many additional topics that every Java programmer should master to be truly proficient. In this regard, the book is a comprehensive primer for learning the Java programming language. After mastering the language by working through this book, the reader can confidently sit for the exam.

This book is *not* a complete reference for Java, as it does not attempt to list every member of every class from the Java SE platform API documentation. The purpose is not to document the Java SE platform API. The emphasis is more on the Java programming language features—their syntax and correct usage through code examples—and less on teaching programming techniques.

The book assumes little background in programming. We believe the exam is accessible to any programmer who works through the book. A Java programmer can easily skip over material that is well understood and concentrate on parts that need reinforcing, whereas a programmer new to Java will find the concepts explained from basic principles.

Each topic is explained and discussed thoroughly with examples, and backed by review questions and exercises to reinforce the concepts. The book is not biased toward any particular platform, but provides platform-specific details where necessary.

Using This Book

The reader can choose a linear or a nonlinear route through the book, depending on his or her programming background. Non-Java programmers wishing to migrate to Java can read Chapter 1, which provides a short introduction to object-oriented programming concepts, and the procedure for compiling and running Java applications. For those preparing for *Java SE 8 Programmer I* exam, the book has a separate appendix (Appendix A) providing all the pertinent information on preparing for and taking the exam.

Cross-references are provided where necessary to indicate the relationships among the various constructs of the language. To understand a language construct, all pertinent details are provided where the construct is covered, but in addition, cross-references are provided to indicate its relationship to other constructs. Sometimes it is necessary to postpone discussion of certain aspects of a topic if they depend on concepts that have not yet been covered in the book. A typical example is the consequences of object-oriented programming concepts (for example, inheritance) on the member declarations that can occur in a class. This approach can result in forward references in the initial chapters of the book.

The table of contents; listings of tables, examples, and figures; and a comprehensive index facilitate locating topics discussed in the book.

In particular, we draw attention to the following features of the book:

Programmer I Exam Objectives

0.1 Exam objectives are stated clearly at the beginning of every chapter.

0.2 The number in front of the objective identifies the exam objective, as defined by Oracle, and can be found in Appendix B.

0.3 The objectives are organized into major sections, detailing the curriculum for the exam.

0.4 The objectives for the *Java SE 8 Programmer I* exam are reproduced verbatim in Appendix B, where for each section of the syllabus, references are included to point the reader to relevant topics in the book.

Supplementary Objectives

- Supplementary objectives cover topics that are *not* on the exam, but which we believe are important for mastering the topics that *are* on the exam.
- Any supplementary objective is listed as a bullet at the beginning of the chapter.

Review Questions

Review questions are provided after every major topic to test and reinforce the material. The review questions predominantly reflect the kind of multiple-choice questions that can be asked on the actual exam. On the exam, the exact number of answers to choose for each question is explicitly stated. The review questions in this book follow that practice.

Many questions on the actual exam contain code snippets with line numbers to indicate that complete implementation is not provided, and that the necessary missing code to compile and run the code snippets can be assumed. The review questions in this book provide complete code implementations where possible, so that the code can be readily compiled and run.

Annotated answers to the review questions are provided in Appendix C.

Example 0.1 *Example Source Code*

We encourage readers to experiment with the code examples to reinforce the material from the book. These examples can be downloaded from the book website (see p. xxxiv).

Java code is presented in a `monospaced font`. Lines of code in the examples or in code snippets are referenced in the text by a number, which is specified by using a single-line comment in the code. For example, in the following code snippet, the call to the method `doSomethingInteresting()` at (1) does something interesting:

```
// ...
doSomethingInteresting();                                      // (1)
// ...
```

Names of classes and interfaces start with an uppercase letter. Names of packages, variables, and methods start with a lowercase letter. Constants are in all uppercase letters. Interface names begin with the prefix `I`, when it makes sense to distinguish them from class names. Coding conventions are followed, except when we have had to deviate from these conventions in the interest of space or clarity.

Chapter Summary

Each chapter concludes with a summary of the topics covered in the chapter, pointing out the major concepts that were introduced.

Programming Exercises

Programming exercises at the end of each chapter provide the opportunity to put concepts into practice. Solutions to the programming exercises are provided in Appendix D.

Mock Exam

The mock exam in Appendix E should be attempted when the reader feels confident about the topics on the exam. It is highly recommended to read Appendix A before attempting the mock exam, as Appendix A contains pertinent information about the questions to expect on the actual exam. Each multiple-choice question in the mock exam explicitly states how many answers are applicable for a given question, as is the case on the actual exam. Annotated answers to the questions in the mock exam are provided in Appendix F.

Java SE Platform API Documentation

A vertical gray bar is used to highlight methods and fields found in the classes of the Java SE Platform API.

Any explanation following the API information is also similarly highlighted.

To obtain the maximum benefit from using this book in preparing for the *Java SE 8 Programmer I* exam, we strongly recommend installing the latest version (Release 8 or newer) of the JDK and its accompanying API documentation. The book focuses solely on Java 8, and does not acknowledge previous versions.

Book Website

This book is backed by a website providing auxiliary material:

`www.ii.uib.no/~khalid/ocajp8/`

The contents of the website include the following:

- Source code for all the examples in the book
- Solutions to the programming exercises in the book
- Annotated answers to the reviews questions in the book
- Annotated answers to the mock exam in the book
- Table of contents, sample chapter, and index from the book
- Errata for the book
- Links to miscellaneous Java resources (e.g., certification, discussion groups, tools)

Information about the Java Standard Edition (SE) and its documentation can be found at the following website:

`www.oracle.com/technetwork/java/javase/overview/index.html`

The current authoritative technical reference for the Java programming language, *The Java® Language Specification: Java SE 8 Edition* (also published by Addison-Wesley), can be found at this website:

`http://docs.oracle.com/javase/specs/index.html`

Request for Feedback

Considerable effort has been made to ensure the accuracy of the content of this book. All code examples (including code fragments) have been compiled and tested on various platforms. In the final analysis, any errors remaining are the sole responsibility of the authors.

Any questions, comments, suggestions, and corrections are welcome. Let us know whether the book was helpful (or not) for your purpose. Any feedback is valuable. The principal author can be reached at the following email address:

`khalid.mughal@uib.no`

Register your copy of *A Programmer's Guide to Java® SE 8 Oracle Certified Associate (OCA)* at informit.com for convenient access to downloads, updates, and corrections as they become available. To start the registration process, go to informit.com/register and log in or create an account. Enter the product ISBN (9780132930215) and click Submit. Once the process is complete, you will find any available bonus content under "Registered Products."

About the Authors

Khalid A. Mughal

Khalid A. Mughal is an associate professor at the Department of Informatics at the University of Bergen, Norway, where he has been responsible for designing and implementing various courses in informatics. Over the years, he has taught programming (primarily Java), software engineering (object-oriented system development), databases (data modeling and database management systems), compiler techniques, web application development, and software security courses. For 15 years, he was responsible for developing and running web-based programming courses in Java, which were offered to off-campus students. He has also given numerous courses and seminars at various levels in object-oriented programming and system development using Java and Java-related technologies, both at the University of Bergen and for the IT industry.

Mughal is the principal author and solely responsible for the contents of this book. He is also the principal author of three books on previous versions of the Java programmer certification—*A Programmer's Guide to Java™ SCJP Certification: A Comprehensive Primer, Third Edition* (0321556054); *A Programmer's Guide to Java™ Certification: A Comprehensive Primer, Second Edition* (0201728281); and *A Programmer's Guide to Java™ Certification* (0201596148)—and three introductory textbooks on programming in Java: *Java Actually: A First Course in Programming* (1844804186); *Java Actually: A Comprehensive Primer in Java Programming* (1844809331); and *Java som første programmeringsspråk/Java as First Programming Language, Third Edition* (8202245540).

Mughal currently works on security issues related to mobile data collection systems for delivering health services in low- and middle-income countries.

Rolf W. Rasmussen

Rolf W. Rasmussen is a system development manager at Vizrt, a company that develops solutions for the TV broadcast industry, including real-time 3D graphic renderers, and content and control systems. Rasmussen works mainly on control and automation systems, video processing, typography, and real-time visualization. He has worked on clean-room implementations of the Java class libraries in the past and is a contributor to the Free Software Foundation.

Over the years, Rasmussen has worked both academically and professionally with numerous programming languages, including Java. He was primarily responsible for developing the review questions and answers, the programming exercises and their solutions, the mock exam, and all the practical aspects related to taking the exam in our three previous books on Java programmer certification. Selected earlier content has been utilized in this book. Together with Mughal, he is also a coauthor of three introductory textbooks on programming in Java.

Acknowledgments

At Addison-Wesley, Greg Doench was again our editor, who effectively managed the process of publishing this book. Regular dialog with him in recent months helped to keep this project on track. Julie Nahil was the in-house contact at Addison-Wesley, who professionally managed the production of the book. Anna Popick was the project editor, who diligently handled the day-to-day project management for this book. Jill Hobbs did a truly marvelous job copy editing the book. The folks at The CIP Group performed the typesetting wizardry necessary to materialize the book. We would like to extend our sincere thanks to Greg, Julie, Anna, Jill, the folks at The CIP Group, and all those behind the scenes at Addison-Wesley, who helped to put this publication on the bookshelf.

For the technical review of the book, we were lucky that Roel De Nijs agreed to take on the task. If you drop in on `CodeRanch.com`, you are bound to find him executing his duties as a Sheriff, especially helping greenhorns find their bearing in the Java certification corrals. He is a freelance Java developer with many IT companies as clients and a multitude of Java certification accolades under his belt (SCJA, SCJP, SCJD, OCAJP7). And not least, he is a Technical Reviewer Par Excellence. Without doubt, Roel has a meticulous eye for detail. It is no exaggeration to say that his exhaustive feedback has been invaluable in improving the quality of this book at all levels. Roel, you have our most sincere thanks for your many excellent comments and suggestions, and above all, for weeding out numerous pesky errors in the manuscript.

Over the years, we have also been lucky to have our own personal manuscript quality controller: Marit Seljeflot Mughal. As diligently as with our previous books, she tirelessly proofread several chapter drafts for this book, and put her finger on many unmentionable mistakes and errors in the manuscript. Her valuable comments and suggestions have also been instrumental in improving the quality of this book. If Marit, who has no IT background, could make sense of the Java jargon we wrote, then we were confident our readers would as well. Our most sincere thanks.

Great effort has been made to eliminate mistakes and errors in this book. We accept full responsibility for any remaining oversights. We hope that when our Dear Readers find any, they will bring them to our attention.

Many family occasions have been missed while working on this book. Without family support, this book would not have seen the light of day. Khalid is ever grateful to his family for their love, support, and understanding—but especially when he is working on a book. Now that this book is out the door, he is off to play with his three grandchildren.

—Khalid A. Mughal

17 May 2016
Bergen, Norway

Basics of Java Programming

1

Programmer I Exam Objectives		
[1.2]	Define the structure of a Java class ○ *See also §3.1, p. 48.*	*§1.2, p. 2*
[1.3]	Create executable Java applications with a main method; run a Java program from the command line; including console output ○ *See also §4.3, p. 107.*	*§1.10, p. 16*
[1.5]	Compare and contrast the features and components of Java such as: platform independence, object orientation, encapsulation, etc.	*§1.12, p. 21*
[2.3]	Know how to read or write to object fields	*§1.3, p. 4*
Supplementary Objectives		
•	Introduce the basic terminology and concepts in object-oriented programming: classes, objects, references, fields, methods, members, inheritance, and associations	*Chapter 1*
•	Format and print values to the terminal window	*§1.11, p. 18*

1.1 Introduction

Before embarking on the road to Java programmer certification, it is important to understand the basic terminology and concepts in object-oriented programming (OOP). In this chapter, the emphasis is on providing an introduction to OOP, rather than exhaustive coverage. In-depth coverage of the concepts follows in subsequent chapters of the book.

Java supports the writing of many different kinds of executables: applications, applets, and servlets. The basic elements of a Java application are introduced in this chapter. The old adage that practice makes perfect is certainly true when learning a programming language. To encourage programming on the computer, the mechanics of compiling and running a Java application are outlined.

1.2 Classes

One of the fundamental ways in which we handle complexity is by using *abstractions*. An abstraction denotes the essential properties and behaviors of an object that differentiate it from other objects. The essence of OOP is modeling abstractions, using classes and objects. The hard part of this endeavor is finding the right abstraction.

A *class* denotes a category of objects, and acts as a blueprint for creating objects. A class models an abstraction by defining the properties and behaviors for the objects representing the abstraction. An *object* exhibits the properties and behaviors defined by its class. The properties of an object of a class are also called *attributes*, and are defined by fields in Java. A *field* in a class is a variable that can store a value that represents a particular property of an object. The behaviors of an object of a class are also known as *operations*, and are defined using *methods* in Java. Fields and methods in a class declaration are collectively called *members*.

An important distinction is made between the *contract* and the *implementation* that a class provides for its objects. The contract defines *which* services are provided, and the implementation defines *how* these services are provided by the class. Clients (i.e., other objects) need to know only the contract of an object, and not its implementation, to avail themselves of the object's services.

As an example, we will implement different versions of a class that models the abstraction of a stack that can push and pop characters. The stack will use an array of characters to store the characters, and a field to indicate the top element in the stack. Using Unified Modeling Language (UML) notation, a class called `CharStack` is graphically depicted in Figure 1.1, which models the abstraction. Both fields and method names are shown in Figure 1.1a.

Figure 1.1 *UML Notation for Classes*

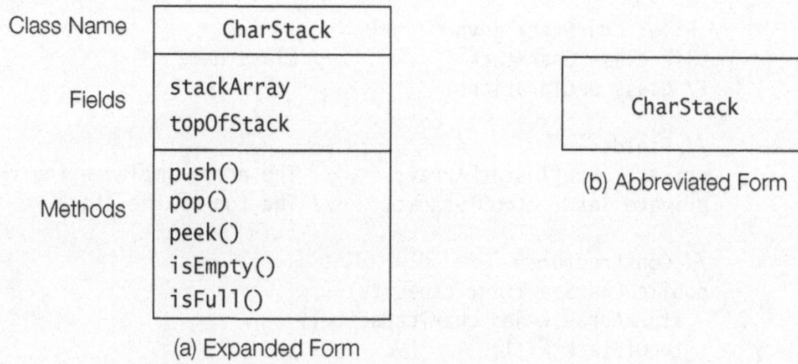

Declaring Members: Fields and Methods

Example 1.1 shows the declaration of the class `CharStack` depicted in Figure 1.1. Its intention is to illustrate the salient features of a class declaration in Java, rather than an effective implementation of stacks. The character sequence `//` in the code indicates the start of a *single-line comment* that can be used to document the code. All characters after this sequence and to the end of the line are ignored by the compiler.

A class declaration contains member declarations that define the fields and the methods of the objects the class represents. In the case of the class `CharStack`, it has two fields declared at (1):

- `stackArray`, which is an array to hold the elements of the stack (in this case, characters)
- `topOfStack`, which denotes the top element of the stack (i.e., the index of the last character stored in the array)

The class `CharStack` has five methods, declared at (3), that implement the essential operations on a stack:

- `push()` pushes a character on to the stack.
- `pop()` removes and returns the top element of the stack.
- `peek()` returns the top element of the stack for inspection.
- `isEmpty()` determines whether the stack is empty.
- `isFull()` determines whether the stack is full.

The class declaration also has a method-like declaration at (2) with the same name as the class. Such declarations are called *constructors*. As we shall see, a constructor is executed when an object is created from the class. However, the implementation details in the example are not important for the present discussion.

Example 1.1 *Basic Elements of a Class Declaration*

```
// File: CharStack.java
public class CharStack {           // Class name
  // Class Declarations:

  // Fields:                                                              (1)
  private char[] stackArray;       // The array implementing the stack
  private int    topOfStack;       // The top of the stack

  // Constructor:                                                         (2)
  public CharStack(int capacity) {
    stackArray = new char[capacity];
    topOfStack = -1;
  }

  // Methods:                                                             (3)
  public void push(char element) { stackArray[++topOfStack] = element; }
  public char pop()              { return stackArray[topOfStack--]; }
  public char peek()             { return stackArray[topOfStack]; }
  public boolean isEmpty()       { return topOfStack == -1; }
  public boolean isFull()        { return topOfStack == stackArray.length - 1; }
}
```

1.3 Objects

Class Instantiation, Reference Values, and References

The process of creating objects from a class is called *instantiation*. An *object* is an instance of a class. The object is constructed using the class as a blueprint and is a concrete instance of the abstraction that the class represents. An object must be created before it can be used in a program.

A *reference value* is returned when an object is created. A reference value denotes a particular object. A *variable* denotes a location in memory where a value can be stored. An *object reference* (or simply *reference*) is a variable that can store a reference value. Thus a reference provides a handle to an object, as it can indirectly denote an object whose reference value it holds. In Java, an object can be manipulated only via its reference value, or equivalently by a reference that holds its reference value.

This setup for manipulating objects requires that a reference be declared, a class be instantiated to create an object, and the reference value of the object created be stored in the reference. These steps are accomplished by a *declaration statement*.

```
CharStack stack1 = new CharStack(10); // Stack length: 10 chars
```

In the preceding declaration statement, the left-hand side of the = operator declares that `stack1` is a reference of class `CharStack`. The reference `stack1`, therefore, can refer to objects of class `CharStack`.

The right-hand side of the = operator creates an object of class CharStack. This step involves using the new operator in conjunction with a call to a constructor of the class (new CharStack(10)). The new operator creates an instance of the CharStack class and returns the reference value of this instance. The = operator (called the *assignment operator*) stores the reference value in the reference stack1 declared on the left-hand side of the assignment operator. The reference stack1 can now be used to manipulate the object whose reference value is stored in it.

Analogously, the following declaration statement declares the reference stack2 to be of class CharStack, creates an object of class CharStack, and assigns its reference value to the reference stack2:

```
CharStack stack2 = new CharStack(5);  // Stack length: 5 chars
```

Each object that is created has its own copy of the fields declared in the class declaration in Example 1.1. That is, the two stack objects, referenced by stack1 and stack2, will have their own stackArray and topOfStack fields.

The purpose of the constructor call on the right-hand side of the new operator is to initialize the newly created object. In this particular case, for each new CharStack object created using the new operator, the constructor at (2) in Example 1.1 creates an array of characters. The length of this array is given by the value of the argument to the constructor. The constructor also initializes the topOfStack field.

Figure 1.2 shows the UML notation for objects. The graphical representation of an object is very similar to that of a class. Figure 1.2 shows the canonical notation, where the name of the reference denoting the object is prefixed to the class name with a colon (:). If the name of the reference is omitted, as in Figure 1.2b, this denotes an anonymous object. Since objects in Java do not have names, but rather are denoted by references, a more elaborate notation is shown in Figure 1.2c, where references of the CharStack class explicitly refer to CharStack objects. In most cases, the more compact notation will suffice.

Figure 1.2 *UML Notation for Objects*

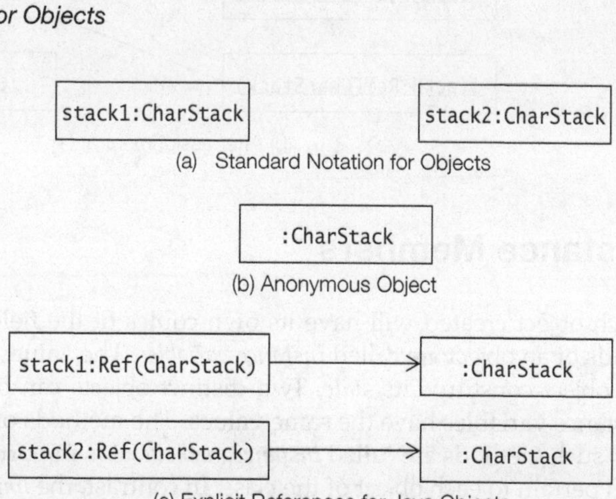

Object Aliases

Several references can refer to the same object, meaning that they store the reference value of the same object. Such references are called *aliases*. The object can be manipulated via any one of its aliases, as each one refers to the same object.

```
// Create two distinct stacks of chars.
CharStack stackA = new CharStack(12); // Stack length: 12 chars
CharStack stackB = new CharStack(6);  // Stack length: 6 chars

stackB = stackA;                      // (1) aliases after assignment
// The stack previously referenced by stackB can now be garbage collected.
```

Two stack objects are created in the preceding code. Before the assignment at (1), the situation is as depicted in Figure 1.3a. After the assignment at (1), the references `stackA` and `stackB` will denote the same stack, as depicted in Figure 1.3b. The *reference value* in `stackA` is assigned to `stackB`. The references `stackA` and `stackB` are aliases after the assignment, as they refer to the same object. What happens to the stack object that was denoted by the reference `stackB` before the assignment? When objects are no longer in use, their memory is, if necessary, reclaimed and reallocated for other objects. This process is called *automatic garbage collection*. Garbage collection in Java is taken care of by the runtime environment.

Figure 1.3 *Aliases*

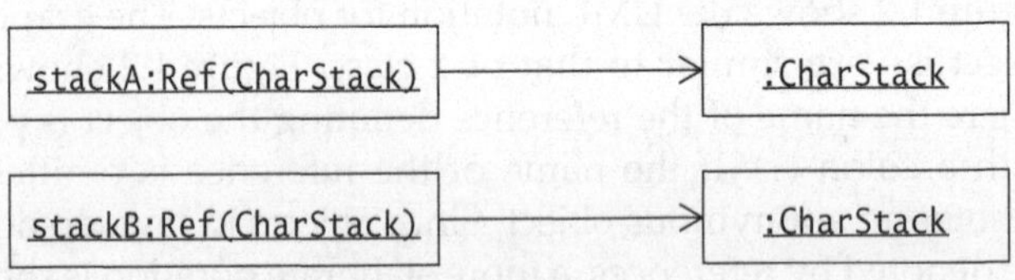

(a) Before assignment at (1)

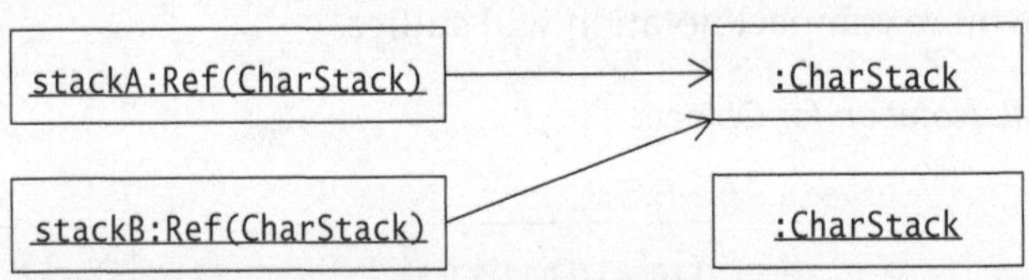

(b) After assignment at (1)

1.4 Instance Members

Each object created will have its own copies of the fields defined in its class. The fields of an object are called *instance variables*. The values of the instance variables in an object constitute its *state*. Two distinct objects can have the same state if their instance variables have the same values. The methods of an object define its behavior; such methods are called *instance methods*. It is important to note that these methods pertain to each object of the class. In contrast, the *implementation* of the methods is shared by all instances of the class. Instance variables and instance methods, which belong to objects, are collectively called *instance members*, to distinguish them from *static members*, which belong to the class only. Static members are discussed in §1.5.

Invoking Methods

Objects communicate by message passing. As a consequence, an object can be made to exhibit a particular behavior by sending the appropriate message to the object. In Java, this is done by *calling* a method on the object using the binary dot (.) operator. A *method call* spells out the complete message: the object that is the receiver of the message, the method to be invoked, and the arguments to be passed to the method, if any. The method invoked on the receiver can also send information back to the sender, via a single return value. The method called must be one that is defined for the object; otherwise, the compiler reports an error.

```
CharStack stack = new CharStack(5);        // Create a stack
stack.push('J');             // (1) Character 'J' pushed
char c = stack.pop();        // (2) One character popped and returned: 'J'
stack.printStackElements(); // (3) Compile-time error: No such method in CharStack
```

The sample code given here invokes methods on the object denoted by the reference `stack`. The method call at (1) pushes one character on the stack, and the method call at (2) pops one character off the stack. Both the `push()` and `pop()` methods are defined in the class `CharStack`. The `push()` method does not return any value, but the `pop()` method returns the character popped. Trying to invoke a method named `printStackElements` on the stack results in a compile-time error, as no such method is defined in the class `CharStack`.

The dot (.) notation can also be used with a reference to access the fields of an object. Use of the dot notation is governed by the *accessibility* of the member. The fields in the class `CharStack` have `private` accessibility, indicating that they are not accessible from outside the class. Thus the following code in a client of the `CharStack` class will not compile:

```
stack.topOfStack++;      // Compile-time error: topOfStack is not visible.
```

1.5 Static Members

In some cases, certain members should belong only to the class; that is, they should not be part of any instance of the class. As an example, suppose a class wants to keep track of how many objects of the class have been created. Defining a counter as an instance variable in the class declaration for tracking the number of objects created does not solve the problem. Each object created will have its own counter field. Which counter should then be updated? The solution is to declare the counter field as being `static`. Such a field is called a *static variable*. It belongs to the class, rather than to any specific object of the class. A static variable is initialized when the class is loaded at runtime. Similarly, a class can have *static methods* that belong to the class, rather than to any specific objects of the class. Static variables and static methods are collectively known as *static members*, and are declared with the keyword `static`.

Figure 1.4 shows the class diagram for the class `CharStack`. It has been augmented by two static members, whose names are underlined. The augmented definition of the `CharStack` class is given in Example 1.2. The field `counter` is a static variable declared at (1). It will be allocated and initialized to the default value `0` when the class is loaded. Each time an object of the `CharStack` class is created, the constructor at (2) is executed. The constructor explicitly increments the counter in the class. The method `getInstanceCount()` at (3) is a static method belonging to the class. It returns the counter value when called.

Figure 1.4 *Class Diagram Showing Static Members of a Class*

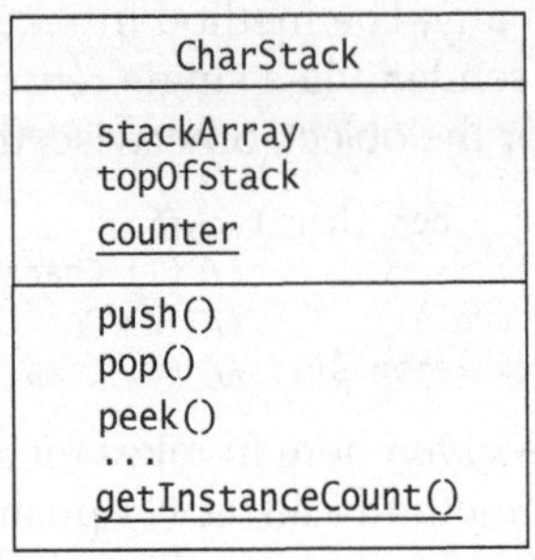

Example 1.2 *Static Members in Class Declaration*

```
// File: CharStack.java
public class CharStack {
  // Instance variables:
  private char[] stackArray;     // The array implementing the stack
  private int    topOfStack;     // The top of the stack

  // Static variable
  private static int counter;                                    // (1)

  // Constructor now increments the counter for each object created.
  public CharStack(int capacity) {                               // (2)
    stackArray = new char[capacity];
    topOfStack = -1;
    counter++;
  }

  // Instance methods:
  public void push(char element) { stackArray[++topOfStack] = element; }
  public char pop()              { return stackArray[topOfStack--]; }
  public char peek()             { return stackArray[topOfStack]; }
  public boolean isEmpty()       { return topOfStack == -1; }
  public boolean isFull()        { return topOfStack == stackArray.length - 1; }

  // Static method                                               (3)
  public static int getInstanceCount() { return counter; }
}
```

Figure 1.5 shows the classification of the members in the class `CharStack`, using the terminology we have introduced so far. Table 1.1 provides a summary of the terminology used in defining members of a class.

Clients can access static members in the class by using the class name. The following code invokes the `getInstanceCount()` method in the class `CharStack`:

```
int count = CharStack.getInstanceCount(); // Class name to invoke static method
```

Static members can also be accessed via object references, although doing so is considered bad style:

```
CharStack myStack = new CharStack(20);
int count = myStack.getInstanceCount();   // Reference invokes static method
```

Static members in a class can be accessed both by the class name and via object references, but instance members can be accessed only by object references.

Figure 1.5 *Members of a Class*

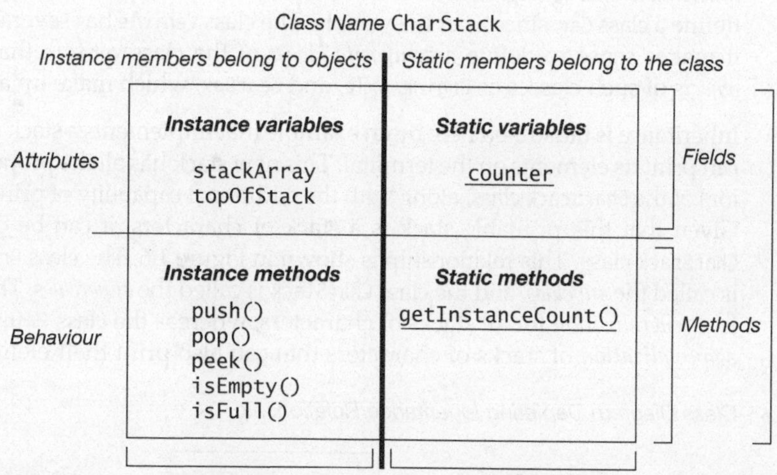

Table 1.1 *Terminology for Class Members*

Instance members	The instance variables and instance methods of an object. They can be accessed or invoked only through an object reference.
Instance variable	A field that is allocated when the class is instantiated (i.e., when an object of the class is created). Also called a *non-static field* or just a *field* when the context is obvious.
Instance method	A method that belongs to an instance of the class. Objects of the same class share its implementation.

Continues

Table 1.1 *Terminology for Class Members (Continued)*

Static members	The static variables and static methods of a class. They can be accessed or invoked either by using the class name or through an object reference.
Static variable	A field that is allocated when the class is loaded. It belongs to the class, and not to any specific object of the class. Also called a *static field* or a *class variable.*
Static method	A method that belongs to the class, and not to any object of the class. Also called a *class method.*

1.6 Inheritance

There are two fundamental mechanisms for building new classes from existing ones: *inheritance* and *aggregation*. It makes sense to *inherit* from an existing class `Vehicle` to define a class `Car`, since a car is a vehicle. The class `Vehicle` has several *parts*; therefore, it makes sense to define a *composite object* of the class `Vehicle` that has *constituent objects* of such classes as `Engine`, `Axle`, and `GearBox`, which make up a vehicle.

Inheritance is illustrated here by an example that implements a stack of characters that can print its elements on the terminal. This new stack has all the properties and behaviors of the `CharStack` class, along with the additional capability of printing its elements. Given that this printable stack is a stack of characters, it can be derived from the `CharStack` class. This relationship is shown in Figure 1.6. The class `PrintableCharStack` is called the *subclass*, and the class `CharStack` is called the *superclass*. The `CharStack` class is a *generalization* for all stacks of characters, whereas the class `PrintableCharStack` is a *specialization* of stacks of characters that can also print their elements.

Figure 1.6 *Class Diagram Depicting Inheritance Relationship*

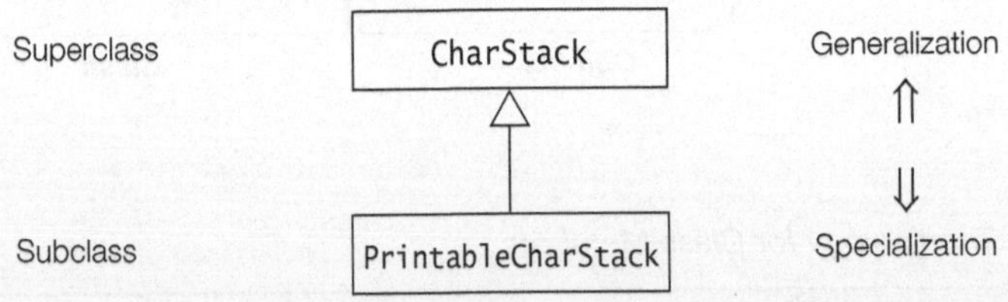

In Java, deriving a new class from an existing class requires the use of the `extends` clause in the subclass declaration. A subclass can *extend* only one superclass. The subclass can inherit members of the superclass. The following code fragment implements the `PrintableCharStack` class:

```
class PrintableCharStack extends CharStack {                    // (1)
  // Instance method
  public void printStackElements() {                            // (2)
    // ... implementation of the method...
  }
```

```
  // The constructor calls the constructor of the superclass explicitly.
  public PrintableCharStack(int capacity) { super(capacity); }      // (3)
}
```

The PrintableCharStack class extends the CharStack class at (1). Implementing the printStackElements() method in the PrintableCharStack class requires access to the field stackArray from the superclass CharStack. However, this field is *private* and, therefore, not accessible in the subclass. The subclass can access these fields if the accessibility of the fields is changed to *protected* in the CharStack class. Example 1.3 uses a version of the class CharStack, which has been modified to support this access. Implementation of the printStackElements() method is shown at (2). The constructor of the PrintableCharStack class at (3) calls the constructor of the superclass CharStack to initialize the stack properly.

Example 1.3 *Defining a Subclass*

```
// File: CharStack.java
public class CharStack {
  // Instance variables
  protected char[] stackArray;  // The array that implements the stack
  protected int    topOfStack;  // The top of the stack

  // The rest of the definition is the same as in Example 1.2.
}
```

```
// File: PrintableCharStack.java
public class PrintableCharStack extends CharStack {                    // (1)

  // Instance method
  public void printStackElements() {                                   // (2)
    for (int i = 0; i <= topOfStack; i++)
      System.out.print(stackArray[i]); // Print each char on terminal
    System.out.println();
  }

  // Constructor calls the constructor of the superclass explicitly.
  PrintableCharStack(int capacity) { super(capacity); }                // (3)
}
```

Objects of the PrintableCharStack class will respond just like the objects of the CharStack class, but they also have the additional functionality defined in the subclass:

```
PrintableCharStack pcStack = new PrintableCharStack(3);
pcStack.push('H');
pcStack.push('i');
pcStack.push('!');
pcStack.printStackElements();    // Prints "Hi!" on the terminal
```

1.7 Associations: Aggregation and Composition

An *association* defines a static relationship between objects of two classes. One such association, called *aggregation*, expresses how an object uses other objects. Java supports aggregation of objects by reference, since objects cannot contain other objects explicitly. The aggregate object usually has fields that denote its constituent objects. A constituent object can be *shared* with other aggregate objects.

For example, an object of class `Airplane` might have a field that denotes an object of class `Pilot`. This `Pilot` object of an `Airplane` object might be shared among other aggregate objects (not necessarily `Airplane` objects) once the pilot has finished duty on one airplane. In fact, the `Pilot` object can still be used even when its `Airplane` object no longer exists. This *aggregation* relationship is depicted by the UML diagram in Figure 1.7 (empty diamond), showing that each object of the `Airplane` class *has* zero or one object of class `Pilot` associated with it.

The aggregate association can be made stronger if the constituent objects cannot be shared with other aggregate objects—for example, an `Airplane` object with two `Wing` objects. The `Wing` objects cannot be shared and can exist only with their `Airplane` object; that is, the `Airplane` object has *ownership* of its `Wing` objects. Conversely, the `Wing` objects are a *part of* their `Airplane` object. This stronger aggregation association is called *composition* and is depicted by the UML diagram in Figure 1.7 (filled diamond), showing that each object of the `Airplane` class *owns* two objects of class `Wing`.

Figure 1.7 *Class Diagram Depicting Associations*

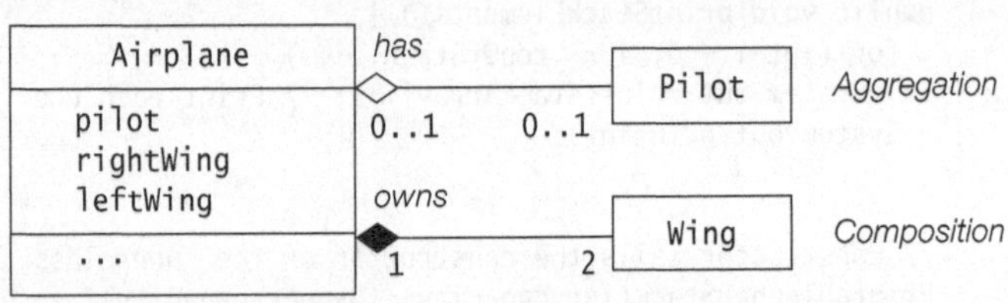

In the case of the `CharStack` class used in the earlier examples, each object of this class has a field to store the reference value of an array object that holds the characters. It would not be a good idea to share this array with other stack objects. The stack owns the array of characters. The relationship between the stack object and its constituent array object can be expressed by composition (Figure 1.8), showing that each object of the `CharStack` class will own one array object of type `char` associated with it.

Figure 1.8 *Class Diagram Depicting Composition*

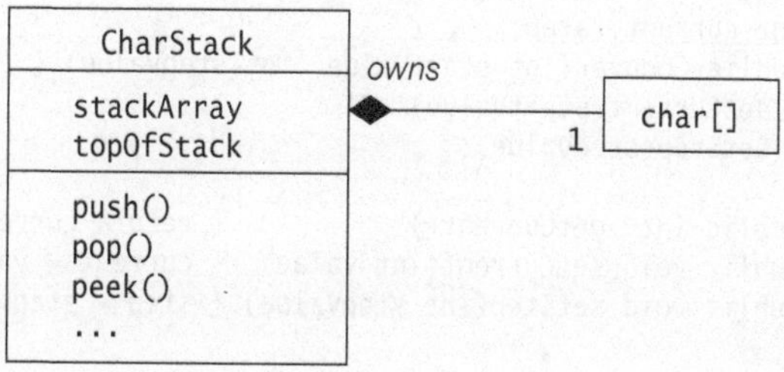

1.8 Tenets of Java

- Code in Java must be encapsulated in classes.
- There are two kinds of values in Java: objects that are instances of classes or arrays, and *atomic* values of primitive data types.
- References store reference values that denote objects, and are used to manipulate objects.
- Objects in Java cannot contain other objects; they can only have references to other objects.
- During execution, reclamation of objects that are no longer in use is managed by the runtime environment.

Review Questions

1.1 Which statement is true about methods?

Select the one correct answer.

(a) A method is an implementation of an abstraction.
(b) A method is an attribute defining the property of a particular abstraction.
(c) A method is a category of objects.
(d) A method is an operation defining the behavior for a particular abstraction.
(e) A method is a blueprint for making operations.

1.2 Which statement is true about objects?

Select the one correct answer.

(a) An object is what classes are instantiated from.
(b) An object is an instance of a class.
(c) An object is a blueprint for creating concrete realization of abstractions.
(d) An object is a reference.
(e) An object is a variable.

1.3 Which is the first line of a constructor declaration in the following code?

```
public class Counter {                                                   // (1)
  int current, step;
  public Counter(int startValue, int stepValue) {                        // (2)
    setCurrent(startValue);                                              // (3)
    setStep(stepValue);
  }
  public int  getCurrent()               { return current; }             // (4)
  public void setCurrent(int value)  { current = value; }               // (5)
  public void setStep(int stepValue) { step = stepValue; }              // (6)
}
```

Select the one correct answer.

(a) (1)
(b) (2)
(c) (3)
(d) (4)
(e) (5)
(f) (6)

1.4 Given that `Thing` is a class, how many objects and how many references are created by the following code?

```
Thing item, stuff;
item = new Thing();
Thing entity = new Thing();
```

Select the two correct answers.

(a) One object is created.
(b) Two objects are created.
(c) Three objects are created.
(d) One reference is created.
(e) Two references are created.
(f) Three references are created.

1.5 Which statement is true about instance members?

Select the one correct answer.

(a) An instance member is also called a static member.
(b) An instance member is always a field.
(c) An instance member is never a method.
(d) An instance member belongs to an instance, not to the class as a whole.
(e) An instance member always represents an operation.

1.6 How do objects communicate in Java?

Select the one correct answer.

(a) They communicate by modifying each other's fields.
(b) They communicate by modifying the static variables of each other's classes.
(c) They communicate by calling each other's instance methods.
(d) They communicate by calling static methods of each other's classes.

1.7 Given the following code, which statements are true?

```
class A {
  protected int value1;
}

class B extends A {
  int value2;
}
```

Select the two correct answers.

(a) Class `A` extends class `B`.
(b) Class `B` is the superclass of class `A`.
(c) Class `A` inherits from class `B`.
(d) Class `B` is a subclass of class `A`.
(e) Objects of class `A` have a field named `value2`.
(f) Objects of class `B` have a field named `value1`.

1.8 Given the following code, which statements express the most accurate association?

```
class Carriage { }

class TrainDriver { }

class Train {
  private Carriage[] carriages;
  private TrainDriver driver;
  Train(TrainDriver trainDriver, int noOfCarriages) {
    carriages = new Carriage[noOfCarriages];
    driver = trainDriver;
  }
  void insertCarriage(Carriage newCarriage) { /* ... */ }
}
```

Select the three correct answers.

(a) A `Train` object *has* an array of `Carriage` objects.
(b) A `Train` object *owns an* array of `Carriage` objects.
(c) A `Train` object *owns* `Carriage` objects.
(d) A `Train` object *has a* `TrainDriver` object.
(e) A `Train` object *owns a* `TrainDriver` object.
(f) A `TrainDriver` object is *part of* a `Train` object.
(g) An array of `Carriage` objects is *part of* a `Train` object.
(h) `Carriage` objects are *part of* a `Train` object.

1.9 Java Programs

A Java *source file* can contain more than one class declaration. Each source file name has the extension `.java`. The JDK (Java Development Kit) enforces the rule that any class in the source file that has `public` accessibility must be declared in its own file, meaning that such a public class must be declared in a source file whose file name comprises the name of this public class with `.java` as its extension. This rule implies that a source file can contain at most one public class. If the source file contains a public class, the file naming rule is enforced by the JDK.

Each class declaration in a source file is compiled into a separate *class file*, containing *Java bytecode*. The name of this file comprises the name of the class with `.class` as its extension. The JDK provides tools for compiling and running programs, as explained in the next section. The classes in the Java SE platform API are already compiled, and the JDK tools know where to find them.

1.10 Sample Java Application

The term *application* is just a synonym for a *program*, referring to source code that is compiled and directly executed. To create an application in Java, the program must have a class that defines a method named `main`, which is the starting point for the execution of any application.

Essential Elements of a Java Application

Example 1.4 is an example of an application in which a client uses the `CharStack` class to reverse a string of characters.

Example 1.4 *An Application*

```
// File: CharStack.java
public class CharStack {
  // Same as in Example 1.2.
}
```

```
// File: Client.java
public class Client {

  public static void main(String[] args) {

    // Create a stack.
    CharStack stack = new CharStack(40);

    // Create a string to push on the stack:
    String str = "!no tis ot nuf era skcatS";
    System.out.println("Original string: " + str);            // (1)
    int length = str.length();

    // Push the string char by char onto the stack:
    for (int i = 0; i < length; i++) {
      stack.push(str.charAt(i));
    }
```

```
      System.out.print("Reversed string: ");                   // (2)
      // Pop and print each char from the stack:
      while (!stack.isEmpty()) { // Check if the stack is not empty.
        System.out.print(stack.pop());
      }
      System.out.println();                                     // (3)
    }
  }
```

Output from the program:

```
Original string: !no tis ot nuf era skcatS
Reversed string: Stacks are fun to sit on!
```

The public class `Client` defines a method with the name `main`. To start the application, the `main()` method in this public class is invoked by the Java interpreter, also called the Java Virtual Machine (JVM). The *method header* of this `main()` method must be declared as shown in the following method stub:

```
public static void main(String[] args)    // Method header
{ /* Implementation */ }
```

The `main()` method has `public` accessibility—that is, it is accessible from any class. The keyword `static` means the method belongs to the class. The keyword `void` indicates that the method does not return any value. The parameter `args` is an array of strings that can be used to pass information to the `main()` method when execution starts.

Compiling and Running an Application

Java source files can be compiled using the Java compiler tool `javac`, which is part of the JDK.

The source file `Client.java` contains the declaration of the `Client` class. This source file can be compiled by giving the following command at the command line (the character `>` is the command prompt):

```
>javac Client.java
```

This command creates the class file `Client.class` containing the Java bytecode for the `Client` class. The `Client` class uses the `CharStack` class, and if the file `CharStack.class` does not already exist, the compiler will also compile the source file `CharStack.java`.

Compiled classes can be executed by the Java interpreter `java`, which is also part of the JDK. To run Example 1.4, give the following command on the command line:

```
>java Client
Original string: !no tis ot nuf era skcatS
Reversed string: Stacks are fun to sit on!
```

Note that only the name of the class is specified, resulting in the execution starting in the `main()` method of the specified class. The application in Example 1.4 terminates when the execution of the `main()` method is completed.

1.11 Program Output

Data produced by a program is called *output*. This output can be sent to different devices. The examples presented in this book send their output to a terminal window, where the output is printed as line of characters with a cursor that advances as characters are printed. A Java program can send its output to the terminal window using an object called *standard out*. This object, which can be accessed using the public static final field `out` in the `System` class, is an object of the class `java.io.PrintStream` that provides methods for printing values. These methods convert values to their string representation and print the resulting string.

Example 1.4 illustrates the process of printing values to the terminal window. The argument in the call to the `println()` method at (1) is first evaluated, and the resulting string is printed to the terminal window. This method always terminates the current line, which results in the cursor being moved to the beginning of the next line:

```
System.out.println("Original string: " + str);              // (1)
```

The `print()` method at (2) prints its argument to the terminal window, but it does not terminate the current line:

```
System.out.print("Reversed string: ");                       // (2)
```

To terminate a line, without printing any values, we can use the no-argument `println()` method:

```
System.out.println();                                        // (3)
```

Formatted Output

To have more control over how the values are printed, we can create formatted output. The following method of the `java.io.PrintStream` class can be used for this purpose:

> `PrintStream printf(String format, Object... args)`
>
> The `String` parameter `format` specifies how formatting will be done. It contains *format specifications* that determine how each subsequent value in the parameter `args` will be formatted and printed. The parameter declaration `Object... args` represents an array of zero or more arguments to be formatted and printed. The resulting string from the formatting will be printed to the *destination stream*. (`System.out` will print to the *standard out* object.)
>
> Any error in the format string will result in a runtime exception.

The following call to the `printf()` method on the standard out object formats and prints three values:

```
System.out.printf("Formatted values|%5d|%8.3f|%5s|%n", // Format string
                  2016, Math.PI, "Hi");              // Values to format
```

At runtime, the following line is printed in the terminal window:

```
Formatted values| 2016|   3.142|   Hi|
```

The format string is the first argument in the method call. It contains four *format specifiers*. The first three are `%5d`, `%8.3f`, and `%5s`, which specify how the three arguments should be processed. The letter in the format specifier indicates the type of value to format. Their location in the format string specifies where the textual representation of the arguments should be inserted. The fourth format specifier, `%n`, is a platform-specific line separator. Its occurrence causes the current line to be terminated, with the cursor moving to the start of the next line. All other text in the format string is fixed, including any other spaces or punctuation, and is printed verbatim.

In the preceding example, the first value is formatted according to the first format specifier, the second value is formatted according to the second format specifier, and so on. The `|` character has been used in the format string to show how many character positions are taken up by the text representation of each value. The output shows that the `int` value was written right-justified, spanning five character positions using the format specifier `%5d`; the `double` value of `Math.PI` took up eight character positions and was rounded to three decimal places using the format specifier `%8.3f`; and the `String` value was written right-justified, spanning five character positions using the format specifier `%5s`. The format specifier `%n` terminates the current line. All other characters in the format string are printed verbatim.

Table 1.2 shows examples of some selected format specifiers that can be used to format values. Their usage is illustrated in Example 1.5, which prints a simple invoice.

At the top of the invoice printed by Example 1.5, the company name is printed at (1) with a format string that contains only fixed text. The date and time of day are printed on the same line, with leading zeros at (2). A header is then printed at (3). The column names `Item`, `Price`, `Quantity`, and `Amount` are positioned appropriately with the format specifications `%-20s`, `%7s`, `%9s`, and `%8s`, respectively.

Beneath the heading, the items purchased are printed at (5), (6), and (7) using the same field widths as the column headings. The format for each item is defined by the format string at (4). The item name is printed with the format string `"%-20s"`, resulting in a 20-character-wide string, left-justified. The item price and the total amount for each type of item are printed as floating-point values using the format specifications `%7.2f` and `%8.2f`, respectively. The quantity is printed as an integer using the format specification `%9d`. The strings are left-justified, while all numbers are right-justified. The character `s` is the conversion code for objects, while floating-point and integer values are printed using the codes `f` and `d`, respectively.

Table 1.2 *Format Specifier Examples*

Parameter value	Format spec	Example value	String printed	Description
Integer value	`"%d"`	`123`	`"123"`	Occupies as many character positions as needed.
	`"%6d"`	`123`	`"   123"`	Occupies six character positions and is right-justified. The printed string is padded with leading spaces, if necessary.
	`"%06d"`	`123`	`"000123"`	Occupies six character positions and is right-justified. The printed string is padded with leading zeros, if necessary.
Floating-point value	`"%f"`	`4.567`	`"4.567000"`	Occupies as many character positions as needed, but always includes six decimal places.
	`"%.2f"`	`4.567`	`"4.57"`	Occupies as many character positions as needed, but includes only two decimal places. The value is rounded in the output, if necessary.
	`"%6.2f"`	`4.567`	`"  4.57"`	Occupies six character positions, including the decimal point, and uses two decimal places. The value is rounded in the output, if necessary.
Any object	`"%s"`	`"Hi!"`	`"Hi!"`	The string representation of the object occupies as many character positions as needed.
	`"%6s"`	`"Hi!"`	`"   Hi!"`	The string representation of the object occupies six character positions and is right-justified.
	`"%-6s"`	`"Hi!"`	`"Hi!   "`	The string representation of the object occupies six character positions and is left-justified.

At (8), the total cost of all items is printed using the format specification `%8.2f`. To position this value correctly under the column `Amount`, we print the string `"Total:"` using the format `%-36s`. The width of 36 characters is found by adding the width of the first three columns of the invoice.

Example 1.5 *Formatted Output*

```
// File: Invoice.java
public class Invoice {
  public static void main(String[] args) {
    System.out.printf("Secure Data Inc.        ");                       // (1)
    System.out.printf("%02d/%02d/%04d, %02d:%02d%n%n",                   // (2)
                      2, 13, 2016, 11, 5);
    System.out.printf("%-20s%7s%9s%8s%n",                                // (3)
                      "Item", "Price", "Quantity", "Amount");

    int quantity = 4;
    double price = 120.25, amount = quantity*price, total = amount;
    String itemFormat = "%-20s%7.2f%9d%8.2f%n";                          // (4)
    System.out.printf(itemFormat,
                      "FlashDrive, 250GB", price, quantity, amount);  // (5)
    quantity = 2;
    price = 455.0; amount = quantity*price; total = total + amount;
    System.out.printf(itemFormat,
                      "Ultra HD, 4TB", price, quantity, amount);      // (6)
    quantity = 1;
    price = 8.50; amount = quantity*price; total = total + amount;
    System.out.printf(itemFormat,
                      "USB 3.0 cable", price, quantity, amount);      // (7)

    System.out.printf("%-36s%8.2f%n", "Total:", total);                  // (8)
  }
}
```

Output from the program:

```
Secure Data Inc.        02/13/2016, 11:05

Item                  Price Quantity  Amount
FlashDrive, 250GB    120.25        4  481.00
Ultra HD, 4TB        455.00        2  910.00
USB 3.0 cable          8.50        1    8.50
Total:                               1399.50
```

1.12 The Java Ecosystem

Since its initial release as Java Development Kit 1.0 (JDK 1.0) in 1996, the name Java has become synonymous with a thriving ecosystem that provides the components and the tools necessary for developing systems for today's multicore world. Its diverse community, comprising a multitude of volunteers, organizations, and corporations, continues to fuel its evolution and grow with its success. Many free open-source technologies now exist that are well proven, mature, and supported, making their adoption less daunting. These tools and frameworks provide support for all phases of the software development life cycle and beyond.

There are three major Java Platforms for the Java programming language:

- Java SE (Standard Edition)
- Java EE (Enterprise Edition)
- Java ME (Micro Edition)

Each platform provides a hardware/operating system–specific JVM and an API (*application programming interface*) to develop applications for that platform. The Java SE platform provides the core functionality of the language. The Java EE platform is a superset of the Java SE platform and, as the most extensive of the three platforms, targets enterprise application development. The Java ME platform is a subset of the Java SE platform, having the smallest footprint, and is suitable for developing mobile and embedded applications. The upshot of this classification is that a Java program developed for one Java platform will not necessary run under the JVM of another Java platform. The JVM must be compatible with the Java platform that was used to develop the program.

The API and the tools for developing and running Java applications are bundled together as JDK. Just the JVM and the runtime libraries are also bundled separately as JRE (Java Runtime Environment).

The subject of this book is Java SE 8. We recommend installing the appropriate JDK for Java SE 8 (or a newer version) depending on the hardware and operating system.

The rest of this section summarizes some of the factors that have contributed to the evolution of Java from an object-oriented programming language to a full-fledged ecosystem for developing all sorts of systems, including large-scale business systems and embedded systems for portable computing devices. A lot of jargon is used in this section, and might be difficult to understand at the first reading, but we recommend coming back after working through the book to appreciate the factors that have contributed to the success of Java.

Object-Oriented Paradigm

The Java programming language supports the object-oriented paradigm, in which the properties of an object and its behavior are encapsulated in the object. The properties and the behavior are represented by the fields and the methods of the object, respectively. The objects communicate through method calls in a procedural manner. Encapsulation ensures that objects are immune to tampering except when manipulated through their public interface. Encapsulation exposes only *what* an object does and not *how* it does it, so that its implementation can be changed with minimum impact on its clients. Some basic concepts of object-oriented programming, such as inheritance and aggregation, were introduced earlier in this chapter, and subsequent chapters will expand on this topic.

Above all, object-oriented system development promotes code reuse where existing objects can be reused to implement new objects. It also facilitates implementation of large systems, allowing their decomposition into manageable subsystems.

Interpreted: The JVM

Java programs are compiled to bytecode that is interpreted by the JVM. Various optimization technologies (e.g., just-in-time [JIT] delivery) have led to the JVM becoming a lean and mean virtual machine with regard to performance, stability, and security. Many other languages, such as Scala, Groovy, and Clojure, now compile to bytecode and seamlessly execute on the JVM. The JVM has thus evolved into an ecosystem in its own right.

Architecture-Neutral and Portable Bytecode

The often-cited slogan "Write once, run everywhere" is true only if a compatible JVM is available for the hardware and software platform. In other words, to run Java SE applications under Windows 10 on a 64-bit hardware architecture, the right JVM must be installed. Fortunately, the JVM has been ported to run under most platforms and operative systems that exist today, including hardware devices such as smart cards, mobile devices, and home appliances.

The specification of the bytecode is architecture neutral, meaning it is independent of any hardware architecture. It is executed by a readily available hardware and operating system–specific JVM. The portability of the Java bytecode thus eases the burden of cross-platform system development.

Simplicity

Language design of Java has been driven by a desire to simplify the programming process. Although Java borrows heavily from the C++ programming language, certain features that were deemed problematic were not incorporated into its design. For example, Java does not have a preprocessor, and it does not allow pointer handling, user-defined operator overloading, or multiple class inheritance.

Java opted for automatic garbage collection, which frees the programmer from dealing with many issues related to memory management, such as memory leaks.

However, the jury is still out on whether the syntax of nested classes or introduction of wild cards for generics can be considered simple.

Dynamic and Distributed

The JVM can dynamically load class libraries from the local file system as well as from machines on the network, when those libraries are needed at runtime. This feature facilitates linking the code as and when necessary during the execution of a program. It is also possible to query programmatically a class or an object at runtime about its meta-information, such as its methods and fields.

Java provides extensive support for networking to build distributed systems, where objects are able to communicate across networks using various communication protocols and technologies, such as Remote Method Invocation (RMI) and socket connections.

Robust and Secure

Java promotes the development of reliable, robust, and secure systems. It is a strong statically typed language: The compiler guarantees runtime execution if the code compiles without errors. Elimination of pointers, runtime index checks for arrays and strings, and automatic garbage collection are some of the features of Java that promote reliability. The exception handling feature of Java is without doubt the main factor that facilitates the development of robust systems.

Java provides multilevel protection from malicious code. The language does not allow direct access to memory. A bytecode verifier determines whether any untrusted code loaded in the JVM is safe. The sandbox model is used to confine and execute any untrusted code, limiting the damage that such code can cause. These features, among others, are provided by a comprehensive Java security model to ensure that application code executes securely in the JVM.

High Performance and Multithreaded

The performance of Java programs has improved significantly with various optimizations that are applied to the bytecode at runtime by the JVM. The JIT feature monitors the program at runtime to identify performance-critical bytecode (called *hotspots*) that can be optimized. Such code is usually translated to machine code to boost performance. The performance achieved by the JVM is a balance between native code execution and interpretation of fully scripted languages, which fortunately is adequate for many applications.

Java has always provided high-level support for multithreading, allowing multiple threads of execution to perform different tasks concurrently in an application. It has risen to the new challenges that have emerged in recent years to harness the increased computing power made available by multicore architectures. Functional programming, in which computation is treated as side-effects–free evaluation of functions, is seen as a boon to meet these challenges. Java 8 brings elements of functional-style programming into the language, providing language constructs (lambda expressions and functional interfaces) and API support (through its Fork & Join Framework and Stream API) to efficiently utilize the many cores to process large amounts of data in parallel.

Review Questions

1.9 Which command from the JDK should be used to compile the following source code contained in a file named `SmallProg.java`?

```
public class SmallProg {
  public static void main(String[] args) { System.out.println("Good luck!"); }
}
```

Select the one correct answer.

(a) `java SmallProg`
(b) `javac SmallProg`
(c) `java SmallProg.java`
(d) `javac SmallProg.java`
(e) `java SmallProg main`

1.10 Which command from the JDK should be used to execute the `main()` method of a class named `SmallProg`?

Select the one correct answer.

(a) `java SmallProg`
(b) `javac SmallProg`
(c) `java SmallProg.java`
(d) `java SmallProg.class`
(e) `java SmallProg.main()`

1.11 Which statement is true about Java?

Select the one correct answer.

(a) A Java program can be executed by any JVM.
(b) Java bytecode cannot be translated to machine code.
(c) Only Java programs can be executed by a JVM.
(d) A Java program can create and destroy objects.
(e) None of the above

Chapter Summary

The following topics were covered in this chapter:

- Essential elements of a Java application
- Accessing object fields and calling methods
- Compiling and running Java applications
- Formatting and printing values to the terminal window

- Basic terminology and concepts in OOP, and how these concepts are supported in Java
- Factors and features of the Java ecosystem that have contributed to its evolution and success

Programming Exercise

1.1 Modify the `Client` class from Example 1.4 to use the `PrintableCharStack` class, rather than the `CharStack` class from Example 1.2. Utilize the `printStackElements()` method from the `PrintableCharStack` class. Is the new program behavior-wise any different from Example 1.4?

Language Fundamentals

2

Programmer I Exam Objectives	
[1.1] Define the scope of variables ○ *See also §4.4, p. 114.*	*§2.4, p. 44*
[2.1] Declare and initialize variables (including casting of primitive data types) ○ *For casting of primitive data types, see §5.6, p. 160.*	*§2.3, p. 40* *§2.4, p. 42*
[2.2] Differentiate between object reference variables and primitive variables	*§2.3, p. 40*
Supplementary Objectives	
• Be able to identify the basic elements of the Java programming language: keywords, identifiers, literals, and primitive data types	*§2.1, p. 28* *§2.2, p. 37*

2.1 Basic Language Elements

Like any other programming language, the Java programming language is defined by *grammar rules* that specify how *syntactically* legal constructs can be formed using the language elements, and by a *semantic definition* that specifies the *meaning* of syntactically legal constructs.

Lexical Tokens

The low-level language elements are called *lexical tokens* (or just *tokens*) and are the building blocks for more complex constructs. Identifiers, numbers, operators, and special characters are all examples of tokens that can be used to build high-level constructs like expressions, statements, methods, and classes.

Identifiers

A name in a program is called an *identifier*. Identifiers can be used to denote classes, methods, variables, and labels.

In Java, an *identifier* is composed of a sequence of characters, where each character can be either a *letter* or a *digit*. However, the first character in an identifier must always be a letter, as explained later.

Since Java programs are written in the Unicode character set (p. 32), characters allowed in identifier names are interpreted according to this character set. Use of the Unicode character set opens up the possibility of writing identifier names in many writing scripts used around the world. As one would expect, the characters `A-Z` and `a-z` are letters, and characters from `0-9` are digits. A *connecting punctuation character* (such as *underscore* _) and any *currency symbol* (such as `$`, `¢`, `¥`, or `£`) are also allowed as letters in identifier names, but these characters should be used judiciously.

Identifiers in Java are *case sensitive*. For example, `price` and `Price` are two different identifiers.

Examples of Legal Identifiers

```
number, Number, sum_$, bingo, $$_100, _007, mål, grüß
```

Examples of Illegal Identifiers

```
48chevy, all@hands, grand-sum
```

The name `48chevy` is not a legal identifier because it starts with a digit. The character `@` is not a legal character in an identifier. It is also not a legal operator, so that `all@hands` cannot be interpreted as a legal expression with two operands. The character `-` is not a legal character in an identifier, but it is a legal operator; thus `grand-sum` could be interpreted as a legal expression with two operands.

Keywords

Keywords are reserved words that are predefined in the language and cannot be used to denote other entities. All Java keywords are lowercase, and incorrect usage results in compile-time errors.

Keywords currently defined in the language are listed in Table 2.1. In addition, three identifiers are reserved as predefined *literals* in the language: the `null` reference, and the boolean literals `true` and `false` (Table 2.2). Keywords currently reserved, but not in use, are listed in Table 2.3. A reserved word cannot be used as an identifier. The index contains references to relevant sections where currently used keywords are explained.

Table 2.1 *Keywords in Java*

abstract	default	if	private	this
assert	do	implements	protected	throw
boolean	double	import	public	throws
break	else	instanceof	return	transient
byte	enum	int	short	try
case	extends	interface	static	void
catch	final	long	strictfp	volatile
char	finally	native	super	while
class	float	new	switch	
continue	for	package	synchronized	

Table 2.2 *Reserved Literals in Java*

null	true	false

Table 2.3 *Reserved Keywords Not Currently in Use*

const	goto

Separators

Separators (also known as *punctuators*) are tokens that have meaning depending on the context in which they are used; they aid the compiler in performing syntax and semantic analysis of a program (Table 2.4). Depending on the context, brackets (`[]`), parentheses (`()`), and the dot operator (`.`) can also be interpreted as *operators* (§5.3, p. 150). See the index entries for these separators for more details.

Table 2.4 *Separators in Java*

{	}	[	]	(	)
.	;	,	...	@	::

Literals

A *literal* denotes a constant value; in other words, the value that a literal represents remains unchanged in the program. Literals represent numerical (integer or floating-point), character, boolean, or string values. In addition, the literal `null` represents the null reference. Table 2.5 shows examples of literals in Java.

Table 2.5 *Examples of Literals*

Integer	`2000`	`0`	`-7`			
Floating-point	`3.14`	`-3.14`	`.5`	`0.5`		
Character	`'a'`	`'A'`	`'0'`	`':'`	`'-'`	`')'`
Boolean	`true`	`false`				
String	`"abba"`	`"3.14"`	`"for"`	`"a piece of the action"`		

Integer Literals

Integer data types comprise the following primitive data types: `int`, `long`, `byte`, and `short` (§2.2, p. 37).

The default data type of an integer literal is always `int`, but it can be specified as `long` by appending the suffix `L` (or `l`) to the integer value. The suffix `L` is often preferred because the suffix `l` and the digit `1` can be hard to distinguish. Without the suffix, the `long` literals `2000L` and `0L` will be interpreted as `int` literals. There is no direct way to specify a `short` or a `byte` literal.

In addition to the decimal number system, integer literals can be specified in the binary (*base* 2, *digits* `0-1`), octal (*base* 8, *digits* `0-7`), and hexadecimal (*base* 16, *digits* `0-9` and `a-f`) number systems. The digits `a` to `f` in the hexadecimal system correspond to decimal values `10` to `15`. Binary, octal, and hexadecimal numbers are specified with `0b` (or `0B`), `0`, and `0x` (or `0X`) as the base or radix prefix, respectively. Examples of decimal, binary, octal, and hexadecimal literals are shown in Table 2.6. Note that the leading `0` (zero) digit is not the uppercase letter `O`. The hexadecimal digits from `a` to `f` can also be specified with the corresponding uppercase forms (`A` to `F`). Negative integers (e.g., `-90`) can be specified by prefixing the minus sign (`-`) to the magnitude of the integer regardless of the number system (e.g., `-0b1011010`, `-0132`, or `-0X5A`). Integer representation is discussed in §5.5, p. 154.

Table 2.6 *Examples of Decimal, Binary, Octal, and Hexadecimal Literals*

Decimal	Binary	Octal	Hexadecimal
`8`	`0b1000`	`010`	`0x8`
`10L`	`0b1010L`	`012L`	`0xaL`
`16`	`0b10000`	`020`	`0x10`
`27`	`0b11011`	`033`	`0x1b`

Table 2.6 *Examples of Decimal, Binary, Octal, and Hexadecimal Literals (Continued)*

Decimal	Binary	Octal	Hexadecimal
90L	0b1011010L	0132L	0x5aL
-90	-0b1011010 or 0b1111111111111111111111 1110100110	-0132 or 037777777646	-0x5a or 0xffffffa6
-1	-0b1 or 0b1111111111111111111111 1111111111	-01 or 037777777777	-0x1 or 0xffffffff
2147483647 (i.e., 2^{31}-1)	0b0111111111111111111111 1111111111	017777777777	0x7fffffff
-2147483648 (i.e., -2^{31})	0b1000000000000000000000 0000000000	020000000000	0x80000000
1125899906842624L (i.e., 2^{50})	0b1000000000000000000000 000000000000000000000000 00000L	040000000000000000L	0x4000000000000L

Floating-Point Literals

Floating-point data types come in two flavors: `float` or `double`.

The default data type of a floating-point literal is `double`, but it can be explicitly designated by appending the suffix `D` (or `d`) to the value. A floating-point literal can also be specified to be a `float` by appending the suffix `F` (or `f`).

Floating-point literals can also be specified in scientific notation, where `E` (or `e`) stands for *exponent*. For example, the `double` literal `194.9E-2` in scientific notation is interpreted as 194.9×10^{-2} (i.e., 1.949).

Examples of `double` *Literals*

```
0.0       0.0d      0D
0.49      .49       .49D
49.0      49.       49D
4.9E+1    4.9E+1D   4.9e1d   4900e-2  .49E2
```

Examples of `float` *Literals*

```
0.0F      0f
0.49F     .49F
49.0F     49.F      49F
4.9E+1F   4900e-2f  .49E2F
```

Note that the decimal point and the exponent are optional, and that at least one digit must be specified. Also, for the examples of `float` literals presented here, the suffix `F` is mandatory; if it was omitted, they would be interpreted as `double` literals.

Underscores in Numerical Literals

The underscore character (_) can be used to improve the readability of numerical literals in the source code. Any number of underscores can be inserted *between the digits* that make up the numerical literal. This rules out underscores adjacent to the sign (+, -), the radix prefix (0b, 0B, 0x, 0X), the decimal point (.), the exponent (e, E), and the data type suffix (l, L, d, D, f, F), as well as before the first digit and after the last digit. Note that octal radix prefix 0 is part of the definition of an octal literal and is therefore considered the first digit of an octal literal.

Underscores in identifiers are treated as letters. For example, the names _XXL and _XXL_ are two distinct legal identifiers. In contrast, underscores are used as a notational convenience for numerical literals, being ignored by the compiler when used in such literals. In other words, a numerical literal can be specified in the source code using underscores between digits, such that 2_0_1_5 and 20__15 represent the same numerical literal 2015 in source code.

Examples of Legal Use of Underscores in Numerical Literals

```
0b0111_1111_1111_1111_1111_1111_1111_1111
0_377_777_777               0xff_ff_ff_ff
-123_456.00                 1_2.345_678e1_2
2009__08__13                49_03_01d
```

Examples of Illegal Use of Underscores in Numerical Literals

```
_0_b_01111111111111111111111111111111_
_0377777777_                _0_x_ffffffff_
+_123456_._00_              _12_._345678_e_12_
_20090813_                  _490301_d_
```

Boolean Literals

The primitive data type boolean represents the truth values *true* and *false* that are denoted by the reserved literals true and false, respectively.

Character Literals

A character literal is quoted in single quotes ('). All character literals have the primitive data type char.

A character literal is represented according to the 16-bit Unicode character set, which subsumes the 8-bit ISO-Latin-1 and the 7-bit ASCII characters. In Table 2.7, note that digits (0 to 9), uppercase letters (A to Z), and lowercase letters (a to z) have contiguous Unicode values. A Unicode character can always be specified as a four-digit hexadecimal number (i.e., 16 bits) with the prefix \u.

Table 2.7 *Examples of Character Literals*

Character literal	Character literal using Unicode value	Character
`' '`	`'\u0020'`	Space
`'0'`	`'\u0030'`	0
`'1'`	`'\u0031'`	1
`'9'`	`'\u0039'`	9
`'A'`	`'\u0041'`	A
`'B'`	`'\u0042'`	B
`'Z'`	`'\u005a'`	Z
`'a'`	`'\u0061'`	a
`'b'`	`'\u0062'`	b
`'z'`	`'\u007a'`	z
`'Ñ'`	`'\u0084'`	Ñ
`'å'`	`'\u008c'`	å
`'ß'`	`'\u00a7'`	ß

Escape Sequences

Certain *escape sequences* define special characters, as shown in Table 2.8. These escape sequences can be single-quoted to define character literals. For example, the character literals `\t` and `\u0009` are equivalent. However, the character literals `\u000a` and `\u000d` should not be used to represent newline and carriage return in the source code. These values are interpreted as line-terminator characters by the compiler, and will cause compile-time errors. You should use the escape sequences `\n` and `\r`, respectively, for correct interpretation of these characters in the source code.

Table 2.8 *Escape Sequences*

Escape sequence	Unicode value	Character
`\b`	`\u0008`	Backspace (BS)
`\t`	`\u0009`	Horizontal tab (HT or TAB)
`\n`	`\u000a`	Linefeed (LF), also known as newline (NL)
`\f`	`\u000c`	Form feed (FF)
`\r`	`\u000d`	Carriage return (CR)
`\'`	`\u0027`	Apostrophe-quote, also known as single quote
`\"`	`\u0022`	Quotation mark, also known as double quote
`\\`	`\u005c`	Backslash

We can also use the escape sequence \ddd to specify a character literal as an octal value, where each digit d can be any octal digit (0–7), as shown in Table 2.9. The number of digits must be three or fewer, and the octal value cannot exceed \377; in other words, only the first 256 characters can be specified with this notation.

Table 2.9 *Examples of Escape Sequence* \ddd

Escape sequence \ddd	Character literal
'\141'	'a'
'\46'	'&'
'\60'	'0'

String Literals

A *string literal* is a sequence of characters that must be enclosed in double quotes and must occur on a single line. All string literals are objects of the class String (§8.4, p. 357).

Escape sequences as well as Unicode values can appear in string literals:

```
"Here comes a tab.\t And here comes another one\u0009!"    (1)
"What's on the menu?"                                       (2)
"\"String literals are double-quoted.\""                    (3)
"Left!\nRight!"                                             (4)
"Don't split                                                (5)
me up!"
```

In (1), the tab character is specified using the escape sequence and the Unicode value, respectively. In (2), the single apostrophe need not be escaped in strings, but it would be if specified as a character literal ('\''). In (3), the double quotes in the string must be escaped. In (4), we use the escape sequence \n to insert a newline. The expression in (5) generates a compile-time error, as the string literal is split over several lines. Printing the strings from (1) to (4) will give the following result:

```
Here comes a tab.    And here comes another one      !
What's on the menu?
"String literals are double-quoted."
Left!
Right!
```

One should also use the escape sequences \n and \r, respectively, for correct interpretation of the characters \u000a (newline) and \u000d (form feed) in string literals.

Whitespace

A *whitespace* is a sequence of spaces, tabs, form feeds, and line terminator characters in a Java source file. Line terminators include the newline, carriage return, or a carriage return–newline sequence.

A Java program is a free-format sequence of characters that is *tokenized* by the compiler—that is, broken into a stream of tokens for further analysis. Separators and operators help to distinguish tokens, but sometimes whitespace has to be inserted explicitly as a separator. For example, the identifier `classRoom` will be interpreted as a single token, unless whitespace is inserted to distinguish the keyword `class` from the identifier `Room`.

Whitespace aids not only in separating tokens, but also in formatting the program so that it is easy to read. The compiler ignores the whitespace once the tokens are identified.

Comments

A program can be documented by inserting comments at relevant places in the source code. These comments are for documentation purposes only and are ignored by the compiler.

Java provides three types of comments that can be used to document a program:

- A single-line comment: `// ... to the end of the line`
- A multiple-line comment: `/* ... */`
- A documentation (Javadoc) comment: `/** ... */`

Single-Line Comment

All characters after the comment-start sequence `//` through to the end of the line constitute a *single-line comment*.

```
// This comment ends at the end of this line.
int age;        // From comment-start sequence to the end of the line is a comment.
```

Multiple-Line Comment

A *multiple-line comment*, as the name suggests, can span several lines. Such a comment starts with the sequence `/*` and ends with the sequence `*/`.

```
/* A comment
   on several
   lines.
*/
```

The comment-start sequences (`//`, `/*`, `/**`) are not treated differently from other characters when occurring within comments, so they are ignored. This means that trying to nest multiple-line comments will result in a compile-time error:

```
/* Formula for alchemy.
   gold = wizard.makeGold(stone);
   /* But it only works on Sundays. */
*/
```

The second occurrence of the comment-start sequence /* is ignored. The last occurrence of the sequence */ in the code is now unmatched, resulting in a syntax error.

Documentation Comment

A *documentation comment* is a special-purpose multiple-line comment that is used by the `javadoc` tool to generate HTML documentation for the program. Documentation comments are usually placed in front of classes, interfaces, methods, and field definitions. Special tags can be used inside a documentation comment to provide more specific information. Such a comment starts with the sequence /** and ends with the sequence */:

```
/**
 *  This class implements a gizmo.
 *  @author K.A.M.
 *  @version 4.0
 */
```

For details on the `javadoc` tool, see the tools documentation provided by the JDK.

Review Questions

2.1 Which of the following is not a legal identifier?

Select the one correct answer.

(a) `a2z`
(b) `ödipus`
(c) `52pickup`
(d) `_class`
(e) `ca$h`
(f) `_8to5`

2.2 Which of the following are not legal literals in Java?

Select the four correct answers.

(a) `0Xbad`
(b) `0B_101_101`
(c) `09`
(d) `+_825`
(e) `1_2e4f`
(f) `'\x'`
(g) `"what\'s your fancy?"`

2.3 Which statement is true?

Select the one correct answer.

(a) `new` and `delete` are keywords in the Java language.
(b) `try`, `catch`, and `thrown` are keywords in the Java language.
(c) `static`, `unsigned`, and `long` are keywords in the Java language.
(d) `exit`, `class`, and `while` are keywords in the Java language.
(e) `return`, `goto`, and `default` are keywords in the Java language.
(f) `for`, `while`, and `next` are keywords in the Java language.

2.4 Which of the following is not a legal comment in Java?

Select the one correct answer.

(a) `/* // */`
(b) `/* */ //`
(c) `// /* */`
(d) `/* /* */`
(e) `/* /* */ */`
(f) `// //`

2.2 Primitive Data Types

Figure 2.1 gives an overview of the primitive data types in Java.

Primitive data types in Java can be divided into three main categories:

- *Integral types*—represent signed integers (`byte`, `short`, `int`, `long`) and unsigned character values (`char`)
- *Floating-point types* (`float`, `double`)—represent fractional signed numbers
- *Boolean type* (`boolean`)—represents logical values

Figure 2.1 *Primitive Data Types in Java*

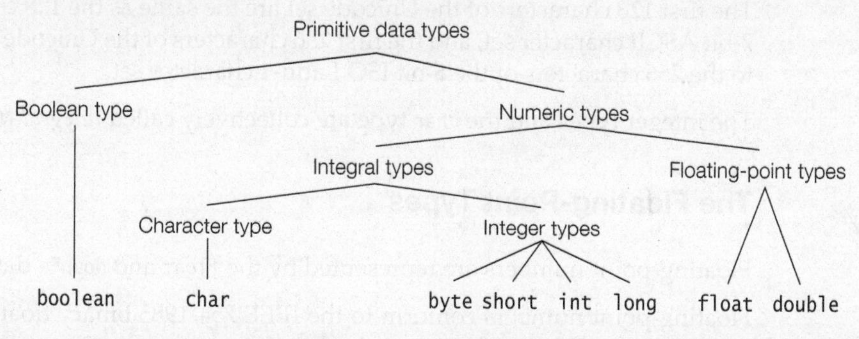

Primitive data values are not objects. Each primitive data type defines the range of values in the data type, and operations on these values are defined by special operators in the language (Chapter 5, p. 143).

Each primitive data type also has a corresponding *wrapper* class that can be used to represent a primitive value as an object. Wrapper classes are discussed in §8.3, p. 346.

The Integer Types

The integer data types are `byte`, `short`, `int`, and `long` (Table 2.10). Their values are signed integers represented by two's complement (§5.5, p. 155).

Table 2.10 *Range of Integer Values*

Data type	Width (bits)	Minimum value MIN_VALUE	Maximum value MAX_VALUE
`byte`	8	-2^7 (-128)	2^7-1 (+127)
`short`	16	-2^{15} (-32768)	2^{15}-1 (+32767)
`int`	32	-2^{31} (-2147483648)	2^{31}-1 (+2147483647)
`long`	64	-2^{63} (-9223372036854775808L)	2^{63}-1 (+9223372036854775807L)

The `char` Type

The data type `char` represents characters (Table 2.11). Their values are unsigned integers that denote all of the 65536 (2^{16}) characters in the 16-bit Unicode character set. This set includes letters, digits, and special characters.

Table 2.11 *Range of Character Values*

Data type	Width (bits)	Minimum Unicode value	Maximum Unicode value
`char`	16	`0x0 (\u0000)`	`0xffff (\uffff)`

The first 128 characters of the Unicode set are the same as the 128 characters of the 7-bit ASCII character set, and the first 256 characters of the Unicode set correspond to the 256 characters of the 8-bit ISO Latin-1 character set.

The integer types and the `char` type are collectively called *integral types*.

The Floating-Point Types

Floating-point numbers are represented by the `float` and `double` data types.

Floating-point numbers conform to the IEEE 754-1985 binary floating-point standard. Table 2.12 shows the range of values for positive floating-point numbers, but these apply equally to negative floating-point numbers with the minus sign (-) as a prefix. Zero can be either `0.0` or `-0.0`.

Table 2.12 *Range of Floating-Point Values*

Data type	Width (bits)	Minimum positive value MIN_VALUE	Maximum positive value MAX_VALUE
`float`	32	`1.401298464324817E-45f`	`3.40282347663852886e+38f`
`double`	64	`4.94065645841246544e-324`	`1.79769313486231570e+308`

Since the size for representation is a finite number of bits, certain floating-point numbers can be represented only as approximations. For example, the value of the expression `(1.0/3.0)` is represented as an approximation due to the finite number of bits used to represent floating-point numbers.

The `boolean` Type

The data type `boolean` represents the two logical values denoted by the literals `true` and `false` (Table 2.13).

Table 2.13 *Boolean Values*

Data type	Width	True value literal	False value literal
`boolean`	not applicable	`true`	`false`

Boolean values are produced by all *relational* (§5.11, p. 180), *conditional* (§5.14, p. 186), and *boolean logical operators* (§5.13, p. 184), and are primarily used to govern the flow of control during program execution.

Table 2.14 summarizes the pertinent facts about the primitive data types: their width or size, which indicates the number of bits required to store a primitive value; their range of legal values, which is specified by the minimum and the maximum values permissible; and the name of the corresponding wrapper class (§8.3, p. 346).

Table 2.14 *Summary of Primitive Data Types*

Data type	Width (bits)	Minimum value, maximum value	Wrapper class
`boolean`	not applicable	`true, false`	`Boolean`
`byte`	8	-2^7, 2^7-1	`Byte`
`short`	16	-2^{15}, 2^{15}-1	`Short`
`char`	16	`0x0, 0xffff`	`Character`
`int`	32	-2^{31}, 2^{31}-1	`Integer`
`long`	64	-2^{63}, 2^{63}-1	`Long`

Continues

Table 2.14 *Summary of Primitive Data Types (Continued)*

Data type	Width (bits)	Minimum value, maximum value	Wrapper class
`float`	32	`±1.40129846432481707e-45f`, `±3.402823476638528860e+38f`	`Float`
`double`	64	`±4.94065645841246544e-324`, `±1.79769313486231570e+308`	`Double`

Review Questions

2.5 Which of the following do not denote a primitive data value in Java?

Select the two correct answers.

(a) `"t"`
(b) `'k'`
(c) `50.5F`
(d) `"hello"`
(e) `false`

2.6 Which of the following primitive data types are not integer types?

Select the three correct answers.

(a) `boolean`
(b) `byte`
(c) `float`
(d) `short`
(e) `double`

2.7 Which integral type in Java has the exact range from `-2147483648` (i.e., -2^{31}) to `2147483647` (i.e., $2^{31}-1$), inclusive?

Select the one correct answer.

(a) `byte`
(b) `short`
(c) `int`
(d) `long`
(e) `char`

2.3 Variable Declarations

A *variable* stores a value of a particular type. A variable has a name, a type, and a value associated with it. In Java, variables can store only values of primitive data types and reference values of objects. Variables that store reference values of objects are called *reference variables* (or *object references* or simply *references*).

Declaring and Initializing Variables

Variable declarations are used to specify the type and the name of variables. This implicitly determines their memory allocation and the values that can be stored in them. Examples of declaring variables that can store primitive values follow:

```
char a, b, c;              // a, b and c are character variables.
double area;               // area is a floating-point variable.
boolean flag;              // flag is a boolean variable.
```

The first declaration is equivalent to the following three declarations:

```
char a;
char b;
char c;
```

A declaration can also be combined with an initialization expression to specify an appropriate initial value for the variable. Such declarations are called *declaration statements*.

```
int i = 10,                // i is an int variable with initial value 10.
    j = 0b101;             // j is an int variable with initial value 5.
long big = 2147483648L;    // big is a long variable with specified initial value.
```

Reference Variables

A *reference variable* can store the reference value of an object, and can be used to manipulate the object denoted by the reference value.

A variable declaration that specifies a *reference type* (i.e., a class, an array, an interface name, or an enum type) declares a reference variable. Analogous to the declaration of variables of primitive data types, the simplest form of reference variable declaration specifies the name and the reference type only. The declaration determines which objects can be referenced by a reference variable. Before we can use a reference variable to manipulate an object, it must be declared and initialized with the reference value of the object.

```
Pizza yummyPizza;   // Variable yummyPizza can reference objects of class Pizza.
Hamburger bigOne,   // Variable bigOne can reference objects of class Hamburger,
          smallOne; // and so can variable smallOne.
```

It is important to note that the preceding declarations do not create any objects of class `Pizza` or `Hamburger`. Rather, they simply create variables that can store reference values of objects of the specified classes.

A declaration can also be combined with an initializer expression to create an object whose reference value can be assigned to the reference variable:

```
Pizza yummyPizza = new Pizza("Hot&Spicy"); // Declaration statement
```

The reference variable `yummyPizza` can reference objects of class `Pizza`. The keyword `new`, together with the *constructor call* `Pizza("Hot&Spicy")`, creates an object of the class `Pizza`. The reference value of this object is assigned to the variable `yummyPizza`. The newly created object of class `Pizza` can now be manipulated through the reference variable `yummyPizza`.

2.4 Initial Values for Variables

This section discusses what value, if any, is assigned to a variable when no explicit initial value is provided in the declaration.

Default Values for Fields

Default values for fields of primitive data types and reference types are listed in Table 2.15. The value assigned depends on the type of the field.

Table 2.15 *Default Values*

Data type	Default value
`boolean`	`false`
`char`	`'\u0000'`
Integer (`byte`, `short`, `int`, `long`)	`0L` for `long`, `0` for others
Floating-point (`float`, `double`)	`0.0F` or `0.0D`
Reference types	`null`

If no explicit initialization is provided for a static variable, it is initialized with the default value of its type when the class is loaded. Similarly, if no initialization is provided for an instance variable, it is initialized with the default value of its type when the class is instantiated. The fields of reference types are always initialized with the `null` reference value if no initialization is provided.

Example 2.1 illustrates the default initialization of fields. Note that static variables are initialized when the class is loaded the first time, and instance variables are initialized accordingly in *every* object created from the class `Light`.

Example 2.1 *Default Values for Fields*

```
public class Light {
  // Static variable
  static int counter;      // Default value 0 when class is loaded

  // Instance variables:
  int     noOfWatts = 100; // Explicitly set to 100
  boolean indicator;       // Implicitly set to default value false
  String  location;        // Implicitly set to default value null

  public static void main(String[] args) {
    Light bulb = new Light();
    System.out.println("Static variable counter:     " + Light.counter);
    System.out.println("Instance variable noOfWatts: " + bulb.noOfWatts);
    System.out.println("Instance variable indicator: " + bulb.indicator);
    System.out.println("Instance variable location:  " + bulb.location);
  }
}
```

Output from the program:

```
Static variable counter:      0
Instance variable noOfWatts: 100
Instance variable indicator: false
Instance variable location:  null
```

Initializing Local Variables of Primitive Data Types

Local variables are variables that are declared in methods, constructors, and blocks (Chapter 3, p. 47). They are *not* initialized implicitly when they are allocated memory at method invocation—that is, when the execution of a method begins. The same applies to local variables in constructors and blocks. Local variables must be explicitly initialized before being used. The compiler will report an error only if an attempt is made to *use* an uninitialized local variable.

Example 2.2 *Flagging Uninitialized Local Variables of Primitive Data Types*

```
public class TooSmartClass {
  public static void main(String[] args) {
    int weight = 10, thePrice;                       // (1) Local variables

    if (weight <  10) thePrice = 1000;
    if (weight >  50) thePrice = 5000;
    if (weight >= 10) thePrice = weight*10;          // (2) Always executed
    System.out.println("The price is: " + thePrice);  // (3) Compile-time error!
  }
}
```

In Example 2.2, the compiler complains that the local variable `thePrice` used in the `println` statement at (3) may not be initialized. However, at runtime, the local variable `thePrice` will get the value `100` in the last `if` statement at (2), before it is used in the `println` statement. The compiler does not perform a rigorous analysis of the program in this regard. It compiles the body of a conditional statement only if it can deduce that the condition is `true`. The program will compile correctly if the variable is initialized in the declaration, or if an unconditional assignment is made to the variable.

Replacing the declaration of the local variables at (1) in Example 2.2 with the following declaration solves the problem:

```
int weight = 10, thePrice = 0;          // (1') Both local variables initialized
```

Initializing Local Reference Variables

Local reference variables are bound by the same initialization rules as local variables of primitive data types.

Example 2.3 *Flagging Uninitialized Local Reference Variables*

```
public class VerySmartClass {
  public static void main(String[] args) {
    String importantMessage;       // Local reference variable

    System.out.println("The message length is: " +
                       importantMessage.length());  // Compile-time error!
  }
}
```

In Example 2.3, the compiler complains that the local variable `importantMessage` used in the `println` statement may not be initialized. If the variable `importantMessage` is set to the value `null`, the program will compile. However, a runtime error (`NullPointerException`) will occur when the code is executed, because the variable `importantMessage` will not denote any object. The golden rule is to ensure that a reference variable, whether local or not, is assigned a reference value denoting an object before it is used—that is, to ensure that it does not have the value `null`.

The program compiles and runs if we replace the declaration with the following declaration of the local variable, which creates a string literal and assigns its reference value to the local reference variable `importantMessage`:

```
String importantMessage = "Initialize before use!";
```

Arrays and their default values are discussed in §3.4, p. 58.

Lifetime of Variables

The lifetime of a variable—that is, the time a variable is accessible during execution—is determined by the context in which it is declared. The lifetime of a variable, which is also called its *scope*, is discussed in more detail in §4.4, p. 114. We distinguish among the lifetimes of variables in three contexts:

- *Instance variables*—members of a class, which are created for each object of the class. In other words, every object of the class will have its own copies of these variables, which are local to the object. The values of these variables at any given time constitute the *state* of the object. Instance variables exist as long as the object they belong to is in use at runtime.

- *Static variables*—members of a class, but which are not created for any specific object of the class and, therefore, belong only to the class (§4.4, p. 114). They are created when the class is loaded at runtime, and exist as long as the class is available at runtime.

- *Local variables* (also called *method automatic variables*)—declared in methods, constructors, and blocks; and created for each execution of the method, constructor, or block. After the execution of the method, constructor, or block completes, local (non-`final`) variables are no longer accessible.

Review Questions

2.8 Which of the following declarations are valid?

Select the three correct answers.

(a) `char a = '\u0061';`
(b) `char 'a' = 'a';`
(c) `char \u0061 = 'a';`
(d) `ch\u0061r a = 'a';`
(e) `ch'a'r a = 'a';`

2.9 Given the following code within a method, which statement is true?

```
int i, j;
j = 5;
```

Select the one correct answer.

(a) Local variable `i` is not declared.
(b) Local variable `j` is not declared.
(c) Local variable `i` is declared but not initialized.
(d) Local variable `j` is declared but not initialized.
(e) Local variable `j` is initialized but not declared.

2.10 In which of these variable declarations will the variable remain uninitialized unless it is explicitly initialized?

Select the one correct answer.

(a) Declaration of an instance variable of type `int`
(b) Declaration of a static variable of type `float`
(c) Declaration of a local variable of type `float`
(d) Declaration of a static variable of type `Object`
(e) Declaration of an instance variable of type `int[]`

2.11 What will be the result of compiling and running the following program?

```
public class Init {

  String title;
  boolean published;

  static int total;
  static double maxPrice;

  public static void main(String[] args) {
    Init initMe = new Init();
    double price;
    if (true)
      price = 100.00;
```

```
    System.out.println("|" + initMe.title + "|" + initMe.published + "|" +
                       Init.total + "|" + Init.maxPrice + "|" + price + "|");
  }
}
```

Select the one correct answer.

(a) The program will fail to compile.
(b) The program will compile, and print `|null|false|0|0.0|0.0|` at runtime.
(c) The program will compile, and print `|null|true|0|0.0|100.0|` at runtime.
(d) The program will compile, and print `| |false|0|0.0|0.0|` at runtime.
(e) The program will compile, and print `|null|false|0|0.0|100.0|` at runtime.

Chapter Summary

The following topics were covered in this chapter:

- Basic language elements: identifiers, keywords, separators, literals, whitespace, and comments
- Primitive data types: integral, floating-point, and boolean
- Notational representation of numbers in decimal, binary, octal, and hexadecimal systems
- Declaration and initialization of variables, including reference variables
- Usage of default values for instance variables and static variables
- Lifetime of instance variables, static variables, and local variables

Programming Exercise

2.1 The following program has several errors. Modify the program so that it will compile and run without errors.

```
// File: Temperature.java
PUBLIC CLASS temperature {
  PUBLIC void main(string args) {
    double fahrenheit = 62.5;
    */ Convert /*
    double celsius = f2c(fahrenheit);
    System.out.println(fahrenheit + 'F' + " = " + Celsius + 'C');
  }

  double f2c(float fahr) {
    RETURN (fahr - 32.0) * 5.0 / 9.0;
  }
}
```

Declarations

3

Programmer I Exam Objectives	
[1.2] Define the structure of a Java class	§3.1, p. 48
[4.1] Declare, instantiate, initialize, and use a one-dimensional array	§3.4, p. 58
[4.2] Declare, instantiate, initialize, and use multi-dimensional array	§3.4, p. 64
[6.1] Create methods with arguments and return values; including overloaded methods ○ *For return statement, see §6.4, p. 224.* ○ *For covariant return, see §7.2, p. 273.* ○ *For overloaded method resolution, see §7.10, p. 316.* ○ *For overriding methods, see §7.2, p. 268.*	§3.2, p. 49 §3.5, p. 72
[6.3] Create and overload constructors; including impact on default constructors ○ *For constructor chaining, see §7.5, p. 282.*	§3.3, p. 53
[6.6] Determine the effect upon object references and primitive values when they are passed into methods that change the values ○ *For conversions in assignment and method invocation contexts, see §5.2, p. 147.*	§3.5, p. 72
[7.4] Use super and this to access objects and constructors ○ *For the* `super` *reference, see §7.4, p. 276.* ○ *For using* `this()` *and* `super()`*, see §7.5, p. 282.*	§3.2, p. 50
Supplementary Objectives	
• Sorting and searching arrays	§3.4, p. 68 §3.4, p. 69
• Declaring and calling methods with a variable arity parameter	§3.6, p. 81
• Passing values to a Java application as program arguments on the command line	§3.7, p. 85
• Basic introduction to declaring and using enum types	§3.8, p. 87

3.1 Class Declarations

A class declaration introduces a new reference type. For the purpose of this book, we will use the following simplified syntax of a class declaration:

```
class_modifiers class class_name
                      extends_clause
                      implements_clause // Class header
{ // Class body
    field_declarations
    method_declarations
    constructor_declarations
}
```

In the class header, the name of the class is preceded by the keyword `class`. In addition, the class header can specify the following information:

- An *accessibility modifier* (§4.5, p. 118)
- Additional *class modifiers* (§4.6, p. 120)
- Any class it *extends* (§7.1, p. 264)
- Any interfaces it *implements* (§7.6, p. 290)

The class body, enclosed in braces (`{}`), can contain *member declarations*. In this book, we discuss the following two kinds of member declarations:

- *Field declarations* (§2.3, p. 40)
- *Method declarations* (§3.2, p. 49)

Members declared `static` belong to the class and are called *static members*. Non-static members belong to the objects of the class and are called *instance members*. In addition, the following declarations can be included in a class body:

- *Constructor declarations* (§3.3, p. 53)

The declarations can appear in any order in the class body. The only mandatory parts of the class declaration syntax are the keyword `class`, the class name, and the class body braces (`{}`), as exemplified by the following class declaration:

```
class X { }
```

To understand which code can be legally declared in a class, we distinguish between *static context* and *non-static context*. A static context is defined by static methods, static field initializers, and static initializer blocks. A non-static context is defined by instance methods, non-static field initializers, instance initializer blocks, and constructors. By *static code*, we mean expressions and statements in a static context; by *non-static code*, we mean expressions and statements in a non-static context. One crucial difference between the two contexts is that static code can refer only to other static members.

3.2 Method Declarations

For the purpose of this book, we will use the following simplified syntax of a method declaration:

method_modifiers return_type method_name
    (formal_parameter_list) throws_clause // Method header
{ // Method body
    local_variable_declarations
    statements
}

In addition to the name of the method, the method header can specify the following information:

- Scope or *accessibility modifier* (§4.7, p. 123)
- Additional *method modifiers* (§4.8, p. 131)
- The *type* of the *return value*, or `void` if the method does not return any value (§6.4, p. 224)
- A *formal parameter list*
- Any *exceptions* thrown by the method, which are specified in a `throws` clause (§6.9, p. 251)

The *formal parameter list* is a comma-separated list of parameters for passing information to the method when the method is invoked by a *method call* (§3.5, p. 72). An empty parameter list must be specified by `( )`. Each parameter is a simple variable declaration consisting of its type and name:

optional_parameter_modifier type parameter_name

The parameter names are local to the method (§4.4, p. 117). The *optional parameter modifier* `final` is discussed in §3.5, p. 80. It is recommended to use the `@param` tag in a Javadoc comment to document the formal parameters of a method.

The *signature* of a method comprises the name of the method and the types of the formal parameters only.

The method body is a *block* containing the *local variable declarations* (§2.3, p. 40) and the *statements* of the method.

The mandatory parts of a method declaration are the return type, the method name, and the method body braces (`{}`), as exemplified by the following method declaration:

```
void noAction() {}
```

Like member variables, member methods can be characterized as one of two types:

- *Instance methods*, which are discussed later in this section
- *Static methods*, which are discussed in §4.8, p. 132

Statements

Statements in Java can be grouped into various categories. Variable declarations with explicit initialization of the variables are called *declaration statements* (§2.3, p. 40, and §3.4, p. 60). Other basic forms of statements are *control flow statements* (§6.1, p. 200) and *expression statements*.

An *expression statement* is an expression terminated by a semicolon. Any value returned by the expression is discarded. Only certain types of expressions have meaning as statements:

- Assignments (§5.6, p. 158)
- Increment and decrement operators (§5.9, p. 176)
- Method calls (§3.5, p. 72)
- Object creation expressions with the `new` operator (§5.17, p. 195)

A solitary semicolon denotes the *empty statement*, which does nothing.

A block, `{}`, is a *compound* statement that can be used to group zero or more local declarations and statements (§4.4, p. 117). Blocks can be nested, since a block is a statement that can contain other statements. A block can be used in any context where a simple statement is permitted. The compound statement that is embodied in a block begins at the left brace, `{`, and ends with a matching right brace, `}`. Such a block must not be confused with an array initializer in declaration statements (§3.4, p. 60).

Labeled statements are discussed in §6.4 on page 220.

Instance Methods and the Object Reference `this`

Instance methods belong to every object of the class and can be invoked only on objects. All members defined in the class, both static and non-static, are accessible in the context of an instance method. The reason is that all instance methods are passed an implicit reference to the *current object*—that is, the object on which the method is being invoked. The current object can be referenced in the body of the instance method by the keyword `this`. In the body of the method, the `this` reference can be used like any other object reference to access members of the object. In fact, the keyword `this` can be used in any non-static context. The `this` reference can be used as a normal reference to reference the current object, but the reference cannot be modified—it is a `final` reference (§4.8, p. 133).

The `this` reference to the current object is useful in situations where a local variable hides, or *shadows*, a field with the same name. In Example 3.1, the two parameters `noOfWatts` and `indicator` in the constructor of the `Light` class have the same names as the fields in the class. The example also declares a local variable `location`, which has the same name as one of the fields. The reference `this` can be used to distinguish the fields from the local variables. At (1), the `this` reference is used to identify the field `noOfWatts`, which is assigned the value of the parameter `noOfWatts`. Without the `this` reference at (2), the value of the parameter `indicator` is assigned back to this parameter, and not to the field by the same name, resulting in a logical error. Similarly at (3), without the `this` reference, it is the local variable `location` that is assigned the value of the parameter `site`, and not the field with the same name.

Example 3.1 *Using the* `this` *Reference*

```
public class Light {
  // Fields:
  int     noOfWatts;        // Wattage
  boolean indicator;        // On or off
  String  location;         // Placement

  // Constructor
  public Light(int noOfWatts, boolean indicator, String site) {
    String location;

    this.noOfWatts = noOfWatts;   // (1) Assignment to field
    indicator = indicator;        // (2) Assignment to parameter
    location = site;              // (3) Assignment to local variable
    this.superfluous();           // (4)
    superfluous();                // equivalent to call at (4)
  }

  public void superfluous() {
    System.out.printf("Current object: %s%n", this); // (5)
  }

  public static void main(String[] args) {
    Light light = new Light(100, true, "loft");
    System.out.println("No. of watts: " + light.noOfWatts);
    System.out.println("Indicator:    " + light.indicator);
    System.out.println("Location:     " + light.location);
  }
}
```

Probable output from the program:

```
Current object: Light@1bc4459
Current object: Light@1bc4459
No. of watts: 100
Indicator:    false
Location:     null
```

If a member is not shadowed by a local declaration, the simple name `member` is considered a short-hand notation for `this.member`. In particular, the `this` reference can be used explicitly to invoke other methods in the class. This usage is illustrated at (4) in Example 3.1, where the method `superfluous()` is called.

If, for some reason, a method needs to pass the current object to another method, it can do so using the `this` reference. This approach is illustrated at (5) in Example 3.1, where the current object is passed to the `printf()` method. The `printf()` method prints the string representation of the current object (which comprises the name of the class of the current object and the hexadecimal representation of the current object's hash code). (The *hash code* of an object is an `int` value that can be used to store and retrieve the object from special data structures called *hash tables*.)

Note that the `this` reference cannot be used in a static context, as static code is not executed in the context of any object.

Method Overloading

Each method has a *signature*, which comprises the name of the method plus the types and order of the parameters in the formal parameter list. Several method implementations may have the same name, as long as the method signatures differ. This practice is called *method overloading*. Because overloaded methods have the same name, their parameter lists must be different.

Rather than inventing new method names, method overloading can be used when the same logical operation requires multiple implementations. The Java SE platform API makes heavy use of method overloading. For example, the class `java.lang.Math` contains an overloaded method `min()`, which returns the minimum of two numeric values.

```
public static double min(double a, double b)
public static float min(float a, float b)
public static int min(int a, int b)
public static long min(long a, long b)
```

In the following examples, five implementations of the method `methodA` are shown:

```
void methodA(int a, double b) { /* ... */ }      // (1)
int  methodA(int a)           { return a; }       // (2)
int  methodA()                { return 1; }       // (3)
long methodA(double a, int b) { return b; }       // (4)
long methodA(int x, double y) { return x; }       // (5) Not OK.
```

The corresponding signatures of the five methods are as follows:

`methodA(int, double)`	1'
`methodA(int)`	2': Number of parameters
`methodA()`	3': Number of parameters
`methodA(double, int)`	4': Order of parameters
`methodA(int, double)`	5': Same as 1'

The first four implementations of the method named `methodA` are overloaded correctly, each time with a different parameter list and, therefore, different signatures. The declaration at (5) has the same signature `methodA(int, double)` as the declaration at (1) and, therefore, is not a valid overloading of this method.

```
void bake(Cake k)  { /* ... */ }                 // (1)
void bake(Pizza p) { /* ... */ }                 // (2)

int    halfIt(int a) { return a/2; }             // (3)
double halfIt(int a) { return a/2.0; }           // (4) Not OK. Same signature.
```

The method named bake is correctly overloaded at (1) and (2), with two different parameter lists. In the implementation, changing just the return type (as shown at (3) and (4) in the preceding example), is not enough to overload a method, and will be flagged as a compile-time error. The parameter list in the declarations must be different.

Only methods declared in the same class and those that are inherited by the class can be overloaded. Overloaded methods should be considered to be individual methods that just happen to have the same name. Methods with the same name are allowed, since methods are identified by their signature. At compile time, the right implementation of an overloaded method is chosen, based on the signature of the method call. Details of method overloading resolution can be found in §7.10 on page 316. Method overloading should not be confused with *method overriding* (§7.2, p. 268).

3.3 Constructors

The main purpose of constructors is to set the initial state of an object, when the object is created by using the new operator.

For the purpose of this book, we will use the following simplified syntax of a constructor:

```
accessibility_modifier class_name (formal_parameter_list)
                                  throws_clause // Constructor header
{ // Constructor body
    local_variable_declarations
    statements
}
```

Constructor declarations are very much like method declarations. However, the following restrictions on constructors should be noted:

- Modifiers other than an accessibility modifier are not permitted in the constructor header. For accessibility modifiers for constructors, see §4.7, p. 123.
- Constructors cannot return a value and, therefore, do not specify a return type, not even void, in the constructor header. But their declaration can use the return statement that does not return a value in the constructor body (§6.4, p. 224).
- The constructor name must be the same as the class name.

Class names and method names exist in different *namespaces*. Thus, there are no name conflicts in Example 3.2, where a method declared at (2) has the same name as the constructor declared at (1). A method must always specify a return type, whereas a constructor does not. However, using such naming schemes is strongly discouraged.

A constructor that has no parameters, like the one at (1) in Example 3.2, is called a *no-argument constructor*.

Example 3.2 *Namespaces*

```
public class Name {

  Name() {                      // (1) No-argument constructor
    System.out.println("Constructor");
  }

  void Name() {                 // (2) Instance method
    System.out.println("Method");
  }

  public static void main(String[] args) {
    new Name().Name();          // (3) Constructor call followed by method call
  }
}
```

Output from the program:

```
Constructor
Method
```

The Default Constructor

If a class does not specify *any* constructors, then a *default constructor* is generated for the class by the compiler. The default constructor is equivalent to the following implementation:

```
class_name() { super(); }   // No parameters. Calls superclass constructor.
```

A default constructor is a no-argument constructor. The only action taken by the default constructor is to call the superclass constructor. This ensures that the inherited state of the object is initialized properly (§7.5, p. 282). In addition, all instance variables in the object are set to the default value of their type, barring those that are initialized by an initialization expression in their declaration.

In the following code, the class `Light` does not specify any constructors:

```
class Light {
  // Fields:
  int     noOfWatts;       // Wattage
  boolean indicator;       // On or off
  String  location;        // Placement

  // No constructors
  //...
}

class Greenhouse {
  // ...
  Light oneLight = new Light();     // (1) Call to default constructor
}
```

In this code, the following default constructor is called when a `Light` object is created by the object creation expression at (1):

```
Light() { super(); }
```

Creating an object using the `new` operator with the default constructor, as at (1), will initialize the fields of the object to their default values (that is, the fields `noOfWatts`, `indicator`, and `location` in a `Light` object will be initialized to `0`, `false`, and `null`, respectively).

A class can choose to provide its own constructors, rather than relying on the default constructor. In the following example, the class `Light` provides a no-argument constructor at (1).

```
class Light {
  // ...
  Light() {                                  // (1) No-argument constructor
    noOfWatts = 50;
    indicator = true;
    location  = "X";
  }
  //...
}

class Greenhouse {
  // ...
  Light extraLight = new Light();    // (2) Call of explicit default constructor
}
```

The no-argument constructor ensures that any object created with the object creation expression `new Light()`, as at (2), will have its fields `noOfWatts`, `indicator`, and `location` initialized to `50`, `true`, and `"X"`, respectively.

If a class defines *any* constructor, it can no longer rely on the default constructor to set the state of its objects. If such a class requires a no-argument constructor, it must provide its own implementation, as in the preceding example. In the next example the class `Light` does not provide a no-argument constructor, but rather includes a non-zero argument constructor at (1). It is called at (2) when an object of the class `Light` is created with the `new` operator. Any attempt to call the default constructor will be flagged as a compile-time error, as shown at (3).

```
class Light {
  // ...
  // Only non-zero argument constructor:
  Light(int noOfWatts, boolean indicator, String location) {          // (1)
    this.noOfWatts = noOfWatts;
    this.indicator = indicator;
    this.location  = location;
  }
  //...
}

class Greenhouse {
  // ...
  Light moreLight  = new Light(100, true, "Greenhouse");// (2) OK
  Light firstLight = new Light();                           // (3) Compile-time error
}
```

Overloaded Constructors

Like methods, constructors can be overloaded. Since the constructors in a class all have the same name as the class, their signatures are differentiated by their parameter lists. In the following example, the class `Light` now provides explicit implementation of the no-argument constructor at (1) and that of a non-zero argument constructor at (2). The constructors are overloaded, as is evident by their signatures. The non-zero argument constructor at (2) is called when an object of the class `Light` is created at (3), and the no-argument constructor is likewise called at (4). Overloading of constructors allows appropriate initialization of objects on creation, depending on the constructor invoked (see chaining of constructors in §7.5, p. 282). It is recommended to use the `@param` tag in a Javadoc comment to document the formal parameters of a constructor.

```
class Light {
  // ...
  // No-argument constructor:
  Light() {                                                    // (1)
    noOfWatts = 50;
    indicator = true;
    location  = "X";
  }

  // Non-zero argument constructor:
  Light(int noOfWatts, boolean indicator, String location) { // (2)
    this.noOfWatts = noOfWatts;
    this.indicator = indicator;
    this.location  = location;
  }
  //...
}
class Greenhouse {
  // ...
  Light moreLight  = new Light(100, true, "Greenhouse");      // (3) OK
  Light firstLight = new Light();                              // (4) OK
}
```

Review Questions

3.1 Which one of these declarations is a valid method declaration?

Select the one correct answer.

(a) `void method1          { /* ... */ }`
(b) `void method2()        { /* ... */ }`
(c) `void method3(void)    { /* ... */ }`
(d) `method4()             { /* ... */ }`
(e) `method5(void)         { /* ... */ }`

3.2 Which statements, when inserted at (1), will not result in compile-time errors?

```
public class ThisUsage {
  int planets;
  static int suns;

  public void gaze() {
    int i;
    // (1) INSERT STATEMENT HERE
  }
}
```

Select the three correct answers.

(a) `i = this.planets;`
(b) `i = this.suns;`
(c) `this = new ThisUsage();`
(d) `this.i = 4;`
(e) `this.suns = planets;`

3.3 Given the following pairs of method declarations, which statements are true?

```
void fly(int distance) {}
int  fly(int time, int speed) { return time*speed; }

void fall(int time) {}
int  fall(int distance) { return distance; }

void glide(int time) {}
void Glide(int time) {}
```

Select the two correct answers.

(a) The first pair of methods will compile, and overload the method name `fly`.
(b) The second pair of methods will compile, and overload the method name `fall`.
(c) The third pair of methods will compile, and overload the method name `glide`.
(d) The first pair of methods will not compile.
(e) The second pair of methods will not compile.
(f) The third pair of methods will not compile.

3.4 Given a class named `Book`, which one of these constructor declarations is valid for the class `Book`?

Select the one correct answer.

(a) `Book(Book b) {}`
(b) `Book Book() {}`
(c) `private final Book() {}`
(d) `void Book() {}`
(e) `public static void Book(String[] args) {}`
(f) `abstract Book() {}`

3.5 Which statements are true?

Select the two correct answers.

(a) A class must define a constructor.
(b) A constructor can be declared `private`.
(c) A constructor can return a value.
(d) A constructor must initialize all fields when a class is instantiated.
(e) A constructor can access the non-static members of a class.

3.6 What will be the result of compiling the following program?

```
public class MyClass {
  long var;

  public void MyClass(long param) { var = param; } // (1)

  public static void main(String[] args) {
    MyClass a, b;
    a = new MyClass();                              // (2)
    b = new MyClass(5);                             // (3)
  }
}
```

Select the one correct answer.

(a) A compile-time error will occur at (1).
(b) A compile-time error will occur at (2).
(c) A compile-time error will occur at (3).
(d) The program will compile without errors.

3.4 Arrays

An *array* is a data structure that defines an indexed collection of a fixed number of homogeneous data elements. This means that all elements in the array have the same data type. A position in the array is indicated by a non-negative integer value called the *index*. An element at a given position in the array is accessed using the index. The size of an array is fixed and cannot be changed after the array has been created.

In Java, arrays are objects. Arrays can be of primitive data types or reference types. In the former case, all elements in the array are of a specific primitive data type. In the latter case, all elements are references of a specific reference type. References in the array can then denote objects of this reference type or its subtypes. Each array object has a `public final` field called `length`, which specifies the array size (i.e., the number of elements the array can accommodate). The first element is always at index 0 and the last element at index $n - 1$, where n is the value of the `length` field in the array.

Simple arrays are *one-dimensional arrays*—that is, a simple list of values. Since arrays can store reference values, the objects referenced can also be array objects. Thus, multidimensional arrays are implemented as *array of arrays*.

Passing array references as parameters is discussed in §3.5, p. 72. Type conversions for array references on assignment and on method invocation are discussed in §7.7, p. 309.

Declaring Array Variables

A one-dimensional array variable declaration has either of the following syntaxes:

element_type`[]` *array_name*`;`

or

element_type array_name`[];`

where *element_type* can be a primitive data type or a reference type. The array variable *array_name* has the type *element_type*`[]`. Note that the array size is not specified. As a consequence, the array variable *array_name* can be assigned the reference value of an array of any length, as long as its elements have *element_type.*

It is important to understand that the declaration does not actually create an array. Instead, it simply declares a *reference* that can refer to an array object. The `[]` notation can also be specified after a variable name to declare it as an array variable, but then it applies to just that variable.

```
int anIntArray[], oneInteger;
Pizza[] mediumPizzas, largePizzas;
```

These two declarations declare `anIntArray` and `mediumPizzas` to be reference variables that can refer to arrays of `int` values and arrays of `Pizza` objects, respectively. The variable `largePizzas` can denote an array of `Pizza` objects, but the variable `oneInteger` cannot denote an array of `int` values—it is a simple variable of the type `int`.

An array variable that is declared as a field in a class, but is not explicitly initialized to any array, will be initialized to the default reference value `null`. This default initialization does *not* apply to *local* reference variables and, therefore, does not apply to local array variables either (§2.4, p. 42). This behavior should not be confused with initialization of the elements of an array during array construction.

Constructing an Array

An array can be constructed for a fixed number of elements of a specific type, using the `new` operator. The reference value of the resulting array can be assigned to an array variable of the corresponding type. The syntax of the *array creation expression* is shown on the right-hand side of the following assignment statement:

array_name `= new` *element_type*`[`*array_size*`];`

The minimum value of *array_size* is 0; in other words zero-length arrays can be constructed in Java. If the array size is negative, a `NegativeArraySizeException` is thrown at runtime.

Given the declarations

```
int anIntArray[], oneInteger;
Pizza[] mediumPizzas, largePizzas;
```

the three arrays in the declarations can be constructed as follows:

```
anIntArray   = new int[10];        // array for 10 integers
mediumPizzas = new Pizza[5];       // array of 5 pizzas
largePizzas  = new Pizza[3];       // array of 3 pizzas
```

The array declaration and construction can be combined.

element_type$_1$`[]` *array_name* `= new` *element_type*$_2$`[`*array_size*`];`

In the preceding syntax, the array type *element_type*$_2$`[]` must be *assignable* to the array type *element_type*$_1$`[]` (§7.7, p. 309). When the array is constructed, all of its elements are initialized to the default value for *element_type*$_2$. This is true for both member and local arrays when they are constructed.

In the next examples, the code constructs the array, and the array elements are implicitly initialized to their default values. For example, all elements of the array `anIntArray` get the value `0`, and all elements of the array `mediumPizzas` get the value `null` when the arrays are constructed.

```
int[] anIntArray = new int[10];              // Default element value: 0
Pizza[] mediumPizzas = new Pizza[5];         // Default element value: null
```

The value of the field `length` in each array is set to the number of elements specified during the construction of the array; for example, `mediumPizzas.length` has the value `5`.

Once an array has been constructed, its elements can also be explicitly initialized individually—for example, in a loop. The examples in the rest of this section make use of a loop to traverse the elements of an array for various purposes.

Initializing an Array

Java provides the means of declaring, constructing, and explicitly initializing an array in one declaration statement:

element_type`[]` *array_name* `= {` *array_initialize_list* `};`

This form of initialization applies to fields as well as to local arrays. The *array_initialize_list* is a comma-separated list of zero or more expressions. Such an array initializer results in the construction and initialization of the array.

```
int[] anIntArray = {13, 49, 267, 15, 215};
```

In this declaration statement, the variable `anIntArray` is declared as a reference to an array of `int`s. The array initializer results in the construction of an array to hold five elements (equal to the length of the list of expressions in the block), where the first element is initialized to the value of the first expression (13), the second element to the value of the second expression (49), and so on.

```
Pizza[] pizzaOrder = { new Pizza(), new Pizza(), null };
```

In this declaration statement, the variable `pizzaOrder` is declared as a reference to an array of `Pizza` objects. The array initializer constructs an array to hold three elements. The initialization code sets the first two elements of the array to refer to two `Pizza` objects, while the last element is initialized to the `null` reference. The reference value of the array of `Pizza` objects is assigned to the reference `pizzaOrder`. Note also that this declaration statement actually creates *three* objects: the array object with three references and the two `Pizza` objects.

The expressions in the *array_initialize_list* are evaluated from left to right, and the array name obviously cannot occur in any of the expressions in the list. In the preceding examples, the *array_initialize_list* is terminated by the right brace, `}`, of the block. The list can also be legally terminated by a comma. The following array has length 2, and not 3:

```
Topping[] pizzaToppings = { new Topping("cheese"), new Topping("tomato"), };
```

The declaration statement at (1) in the following code defines an array of four `String` objects, while the declaration statement at (2) shows that a `String` object is not the same as an array of `char`.

```
// Array with 4 String objects:
String[] pets = {"crocodiles", "elephants", "crocophants", "elediles"}; // (1)

// Array of 3 characters:
char[] charArray = {'a', 'h', 'a'};    // (2) Not the same as "aha"
```

Using an Array

The array object is referenced by the array name, but individual array elements are accessed by specifying an index with the `[]` operator. The array element access expression has the following syntax:

array_name `[`*index_expression*`]`

Each individual element is treated as a simple variable of the element type. The *index* is specified by the *index_expression*, whose value should be promotable to an `int` value; otherwise, a compile-time error is flagged. Since the lower bound of an array index is always `0`, the upper bound is 1 less than the array size—that is, *array_name*`.length-1`. The `i`th element in the array has index `(i-1)`. At runtime, the index value is automatically checked to ensure that it is within the array index bounds. If the index value is less than `0`, or greater than or equal to *array_name*`.length`, an `ArrayIndexOutOfBoundsException` is thrown. A program can either check the index explicitly or catch the runtime exception (§6.5, p. 230), but an illegal index is typically an indication of a programming error.

In the array element access expression, the *array_name* can be any expression that returns a reference to an array. For example, the expression on the right-hand side of the following assignment statement returns the character 'H' at index 1 in the character array returned by a call to the toCharArray() method of the String class:

```
char letter = "AHA".toCharArray()[1];      // 'H'
```

The array operator [] is used to declare array types (Topping[]), specify the array size (new Topping[3]), and access array elements (toppings[1]). This operator is not used when the array reference is manipulated, such as in an array reference assignment (§7.9, p. 312), or when the array reference is passed as an actual parameter in a method call (§3.5, p. 77).

Example 3.3 shows traversal of arrays using for loops (§6.3, p. 215 and p. 217). A for(;;) loop at (3) in the main() method initializes the local array trialArray declared at (2) five times with pseudo-random numbers (from 0.0 to 100.0), by calling the method randomize() declared at (5). The minimum value in the array is found by calling the method findMinimum() declared at (6), and is stored in the array storeMinimum declared at (1). Both of these methods also use a for(;;) loop. The loop variable is initialized to a start value—0 in (3) and (5), and 1 in (6). The loop condition tests whether the loop variable is less than the length of the array; this guarantees that the loop will terminate when the last element has been accessed. The loop variable is incremented after each iteration to access the next element.

A for(:) loop at (4) in the main() method is used to print the minimum values from the trials, as elements are read consecutively from the array, without keeping track of an index value.

Example 3.3 *Using Arrays*

```
public class Trials {
  public static void main(String[] args) {
    // Declare and construct the local arrays:
    double[] storeMinimum = new double[5];               // (1)
    double[] trialArray = new double[15];                // (2)
    for (int i = 0; i < storeMinimum.length; ++i) {      // (3)
      // Initialize the array.
      randomize(trialArray);

      // Find and store the minimum value.
      storeMinimum[i] = findMinimum(trialArray);
    }

    // Print the minimum values:                            (4)
    for (double minValue : storeMinimum)
      System.out.printf("%.4f%n", minValue);
  }

  public static void randomize(double[] valArray) {      // (5)
    for (int i = 0; i < valArray.length; ++i)
      valArray[i] = Math.random() * 100.0;
  }
```

```
    public static double findMinimum(double[] valArray) {  // (6)
      // Assume the array has at least one element.
      double minValue = valArray[0];
      for (int i = 1; i < valArray.length; ++i)
        minValue = Math.min(minValue, valArray[i]);
      return minValue;
    }
}
```

Probable output from the program:

```
6.9330
2.7819
6.7427
18.0849
26.2462
```

Anonymous Arrays

As shown earlier in this section, the following declaration statement can be used to construct arrays using an array creation expression:

`element_type1[] array_name = new element_type2[array_size];     // (1)`

```
int[] intArray = new int[5];
```

The size of the array is specified in the array creation expression, which creates the array and initializes the array elements to their default values. By comparison, the following declaration statement both creates the array and initializes the array elements to specific values given in the array initializer:

`element_type[] array_name = { array_initialize_list };     // (2)`

```
int[] intArray = {3, 5, 2, 8, 6};
```

However, the array initializer is *not* an expression. Java has another array creation expression, called an *anonymous array*, which allows the concept of the array creation expression from (1) to be combined with the array initializer from (2), so as to create and initialize an array object:

`new element_type[] { array_initialize_list }`

```
new int[] {3, 5, 2, 8, 6}
```

This construct has enough information to create a nameless array of a specific type. Neither the name of the array nor the size of the array is specified. The construct returns the reference value of the newly created array, which can be assigned to references and passed as argument in method calls. In particular, the following declaration statements are equivalent:

```
int[] intArray = {3, 5, 2, 8, 6};                                  // (1)
int[] intArray = new int[] {3, 5, 2, 8, 6};                        // (2)
```

In (1), an array initializer is used to create and initialize the elements. In (2), an anonymous array expression is used. It is tempting to use the array initializer as an expression—for example, in an assignment statement, as a shortcut for assigning values to array elements in one go. However, this is illegal; instead, an anonymous array expression should be used. The concept of the anonymous array combines the definition and the creation of the array into one operation.

```
int[] daysInMonth;
daysInMonth = {31, 28, 31, 30, 31, 30,
               31, 31, 30, 31, 30, 31};                        // Compile-time error
daysInMonth = new int[] {31, 28, 31, 30, 31, 30, 31, 31, 30, 31, 30, 31}; // OK
```

In Example 3.4, an anonymous array is constructed at (1), and passed as an actual parameter to the static method `findMinimum()` defined at (2). Note that no array name or array size is specified for the anonymous array.

Example 3.4 *Using Anonymous Arrays*

```
public class AnonArray {
  public static void main(String[] args) {
    System.out.println("Minimum value: " +
        findMinimum(new int[] {3, 5, 2, 8, 6}));                    // (1)
  }

  public static int findMinimum(int[] dataSeq) {                     // (2)
    // Assume the array has at least one element.
    int min = dataSeq[0];
    for (int index = 1; index < dataSeq.length; ++index)
      if (dataSeq[index] < min)
        min = dataSeq[index];
    return min;
  }
}
```

Output from the program:

```
Minimum value: 2
```

Multidimensional Arrays

Since an array element can be an object reference and arrays are objects, array elements can themselves refer to other arrays. In Java, an array of arrays can be defined as follows:

element_type`[][]...[]` *array_name*;

or

element_type array_name`[][]...[]`;

In fact, the sequence of square bracket pairs, `[]`, indicating the number of dimensions, can be distributed as a postfix to both the element type and the array name. Arrays of arrays are often called *multidimensional arrays*.

The following declarations are all equivalent:

```
int[][] mXnArray;    // 2-dimensional array
int[]   mXnArray[];  // 2-dimensional array
int     mXnArray[][]; // 2-dimensional array
```

It is customary to combine the declaration with the construction of the multi-dimensional array.

```
int[][] mXnArray = new int[4][5];    // 4 x 5 matrix of ints
```

The previous declaration constructs an array `mXnArray` of four elements, where each element is an array (row) of five `int` values. The concept of rows and columns is often used to describe the dimensions of a 2-dimensional array, which is often called a *matrix*. However, such an interpretation is not dictated by the Java language.

Each row in the previous matrix is denoted by `mXnArray[i]`, where `0 ≤ i < 4`. Each element in the `i`th row, `mXnArray[i]`, is accessed by `mXnArray[i][j]`, where `0 ≤ j < 5`. The number of rows is given by `mXnArray.length`, in this case `4`, and the number of values in the `i`th row is given by `mXnArray[i].length`, in this case `5` for all the rows, where `0 ≤ i < 4`.

Multidimensional arrays can also be constructed and explicitly initialized using the array initializers discussed for simple arrays. Note that each row is an array that uses an array initializer to specify its values:

```
double[][] identityMatrix = {
  {1.0, 0.0, 0.0, 0.0 }, // 1. row
  {0.0, 1.0, 0.0, 0.0 }, // 2. row
  {0.0, 0.0, 1.0, 0.0 }, // 3. row
  {0.0, 0.0, 0.0, 1.0 }  // 4. row
}; // 4 x 4 floating-point matrix
```

Arrays in a multidimensional array need not have the same length; when they do not, they are called *ragged arrays*. The array of arrays `pizzaGalore` in the following code has five rows; the first four rows have different lengths but the fifth row is left unconstructed:

```
Pizza[][] pizzaGalore = {
  { new Pizza(), null, new Pizza() },    // 1. row is an array of 3 elements.
  { null, new Pizza()},                  // 2. row is an array of 2 elements.
  new Pizza[1],                          // 3. row is an array of 1 element.
  {},                                    // 4. row is an array of 0 elements.
  null                                   // 5. row is not constructed.
};
```

When constructing multidimensional arrays with the `new` operator, the length of the deeply nested arrays may be omitted. In such a case, these arrays are left unconstructed. For example, an array of arrays to represent a room on a floor in a hotel on a street in a city can have the type `HotelRoom[][][][]`. From left to right, the square brackets represent indices for street, hotel, floor, and room, respectively. This 4-dimensional array of arrays can be constructed piecemeal, starting with the leftmost dimension and proceeding to the rightmost successively.

```
HotelRoom[][][][] rooms = new HotelRoom[10][5][][];  // Just streets and hotels.
```

The preceding declaration constructs the array of arrays `rooms` partially with ten streets, where each street has five hotels. Floors and rooms can be added to a particular hotel on a particular street:

```
rooms[0][0]          = new HotelRoom[3][]; // 3 floors in 1st hotel on 1st street.
rooms[0][0][0]       = new HotelRoom[8];   // 8 rooms on 1st floor in this hotel.
rooms[0][0][0][0] = new HotelRoom();       // Initializes 1st room on this floor.
```

The next code snippet constructs an array of arrays `matrix`, where the first row has one element, the second row has two elements, and the third row has three elements. Note that the outer array is constructed first. The second dimension is constructed in a loop that constructs the array in each row. The elements in the multidimensional array will be implicitly initialized to the default `double` value (`0.0D`). In Figure 3.1, the array of arrays `matrix` is depicted after the elements have been explicitly initialized.

```
double[][] matrix = new double[3][];         // Number of rows.

for (int i = 0; i < matrix.length; ++i)
  matrix[i] = new double[i + 1];             // Construct a row.
```

Two other ways of initializing such an array of arrays are shown next. The first approach uses array initializers, and the second uses an anonymous array of arrays.

```
double[][] matrix2 = {     // Using array initializers.
  {0.0},                   // 1. row
  {0.0, 0.0},              // 2. row
  {0.0, 0.0, 0.0}          // 3. row
};

double[][] matrix3 = new double[][] { // Using an anonymous array of arrays.
  {0.0},                   // 1. row
  {0.0, 0.0},              // 2. row
  {0.0, 0.0, 0.0}          // 3. row
};
```

The type of the variable `matrix` is `double[][]`, a two-dimensional array of `double` values. The type of the variable `matrix[i]` (where $0 \le$ `i`< `matrix.length`) is `double[]`, a one-dimensional array of `double` values. The type of the variable `matrix[i][j]` (where $0 \le$ `i`< `matrix.length` and $0 \le$ `j`< `matrix[i].length`) is `double`, a simple variable of type `double`.

Nested loops are a natural match for manipulating multidimensional arrays. In Example 3.5, a rectangular 4×3 `int` matrix is declared and constructed at (1). The program finds the minimum value in the matrix. The outer loop at (2) traverses the rows (`mXnArray[i]`, where $0 \le$ `i`< `mXnArray.length`), and the inner loop at (3) traverses the elements in each row in turn (`mXnArray[i][j]`, where $0 \le$ `j`< `mXnArray[i].length`). The outer loop is executed `mXnArray.length` times, or 4 times, and the inner loop is

Figure 3.1 *Array of Arrays*

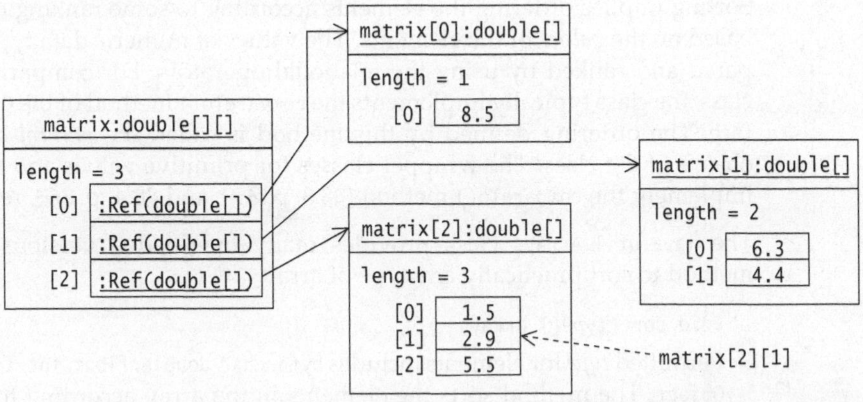

executed (`mXnArray.length`) × (`mXnArray[i].length`), or 12 times, since all rows have the same length 3.

The `for(:)` loop also provides a safe and convenient way of traversing an array. Several examples of its use are provided in §6.3, p. 217.

Example 3.5 *Using Multidimensional Arrays*

```
public class MultiArrays {

  public static void main(String[] args) {
    // Declare and construct the M X N matrix.
    int[][] mXnArray = {                                  // (1)
        {16,  7, 12}, // 1. row
        { 9, 20, 18}, // 2. row
        {14, 11,  5}, // 3. row
        { 8,  5, 10}  // 4. row
    }; // 4 x 3 int matrix

    // Find the minimum value in a M X N matrix:
    int min = mXnArray[0][0];
    for (int i = 0; i < mXnArray.length; ++i)             // (2)
      // Find min in mXnArray[i], in the row given by index i:
      for (int j = 0; j < mXnArray[i].length; ++j)        // (3)
        min = Math.min(min, mXnArray[i][j]);

    System.out.println("Minimum value: " + min);
  }
}
```

Output from the program:

```
Minimum value: 5
```

Sorting Arrays

Sorting implies ordering the elements according to some ranking criteria, usually based on the *values* of the elements. The values of numeric data types can be compared and ranked by using the relational operators. For comparing objects of a class, the class typically implements the `compareTo()` method of the `Comparable` interface. The ordering defined by this method is called the *natural ordering* for the objects of the class. The wrapper classes for primitive values and the `String` class implement the `compareTo()` method (§8.3, p. 350, and §8.4, p. 363, respectively).

The `java.util.Arrays` class provides many overloaded versions of the `sort()` method to sort practically any type of array.

> `void sort(`*`type`*`[] array)`
>
> Permitted *type* for elements includes `byte`, `char`, `double`, `float`, `int`, `long`, `short`, and `Object`. The method sorts the elements in the array according to their *natural ordering*. In the case of an array of objects being passed as argument, the *objects* must be *mutually comparable*; that is, it should be possible to compare any two objects in the array according to the natural ordering defined by the `compareTo()` method of the `Comparable` interface.

An appropriate `import` statement should be included in the source code to access the `java.util.Arrays` class. In the next code snippet, an array of strings is sorted according to natural ordering for strings—that is, based on the Unicode values of the characters in the strings:

```
String[] strArray =  {"biggest", "big", "bigger", "Bigfoot"};
Arrays.sort(strArray);    // Natural ordering: [Bigfoot, big, bigger, biggest]
```

The next examples illustrate sorting an array of primitive values (`int`) at (1), and an array of type `Object` containing mutually comparable elements (`String`) at (2). In (3), the numerical values are autoboxed into their corresponding wrapper classes (§8.3, p. 346), but the objects of different wrapper classes and the `String` class are not mutually comparable. In (4), the numerical values are also autoboxed into their corresponding wrapper classes, but again the objects of different wrapper classes are not mutually comparable. A `ClassCastException` is thrown when the elements are not mutually comparable.

```
int[] intArray = {5, 3, 7, 1};                 // int
Arrays.sort(intArray);                         // (1) Natural ordering: [1, 3, 5, 7]

Object[] objArray1 = {"I", "am", "OK"};        // String
Arrays.sort(objArray1);                        // (2) Natural ordering: [I, OK, am]

Object[] objArray2 = {23, "ten", 3.14};        // Not mutually comparable
Arrays.sort(objArray2);                        // (3) ClassCastException

Number[] numbers = {23, 3.14, 10L};            // Not mutually comparable
Arrays.sort(numbers);                          // (4) ClassCastException
```

Searching Arrays

A common operation on an array is to search the array for a given element, called the *key*. The `java.util.Arrays` class provides overloaded versions of the `binarySearch()` method to search in practically any type of array that is *sorted*.

> `int binarySearch(`*type*`[] array, `*type*` key)`
>
> Permitted *type* for elements include `byte`, `char`, `double`, `float`, `int`, `long`, `short`, and `Object`. The array must be sorted in ascending order before calling this method, or the results are unpredictable. In the case where an array of objects is passed as argument, the *objects* must be sorted in ascending order according to their *natural ordering*, as defined by the `Comparable` interface.
>
> The method returns the index to the key in the sorted array, if the key exists. The index is then guaranteed to be greater or equal to 0. If the key is not found, a negative index is returned, corresponding to –(*insertion point* + *1*), where *insertion point* is the index of the element where the key would have been found, if it had been in the array. If there are duplicate elements equal to the key, there is no guarantee which duplicate's index will be returned. The elements and the key must be *mutually comparable*.

An appropriate `import` statement should be included in the source code to access the `java.util.Arrays` class. In the code that follows, the return value –3 indicates that the key would have been found at index 2 had it been in the list:

```
// Sorted String array (natural ordering): [Bigfoot, big, bigger, biggest]
// Search in natural ordering:
int index1 = Arrays.binarySearch(strArray, "bigger");   // Successful:    2
int index2 = Arrays.binarySearch(strArray, "bigfeet");  // Unsuccessful: -3
int index3 = Arrays.binarySearch(strArray, "bigmouth"); // Unsuccessful: -5
```

Results are unpredictable if the array is not sorted, or if the ordering used in the search is not the same as the sort ordering. Searching in the `strArray` using natural ordering when the array is sorted in reverse natural ordering gives the wrong result:

```
// Sorted String array (inverse natural ordering): [biggest, bigger, big, Bigfoot]
// Search in natural ordering:
int index4 = Arrays.binarySearch(strArray, "big");  //  -1 (INCORRECT)
```

A `ClassCastException` is thrown if the key and the elements are not mutually comparable:

```
int index5 = Arrays.binarySearch(strArray, 4); // Key: 4 => ClassCastException
```

However, this incompatibility is caught at compile time in the case of arrays with primitive values:

```
// Sorted int array (natural ordering): [1, 3, 5, 7]
int index6 = Arrays.binarySearch(intArray, 4.5);//Key: 4.5 => compile-time error!
```

The method `binarySearch()` derives its name from the divide-and-conquer algorithm that it uses to perform the search. It repeatedly divides the remaining elements to be searched into two halves and selects the half containing the key to continue the search in, until either the key is found or there are no more elements left to search.

Review Questions

3.7 Given the following declaration, which expression returns the size of the array, assuming that the `array` reference has been properly initialized?

```
int[] array;
```

Select the one correct answer.

(a) `array[].length()`
(b) `array.length()`
(c) `array[].length`
(d) `array.length`
(e) `array[].size()`
(f) `array.size()`
(g) `array[].size`
(h) `array.size`

3.8 Is it possible to create arrays of length zero?

Select the one correct answer.

(a) Yes, you can create arrays of any type with length zero.
(b) Yes, but only for primitive data types.
(c) Yes, but only for arrays of reference types.
(d) No, you cannot create zero-length arrays, but the `main()` method may be passed a zero-length array of `Strings` when no program arguments are specified.
(e) No, it is not possible to create arrays of length zero in Java.

3.9 Which one of the following array declaration statements is not legal?

Select the one correct answer.

(a) `int []a[] = new int [4][4];`
(b) `int a[][] = new int [4][4];`
(c) `int a[][] = new int [][4];`
(d) `int []a[] = new int [4][];`
(e) `int [][]a = new int [4][4];`

3.10 Which of these array declaration statements are not legal?

Select the two correct answers.

(a) `int[] i[] = { { 1, 2 }, { 1 }, {}, { 1, 2, 3 } };`
(b) `int i[] = new int[2] {1, 2};`
(c) `int i[][] = new int[][] { {1, 2, 3}, {4, 5, 6} };`
(d) `int i[][] = { { 1, 2 }, new int[ 2 ] };`
(e) `int i[4] = { 1, 2, 3, 4 };`

3.11 What would be the result of compiling and running the following program?

```
public class MyClass {
  public static void main(String[] args) {
    int size = 20;
    int[] arr = new int[ size ];

    for (int i = 0; i < size; ++i) {
      System.out.println(arr[i]);
    }
  }
}
```

Select the one correct answer.

(a) The code will not compile, because the array type `int[]` is incorrect.
(b) The program will compile, but will throw an `ArrayIndexOutOfBoundsException` when run.
(c) The program will compile and run without error, but will produce no output.
(d) The program will compile and run without error, and will print the numbers 0 through 19.
(e) The program will compile and run without error, and will print `0` twenty times.
(f) The program will compile and run without error, and will print `null` twenty times.

3.12 What would be the result of compiling and running the following program?

```
public class DefaultValuesTest {
  int[] ia = new int[1];
  boolean b;
  int i;
  Object o;

  public static void main(String[] args) {
    DefaultValuesTest instance = new DefaultValuesTest();
    instance.print();
  }

  public void print() {
    System.out.println(ia[0] + " " + b + " " + i + " " + o);
  }
}
```

Select the one correct answer.

(a) The program will fail to compile because of uninitialized variables.
(b) The program will throw a `java.lang.NullPointerException` when run.
(c) The program will print `0 false NaN null`.
(d) The program will print `0 false 0 null`.
(e) The program will print `null 0 0 null`.
(f) The program will print `null false 0 null`.

3.5 Parameter Passing

Objects communicate by calling methods on each other. A *method call* is used to invoke a method on an object. Parameters in the method call provide one way of exchanging information between the caller object and the callee object (which need not be different).

Declaring methods is discussed in §3.2, p. 49. Invoking static methods on classes is discussed in §4.8, p. 132.

The syntax of a method call can be any one of the following:

object_reference.method_name(actual_parameter_list)

class_name.static_method_name(actual_parameter_list)

method_name(actual_parameter_list)

The *object_reference* must be an expression that evaluates to a reference value denoting the object on which the method is called. If the caller and the callee are the same, *object reference* can be omitted (see the discussion of the `this` reference in §3.2, p. 50). The *class_name* can be the *fully qualified name* (§4.2, p. 97) of the class. The *actual_parameter_list* is *comma separated* if there is more than one parameter. The parentheses are mandatory even if the actual parameter list is empty. This distinguishes the method call from field access. One can specify fully qualified names for classes and packages using the dot operator (`.`).

```
objRef.doIt(time, place);            // Explicit object reference
int i = java.lang.Math.abs(-1);      // Fully qualified class name
int j = Math.abs(-1);                // Simple class name
someMethod(ofValue);                 // Object or class implicitly implied
someObjRef.make().make().make();     // make() returns a reference value
```

The dot operator (`.`) has left associativity. In the last code line, the first call of the `make()` method returns a reference value that denotes the object on which to execute the next call, and so on. This is an example of *call chaining*.

Each *actual parameter* (also called an *argument*) is an expression that is evaluated, and whose value is passed to the method when the method is invoked. Its value can vary from invocation to invocation. *Formal parameters* are parameters defined in the *method declaration* (§3.2, p. 49) and are local to the method (§2.4, p. 44).

In Java, all parameters are *passed by value*—that is, an actual parameter is evaluated and its value is assigned to the corresponding formal parameter. Table 3.1 summarizes the value that is passed depending on the type of the parameters. In the case of primitive data types, the data value of the actual parameter is passed. If the actual parameter is a reference to an object, the reference value of the denoted object is passed and not the object itself. Analogously, if the actual parameter is an array element of a primitive data type, its data value is passed, and if the array element is a reference to an object, then its reference value is passed.

Table 3.1 *Parameter Passing by Value*

Data type of the formal parameter	Value passed
Primitive data type	Primitive data value of the actual parameter
Reference type (i.e., class, interface, array, or enum type)	Reference value of the actual parameter

It should also be stressed that each invocation of a method has its own copies of the formal parameters, as is the case for any local variables in the method (§6.5, p. 230).

The order of evaluation in the actual parameter list is always *from left to right*. The evaluation of an actual parameter can be influenced by an earlier evaluation of an actual parameter. Given the following declaration:

```
int i = 4;
```

the method call

```
leftRight(i++, i);
```

is effectively the same as

```
leftRight(4, 5);
```

and not the same as

```
leftRight(4, 4);
```

An overview of the conversions that can take place in a method invocation context is provided in §5.2, p. 148. Method invocation conversions for primitive values are discussed in the next subsection (p. 73), and those for reference types are discussed in §7.10, p. 315. Calling variable arity methods is discussed in §3.6, p. 81.

For the sake of simplicity, the examples in subsequent sections primarily show method invocation on the same object or the same class. The parameter passing mechanism is no different when different objects or classes are involved.

Passing Primitive Data Values

An actual parameter is an expression that is evaluated first, with the resulting value then being assigned to the corresponding formal parameter at method invocation. The use of this value in the method has no influence on the actual parameter. In particular, when the actual parameter is a variable of a primitive data type, the value of the variable is copied to the formal parameter at method invocation. Since formal parameters are local to the method, any changes made to the formal parameter will not be reflected in the actual parameter after the call completes.

Legal type conversions between actual parameters and formal parameters of *primitive data types* are summarized here from Table 5.1, p. 147:

- Widening primitive conversion
- Unboxing conversion, followed by an optional widening primitive conversion

These conversions are illustrated by invoking the following method

```
static void doIt(long i) { /* ... */ }
```

with the following code:

```
Integer intRef = 34;
Long longRef = 34L;
doIt(34);         // (1) Primitive widening conversion: long <-- int
doIt(longRef);    // (2) Unboxing: long <-- Long
doIt(intRef);     // (3) Unboxing, followed by primitive widening conversion:
                  //     long <-- int <-- Integer
```

However, for parameter passing, there are no implicit narrowing conversions for integer constant expressions (§5.2, p. 148).

Example 3.6 *Passing Primitive Values*

```
public class CustomerOne {
  public static void main (String[] args) {
    PizzaFactory pizzaHouse = new PizzaFactory();
    int pricePrPizza = 15;
    System.out.println("Value of pricePrPizza before call: " + pricePrPizza);
    double totPrice = pizzaHouse.calcPrice(4, pricePrPizza);             // (1)
    System.out.println("Value of pricePrPizza after call: " + pricePrPizza);
  }
}

class PizzaFactory {
  public double calcPrice(int numberOfPizzas, double pizzaPrice) {       // (2)
    pizzaPrice = pizzaPrice / 2.0;          // Changes price.
    System.out.println("Changed pizza price in the method: " + pizzaPrice);
    return numberOfPizzas * pizzaPrice;
  }
}
```

Output from the program:

```
Value of pricePrPizza before call: 15
Changed pizza price in the method: 7.5
Value of pricePrPizza after call: 15
```

In Example 3.6, the method `calcPrice()` is defined in the class `PizzaFactory` at (2). It is called from the `CustomerOne.main()` method at (1). The value of the first actual parameter, `4`, is copied to the `int` formal parameter `numberOfPizzas`. Note that the second actual parameter `pricePrPizza` is of the type `int`, while the corresponding formal parameter `pizzaPrice` is of the type `double`. Before the value of the actual parameter `pricePrPizza` is copied to the formal parameter `pizzaPrice`, it is implicitly widened to a `double`. The passing of primitive values is illustrated in Figure 3.2.

The value of the formal parameter `pizzaPrice` is changed in the `calcPrice()` method, but this does not affect the value of the actual parameter `pricePrPizza` on

Figure 3.2 *Parameter Passing: Primitive Data Values*

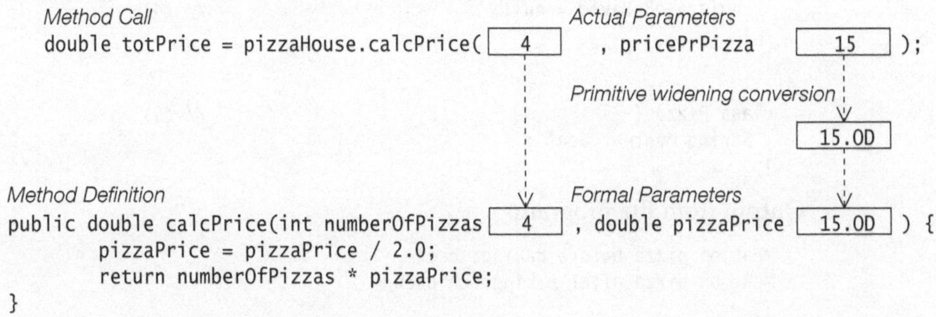

return: It still has the value `15`. The bottom line is that the formal parameter is a local variable, and changing its value does not affect the value of the actual parameter.

Passing Reference Values

If the actual parameter expression evaluates to a reference value, the resulting reference value is assigned to the corresponding formal parameter reference at method invocation. In particular, if an actual parameter is a reference to an object, the reference value stored in the actual parameter is passed. Consequently, both the actual parameter and the formal parameter are aliases to the object denoted by this reference value during the invocation of the method. In particular, this implies that changes made to the object via the formal parameter *will* be apparent after the call returns.

Type conversions between actual and formal parameters of reference types are discussed in §7.10, p. 315.

In Example 3.7, a `Pizza` object is created at (1). Any object of the class `Pizza` created using the class declaration at (5) always results in a beef pizza. In the call to the `bake()` method at (2), the reference value of the object referenced by the actual parameter `favoritePizza` is assigned to the formal parameter `pizzaToBeBaked` in the declaration of the `bake()` method at (3).

Example 3.7 *Passing Reference Values*

```
public class CustomerTwo {
  public static void main (String[] args) {
    Pizza favoritePizza = new Pizza();                    // (1)
    System.out.println("Meat on pizza before baking: " + favoritePizza.meat);
    bake(favoritePizza);                                  // (2)
    System.out.println("Meat on pizza after baking: " + favoritePizza.meat);
  }
```

```
    public static void bake(Pizza pizzaToBeBaked) {  // (3)
      pizzaToBeBaked.meat = "chicken";  // Change the meat on the pizza.
      pizzaToBeBaked = null;                          // (4)
    }
  }

  class Pizza {                                       // (5)
    String meat = "beef";
  }
```

Output from the program:

```
Meat on pizza before baking: beef
Meat on pizza after baking: chicken
```

One particular consequence of passing reference values to formal parameters is that any changes made to the object via formal parameters will be reflected back in the calling method when the call returns. In this case, the reference `favoritePizza` will show that chicken has been substituted for beef on the pizza. Setting the formal parameter `pizzaToBeBaked` to `null` at (4) does not change the reference value in the actual parameter `favoritePizza`. The situation at method invocation, and just before the return from method `bake()`, is illustrated in Figure 3.3.

Figure 3.3 *Parameter Passing: Reference Values*

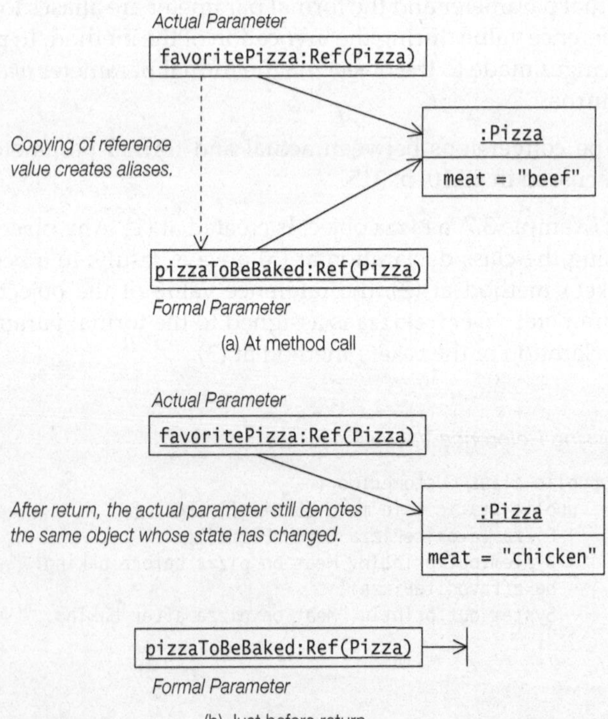

In summary, the formal parameter can only change the *state* of the object whose reference value was passed to the method.

The parameter passing strategy in Java is *call by value* and not *call by reference*, regardless of the type of the parameter. Call by reference would have allowed values in the actual parameters to be changed via formal parameters; that is, the value in `pricePrPizza` would be halved in Example 3.6 and `favoritePizza` would be set to `null` in Example 3.7. However, this cannot be directly implemented in Java.

Passing Arrays

The discussion of passing reference values in the previous section is equally valid for arrays, as arrays are objects in Java. Method invocation conversions for array types are discussed along with those for other reference types in §7.10, p. 315.

In Example 3.8, the idea is to repeatedly swap neighboring elements in an integer array until the largest element in the array *percolates* to the last position in the array.

Example 3.8 *Passing Arrays*

```
public class Percolate {

  public static void main (String[] args) {
    int[] dataSeq = {8,4,6,2,1};    // Create and initialize an array.

    // Write array before percolation:
    printIntArray(dataSeq);

    // Percolate:
    for (int index = 1; index < dataSeq.length; ++index)
      if (dataSeq[index-1] > dataSeq[index])
        swap(dataSeq, index-1, index);                         // (1)

    // Write array after percolation:
    printIntArray(dataSeq);
  }

  public static void swap(int[] intArray, int i, int j) { // (2)
    int tmp = intArray[i]; intArray[i] = intArray[j]; intArray[j] = tmp;
  }

  public static void swap(int v1, int v2) {               // (3) Logical error!
    int tmp = v1; v1 = v2; v2 = tmp;
  }

  public static void printIntArray(int[] array) {         // (4)
    for (int value : array)
      System.out.print(" " + value);
    System.out.println();
  }
}
```

Output from the program:

```
8 4 6 2 1
4 6 2 1 8
```

Note that in the declaration of the method `swap()` at (2), the formal parameter `intArray` is of the array type `int[]`. The `swap()` method is called in the `main()` method at (1), where one of the actual parameters is the array variable `dataSeq`. The reference value of the array variable `dataSeq` is assigned to the array variable `intArray` at method invocation. After return from the call to the `swap()` method, the array variable `dataSeq` will reflect the changes made to the array via the corresponding formal parameter. This situation is depicted in Figure 3.4 at the first call and return from the `swap()` method, indicating how the values of the elements at indices `0` and `1` in the array have been swapped.

However, the declaration of the `swap()` method at (3) will *not* swap two values. The method call

```
swap(dataSeq[index-1], dataSeq[index]);
```

will have no effect on the array elements, as the swapping is done on the values of the formal parameters.

Figure 3.4 *Parameter Passing: Arrays*

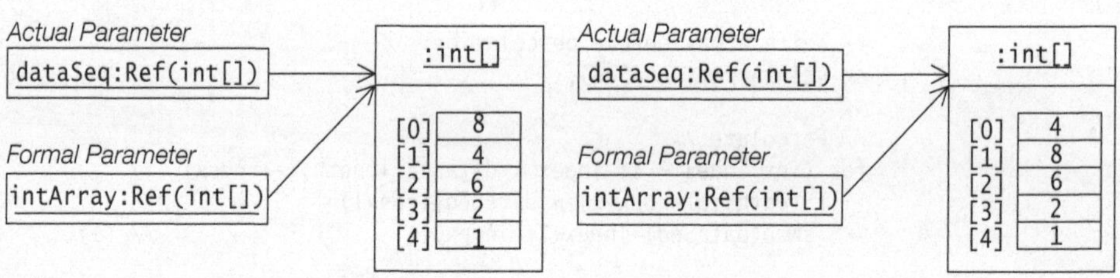

(a) At first call to the `swap()` method (b) Just before first return from the `swap()` method

The method `printIntArray()` at (4) also has a formal parameter of array type `int[]`. Note that the formal parameter is specified as an array reference using the `[]` notation, but this notation is not used when an array is passed as an actual parameter.

Array Elements as Actual Parameters

Array elements, like other variables, can store values of primitive data types or reference values of objects. In the latter case, they can also be arrays—that is, arrays of arrays (§3.4, p. 63). If an array element is of a primitive data type, its data value is passed; if it is a reference to an object, the reference value is passed. The method invocation conversions apply to the values of array elements as well.

Example 3.9 *Array Elements as Primitive Data Values*

```
public class FindMinimum {

  public static void main(String[] args) {
    int[] dataSeq = {6,4,8,2,1};

    int minValue = dataSeq[0];
    for (int index = 1; index < dataSeq.length; ++index)
      minValue = minimum(minValue, dataSeq[index]);              // (1)

    System.out.println("Minimum value: " + minValue);
  }

  public static int minimum(int i, int j) {                    // (2)
    return (i <= j) ? i : j;
  }
}
```

Output from the program:

```
Minimum value: 1
```

In Example 3.9, the value of all but one element of the array `dataSeq` is retrieved and passed consecutively at (1) to the formal parameter `j` of the `minimum()` method defined at (2). The discussion in §3.5, p. 73, on passing primitive values also applies to array elements that have primitive values.

In Example 3.10, the formal parameter `seq` of the `findMinimum()` method defined at (4) is an array variable. The variable `matrix` denotes an array of arrays declared at (1) simulating a multidimensional array, which has three rows, where each row is a simple array. The first row, denoted by `matrix[0]`, is passed to the `findMinimum()` method in the call at (2). Each remaining row is passed by its reference value in the call to the `findMinimum()` method at (3).

Example 3.10 *Array Elements as Reference Values*

```
public class FindMinimumMxN {

  public static void main(String[] args) {
    int[][] matrix = { {8,4},{6,3,2},{7} };                   // (1)

    int min = findMinimum(matrix[0]);                         // (2)
    for (int i = 1; i < matrix.length; ++i) {
      int minInRow = findMinimum(matrix[i]);                  // (3)
      min = Math.min(min, minInRow);
    }
    System.out.println("Minimum value in matrix: " + min);
  }
```

```
  public static int findMinimum(int[] seq) {                    // (4)
    int min = seq[0];
    for (int i = 1; i < seq.length; ++i)
      min = Math.min(min, seq[i]);
    return min;
  }
}
```

Output from the program:

```
Minimum value in matrix: 2
```

`final` Parameters

A formal parameter can be declared with the keyword `final` preceding the parameter declaration in the method declaration. A `final` parameter is also known as a *blank final variable*; that is, it is blank (uninitialized) until a value is assigned to it, (e.g., at method invocation) and then the value in the variable cannot be changed during the lifetime of the variable (see also the discussion in §4.8, p. 133). The compiler can treat `final` variables as constants for code optimization purposes. Declaring parameters as `final` prevents their values from being changed inadvertently. A formal parameter's declaration as `final` does not affect the caller's code.

The declaration of the method `calcPrice()` from Example 3.6 is shown next, with the formal parameter `pizzaPrice` declared as `final`:

```
public double calcPrice(int numberOfPizzas, final double pizzaPrice) {  // (2')
  pizzaPrice = pizzaPrice/2.0;                            // (3) Not allowed
  return numberOfPizzas * pizzaPrice;
}
```

If this declaration of the `calcPrice()` method is compiled, the compiler will not allow the value of the `final` parameter `pizzaPrice` to be changed at (3) in the body of the method.

As another example, the declaration of the method `bake()` from Example 3.7 is shown here, with the formal parameter `pizzaToBeBaked` declared as `final`:

```
public static void bake(final Pizza pizzaToBeBaked) { // (3)
  pizzaToBeBaked.meat = "chicken";                    // (3a) Allowed
  pizzaToBeBaked = null;                              // (4) Not allowed
}
```

If this declaration of the `bake()` method is compiled, the compiler will not allow the reference value of the `final` parameter `pizzaToBeBaked` to be changed at (4) in the body of the method. Note that this applies to the reference value in the `final` parameter, but not to the object denoted by this parameter. The state of the object can be changed as before, as shown at (3a).

3.6 Variable Arity Methods

A *fixed arity* method must be called with the same number of actual parameters (also called *arguments*) as the number of formal parameters specified in its declaration. If the method declaration specifies two formal parameters, every call of this method must specify exactly two arguments. We say that the arity of this method is 2. In other words, the arity of such a method is fixed, and it is equal to the number of formal parameters specified in the method declaration.

Java also allows declaration of *variable arity* methods, meaning that the number of arguments in its call can be *varied*. As we shall see, invocations of such a method may contain more actual parameters than formal parameters. Variable arity methods are heavily employed in formatting text representation of values, as demonstrated by the variable arity method `System.out.printf()` that is used in many examples for this purpose.

The *last* formal parameter in a variable arity method declaration is declared as follows:

type... *formal_parameter_name*

The ellipsis (...) is specified between the *type* and the *formal_parameter_name*. The *type* can be a primitive type, a reference type, or a type parameter. Whitespace can be specified on both sides of the ellipsis. Such a parameter is usually called a *variable arity parameter* (also known as *varargs*).

Apart from the variable arity parameter, a variable arity method is identical to a fixed arity method. The method `publish()` is a variable arity method:

```
public static void publish(int n, String... data) {      // (int, String[])
  System.out.println("n: " + n + ", data size: " + data.length);
}
```

The variable arity parameter in a variable arity method is always interpreted as having an array type:

type`[]`

In the body of the `publish()` method, the variable arity parameter `data` has the type `String[]`, so it is a simple array of `String`s.

Only *one* variable arity parameter is permitted in the formal parameter list, and it is always the *last* parameter in the formal parameter list. Given that the method declaration has n formal parameters, and the method call has k actual parameters, k must be equal to or greater than $n - 1$. The last $k - n + 1$ actual parameters are evaluated and stored in an array whose reference value is passed as the value of the actual parameter. In the case of the `publish()` method, n is equal to 2, so k can be 1, 2, 3, and so on. The following invocations of the `publish()` method show which arguments are passed in each method call:

```
publish(1);                    // (1, new String[] {})
publish(2, "two");             // (2, new String[] {"two"})
publish(3, "two", "three");    // (3, new String[] {"two", "three"})
```

Each method call results in an implicit array being created and passed as an argument. This array can contain zero or more argument values that do *not* correspond to the formal parameters preceding the variable arity parameter. This array is referenced by the variable arity parameter data in the method declaration. The preceding calls would result in the publish() method printing the following output:

```
n: 1, data size: 0
n: 2, data size: 1
n: 3, data size: 2
```

To overload a variable arity method, it is not enough to change the type of the variable arity parameter to an explicit array type. The compiler will complain if an attempt is made to overload the method transmit(), as shown in the following code:

```
public static void transmit(String... data) { }  // Compile-time error!
public static void transmit(String[] data)  { }  // Compile-time error!
```

These declarations would result in two methods with equivalent signatures in the same class, which is not permitted.

Overloading and overriding of methods with variable arity are discussed in §7.10, p. 316.

Calling a Variable Arity Method

Example 3.11 illustrates various aspects of calling a variable arity method. The method flexiPrint() in the VarargsDemo class has a variable arity parameter:

```
public static void flexiPrint(Object... data) { // Object[]
  //...
}
```

The variable arity method prints the name of the Class object representing the *actual array* that is passed at runtime. It prints the number of elements in this array as well as the text representation of each element in the array.

The method flexiPrint() is called in the main() method. First with the values of primitive types and Strings ((1) to (8)), then it is called with the program arguments (p. 85) supplied in the command line, ((9) to (11)).

Compiling the program results in a *warning* at (9), which we ignore for the time being. The program can still be run, as shown in Example 3.11. The numbers at the end of the lines in the output relate to numbers in the code, and are not printed by the program.

Example 3.11 *Calling a Variable Arity Method*

```
public class VarargsDemo {
  public static void flexiPrint(Object... data) { // Object[]
    // Print the name of the Class object for the varargs parameter.
    System.out.print("Type: " + data.getClass().getName());

    System.out.println("  No. of elements: " + data.length);

    System.out.print("Element values: ");
    for(Object element : data)
      System.out.print(element + " ");
    System.out.println();
  }

  public static void main(String... args) {
    int    day       = 13;
    String monthName = "August";
    int    year      = 2009;

    // Passing primitives and non-array types:
    flexiPrint();                        // (1) new Object[] {}
    flexiPrint(day);                     // (2) new Object[] {Integer.valueOf(day)}
    flexiPrint(day, monthName);          // (3) new Object[] {Integer.valueOf(day),
                                         //                   monthName}
    flexiPrint(day, monthName, year);    // (4) new Object[] {Integer.valueOf(day),
                                         //                   monthName,
                                         //                   Integer.valueOf(year)}
    System.out.println();

    // Passing an array type:
    Object[] dateInfo = {day,            // (5) new Object[] {Integer.valueOf(day),
                         monthName,      //                   monthName,
                         year};          //                   Integer.valueOf(year)}
    flexiPrint(dateInfo);                // (6) Non-varargs call
    flexiPrint((Object) dateInfo);       // (7) new Object[] {(Object) dateInfo}
    flexiPrint(new Object[]{dateInfo});// (8) Non-varargs call
    System.out.println();

    // Explicit varargs or non-varargs call:
    flexiPrint(args);                    // (9) Warning!
    flexiPrint((Object) args);           // (10) Explicit varargs call
    flexiPrint((Object[]) args);         // (11) Explicit non-varargs call
  }
}
```

Compiling the program:

```
>javac VarargsDemo.java
VarargsDemo.java:41: warning: non-varargs call of varargs method with inexact
argument type for last parameter;
    flexiPrint(args);                    // (9) Warning!
               ^
  cast to Object for a varargs call
  cast to Object[] for a non-varargs call and to suppress this warning
1 warning
```

Running the program:

```
>java VarargsDemo To arg or not to arg
Type: [Ljava.lang.Object;  No. of elements: 0              (1)
Element values:
Type: [Ljava.lang.Object;  No. of elements: 1              (2)
Element values: 13
Type: [Ljava.lang.Object;  No. of elements: 2              (3)
Element values: 13 August
Type: [Ljava.lang.Object;  No. of elements: 3              (4)
Element values: 13 August 2009

Type: [Ljava.lang.Object;  No. of elements: 3              (6)
Element values: 13 August 2009
Type: [Ljava.lang.Object;  No. of elements: 1              (7)
Element values: [Ljava.lang.Object;@1eed786
Type: [Ljava.lang.Object;  No. of elements: 1              (8)
Element values: [Ljava.lang.Object;@1eed786

Type: [Ljava.lang.String;  No. of elements: 6              (9)
Element values: To arg or not to arg
Type: [Ljava.lang.Object;  No. of elements: 1              (10)
Element values: [Ljava.lang.String;@187aeca
Type: [Ljava.lang.String;  No. of elements: 6              (11)
Element values: To arg or not to arg
```

Variable Arity and Fixed Arity Method Calls

The calls in (1) to (4) in Example 3.11 are all *variable arity calls*, as an implicit `Object` array is created, in which the values of the actual parameters are stored. The reference value of this array is passed to the method. The printout shows that the type of the parameter is actually an array of `Objects` (`[Ljava.lang.Object;`).

The call at (6) differs from the previous calls, in that the actual parameter is an array that has the *same* type (`Object[]`) as the variable arity parameter, without having to create an implicit array. In such a case, *no* implicit array is created, and the reference value of the array `dateInfo` is passed to the method. See also the result from this call at (6) in the output. The call at (6) is a *fixed arity call* (also called a *non-varargs call*), where no implicit array is created:

```
flexiPrint(dateInfo);                // (6) Non-varargs call
```

However, if the actual parameter is cast to the type `Object` as in (7), a *variable arity* call is executed:

```
flexiPrint((Object) dateInfo);       // (7) new Object[] {(Object) dateInfo}
```

The type of the actual argument is now *not* the same as that of the variable arity parameter, resulting in an array of the type `Object[]` being created, in which the array `dateInfo` is stored as an element. The printout at (7) shows that only the text representation of the `dateInfo` array is printed, and not its elements, as it is the sole element of the implicit array.

The call at (8) is a *fixed arity* call, for the same reason as the call in (6). Now, however, the array `dateInfo` is explicitly stored as an element in an array of the type `Object[]` that matches the type of the variable arity parameter:

```
flexiPrint(new Object[]{dateInfo});// (8) Non-varargs call
```

The output from (8) is the same as the output from (7), where the array `dateInfo` was passed as an element in an implicitly created array of type `Object[]`.

The compiler issues a *warning* for the call at (9):

```
flexiPrint(args);                    // (9) Warning!
```

The actual parameter `args` is an array of the type `String[]`, which is a *subtype* of `Object[]`—the type of the variable arity parameter. The array `args` can be passed in a fixed arity call as an array of the type `String[]`, or in a variable arity call as *an element* in an implicitly created array of the type `Object[]`. *Both* calls are feasible and valid in this case. Note that the compiler chooses a fixed arity call rather than a variable arity call, but also issues a warning. The result at (9) confirms this course of action.

The array `args` of the type `String[]` is explicitly passed as an `Object` in a variable arity call at (10), similar to the call at (7):

```
flexiPrint((Object) args);           // (10) Explicit varargs call
```

The array `args` of type `String[]` is explicitly passed as an array of the type `Object[]` in a fixed arity call at (11). This call is equivalent to the call at (9), where the widening reference conversion is implicit, but now without a warning at compile time. The two calls print the same information, as is evident from the output at (9) and (11):

```
flexiPrint((Object[]) args);         // (11) Explicit non-varargs call
```

3.7 The `main()` Method

The mechanics of compiling and running Java applications using the JDK are outlined in §1.10, p. 16. The `java` command executes a method called `main` in the class specified on the command line. Any class can have a `main()` method, but only the `main()` method of the class specified in the `java` command starts the execution of a Java application.

The `main()` method must have `public` accessibility so that the JVM can call this method (§4.7, p. 123). It is a `static` method belonging to the class, so that no object of the class is required to start the execution (§4.8, p. 132). It does not return a value; that is, it is declared as `void` (§6.4, p. 224). It always has an array of `String` objects as its only formal parameter. This array contains any arguments passed to the program on the command line (see the next subsection). The following method header declarations fit the bill, and any one of them can be used for the `main()` method:

```
public static void main(String[] args)    // Method header
public static void main(String... args)   // Method header
```

The three modifiers can occur in any order in the method header. The requirements given in these examples do not exclude specification of additional modifiers (§4.8, p. 131) or any throws clause (§6.9, p. 251). The main() method can also be overloaded like any other method (§3.2, p. 52). The JVM ensures that the main() method having the previously mentioned method header is the starting point of program execution.

Program Arguments

Any arguments passed to the program on the command line can be accessed in the main() method of the class specified on the command line:

```
>java Colors red green blue
```

These arguments are called *program arguments*. Note that the command name, java, and the class name Colors are not passed to the main() method of the class Colors, nor are any other options that are specified on the command line passed to this method.

Since the formal parameter of the main() method is an array of String objects, individual String elements in the array can be accessed by using the [] operator.

In Example 3.12, the three arguments red, green, and blue can be accessed in the main() method of the Colors class as args[0], args[1], and args[2], respectively. The total number of arguments is given by the field length of the String array args. Note that program arguments can be passed only as strings, and must be explicitly converted to other values by the program, if necessary.

When no arguments are specified on the command line, an array of zero String elements is created and passed to the main() method. Thus the reference value of the formal parameter in the main() method is never null.

Program arguments supply information to the application, which can be used to tailor the runtime behavior of the application according to user requirements.

Example 3.12 *Passing Program Arguments*

```
public class Colors {
  public static void main(String[] args) {
    System.out.println("No. of program arguments: " + args.length);
    for (int i = 0; i < args.length; i++)
      System.out.println("Argument no. " + i + " (" + args[i] + ") has " +
                         args[i].length() + " characters.");
  }
}
```

Running the program:

```
>java Colors red green blue
No. of program arguments: 3
Argument no. 0 (red) has 3 characters.
Argument no. 1 (green) has 5 characters.
Argument no. 2 (blue) has 4 characters.
```

3.8 Enumerated Types

In this section we provide a basic introduction to enumerated types. An *enumerated type* defines *a finite set of symbolic names and their values*. These symbolic names are usually called *enum constants* or *named constants*.

One way to define constants is to declare them as `final`, `static` variables in a class (or interface) declaration:

```
public class MachineState {
  public static final int BUSY = 1;
  public static final int IDLE = 0;
  public static final int BLOCKED = -1;
}
```

Such constants are not type-safe, as *any* `int` value can be used where we need to use a constant declared in the `MachineState` class. Such a constant must be qualified by the class (or interface) name, unless the class is extended (or the interface is implemented). When such a constant is printed, only its value (for example, `0`), and not its name (for example, `IDLE`), is printed. A constant also needs recompiling if its value is changed, as the values of such constants are compiled into the client code.

An enumerated type in Java is a special kind of class type that is much more powerful than the approach outlined earlier for defining collections of named constants.

Declaring Type-safe Enums

The canonical form of declaring an *enum type* is shown here:

```
public enum MachineState          // Enum header
{                                 // Enum body
  BUSY, IDLE, BLOCKED             // Enum constants
}
```

The keyword `enum` is used to declare an enum type, as opposed to the keyword `class` for a class declaration. The basic notation requires the *enum type name* in enum header, and *a comma-separated list of enum constants* can be specified in the enum body. Optionally, an access modifier can also be specified in the enum header, as for a (top-level) class. In the example enum declaration, the name of the enum type is `MachineState`. It defines three enum constants with explicit names. An enum constant can be any legal Java identifier, but the convention is to use uppercase letters in the name. Essentially, an enum declaration defines a *reference type* that has a *finite number of permissible values* referenced by the enum constants, and the compiler ensures they are used in a type-safe manner.

Other member declarations can be specified in the body of an enum type, but the canonical form suffices for the purpose of this book. Analogous to a class declaration, an enum type is compiled to Java bytecode that is placed in a separate class file.

The enum types `java.time.Month` and `java.time.DayOfWeek` are two examples of enum types from the Java SE platform API. As we would expect, the `Month` enum type represents the months from `JANUARY` to `DECEMBER`, and the `DayOfWeek` enum type represents the days of the week from `MONDAY` to `SUNDAY`. Examples of their usage can be found in §11.2, p. 462.

Some additional examples of enum types follow:

```
public enum MarchingOrders { LEFT, RIGHT }

public enum TrafficLightState { RED, YELLOW, GREEN }

enum MealType { BREAKFAST, LUNCH, DINNER }
```

Using Type-safe Enums

Example 3.13 illustrates the use of enum constants. An enum type is essentially used in the same way as any other reference type. Enum constants are actually `public`, `static`, `final` fields of the enum type, and they are implicitly initialized with instances of the enum type when the enum type is loaded at runtime. Since the enum constants are static members, they can be accessed using the name of the enum type—analogous to accessing static members in a class or an interface.

Example 3.13 shows a machine client that uses a machine whose state is an enum constant. In this example, we see that an enum constant can be passed as an argument, as shown as (1), and we can declare references whose type is an enum type, as shown as (3), but we *cannot* create new constants (that is, objects) of the enum type `MachineState`. An attempt to do so, at (5), results in a compile-time error.

The string representation of an enum constant is its name, as shown at (4). Note that it is not possible to pass a type of value other than a `MachineState` enum constant in the call to the method `setState()` of the `Machine` class, as shown at (2).

Example 3.13 *Using Enums*

```
// File: MachineState.java
public enum MachineState { BUSY, IDLE, BLOCKED }
```

```
// File: Machine.java
public class Machine {

  private MachineState state;

  public void setState(MachineState state) { this.state = state; }
  public MachineState getState() { return this.state; }
}
```

```
// File: MachineClient.java
public class MachineClient {
  public static void main(String[] args) {
```

```
        Machine machine = new Machine();
        machine.setState(MachineState.IDLE);           // (1) Passed as a value.
        // machine.setState(1);                        // (2) Compile-time error!

        MachineState state = machine.getState();       // (3) Declaring a reference.
        System.out.println(
          "Current machine state: " + state            // (4) Printing the enum name.
        );

        // MachineState newState = new MachineState(); // (5) Compile-time error!

        System.out.println("All machine states:");
        for (MachineState ms : MachineState.values()) { // (6) Traversing over enum
          System.out.println(ms + ":" + ms.ordinal());  //     contants.
        }

        System.out.println("Comparison:");
        MachineState state1 = MachineState.BUSY;
        MachineState state2 = state1;
        MachineState state3 = MachineState.BLOCKED;

        System.out.println(state1 + " == " + state2 + ": " +
                           (state1 == state2));                        // (7)
        System.out.println(state1 + " is equal to " + state2 + ": " +
                           (state1.equals(state2)));                   // (8)
        System.out.println(state1 + " is less than " + state3 + ": " +
                           (state1.compareTo(state3) < 0));            // (9)
    }
}
```

Output from the program:

```
Current machine state: IDLE
All machine states:
BUSY:0
IDLE:1
BLOCKED:2
Comparison:
BUSY == BUSY: true
BUSY is equal to BUSY: true
BUSY is less than BLOCKED: true
```

Selected Methods for Enum Types

All enum types implicitly have the following useful method:

> `static EnumTypeName[] values()`
>
> Returns an array containing the enum constants of this enum type, *in the order they are specified*.

The loop at (6) in Example 3.13 illustrates traversing over all the `MachineState` enum constants in the order they are specified. An array containing all the `MachineState` constants is obtained by calling the static method `values()` on the enum type.

All enum types are subtypes of the `java.lang.Enum` class, which provides the default behavior. All enum types inherit the following selected methods from the `java.lang.Enum` class:

`final boolean equals(Object other)`

This method returns `true` if the specified object is equal to this enum constant.

`final int compareTo(E other)`

The *natural order* of the enum constants in an enum type is based on their *ordinal values* (see the `ordinal()` method next). The `compareTo()` method of the `Comparable` interface returns the value zero if this enum constant is equal to the other enum constant, a value less than zero if this enum constant is less than the other enum constant, or a value greater than zero if this enum constant is greater than the other enum constant.

`final int ordinal()`

This method returns the *ordinal value* of this enum constant (that is, its position in its enum type declaration). The first enum constant is assigned an ordinal value of zero. If the ordinal value of an enum constant is less than the ordinal value of another enum constant of the same enum type, the former occurs before the latter in the enum type declaration.

Note that the equality test implemented by the `equals()` method is based on reference equality (`==`) of the enum constants, not on value equality. An enum type has a finite number of distinct objects. Comparing two enum references for equality means determining whether they store the reference value of the same enum constant—in other words, whether the references are aliases. Thus, for any two enum references `state1` and `state2`, the expressions `state1.equals(state2)` and `state1 == state2` are equivalent, as shown at (7) and (8) in Example 3.13.

The ordinal value of the constants in an enum type determines the result of comparing such constants with the `compareTo()` method, as shown at (9) in Example 3.13.

Review Questions

3.13 What will the following program print when run?

```
public class ParameterPass {
  public static void main(String[] args) {
    int i = 0;
    addTwo(i++);
    System.out.println(i);
  }

  static void addTwo(int i) {
    i += 2;
  }
}
```

Select the one correct answer.

(a) 0
(b) 1
(c) 2
(d) 3

3.14 What will be the result of compiling and running the following program?

```
public class Passing {
  public static void main(String[] args) {
    int a = 0; int b = 0;
    int[] bArr = new int[1]; bArr[0] = b;

    inc1(a); inc2(bArr);

    System.out.println("a=" + a + " b=" + b + " bArr[0]=" + bArr[0]);
  }

  public static void inc1(int x) { x++; }

  public static void inc2(int[] x) { x[0]++; }
}
```

Select the one correct answer.

(a) The code will fail to compile, since `x[0]++;` is not a legal statement.
(b) The code will compile and will print `a=1 b=1 bArr[0]=1` at runtime.
(c) The code will compile and will print `a=0 b=1 bArr[0]=1` at runtime.
(d) The code will compile and will print `a=0 b=0 bArr[0]=1` at runtime.
(e) The code will compile and will print `a=0 b=0 bArr[0]=0` at runtime.

3.15 Which statements, when inserted at (1), will result in a compile-time error?

```
public class ParameterUse {
  static void main(String[] args) {
    int a = 0;
    final int b = 1;
    int[] c = { 2 };
    final int[] d = { 3 };
    useArgs(a, b, c, d);
  }

  static void useArgs(final int a, int b, final int[] c, int[] d) {
    // (1) INSERT STATEMENT HERE.
  }
}
```

Select the two correct answers.

(a) `a++;`
(b) `b++;`
(c) `b = a;`
(d) `c[0]++;`
(e) `d[0]++;`
(f) `c = d;`

3.16 Which of the following method declarations are valid declarations?

Select the three correct answers.

(a) `void compute(int... is) { }`
(b) `void compute(int is...) { }`
(c) `void compute(int... is, int i, String... ss) { }`
(d) `void compute(String... ds) { }`
(e) `void compute(String... ss, int len) { }`
(f) `void compute(char[] ca, int... is) { }`

3.17 Given the following code:

```
public class RQ810A40 {
  static void print(Object... obj) {
    System.out.println("Object...: " + obj[0]);
  }
  public static void main(String[] args) {
    // (1) INSERT METHOD CALL HERE.
  }
}
```

Which method call, when inserted at (1), will not result in the following output from the program:

```
Object...: 9
```

Select the one correct answer.

(a) `print("9", "1", "1");`
(b) `print(9, 1, 1);`
(c) `print(new int[] {9, 1, 1});`
(d) `print(new Integer[] {9, 1, 1});`
(e) `print(new String[] {"9", "1", "1"});`
(f) `print(new Object[] {"9", "1", "1"});`
(g) None of the above.

Chapter Summary

The following topics were covered in this chapter:

- An overview of declarations that can be specified in a class
- Declaration of methods, usage of the `this` reference in an instance method, and method overloading
- Declaration of constructors, usage of the default constructor, and overloading of constructors
- Explanation of declaration, construction, initialization, and usage of both one-dimensional and multidimensional arrays, including anonymous arrays
- Sorting and searching arrays

- Parameter passing, both primitive values and object references, including arrays and array elements; and declaring `final` parameters
- Declaring and calling methods with variable arity
- Declaration of the `main()` method whose execution starts the application
- Passing program arguments to the `main()` method
- Declaring and using simple enum types

Programming Exercise

3.1 Write a program to grade a short multiple-choice quiz. The correct answers for the quiz are

```
1. C    5. B
2. A    6. C
3. B    7. C
4. D    8. A
```

Assume that the passing marks are at least 5 out of 8. The program stores the correct answers in an array. The submitted answers are specified as program arguments. Let `X` represent a question that was not answered on the quiz. Use an enum type to represent the result of answering a question.

Example of running the program:

```
>java QuizGrader C B B D B C A X
Question  Submitted Ans. Correct Ans.  Result
    1          C              C        CORRECT
    2          B              A          WRONG
    3          B              B        CORRECT
    4          D              D        CORRECT
    5          B              B        CORRECT
    6          C              C        CORRECT
    7          A              C          WRONG
    8          X              A     UNANSWERED
No. of correct answers:       5
No. of wrong answers:         2
No. of questions unanswered: 1
The candidate PASSED.
```

Access Control

4

Programmer I Exam Objectives		
[1.1]	Define the scope of variables ○ *See also §2.4, p. 44.*	*§4.4, p. 114*
[1.3]	Create executable Java applications with a main method; run a Java program from the command line; including console output ○ *See also §1.10, p. 16.*	*§4.3, p. 107*
[1.4]	Import other Java packages to make them accessible in your code	*§4.2, p. 97*
[6.2]	Apply the static keyword to methods and fields	*§4.8, p. 132*
[6.4]	Apply access modifiers	*§4.5, p. 118* *§4.7, p. 123*
[7.5]	Use abstract classes and interfaces ○ *For interfaces, see §7.6, p. 290.*	*§4.6, p. 120*
Supplementary Objectives		
•	Structure of a Java source file	*§4.1, p. 96*
•	Creating Java packages	*§4.2, p. 97*
•	Other modifiers for classes and members	*§4.6, p. 120* *§4.8, p. 131*

4.1 Java Source File Structure

The structure of a skeletal Java source file is depicted in Figure 4.1. A Java source file can have the following elements that, if present, must be specified in the following order:

1. An optional `package` declaration to specify a package name. Packages are discussed in §4.2.
2. Zero or more `import` declarations. Since `import` declarations introduce type or static member names in the source code, they must be placed before any type declarations. Both type and static `import` declarations are discussed in §4.2.
3. Any number of *top-level* type declarations. Class, enum, and interface declarations are collectively known as *type declarations*. Since these declarations belong to the same package, they are said to be defined at the *top level*, which is the package level.

   The type declarations can be defined in any order. Technically, a source file need not have any such declarations, but that is hardly useful.

   The JDK imposes the restriction that at most one `public` class declaration per source file can be defined. If a `public` class is defined, the file name must match this `public` class. For example, if the `public` class name is `NewApp`, the file name must be `NewApp.java`.

   Classes are discussed in §3.1, p. 48; enums are discussed in §3.8, p. 87; and interfaces are discussed in §7.6, p. 290.

Note that except for the `package` and the `import` statements, all code is encapsulated in classes, interfaces, and enums. No such restriction applies to comments and whitespace.

Figure 4.1 *Java Source File Structure*

```
// File: NewApp.java

// PART 1: (OPTIONAL) package declaration
package com.company.project.fragilepackage;

// PART 2: (ZERO OR MORE) import declarations
import java.io.*;
import java.util.*;
import static java.lang.Math.*;

// PART 3: (ZERO OR MORE) top-level declarations
public class NewApp { }
class A { }
interface IX { }
class B { }
enum C { }
// end of file
```

4.2 Packages

A package in Java is an encapsulation mechanism that can be used to group related classes, interfaces, enums, and subpackages.

Figure 4.2 shows an example of a package hierarchy, comprising a package called `wizard` that contains two other packages: pandorasbox and `spells`. The package `pandorasbox` has a class called `Clown` that implements an interface called `Magic`, also found in the same package. In addition, the package `pandorasbox` has a class called `LovePotion` and a subpackage called `artifacts` containing a class called `Ailment`. The package `spells` has two classes: `Baldness` and `LovePotion`. The class `Baldness` is a subclass of class `Ailment` found in the subpackage `artifacts` in the package `pandorasbox`.

The dot (`.`) notation is used to uniquely identify package members in the package hierarchy. The class `wizard.pandorasbox.LovePotion`, for example, is different from the class `wizard.spells.LovePotion`. The `Ailment` class can be easily identified by the name `wizard.pandorasbox.artifacts.Ailment`, which is known as the *fully qualified name* of the type. Note that the fully qualified name of the type in a named package comprises the fully qualified name of the package and the simple name of the type. The *simple type name* `Ailment` and the *fully qualified package name* `wizard.pandorasbox.artifacts` together define the *fully qualified type name* `wizard.pandorasbox.artifacts.Ailment`. Analogously, the fully qualified name of a *subpackage* comprises the fully qualified name of the parent package and the simple name of the subpackage.

Java programming environments usually map the fully qualified name of packages to the underlying (hierarchical) file system. For example, on a Unix system, the class file `LovePotion.class` corresponding to the fully qualified name `wizard.pandorasbox.LovePotion` would be found under the directory `wizard/pandorasbox`.

Figure 4.2 *Package Hierarchy*

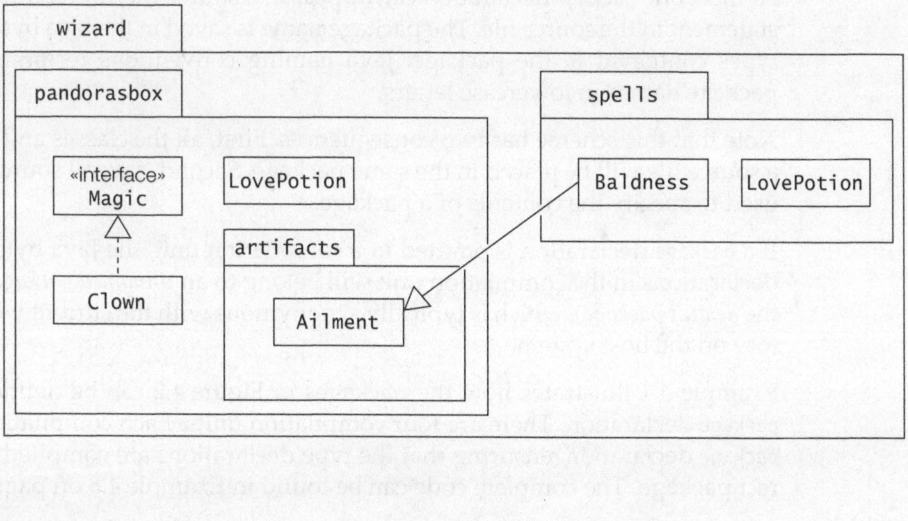

Conventionally, a global naming scheme based on the Internet domain names is used to uniquely identify packages. If the package `wizard` was implemented by a company called Sorcerers Limited that owns the domain `sorcerersltd.com`, its fully qualified name would be

```
com.sorcerersltd.wizard
```

Because domain names are unique, packages with this naming scheme are globally identifiable. It is not advisable to use the top-level package names `java` and `sun`, as these are reserved for the Java designers.

The subpackage `wizard.pandorasbox.artifacts` could easily have been placed elsewhere, as long as it was uniquely identified. Subpackages in a package do not affect the accessibility of the other package members. For all intents and purposes, subpackages are more an *organizational* feature rather than a language feature. Accessibility of members in a package is discussed in §4.4. Accessibility of members defined in type declarations is discussed in §4.7.

Defining Packages

A package hierarchy represents an organization of the Java classes and interfaces. It does *not* represent the *source code* organization of the classes and interfaces. The source code is of no consequence in this regard. Each Java source file (also called *compilation unit*) can contain zero or more type declarations, but the compiler produces a separate *class* file containing the Java bytecode for each of them. A type declaration can indicate that its Java bytecode should be placed in a particular package, using a `package` declaration.

The `package` statement has the following syntax:

`package` *fully_qualified_package_name*;

At most one `package` declaration can appear in a source file, and it must be the first statement in the source file. The package name is saved in the Java bytecode for the types contained in the package. Java naming conventions recommend writing package names in lowercase letters.

Note that this scheme has two consequences. First, all the classes and interfaces in a source file will be placed in the same package. Second, several source files can be used to specify the contents of a package.

If a `package` declaration is omitted in a compilation unit, the Java bytecode for the declarations in the compilation unit will belong to an *unnamed package* (also called the *default package*), which is typically synonymous with the current working directory on the host system.

Example 4.1 illustrates how the packages in Figure 4.2 can be defined using the `package` declaration. There are four compilation units. Each compilation unit has a `package` declaration, ensuring that the type declarations are compiled into the correct package. The complete code can be found in Example 4.8 on page 118.

Example 4.1 *Defining Packages and Using Type Import*

```
// File name: Clown.java
package wizard.pandorasbox;                       // Package declaration

import wizard.pandorasbox.artifacts.Ailment; // Importing specific class

public class Clown implements Magic { /* ... */ }

interface Magic { /* ... */ }
```

```
// File name: LovePotion.java
package wizard.pandorasbox;                       // Package declaration

public class LovePotion { /* ... */
```

```
// File name: Ailment.java
package wizard.pandorasbox.artifacts;             // Package declaration

public class Ailment { /* ... */ }
```

```
// File name: Baldness.java
package wizard.spells;                            // Package declaration

import wizard.pandorasbox.*;                      // (1) Type-import-on-demand
import wizard.pandorasbox.artifacts.*;            // (2) Import from subpackage

public class Baldness extends Ailment {           // Simple name for Ailment
  wizard.pandorasbox.LovePotion tlcOne;           // (3) Fully qualified class name
  LovePotion tlcTwo;                              // Class in same package
  // ...
}

class LovePotion { /* ... */ }
```

Using Packages

The import facility in Java makes it easier to use the contents of packages. This subsection discusses importing *reference types* and *static members of reference types* from packages.

Importing Reference Types

The accessibility of types (classes, interfaces, and enums) in a package determines their access from other packages. Given a reference type that is accessible from outside a package, the reference type can be accessed in two ways. One way is to use the fully qualified name of the type. However, writing long names can become tedious. The second way is to use the `import` declaration that provides a shorthand notation for specifying the name of the type, often called *type import*.

The `import` declarations must be the first statement after any `package` declaration in a source file. The simple form of the `import` declaration has the following syntax:

`import` *fully_qualified_type_name*;

This is called *single-type-import*. As the name implies, such an `import` declaration provides a shorthand notation for a single type. The *simple* name of the type (that is, its identifier) can now be used to access this particular type. Given the `import` declaration

```
import wizard.pandorasbox.Clown;
```

the simple name `Clown` can be used in the source file to refer to this class.

Alternatively, the following form of the `import` declaration can be used:

`import` *fully_qualified_package_name*`.*`;

This is called *type-import-on-demand*. It allows any type from the specified package to be accessed by its simple name.

An `import` declaration does not recursively import subpackages. The declaration also does not result in inclusion of the source code of the types; rather, it simply imports type names (that is, it makes type names available to the code in a compilation unit).

All compilation units implicitly import the `java.lang` package (§8.1, p. 342). This is the reason why we can refer to the class `String` by its simple name, and need not use its fully qualified name `java.lang.String` all the time.

Example 4.1 shows several usages of the `import` statement. Here we will draw attention to the class `Baldness` in the file `Baldness.java`. This class relies on two classes that have the same simple name `LovePotion` but are in different packages: `wizard.pandorasbox` and `wizard.spells`, respectively. To distinguish between the two classes, we can use their fully qualified names. However, since one of them is in the same package as the class `Baldness`, it is enough to fully qualify the class from the other package. This solution is used in Example 4.1 at (3). Note that the import of the `wizard.pandorasbox` package at (1) becomes redundant. Such name conflicts can usually be resolved by using variations of the `import` statement together with fully qualified names.

The class `Baldness` extends the class `Ailment`, which is in the subpackage `artifacts` of the `wizard.pandorasbox` package. The `import` declaration at (2) is used to import the types from the subpackage `artifacts`.

The following example shows how a single-type-import declaration can be used to disambiguate a type name when access to the type is ambiguous by its simple name. The following `import` statement allows the simple name `List` to be used as shorthand for the `java.awt.List` type as expected:

```
import java.awt.*;             // imports all reference types from java.awt
```

Given the two `import` declarations

```
import java.awt.*;             // imports all type names from java.awt
import java.util.*;            // imports all type names from java.util
```

the simple name `List` is now ambiguous, because both the types `java.util.List` and `java.awt.List` match.

Adding a single-type-import declaration for the `java.awt.List` type allows the simple name `List` to be used as a shorthand notation for this type:

```
import java.awt.*;             // imports all type names from java.awt
import java.util.*;            // imports all type names from java.util
import java.awt.List;          // imports the type List from java.awt explicitly
```

Importing Static Members of Reference Types

Analogous to the type import facility, Java also allows import of *static* members of reference types from packages, often called *static import*.

Static import allows accessible static members declared in a type to be imported, so that they can be used by their simple names, and therefore need not be qualified. The import applies to the whole compilation unit, and importing from the unnamed package is not permissible.

The two forms of static import are shown here:

```
// Single-static-import: imports a specific static member from the designated type
import static fully_qualified_type_name.static_member_name;

// Static-import-on-demand: imports all static members in the designated type
import static fully_qualified_type_name.*;
```

Both forms require the use of the keyword `import` followed by the keyword `static`, although the feature is called *static import*. In both cases, the *fully qualified name of the reference type* we are importing from is required.

The first form allows *single static import* of individual static members, and is demonstrated in Example 4.2. The constant `PI`, which is a static field in the class `java.lang.Math`, is imported at (1). Note the use of the fully qualified name of the type in the static import statement. The static method named `sqrt` from the class `java.lang.Math` is imported at (2). Only the *name* of the static method is specified in the static import statement; no parameters are listed. Use of any other static member from the `Math` class requires that the fully qualified name of the class be specified. Since types from the `java.lang` package are imported implicitly, the fully qualified name of the `Math` class is not necessary, as shown at (3).

Static import on demand is easily demonstrated by replacing the two `import` statements in Example 4.2 by the following `import` statement:

```
import static java.lang.Math.*;
```

We can also dispense with the use of the class name `Math` in (3), as all static members from the `Math` class are now imported:

```
double hypotenuse = hypot(x, y);   // (3') Type name can now be omitted.
```

Example 4.2 *Single Static Import*

```
import static java.lang.Math.PI;            // (1) Static field
import static java.lang.Math.sqrt;          // (2) Static method
// Only specified static members are imported.

public class Calculate3 {
  public static void main(String[] args) {
    double x = 3.0, y = 4.0;
    double squareroot = sqrt(y);            // Simple name of static method
    double hypotenuse = Math.hypot(x, y);   // (3) Requires type name
    double area = PI * y * y;               // Simple name of static field
    System.out.printf("Square root: %.2f, hypotenuse: %.2f, area: %.2f%n",
                        squareroot, hypotenuse, area);
  }
}
```

Output from the program:

```
Square root: 2.00, hypotenuse: 5.00, area: 50.27
```

Example 4.3 illustrates how static import can be used to access interface constants (§7.6, p. 302). The static `import` statement at (1) allows the interface constants in the package `mypkg` to be accessed by their simple names. The static import facility avoids the `MyFactory` class having to *implement* the interface so as to access the constants by their simple name (often referred to as the *interface constant antipattern*):

```
public class MyFactory implements mypkg.IMachineState {
 // ...
}
```

Example 4.3 *Avoiding the Interface Constant Antipattern*

```
package mypkg;

public interface IMachineState {
  // Fields are public, static and final.
  int BUSY = 1;
  int IDLE = 0;
  int BLOCKED = -1;
}
```

```
import static mypkg.IMachineState.*;    // (1) Static import interface constants

public class MyFactory {
  public static void main(String[] args) {
    int[] states = { IDLE, BUSY, IDLE, BLOCKED };
    for (int s : states)
      System.out.print(s + " ");
  }
}
```

Output from the program:

```
0 1 0 -1
```

Static import is ideal for importing enum constants from packages, as such constants are static members of an enum type. Example 4.4 combines type and static imports. The enum constants can be accessed at (5) using their simple names because of the static import statement at (2). The type import at (1) is required to access the enum type State by its simple name at (4) and (6).

Example 4.4 *Importing Enum Constants*

```
package mypkg;

public enum State { BUSY, IDLE, BLOCKED }
```

```
// File: Factory.java (in unnamed package)
import mypkg.State;                  // (1) Single type import

import static mypkg.State.*;         // (2) Static import on demand
import static java.lang.System.out;  // (3) Single static import

public class Factory {
  public static void main(String[] args) {
    State[] states = {               // (4) Using type import implied by (1)
        IDLE, BUSY, IDLE, BLOCKED    // (5) Using static import implied by (2)
    };
    for (State s : states)           // (6) Using type import implied by (1)
      out.print(s + " ");            // (7) Using static import implied by (3)
  }
}
```

Output from the program:

```
IDLE BUSY IDLE BLOCKED
```

Identifiers in a class can *shadow* static members that are imported. Example 4.5 illustrates the case where the parameter out of the method writeInfo() has the same name as the statically imported field java.lang.System.out. The type of the parameter is ShadowImport and that of the statically imported field is PrintStream. Both classes

PrintStream and ShadowImport define the method println() that is called in the program. The only way to access the imported field out in the method writeInfo() is to use its fully qualified name.

Example 4.5 *Shadowing Static Import*

```
import static java.lang.System.out;        // (1) Static import

public class ShadowImport {

  public static void main(String[] args) {
    out.println("Calling println() in java.lang.System.out");
    ShadowImport sbi = new ShadowImport();
    writeInfo(sbi);
  }

  // Parameter shadows java.lang.System.out:
  public static void writeInfo(ShadowImport out) {
    out.println("Calling println() in the parameter out");
    System.out.println("Calling println() in java.lang.System.out"); // Qualify
  }

  public void println(String msg) {
    out.println(msg + " of type ShadowImport");
  }
}
```

Output from the program:

```
Calling println() in java.lang.System.out
Calling println() in the parameter out of type ShadowImport
Calling println() in java.lang.System.out
```

The next code snippet illustrates a common conflict that occurs when a static field with the same name is imported by *several* static import statements. This conflict is readily resolved by using the fully qualified name of the field. In the case shown here, we can use the simple name of class in which the field is declared, as the java.lang package is implicitly imported by all compilation units.

```
import static java.lang.Integer.MAX_VALUE;
import static java.lang.Double.MAX_VALUE;

public class StaticFieldConflict {
  public static void main(String[] args) {
    System.out.println(MAX_VALUE);           // (1) Ambiguous! Compile-time error!
    System.out.println(Integer.MAX_VALUE);   // OK
    System.out.println(Double.MAX_VALUE);    // OK
  }
}
```

Conflicts can also occur when a static method with the same signature is imported by several static import statements. In Example 4.6, a method named binarySearch is imported 21 times by the static import statements. This method is overloaded twice in the `java.util.Collections` class and 18 times in the `java.util.Arrays` class, in addition to one declaration in the `mypkg.Auxiliary` class. The classes `java.util.Arrays` and `mypkg.Auxiliary` have a declaration of this method with the *same signature* that matches the method call at (2), resulting in a signature conflict that is flagged as a compile-time error. The conflict can again be resolved by specifying the fully qualified name of the method.

If the static import statement at (1) is removed, there is no conflict, as only the class `java.util.Arrays` has a method that matches the method call at (2). If the declaration of the method `binarySearch()` at (3) is allowed, there is also *no* conflict, as this method declaration will *shadow* the imported method whose signature it matches.

Example 4.6 *Conflict in Importing Static Method with the Same Signature*

```
package mypkg;

public class Auxiliary {
  public static int binarySearch(int[] a, int key) { // Same in java.util.Arrays
    // Implementation is omitted.
    return -1;
  }
}
```

```
// File: MultipleStaticImport.java (in unnamed package)
import static java.util.Collections.binarySearch;  //    2 overloaded methods
import static java.util.Arrays.binarySearch;       // + 18 overloaded methods
import static mypkg.Auxiliary.binarySearch; // (1) Causes signature conflict

public class MultipleStaticImport {
  public static void main(String[] args) {
    int index = binarySearch(new int[] {10, 50, 100}, 50); // (2) Ambiguous!
    System.out.println(index);
  }

//public static int binarySearch(int[] a, int key) {     // (3)
//  return -1;
//}
}
```

Compiling Code into Packages

Conventions for specifying pathnames vary on different platforms. In this chapter, we will use pathname conventions used on a Unix platform. While trying out the examples in this section, attention should be paid to platform dependencies in this regard—especially the fact that the *separator characters* in *file paths* for the Unix and Windows platforms are / and \, respectively.

As mentioned earlier, a package can be mapped on a hierarchical file system. We can think of a package name as a pathname in the file system. Referring to Example 4.1, the package name `wizard.pandorasbox` corresponds to the pathname `wizard/pandorasbox`. The Java bytecode for all types declared in the source files `Clown.java` and `LovePotion.java` will be placed in the *package directory* with the pathname `wizard/pandorasbox`, as these source files have the following `package` declaration:

```
package wizard.pandorasbox;
```

The *location* in the file system where the package directory should be created is specified using the `-d` option (`d` for *destination*) of the `javac` command. The term *destination directory* is a synonym for this location in the file system. The compiler will create the package directory with the pathname `wizard/pandorasbox` (including any subdirectories required) *under* the specified location, and place the Java bytecode for the types declared in the source files `Clown.java` and `LovePotion.java` inside the package directory.

Assuming that the current directory (`.`) is the directory `/pgjc/work`, and the four source files in Example 4.1 are found in this directory, the following command issued in the current directory will create a file hierarchy under this directory (Figure 4.3) that mirrors the package hierarchy in Figure 4.2:

```
>javac -d . Clown.java LovePotion.java Ailment.java Baldness.java
```

Note the subdirectories that are created for a fully qualified package name, and where the class files are located. In this command line, the space between the `-d` option and its argument is mandatory.

We can specify any *relative* pathname that designates the destination directory, or its *absolute* pathname:

```
>javac -d /pgjc/work Clown.java LovePotion.java Ailment.java Baldness.java
```

We can, of course, specify destinations other than the current directory where the class files with the bytecode should be stored. The following command in the current directory `/pgjc/work` will create the necessary packages with the class files under the destination directory `/pgjc/myapp`:

```
>javac -d ../myapp Clown.java LovePotion.java Ailment.java Baldness.java
```

Without the `-d` option, the default behavior of the `javac` compiler is to place all class files directly under the current directory (where the source files are located), rather than in the appropriate subdirectories corresponding to the packages.

The compiler will report an error if there is any problem with the destination directory specified with the `-d` option (e.g., if it does not exist or does not have the right file permissions).

Running Code from Packages

Referring to Example 4.1, if the current directory has the absolute pathname `/pgjc/work` and we want to run `Clown.class` in the directory with the pathname `./wizard/`

Figure 4.3 *File Hierarchy*

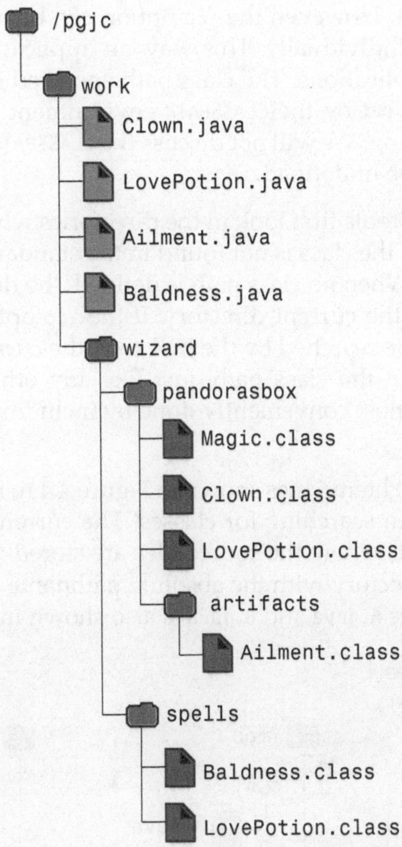

pandorasbox, the *fully qualified name* of the Clown class *must* be specified in the java command:

```
>java wizard.pandorasbox.Clown
```

This will load the bytecode of the class Clown from the file with the pathname ./wizard/pandorasbox/Clown.class, and start the execution of its main() method.

4.3 Searching for Classes

The documentation for the JDK tools explains how to organize packages in more elaborate schemes. In particular, the CLASSPATH environment variable can be used to specify the *class search path* (usually abbreviated to just *class path*), which are *pathnames* or *locations* in the file system where JDK tools should look when searching for classes and other resource files. Alternatively, the -classpath option (often abbreviated to -cp) of the JDK tool commands can be used for the same purpose.

The CLASSPATH environment variable is not recommended for this purpose, as its class path value affects *all* Java applications on the host platform, and any application can modify it. However, the -cp option can be used to set the class path for each application individually. This way, an application cannot modify the class path for other applications. The class path specified in the -cp option supersedes the path or paths set by the CLASSPATH environment variable while the JDK tool command is running. We will not discuss the CLASSPATH environment variable here, and assume it to be undefined.

Basically, the JDK tools first look in the directories where the Java standard libraries are installed. If the class is not found in the standard libraries, the tool searches in the class path. When no class path is defined, the default value of the class path is assumed to be the current directory. If the -cp option is used and the current directory should be searched by the JDK tool, the current directory must be specified as an entry in the class path, just like any other directory that should be searched. This is most conveniently done by including '.' as one of the entries in the class path.

We will use the file hierarchies shown in Figure 4.4 to illustrate some of the intricacies involved when searching for classes. The current directory has the absolute pathname /top/src, where the source files are stored. The package pkg will be created under the directory with the absolute pathname /top/bin. The source code in the two source files A.java and B.java is also shown in Figure 4.4.

Figure 4.4 *Searching for Classes*

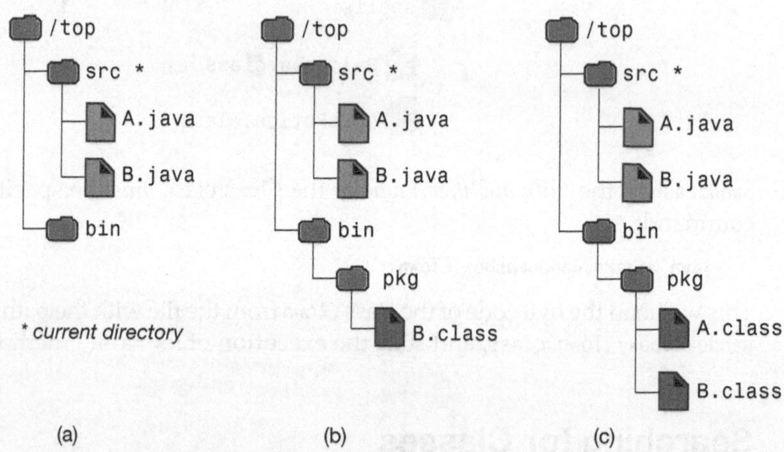


```
// File: A.java
package pkg;
class A { B b; } // A uses B
```

```
// File: B.java
package pkg;
class B { }
```

The file hierarchy before any files are compiled is shown in Figure 4.4a. Since the class B does not use any other classes, we compile it first with the following command, resulting in the file hierarchy shown in Figure 4.4b:

```
>javac -d ../bin B.java
```

Next, we try to compile the file A.java, and get the following results:

```
>javac -d ../bin A.java
A.java:3: cannot find symbol
symbol  : class B
location: class pkg.A
public class A { B b; }
                 ^
1 error
```

The compiler cannot find the class B—that is, the file B.class containing the Java bytecode for the class B. In Figure 4.4b, we can see that it is in the package pkg under the directory bin, but the compiler cannot find it. This is hardly surprising, as there is no bytecode file for the class B in the current directory, which is the default value of the class path. The following command sets the value of the class path to be /top/bin, and compilation is successful (Figure 4.4c):

```
>javac -cp /top/bin -d ../bin A.java
```

It is very important to understand that when we want the JDK tool to search in a *named package*, it is the *location* of the package that is specified; in other words, the class path indicates the directory that *contains* the first element of the fully qualified package name. In Figure 4.4c, the package pkg is contained under the directory whose absolute path is /top/bin. The following command will *not* work, as the directory /top/bin/pkg does *not* contain a package with the name pkg that has a class B:

```
>javac -cp /top/bin/pkg -d ../bin A.java
```

Also, the compiler is not using the class path to find the source file(s) that are specified in the command line. In the preceding command, the source file has the relative pathname ./A.java. Consequently, the compiler looks for the source file in the current directory. The class path is used to find the classes used by the class A.

Given the file hierarchy in Figure 4.3, the following -cp option sets the class path so that *all* packages (wizard.pandorasbox, wizard.pandorasbox.artifacts, wizard.spells) in Figure 4.3 will be searched, as all packages are located under the specified directory:

```
-cp /pgjc/work
```

However, the following -cp option will not help in finding *any* of the packages in Figure 4.3, as none of the *packages* are located under the specified directory:

```
>java -cp /pgjc/work/wizard pandorasbox.Clown
```

This command also illustrates an important point about package names: The *fully qualified package name* should not be split. The package name for the class wizard.pandorasbox.Clown is wizard.pandorasbox, and must be specified fully. The following command will search all packages in Figure 4.3 for classes that are used by the class `wizard.pandorasbox.Clown`:

```
>java -cp /pgjc/work wizard.pandorasbox.Clown
```

The class path can specify several *entries* (i.e., several locations), and the JDK tool searches them in the order they are specified, from left to right.

```
-cp /pgjc/work:/top/bin:.
```

We have used the path-separator character `':'` for Unix platforms to separate the entries, and also included the current directory (`.`) as an entry. There should be no whitespace on either side of the path-separator character.

The search in the class path entries stops once the required class file is found. Therefore, the order in which entries are specified can be significant. If a class `B` is found in a package `pkg` located under the directory `/ext/lib1`, and also in a package `pkg` located under the directory `/ext/lib2`, the order in which the entries are specified in the two `-cp` options shown next is significant. They will result in the class `pkg.B` being found under `/ext/lib1` and `/ext/lib2`, respectively.

```
-cp /ext/lib1:/ext/lib2
-cp /ext/lib2:/ext/lib1
```

The examples so far have used absolute pathnames for class path entries. We can, of course, use relative pathnames as well. If the current directory has the absolute pathname `/pgjc/work` in Figure 4.3, the following command will search the packages under the current directory:

```
>java -cp . wizard.pandorasbox.Clown
```

If the current directory has the absolute pathname `/top/src` in Figure 4.4, the following command will compile the file `./A.java`:

```
>javac -cp ../bin -d ../bin A.java
```

If the name of an entry in the class path includes whitespace, the name should be double quoted so that it will be interpreted correctly:

```
-cp "../new bin"
```

Review Questions

4.1 Given the source file `A.java`:

```
// File: A.java
package net.alphabet;
import java.util.ArrayList;
public class A {}
class B {}
```

Select the two correct answers.

(a) Both class `A` and class `B` will be placed in the package `net.alphabet`.
(b) Only class `A` will be placed in the package `net.alphabet`. Class `B` will be placed in the default package.
(c) Both class `A` and class `B` can access the imported class `java.util.ArrayList` by its simple name.
(d) Only class `A` can access the imported class `java.util.ArrayList` by its simple name.

4.2 Which import statement, when inserted independently at (1), will make the code compile?

```
// File: Window.java
package app;

public class Window {
  final static String frame = "Top-frame";
}
```

```
// File: Canvas.java
package app;

// (1) INSERT IMPORT STATEMENT HERE.

public class Canvas {
  private String str = frame;
}
```

Select the one correct answer.

(a) `import app.*;`
(b) `import app.Window;`
(c) `import java.lang.*;`
(d) `import java.lang.String;`
(e) `import static app.Window.frame;`

4.3 Which import statements, when inserted independently at (1), will make the code compile?

```
// File: Window.java
package mainpkg.subpkg1;
public class Window {}
```

```
// File: Window.java
package mainpkg.subpkg2;
public class Window {}
```

```
// File: Screen.java
package mainpkg;
// (1) INSERT IMPORT STATEMENTS HERE.
public class Screen {
  private Window win;
}
```

Select the four correct answers.

(a) `import mainpkg.*;`

(b) `import mainpkg.subpkg1.*;`

(c) `import mainpkg.subpkg2.*;`

(d)
```
import mainpkg.subpkg1.*;
import mainpkg.subpkg2.Window;
```

(e)
```
import mainpkg.subpkg1.Window;
import mainpkg.subpkg2.*;
```

(f)
```
import mainpkg.subpkg1.*;
import mainpkg.subpkg2.*;
```

(g)
```
import mainpkg.subpkg1.Window;
import mainpkg.subpkg2.Window;
```

4.4 Given the following code:

```
// (1) INSERT ONE IMPORT STATEMENT HERE
public class RQ700A20 {
  public static void main(String[] args) {
    System.out.println(sqrt(49));
  }
}
```

Which import statements, when inserted independently at (1), will make the program print 7, when the program is compiled and run?

Select the two correct answers.

(a) `import static Math.*;`

(b) `import static Math.sqrt;`

(c) `import static java.lang.Math.sqrt;`

(d) `import static java.lang.Math.sqrt();`

(e) `import static java.lang.Math.*;`

4.5 Given the source file `A.java`:

```
package top.sub;
public class A {}
```

and the following directory hierarchy:

```
/proj
   |--- src
   |       |--- top
   |               |--- sub
   |                       |--- A.java
   |--- bin
```

Assuming that the current directory is `/proj/src`, which of the following statements are true?

Select the three correct answers.

(a) The following command will compile, and place the bytecode of the class `top.sub.A` under `/proj/bin`:
`javac -d . top/sub/A.java`

(b) The following command will compile, and place the bytecode of the class `top.sub.A` under `/proj/bin`:
`javac -d /proj/bin top/sub/A.java`

(c) The following command will compile, and place the bytecode of the class `top.sub.A` under `/proj/bin`:
`javac -D /proj/bin ./top/sub/A.java`

(d) The following command will compile, and place the bytecode of the class `top.sub.A` under `/proj/bin`:
`javac -d ../bin top/sub/A.java`

(e) After successful compilation, the absolute pathname of the file `A.class` will be:
`/proj/bin/A.class`

(f) After successful compilation, the absolute pathname of the file `A.class` will be:
`/proj/bin/top/sub/A.class`

4.6 Given the following directory structure:

```
/top
   |--- wrk
          |--- pkg
                 |--- A.java
                 |--- B.java
```

Assume that the two files `A.java` and `B.java` contain the following code, respectively:

```
// File: A.java
package pkg;
class A { B b; }
```

```
// File: B.java
package pkg;
class B {...}
```

For which combinations of current directory and command is the compilation successful?

Select the two correct answers.

(a) `Current directory: /top/wrk`
`Command: javac -cp .:pkg A.java`

(b) `Current directory: /top/wrk`
`Command: javac -cp . pkg/A.java`

(c) `Current directory: /top/wrk`
`Command: javac -cp pkg A.java`

(d) `Current directory: /top/wrk`
`Command: javac -cp .:pkg pkg/A.java`

(e) `Current directory: /top/wrk/pkg`
`Command: javac A.java`

(f) `Current directory: /top/wrk/pkg`
`Command: javac -cp . A.java`

4.7 Given the following directory structure:

```
/proj
   |--- src
   |       |--- A.java
   |
   |
   |--- bin
           |--- top
                   |--- sub
                           |--- A.class
```

Assume that the current directory is `/proj/src`. Which class path specifications will find the file `A.class` of the class `top.sub.A` declared in the file `/proj/src/A.java`?

Select the two correct answers.

(a) `-cp /proj/bin/top`
(b) `-cp /proj/bin/top/sub`
(c) `-cp /proj/bin/top/sub/A.class`
(d) `-cp .:../bin`
(e) `-cp /proj`
(f) `-cp /proj/bin`

4.4 Scope Rules

Java provides explicit accessibility modifiers to control the accessibility of members in a class by external clients (§4.7, p. 123), but in two areas access is governed by specific scope rules:

- Class scope for members: how member declarations are accessed within the class.
- Block scope for local variables: how local variable declarations are accessed within a block.

Class Scope for Members

Class scope concerns accessing members (including inherited ones) from code within a class. Table 4.1 gives an overview of how static and non-static code in a class can access members of the class, including those that are inherited. Table 4.1 assumes the following declarations:

```
class SuperName {
  int instanceVarInSuper;
  static int staticVarInSuper;

  void instanceMethodInSuper()      { /* ... */ }
  static void staticMethodInSuper() { /* ... */ }
  // ...
}

class ClassName extends SuperName {
  int instanceVar;
  static int staticVar;

  void instanceMethod()      { /* ... */ }
  static void staticMethod() { /* ... */ }
  // ...
}
```

Table 4.1 *Accessing Members within a Class*

Member declarations	Non-static code in the class `ClassName` can refer to the member as	Static code in the class `ClassName` can refer to the member as

Instance variables	`instanceVar`
	`this.instanceVar`
	`instanceVarInSuper`
	`this.instanceVarInSuper`
	`super.instanceVarInSuper`
		Not possible

Instance methods	`instanceMethod()`
	`this.instanceMethod()`
	`instanceMethodInSuper()`
	`this.instanceMethodInSuper()`
	`super.instanceMethodInSuper()`
		Not possible

Static variables	`staticVar`
	`this.staticVar`
	`ClassName.staticVar`
	`staticVarInSuper`
	`this.staticVarInSuper`
	`super.staticVarInSuper`
	`ClassName.staticVarInSuper`
	`SuperName.staticVarInSuper`
		`staticVar`
		
		`ClassName.staticVar`
		`staticVarInSuper`
		
		`ClassName.staticVarInSuper`
		`SuperName.staticVarInSuper`

Static methods	`staticMethod()`
	`this.staticMethod()`
	`ClassName.staticMethod()`
	`staticMethodInSuper()`
	`this.staticMethodInSuper()`
	`super.staticMethodInSuper()`
	`ClassName.staticMethodInSuper()`
	`SuperName.staticMethodInSuper()`
		`staticMethod()`
		
		`ClassName.staticMethod()`
		`staticMethodInSuper()`
		
		`ClassName.staticMethodInSuper()`
		`SuperName.staticMethodInSuper()`

The golden rule is that static code can only access other static members by their simple names. Static code is not executed in the context of an object, so the references `this` and `super` are not available. An object has knowledge of its class, so static members are always accessible in a non-static context.

Note that using the class name to access static members within the class is no different from how external clients access these static members.

The following factors can all influence the scope of a member declaration:

- Shadowing of a field declaration, either by local variables (§4.4, p. 117) or by declarations in the subclass (§7.3, p. 275)
- Overriding an instance method from a superclass (§7.2, p. 268)
- Hiding a static method declared in a superclass (§7.3, p. 275)

Within a class, references of the class can be declared and used to access *all* members in the class, regardless of their accessibility modifiers. In Example 4.7, the method `duplicateLight` at (1) in the class `Light` has the parameter `oldLight` and the local variable `newLight` that are references of the class `Light`. Even though the fields of the class are `private`, they are accessible through the two references (`oldLight` and `newLight`) in the method `duplicateLight()` as shown at (2), (3), and (4).

Example 4.7 *Class Scope*

```
class Light {
  // Instance variables:
  private int     noOfWatts;        // Wattage
  private boolean indicator;        // On or off
  private String  location;         // Placement

  // Instance methods:
  public void switchOn()  { indicator = true; }
  public void switchOff() { indicator = false; }
  public boolean isOn()   { return indicator; }

  public static Light duplicateLight(Light oldLight) {     // (1)
    Light newLight = new Light();
    newLight.noOfWatts = oldLight.noOfWatts;               // (2)
    newLight.indicator = oldLight.indicator;               // (3)
    newLight.location  = oldLight.location;                // (4)
    return newLight;
  }
}
```

Block Scope for Local Variables

Declarations and statements can be grouped into a *block* using braces, {}. Blocks can be nested, and scope rules apply to local variable declarations in such blocks. A local declaration can appear anywhere in a block. The general rule is that a variable declared in a block is *in scope* inside the block in which it is declared, but it is not accessible outside of this block. It is not possible to redeclare a variable if a local variable of the same name is already declared in the current scope.

Local variables of a method include the formal parameters of the method and variables that are declared in the method body. The local variables in a method are created each time the method is invoked, and are therefore distinct from local variables in other invocations of the same method that might be executing (§6.5, p. 230).

Figure 4.5 illustrates *block scope* (also known as *lexical scope*) for local variables. A method body is a block. Parameters cannot be redeclared in the method body, as shown at (1) in Block 1.

A local variable—already declared in an enclosing block and, therefore, visible in a nested block—cannot be redeclared in the nested block. These cases are shown at (3), (5), and (6).

Figure 4.5 *Block Scope*

```
public static void main(String args[]) {              // Block 1
//  String args = "";       // (1) Cannot redeclare parameters.
    char digit = 'z';
  for (int index = 0; index < 10; ++index) {          // Block 2
      switch(digit) {                                 // Block 3
          case 'a':
              int i;        // (2)
          default:
          //  int i;        // (3) Already declared in the same block
      } // end switch
      if (true) {                                     // Block 4
          int i;            // (4) OK
      //  int digit;        // (5) Already declared in enclosing Block 1
      //  int index;        // (6) Already declared in enclosing Block 2
      } // end if
  } // end for
  int index;                // (7) OK
} // end main
```

A local variable in a block can be redeclared in another block if the blocks are *disjoint*—that is, they do not overlap. This is the case for variable `i` at (2) in Block 3 and at (4) in Block 4, as these two blocks are disjoint.

The scope of a local variable declaration begins from where it is declared in the block and ends where this block terminates. The scope of the loop variable `index` is the entire Block 2. Even though Block 2 is nested in Block 1, the declaration of the variable `index` at (7) in Block 1 is valid. The scope of the variable `index` at (7) spans from its declaration to the end of Block 1, and it does not overlap with that of the loop variable `index` in Block 2.

4.5 Accessibility Modifiers for Top-Level Type Declarations

The accessibility modifier `public` can be used to declare top-level types (that is, classes, enums, and interfaces) in a package to be accessible from everywhere, both inside their own package and inside other packages. If the accessibility modifier is omitted, they will be accessible only in their own package and not in any other packages or subpackages. This is called *package* or *default accessibility*.

Example 4.8 *Accessibility Modifiers for Classes and Interfaces*

```
// File: Clown.java
package wizard.pandorasbox;                        // Package declaration

import wizard.pandorasbox.artifacts.Ailment; // Importing class Ailment

public class Clown implements Magic {          // (1)
  LovePotion tlc;                              // Class in same package
  Ailment problem;                             // Simple class name
  Clown() {
    tlc = new LovePotion("passion");
    problem = new Ailment("flu");              // Simple class name
  }
  @Override public void levitate()  {          // (2)
    System.out.println("Levitating");
  }
  public void mixPotion() { System.out.println("Mixing " + tlc); }
  public void healAilment() { System.out.println("Healing " + problem); }

  public static void main(String[] args) {
    Clown joker = new Clown();
    joker.levitate();
    joker.mixPotion();
    joker.healAilment();
  }
}

interface Magic { void levitate(); }           // (3)
```

```
// File: LovePotion.java
package wizard.pandorasbox;                 // Package declaration

public class LovePotion {                   // (4) Accessible outside package
  String potionName;
  public LovePotion(String name) { potionName = name; }
  public String toString() { return potionName; }
}
```

```
// File: Ailment.java
package wizard.pandorasbox.artifacts;       // Package declaration

public class Ailment {                      // Accessible outside package
  String ailmentName;
  public Ailment(String name) { ailmentName = name; }
  public String toString() { return ailmentName; }
}
```

```
// File: Baldness.java
package wizard.spells;                      // Package declaration

import wizard.pandorasbox.*;                // Redundant
import wizard.pandorasbox.artifacts.*;      // Import of subpackage

public class Baldness extends Ailment {     // Simple name for Ailment
  wizard.pandorasbox.LovePotion tlcOne;     // Fully qualified name
  LovePotion tlcTwo;                        // Class in same package
  Baldness(String name) {
    super(name);
    tlcOne = new wizard.pandorasbox.        // Fully qualified name
                 LovePotion("romance");
    tlcTwo = new LovePotion();              // Class in same package
  }
}

class LovePotion /* implements Magic */ {   // (5) Magic is not accessible
  // @Override public void levitate() {}    // (6) Cannot override method
}
```

Compiling and running the program from the current directory gives the following results:

```
>javac -d . Clown.java LovePotion.java Ailment.java Baldness.java
>java wizard.pandorasbox.Clown
Levitating
Mixing passion
Healing flu
```

In Example 4.8, the class `Clown` at (1) and the interface `Magic` at (3) are placed in a package called `wizard.pandorasbox`. The `public` class `Clown` is accessible from everywhere. The `Magic` interface has default accessibility, and can be accessed only within the package `wizard.pandorasbox`. It is not accessible from other packages, not even from subpackages.

The class `LovePotion` at (4) is also placed in the package called `wizard.pandorasbox`. The class has `public` accessibility and, therefore, is accessible from other packages. The two files `Clown.java` and `LovePotion.java` demonstrate how several compilation units can be used to group classes in the same package.

In the file `Clown.java`, the class `Clown` at (1) implements the interface `Magic` at (3) from the same package. We have used the annotation `@Override` in front of the declaration of the `levitate()` method at (2) so that the compiler can aid in checking that this method is declared correctly as required by the interface `Magic`.

In the file `Baldness.java`, the class `LovePotion` at (5) wishes to implement the interface `Magic` at (3) from the package `wizard.pandorasbox`, but cannot do so, although the source file imports from this package. The reason is that the interface `Magic` has default accessibility and can, therefore, be accessed only within the package `wizard.pandorasbox`. The method `levitate()` of the `Magic` interface therefore cannot be overridden in class `LovePotion` at (6).

Just because a reference type is accessible does not necessarily mean that members of the type are also accessible. Member accessibility is governed separately from type accessibility, as explained in §4.7, p. 123. Table 4.2 gives a summary of accessibility modifiers for top-level types.

Table 4.2 *Summary of Accessibility Modifiers for Top-Level Types*

Modifiers	Top-level types
No modifier	Accessible in its own package (*package accessibility*)
`public`	Accessible anywhere

4.6 Non-Accessibility Modifiers for Classes

The non-accessibility modifiers `abstract` and `final` can be applied to top-level classes.

`abstract` Classes

A class can be declared with the keyword `abstract` to indicate that it cannot be instantiated. A class might choose to do this if the abstraction it represents is so general that it needs to be specialized to be of practical use. The class `Vehicle` might be specified as `abstract` to represent the general abstraction of a vehicle, as creating instances of the class would not make much sense. Creating instances of non-abstract subclasses, like Car and Bus, would make more sense, as this would make the abstraction more concrete.

Any *normal class* (that is, a class declared with the keyword class) can be declared as abstract. However, if such a class has one or more abstract methods (§4.8, p. 136), it must be declared as abstract. Obviously, such classes cannot be instantiated, as their implementation might be only partial. A class might choose this strategy to dictate certain behavior, but allow its subclasses the freedom to provide the relevant implementation. In other words, subclasses of the abstract class have to take a stand and provide implementations of any inherited abstract methods before instances can be created. A subclass that does not provide an implementation of its inherited abstract methods must also be declared as abstract or the code will not compile.

In Example 4.9, the declaration of the abstract class Light has an abstract method named kwhPrice at (1). This forces its *concrete* (i.e., non-abstract) subclasses to provide an implementation for this method. Such a class provides implementations of all its methods. The concrete subclass TubeLight provides an implementation for the method kwhPrice() at (2). The class Factory creates an instance of the class TubeLight at (3). References of an abstract class can be declared, as shown at (4), but an abstract class cannot be instantiated, as shown at (5). References of an abstract class can refer to objects of the subclasses, as shown at (6).

Example 4.9 *Abstract Classes*

```
abstract class Light {
  // Fields:
  int     noOfWatts;         // Wattage
  boolean indicator;         // On or off
  String  location;          // Placement

  // Instance methods:
  public void switchOn()  { indicator = true; }
  public void switchOff() { indicator = false; }
  public boolean isOn()   { return indicator; }

  // Abstract instance method
  public abstract double kwhPrice();                    // (1) No method body
}
//______________________________________________________________________
class TubeLight extends Light {
  // Field
  int tubeLength;

  // Implementation of inherited abstract method.
  @Override public double kwhPrice() { return 2.75; } // (2)
}
//______________________________________________________________________
```

```
public class Factory {
  public static void main(String[] args) {
    TubeLight cellarLight = new TubeLight();           // (3) OK
    Light nightLight;                                  // (4) OK
//  Light tableLight = new Light();                    // (5) Compile-time error
    nightLight = new TubeLight();                      // (6) OK
    System.out.println("KWH price: $" + nightLight.kwhPrice());
  }
}
```

Output from the program:

```
KWH price: $2.75
```

`final` Classes

A class can be declared as `final` to indicate that it cannot be extended; that is, one cannot declare subclasses of a `final` class. This implies that one cannot override any methods declared in such a class. In other words, the class behavior cannot be changed by extending the class. A `final` class marks the lower boundary of its *implementation inheritance hierarchy* (§7.1, p. 264). Only a *concrete* class can be declared as `final`.

A `final` class must be complete, whereas an `abstract` class is considered incomplete. Classes, therefore, cannot be both `final` and `abstract` at the same time. Interfaces are inherently `abstract`, as they can specify methods that are abstract, and therefore cannot be declared as `final`. A `final` class and an interface represent two extremes when it comes to providing an implementation. An `abstract` class represents a compromise between these two extremes. Table 4.3 provides a summary of non-accessibility modifiers for classes.

The Java SE platform API includes many `final` classes—for example, the `java.lang.String` class and the wrapper classes for primitive values.

If it is decided that the class `TubeLight` in Example 4.9 may not be extended, it can be declared as `final`:

```
final class TubeLight extends Light {
  // ...
}
```

Discussion of `final` methods, fields, and local variables can be found in §4.8, p. 133.

Table 4.3 *Summary of Non-Accessibility Modifiers for Classes*

Modifier	Classes
`abstract`	A non-`final` class can be declared as `abstract`. A class with an `abstract` method must be declared as `abstract`. An `abstract` class cannot be instantiated.
`final`	A non-`abstract` class can be declared as `final`. A class with a `final` method need not be declared as `final`. A `final` class cannot be extended.

Review Questions

4.8 Given the following class, which of these alternatives are valid ways of referring to the class from outside of the package `net.basemaster`?

```
package net.basemaster;

public class Base {
  // ...
}
```

Select the two correct answers.

(a) By simply referring to the class as `Base`
(b) By simply referring to the class as `basemaster.Base`
(c) By simply referring to the class as `net.basemaster.Base`
(d) By importing with `net.basemaster.*`, and referring to the class as `Base`
(e) By importing with `net.*`, and referring to the class as `basemaster.Base`

4.9 Which one of the following class declarations is a valid declaration of a class that cannot be instantiated?

Select the one correct answer.

(a) `class Ghost          { abstract void haunt(); }`
(b) `abstract class Ghost { void haunt(); }`
(c) `abstract class Ghost { void haunt() {}; }`
(d) `abstract Ghost       { abstract void haunt(); }`
(e) `abstract class Ghost { abstract haunt(); }`

4.10 Which one of the following class declarations is a valid declaration of a class that cannot be extended?

Select the one correct answer.

(a) `class Link { }`
(b) `abstract class Link { }`
(c) `native class Link { }`
(d) `final class Link { }`
(e) `abstract final class Link { }`

4.7 Member Accessibility Modifiers

By specifying member accessibility modifiers, a class can control which information is accessible to clients (that is, other classes). These modifiers help a class to define a *contract* so that clients know exactly which services are offered by the class.

The accessibility of members can be one of the following:

- `public`
- `protected`
- *Default accessibility* (also known as *package accessibility*), meaning that no accessibility modifier is specified
- `private`

In the following discussion of accessibility modifiers for members of a class, keep in mind that the member accessibility modifier has meaning only if the class (or one of its subclasses) is accessible to the client. Also, note that only one accessibility modifier can be specified for a member.

The discussion in this section applies to both instance and static members of top-level classes. It applies equally to *constructors* as well.

In UML notation, the prefixes `+`, `#`, and `-`, when applied to a member name, indicate `public`, `protected`, and `private` member accessibility, respectively. No prefix indicates default or package accessibility.

`public` Members

Public accessibility is the least restrictive of all the accessibility modifiers. A `public` member is accessible from anywhere, both in the package containing its class and in other packages where this class is visible.

Example 4.10 contains two source files, shown at (1) and (6). The package hierarchy defined by the source files is depicted in Figure 4.6, showing the two packages, `packageA` and `packageB`, containing their respective classes. The classes in `packageB` use classes from `packageA`. The class `SuperclassA` in `packageA` has two subclasses: `SubclassA` in `packageA` and `SubclassB` in `packageB`.

Figure 4.6 *Public Accessibility for Members*

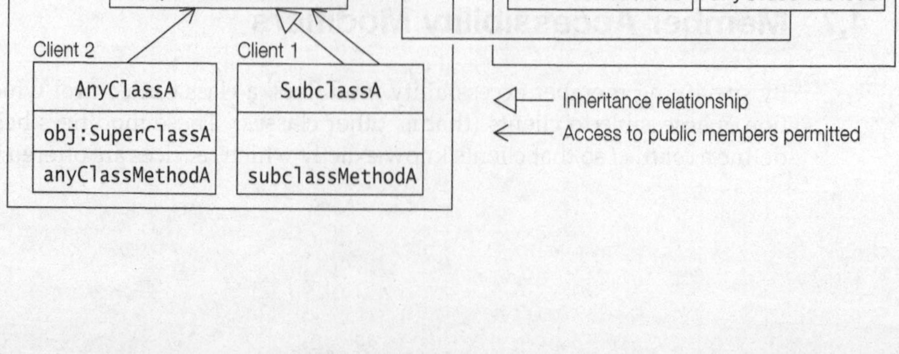

Example 4.10 *Public Accessibility of Members*

```
// File: SuperclassA.java                                  (1)
package packageA;

public class SuperclassA {
  public int superclassVarA;                               // (2)
  public void superclassMethodA() {/*...*/}                // (3)
}

class SubclassA extends SuperclassA {
  void subclassMethodA() { superclassVarA = 10; }          // (4) OK
}

class AnyClassA {
  SuperclassA obj = new SuperclassA();
  void anyClassMethodA() {
    obj.superclassMethodA();                               // (5) OK
  }
}
```

```
// File: SubclassB.java                                    (6)
package packageB;
import packageA.*;

public class SubclassB extends SuperclassA {
  void subclassMethodB() { superclassMethodA(); }          // (7) OK
}

class AnyClassB {
  SuperclassA obj = new SuperclassA();
  void anyClassMethodB() {
    obj.superclassVarA = 20;                               // (8) OK
  }
}
```

Accessibility is illustrated in Example 4.10 by the accessibility modifiers for the field `superclassVarA` and the method `superclassMethodA()` at (2) and (3), respectively, defined in the class `SuperclassA`. These members are accessed from four different clients in Example 4.10.

- Client 1: From a subclass in the same package, which accesses an inherited field from the class `SuperclassA`. `SubclassA` is such a client, and does this at (4).
- Client 2: From a non-subclass in the same package, which invokes a method on an instance of the `SuperclassA` class. `AnyClassA` is such a client, and does this at (5).

- Client 3: From a subclass in another package, which invokes an inherited method from the class `SuperclassA`. `SubclassB` is such a client, and does this at (7).
- Client 4: From a non-subclass in another package, which accesses a field in an instance of the `SuperclassA` class. `AnyClassB` is such a client, and does this at (8).

In Example 4.10, the field `superclassVarA` and the method `superclassMethodA()` have public accessibility in the `SuperclassA` class, and are accessible by all four of these clients. Subclasses can access their inherited public members by their simple names, and all clients can access public members in an instance of the `SuperclassA` class. Public accessibility is depicted in Figure 4.6.

`protected` Members

A protected member is accessible in all classes in the same package, and by all subclasses of its class in any package where this class is visible. In other words, non-subclasses in other packages cannot access protected members from other packages. This kind of accessibility is more restrictive than public member accessibility.

In Example 4.10, if the field `superclassVarA` and the method `superclassMethodA()` of the class `SuperclassA` have protected accessibility, they are accessible within `packageA`, and only accessible by subclasses in any other packages.

```
public class SuperclassA {
  protected int superclassVarA;                          // (2) Protected member
  protected void superclassMethodA() {/*...*/}           // (3) Protected member
}
```

Client 4 in `packageB` cannot access these members, as shown in Figure 4.7.

An important caveat is that a subclass in another package can access only protected members in the superclass via references of its own type or its subtypes. The following new declaration of `SubclassB` in `packageB` from Example 4.10 illustrates the point:

```
// File: SubclassB.java
package packageB;
import packageA.*;
public class SubclassB extends SuperclassA {        // In packageB
  SuperclassA objRefA = new SuperclassA();          // (1)
  void subclassMethodB(SubclassB objRefB) {
    objRefB.superclassMethodA();                    // (2) OK
    objRefB.superclassVarA = 5;                     // (3) OK
    objRefA.superclassMethodA();                    // (4) Not OK
    objRefA.superclassVarA = 10;                    // (5) Not OK
  }
}
```

Figure 4.7 *Protected Accessibility for Members*

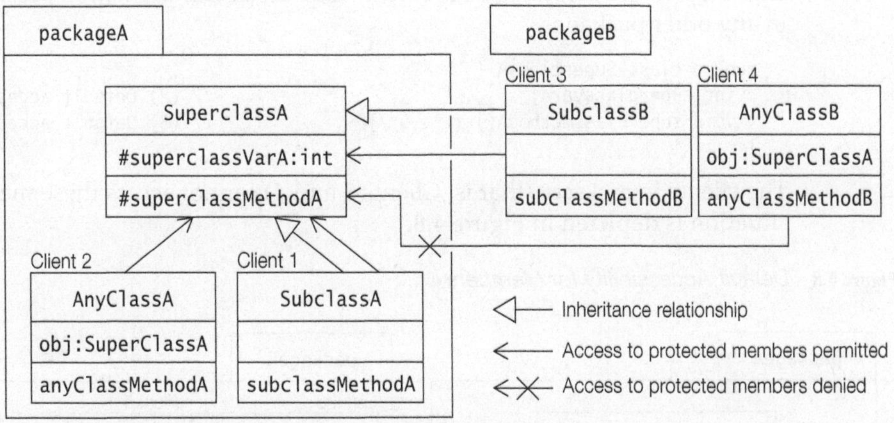

The class `SubclassB` declares the field `objRefA` of type `SuperclassA` at (1). The method `subclassMethodB()` has the formal parameter `objRefB` of type `SubclassB`. Access is permitted to a protected member of `SuperclassA` in `packageA` by a reference of the subclass, as shown at (2) and (3), but not by a reference of its superclass, as shown at (4) and (5). Access to the field `superclassVarA` and the call to the method `superclassMethodA()` occur in `SubclassB`. These members are declared in `SuperclassA`. `SubclassB` is not involved in the implementation of `SuperclassA`, which is the type of the reference `objRefA`. Hence, access to protected members at (4) and (5) is not permitted as these are not members of an object that can be guaranteed to be implemented by the code accessing them.

Accessibility to protected members of the superclass would also be permitted via any reference whose type is a subclass of `SubclassB`. The previously mentioned restriction helps to ensure that subclasses in packages different from their superclass can access protected members of the superclass only in their part of the implementation inheritance hierarchy. In other words, a protected member of a superclass is accessible in a subclass that is in another package only if the member is inherited by an object of the subclass (or by an object of a subclass of this subclass).

Default Accessibility for Members

When no member accessibility modifier is specified, the member is accessible only to other classes in its own class's package. Even if its class is visible in another (possibly nested) package, the member is not accessible elsewhere. Default member accessibility is more restrictive than protected member accessibility.

In Example 4.10, if the field `superclassVarA` and the method `superclassMethodA()` are defined with no accessibility modifier, they are accessible within `packageA`, but not in any other packages.

```
public class SuperclassA {
  int superclassVarA;                                    // (2) Default accessibility
  void superclassMethodA() {/*...*/}                     // (3) Default accessibility
}
```

The clients in `packageB` (that is, Clients 3 and 4) cannot access these members. This situation is depicted in Figure 4.8.

Figure 4.8 *Default Accessibility for Members*

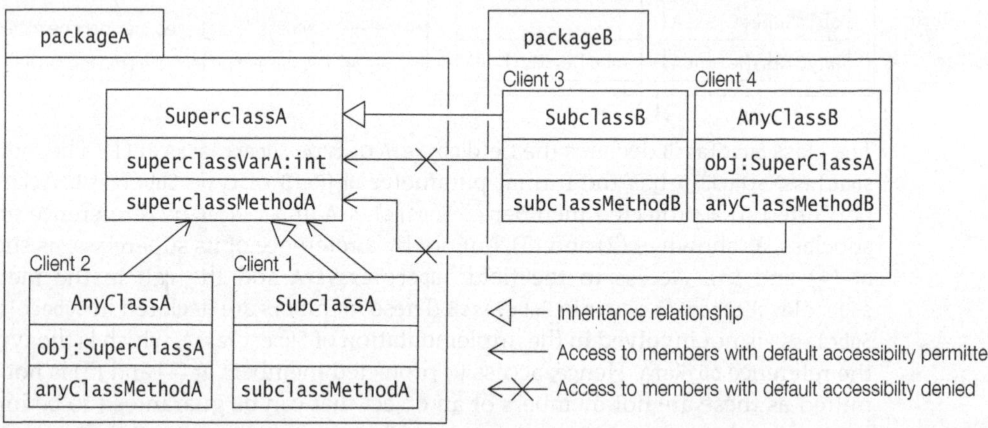

`private` Members

The `private` modifier is the most restrictive of all the accessibility modifiers. Private members are not accessible from any other classes. This also applies to subclasses, whether they are in the same package or not. Since they are not accessible by their simple names in a subclass, they are also not inherited by the subclass. A standard design strategy for a class is to make all fields private and provide public accessor methods for them. Auxiliary methods are often declared as `private`, as they do not concern any client.

In Example 4.10, if the field `superclassVarA` and the method `superclassMethodA()` have private accessibility, they are not accessible by any other clients.

```
public class SuperclassA {
  private int superclassVarA;                       // (2) Private member
  private void superclassMethodA() {/*...*/}        // (3) Private member
}
```

None of the clients in Figure 4.9 can access these members. Table 4.4 provides a summary of accessibility modifiers for members.

Figure 4.9 *Private Accessibility for Members*

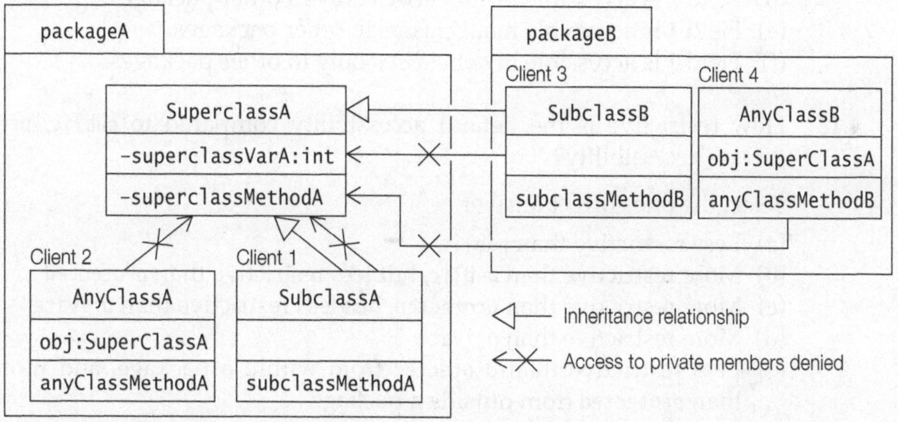

Table 4.4 *Summary of Accessibility Modifiers for Members*

Modifier	Members
`public`	Accessible everywhere.
`protected`	Accessible by any class in the same package as its class, and accessible only by subclasses of its class in other packages.
No modifier	Only accessible by classes, including subclasses, in the same package as its class (package or default accessibility).
`private`	Only accessible in its own class and not anywhere else.

Review Questions

4.11 Given the following declaration of a class, which field is accessible from outside the package `com.corporation.project`?

```
package com.corporation.project;

public class MyClass {
            int i;
  public    int j;
  protected int k;
  private   int l;
}
```

Select the one correct answer.

(a) Field `i` is accessible in all classes in other packages.
(b) Field `j` is accessible in all classes in other packages.

(c) Field k is accessible in all classes in other packages.
(d) Field k is accessible in subclasses only in other packages.
(e) Field l is accessible in all classes in other packages.
(f) Field l is accessible in subclasses only in other packages.

4.12 How restrictive is the default accessibility compared to public, protected, and private accessibility?

Select the one correct answer

(a) Less restrictive than public
(b) More restrictive than public, but less restrictive than protected
(c) More restrictive than protected, but less restrictive than private
(d) More restrictive than private
(e) Less restrictive than protected from within a package, and more restrictive than protected from outside a package

4.13 Which statement is true about the accessibility of members?

Select the one correct answer.

(a) A private member is always accessible within the same package.
(b) A private member can be accessed only within the class of the member.
(c) A member with default accessibility can be accessed by any subclass of the class in which it is declared.
(d) A private member cannot be accessed at all.
(e) Package/default accessibility for a member can be declared using the keyword default.

4.14 Which lines that are marked will compile in the following code?

```
// File name: A.java
package packageA;

public class A {
  protected int pf;
}
```

```
// File name: B.java
package packageB;
import packageA.A;

public class B extends A {
  void action(A obj1, B obj2, C obj3) {
    pf = 10;                    // (1)
    obj1.pf = 10;               // (2)
    obj2.pf = 10;               // (3)
    obj3.pf = 10;               // (4)
  }
}
```

```
class C extends B {
  void action(A obj1, B obj2, C obj3) {
    pf = 10;                  // (5)
    obj1.pf = 10;             // (6)
    obj2.pf = 10;             // (7)
    obj3.pf = 10;             // (8)
  }
}

class D {
  void action(A obj1, B obj2, C obj3) {
    pf = 10;                  // (9)
    obj1.pf = 10;             // (10)
    obj2.pf = 10;             // (11)
    obj3.pf = 10;             // (12)
  }
}
```

Select the five correct answers.

(a) (1)
(b) (2)
(c) (3)
(d) (4)
(e) (5)
(f) (6)
(g) (7)
(h) (8)
(i) (9)
(j) (10)
(k) (11)
(l) (12)

4.8 Non-Accessibility Modifiers for Members

The following keywords can be used to specify certain aspects of members in a type declaration:

- `static`
- `final`
- `abstract`
- `synchronized`
- `native`
- `transient`
- `volatile`

static Members

Static members belong to the class in which they are declared and are not part of any instance of the class. The declaration of static members is prefixed by the keyword `static` to distinguish them from instance members. Depending on the accessibility modifiers of the static members in a class, clients can access these members by using the class name or through object references of the class. The class need not be instantiated to access its static members.

Static variables (also called *class variables*) exist only in the class in which they are defined. They are not instantiated when an instance of the class is created. In other words, the values of these variables are not a part of the state of any object. When the class is loaded, static variables are initialized to their default values if no explicit initialization expression is specified.

Static methods are also known as *class methods*. A static method in a class can directly access other static members in the class. It cannot access instance (i.e., non-static) members of the class directly, as there is no notion of an object associated with a static method.

A typical static method might perform some task on behalf of the whole class or for objects of the class. In Example 4.11, the static variable `counter` keeps track of the number of instances of the `Light` class that have been created. The example shows that the static method `writeCount()` can access static members directly, as shown at (2), but not non-static members, as shown at (3). The static variable `counter` at (1) will be initialized to the default value `0` when the class is loaded at runtime. The `main()` method at (4) in the class `Warehouse` shows how static members of the class `Light` can be accessed using the class name and via object references of the type `Light`.

A summary of how static members are accessed in static and non-static code is given in Table 4.1, p. 115.

Example 4.11 *Accessing Static Members*

```
class Light {
  // Fields:
  int     noOfWatts;       // Wattage
  boolean indicator;       // On or off
  String  location;        // Placement

  // Static variable
  static int counter;      // Number of Light objects created            (1)

  // Non-zero argument constructor
  Light(int noOfWatts, boolean indicator, String location) {
    this.noOfWatts = noOfWatts;
    this.indicator = indicator;
    this.location  = location;
    ++counter;            // Increment counter.
  }
```

```
    // Static method
    public static void writeCount() {
      System.out.println("Number of lights: " + counter);       // (2)
      // Compile-time error. Field noOfWatts is not accessible:
      // System.out.println("Number of Watts: " + noOfWatts);   // (3)
    }
  }
  //______________________________________________________________
  public class Warehouse {
    public static void main(String[] args) {                    // (4)

      Light.writeCount();                          // Invoked using class name
      Light light1 = new Light(100, true, "basement"); // Create an object
      System.out.println(
          "Value of counter: " + Light.counter     // Accessed via class name
      );
      Light light2 = new Light(200, false, "garage");  // Create another object
      light2.writeCount();                          // Invoked using reference
      Light light3 = new Light(300, true, "kitchen");  // Create another object
      System.out.println(
          "Value of counter: " + light3.counter    // Accessed via reference
      );
    }
  }
```

Output from the program:

```
Number of lights: 0
Value of counter: 1
Number of lights: 2
Value of counter: 3
```

`final` Members

A `final` variable is a constant despite being called a variable. Its value cannot be changed once it has been initialized. Instance and static variables can be declared as `final`. Note that the keyword `final` can also be applied to local variables, including formal parameters of a method. Declaring a variable as `final` has the following implications:

- A `final` variable of a primitive data type cannot change its value once it has been initialized.
- A `final` variable of a reference type cannot change its reference value once it has been initialized. This effectively means that a `final` reference will always refer to the same object. However, the keyword `final` has no bearing on whether the *state of the object* denoted by the reference can be changed.
- After the constructor exits, the `final` fields of a object are all guaranteed to be initialized. The compiler ensures that the class provides the appropriate code to initialize the `final` fields.

A `final` variable must be explicitly initialized only once with an initializer expression, either in its declaration or in an initializer block (§9.7, p. 399). A `final` instance variable can also be initialized in a constructor.

Note that a `final` local variable need not be initialized in its declaration, but it must be initialized in the code once before it is used. These variables are also known as *blank final variables*. For a discussion of `final` parameters, see §3.5, p. 80.

A `final` method in a class is a *concrete* method (that is, has an implementation) and cannot be overridden in any subclass (§7.2, p. 268).

Variables declared as `final` ensure that values cannot be changed and methods declared as `final` ensure that behavior cannot be changed. Classes declared as `final` are discussed in §4.6, p. 122.

The compiler may be able to perform code optimizations for `final` members, because certain assumptions can be made about such members.

Static final variables are commonly used to define *manifest constants* (also called *named constants*)—for example, `Integer.MAX_VALUE`, which is the maximum `int` value. Variables defined in an interface are implicitly `final` (§7.6, p. 290).

In Example 4.12, the class `Light` defines two `public static final` variables at (1) and (2). The `public static final` variable `KWH_PRICE` is initialized in the declaration at (1), and the `public static final` variable `MANUFACTURER` is initialized in the `static` initializer block at (3). An attempt to change the value of the `public static final` variable `KWH_PRICE` at (9) results in a compile-time error.

The class `Light` also defines two `final` instance variables at (4) and (5). The `final` instance variable `color` is initialized in the instance initializer block at (6), and the `final` instance variable `energyRating` is initialized in the constructor at (7).

The class `Light` also defines a `final` method at (8). The subclass `TubeLight` attempts to override the `final` method `setWatts()` from the superclass `Light` at (10), which is not permitted.

The class `Warehouse` also defines a `final` local reference `workLight` at (11). The state of the object denoted by the reference `workLight` is changed at (12), but its reference value cannot be changed as attempted at (13). Another `final` local reference `alarmLight` is declared at (14), but it is not initialized. The compiler reports an error when an attempt is made to use this reference at (15).

Example 4.12 *Using* `final` *Modifier*

```
class Light {
  // Static final variables
  public static final double KWH_PRICE = 3.25;    // (1)
  public static final String MANUFACTURER;        // (2)
```

```
  static {                                    // Static initializer block
    MANUFACTURER = "Ozam";                    // (3) Initializes (2)
  }

  // Instance variables
  int noOfWatts;
  final String color;                         // (4)
  final String energyRating;                  // (5)

  {                                           // Instance initializer block
    color = "off white";                      // (6) Initializes (4)
  }

  // Constructor
  Light() {
    energyRating = "A++";                     // (7) Initializes (5)
  }

  // Final instance method                       (8)
  final public void setWatts(int watt) {
    noOfWatts = watt;
  }

  public void setKWH() {
    // KWH_PRICE = 4.10;                  // (9) Not OK. Cannot be changed.
  }
}
//______________________________________________________________________________
class TubeLight extends Light {
  // Final method in superclass cannot be overridden.
  // This method will not compile.
  /*
   @Override
   public void setWatts(int watt) {       // (10) Attempt to override.
        noOfWatts = 2*watt;
   }
  */
}
//______________________________________________________________________________
public class Warehouse {
  public static void main(String[] args) {

    final Light workLight = new Light(); // (11) Final local variable.
    workLight.setWatts(100);             // (12) OK. Changing object state.
//  workLight = new Light();             // (13) Not OK. Changing final reference.

    final Light alarmLight;              // (14) Not initialized.
//  alarmLight.setWatts(200);            // (15) Not OK.

    System.out.println("KWH_PRICE:    " + Light.KWH_PRICE);
    System.out.println("MANUFACTURER: " + Light.MANUFACTURER);
    System.out.println("noOfWatts:    " + workLight.noOfWatts);
    System.out.println("color:        " + workLight.color);
    System.out.println("energyRating: " + workLight.energyRating);
  }
}
```

Output from the program:

```
KWH_PRICE:    3.25
MANUFACTURER: Ozam
noOfWatts:    100
color:        off white
energyRating: A++
```

abstract Methods

An abstract method in an abstract class has the following syntax:

accessibility_modifier `abstract` *return_type method_name* (*formal_parameter_list*) *throws_clause*;

An abstract method does not have an implementation; that is, no method body is defined for an abstract method, and only the *method header* is provided in the class declaration. The keyword `abstract` is mandatory in the header of an abstract method declared in a class. Its class is then incomplete and must be explicitly declared as `abstract` (§4.6, p. 120). Subclasses of an abstract class must then provide the method implementation; otherwise, they must also be declared as `abstract`. The accessibility of an abstract method declared in a top-level class cannot be `private`, as subclasses would not be able to override the method and provide an implementation. See §4.6, where Example 4.9 also illustrates the use of abstract methods.

Only an instance method can be declared as `abstract`. Since static methods cannot be overridden, declaring an `abstract` static method makes no sense, and the compiler will report an error. A `final` method cannot be `abstract` (i.e., cannot be incomplete), and vice versa. The keyword `abstract` can be specified only in combination with the `public` or `protected` accessibility modifier.

Abstract methods specified in a top-level interface are implicitly `abstract`, and the keyword `abstract` is seldom specified in their method headers. These methods can have only `public` accessibility. See §7.6, p. 291, for a discussion of abstract methods in top-level interfaces.

synchronized Methods

A thread is an independent path of execution in a program. Several threads can be executing in a program. They might try to execute several methods on the same object simultaneously. Methods can be declared as `synchronized` if it is desired that only one thread at a time be able to execute a method of the object. Their execution is then mutually exclusive among all threads. At any given time, at most one thread can be executing a `synchronized` method on an object. This discussion also applies to static `synchronized` methods of a class.

In Example 4.13, both the `push()` method, declared at (1), and the `pop()` method, declared at (2), are `synchronized` in the class `StackImpl`. Only one thread at a time can execute a `synchronized` method in an object of the class `StackImpl`. Consequently, it is not possible for the state of an object of the class `StackImpl` to be corrupted, for example, while one thread is pushing an element and another is attempting to pop the stack.

Example 4.13 *Synchronized Methods*

```
class StackImpl {                          // Non-generic partial implementation
  private Object[] stackArray;
  private int topOfStack;
  // ...
  synchronized public void push(Object elem) { // (1)
    stackArray[++topOfStack] = elem;
  }

  synchronized public Object pop() {           // (2)
    Object obj = stackArray[topOfStack];
    stackArray[topOfStack] = null;
    topOfStack--;
    return obj;
  }

  // Other methods, etc.
  public Object peek() { return stackArray[topOfStack]; }
}
```

`native` Methods

Native methods are methods whose implementation is not defined in Java but rather in another programming language, such as C or C++. Such a method can be declared as a member in a Java class declaration. Since its implementation appears elsewhere, only the method header is specified in the class declaration. The keyword `native` is mandatory in the method header. A native method can also specify checked exceptions in a `throws` clause (§6.9, p. 251), but the compiler cannot check them, since the method is not implemented in Java.

The Java Native Interface (JNI) is a special API that allows Java methods to invoke native functions implemented in C.

In the following example, a `native` method in the class `Native` is declared at (2). The class also uses a static initializer block to load the native library when the class is loaded. Clients of the `Native` class can call the `native` method like any another method, as at (3).

```
class Native {

  /*
   * The static block ensures that the native method library
   * is loaded before the native method is called.
   */
  static {
    System.loadLibrary("NativeMethodLib");  // (1) Load native library.
  }

  native void nativeMethod();               // (2) Native method header.
  // ...

}

class Client {
  //...
  public static void main(String[] args) {
    Native trueNative = new Native();
    trueNative.nativeMethod();              // (3) Native method call.
  }
  //...
}
```

`transient` Fields

Often it is desirable to save the state of an object—for example, on a file. Such objects are said to be *persistent*. In Java, the state of an object can be stored using serialization. Serialization transforms objects into an output format that is conducive for storing objects. Objects can later be retrieved in the same state as when they were serialized, meaning that all fields included in the serialization will have the same values as at the time of serialization.

Sometimes the value of a field in an object should not be saved, in which case the field can be specified as `transient` in the class declaration. This designation implies that its value should not be saved when objects of the class are written to persistent storage. In the following example, the field `currentTemperature` is declared as `transient` at (1), because the current temperature is most likely to have changed when the object is restored at a later date. However, the value of the field `mass`, declared at (2), is likely to remain unchanged. When objects of the class `Experiment` are serialized, the value of the field `currentTemperature` will not be saved, but that of the field `mass` will be, as part of the state of the serialized object.

```
class Experiment implements Serializable {
  // ...

  // The value of currentTemperature will not persist.
  transient int currentTemperature;      // (1) Transient value.

  double mass;                           // (2) Persistent value.

}
```

Specifying the `transient` modifier for static variables is redundant and, therefore, discouraged. Static variables are not part of the persistent state of a serialized object.

`volatile` Fields

During execution, compiled code might cache the values of fields for efficiency reasons. Since multiple threads can access the same field, it is vital that caching is not allowed to cause inconsistencies when reading and writing the value in the field. The `volatile` modifier can be used to inform the compiler that it should not attempt to perform optimizations on the field, which could cause unpredictable results when the field is accessed by multiple threads.

In the simple example that follows, the value of the field `clockReading` might be changed unexpectedly by another thread while one thread is performing a task that involves always using the current value of the field `clockReading`. Declaring the field as `volatile` ensures that a write operation will always be performed on the master field variable, and a read operation will always return the correct current value.

```
class VitalControl {
  // ...
  volatile long clockReading;
  // Two successive reads might give different results.
}
```

Table 4.5 provides a summary of non-accessibility modifiers for members.

Table 4.5 *Summary of Non-Accessibility Modifiers for Members*

Modifier	Fields	Methods
`static`	Defines a class variable.	Defines a class method.
`final`	Defines a constant.	The method cannot be overridden.
`abstract`	Not applicable.	No method body is defined. Its class must also be designated as `abstract`.
`synchronized`	Not applicable.	Only one thread at a time can execute the method.
`native`	Not applicable.	Declares that the method is implemented in another language.
`transient`	The value in the field will not be included when the object is serialized.	Not applicable.
`volatile`	The compiler will not attempt to optimize access to the value in the field.	Not applicable.

Review Questions

4.15 Which statements about the use of modifiers are true?

Select the two correct answers.

(a) If no accessibility modifier (`public`, `protected`, or `private`) is specified for a member declaration, the member is accessible only by classes in the package of its class and by subclasses of its class in any package.
(b) You cannot specify accessibility of local variables. They are accessible only within the block in which they are declared.
(c) Subclasses of a class must reside in the same package as the class they extend.
(d) Local variables can be declared as `static`.
(e) The objects themselves do not have any accessibility modifiers; only field references do.

4.16 Given the following source code, which comment line can be uncommented without introducing errors?

```
abstract class MyClass {
  abstract void f();
  final    void g() {}
//final    void h() {}                              // (1)

  protected static int i;
  private          int j;
}

final class MyOtherClass extends MyClass {
//MyOtherClass(int n) { m = n; }                    // (2)

  public static void main(String[] args) {
    MyClass mc = new MyOtherClass();
  }

  void f() {}
  void h() {}
//void k() { i++; }                                 // (3)
//void l() { j++; }                                 // (4)

  int m;
}
```

Select the one correct answer.

(a) (1)
(b) (2)
(c) (3)
(d) (4)

4.17 Which statement is true?

Select the one correct answer.

(a) A static method can call other non-static methods in the same class by using the `this` keyword.
(b) A class may contain both static and non-static variables, and both static and non-static methods.
(c) Each object of a class has its own instance of the static variables declared in the class.
(d) Instance methods may access local variables of static methods.
(e) All methods in a class are implicitly passed the `this` reference as an argument, when invoked.

4.18 Which one of these is not a legal member declaration within a class?

Select the one correct answer.

(a) `static int a;`
(b) `final Object[] fudge = { null };`
(c) `abstract int t;`
(d) `native void sneeze();`
(e) `static final private double PI = 3.14159265358979323846;`

4.19 Which statements about modifiers are true?

Select the two correct answers.

(a) Abstract classes can declare `final` methods.
(b) Fields can be declared as `native`.
(c) Non-`abstract` methods can be declared in `abstract` classes.
(d) Classes can be declared as `native`.
(e) Abstract classes can be declared as `final`.

4.20 Which statement is true?

Select the one correct answer.

(a) The values of `transient` fields will not be saved during serialization.
(b) Constructors can be declared as `abstract`.
(c) The initial state of an array object constructed with the statement `int[] a = new int[10]` will depend on whether the array variable a is a local variable or a field.
(d) A subclass of a class with an `abstract` method must provide an implementation for the `abstract` method.
(e) Only static methods can access static members.

Chapter Summary

The following topics were covered in this chapter:

- The structure of a Java source file
- Defining, using, and deploying packages
- Class scope for members, and block scope for local variables
- Accessibility (default, `public`) and other modifiers (`abstract`, `final`) for reference types
- Applicability of member accessibility (default, `public`, `protected`, `private`) and other member modifiers (`static`, `final`, `abstract`, `synchronized`, `native`, `transient`, `volatile`)

Programming Exercise

4.1 Design a class for a bank database. The database should support the following operations:

- Deposit a certain amount into an account
- Withdraw a certain amount from an account
- Get the balance (i.e., the current amount) in an account
- Transfer an amount from one account to another

The amount in the transactions is a value of type `double`. The accounts are identified by instances of the class `Account` that is in the package `com.megabankcorp.records`. The database class should be placed in a package called `com.megabankcorp.system`.

The deposit, withdraw, and balance operations should not have any implementation, but should allow subclasses to provide the implementation. The transfer operation should use the deposit and withdraw operations to implement the transfer. It should not be possible to alter this operation in any subclass, and only classes within the package `com.megabankcorp.system` should be allowed to use this operation. The deposit and withdraw operations should be accessible in all packages. The balance operation should be accessible only in subclasses and classes within the package `com.megabankcorp.system`.

Operators and Expressions

5

Programmer I Exam Objectives	
[2.1] Declare and initialize variables (including casting of primitive data types) ○ *For declaring and initializing variables, see §2.3, p. 40, and §2.4, p. 42.*	*§5.6, p. 160*
[3.1] Use Java operators; including parentheses to override operator precedence	*§5.3, p. 150* *§5.4, p. 152* *§5.6–§5.17*
[3.2] Test equality between Strings and other objects using == and equals() ○ *For String equality, see §8.4, p. 357.* ○ *For String comparison, see §8.4, p. 363.*	*§5.12, p. 181*
[3.3] Create if and if/else and ternary constructs ○ *For if and if/else statements, see §6.2, p. 200.*	*§5.16, p. 194*
[6.6] Determine the effect upon object references and primitive values when they are passed into methods that change the values ○ *For parameter passing, see §3.5, p. 72.*	*§5.2, p. 147*
Supplementary Objectives	
• Distinguish between conversion categories and conversion contexts, and understand which conversions are permissible in each conversion context	*§5.1, p. 144* *§5.2, p. 147*
• Represent integers in different number systems and in memory	*§5.5, p. 154*

5.1 Conversions

In this section we first discuss the different kinds of type conversions that can be applied to values; in the next section we discuss the contexts in which these conversions are permitted. Some type conversions must be explicitly stated in the program, while others are performed implicitly. Some type conversions can be checked at compile time to guarantee their validity at runtime, while others will require an extra check at runtime.

Widening and Narrowing Primitive Conversions

For the primitive data types, the value of a *narrower* data type can be converted to a value of a *wider* data type. This is called a *widening primitive conversion*. Widening conversions from one primitive type to the next wider primitive type are summarized in Figure 5.1. The conversions shown are transitive. For example, an `int` can be directly converted to a `double` without first having to convert it to a `long` and a `float`.

Note that the target type of a widening primitive conversion has a *wider range* of values than the source type—for example, the range of the `long` type subsumes the range of the `int` type. In widening conversions between *integral* types, the source value remains intact, with no loss of magnitude information. However, a widening conversion from an `int` or a `long` value to a `float` value, or from a `long` value to a `double` value, may result in a *loss of precision*. The floating-point value in the target type is then a correctly rounded approximation of the integer value. Note that precision relates to the number of significant bits in the value, and must not be confused with *magnitude*, which relates how big a value can be represented.

Figure 5.1 *Widening Primitive Conversions*

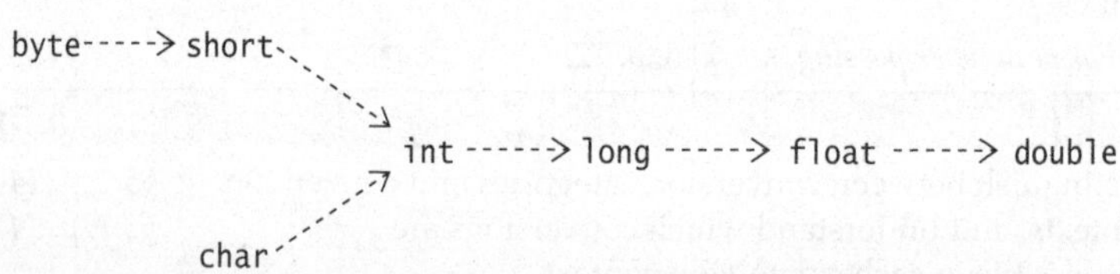

Converting from a wider primitive type to a narrower primitive type is called a *narrowing primitive conversion*; it can result in loss of magnitude information, and possibly in a loss of precision as well. Any conversion that is not a widening primitive conversion according to Figure 5.1 is a narrowing primitive conversion. The target type of a narrowing primitive conversion has a *narrower range* of values than the source type—for example, the range of the `int` type does not include all the values in the range of the `long` type.

Note that all conversions between `char` and the two integer types `byte` and `short` are considered narrowing primitive conversions. The reason is that the conversions between the unsigned type `char` and the signed types `byte` or `short` can result in loss of information. These narrowing conversions are done in two steps: first converting the source value to the `int` type, and then converting the `int` value to the target type.

Widening primitive conversions are usually done implicitly, whereas narrowing primitive conversions usually require a *cast* (§5.2, p. 148). It is not illegal to use a cast for a widening conversion. However, the compiler will flag any conversion that requires a cast if none has been specified. Regardless of any loss of magnitude or precision, widening and narrowing primitive conversions *never* result in a runtime exception.

Ample examples of widening and narrowing primitive conversions can be found in this chapter.

Widening and Narrowing Reference Conversions

The *subtype–supertype* relationship between reference types determines which conversions are permissible between them. Conversions *up* the *type hierarchy* are called *widening reference conversions* (also called *upcasting*). Such a conversion converts from a subtype to a supertype:

```
Object obj = "Upcast me";  // Widening: Object <----- String
```

Conversions *down* the type hierarchy represent *narrowing reference conversions* (also called *downcasting*):

```
String str = (String) obj; // Narrowing requires cast: String <----- Object
```

A subtype is a *narrower* type than its supertype in the sense that it is a specialization of its supertype. Contexts under which reference conversions can occur are discussed in §7.8, p. 311.

Widening reference conversions are usually done implicitly, whereas narrowing reference conversions usually require a cast, as illustrated in the second declaration statement in this subsection. The compiler will reject casts that are not legal or issue an *unchecked warning* under certain circumstances if type safety cannot be guaranteed.

Widening reference conversions do not require any runtime checks and never result in an exception during execution. This is not the case for narrowing reference conversions, which require a runtime check and can throw a `ClassCastException` if the conversion is not legal.

Boxing and Unboxing Conversions

Boxing and unboxing conversions allow interoperability between primitive values and their representation as objects of the wrapper types (§8.3, p. 346).

A *boxing conversion* converts the value of a primitive type to a corresponding value of its wrapper type. If `p` is a value of a *primitiveType*, boxing conversion converts `p` into a reference `r` of the corresponding *WrapperType*, such that `r.`*primitiveType*`Value() == p`. In the code that follows, the `int` value `10` results in an object of the type `Integer` implicitly being created; this object contains the `int` value `10`. We say that the `int` value `10` has been *boxed* in an object of the wrapper type `Integer`. The terminology *autoboxed* is also used for this conversion.

```
Integer iRef = 10;                          // Boxing: Integer <----- int
System.out.println(iRef.intValue() == 10);  // true
```

An *unboxing conversion* converts the value of a wrapper type to a value of its corresponding primitive type. If `r` is a reference of a *WrapperType*, an unboxing conversion converts the reference `r` into `r.`*primitiveType*`Value()`, where *primitiveType* is the primitive type corresponding to the *WrapperType*. In the next code snippet, the value in the `Integer` object referenced by `iRef` is implicitly converted to the `int` type. We say that the wrapper object has been *unboxed* to its corresponding primitive type.

```
int i = iRef;                               // Unboxing: int <----- Integer
System.out.println(iRef.intValue() == i);   // true
```

Note that both boxing and unboxing are done implicitly in the right context. Boxing allows primitive values to be used where an object of their wrapper type is expected, and unboxing allows the converse. Unboxing makes it possible to use a `Boolean` wrapper object as a `boolean` value in a boolean expression, and to use an integral wrapper object as an integral primitive value in an arithmetic expression. Unboxing a wrapper reference that has the `null` value results in a `NullPointerException`. Ample examples of boxing and unboxing can be found in this chapter and in §7.8, p. 311.

Other Conversions

We briefly mention some other conversions, and identify where they are covered in this book.

- *Identity conversions* are always permitted, as they allow conversions from a type to that same type. An identity conversion is always permitted.

```
int i = (int) 10;                   // int <---- int
String str = (String) "Hi";         // String <---- String
```

- *String conversions* allow a value of any other type to be converted to a `String` type in the context of the string concatenation operator `+` (§5.8, p. 174).

- *Unchecked conversions* are permitted to facilitate operability between legacy and generic code (§10.1, p. 416).

5.2 Type Conversion Contexts

Selected conversion contexts and the conversions that are applicable in these contexts are summarized in Table 5.1. The conversions shown in each context occur *implicitly*, without the program having to take any special action. For other conversion contexts, see §5.1, p. 146.

Table 5.1 *Selected Conversion Contexts and Conversion Categories*

Conversion categories	Conversion contexts			
	Assignment	Method invocation	Casting	Numeric promotion
Widening/ narrowing *primitive* conversions	Widening Narrowing for *constant expressions* of non-`long` integral type, with optional boxing	Widening	Both	Widening
Widening/ narrowing *reference* conversions	Widening	Widening	Both, followed by optional unchecked conversion	Not applicable
Boxing/ unboxing conversions	Unboxing, followed by optional widening *primitive* conversion Boxing, followed by optional widening *reference* conversion	Unboxing, followed by optional widening *primitive* conversion Boxing, followed by optional widening *reference* conversion	Both	Unboxing, followed by optional widening *primitive* conversion

Assignment Context

Assignment conversions that can occur in an assignment context are shown in the second column of Table 5.1. An assignment conversion converts the type of an expression to the type of a target variable.

An expression (or its value) is *assignable* to the target variable, if the type of the expression can be converted to the type of the target variable by an assignment conversion. Equivalently, the type of the expression is *assignment compatible* with the type of the target variable.

For assignment conversion involving primitive data types, see §5.6, p. 158. Note the special case where a narrowing conversion occurs when assigning a non-`long` integer constant expression:

```
byte b = 10;   // Narrowing conversion: byte <--- int
```

For assignment conversions involving reference types, see §7.8, p. 311.

Method Invocation Context

Method invocation conversions that can occur in a method invocation context are shown in the third column of Table 5.1. Note that method invocation and assignment conversions differ in one respect: Method invocation conversions do not include the implicit narrowing conversion performed for non-`long` integral constant expressions.

```
// Assignment: (1) Implicit narrowing followed by (2) boxing.
Character space1 = 32;      // Character <-(2)-- char <-(1)-- int

// Invocation of method with signature: valueOf(char)
Character space2 = Character.valueOf(32);        // Compile-time error!
                                                  // Call signature: valueOf(int)
Character space3 = Character.valueOf((char)32); // OK!
                                                  // Call signature: valueOf(char)
```

A method invocation conversion involves converting each argument value in a method or constructor call to the type of the corresponding formal parameter in the method or constructor declaration.

Method invocation conversions involving parameters of primitive data types are discussed in §3.5, p. 73, and those involving reference types are discussed in §7.8, p. 311.

Casting Context of the Unary Type Cast Operator: (*type*)

Java, being a *strongly typed* language, checks for *type compatibility* (i.e., it checks if a type can substitute for another type in a given context) at compile time. However, some checks are possible only at runtime (e.g., which type of object a reference actually denotes during execution). In cases where an operator would have incompatible operands (e.g., assigning a `double` to an `int`), Java demands that a *type cast* be used to *explicitly* indicate the type conversion. The type cast construct has the following syntax:

(*type*) *expression*

The *cast operator* (*type*) is applied to the value of the *expression*. At runtime, a cast results in a new value of *type*, which best represents the value of the *expression* in the old type. We use the term *casting* to mean applying the cast operator for *explicit* type conversion.

However, in the context of casting, *implicit* casting conversions can take place. These casting conversions are shown in the fourth column of Table 5.1. Casting conversions include more conversion categories than the assignment or the method invocation conversions. In the code that follows, the comments indicate the category of the conversion that takes place because of the cast operator on the right-hand side of each assignment—although casts are only necessary for the sake of the assignment at (1) and (2).

```
long l = (long) 10;    // Widening primitive conversion: long <--- int
int i = (int) l;       // (1) Narrowing primitive conversion: int <--- long
Object obj = (Object) "7Up"; // Widening ref conversion: Object <--- String
String str = (String) obj;   // (2) Narrowing ref conversion: String <--- Object
Integer iRef = (Integer) i;  // Boxing: Integer <--- int
i = (int) iRef;              // Unboxing: int <--- Integer
```

A casting conversion is applied to the value of the operand *expression* of a cast operator. Casting can be applied to primitive values as well as references. Casting between primitive data types and reference types is not permitted, except where boxing and unboxing is applicable. Boolean values cannot be cast to other data values, and vice versa. The reference literal `null` can be cast to any reference type.

Examples of casting between primitive data types are provided in this chapter. Casting reference values is discussed in §7.11, p. 320.

Numeric Promotion Context

Numeric operators allow only operands of certain types. Numeric promotion results in conversions being applied to the operands to convert them to permissible types. *Numeric promotion conversions* that can occur in a numeric promotion context are shown in the fifth column of Table 5.1. Permissible conversion categories are widening primitive conversions and unboxing conversions. A distinction is made between unary and binary numeric promotion.

Unary Numeric Promotion

Unary numeric promotion proceeds as follows:

- If the single operand is of type `Byte`, `Short`, `Character`, or `Integer`, it is unboxed. If the resulting value is narrower than `int`, it is promoted to a value of type `int` by a widening conversion.
- Otherwise, if the single operand is of type `Long`, `Float`, or `Double`, it is unboxed.
- Otherwise, if the single operand is of a type narrower than `int`, its value is promoted to a value of type `int` by a widening conversion.
- Otherwise, the operand remains unchanged.

In other words, unary numeric promotion results in an operand value that is either `int` or wider.

Unary numeric promotion is applied in the following expressions:

- Operand of the unary arithmetic operators `+` and `-` (§5.7, p. 163)
- Array creation expression; for example, `new int[20]`, where the dimension expression (in this case `20`) must evaluate to an `int` value (§3.4, p. 59)
- Indexing array elements; for example, `objArray['a']`, where the index expression (in this case `'a'`) must evaluate to an `int` value (§3.4, p. 61)

Binary Numeric Promotion

Binary numeric promotion implicitly applies appropriate widening primitive conversions so that a pair of operands have the widest numeric type of the two, which is always at least `int`. If `T` is the widest numeric type of the two operands after any unboxing conversions have been performed, the operands are promoted as follows during binary numeric promotion:

> If `T` is wider than `int`, both operands are converted to `T`; otherwise, both operands are converted to `int`.

This means that the resulting type of the operands is at least `int`.

Binary numeric promotion is applied in the following expressions:

- Operands of the arithmetic operators `*`, `/`, `%`, `+`, and `-` (§5.7, p. 163)
- Operands of the relational operators `<`, `<=`, `>`, and `>=` (§5.11, p. 180)
- Operands of the numerical equality operators `==` and `!=` (§5.12, p. 181)
- Operands of the conditional operator `? :`, under certain circumstances (§5.16, p. 194)

5.3 Precedence and Associativity Rules for Operators

Precedence and associativity rules are necessary for deterministic evaluation of expressions. The operators are summarized in Table 5.2. The majority of them are discussed in subsequent sections in this chapter. See also the index entries for these operators.

The following remarks apply to Table 5.2:

- The operators are shown with decreasing precedence from the top of the table.
- Operators within the same row have the same precedence.
- Parentheses, `( )`, can be used to override precedence and associativity.
- The *unary operators*, which require one operand, include the following: the postfix increment (`++`) and decrement (`--`) operators from the first row, all the prefix

operators (+, -, ++, --, ~, !) in the second row, and the prefix operators (object creation operator new, cast operator (*type*)) in the third row.

- The conditional operator (? :) is *ternary*—that is, it requires three operands.
- All operators not identified previously as unary or ternary are *binary*—that is, they require two operands.
- All binary operators, except for the relational and assignment operators, associate from left to right. The relational operators are nonassociative.
- Except for unary postfix increment and decrement operators, all unary operators, all assignment operators, and the ternary conditional operator associate from right to left.

Depending on the context, brackets ([]), parentheses (()), colon (:) and the dot operator (.) can also be interpreted as *separators* (§2.1, p. 29). See the index entries for these separators for more details.

Table 5.2 *Operator Summary*

Operator	Syntax
Array element access, member access, method invocation	[*expression*] . (*args*)
Unary postfix operators	*expression*++ *expression*--
Unary prefix operators	~ ! ++*expression* --*expression* +*expression* -*expression*
Unary prefix creation and cast	new (*type*)
Multiplicative	* / %
Additive	+ -
Shift	<< >> >>>
Relational	< <= > >= instanceof
Equality	== !=
Bitwise/logical AND	&
Bitwise/logical XOR	^
Bitwise/logical OR	|
Conditional AND	&&
Conditional OR	||
Conditional	?:
Arrow operator	->
Assignment	= += -= *= /= %= <<= >>= >>>= &= ^= |=

Precedence rules are used to determine which operator should be applied first if there are two operators with different precedence, and these operators follow each other in the expression. In such a case, the operator with the highest precedence is applied first.

The expression `2 + 3 * 4` is evaluated as `2 + (3 * 4)` (with the result `14`) since `*` has higher precedence than `+`.

Associativity rules are used to determine which operator should be applied first if there are two operators with the same precedence, and these operators follow each other in the expression.

Left associativity implies grouping from left to right: The expression `7 - 4 + 2` is interpreted as `((7 - 4) + 2)`, since the binary operators `+` and `-` both have same precedence and left associativity.

Right associativity implies grouping from right to left: The expression `- - 4` is interpreted as `(- (- 4))` (with the result `4`), since the unary operator `-` has right associativity.

The precedence and associativity rules together determine the *evaluation order of the operators*.

5.4 Evaluation Order of Operands

To understand the result returned by an operator, it is important to understand the *evaluation order of its operands*. In general, the operands of operators are evaluated from left to right. The evaluation order also respects any parentheses, and the precedence and associativity rules of operators.

Examples illustrating how the operand evaluation order influences the result returned by an operator, can be found in §5.6 and §5.9.

Left-Hand Operand Evaluation First

The left-hand operand of a binary operator is fully evaluated before the right-hand operand is evaluated.

The evaluation of the left-hand operand can have side effects that can influence the value of the right-hand operand. For example, in the code

```
int b = 10;
System.out.println((b=3) + b);
```

the value printed will be `6` and not `13`. The evaluation proceeds as follows:

```
(b=3) + b
  3   + b       b is assigned the value 3
  3   + 3
  6
```

If evaluation of the left-hand operand of a binary operator throws an exception (§6.5, p. 230), we cannot rely on the presumption that the right-hand operand has been evaluated.

Operand Evaluation before Operation Execution

Java guarantees that *all* operands of an operator are fully evaluated *before* the actual operation is performed. This rule does not apply to the short-circuit conditional operators &&, ||, and ?:.

This rule also applies to operators that throw an exception (the integer division operator / and the integer remainder operator %). The operation is performed only if the operands evaluate normally. Any side effects of the right-hand operand will have been effectuated before the operator throws an exception.

Example 5.1 illustrates the evaluation order of the operands and precedence rules for arithmetic expressions. We use the `eval()` method at (3) in Example 5.1 to demonstrate integer expression evaluation. The first argument to this method is the operand value that is returned by the method, and the second argument is a string to identify the evaluation order.

The argument to the `println()` method in the statement at (1) is an integer expression to evaluate 2 + 3 * 4. The evaluation of each operand in the expression at (1) results in a call of the `eval()` method declared at (3).

```
out.println(eval(j++, " + ") + eval(j++, " * ") * eval(j, "\n"));  // (1)
```

The output from Example 5.1 shows that the operands were evaluated first, from left to right, before operator execution, and that the expression was evaluated as `(2 + (3 * 4))`, respecting the precedence rules for arithmetic expression evaluation. Note how the value of variable `j` changes successively from left to right as the first two operands are evaluated.

Example 5.1 *Evaluation Order of Operands and Arguments*

```
import static java.lang.System.out;

public class EvalOrder{
  public static void main(String[] args){

    int j = 2;
    out.println("Evaluation order of operands:");
    out.println(eval(j++, " + ") + eval(j++, " * ") * eval(j, "\n"));    // (1)

    int i = 1;
    out.println("Evaluation order of arguments:");
    add3(eval(i++, ", "), eval(i++, ", "), eval(i, "\n")); // (2) Three arguments.
  }

  public static int eval(int operand, String str) {      // (3)
    out.print(operand + str);           // Print int operand and String str.
    return operand;                     // Return int operand.
  }
```

```
  public static void add3(int operand1, int operand2, int operand3) {    // (4)
    out.print(operand1 + operand2 + operand3);
  }
}
```

Output from the program:

```
Evaluation order of operands:
2 + 3 * 4
14
Evaluation order of arguments:
1, 2, 3
6
```

Left-to-Right Evaluation of Argument Lists

In a method or constructor invocation, each argument expression in the argument list is fully evaluated before any argument expression to its right.

If evaluation of an argument expression does not complete normally, we cannot presume that any argument expression to its right has been evaluated.

We can use the `add3()` method at (4) in Example 5.1, which takes three arguments, to demonstrate the order in which the arguments in a method call are evaluated. The method call at (2)

```
add3(eval(i++, ", "), eval(i++, ", "), eval(i, "\n")); // (2) Three arguments.
```

results in the following output, clearly indicating that the arguments were evaluated from left to right, before being passed to the method:

```
1, 2, 3
6
```

Note how the value of variable `i` changes successively from left to right as the first two arguments are evaluated.

5.5 Representing Integers

Integer data types in Java represent *signed* integer values, meaning both positive and negative integer values. The values of `char` type can effectively be regarded as *unsigned* 16-bit integers.

Values of type `byte` are represented as shown in Table 5.3. A value of type `byte` requires 8 bits. With 8 bits, we can represent 2^8 or 256 values. Java uses two's complement (explained later) to store signed values of integer data types. For the `byte` data type, this means values are in the range –128 (i.e., -2^7) to +127 (i.e., 2^7-1), inclusive.

Bits in an integral value are usually numbered from right to left, starting with the least significant bit 0 (also called the *rightmost bit*). The representation of the signed types sets the most significant bit to 1, indicating negative values. Adding 1 to the maximum int value 2147483647 results in the minimum value -2147483648, such that the values wrap around for integers and no overflow or underflow is indicated.

Table 5.3 *Representing Signed* byte *Values Using Two's Complement*

Decimal value	Binary representation (8 bit)	Binary value with prefix 0b	Octal value with prefix 0	Hexadecimal value with prefix 0x
127	01111111	0b1111111	0177	0x7f
126	01111110	0b1111110	0176	0x7e
...	...	...	...	...
41	00101001	0b101001	051	0x29
...	...	...	...	...
2	00000010	0b10	02	0x2
1	00000001	0b1	01	0x1
0	00000000	0b0	00	0x0
-1	11111111	0b11111111	0377	0xff
-2	11111110	0b11111110	0376	0xfe
...	...	...	...	...
-41	11010111	0b11010111	0327	0xd7
...	...	...	...	...
–127	10000001	0b10000001	0201	0x81
–128	10000000	0b10000000	0200	0x80

Calculating Two's Complement

Before we look at the two's complement, we need to understand the one's complement. The one's complement of a binary integer is computed by inverting the bits in the number. Thus, the one's complement of the binary number 00101001 is 11010110. The one's complement of a binary number N_2 is denoted as $\sim N_2$. The following relations hold between a binary integer N_2, its one's complement $\sim N_2$, and its two's complement $-N_2$:

$$-N_2 = \sim N_2 + 1$$

$$0 = -N_2 + N_2$$

If N_2 is a positive binary integer, then $-N_2$ denotes its negative binary value, and vice versa. The second relation states that adding a binary integer N_2 to its two's complement $-N_2$ equals 0.

Given a positive `byte` value, say `41`, the binary representation of `-41` can be found as follows:

	Binary representation	Decimal value
Given a value, N_2:	00101001	41
Form one's complement, $\sim N_2$:	11010110	
Add 1:	00000001	
Result is two's complement, $-N_2$:	11010111	–41

Adding a number N_2 to its two's complement $-N_2$ gives 0, and the carry bit from the addition of the most significant bits (after any necessary extension of the operands) is ignored:

	Binary representation	Decimal value
Given a value, N_2:	00101001	41
Add two's complement, $\sim N_2$:	11010111	-41
Sum:	00000000	0

Subtraction between two integers is also computed as addition with two's complement:

$N_2 - M_2 = N_2 + (-M_2)$

For example, the expression $41_{10} - 3_{10}$ (with the correct result 38_{10}) is computed as follows:

	Binary representation	Decimal value
Given a value, N_2:	00101001	41
Add $-M_2$ (i.e., subtract M_2):	11111101	–3
Result:	00100110	38

The previous discussion of `byte` values applies equally to values of other integer types: `short`, `int`, and `long`. These types have their values represented by two's complement in 16, 32, and 64 bits, respectively.

Converting Binary Numbers to Decimals

A binary number can be converted to its equivalent decimal value by computing the *positional values* of its digits. Each digit in the binary number contributes to the final decimal value by virtue of its position, starting with position 0 (units) for the rightmost digit in the number. The positional value of each digit is given by

$digit \times base^{position}$

The number 101001_2 corresponds to 41_{10} in the decimal number system:

$$\begin{aligned}\mathbf{101001_2} &= \mathbf{1} \times 2^5 + \mathbf{0} \times 2^4 + \mathbf{1} \times 2^3 + \mathbf{0} \times 2^2 + \mathbf{0} \times 2^1 + \mathbf{1} \times 2^0 \\ &= 32 + 0 + 8 + 0 + 0 + 1 \\ &= \mathbf{41_{10}}\end{aligned}$$

The same technique can be used to convert a number from any base, for example, octal (base 8) or hexadecimal (base 16), to its equivalent representation in the decimal number system.

Converting Decimals to Binary Numbers

To convert decimals to binaries, we reverse the process outlined previously for converting a binary to a decimal.

$\mathbf{41_{10}} =$	20×2	$+\,\mathbf{1}$	Dividing 41 by the base 2, gives the quotient 20 and remainder 1.
$20_{10} =$	10×2	$+\,\mathbf{0}$	We again divide the current quotient 20 by the base 2.
$10_{10} =$	5×2	$+\,\mathbf{0}$	
$5_{10} =$	2×2	$+\,\mathbf{1}$	We repeat this procedure until ...
$2_{10} =$	1×2	$+\,\mathbf{0}$	
$1_{10} =$	0×2	$+\,\mathbf{1}$	... the quotient is 0.

$\mathbf{41_{10}} = \mathbf{101001_2}$

The divisor used in these steps is the base of the target number system (binary, base 2). The binary value, 101001_2, is represented by the remainders, *with the last remainder as the leftmost bit*.

Analogously, we can apply this procedure for converting an octal (base 8) or hexadecimal (base 16) number to its binary equivalent.

Relationships among Binary, Octal, and Hexadecimal Numbers

We need 3 bits to represent all the octal digits ($8 = 2^3$) and 4 bits to represent all the hexadecimal digits ($16 = 2^4$). We can use this fact to convert among the binary, octal, and hexadecimal systems, as shown in Figure 5.2.

The procedure for converting an octal to a binary is shown by the arrow marked (a). We can convert an octal number to its equivalent binary number by replacing each digit in the octal number by its 3-bit equivalent binary value.

Analogously, we can convert a hexadecimal number to its equivalent binary number by replacing each digit in the hexadecimal number by its 4-bit equivalent binary value, as shown by the arrow marked (b).

To convert a binary to its octal equivalent, we reverse the procedure outlined earlier (arrow marked (c) in Figure 5.2). The bits in the binary number are grouped into 3-bit groups from right to left. Each such group is replaced by its equivalent octal digit. Analogously, we can convert a binary to a hexadecimal number by replacing each 4-bit group by its equivalent hexadecimal digit (arrow marked (d) in Figure 5.2).

Figure 5.2 *Converting among Binary, Octal, and Hexadecimal Numbers*

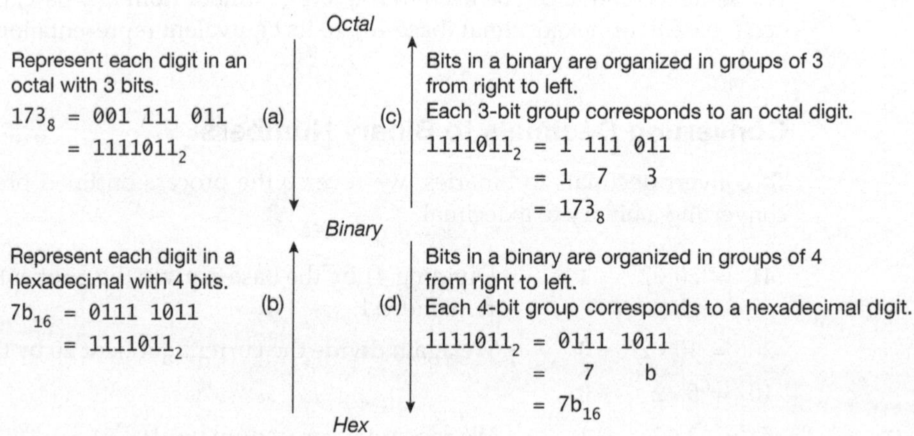

5.6 The Simple Assignment Operator =

The assignment statement has the following syntax:

variable = *expression*

which can be read as "the target, *variable*, gets the value of the source, *expression*." The previous value of the target variable is overwritten by the assignment operator =.

The target *variable* and the source *expression* must be assignment compatible. The target variable must also have been declared. Since variables can store either primitive values or reference values, *expression* evaluates to either a primitive value or a reference value.

Assigning Primitive Values

The following examples illustrate assignment of primitive values:

```
int j, k;
j = 0b10;            // j gets the value 2.
j = 5;               // j gets the value 5. Previous value is overwritten.
k = j;               // k gets the value 5.
```

The assignment operator has the lowest precedence, so that the expression on the right-hand side is evaluated before the assignment is done.

```
int i;
i = 5;               // i gets the value 5.
i = i + 1;           // i gets the value 6. + has higher precedence than =.
i = 20 - i * 2;      // i gets the value 8: (20 - (i * 2))
```

Assigning References

Copying reference values by assignment creates aliases, which are discussed in §1.3, p. 6. The following example recapitulates that discussion:

```
Pizza pizza1 = new Pizza("Hot&Spicy");
Pizza pizza2 = new Pizza("Sweet&Sour");

pizza2 = pizza1;
```

The variable `pizza1` is a reference to a pizza that is hot and spicy, and `pizza2` is a reference to a pizza that is sweet and sour. Assigning `pizza1` to `pizza2` means that `pizza2` now refers to the same pizza as `pizza1`, the hot and spicy one. After the assignment, these variables are aliases and either one can be used to manipulate the hot and spicy `Pizza` object.

Assigning a reference value does *not* create a copy of the source object denoted by the reference variable on the right-hand side. It merely assigns the reference value of the variable on the right-hand side to the variable on the left-hand side, so that they denote the same object. Reference assignment also does not copy the *state* of the source object to any object denoted by the reference variable on the left-hand side.

A more detailed discussion of reference assignment can be found in §7.8, p. 311.

Multiple Assignments

The assignment statement is an *expression statement*, which means that application of the binary assignment operator returns the value of the expression on the *right-hand* side.

```
int j, k;
j = 10;            // j gets the value 10, which is returned
k = j;             // k gets the value of j, which is 10, and this value is returned
```

The last two assignments can be written as multiple assignments, illustrating the right associativity of the assignment operator:

```
k = j = 10;      // (k = (j = 10))
```

Multiple assignments are equally valid with references:

```
Pizza pizzaOne, pizzaTwo;
pizzaOne = pizzaTwo = new Pizza("Supreme"); // Aliases
```

The following example shows the effect of operand evaluation order:

```
int[] a = {10, 20, 30, 40, 50}; // An array of int
int index = 4;
a[index] = index = 2;                 // (1)
```

What is the value of `index`, and which array element `a[index]` is assigned a value in the multiple assignment statement at (1)? The evaluation proceeds as follows:

```
a[index] = index = 2;
a[4]     = index = 2;
a[4]     = (index = 2);          // index gets the value 2. = is right associative.
a[4]     =        2;             // The value of a[4] is changed from 50 to 2.
```

The following declaration statement will not compile, as the variable `v2` has not been declared:

```
int v1 = v2 = 2016;                 // Only v1 is declared. Compile-time error!
```

Type Conversions in an Assignment Context

If the target and the source have the same type in an assignment, then, obviously, the source and the target are assignment compatible and the source value need not be converted. Otherwise, if a widening primitive conversion is permissible, then the widening conversion is applied implicitly; that is, the source type is converted to the target type in an assignment context.

```
// Widening Primitive Conversions
int    smallOne = 1234;                // No widening necessary.
long   bigOne   = 2000;                // Widening: int to long.
double largeOne = bigOne;              // Widening: long to double.
double hugeOne  = (double) bigOne;     // Cast redundant but allowed.
```

A widening primitive conversion can result in loss of *precision*. In the next example, the precision of the least significant bits of the `long` value may be lost when it is converting to a `float` value:

```
long bigInteger = 98765432112345678L;
float fpNum = bigInteger;  // Widening but loss of precision: 9.8765436E16
```

Additionally, implicit narrowing primitive conversions on assignment can occur in cases where *all* of the following conditions are fulfilled:

- The source is a *constant expression* of either `byte`, `short`, `char`, or `int` type.
- The target type is either `byte`, `short`, or `char` type.

- The value of the source is determined to be in the range of the target type at compile time.

A *constant expression* is an expression that denotes either a primitive or a `String` literal, and is composed of operands that can be only *literals* or *constant variables*, and operators that can be evaluated only at compile time (for example, arithmetic and numerical comparison operators, but not increment/decrement operators and method calls). A *constant variable* is a `final` variable of either a primitive type or `String` type that is initialized with a constant expression.

```
int result = 100;                    // Not a constant variable. Not declared final.
final char finalGrade = 'A';         // Constant variable.
System.out.printf("%d%n%s%n%d%n%.2f%n%b%n%d%n%d%n",
    2106,                            // Constant expression.
    "Trust " + "me!",                // Constant expression.
    2 + 3 * 4,                       // Constant expression.
    Math.PI * Math.PI * 10.0,        // Constant expression.
    finalGrade == 'A',               // Constant expression.
    Math.min(2015, 2016),            // Not constant expression. Method call.
    ++result                         // Not constant expression. Increment operator.
);
```

Here are some examples that illustrate how the conditions mentioned previously affect narrowing primitive conversions:

```
// Conditions fulfilled for implicit narrowing primitive conversions.
short s1 = 10;        // int value in range.
short s2 = 'a';       // char value in range.
char c1 = 32;         // int value in range.
char c2 = (byte)35;   // byte value in range. (int value in range, without cast.)
byte b1 = 40;         // int value in range.
byte b2 = (short)40;  // short value in range. (int value in range, without cast.)
final int i1 = 20;    // Constant variable
byte b3 = i1;         // final value of i1 in range.
```

All other narrowing primitive conversions will produce a compile-time error on assignment and will explicitly require a cast. Here are some examples:

```
// Conditions not fulfilled for implicit narrowing primitive conversions.
// A cast is required.
int i2 = -20;             // i2 is not a constant variable. i2 is not final.
final int i3 = i2;        // i3 is not a constant variable, since i2 is not.
final int i4 = 200;       // i4 is a constant variable.
final int i5;             // i5 is not a constant variable.
short s3 = (short) i2;    // Not constant expression.
char  c3 = (char)  i3;    // Final value of i3 not determinable at compile time.
char  c4 = (char)  i2;    // Not constant expression.
byte  b4 = (byte)  128;   // int value not in range.
byte  b5 = (byte)  i4;    // Value of constant variable i4 is not in range.
i5 = 100;                 // Initialized at runtime.
short s4 = (short) i5;    // Final value of i5 not determinable at compile time.
```

Floating-point values are truncated when cast to integral values.

```
// The value is truncated to fit the size of the target type.
float huge   = (float) 1.7976931348623157d;  // double to float.
```

```
long  giant  = (long)  4415961481999.03D;     // (1) double to long.
int   big    = (int)   giant;                 // (2) long to int.
short small  = (short) big;                   // (3) int to short.
byte  tiny   = (byte)  small;                 // (4) short to byte.
char  symbol = (char)  112.5F;                // (5) float to char.
```

Table 5.4 shows how the values are truncated for assignments from (1) to (5).

Table 5.4 *Examples of Truncated Values*

Binary	Decimal	
0000000000000000000001000000010000101011110100001100001100001111	4415961481999	(1)
00101011110100001100001100001111	735101711	(2)
1100001100001111	-15601	(3)
00001111	15	(4)
0000000001110000	'p'	(5)

The discussion of numeric assignment conversions also applies to numeric parameter values at method invocation (§3.5, p. 73), except for the narrowing conversions, which always require a cast.

The following examples illustrate boxing and unboxing in an assignment context:

```
Boolean    boolRef = true; // Boxing.
Byte       bRef =  2;      // Constant in range: narrowing, then boxing.
// Byte  bRef2 =  257;     // Constant not in range. Compile-time error!

short s = 10;              // Narrowing from int to short.
// Integer   iRef1 = s;    // short not assignable to Integer.
Integer iRef3 = (int) s;   // Explicit widening with cast to int and boxing

boolean bv1 = boolRef;     // Unboxing.
byte b1 = bRef;            // Unboxing.
int  iVal = bRef;          // Unboxing and widening.

Integer iRefVal = null;              // Always allowed.
// int j = iRefVal;                  // NullPointerException at runtime.
if (iRef3 != null) iVal = iRef3;  // Avoid exception at runtime.
```

Review Questions

5.1 Given the following declaration:

```
char c = 'A';
```

What is the simplest way to convert the character value in c to an int?

Select the one correct answer.

(a) `int i = c;`
(b) `int i = (int) c;`
(c) `int i = Character.getNumericValue(c);`

5.2 What will be the result of compiling and running the following program?

```
public class Assignment {
  public static void main(String[] args) {
    int a, b, c;
    b = 10;
    a = b = c = 20;
    System.out.println(a);
  }
}
```

Select the one correct answer.

(a) The program will fail to compile, since the compiler will report that the variable `c` in the multiple assignment statement `a = b = c = 20;` has not been initialized.
(b) The program will fail to compile, because the multiple assignment statement `a = b = c = 20;` is illegal.
(c) The code will compile, and print `10` at runtime.
(d) The code will compile, and print `20` at runtime.

5.3 What will be the result of compiling and running the following program?

```
public class MyClass {
  public static void main(String[] args) {
    String a, b, c;
    c = new String("mouse");
    a = new String("cat");
    b = a;
    a = new String("dog");
    c = b;

    System.out.println(c);
  }
}
```

Select the one correct answer.

(a) The program will fail to compile.
(b) The program will print `mouse` at runtime.
(c) The program will print `cat` at runtime.
(d) The program will print `dog` at runtime.
(e) The program will randomly print either `cat` or `dog` at runtime.

5.7 Arithmetic Operators: *, /, %, +, -

Arithmetic operators are used to construct mathematical expressions as in algebra. Their operands are of numeric type (which includes the `char` type).

Arithmetic Operator Precedence and Associativity

In Table 5.5, the precedence of the operators appears in decreasing order, starting from the top row, which has the highest precedence. Unary subtraction has higher precedence than multiplication. The operators in the same row have the same precedence. Binary multiplication, division, and remainder operators have the same precedence. The unary operators have right associativity, and the binary operators have left associativity.

Table 5.5 *Arithmetic Operators*

Unary	+ *Addition*	- *Subtraction*	
Binary	* *Multiplication*	/ *Division*	% *Remainder*
	+ *Addition*	- *Subtraction*	

Evaluation Order in Arithmetic Expressions

Java guarantees that the operands are fully evaluated from left to right before an arithmetic binary operator is applied. If evaluation of an operand results in an error, the subsequent operands will not be evaluated.

In the expression `a + b * c`, the operand `a` will always be fully evaluated before the operand `b`, which will always be fully evaluated before the operand `c`. However, the multiplication operator `*` will be applied before the addition operator `+`, respecting the precedence rules. Note that `a`, `b`, and `c` are arbitrary arithmetic expressions that have been determined to be the operands of the operators.

Example 5.1, p. 153, illustrates the evaluation order and precedence rules for arithmetic expressions.

Range of Numeric Values

As we have seen, all numeric types have a range of valid values (§2.2, p. 37). This range is given by the constants named `MAX_VALUE` and `MIN_VALUE`, which are defined in each numeric wrapper type.

The arithmetic operators are overloaded, meaning that the operation of an operator varies depending on the type of its operands. Floating-point arithmetic is performed if any operand of an operator is of floating-point type; otherwise, integer arithmetic is performed.

Values that are out of range or are the results of invalid expressions are handled differently depending on whether integer or floating-point arithmetic is performed.

Integer Arithmetic

Integer arithmetic always returns a value that is in range, except in the case of integer division by zero and remainder by zero, which cause an `ArithmeticException` (see the later discussion of the division operator `/` and the remainder operator `%`). A valid value does not necessarily mean that the result is correct, as demonstrated by the following examples:

```
int tooBig   = Integer.MAX_VALUE + 1;    // -2147483648 which is Integer.MIN_VALUE.
int tooSmall = Integer.MIN_VALUE - 1;    // 2147483647 which is Integer.MAX_VALUE.
```

These results should be values that are out of range. However, integer arithmetic *wraps round* if the result is out of range; that is, the result is reduced modulo in the range of the result type. To avoid wrapping round of out-of-range values, programs should either use explicit checks or a wider type. If the type `long` is used in the earlier examples, the results would be correct in the `long` range:

```
long notTooBig   = Integer.MAX_VALUE + 1L;   //  2147483648L in range.
long notTooSmall = Integer.MIN_VALUE - 1L;   // -2147483649L in range.
```

Floating-Point Arithmetic

Certain floating-point operations result in values that are out of range. Typically, adding or multiplying two very large floating-point numbers can result in an out-of-range value that is represented by *infinity* (Figure 5.3). Attempting floating-point division by zero also returns infinity. The following examples show how this value is printed as signed infinity:

```
System.out.println( 4.0 / 0.0);          // Prints:  Infinity
System.out.println(-4.0 / 0.0);          // Prints: -Infinity
```

Both positive and negative infinity represent *overflow* to infinity; that is, the value is too large to be represented as a `double` or `float` (Figure 5.3). Signed infinity is represented by the named constants `POSITIVE_INFINITY` and `NEGATIVE_INFINITY` in the wrapper classes `java.lang.Float` and `java.lang.Double`. A value can be compared with these constants to detect overflow.

Floating-point arithmetic can also result in *underflow* to zero, when the value is too small to be represented as a `double` or `float` (Figure 5.3). Underflow occurs in the following situations:

- The result is between `Double.MIN_VALUE` (or `Float.MIN_VALUE`) and zero, as with the result of `(5.1E-324 - 4.9E-324)`. Underflow then returns positive zero `0.0` (or `0.0F`).
- The result is between `-Double.MIN_VALUE` (or `-Float.MIN_VALUE`) and zero, as with the result of `(-Double.MIN_VALUE * 1E-1)`. Underflow then returns negative zero `-0.0` (or `-0.0F`).

Negative zero compares equal to positive zero; in other words, `(-0.0 == 0.0)` is `true`.

Figure 5.3 *Overflow and Underflow in Floating-Point Arithmetic*

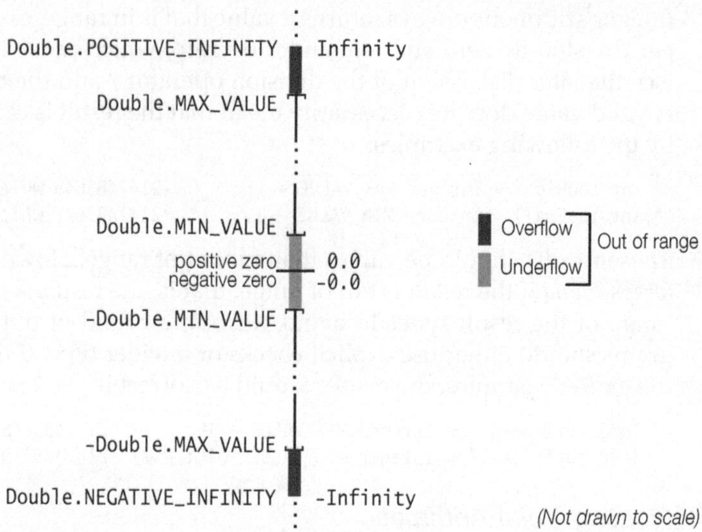

Certain operations have no mathematical result, and are represented by *NaN* (*Not a Number*). For example, calculating the square root of -1 results in NaN. Another example is (floating-point) dividing zero by zero:

```
System.out.println(0.0 / 0.0);          // Prints: NaN
```

NaN is represented by the constant named `NaN` in the wrapper classes `java.lang.Float` and `java.lang.Double`. Any operation involving NaN produces NaN. Any comparison (except inequality `!=`) involving NaN and any other value (including NaN) returns `false`. An inequality comparison of NaN with another value (including NaN) always returns `true`. However, the recommended way of checking a value for NaN is to use the static method `isNaN()` defined in both wrapper classes, `java.lang.Float` and `java.lang.Double`.

Strict Floating-Point Arithmetic: `strictfp`

Although floating-point arithmetic in Java is defined in accordance with the IEEE-754 32-bit (`float`) and 64-bit (`double`) standard formats, the language does allow JVM implementations to use other extended formats for intermediate results. This means that floating-point arithmetic can give different results on such JVMs, with possible loss of precision. Such a behavior is termed *non-strict*, in contrast to being *strict* and adhering to the standard formats.

To ensure that identical results are produced on all JVMs, the keyword `strictfp` can be used to enforce strict behavior for floating-point arithmetic. The modifier `strictfp` can be applied to classes, interfaces, and methods. A `strictfp` method ensures that all code in the method is executed strictly. If a class or interface is declared to be `strictfp`, then all code (in methods, initializers, and nested classes and interfaces) is executed strictly. If the expression is determined to be in a strictfp construct, it is executed strictly. Strictness, however, is not inherited by the subclasses or subinterfaces. Constant expressions are always evaluated strictly at compile time.

Unary Arithmetic Operators: -, +

The unary operators have the highest precedence of all the arithmetic operators. The unary operator - negates the numeric value of its operand. The following example illustrates the right associativity of the unary operators:

```
int value = - -10;                    // (-(-10)) is 10
```

Notice the blank needed to separate the unary operators; otherwise, these would be interpreted as the decrement operator -- (§5.9, p. 176), which would result in a compile-time error because a literal cannot be decremented. The unary operator + has no effect on the evaluation of the operand value.

Multiplicative Binary Operators: *, /, %

*Multiplication Operator: **

The multiplication operator * multiplies two numbers.

```
int    sameSigns     = -4    * -8;   // result:  32
double oppositeSigns =  4    * -8.0; // Widening of int 4 to double. result: -32.0
int    zero          =  0    * -0;   // result:   0
```

Division Operator: /

The division operator / is overloaded. If its operands are integral, the operation results in *integer division*.

```
int    i1 = 4  / 5;    // result: 0
int    i2 = 8  / 8;    // result: 1
double d1 = 12 / 8;    // result: 1.0; integer division, then widening conversion
```

Integer division always returns the quotient as an integer value; that is, the result is truncated toward zero. Note that the division performed is integer division if the operands have integral values, even if the result will be stored in a floating-point type. The integer value is subjected to a widening conversion in the assignment context.

An ArithmeticException is thrown when integer division with zero is attempted, meaning that integer division by zero is an illegal operation.

If any of the operands is a floating-point type, the operation performs *floating-point division*, where relevant operand values undergo binary numeric promotion:

```
double d2 = 4.0 / 8;        // result: 0.5
double d3 = 8 / 8.0;        // result: 1.0
```

```
float d4   = 12.0F / 8;     // result: 1.5F

double result1 = 12.0 / 4.0 * 3.0;          // ((12.0 / 4.0) * 3.0) which is 9.0
double result2 = 12.0 * 3.0 / 4.0;          // ((12.0 * 3.0) / 4.0) which is 9.0
```

Remainder Operator: %

In mathematics, when we divide a number (the *dividend*) by another number (the *divisor*), the result can be expressed in terms of a *quotient* and a *remainder*. For example, when 7 is divided by 5, the quotient is 1 and the remainder is 2. The remainder operator % returns the remainder of the division performed on the operands.

```
int quotient  = 7 / 5;   // Integer division operation: 1
int remainder = 7 % 5;   // Integer remainder operation: 2
```

For *integer remainder operation*, where only integer operands are involved, evaluation of the expression (x % y) always satisfies the following relation:

$x == (x \ / \ y) * y + (x \ \% \ y)$

In other words, the right-hand side yields a value that is always equal to the value of the dividend. The following examples show how we can calculate the remainder so that this relation is satisfied:

Calculating (7 % 5):

```
 7 == (7 / 5) * 5 + (7 % 5)
   == (  1  ) * 5 + (7 % 5)
   ==             5 + (7 % 5)
 2 ==                 (7 % 5)
```

(7 % 5) is equal to 2

Calculating (7 % -5):

```
 7 == (7 / -5) * -5 + (7 % -5)
   == (  -1  ) * -5 + (7 % -5)
   ==                5 + (7 % -5)
 2 ==                    (7 % -5)
```

(7 % -5) is equal to 2

Calculating (-7 % 5):

```
-7 == (-7 / 5) * 5 + (-7 % 5)
   == (  -1  ) * 5 + (-7 % 5)
   ==               -5 + (-7 % 5)
-2 ==                    (-7 % 5)
```

(-7 % 5) is equal to -2

Calculating (-7 % -5):

```
-7 == (-7 / -5) * -5 + (-7 % -5)
   == (   1   ) * -5 + (-7 % -5)
   ==                 -5 + (-7 % -5)
-2 ==                      (-7 % -5)
```

(-7 % -5) is equal to -2

The remainder can be negative only if the dividend is negative, and the sign of the divisor is irrelevant. A shortcut to evaluating the remainder involving negative operands is the following: ignore the signs of the operands, calculate the remainder, and negate the remainder if the dividend is negative.

```
int  r0 =  7  %  7;     // 0
int  r1 =  7  %  5;     // 2
long r2 =  7L % -5L;    // 2L
int  r3 = -7  %  5;     // -2
long r4 = -7L % -5L;    // -2L
boolean relation = -7L == (-7L / -5L) * -5L + r4;  // true
```

An `ArithmeticException` is thrown if the divisor evaluates to zero.

Note that the remainder operator accepts not only integral operands, but also floating-point operands. The *floating-point remainder* r is defined by the relation

$r == a - (b * q)$

where a and b are the dividend and the divisor, respectively, and q is the *integer* quotient of (a/b). The following examples illustrate a floating-point remainder operation:

```
double  dr0 =  7.0  %  7.0;    //  0.0
float   fr1 =  7.0F %  5.0F;   //  2.0F
double  dr1 =  7.0  % -5.0;    //  2.0
float   fr2 = -7.0F %  5.0F;   // -2.0F
double  dr2 = -7.0  % -5.0;    // -2.0
boolean fpRelation = dr2  == (-7.0) - (-5.0) * (long)(-7.0 / -5.0);  // true
float   fr3 = -7.0F %  0.0F;   // NaN
```

Additive Binary Operators: +, -

The addition operator + and the subtraction operator - behave as their names imply: They add and subtract values, respectively. The binary operator + also acts as *string concatenation* if any of its operands is a string (§5.8, p. 174).

Additive operators have lower precedence than all the other arithmetic operators. Table 5.6 includes examples that show how precedence and associativity are used in arithmetic expression evaluation.

Table 5.6 *Examples of Arithmetic Expression Evaluation*

Arithmetic expression	Evaluation	Result when printed
3 + 2 - 1	((3 + 2) - 1)	4
2 + 6 * 7	(2 + (6 * 7))	44
-5 + 7 - -6	(((-5) + 7) - (-6))	8
2 + 4 / 5	(2 + (4 / 5))	2
13 % 5	(13 % 5)	3
11.5 % 2.5	(11.5 % 2.5)	1.5
10 / 0		ArithmeticException
2 + 4.0 / 5	(2.0 + (4.0 / 5.0))	2.8
4.0 / 0.0	(4.0 / 0.0)	Infinity
-4.0 / 0.0	((-4.0) / 0.0)	-Infinity
0.0 / 0.0	(0.0 / 0.0)	NaN

Numeric Promotions in Arithmetic Expressions

Unary numeric promotion is applied to the single operand of the unary arithmetic operators `-` and `+`. When a unary arithmetic operator is applied to an operand whose type is narrower than `int`, the operand is promoted to a value of type `int`, with the operation resulting in an `int` value. If the conditions for implicit narrowing conversion are not fulfilled (p. 160), assigning the `int` result to a variable of a narrower type will require a cast. This is demonstrated by the following example, where the `byte` operand `b` is promoted to an `int` in the expression `(-b)`:

```
byte b = 3;            // int literal in range. Narrowing conversion.
b = (byte) -b;         // Cast required on assignment.
```

Binary numeric promotion is applied to operands of binary arithmetic operators. Its application leads to type promotion for the operands, as explained in §5.2, p. 149. The result is of the promoted type, which is always type `int` or wider. For the expression at (1) in Example 5.2, numeric promotions proceed as shown in Figure 5.4. Note the integer division performed in evaluating the subexpression `(c / s)`.

Figure 5.4 *Numeric Promotion in Arithmetic Expressions*

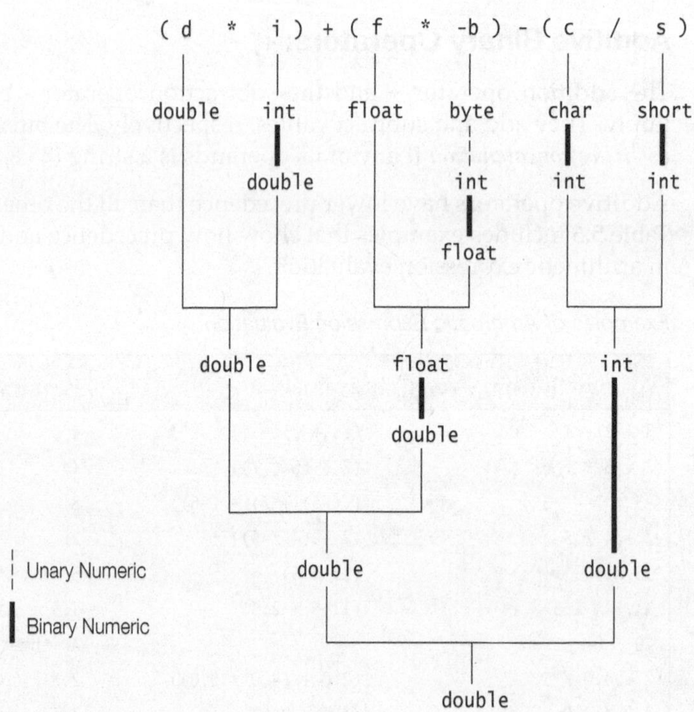

Example 5.2 *Numeric Promotion in Arithmetic Expressions*

```
public class NumPromotion {
  public static void main(String[] args) {
    byte   b = 32;
    char   c = 'z';                    // Unicode value 122 (\u007a)
    short  s = 256;
    int    i = 10000;
    float  f = 3.5F;
    double d = 0.5;
    double v = (d * i) + (f * -b) - (c / s);     // (1) 4888.0D
    System.out.println("Value of v: " + v);
  }
}
```

Output from the program:

```
Value of v: 4888.0
```

In addition to the binary numeric promotions in arithmetic expression evaluation, the resulting value can undergo an implicit widening conversion if assigned to a variable. In the first two declaration statements that follow, only assignment conversions take place. Numeric promotions take place in the evaluation of the right-hand expression in the other declaration statements.

```
Byte   b = 10;      // Constant in range: narrowing and boxing on assignment.
Short  s = 20;      // Constant in range: narrowing and boxing on assignment.
char   c = 'z';     // 122 (\u007a)
int    i = s * b;   // Values in s and b promoted to int: unboxing, widening.
long   n = 20L + s; // Value in s promoted to long: unboxing, widening.
float  r = s + c;   // Value in s is unboxed. This short value and the char
                    // value in c are promoted to int, followed by implicit
                    // widening conversion of int to float on assignment.
double d = r + i;   // Value in i promoted to float, followed by implicit
                    // widening conversion of float to double on assignment.
```

Binary numeric promotion for operands of binary operators implies that each operand of a binary operator is promoted to type int or a broader numeric type, if necessary. As with unary operators, care must be exercised in assigning the value resulting from applying a binary operator to operands of these types.

```
short h = 40;            // OK: int converted to short. Implicit narrowing.
h = h + 2;               // Error: cannot assign an int to short.
```

The value of the expression `h + 2` is of type `int`. Although the result of the expression is in the range of `short`, this cannot be determined at compile time. The assignment requires a cast.

```
h = (short) (h + 2);  // OK
```

Notice that applying the cast operator `(short)` to the individual operands does not work:

```
h = (short) h + (short) 2;     // The resulting value should be cast.
```

Neither does the following approach, which results in a compile-time error:

```
h = (short) h + 2;                  // The resulting value should be cast.
```

In this case, binary numeric promotion leads to an `int` value as the result of evaluating the expression on the right-hand side and, therefore, requires an additional cast to narrow it to a `short` value.

Arithmetic Compound Assignment Operators: *=, /=, %=, +=, -=

A compound assignment operator has the following syntax:

variable op= expression

and the following semantics:

variable = (*type*) ((*variable*) *op* (*expression*))

The type of the *variable* is *type* and the *variable* is evaluated only once. Note the cast and the parentheses implied in the semantics. Here *op=* can be any of the compound assignment operators specified in Table 5.2. The compound assignment operators have the lowest precedence of all the operators in Java, allowing the expression on the right-hand side to be evaluated before the assignment. Table 5.7 defines the arithmetic compound assignment operators.

Table 5.7 *Arithmetic Compound Assignment Operators*

Expression	Given T as the numeric type of x, the expression is evaluated as:
`x *= a`	`x = (T) ((x) * (a))`
`x /= a`	`x = (T) ((x) / (a))`
`x %= a`	`x = (T) ((x) % (a))`
`x += a`	`x = (T) ((x) + (a))`
`x -= a`	`x = (T) ((x) - (a))`

The implied cast operator, (T), in the compound assignments becomes necessary when the result must be narrowed to the target type. This is illustrated by the following examples:

```
int i = 2;
i *= i + 4;             // (1) Evaluated as i = (int) ((i) * (i + 4)).

Integer iRef = 2;
iRef *= iRef + 4;       // (2) Evaluated as iRef = (Integer) ((iRef) * (iRef + 4)).

byte b = 2;
b += 10;                // (3) Evaluated as b = (byte) (b + 10).
b = b + 10;             // (4) Will not compile. Cast is required.
```

At (1) the source `int` value is assigned to the target `int` variable, and the cast operator `(int)` in this case is an *identity conversion* (i.e., conversion from a type to the same type). Such casts are permitted. The assignment at (2) entails unboxing to evaluate the expression on the right-hand side, followed by boxing to assign the `int` value. However, at (3), as the source value is an `int` value because the `byte` value in `b` is promoted to `int` to carry out the addition, assigning it to a target `byte` variable requires an implicit narrowing conversion. The situation at (4) with simple assignment will not compile, because implicit narrowing conversion is not applicable.

The *variable* is evaluated only once in the expression, not twice, as one might infer from the definition of the compound assignment operator. In the following assignment, `a[i]` is evaluated just once:

```
int[] a = new int[] { 2015, 2016, 2017 };
int i = 2;
a[i] += 1;       // Evaluates as a[2] = a[2] + 1, and a[2] gets the value 2018.
```

Implicit narrowing conversions are also applied to increment and decrement operators (§5.9, p. 176).

Boolean logical compound assignment operators are covered in §5.13, p. 184.

Review Questions

5.4 Which of the following expressions will be evaluated using floating-point arithmetic?

Select the three correct answers.

(a) 2.0 * 3.0
(b) 2 * 3
(c) 2/3 + 5/7
(d) 2.4 + 1.6
(e) 0x10 * 1L * 300.0

5.5 What is the value of the expression `(1 / 2 + 3 / 2 + 0.1)`?

Select the one correct answer.

(a) 1
(b) 1.1
(c) 1.6
(d) 2
(e) 2.1

5.6 What will be the result of compiling and running the following program?

```
public class Integers {
  public static void main(String[] args) {
    System.out.println(0x10 + 10 + 010 + 0b10);
  }
}
```

Select the one correct answer.

(a) The program will not compile.
(b) When run, the program will print `28`.
(c) When run, the program will print `30`.
(d) When run, the program will print `34`.
(e) When run, the program will print `36`.
(f) When run, the program will print `10101010`.

5.7 Which of the following expressions are valid?

Select the three correct answers.

(a) (- 1 -)
(b) (+ + 1)
(c) (+-+-+-1)
(d) (--1)
(e) (1 * * 1)
(f) (- -1)

5.8 What is the value of evaluating the following expression: (- `-1-3 * 10 / 5-1`)?

Select the one correct answer.

(a) –8
(b) –6
(c) 7
(d) 8
(e) 10
(f) None of the above

5.9 Which of these assignments are valid?

Select the four correct answers.

(a) `short s = 12;`
(b) `long l = 012;`
(c) `int other = (int) true;`
(d) `float f = -123;`
(e) `double d = 0x12345678;`

5.8 The Binary String Concatenation Operator +

The binary operator + is overloaded in the sense that the operation performed is determined by the type of the operands. When one of the operands is a `String` object, a string concatenation is performed rather than numeric addition. String concatenation results in a newly created `String` object in which the characters in the string representation of the left-hand operand precede the characters in the string representation of the right-hand operand. It might be necessary to perform a *string conversion* on the non-String operand before the string concatenation can be performed. The String class is discussed in §8.4, p. 357.

A *string conversion* is performed on the non-String operand as follows:

- For an operand of a primitive data type, its value is converted to a string representation.
- For all reference value operands, a string representation is constructed by calling the no-argument toString() method on the referred object. Most classes override this method from the Object class so as to provide a more meaningful string representation of their objects. Discussion of the toString() method can be found in §8.2, p. 342.
- Values like true, false, and null have string representations that correspond to their names. A reference variable with the value null also has the string representation "null" in this context.

The operator + is left associative and has the same precedence level as the additive operators, whether it is performed as a string concatenation or as a numeric addition.

```
String strVal = "" + 2016;                        // (1) "2016"
String theName = " Uranium";
theName = " Pure" + theName;                      // (2) " Pure Uranium"
String trademark1 = 100 + "%" + theName;          // (3) "100% Pure Uranium"
```

Since the + operator is left-associative, the evaluation in (3) proceeds as follows: The int value 100 is concatenated with the string literal "%", followed by concatenation with the contents of the String object referred to by theName reference.

Note that using the character literal '%', instead of the string literal "%" in line (2), does not give the same result:

```
String trademark2 = 100 + '%' + theName;          // (4) "137 Pure Uranium"
```

Integer addition is performed by the first + operator: 100 + '%'; that is, (100 + 37).

Caution should be exercised because the + operator might not be applied as intended, as shown by the following example:

```
System.out.println("We can put two and two together and get " + 2 + 2);   // (5)
```

This statement prints "We can put two and two together and get 22". String concatenation proceeds from left to right: The String literal is concatenated with the first int literal 2, followed by concatenation with the second int literal 2. Both occurrences of the + operator are treated as string concatenation. To convey the intended meaning of the sentence, parentheses are necessary:

```
System.out.println("We can put two and two together and get " + (2 + 2)); // (6)
```

This statement prints "We can put two and two together and get 4", since the parentheses enforce integer addition in the expression (2 + 2) before string concatenation is performed with the contents of the String operand.

The following statement will print the correct result, even without the parentheses, because the * operator has higher precedence than the + operator:

```
System.out.println("2 * 2 = " + 2 * 2);          // (7) 2 * 2 = 4
```

Creation of temporary String objects might be necessary to store the results of performing successive string concatenations in a String-valued expression. For a String-valued *constant expression* ((1), (5), (6) and (7) in the preceding examples), the compiler computes such an expression at compile time, and the result is treated as a string literal in the program. The compiler uses a *string builder* to avoid the overhead of temporary String objects when applying the string concatenation operator (+) in String-valued non-constant expressions ((2), (3) and (4) in the preceding examples), as explained in §8.5, p. 378.

5.9 Variable Increment and Decrement Operators: ++, --

Variable increment (++) and decrement (--) operators come in two flavors: *prefix* and *postfix*. These unary operators have the side effect of changing the value of the arithmetic operand, which must evaluate to a variable. Depending on the operator used, the variable is either incremented or decremented by 1.

These operators cannot be applied to a variable that is declared final and that has been initialized, as the side effect would change the value in such a variable.

These operators are very useful for updating variables in loops where only the side effect of the operator is of interest.

The Increment Operator ++

The prefix increment operator has the following semantics: ++i adds 1 to the value in i, and stores the new value in i. It returns the *new* value as the value of the expression. It is equivalent to the following statements:

```
i += 1;
result = i;
return result;
```

The postfix increment operator has the following semantics: j++ adds 1 to the value in j, and stores the new value in j. It returns the *original* value that was in j as the value of the expression. It is equivalent to the following statements:

```
result = j;
j += 1;
return result;
```

The Decrement Operator --

The prefix decrement operator has the following semantics: --i subtracts 1 from the value of i, and stores the new value in i. It returns the *new* value as the value of the expression. It is equivalent to the following statements:

```
i -= 1;
result = i;
return result;
```

The postfix decrement operator has the following semantics: `j--` subtracts 1 from the value of `j`, and stores the new value in `j`. It returns the *original* value that was in `j` as the value of the expression. It is equivalent to the following statements:

```
result = j;
j -= 1;
return result;
```

This behavior of decrement and increment operators applies to any variable whose type is a numeric primitive type or its corresponding numeric wrapper type. Necessary numeric promotions are performed on the value 1 and the value of the variable. Before the new value is assigned to the variable, it is subjected to any narrowing primitive conversion and/or boxing that might be necessary.

Here are some examples that illustrate the behavior of increment and decrement operators:

```
// (1) Prefix order: increment/decrement operand before use.
int i = 10;
int k = ++i + --i;  // ((++i) + (--i)). k gets the value 21 and i becomes 10.
--i;                // Only side effect utilized. i is 9. (expression statement)

Integer iRef = 11;  // Boxing on assignment
--iRef;             // Only side effect utilized. iRef refers to an Integer
                    // object with the value 10. (expression statement)
k = ++iRef + --iRef;// ((++iRef) + (--iRef)). k gets the value 21 and
                    // iRef refers to an Integer object with the value 10.

// (2) Postfix order: increment/decrement operand after use.
long j = 10;
long n = j++ + j--; // ((j++) + (j--)). n gets the value 21L and j becomes 10L.
j++;                // Only side effect utilized. j is 11L. (expression statement)
```

An increment or decrement operator, together with its operand, can be used as an *expression statement* (§3.2, p. 50).

Execution of the assignment in the second declaration statement under (1) proceeds as follows:

`k = ((++i) + (--i))`	Operands are evaluated from left to right.
`k = ( 11   + (--i))`	Side effect: `i += 1`, `i` gets the value 11.
`k = ( 11   +  10)`	Side effect: `i -= 1`, `i` gets the value 10.
`k = 21`	

Execution of the expression statement `--iRef;` under (1) proceeds as follows:

- The value in the `Integer` object referred to by the reference `iRef` is unboxed, resulting in the `int` value 11.
- The value 11 is decremented, resulting in the value 10.

- The value 10 is boxed in an Integer object, and this object's reference value is assigned to the reference iRef.
- The int value 10 of the expression statement is discarded.

Expressions where variables are modified multiple times during the evaluation should be avoided, because the order of evaluation is not always immediately apparent.

We cannot associate increment and decrement operators. Given that a is a variable, we cannot write (++(++a)). The reason is that any operand to ++ must evaluate to a variable, but the evaluation of (++a) results in a value.

In the next example, both binary numeric promotion and an implicit narrowing conversion are performed to achieve the side effect of modifying the value of the operand. The int value of the expression (++b) (that is, 11), is assigned to the int variable i. The side effect of incrementing the value of the byte variable b requires binary numeric promotion to perform int addition, followed by an implicit narrowing conversion of the int value to byte to perform the assignment.

```
byte b = 10;
int  i = ++b;          // i is 11, and so is b.
```

The following example illustrates applying the increment operator to a floating-point operand. The side effect of the ++ operator is overwritten by the assignment.

```
double x = 4.5;
x = x + ++x;           // x gets the value 10.0.
```

Review Questions

5.10 Which statements are true?

Select the three correct answers.

(a) The expression (1 + 2 + "3") evaluates to the string "33".
(b) The expression ("1" + 2 + 3) evaluates to the string "15".
(c) The expression (4 + 1.0f) evaluates to the float value 5.0f.
(d) The expression (10/9) evaluates to the int value 1.
(e) The expression ('a' + 1) evaluates to the char value 'b'.

5.11 What happens when you try to compile and run the following program?

```
public class Prog1 {
  public static void main(String[] args) {
    int k = 1;
    int i = ++k + k++ + + k;     // (1)
    System.out.println(i);
  }
}
```

Select the one correct answer.

(a) The program will not compile, because of errors in the expression at (1).
(b) The program will compile and print the value 3 at runtime.
(c) The program will compile and print the value 4 at runtime.
(d) The program will compile and print the value 7 at runtime.
(e) The program will compile and print the value 8 at runtime.

5.12 Which is the first line that will cause a compile-time error in the following program?

```
public class MyClass {
  public static void main(String[] args) {
    char c;
    int i;
    c = 'a'; // (1)
    i = c;   // (2)
    i++;     // (3)
    c = i;   // (4)
    c++;     // (5)
  }
}
```

Select the one correct answer.

(a) (1)
(b) (2)
(c) (3)
(d) (4)
(e) (5)
(f) None of the above. The compiler will not report any errors.

5.13 What is the result of compiling and running the following program?

```
public class Cast {
  public static void main(String[] args) {
    byte b = 128;
    int  i = b;
    System.out.println(i);
  }
}
```

Select the one correct answer.

(a) The program will not compile, because a `byte` value cannot be assigned to an `int` variable without using a cast.
(b) The program will compile, and print `128` at runtime.
(c) The program will not compile, because the value `128` is not in the range of values for the `byte` type.
(d) The program will compile, but will throw a `ClassCastException` at runtime.
(e) The program will compile, and print `255` at runtime.

5.14 What will be the result of compiling and running the following program?

```
public class EvaluationOrder {
  public static void main(String[] args) {
    int[] array = { 4, 8, 16 };
    int i = 1;
    array[++i] = --i;
    System.out.println(array[0] + array[1] + array[2]);
  }
}
```

Select the one correct answer.

(a) 13
(b) 14
(c) 20
(d) 21
(e) 24

5.10 Boolean Expressions

As the name implies, a boolean expression has the `boolean` data type and can evaluate to only the values `true` or `false`. Boolean expressions, when used as conditionals in control statements, allow the program flow to be controlled during execution.

Boolean expressions can be formed using *relational operators* (§5.11, p. 180), *equality operators* (§5.12, p. 181), *boolean logical operators* (§5.13, p. 184), *conditional operators* (§5.14, p. 186), the *assignment operator* (§5.6, p. 158), and the `instanceof` operator (§7.11, p. 321).

5.11 Relational Operators: <, <=, >, >=

Given that `a` and `b` represent numeric expressions, the relational (also called *comparison*) operators are defined as shown in Table 5.8.

Table 5.8 *Relational Operators*

`a < b`	a less than b?
`a <= b`	a less than or equal to b?
`a > b`	a greater than b?
`a >= b`	a greater than or equal to b?

All relational operators are binary operators and their operands are numeric expressions. Binary numeric promotion is applied to the operands of these operators. The evaluation results in a `boolean` value. Relational operators have precedence lower than arithmetic operators, but higher than that of the assignment operators.

```
double hours = 45.5;
Double time = 18.0;                // Boxing of double value.
boolean overtime = hours >= 35; // true. Binary numeric promotion: double <-- int.
boolean beforeMidnight = time < 24.0;// true. Unboxing of value in time reference.
char letterA = 'A';
boolean order = letterA < 'a';  // true. Binary numeric promotion: int <-- char.
```

Relational operators are nonassociative. Mathematical expressions like $a \leq b \leq c$ must be written using relational and boolean logical / conditional operators.

```
int a = 1, b = 7, c = 10;
boolean illegal = a <= b <= c;      // (1) Illegal.
boolean valid2 = a <= b && b <= c;  // (2) OK.
```

Since relational operators have left associativity, the evaluation of the expression `a <= b <= c` at (1) in these examples would proceed as follows: `((a <= b) <= c)`. Evaluation of `(a <= b)` would yield a `boolean` value that is not permitted as an operand of a relational operator; that is, (*boolean value* `<= c`) would be illegal.

5.12 Equality

We distinguish between primitive data equality, object reference equality, and object value equality.

The equality operators have lower precedence than the relational operators, but higher precedence than the assignment operators.

Primitive Data Value Equality: ==, !=

Given that `a` and `b` represent operands of primitive data types, the primitive data value equality operators are defined as shown in Table 5.9.

Table 5.9 *Primitive Data Value Equality Operators*

`a == b`	Determines whether `a` and `b` are equal—that is, have the same primitive value. (Equality)
`a != b`	Determines whether `a` and `b` are not equal—that is, do not have the same primitive value. (Inequality)

The equality operator == and the inequality operator `!=` can be used to compare primitive data values, including `boolean` values. Binary numeric promotion is applied to the non-boolean operands of these equality operators.

```
int year = 2002;
boolean isEven  = year % 2 == 0;        // true.
boolean compare = '1' == 1;             // false. Binary numeric promotion applied.
boolean test    = compare == false;  // true.
```

Care must be exercised when comparing floating-point numbers for equality, as an infinite number of floating-point values can be stored only as approximations in a finite number of bits. For example, the expression `(1.0 - 2.0/3.0 == 1.0/3.0)` returns `false`, although mathematically the result should be true.

Analogous to the discussion for relational operators, mathematical expressions like $a = b = c$ must be written using relational and logical/conditional operators. Since equality operators have left associativity, the evaluation of the expression `a == b == c` would proceed as follows: `((a == b) == c)`. Evaluation of `(a == b)` would yield a `boolean` value that *is* permitted as an operand of a data value equality operator, but `(`*boolean value* `== c)` would be illegal if `c` had a numeric type. This problem is illustrated in the following examples. The expression at (1) is illegal, but those at (2) and (3) are legal.

```
int a, b, c;
a = b = c = 5;
boolean illegal = a == b == c;                // (1) Illegal.
boolean valid2 = a == b && b == c;            // (2) Legal.
boolean valid3 = a == b == true;              // (3) Legal.
```

Object Reference Equality: ==, !=

The equality operator `==` and the inequality operator `!=` can be applied to reference variables to test whether they refer to the same object. Given that `r` and `s` are reference variables, the reference equality operators are defined as shown in Table 5.10.

Table 5.10 *Reference Equality Operators*

`r == s`	Determines whether `r` and `s` are equal—that is, have the same reference value and therefore refer to the same object (also called *aliases*). (Equality)
`r != s`	Determines whether `r` and `s` are not equal—that is, do not have the same reference value and therefore refer to different objects. (Inequality)

The operands must be cast compatible: It must be possible to cast the reference value of the one into the other's type; otherwise, it is a compile-time error. Casting of references is discussed in §7.8, p. 311.

```
Pizza pizzaA = new Pizza("Sweet&Sour");       // new object
Pizza pizzaB = new Pizza("Sweet&Sour");       // new object
Pizza pizzaC = new Pizza("Hot&Spicy");        // new object

String banner = "Come and get it!";           // new object

boolean test  = banner == pizzaA;             // (1) Compile-time error
boolean test1 = pizzaA == pizzaB;             // false
boolean test2 = pizzaA == pizzaC;             // false

pizzaA = pizzaB;                            // Denote the same object; are aliases
boolean test3 = pizzaA == pizzaB;           // true
```

The comparison `banner == pizzaA` in (1) is illegal, because the `String` and `Pizza` types are not related and therefore the reference value of one type cannot be cast to the other type. The values of `test1` and `test2` are `false` because the three references denote different objects, regardless of the fact that pizzaA and pizzaB are both sweet and sour pizzas. The value of test3 is true because now both pizzaA and pizzaB denote the same object.

The equality and inequality operators are applied to object references to check whether two references denote the same object. The state of the objects that the references denote is not compared. This is the same as testing whether the references are aliases, meaning that they denote the same object.

The null literal can be assigned to any reference variable, and the reference value in a reference variable can be compared for equality with the null literal. The comparison can be used to avoid inadvertent use of a reference variable that does not denote any object.

```
if (objRef != null) {
    // ... use objRef ...
}
```

Note that only when the type of *both* operands is either a reference type or the null type, do these operators test for object reference equality. Otherwise, they test for primitive data equality (see also §8.3, p. 350). In the following code snippet, binary numeric promotion involving unboxing is performed at (2):

```
Integer iRef = 10;
boolean b1 = iRef == null;            // (1) Object reference equality
boolean b2 = iRef == 10;              // (2) Primitive data equality
boolean b3 = null == 10;              // Compile-time error!
```

Object Value Equality

The Object class provides the method public boolean equals(Object obj), which can be *overridden* (§7.2, p. 268) to give the right semantics of *object value equality*. The default implementation of this method in the Object class returns true only if the object is compared with itself, as if the equality operator == had been used to compare aliases of an object. Consequently, if a class does not override the semantics of the equals() method from the Object class, object value equality is the same as object reference equality.

Certain classes in the standard API override the equals() method, such as java.lang.String and the wrapper classes for the primitive data types. For two String objects, value equality means they contain identical character sequences. For the wrapper classes, value equality means that the wrapper objects have the same primitive value and are of the same wrapper type (see also §8.3, p. 350).

```
// Equality for String objects means identical character sequences.
String movie1 = new String("The Revenge of the Exception Handler");
String movie2 = new String("High Noon at the Java Corral");
String movie3 = new String("The Revenge of the Exception Handler");
boolean test0 = movie1.equals(movie2);             // false.
boolean test1 = movie1.equals(movie3);             // true.
```

```
// Equality for wrapper classes means same type and same primitive value.
        Boolean flag1 = true;                          // Boxing.
        Boolean flag2 = false;                         // Boxing.
        boolean test2 = flag1.equals("true");          // false. Not same type.
        boolean test3 = flag1.equals(!flag2);          // true. Same type and value.

        Integer iRef = 100;                            // Boxing.
        Short sRef = 100;                              // Boxing.
        boolean test4 = iRef.equals(100);              // true. Same type and value.
        boolean test5 = iRef.equals(sRef);             // false. Not same type.
        boolean test6 = iRef.equals(3.14);             // false. Not same type.

// The Pizza class does not override the equals() method, so we can use either
// equals() method inherited from the Object class or equality operator ==.
        Pizza pizza1 = new Pizza("VeggiesDelight");
        Pizza pizza2 = new Pizza("VeggiesDelight");
        Pizza pizza3 = new Pizza("CheeseDelight");
        boolean test7 = pizza1.equals(pizza2);         // false.
        boolean test8 = pizza1.equals(pizza3);         // false.
        boolean test9 = pizza1 == pizza2;              // false.
        pizza1 = pizza2;                               // Creates aliases.
        boolean test10 = pizza1.equals(pizza2);        // true.
        boolean test11 = pizza1 == pizza2;             // true.
```

5.13 Boolean Logical Operators: !, ^, &, |

Boolean logical operators include the unary operator ! (*logical complement*) and the binary operators & (*logical* AND), | (*logical inclusive* OR), and ^ (*logical exclusive* OR, also called *logical* XOR). These operators can be applied to boolean or Boolean operands, returning a boolean value. The operators &, |, and ^ can also be applied to integral operands to perform *bitwise* logical operations, but are not in the scope of this book.

Given that x and y represent boolean expressions, the boolean logical operators are defined in Table 5.11. The precedence of the operators decreases from left to right in the table.

These operators always evaluate both the operands, unlike their counterpart conditional operators && and || (§5.14, p. 186). Unboxing is applied to the operand values, if necessary. Truth values for boolean logical operators are shown in Table 5.11.

Table 5.11 *Truth Values for Boolean Logical Operators*

x	y	Complement !x	AND x & y	XOR x ^ y	OR x | y
true	true	false	true	false	true
true	false	false	false	true	true
false	true	true	false	true	true
false	false	true	false	false	false

Operand Evaluation for Boolean Logical Operators

In the evaluation of boolean expressions involving boolean logical AND, XOR, and OR operators, both the operands are evaluated. The order of operand evaluation is always from left to right.

```
if (i > 0 & i++ < 10) {/*...*/} // i will be incremented, regardless of value in i.
```

The binary boolean logical operators have precedence lower than the arithmetic and relational operators, but higher precedence than the assignment, conditional AND, and OR operators (§5.14, p. 186). This is illustrated in the following examples:

```
boolean b1, b2, b3 = false, b4 = false;
Boolean b5 = true;
b1 = 4 == 2 & 1 < 4;              // false, evaluated as (b1 = ((4 == 2) & (1 < 4)))
b2 = b1 | !(2.5 >= 8);            // true
b3 = b3 ^ b5;                     // true, unboxing conversion on b5
b4 = b4 | b1 & b2;                // false
```

Here, the order of evaluation is illustrated for the last expression statement:

```
   (b4 = (b4 | (b1 & b2)))
⇒ (b4 = (false | (b1 & b2)))
⇒ (b4 = (false | (false & b2)))
⇒ (b4 = (false | (false & true)))
⇒ (b4 = (false | false))
⇒ (b4 = false)
⇒ false
```

Note that b2 was evaluated although, strictly speaking, it was not necessary. This behavior is guaranteed for boolean logical operators.

Boolean Logical Compound Assignment Operators: &=, ^=, |=

Compound assignment operators for the boolean logical operators are defined in Table 5.12. The left-hand operand must be a boolean variable, and the right-hand operand must be a boolean expression. An identity conversion is applied implicitly on assignment. These operators can also be applied to integral operands to perform *bitwise* compound assignments, but are not covered in this book. See also the discussion on arithmetic compound assignment operators in §5.7, p. 172.

Table 5.12 *Boolean Logical Compound Assignment Operators*

Expression	Given a and b are of type boolean or Boolean, the expression is evaluated as:
b &= a	b = (b & (a))
b ^= a	b = (b ^ (a))
b |= a	b = (b | (a))

Here are some examples to illustrate the behavior of boolean logical compound assignment operators:

```
boolean b1 = false, b2 = true, b3 = false;
Boolean b4 = false;
b1 |= true;               // true
b4 ^= b1;                 // (1) true, unboxing in (b4 ^ (b1)), boxing on assignment
b3 &= b1 | b2;            // (2) false, b3 = (b3 & (b1 | b2))
b3 = b3 & b1 | b2;        // (3) true,  b3 = ((b3 & b1) | b2)
```

The assignment at (1) entails unboxing to evaluate the expression on the right-hand side, followed by boxing to assign the boolean result. It is also instructive to compare how the assignments at (2) and (3) are performed, as they lead to different results with the same values of the operands, showing how the precedence affects the evaluation.

5.14 Conditional Operators: &&, ||

The conditional operators && and || are similar to their counterpart logical operators & and |, except that their evaluation is *short-circuited*. Given that x and y represent values of boolean or Boolean expressions, the conditional operators are defined in Table 5.13. In the table, the operators are listed in decreasing precedence order.

Table 5.13 *Conditional Operators*

Conditional AND	x && y	true if both operands are true; otherwise, false.
Conditional OR	x || y	true if either or both operands are true; otherwise, false.

Unlike their logical counterparts & and |, which can also be applied to integral operands for bitwise operations, the conditional operators && and || can be applied only to boolean operands. Their evaluation results in a boolean value. Truth values for conditional operators are shown in Table 5.14. Not surprisingly, the conditional operators have the same truth values as their counterpart logical operators. However, unlike with their logical counterparts, there are no compound assignment operators for the conditional operators.

Table 5.14 *Truth Values for Conditional Operators*

x	y	AND x && y	OR x || y
true	true	true	true
true	false	false	true
false	true	false	true
false	false	false	false

Short-Circuit Evaluation

In evaluation of boolean expressions involving conditional AND and OR, the left-hand operand is evaluated before the right-hand operand, and the evaluation is short-circuited (i.e., if the result of the boolean expression can be determined from the left-hand operand, the right-hand operand is not evaluated). In other words, the right-hand operand is evaluated conditionally.

The binary conditional operators have lower precedence than the arithmetic, relational, and logical operators, but higher precedence than the assignment operators. Unboxing of the operand value takes place when necessary, before the operation is performed. The following examples illustrate usage of conditional operators:

```
Boolean b1 = 4 == 2 && 1 < 4;     // false, short-circuit evaluated as
                                  // (b1 = ((4 == 2) && (1 < 4)))
boolean b2 = !b1 || 2.5 > 8;      // true, short-circuit evaluated as
                                  // (b2 = ((!b1) || (2.5 > 8)))
Boolean b3 = !(b1 && b2);         // true
boolean b4 = b1 || !b3 && b2;     // false, short-circuit evaluated as
                                  // (b4 = (b1 || ((!b3) && b2)))
```

The order of evaluation for computing the value stored in the boolean variable b4 proceeds as follows:

```
   (b4 = (b1 || ((!b3) && b2)))
⇒ (b4 = (false || ((!b3) && b2)))
⇒ (b4 = (false || ((!true) && b2)))
⇒ (b4 = (false || ((false) && b2)))
⇒ (b4 = (false || false))
⇒ (b4 = false)
```

Note that b2 is not evaluated, short-circuiting the evaluation. Example 5.3 illustrates the short-circuit evaluation of the initialization expressions in the declaration statements given in the earlier code snippet. In addition, it shows an evaluation (see the declaration of b5) involving boolean logical operators that always evaluate both operands. See also Example 5.1, p. 153, which uses a similar approach to illustrate the order of operand evaluation in arithmetic expressions.

Example 5.3 *Short-Circuit Evaluation Involving Conditional Operators*

```
public class ShortCircuit {
  public static void main(String[] args) {
    // Boolean b1 = 4 == 2 && 1 < 4;
    Boolean b1 = operandEval(1, 4 == 2) && operandEval(2, 1 < 4);
    System.out.println();
    System.out.println("Value of b1: " + b1);

    // boolean b2 = !b1 || 2.5 > 8;
    boolean b2 = !operandEval(1, b1) || operandEval(2, 2.5 > 8);
    System.out.println();
    System.out.println("Value of b2: " + b2);
```

```
        // Boolean b3 = !(b1 && b2);
        Boolean b3 = !(operandEval(1, b1) && operandEval(2, b2));
        System.out.println();
        System.out.println("Value of b3: " + b3);

        // boolean b4 = b1 || !b3 && b2;
        boolean b4 = operandEval(1, b1) || !operandEval(2, b3) && operandEval(3, b2);
        System.out.println();
        System.out.println("Value of b4: " + b4);

        // boolean b5 = b1 | !b3 & b2;     // Using boolean logical operators
        boolean b5 = operandEval(1, b1) | !operandEval(2, b3) & operandEval(3, b2);
        System.out.println();
        System.out.println("Value of b5: " + b5);
      }

      static boolean operandEval(int opNum, boolean operand) {                // (1)
        System.out.print(opNum);
        return operand;
      }
    }
```

Output from the program:

```
1
Value of b1: false
1
Value of b2: true
1
Value of b3: true
12
Value of b4: false
123
Value of b5: false
```

Short-circuit evaluation can be used to ensure that a reference variable denotes an object before it is used.

```
if (objRef != null && objRef.equals(other)) { /*...*/ }
```

The method call is now conditionally dependent on the left-hand operand and will not be executed if the variable `objRef` has the `null` reference. If we use the logical `&` operator and the variable `objRef` has the `null` reference, evaluation of the right-hand operand will result in a `NullPointerException`.

In summary, we employ the conditional operators `&&` and `||` if the evaluation of the right-hand operand is conditionally dependent on the left-hand operand. We use the boolean logical operators `&` and `|` if both operands must be evaluated. The subtlety of conditional operators is illustrated by the following examples:

```
if (i > 0 && i++ < 10) {/*...*/}   // i is not incremented if i > 0 is false.
if (i > 0 || i++ < 10) {/*...*/}   // i is not incremented if i > 0 is true.
```

5.15 Integer Bitwise Operators: ~, &, |, ^

A review of integer representation (§5.5, p. 154) is recommended before continuing with this section on how integer bitwise operators can be applied to values of *integral* data types.

Integer bitwise operators include the unary operator ~ (*bitwise complement*) and the binary operators & (*bitwise* AND), | (*bitwise inclusive* OR), and ^ (*bitwise exclusive* OR, also known as *bitwise* XOR). The operators &, |, and ^ are overloaded, as they can be applied to `boolean` or `Boolean` operands to perform *boolean* logical operations (§5.13, p. 184). Although the integer bitwise operators are not on the OCAJP 8 exam, they are included here to contrast their evaluation with that of their boolean counterparts.

The binary bitwise operators perform bitwise operations between corresponding individual bit values in the operands. Unary numeric promotion is applied to the operand of the unary bitwise complement operator ~, and binary numeric promotion is applied to the operands of the binary bitwise operators. The result is a new integer value of the promoted type, which can be either `int` or `long`.

Given that `A` and `B` are corresponding bit values (either `0` or `1`) in the left-hand and right-hand operands, respectively, these bitwise operators are defined as shown in Table 5.15. The operators are listed in decreasing precedence order.

Table 5.15 *Integer Bitwise Operators*

Operator name	Notation	Effect on each bit of the binary representation
Bitwise complement	`~A`	Invert the bit value: 1 to 0, 0 to 1
Bitwise AND	`A & B`	1 if both bits are 1; otherwise 0
Bitwise OR	`A | B`	1 if either or both bits are 1; otherwise 0
Bitwise XOR	`A ^ B`	1 if and only if one of the bits is 1; otherwise 0

The result of applying bitwise operators between two corresponding bits in the operands is shown in Table 5.16, where `A` and `B` are corresponding bit values in the left-hand right-hand operands, respectively. Table 5.16 is analogous to Table 5.11 for boolean logical operators, if we consider bit value `1` to represent `true` and bit value `0` to represent `false`.

Table 5.16 *Result Table for Bitwise Operators*

A	B	Complement ~A	AND A & B	XOR A ^ B	OR A | B
1	1	0	1	0	1
1	0	0	0	1	1
0	1	1	0	1	1
0	0	1	0	0	0

Examples of Bitwise Operator Application

```
char v1 = ')';                 // Unicode value 41
byte v2 = 13;

int result1 = ~v1;       // -42
int result2 = v1 & v2;   // 9
int result3 = v1 | v2;   // 45
int result4 = v1 ^ v2;   // 36
```

Table 5.17 shows how the result is calculated. Unary and binary numeric promotions are applied first, converting the operands to `int` in these cases. Note that the operator semantics is applied to corresponding individual bits—that is, first bit of left-hand operand and first bit of right-hand operand, second bit of left-hand operand and second bit of right-hand operand, and so on.

Table 5.17 *Examples of Bitwise Operations*

~v1	v1 & v2	v1 | v2	v1 ^ v2
~ 0...0010 1001	0...0010 1001	0...0010 1001	0...0010 1001
	& 0...0000 1101	| 0...0000 1101	^ 0...0000 1101
= 1...1101 0110	= 0...0000 1001	= 0...0010 1101	= 0...0010 0100
= 0xffffffd6	= 0x00000009	= 0x0000002d	= 0x00000024
= -42	= 9	= 45	= 36

It is instructive to run examples and print the result of a bitwise operation in different notations, as shown in Example 5.4. The integer bitwise operators support a programming technique called *bit masking*. The value `v2` is usually called a *bit mask*. Depending on the bitwise operation performed on the value `v1` and the mask `v2`, we see how the resulting value reflects the bitwise operation performed between the individual corresponding bits of the value `v1` and the mask `v2`. By choosing appropriate values for the bits in the mask `v2` and the right bitwise operation, it is possible to extract, set, and toggle specific bits in the value `v1`.

Methods for converting integers to strings in different notations can be found in the `Integer` class (§8.3, p. 353). Converting integers to different number systems is discussed in §5.5, p. 154.

Example 5.4 *Bitwise Operations*

```
public class BitOperations {
  public static void main(String[] args) {
    char v1 = ')';                      // Unicode value 41
    byte v2 = 13;
    printIntToStr("v1:", v1);           // 41
    printIntToStr("v2:", v2);           // 13
    printIntToStr("~v1:", ~v1);         // -42
    printIntToStr("v1 & v2:", v1 & v2); // 9
    printIntToStr("v1 | v2:", v1 | v2); // 45
    printIntToStr("v1 ^ v2:", v1 ^ v2); // 36
  }

  public static void printIntToStr(String label, int result) {
    System.out.println(label);
    System.out.println("    Binary:  " + Integer.toBinaryString(result));
    System.out.println("    Hex:     " + Integer.toHexString(result));
    System.out.println("    Decimal: " + result);
  }
}
```

Output from the program:

```
v1:
    Binary:  101001
    Hex:     29
    Decimal: 41
v2:
    Binary:  1101
    Hex:     d
    Decimal: 13
~v1:
    Binary:  11111111111111111111111111010110
    Hex:     ffffffd6
    Decimal: -42
v1 & v2:
    Binary:  1001
    Hex:     9
    Decimal: 9
v1 | v2:
    Binary:  101101
    Hex:     2d
    Decimal: 45
v1 ^ v2:
    Binary:  100100
    Hex:     24
    Decimal: 36
```

Bitwise Compound Assignment Operators: &=, ^=, |=

Bitwise compound assignment operators for the bitwise operators are defined in Table 5.18. Type conversions for these operators, when applied to integral operands, are the same as for other compound assignment operators: an implicit narrowing conversion is performed on assignment when the destination data type is either `byte`, `short`, or `char`. These operators can also be applied to boolean operands to perform logical compound assignments (§5.13, p. 185).

Table 5.18 *Bitwise Compound Assignment Operators*

Expression	Given T is the integral type of b, the expression is evaluated as:
`b &= a`	`b = (T) ((b) & (a))`
`b ^= a`	`b = (T) ((b) ^ (a))`
`b |= a`	`b = (T) ((b) | (a))`

Examples of Bitwise Compound Assignment

```
int  v0 = -42;
char v1 = ')';  // 41
byte v2 = 13;

v0 &= 15;        //     1...1101 0110 & 0...0000 1111 => 0...0000 0110 (= 6)
v1 |= v2;        // (1) 0...0010 1001 | 0...0000 1101 => 0...0010 1101 (= 45, '-')
```

At (1) in these examples, both the `char` value in `v1` and the `byte` value in `v2` are first promoted to `int`. The result is implicitly narrowed to the destination type `char` on assignment.

Review Questions

5.15 Which of the following expressions evaluate to `true`?

Select the two correct answers.

(a) `(false | true)`
(b) `(null != null)`
(c) `(4 <= 4)`
(d) `(!true)`
(e) `(true & false)`

5.16 Which of the following statements are true?

Select the two correct answers.

(a) The remainder operator `%` can be used only with integral operands.
(b) Short-circuit evaluation occurs with boolean logical operators.
(c) The arithmetic operators `*`, `/`, and `%` have the same level of precedence.
(d) A `short` value ranges from `-128` to `+127`, inclusive.
(e) `(+15)` is a legal expression.

5.17 Which statements are true about the lines of output printed by the following program?

```
public class BoolOp {
  static void op(boolean a, boolean b) {
    boolean c = a != b;
    boolean d = a ^ b;
    boolean e = c == d;
    System.out.println(e);
  }

  public static void main(String[] args) {
    op(false, false);
    op(true, false);
    op(false, true);
    op(true, true);
  }
}
```

Select the three correct answers.

(a) All lines printed are the same.
(b) At least one line contains `false`.
(c) At least one line contains `true`.
(d) The first line contains `false`.
(e) The last line contains `true`.

5.18 What is the result of running the following program?

```
public class OperandOrder {
  public static void main(String[] args) {
    int i = 0;
    int[] a = {3, 6};
    a[i] = i = 9;
    System.out.println(i + " " + a[0] + " " + a[1]);
  }
}
```

Select the one correct answer.

(a) When run, the program throws an `ArrayIndexOutOfBoundsException`.
(b) When run, the program will print `9 9 6`.
(c) When run, the program will print `9 0 6`.
(d) When run, the program will print `9 3 6`.
(e) When run, the program will print `9 3 9`.

5.19 Which statements are true about the output from the following program?

```
public class Logic {
  public static void main(String[] args) {
    int i = 0;
    int j = 0;

    boolean t = true;
    boolean r;
```

```
        r = (t &  0 < (i+=1));
        r = (t && 0 < (i+=2));
        r = (t |  0 < (j+=1));
        r = (t || 0 < (j+=2));
        System.out.println(i + " " + j);
    }
}
```

Select the two correct answers.

(a) The first digit printed is 1.
(b) The first digit printed is 2.
(c) The first digit printed is 3.
(d) The second digit printed is 1.
(e) The second digit printed is 2.
(f) The second digit printed is 3.

5.16 The Conditional Operator: `?:`

The ternary conditional operator `?:` allows *conditional expressions* to be defined. The conditional expression has the following syntax:

condition ? $expression_1$: $expression_2$

It is called ternary because it has three operands. If the boolean expression *condition* is `true`, then $expression_1$ is evaluated; otherwise, $expression_2$ is evaluated. Both $expression_1$ and $expression_2$ must evaluate to values that can be converted to the *type* of the conditional expression. This type is determined from the types of the two expressions. The value of the expression evaluated is converted to the type of the conditional expression, and may involve autoboxing and unboxing.

Evaluation of a conditional expression is an example of short-circuit evaluation. As only one of the two expressions is evaluated, one should be wary of any side effects in a conditional expression.

In the following code snippet at (1), both expressions in the conditional expression are of type `byte`. The type of the conditional expression is therefore `byte`. That a value of type `byte` can be converted to an `int` by an implicit widening numeric conversion to be assignment compatible with the `int` variable `daysInFebruary` is secondary in determining the type of the conditional expression. Note that the conditional operator at (1) has higher precedence than the assignment operator `=`, making it unnecessary to enclose the conditional expression in parentheses.

```
boolean leapYear = false;
byte v29 = 29;
byte v28 = 28;
int daysInFebruary = leapYear ? v29 : v28;    // (1)
```

The following examples illustrate the use of conditional expressions. The type of the conditional expression at (2) is `int`, and no conversion of any expression value is necessary. The type of the conditional expression at (3) is `double`, due to binary numeric promotion: The `int` value of the first expressions is promoted to a `double`. The compiler reports an error because a `double` cannot be assigned to an `int` variable. The type of the conditional expression at (4) is also `double` as in (3), but now the `double` value is assignment compatible with the `double` variable `minDoubleValue`.

```
int i = 3;
int j = 4;
int minValue1 = i < j ? i : j;                       // (2) int
int minValue2 = i < j ? i : Double.MIN_VALUE;        // (3) double. Not OK.
double minDoubleValue = i < j ? i : Double.MIN_VALUE; // (4) double
```

In the following code snippet in (5), the primitive values of the expressions can be boxed and assigned to an `Object` reference. In (6), the `int` value of the first expression can be boxed in an `Integer`. The `println()` method creates and prints a string representation of any object whose reference value is passed as parameter.

```
// Assume i and j are of type int and initialized correctly.
Object obj = i < j ? i : true;          // (5) value of i boxed in Integer or
                                        //     literal true boxed in Boolean
System.out.println(i < j ? i : "Hi"); // (6) value of i boxed in Integer or
                                        //     String object "Hi"
```

The conditional expression is *not* an expression statement. The following code will not compile:

```
(i < j) ? i : j;    // Compile-time error!
```

The conditional expression can be nested, and the conditional operator associates from right to left.

`a?b:c?d:e?f:g` evaluates as `(a?b:(c?d:(e?f:g)))`

The value of this conditional expression is `g` if, and only if, `a`, `c`, and `e` are `false`. A nested conditional expression is used in the next example. As a convention, the condition in a conditional expression is enclosed in parentheses to aid reading the code. Typically, a conditional expression is used when it makes the code easier to read, especially when the expressions are short and without side effects.

```
int n = 3;
String msg = (n==0) ? "no cookies." : (n==1) ? "one cookie." : "many cookies.";
System.out.println("You get " + msg); // You get many cookies.
```

The conditional operator is the expression equivalent of the `if-else` statement (§6.2, p. 201).

5.17 Other Operators: `new`, `[]`, `instanceof`, `->`

The `new` operator is used to create objects, such as instances of classes and arrays. It is used with a constructor call to instantiate classes (§3.3, p. 53) and with the `[]` notation to create arrays (§3.4, p. 59). It is also used to instantiate anonymous arrays (§3.4, p. 63).

```
Pizza onePizza = new Pizza();         // Create an instance of the Pizza class.
```

The [] notation is used to declare and construct arrays, and is also to access array elements (§3.4, p. 58).

```
int[] anArray = new int[5];// Declare and construct an int array of 5 elements.
anArray[4] = anArray[3];   // Element at index 4 gets value of element at index 3.
```

The boolean, binary, and infix operator `instanceof` is used to test the type of an object (§7.11, p. 320).

```
Pizza myPizza = new Pizza();
boolean test1 = myPizza instanceof Pizza; // true.
boolean test2 = "Pizza" instanceof Pizza; // Compile error. String is not Pizza.
boolean test3 = null instanceof Pizza; // Always false. null is not an instance.
```

The arrow operator -> is used in the definition of a lambda expression (§10.2, p. 444).

```
java.util.function.Predicate<String> predicate = str -> str.length() % 2 == 0;
boolean test4 = predicate.test("The lambda strikes back!");     // true.
```

Review Questions

5.20 Which of the following are not operators in Java?

Select the two correct answers.

(a) `%`
(b) `&&`
(c) `%=`
(d) `&&=`
(e) `<=`
(f) `%%`
(g) `->`

5.21 Which statements when inserted at (1) will not result in a compile-time error?

```
public class RQ05A200 {
  public static void main(String[] args) {
    int i = 20;
    int j = 30;
    // (1) INSERT STATEMENT HERE.
  }
}
```

Select the three correct answers.

(a) `int result1 = i < j ? i : j * 10D;`
(b) `int result2 = i< j ? { ++i } : { ++j };`
(c) `Number number = i < j ? i : j * 10D;`
(d) `System.out.println(i < j ? i);`
(e) `System.out.println(i < j ? ++i : ++j);`
(f) `System.out.println(i == j ? i == j : "i not equal to j");`

5.22 Which statements are true about the following code?

```
public class RQ05A100 {
  public static void main(String[] args) {
    int n1 = 10, n2 = 10;
    int m1 = 20, m2 = 30;
    int result = n1 != n2? n1 : m1 != m2? m1 : m2;
    System.out.println(result);
  }
}
```

Select the one correct answer.

(a) The program will not compile.
(b) When run, the program throws an `ArithmeticException` at runtime.
(c) When run, the program will print `10`.
(d) When run, the program will print `20`.
(e) When run, the program will print `30`.

Chapter Summary

The following topics were covered in this chapter:

- Type conversion categories and conversion contexts, and which conversions are permissible in each conversion context.
- Defining and evaluating arithmetic and boolean expressions, and the order in which operands and operators are evaluated.
- Representing integers in different number systems and in memory.
- Operators in Java, including precedence and associativity rules.

Programming Exercise

5.1 The following program is supposed to calculate and print the time it takes for light to travel from the sun to the earth. It contains some logical errors. Fix the program so that it will compile, compute, and print the correct result when run.

```
// File: Sunlight.java
public class Sunlight {
  public static void main(String[] args) {
    // Distance from sun (150 million kilometers)
    int kmFromSun = 150_000_000;

    int lightSpeed = 299_792_458; // meters per second

    // Convert distance to meters.
    int mFromSun = kmFromSun * 1000;
```

```
    int seconds = mFromSun / lightSpeed;

    System.out.print("Light will use ");
    printTime(seconds);
    System.out.println(" to travel from the sun to the earth.");
  }

  public static void printTime(int sec) {
    int min = sec / 60;
    sec = sec - (min * 60);
    System.out.print(min + " minute(s) and " + sec + " second(s)");
  }
}
```

Control Flow

6

Programmer I Exam Objectives	
[3.3] Create if and if/else and ternary constructs ○ *For ternary construct, see §5.16, p. 194.*	§6.2, p. 200
[3.4] Use a switch statement	§6.2, p. 203
[5.1] Create and use while loops	§6.3, p. 213
[5.2] Create and use for loops including the enhanced for loop	§6.3, p. 215 §6.3, p. 217
[5.3] Create and use do/while loops	§6.3, p. 214
[5.4] Compare loop constructs	§6.3, p. 213
[5.5] Use break and continue	§6.4, p. 219
[6.1] Create methods with arguments and return values; including overloaded methods ○ *For method declarations, see §3.2, p. 49.* ○ *For parameter passing, see §3.5, p. 72.* ○ *For covariant return, see §7.2, p. 273.*	§6.4, p. 224
[8.1] Differentiate among checked exceptions, unchecked exceptions, and Errors	§6.6, p. 237
[8.2] Create a try-catch block and determine how exceptions alter normal program flow	§6.7, p. 238
[8.3] Describe the advantages of exception handling	§6.10, p. 254
[8.4] Create and invoke a method that throws an exception	§6.8, p. 249 §6.9, p. 251
[8.5] Recognize common exception classes (such as NullPointerException, ArithmeticException, ArrayIndexOutOfBoundsException, ClassCastException)	§6.6, p. 233
Supplementary Objectives	
• Understand method execution and exception propagation through the JVM stack	§6.5, p. 230

6.1 Overview of Control Flow Statements

Control flow statements govern *the flow of control* in a program during execution, meaning the order in which statements are executed in a running program. There are three main categories of control flow statements:

- *Selection* statements: `if`, `if-else`, and `switch`.
- *Iteration* statements: `while`, `do-while`, basic `for`, and enhanced `for`.
- *Transfer* statements: `break`, `continue`, `return`, `try-catch-finally`, `throw`, and `assert`.

Only the basic form of the `try-catch-finally` construct is covered here, and the `assert` facility is not in the scope of this book.

6.2 Selection Statements

Java provides selection statements that allow the program to choose between alternative actions during execution. The choice is based on criteria specified in the selection statement. These selection statements are

- Simple `if` statement
- `if-else` statement
- `switch` statement

The Simple `if` Statement

The simple `if` statement has the following syntax:

```
if (condition)
  statement
```

It is used to decide whether an action is to be performed or not, based on a *condition*. The action to be performed is specified by *statement*, which can be a single statement or a code block. The *condition* must evaluate to a `boolean` or `Boolean` value. In the latter case, the `Boolean` value is unboxed to the corresponding `boolean` value.

The semantics of the simple `if` statement are straightforward. The *condition* is evaluated first. If its value is `true`, *statement* (called the `if` block) is executed and then execution continues with the rest of the program. If the value is `false`, the `if` block is skipped and execution continues with the rest of the program. The semantics are illustrated by the activity diagram in Figure 6.1a.

In the following examples of the `if` statement, it is assumed that the variables and the methods have been appropriately defined:

```
if (emergency)              // emergency is a boolean variable
  operate();

if (temperature > critical)
  soundAlarm();

if (isLeapYear() && endOfCentury())
  celebrate();

if (catIsAway()) {          // Block
  getFishingRod();
  goFishing();
}
```

Figure 6.1 *Activity Diagram for* `if` *Statements*

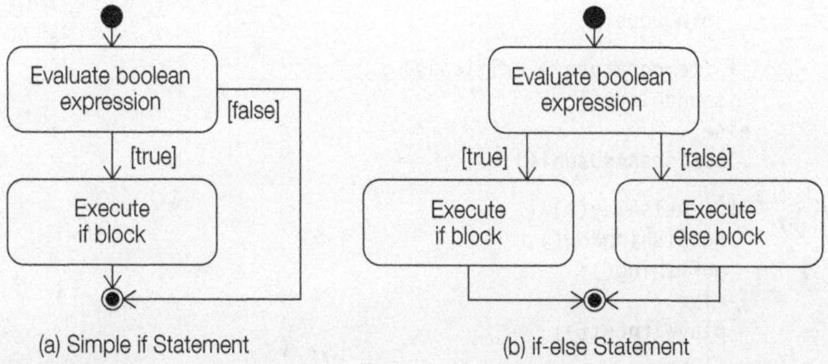

Note that *statement* can be a *block*, and the block notation is necessary if more than one statement is to be executed when the *condition* is `true`.

Since the *condition* evaluates to a `boolean` value, it avoids a common programming error: using an expression of the form `(a=b)` as the condition, where inadvertently an assignment operator is used instead of a relational operator. The compiler will flag this as an error, unless both `a` and `b` are boolean.

Note that the `if` block can be any valid statement. In particular, it can be the empty statement (`;`) or the empty block (`{}`). A common programming error is inadvertent use of the empty statement.

```
if (emergency); // Empty if block
  operate();    // Executed regardless of whether it was an emergency
```

The `if-else` Statement

The `if-else` statement is used to decide between two actions, based on a *condition*. It has the following syntax:

```
if (condition)
  statement₁
else
  statement₂
```

The *condition* is evaluated first. If its value is `true` (or unboxed to `true`), *statement*$_1$ (the `if` block) is executed and then execution continues with the rest of the program. If the value is `false` (or unboxed to `false`), *statement*$_2$ (the `else` block) is executed and then execution continues with the rest of the program. In other words, one of two mutually exclusive actions is performed. The `else` clause is optional; if omitted, the construct is equivalent to the simple `if` statement. The semantics are illustrated by the activity diagram in Figure 6.1b.

In the following examples of the `if-else` statement, it is assumed that all variables and methods have been appropriately defined:

```
if (emergency)
  operate();
else
  joinQueue();

if (temperature > critical)
  soundAlarm();
else
  businessAsUsual();

if (catIsAway()) {
  getFishingRod();
  goFishing();
} else
  playWithCat();
```

Since actions can be arbitrary statements, the `if` statements can be nested.

```
if (temperature >= upperLimit) {        // (1)
  if (danger)                           // (2) Simple if.
    soundAlarm();
  if (critical)                         // (3)
    evacuate();
  else                                  // Goes with if at (3).
    turnHeaterOff();
} else                                  // Goes with if at (1).
    turnHeaterOn();
```

The use of the block notation, {}, can be critical to the execution of `if` statements. The `if` statements (A) and (B) in the following examples do *not* have the same meaning. The `if` statements (B) and (C) are the same, with extra indentation used in (C) to make the meaning evident. Leaving out the block notation in this case could have catastrophic consequences: The heater could be turned on when the temperature is above the upper limit.

```
// (A):
if (temperature > upperLimit) {         // (1) Block notation.
  if (danger) soundAlarm();             // (2)
} else                                  // Goes with if at (1).
  turnHeaterOn();

// (B):
if (temperature > upperLimit)           // (1) Without block notation.
```

```
    if (danger) soundAlarm();                 // (2)
  else turnHeaterOn();                        // Goes with if at (2).

  // (C):
  if (temperature > upperLimit)               // (1)
    if (danger)                               // (2)
      soundAlarm();
    else                                      // Goes with if at (2).
      turnHeaterOn();
```

The rule for matching an `else` clause is that an `else` clause always refers to the nearest `if` that is not already associated with another `else` clause. Block notation and proper indentation can be used to make the meaning obvious.

Cascading `if-else` statements comprise a sequence of nested `if-else` statements where the `if` block of the next `if-else` statement is joined to the `else` clause of the previous one. The decision to execute a block is then based on all the conditions evaluated so far.

```
if (temperature >= upperLimit) {                               // (1)
  soundAlarm();
  turnHeaterOff();
} else if (temperature < lowerLimit) {                         // (2)
  soundAlarm();
  turnHeaterOn();
} else if (temperature == (upperLimit-lowerLimit)/2) {         // (3)
  doingFine();
} else                                                         // (4)
  noCauseToWorry();
```

The block corresponding to the first `if` condition that evaluates to `true` is executed, and the remaining `if` statements are skipped. In the preceding example, the block at (3) will execute only if the conditions at (1) and (2) are `false` and the condition at (3) is `true`. If none of the conditions is `true`, the block associated with the last `else` clause is executed. If there is no last `else` clause, no actions are performed.

The `switch` Statement

Conceptually, the `switch` statement can be used to choose one among many alternative actions, based on the value of an expression. Its general form is as follows:

```
switch (switch_expression) {
  case label_1: statement_1
  case label_2: statement_2
  ...
  case label_n: statement_n
  default:      statement
} // end switch
```

The syntax of the `switch` statement comprises a `switch` expression followed by the `switch` body, which is a block of statements. The `switch` expression must evaluate to a value of the following types:

- One of the following primitive data types: `char`, `byte`, `short`, or `int`
- One of the following wrapper types: `Character`, `Byte`, `Short`, or `Integer`
- `String` type
- An enumerated type

Note that the type of the `switch` expression cannot be `boolean`, `long`, or floating-point. The statements in the `switch` body can be labeled, thereby defining entry points in the `switch` body where control can be transferred depending on the value of the `switch` expression. The execution of the `switch` statement is as follows:

- The `switch` expression is evaluated first. If the value is a wrapper type, an unboxing conversion is performed.
- The value of the `switch` expression is compared with the `case` labels. Control is transferred to the *statement* associated with the `case` label that is equal to the value of the `switch` expression. After execution of the associated statement, control *falls through* to the *next* statement unless this was the last statement declared or control was transferred out of the `switch` statement.
- If no `case` label is equal to the value of the `switch` expression, the statement associated with the `default` label is executed. After execution of the associated statement, control *falls through* to the *next* statement unless this was the last statement declared or control was transferred out of the `switch` statement.

Figure 6.2 illustrates the flow of control through a `switch` statement where the `default` label is declared last.

Figure 6.2 *Activity Diagram for a `switch` Statement*

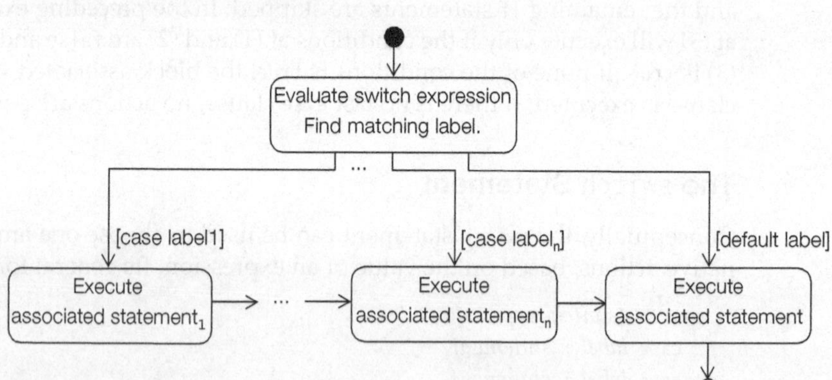

All labels (including the `default` label) are optional, and can be defined in any order in the `switch` body. At most one `default` label can be present in a `switch` statement. If no valid `case` labels are found and the `default` label is omitted, the whole `switch` statement is skipped.

The case labels are constant expressions whose values must be unique, meaning no duplicate values are allowed. In fact, a case label must be a compile-time constant expression whose value is *assignable* to the type of the switch expression (§5.2, p. 147). In particular, all case label values must be in the range of the type of the switch expression. The type of the case label cannot be boolean, long, or floating-point.

The compiler is able to generate efficient code for a switch statement, as this statement only tests for *equality* between the switch expression and the constant value of the case labels, so as to determine which code to execute at runtime. In contrast, a sequence of if statements determines the flow of control at runtime, based on arbitrary conditions whose value might be possible to determine only at runtime.

In Example 6.1, depending on the value of the howMuchAdvice parameter, different advice is printed in the switch statement at (1) in the method dispenseAdvice(). The example shows the output when the value of the howMuchAdvice parameter is LOTS_OF_ADVICE. In the switch statement, the associated statement at (2) is executed, giving one piece of advice. Control then falls through to the statement at (3), giving the second advice. Control next falls through to (4), dispensing the third piece of advice, and finally execution of the break statement at (5) causes control to exit the switch statement. Without the break statement at (5), control would continue to fall through the remaining statements—in this case, to the statement at (6) being executed. Execution of the break statement in a switch body transfers control out of the switch statement (§6.4, p. 221). If the parameter howMuchAdvice has the value MORE_ADVICE, then the advice at both (3) and (4) is given. The value LITTLE_ADVICE results in only one piece of advice at (4) being given. Any other value results in the default action, which announces that there is no advice.

The associated statement of a case label can be a *list* of statements (which need *not* be a statement block). The case label is prefixed to the first statement in each case. This is illustrated by the associated statement for the case label LITTLE_ADVICE in Example 6.1, which comprises statements (4) and (5).

Example 6.1 *Fall-Through in a* switch *Statement*

```
public class Advice {

  private static final int LITTLE_ADVICE = 0;
  private static final int MORE_ADVICE = 1;
  private static final int LOTS_OF_ADVICE = 2;

  public static void main(String[] args) {
    dispenseAdvice(LOTS_OF_ADVICE);
  }

  public static void dispenseAdvice(int howMuchAdvice) {
    switch (howMuchAdvice) {                    // (1)
      case LOTS_OF_ADVICE:
        System.out.println("See no evil.");    // (2)
      case MORE_ADVICE:
        System.out.println("Speak no evil."); // (3)
```

```
         case LITTLE_ADVICE:
           System.out.println("Hear no evil.");  // (4)
           break;                                // (5)
         default:
           System.out.println("No advice.");     // (6)
       }
     }
   }
```

Output from the program:

```
See no evil.
Speak no evil.
Hear no evil.
```

Example 6.2 makes use of a break statement inside a switch statement to convert a char value representing a digit to the corresponding word in English. Note that the break statement is the last statement in the list of statements associated with each case label. It is easy to think that the break statement is a part of the switch statement syntax, but technically it is not.

Example 6.2 *Using* break *in a* switch *Statement*

```
public class Digits {

  public static void main(String[] args) {
    System.out.println(digitToString('7') + " " + digitToString('8') + " " +
                       digitToString('6'));
    System.out.println(digitToString('2') + " " + digitToString('a') + " " +
        digitToString('5'));
  }

  public static String digitToString(char digit) {
    String str = "";
    switch(digit) {
      case '1': str = "one";   break;
      case '2': str = "two";   break;
      case '3': str = "three"; break;
      case '4': str = "four";  break;
      case '5': str = "five";  break;
      case '6': str = "six";   break;
      case '7': str = "seven"; break;
      case '8': str = "eight"; break;
      case '9': str = "nine";  break;
      case '0': str = "zero";  break;
      default:  System.out.println(digit + " is not a digit!");
    }
    return str;
  }
}
```

Output from the program:

```
seven eight six
a is not a digit!
two  five
```

Several case labels can prefix the same statement. They will all result in the associated statement being executed. This behavior is illustrated in Example 6.3 for the switch statement at (1).

The first statement in the switch body must have a case or default label, or otherwise it will be unreachable. This statement will never be executed, because control can never be transferred to it. The compiler will flag this as an error. An empty switch block is perfectly legal, but not of much use.

Since each action associated with a case label can be an arbitrary statement, it can be another switch statement. In other words, switch statements can be nested. Since a switch statement defines its own local block, the case labels in an inner block do not conflict with any case labels in an outer block. Labels can be redefined in nested blocks; in contrast, variables cannot be redeclared in nested blocks (§4.4, p. 117). In Example 6.3, an inner switch statement is defined at (2), which allows further refinement of the action to take on the value of the switch expression in cases where multiple labels are used in the outer switch statement. A break statement terminates the innermost switch statement in which it is executed.

Example 6.3 *Nested* switch *Statement*

```
public class Seasons {

  public static void main(String[] args) {
    int monthNumber = 11;
    switch(monthNumber) {                                     // (1) Outer
      case 12: case 1: case 2:
        System.out.println("Snow in the winter.");
        break;
      case 3: case 4: case 5:
        System.out.println("Green grass in the spring.");
        break;
      case 6: case 7: case 8:
        System.out.println("Sunshine in the summer.");
        break;
      case 9: case 10: case 11:                               // (2)
        switch(monthNumber) { // Nested switch                   (3) Inner
          case 10:
            System.out.println("Halloween.");
            break;
          case 11:
            System.out.println("Thanksgiving.");
            break;
        } // End nested switch
```

```
        // Always printed for case labels 9, 10, 11
        System.out.println("Yellow leaves in the fall.");     // (4)
        break;
      default:
        System.out.println(monthNumber + " is not a valid month.");
    }
  }
}
```

Output from the program:

```
Thanksgiving.
Yellow leaves in the fall.
```

Example 6.4 illustrates using strings in a `switch` statement. The thing to note is what constitutes a constant string expression that can be used as a case label. The case labels in (3), (4), (5), and (6) are all valid *constant string expressions*, as the compiler can figure out their values at compile time. String literals, used in (3) and (6), and constant field values, declared in (1) and (2a), and used in (4) and (5), are all valid case labels. In contrast, the `HOT` reference from declarations (2b) and (2c) cannot be used as a case label. From the declaration in (2a), the compiler cannot guarantee that the value of the reference will not change at runtime. From the declaration in (2c), it cannot deduce the value at compile time, as the constructor must be run to construct the value.

Switching on strings is essentially based on equality comparison of integer values that are hash values of strings, followed by an object equality test to rule out the possibility of collision between two different strings having the same hash value. Switching on strings should be used judiciously, as it is less efficient than switching on integers. Switching on strings is not advisable if the values being switched on are not already strings.

Example 6.4 *Strings in* `switch` *Statement*

```
public class SwitchingOnAString {
  public static final String MEDIUM = "Medium";        // (1)
  public static final String HOT = "Hot";              // (2a)
//public static       String HOT = "Hot";              // (2b) Not OK as case lablel
//public static final String HOT = new String("Hot");// (2c) Not OK as case lablel

  public static void main(String[] args) {
    String spiceLevel = "Medium_Hot";
    switch (spiceLevel) {
      case "Mild":                                     // (3)
      case MEDIUM + "_" + HOT:                         // (4)
        System.out.println("Enjoy your meal!");
        break;
      case HOT:                                        // (5)
        System.out.println("Have fun!");
        break;
```

```
        case "Suicide":                              // (6)
          System.out.println("Good luck!");
          break;
        default:
          System.out.println("You being funny?");
      }
    }
  }
```

Output from the program:

```
Enjoy your meal!
```

Example 6.5 illustrates the use of enum types in a switch statement. The enum type SpiceGrade is defined at (1). The type of the switch expression is SpiceGrade. Note that the enum constants are *not* specified with their fully qualified name (see (2a)). Using the fully qualified name results in a compile-time error, as shown at (2b). Only enum constants that have the same enum type as the switch expression can be specified as case label values.

The semantics of the switch statement are the same as described earlier. However, if a switch expression evaluates to the null reference, a NullPointerException will be thrown. Switching on enumerated values is essentially based on equality comparison of unique integer values that are ordinal values assigned by the compiler to the constants of an enum type.

Example 6.5 *Enums in* switch *Statement*

```
enum SpiceGrade {                                    // (1)
    MILD, MEDIUM_HOT, HOT, SUICIDE;
}

public class SwitchingFun {

  public static void main(String[] args) {
    SpiceGrade spicing = SpiceGrade.HOT;
    switch (spicing) {
      case HOT:                                      // (2a) OK!
//    case SpiceGrade.HOT:                           // (2b) Compile-time error!
        System.out.println("Have fun!");
        break;
      case SUICIDE:
        System.out.println("Good luck!");
        break;
      default:                                       // Can only be MILD or MEDIUM_HOT.
        System.out.println("Enjoy you meal!");
    }
  }
}
```

Output from the program:

```
Have fun!
```

Review Questions

6.1 What will be the result of attempting to compile and run the following class?

```
public class IfTest {
  public static void main(String[] args) {
    if (true)
    if (false)
    System.out.println("a");
    else
    System.out.println("b");
  }
}
```

Select the one correct answer.

(a) The code will fail to compile because the syntax of the `if` statement is incorrect.
(b) The code will fail to compile because the compiler will not be able to determine which `if` statement the `else` clause belongs to.
(c) The code will compile correctly, and display the letter `a` at runtime.
(d) The code will compile correctly, and display the letter `b` at runtime.
(e) The code will compile correctly, but will not display any output.

6.2 Which of the following statements are true?

Select the three correct answers.

(a) The condition in an `if` statement can have method calls.
(b) If `a` and `b` are of type `boolean` or `Boolean`, the expression `(a = b)` can be the condition of an `if` statement.
(c) An `if` statement can have either an `if` clause or an `else` clause.
(d) The statement `if (false) ; else ;` is illegal.
(e) Only expressions that evaluate or can be unboxed to a `boolean` value can be used as the condition in an `if` statement.

6.3 What, if anything, is wrong with the following code?

```
void test(int x) {
  switch (x) {
    case 1:
    case 2:
    case 0:
    default:
    case 4:
  }
}
```

Select the one correct answer.

(a) The variable `x` does not have the right type for a `switch` expression.
(b) The `case` label `0` must precede the case label `1`.

(c) Each case section must end with a break statement.
(d) The default label must be the last label in the switch statement.
(e) The body of the switch statement must contain at least one statement.
(f) There is nothing wrong with the code.

6.4 What will be the result of attempting to compile and run the following program?

```
public class Switching {
  public static void main(String[] args) {
    final int iLoc = 3;
    switch (6) {
      case 1:
      case iLoc:
      case 2 * iLoc:
        System.out.println("I am not OK.");
      default:
        System.out.println("You are OK.");
      case 4:
        System.out.println("It's OK.");
    }
  }
}
```

Select the one correct answer.

(a) The code will fail to compile because of the case label value 2 * iLoc.
(b) The code will fail to compile because the default label is not specified last in the switch statement.
(c) The code will compile correctly and will print the following at runtime:
```
I am not OK.
You are OK.
It's OK.
```
(d) The code will compile correctly and will print the following at runtime:
```
You are OK.
It's OK.
```
(e) The code will compile correctly and will print the following at runtime:
```
It's OK.
```

6.5 What will be the result of attempting to compile and run the following program?

```
public class MoreSwitching {
  public static void main(String[] args) {
    final int iLoc = 3;
    Integer iRef = 5;
    switch (iRef) {
      default:
        System.out.println("You are OK.");
      case 1:
      case iLoc:
      case 2 * iLoc:
        System.out.println("I am not OK.");
        break;
```

```
      case 4:
        System.out.println("It's OK.");
      }
    }
  }
```

Select the one correct answer.

(a) The code will fail to compile because the type of the `switch` expression is not valid.

(b) The code will compile correctly and will print the following at runtime:
```
You are OK.
I am not OK.
```

(c) The code will compile correctly and will print the following at runtime:
```
You are OK.
I am not OK.
It's OK.
```

(d) The code will compile correctly and will print the following at runtime:
```
It's OK.
```

6.6 Which case label declaration can be inserted at (1) so that the following program will compile, run, and print `Hi, TomTom!`?

```
public class Switcheroo {
  public static void main(String[] args) {
    final String TOM1 = "Tom";
          String TOM2 = "Tom";
    final String TOM3 = new String("Tom");
    switch ("TomTom") {
      default:
        System.out.println("Whatever!");
        break;
//      (1) INSERT case LABEL DECLARATION HERE.
        System.out.println("Hi, TomTom!");
    }
  }
}
```

Select the four correct answers.

(a) `case "TomTom":`
(b) `case TOM1 + TOM1:`
(c) `case TOM1 + TOM2:`
(d) `case TOM1 + TOM3:`
(e) `case TOM2 + TOM3:`
(f) `case "Tom" + TOM1:`
(g) `case "Tom" + TOM2:`
(h) `case "Tom" + TOM3:`
(i) `case 'T' + 'o' + 'm' + TOM1:`
(j) `case "T" + 'o' + 'm' + TOM1:`

6.3 Iteration Statements

Loops allow a block of statements to be executed repeatedly (that is, iterated). A boolean condition (called the *loop condition*) is commonly used to determine when to terminate the loop. The statements executed in the loop constitute the *loop body*. The loop body can be a single statement or a block.

Java provides three language constructs for loop construction:

- The `while` statement
- The `do-while` statement
- The basic `for` statement

These loops differ in the order in which they execute the loop body and test the loop condition. The `while` loop and the basic `for` loop test the loop condition *before* executing the loop body, whereas the `do-while` loop tests the loop condition *after* execution of the loop body.

In addition to the basic `for` loop, a specialized loop called the *enhanced* `for` loop (also called the *for-each* loop) simplifies iterating over arrays and collections. We will use the notations `for(;;)` and `for(:)` to designate the basic `for` loop and the enhanced `for` loop, respectively.

The `while` Statement

The syntax of the `while` loop is

```
while (loop_condition)
  loop_body
```

The *loop condition* is evaluated before executing the *loop body*. The `while` statement executes the *loop body* as long as the *loop condition* is `true`. When the *loop condition* becomes `false`, the loop is terminated and execution continues with the statement immediately following the loop. If the *loop condition* is `false` to begin with, the *loop body* is not executed at all. In other words, a `while` loop can execute zero or more times. The *loop condition* must evaluate to a `boolean` or a `Boolean` value. In the latter case, the reference value is unboxed to a `boolean` value. The flow of control in a `while` statement is shown in Figure 6.3.

Figure 6.3 *Activity Diagram for the* `while` *Statement*

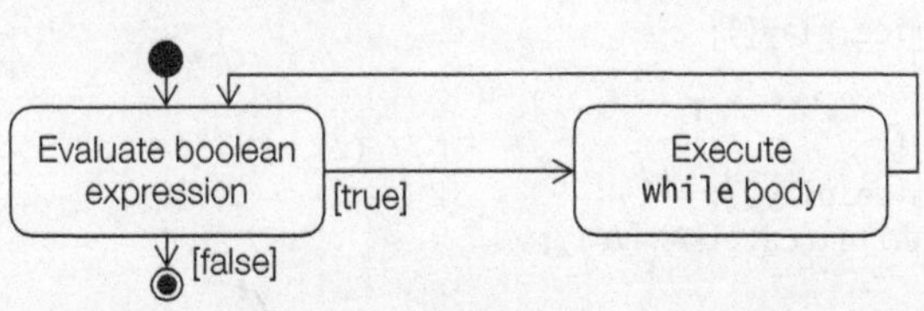

The `while` statement is normally used when the number of iterations is not known.

```
while (noSignOfLife())
  keepLooking();
```

Since the *loop body* can be any valid statement, inadvertently terminating each line with the empty statement (;) can give unintended results. Always using a block statement as the *loop body* helps to avoid such problems.

```
while (noSignOfLife());         // Empty statement as loop body!
  keepLooking();                // Statement not in the loop body.
```

The `do-while` Statement

The syntax of the `do-while` loop is

```
do
   loop_body
while (loop_condition);
```

In a `do-while` statement, the *loop condition* is evaluated *after* executing the *loop body*. The *loop condition* must evaluate to a `boolean` or `Boolean` value. The value of the *loop condition* is subjected to unboxing if it is of the type `Boolean`. The `do-while` statement executes the *loop body* until the *loop condition* becomes `false`. When the *loop condition* becomes `false`, the loop is terminated and execution continues with the statement immediately following the loop. Note that the *loop body* is executed at least once. Figure 6.4 illustrates the flow of control in a `do-while` statement.

Figure 6.4 *Activity Diagram for the* `do-while` *Statement*

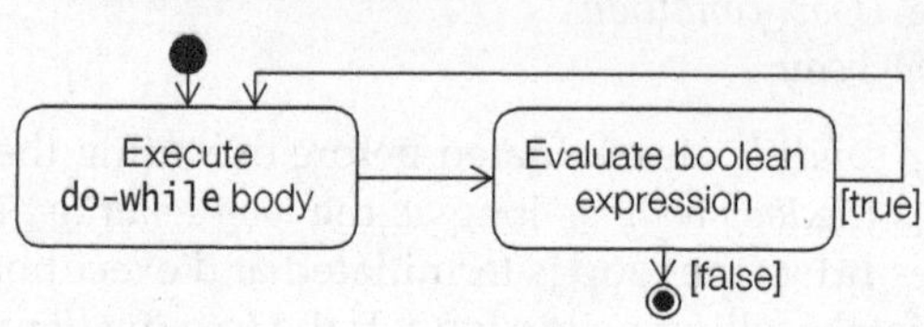

The *loop body* in a `do-while` loop is invariably a statement block. It is instructive to compare the `while` and `do-while` loops. In the examples that follow, the mice might never get to play if the cat is not away, as in the loop at (1). The mice do get to play at least once (at the peril of losing their life) in the loop at (2).

```
while (cat.isAway()) {          // (1)
  mice.play();
}

do {                            // (2)
  mice.play();
} while (cat.isAway());
```

The for(;;) Statement

The `for(;;)` loop is the most general of all the loops. It is mostly used for counter-controlled loops, in which the number of iterations is known beforehand.

The syntax of the loop is as follows:

```
for (initialization; loop_condition; update_expression)
    loop_body
```

The *initialization* usually declares and initializes a loop variable that controls the execution of the *loop body*. The *loop condition* must evaluate to a `boolean` or `Boolean` value. In the latter case, the reference value is converted to a `boolean` value by unboxing. The *loop condition* usually involves the loop variable, and if the loop condition is `true`, the loop body is executed; otherwise, execution continues with the statement following the `for(;;)` loop. After each iteration (that is, execution of the loop body), the *update expression* is executed. This usually modifies the value of the loop variable to ensure eventual loop termination. The *loop condition* is then tested to determine whether the loop body should be executed again. Note that the *initialization* is executed only once, on entry into the loop. The semantics of the `for(;;)` loop are illustrated in Figure 6.5, and are summarized by the following equivalent `while` loop code template:

```
initialization
while (loop_condition) {
  loop_body
  update_expression
}
```

Figure 6.5 *Activity Diagram for the* `for` *Statement*

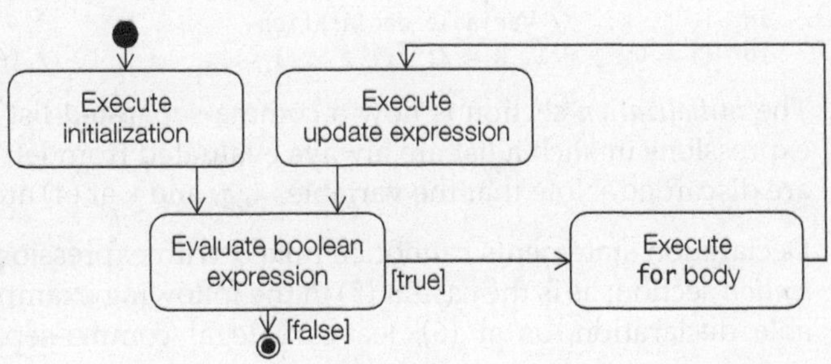

The following code creates an `int` array and sums the values in the array:

```
int sum = 0;
int[] array = {12, 23, 5, 7, 19};
for (int index = 0; index < array.length; index++)   // (1)
  sum += array[index];
```

The loop variable `index` is declared and initialized in the *initialization* section of the loop. It is incremented in the *update expression* section. This loop is an example of a *forward* `for(;;)` loop, where the loop variable is incremented.

The next code snippet is an example of a *backward* `for(;;)` loop, where the loop variable is decremented to sum the values in the array:

```
int sum = 0;
int[] array = {12, 23, 5, 7, 19};
for (int index = array.length - 1; index >= 0; index--)
  sum += array[index];
```

It is instructive to compare the specification of the loop header in the forward and backward `for(;;)` loops in these examples.

The `for(;;)` loop defines a local block so that the *scope* of this declaration is the `for(;;)` block, which comprises the *initialization*, the *loop condition*, the *loop body*, and the *update expression* sections. Any variable declared in the `for(;;)` block, therefore, is not accessible after the `for(;;)` loop terminates. The loop at (1) earlier showed how a declaration statement can be specified in the *initialization* section. Such a declaration statement can also specify a comma-separated list of variables:

```
for (int i = 0, j = 1, k = 2; ... ; ...) ...;      // (2)
```

The variables `i`, `j`, and `k` in the declaration statement all have type `int`. All variables declared in the *initialization* section are local variables in the `for(;;)` block and obey the scope rules for local blocks. The following code will not compile, however, as variable declarations of different types (in this case, `int` and `String`) require declaration statements that are terminated by semicolons:

```
for (int i = 0, String str = "@"; ... ; ...) ...;  // (3) Compile-time error
```

The *initialization* section can also be a comma-separated list of *expression* statements (§3.2, p. 50). Any value returned by an expression statement is discarded. For example, the loop at (2) can be rewritten by factoring out the variable declaration:

```
int i, j, k;  // Variable declaration
for (i = 0, j = 1, k = 2; ... ; ...) ...;          // (4) Only initialization
```

The *initialization* section is now a comma-separated list of three expressions. The expressions in such a list are always evaluated from left to right, and their values are discarded. Note that the variables `i`, `j`, and `k` at (4) are not local to the loop.

Declaration statements cannot be mixed with expression statements in the *initialization* section, as is the case at (5) in the following example. Factoring out the variable declaration, as at (6), leaves a legal comma-separated list of expression statements.

```
// (5) Not legal and ugly:
for (int i = 0, System.out.println("This won't do!"); flag; i++) { // Error!
  // loop body
}

// (6) Legal, but still ugly:
int i;                                              // Declaration factored out.
for (i = 0, System.out.println("This is legal!"); flag; i++) {      // OK.
  // loop body
}
```

The *update expression* can also be a comma-separated list of expression statements. The following code specifies a `for(;;)` loop that has a comma-separated list of three variables in the *initialization* section, and a comma-separated list of two expressions in the *update expression* section:

```
// Legal usage but not recommended.
int[][] sqMatrix = { {3, 4, 6}, {5, 7, 4}, {5, 8, 9} };
for (int i = 0, j = sqMatrix[0].length - 1, asymDiagonal = 0;  // initialization
     i < sqMatrix.length;                                       // loop condition
     i++, j--)                                                 // update expression
  asymDiagonal += sqMatrix[i][j];                              // loop body
```

All sections in the `for(;;)` header are optional. Any or all of them can be left empty, but the two semicolons are mandatory. In particular, leaving out the *loop condition* signifies that the loop condition is `true`. The "crab", `(;;)`, can be used to construct an infinite loop, where termination is presumably achieved through code in the loop body (see the next section on transfer statements):

```
for (;;) doProgramming();          // Infinite loop
```

The `for(:)` Statement

The enhanced `for` loop is convenient when we need to iterate over an array or a collection, especially when some operation needs to be performed on each element of the array or collection. In this section we discuss iterating over arrays; in §10.1, p. 423, we take a look at the `for(:)` loop for iterating over `ArrayList`s.

Earlier in this chapter we used a `for(;;)` loop to sum the values of elements in an `int` array:

```
int sum = 0;
int[] intArray = {12, 23, 5, 7, 19};
for (int index = 0; index < intArray.length; index++) { // (1) using for(;;) loop
  sum += intArray[index];
}
```

The `for(;;)` loop at (1) is rewritten using the `for(:)` loop in Figure 6.6.

Figure 6.6 *Enhanced* `for` *Statement*

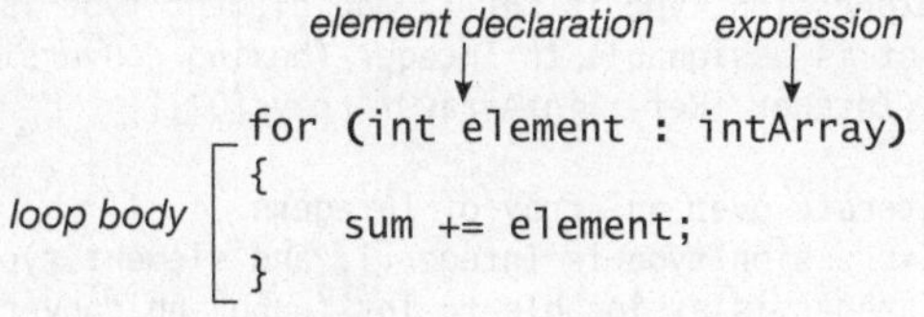

The body of the loop is executed for each element in the array, where the variable `element` successively denotes the current element in the array `intArray`. When the loop terminates, the variable `sum` will contain the sum of all elements in the array. We do not care about the *position* of the elements in the array, just that the loop iterates over *all* elements of the array.

From Figure 6.6 we see that the `for(:)` loop header has two parts. The *expression* must evaluate to a reference value that refers to an array—that is, the array we want to iterate over. The array can be an array of primitive values or objects, or even an array of arrays. The *expression* is evaluated only once. The *element declaration* specifies a local variable that can be assigned a value of the element type of the array. The type of the array `intArray` in Figure 6.6 is `int[]`, and the element type is `int`. The element variable of type `int` can be assigned `int` values from the array of `int`. However, this assignment might require either a boxing or an unboxing conversion, with optional widening conversion.

The element variable is local to the loop block and is not accessible after the loop terminates. Also, changing the value of the current variable does *not* change any value in the array. The *loop body*, which can be a simple statement or a statement block, is executed for each element in the array and there is no danger of any out-of-bounds errors.

The `for(:)` loop has its limitations. Specifically, we cannot change element values, and this kind of loop does not provide any provision for positional access using an index. The `for(:)` loop only increments by one and always in a forward direction. It does not allow iterations over several arrays simultaneously. Under such circumstances, the `for(;;)` loop can be more convenient.

Here are some code examples of legal `for(:)` loops:

```
// Some 1-dim arrays:
int[]     intArray =    {10, 20, 30};
Integer[] intObjArray = {10, 20, 30};
String[]  strArray =    {"one", "two"};

// Some 2-dim arrays:
Object[][] objArrayOfArrays = {intObjArray, strArray};
Number[][] numArrayOfArrays = {{1.5, 2.5}, intObjArray, {100L, 200L}};
int[][]    intArrayOfArrays = {{20}, intArray, {40}};

// Iterate over an array of Strings.
// Expression type is String[], and element type is String.
// String is assignable to Object (widening conversion).
for (Object obj : strArray) {}

// Iterate over an array of ints.
// Expression type is int[], and element type is int.
// int is assignable to Integer (boxing conversion)
for (Integer iRef : intArrayOfArrays[0]){}

// Iterate over an array of Integers.
// Expression type is Integer[], and element type is Integer.
// Integer is assignable to int (unboxing conversion)
for (int i : intObjArray){}

// Iterate over a 2-dim array of ints.
// Outer loop: expression type is int[][], and element type is int[].
// Inner loop: expression type is int[], and element type is int.
for (int[] row : intArrayOfArrays)
  for (int val : row) {}
```

```
// Iterate over a 2-dim array of Numbers.
// Outer loop: expression type is Number[][], and element type is Number[].
// Outer loop: Number[] is assignable to Object[] (widening conversion).
// Inner loop: expression type is Object[], and element type is Object.
for (Object[] row : numArrayOfArrays)
  for (Object obj : row) {}

// Outer loop: expression type is Integer[][], and element type is Integer[].
// Outer loop: Integer[] is assignable to Number[].
// Inner loop: expression type is int[], and element type is int.
// Inner loop: int is assignable to double.
for (Number[] row : new Integer[][] {intObjArray, intObjArray, intObjArray})
  for (double num : new int[] {}) {}
```

Here are some code examples of for(:) loops that are not legal:

```
// Expression type is Number[][], and element type is Number[].
// Number[] is not assignable to Number.
for (Number num : numArrayOfArrays) {}        // Compile-time error.

// Expression type is Number[], and element type is Number.
// Number is not assignable to int.
for (int row : numArrayOfArrays[0]) {}        // Compile-time error.

// Outer loop: expression type is int[][], and element type is int[].
// int[] is not assignable to Integer[].
for (Integer[] row : intArrayOfArrays)        // Compile-time error.
  for (int val : row) {}

// Expression type is Object[][], and element type is Object[].
// Object[] is not assignable to Integer[].
for (Integer[] row : objArrayOfArrays) {}     // Compile-time error.

// Outer loop: expression type is String[], and element type is String.
// Inner loop: expression type is String, which is not legal here. Not an array.
for (String str : strArray)
  for (char val : str) {}                     // Compile-time error.
```

When using the for(:) loop to iterate over an array, the two main causes of errors are an expression in the loop header that does not represent an array and/or an element type of the array that is not assignable to the local variable declared in the loop header.

6.4 Transfer Statements

Java provides six language constructs for transferring control in a program:

- break
- continue
- return

- `try-catch-finally`
- `throw`
- `assert`

This section discusses the first three statements. Except for the `assert` statement (not on the OCAJP8 exam), the remaining statements are discussed in subsequent sections.

Note that Java does not have a `goto` statement, although `goto` is a reserved word.

Labeled Statements

A statement may have a *label*:

label : *statement*

A label is any valid identifier; it always immediately precedes the statement. Label names exist in their own namespace, so that they do not conflict with names of packages, classes, interfaces, methods, fields, and local variables. The scope of a label is the statement prefixed by the label, meaning that it cannot be redeclared as a label inside the labeled statement—analogous to the scope of local variables.

```
L1: if (i > 0) {
  L1: System.out.println(i);    // (1) Not OK. Label redeclared.
}

L1: while (i < 0) {             // (2) OK.
  L2: System.out.println(i);
}

L1: {                           // (3) OK. Labeled block.
  int j = 10;
  System.out.println(j);
}

L1: try {                       // (4) OK. Labeled try-catch-finally block.
  int j = 10, k = 0;
  L2: System.out.println(j/k);
} catch (ArithmeticException ae) {
  L3: ae.printStackTrace();
} finally {
  L4: System.out.println("Finally done.");
}
```

A statement can have multiple labels:

```
LabelA: LabelB: System.out.println("Mutliple labels. Use judiciously.");
```

A declaration statement cannot have a label:

```
L0: int i = 0;                  // Compile-time error!
```

A labeled statement is executed as if it was unlabeled, unless it is the `break` or `continue` statement. This behavior is discussed in the next two subsections.

The break Statement

The `break` statement comes in two forms: *unlabeled* and *labeled*.

```
break;              // the unlabeled form
break label;        // the labeled form
```

The unlabeled `break` statement terminates loops (`for(;;)`, `for(:)`, `while`, `do-while`) and `switch` statements, and transfers control out of the current context (i.e., the closest enclosing block). The rest of the statement body is skipped, and execution continues after the enclosing statement.

In Example 6.6, the `break` statement at (1) is used to terminate a `for(;;)` loop. Control is transferred to (2) when the value of `i` is equal to `4` at (1), skipping the rest of the loop body and terminating the loop.

Example 6.6 also shows that the unlabeled `break` statement terminates only the innermost loop or `switch` statement that contains the `break` statement. The `break` statement at (3) terminates the inner `for(;;)` loop when `j` is equal to `2`, and execution continues in the outer `switch` statement at (4) after the `for(;;)` loop.

Example 6.6 *The* `break` *Statement*

```
class BreakOut {

  public static void main(String[] args) {
    System.out.println("i     sqrt(i)");
    for (int i = 1; i <= 5; ++i) {
      if (i == 4)
        break;                              // (1) Terminate loop. Control to (2).
      // Rest of loop body skipped when i gets the value 4.
      System.out.printf("%d    %.2f%n", i, Math.sqrt(i));
    } // end for
    // (2) Continue here.
    int n = 2;
    switch (n) {
      case 1:
        System.out.println(n);
        break;
      case 2:
        System.out.println("Inner for(;;) loop: ");
        for (int j = 0; j <= n; j++) {
          if (j == 2)
            break;                          // (3) Terminate loop. Control to (4).
          System.out.println("j = " + j);
        }
      default:
        System.out.println("default: n = " + n); // (4) Continue here.
    }
  }
}
```

Output from the program:

```
i    sqrt(i)
1    1.00
2    1.41
3    1.73
Inner for(;;) loop:
j = 0
j = 1
default: n = 2
```

A labeled break statement can be used to terminate *any* labeled statement that contains the break statement. Control is then transferred to the statement following the enclosing labeled statement. In the case of a labeled block, the rest of the block is skipped and execution continues with the statement following the block:

```
out:                          // Label.
{                             // (1) Labeled block.
  // ...
  if (j == 10) break out;     // (2) Terminate block. Control to (3).
  System.out.println(j);      // Rest of the block not executed if j == 10.
  // ...
}
// (3) Continue here.
```

In Example 6.7, the program continues to add the elements below the diagonal of a square matrix until the sum is greater than 10. Two nested for loops are defined at (1) and (2). The outer loop is labeled outer at (1). The unlabeled break statement at (3) transfers control to (5) when it is executed; that is, it terminates the inner loop and control is transferred to the statement after the inner loop. The labeled break statement at (4) transfers control to (6) when it is executed; that is, it terminates both the inner and the outer loop, transferring control to the statement after the loop labeled outer.

Example 6.7 *Labeled* break *Statement*

```
class LabeledBreakOut {
  public static void main(String[] args) {
    int[][] squareMatrix = {{4, 3, 5}, {2, 1, 6}, {9, 7, 8}};
    int sum = 0;
    outer: for (int i = 0; i < squareMatrix.length; ++i){   // (1) label
        for (int j = 0; j < squareMatrix[i].length; ++j) {  // (2)
          if (j == i) break;          // (3) Terminate inner loop. Control to (5).
          System.out.println("Element[" + i + ", " + j + "]: " +
                              squareMatrix[i][j]);
          sum += squareMatrix[i][j];
          if (sum > 10) break outer; // (4) Terminate both loops. Control to (6).
        } // end inner loop
        // (5) Continue with update expression in the outer loop header.
      } // end outer loop
    // (6) Continue here.
    System.out.println("sum: " + sum);
  }
}
```

Output from the program:

```
Element[1, 0]: 2
Element[2, 0]: 9
sum: 11
```

The `continue` Statement

Like the `break` statement, the `continue` statement comes in two forms: *unlabeled* and *labeled*.

```
continue;              // the unlabeled form
continue label;        // the labeled form
```

The `continue` statement can be used only in a `for(;;)`, `for(:)`, `while`, or `do-while` loop to prematurely stop the current iteration of the loop body and proceed with the next iteration, if possible. In the case of the `while` and `do-while` loops, the rest of the loop body is skipped—that is, the current iteration is stopped, with execution continuing with the *loop condition*. In the case of the `for(;;)` loop, the rest of the loop body is skipped, with execution continuing with the *update expression*.

In Example 6.8, an unlabeled `continue` statement is used to skip an iteration in a `for(;;)` loop. Control is transferred to (2) when the value of `i` is equal to `4` at (1), skipping the rest of the loop body and continuing with the *update expression* in the `for(;;)` statement.

Example 6.8 `continue` *Statement*

```
class Skip {
  public static void main(String[] args) {
    System.out.println("i     sqrt(i)");
    for (int i = 1; i <= 5; ++i) {
      if (i == 4) continue;              // (1) Control to (2).
      // Rest of loop body skipped when i has the value 4.
      System.out.printf("%d    %.2f%n", i, Math.sqrt(i));
      // (2) Continue with update expression in the loop header.
    } // end for
  }
}
```

Output from the program:

```
i    sqrt(i)
1    1.00
2    1.41
3    1.73
5    2.24
```

A labeled continue statement must occur within a labeled loop that has the same label. Execution of the labeled continue statement then transfers control to the end of that enclosing labeled loop. In Example 6.9, the unlabeled continue statement at (3) transfers control to (5) when it is executed; that is, the rest of the loop body is skipped and execution continues with the update expression in the inner loop. The labeled continue statement at (4) transfers control to (6) when it is executed; that is, it terminates the inner loop but execution continues with the update expression in the loop labeled outer. It is instructive to compare the output from Example 6.7 (labeled break) and that from Example 6.9 (labeled continue).

Example 6.9 *Labeled* continue *Statement*

```
class LabeledSkip {
  public static void main(String[] args) {
    int[][] squareMatrix = {{4, 3, 5}, {2, 1, 6}, {9, 7, 8}};
    int sum = 0;
    outer: for (int i = 0; i < squareMatrix.length; ++i){   // (1) label
        for (int j = 0; j < squareMatrix[i].length; ++j) {  // (2)
          if (j == i) continue;                             // (3) Control to (5).
          System.out.println("Element[" + i + ", " + j + "]: " +
              squareMatrix[i][j]);
          sum += squareMatrix[i][j];
          if (sum > 10) continue outer;                     // (4) Control to (6).
          // (5) Continue with update expression in the inner loop header.
        } // end inner loop
        // (6) Continue with update expression in the outer loop header.
      } // end outer loop
    System.out.println("sum: " + sum);
  }
}
```

Output from the program:

```
Element[0, 1]: 3
Element[0, 2]: 5
Element[1, 0]: 2
Element[1, 2]: 6
Element[2, 0]: 9
sum: 25
```

The return Statement

The return statement is used to stop execution of a method (or a constructor) and transfer control back to the calling code (also called the *caller* or *invoker*). The usage of the two forms of the return statement is dictated by whether that statement is used in a void or a non-void method (Table 6.1). The first form does not return any value to the calling code, but the second form does. Note that the keyword void does not represent any type.

In Table 6.1, the *expression* must evaluate to a primitive value or a reference value, and its type must be *assignable* to the *return type* specified in the method header

(§5.6, p. 158, and §7.9, p. 312). See also the discussion on covariant return in connection with method overriding in §7.2, p. 268.

As can be seen from Table 6.1, a `void` method need not have a `return` statement—in which case the control typically returns to the caller after the last statement in the method's body has been executed. However, a `void` method can specify only the first form of the `return` statement. This form of the `return` statement can also be used in constructors, as they likewise do not return a value.

Table 6.1 also shows that the first form of the `return` statement is not allowed in a non-`void` method. The second form of the return statement is mandatory in a non-`void` method, if the method execution is not terminated programmatically—for example, by throwing an exception. Example 6.10 illustrates the use of the `return` statement summarized in Table 6.1. A recommended best practice is to document the value returned by a method in a Javadoc comment using the `@return` tag.

Table 6.1 *The `return` Statement*

Form of `return` statement	In `void` method/ constructor	In non-`void` method
`return;`	Optional	Not allowed
`return` *expression*;	Not allowed	Mandatory, if the method is not terminated explicitly

Example 6.10 *The `return` Statement*

```
public class ReturnDemo {

  public static void main (String[] args) { // (1) void method can use return.
    if (args.length == 0) return;
    output(checkValue(args.length));
  }

  static void output(int value) {  // (2) void method need not use return.
    System.out.println(value);
    return 'a';                    // Not OK. Cannot return a value.
  }

  static int checkValue(int i) {   // (3) Non-void method: Any return statement
                                   //     must return a value.
    if (i > 3)
      return i;                    // OK.
    else
      return 2.0;                  // Not OK. double not assignable to int.
  }

  static int absentMinded() {      // (4) Non-void method.
    throw new RuntimeException();  // OK: No return statement provided, but
                                   // method terminates by throwing an exception.
  }
}
```

Review Questions

6.7 What will be the result of attempting to compile and run the following code?

```
class MyClass {
  public static void main(String[] args) {
    boolean b = false;
    int i = 1;
    do {
      i++;
      b = ! b;
    } while (b);
    System.out.println(i);
  }
}
```

Select the one correct answer.

(a) The code will fail to compile because `b` is an invalid condition for the `do-while` statement.
(b) The code will fail to compile because the assignment `b = ! b` is not allowed.
(c) The code will compile without error, and will print `1` at runtime.
(d) The code will compile without error, and will print `2` at runtime.
(e) The code will compile without error, and will print `3` at runtime.

6.8 What will be the output when running the following program?

```
public class StillMyClass {
  public static void main(String[] args) {
    int i = 0;
    int j;
    for (j = 0; j < 10; ++j) { i++; }
    System.out.println(i + " " + j);
  }
}
```

Select the two correct answers.

(a) The first number printed will be `9`.
(b) The first number printed will be `10`.
(c) The first number printed will be `11`.
(d) The second number printed will be `9`.
(e) The second number printed will be `10`.
(f) The second number printed will be `11`.

6.9 Which of the following `for` statements is valid?

Select the one correct answer.

(a) `int j = 10; for (int i = 0, j += 90; i < j; i++) { j--; }`
(b) `for (int i = 10; i = 0; i--) {}`

(c) `for (int i = 0, j = 100; i < j; i++, --j) {;}`
(d) `int i, j; for (j = 100; i < j; j--) { i += 2; }`
(e) `int i = 100; for ((i > 0); i--) {}`

6.10 What will be the result of attempting to compile and run the following program?

```
class AnotherClass {
  public static void main(String[] args) {
    int i = 0;
    for (; i < 10; i++) ;          // (1)
    for (i = 0;; i++) break;       // (2)
    for (i = 0; i < 10;) i++;      // (3)
    for (;;) ;                     // (4)
  }
}
```

Select the one correct answer.

(a) The code will fail to compile because of errors in the `for` loop at (1).
(b) The code will fail to compile because of errors in the `for` loop at (2).
(c) The code will fail to compile because of errors in the `for` loop at (3).
(d) The code will fail to compile because of errors in the `for` loop at (4).
(e) The code will compile without error, and the program will run and terminate without any output.
(f) The code will compile without error, but will never terminate when run.

6.11 Which of the following statements are valid when occurring on their own?

Select the three correct answers.

(a) `while () break;`
(b) `do { break; } while (true);`
(c) `if (true) { break; }`
(d) `switch (1) { default: break; }`
(e) `for (;true;) break;`

6.12 Given the following code fragment, which of the following lines will be a part of the output?

```
outer:
for (int i = 0; i < 3; i++) {
  for (int j = 0; j < 2; j++) {
    if (i == j) {
      continue outer;
    }
    System.out.println("i=" + i + ", j=" + j);
  }
}
```

Select the two correct answers.

(a) `i=1, j=0`
(b) `i=0, j=1`
(c) `i=1, j=2`
(d) `i=2, j=1`
(e) `i=2, j=2`
(f) `i=3, j=3`
(g) `i=3, j=2`

6.13 What will be the result of attempting to compile and run the following code?

```
class MyClass {
  public static void main(String[] args) {
    for (int i = 0; i < 10; i++) {
      switch(i) {
        case 0:
          System.out.println(i);
      }
      if (i) {
        System.out.println(i);
      }
    }
  }
}
```

Select the one correct answer.

(a) The code will fail to compile because of an illegal `switch` expression in the `switch` statement.
(b) The code will fail to compile because of an illegal condition in the `if` statement.
(c) The code will compile without error, and will print the numbers 0 through 10 at runtime.
(d) The code will compile without error, and will print the number 0 at runtime.
(e) The code will compile without error, and will print the number 0 twice at runtime.
(f) The code will compile without error, and will print the numbers 1 through 10 at runtime.

6.14 Which declarations, when inserted at (1), will result in the program compiling and printing 90 at runtime?

```
public class RQ400A10 {
  public static void main(String[] args) {
    // (1) INSERT DECLARATION HERE
    int sum = 0;
    for (int i : nums)
      sum += i;
    System.out.println(sum);
  }
}
```

Select the two correct answers.

(a) `Object[] nums = {20, 30, 40};`
(b) `Number[] nums = {20, 30, 40};`
(c) `Integer[] nums = {20, 30, 40};`
(d) `int[] nums = {20, 30, 40};`
(e) None of the above

6.15 Which method declarations, when inserted at (1), will result in the program compiling and printing 90 when run?

```
public class RQ400A30 {
  public static void main(String[] args) {
    doIt();
  }
  // (1) INSERT METHOD DECLARATION HERE.
}
```

Select the two correct answers.

(a)
```
public static void doIt() {
  int[] nums = {20, 30, 40};
  for (int sum = 0, i : nums)
    sum += i;
  System.out.println(sum);
}
```
(b)
```
public static void doIt() {
  for (int sum = 0, i : {20, 30, 40})
    sum += i;
  System.out.println(sum);
}
```
(c)
```
public static void doIt() {
  int sum = 0;
  for (int i : {20, 30, 40})
    sum += i;
  System.out.println(sum);
}
```
(d)
```
public static void doIt() {
  int sum = 0;
  for (int i : new int[] {20, 30, 40})
    sum += i;
  System.out.println(sum);
}
```
(e)
```
public static void doIt() {
  int[] nums = {20, 30, 40};
  int sum = 0;
  for (int i : nums)
    sum += i;
  System.out.println(sum);
}
```

6.5 Stack-Based Execution and Exception Propagation

An exception in Java signals the occurrence of an error situation due to the violation of some semantic constraint of the Java programming language during execution—for example, a requested file cannot be found, an array index is out of bounds, or a network link failed. Explicit checks in the code for such situations can easily result in incomprehensible code. Java provides an exception handling mechanism for systematically dealing with such error situations.

The exception mechanism is built around the *throw-and-catch* paradigm. To *throw* an exception is to signal that an unexpected condition has occurred. To *catch* an exception is to take appropriate action to deal with the exception. An exception is caught by an *exception handler*, and the exception need not be caught in the same context in which it was thrown. The runtime behavior of the program determines which exceptions are thrown and how they are caught. The throw-and-catch principle is embedded in the `try-catch-finally` construct.

Several threads can be executing at the same time in the JVM. Each thread has its own *JVM stack* (also called a *runtime stack*, *call stack*, and *invocation stack* in the literature) that is used to handle execution of methods. Each element on the stack (called an *activation frame* or a *stack frame*) corresponds to a method call. Each new call results in a new activation frame being pushed on the stack, which stores all the pertinent information such as the local variables. The method with the activation frame on the top of the stack is the one currently executing. When this method finishes executing, its activation frame is popped from the top of the stack. Execution then continues in the method corresponding to the activation frame that is now uncovered on the top of the stack. The methods on the stack are said to be *active*, as their execution has not completed. At any given time, the active methods on a JVM stack make up what is called the *stack trace* of a thread's execution.

Example 6.11 is a simple program to illustrate method execution. It calculates the average for a list of integers, given the sum of all the integers and the number of integers. It uses three methods:

- The method `main()` calls the method `printAverage()` with parameters giving the total sum of the integers and the total number of integers, (1).
- The method `printAverage()` in turn calls the method `computeAverage()`, (3).
- The method `computeAverage()` uses integer division to calculate the average and returns the result, (7).

Example 6.11 *Method Execution*

```
public class Average1 {

  public static void main(String[] args) {
    printAverage(100, 20);                                        // (1)
    System.out.println("Exit main().");                           // (2)
  }
```

```
  public static void printAverage(int totalSum, int totalNumber) {
    int average = computeAverage(totalSum, totalNumber);           // (3)
    System.out.println("Average = " +                              // (4)
        totalSum + " / " + totalNumber + " = " + average);
    System.out.println("Exit printAverage().");                    // (5)
  }

  public static int computeAverage(int sum, int number) {
    System.out.println("Computing average.");                      // (6)
    return sum/number;                                             // (7)
  }
}
```

Output of program execution:

```
Computing average.
Average = 100 / 20 = 5
Exit printAverage().
Exit main().
```

Execution of Example 6.11 is illustrated in Figure 6.7. Each method execution is shown as a box with the local variables declared in the method. The height of the box indicates how long a method is active. Before the call to the method `System.out.println()`

Figure 6.7 *Method Execution*

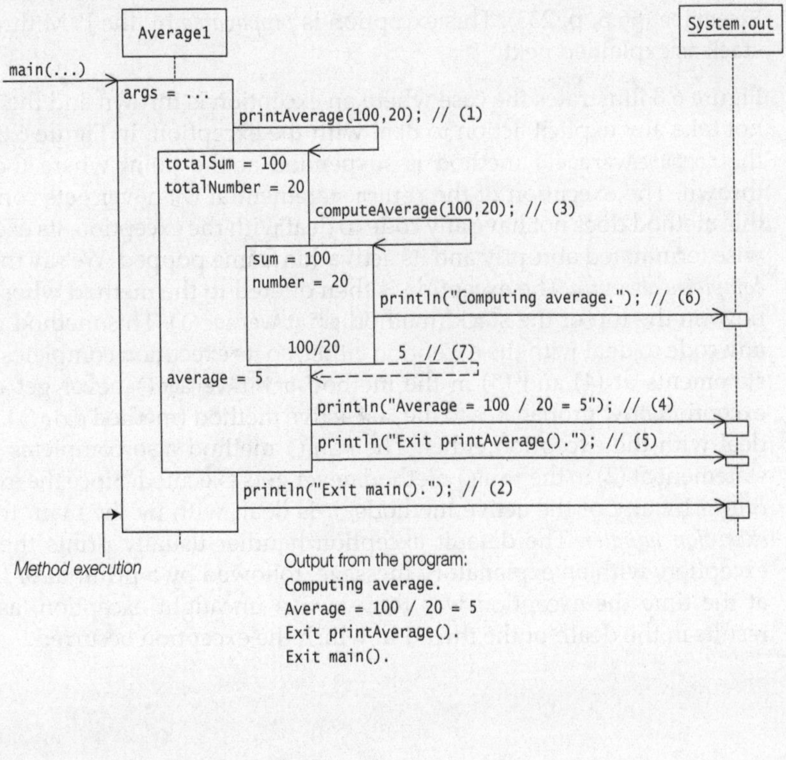

at (6) in Figure 6.7, the stack trace comprises the three active methods: `main()`, `printAverage()`, and `computeAverage()`. The result 5 from the method `computeAverage()` is returned at (7) in Figure 6.7. The output from the program corresponds with the sequence of method calls in Figure 6.7. As the program terminates normally, this program behavior is called *normal execution*.

If the method call at (1) in Example 6.11

```
printAverage(100, 20);                              // (1)
```

is replaced with

```
printAverage(100, 0);                               // (1)
```

and the program is run again, the output is as follows:

```
Computing average.
Exception in thread "main" java.lang.ArithmeticException: / by zero
        at Average1.computeAverage(Average1.java:18)
        at Average1.printAverage(Average1.java:10)
        at Average1.main(Average1.java:5)
```

Figure 6.8 illustrates the program execution when the method `printAverage()` is called with the arguments `100` and `0` at (1). All goes well until the `return` statement at (7) in the method `computeAverage()` is executed. An error condition occurs in calculating the expression `sum/number`, because integer division by 0 is an illegal operation. This error condition is signaled by the JVM by *throwing* an `ArithmeticException` (§6.6, p. 233). This exception is *propagated* by the JVM through the JVM stack as explained next.

Figure 6.8 illustrates the case where an exception is thrown and the program does not take any explicit action to deal with the exception. In Figure 6.8, execution of the `computeAverage()` method is suspended at the point where the exception is thrown. The execution of the `return` statement at (7) never gets completed. Since this method does not have any code to deal with the exception, its execution is likewise terminated abruptly and its activation frame popped. We say that the method *completes abruptly*. The exception is then offered to the method whose activation is now on the top of the stack (method `printAverage()`). This method does not have any code to deal with the exception either, so its execution completes abruptly. The statements at (4) and (5) in the method `printAverage()` never get executed. The exception now propagates to the last active method (method `main()`). This does not deal with the exception either. The `main()` method also completes abruptly. The statement at (2) in the `main()` method never gets executed. Since the exception is not *caught* by any of the active methods, it is dealt with by the main thread's *default exception handler*. The default exception handler usually prints the name of the exception, with an explanatory message, followed by a printout of the stack trace at the time the exception was thrown. An uncaught exception, as in this case, results in the death of the thread in which the exception occurred.

Figure 6.8 *Exception Propagation*

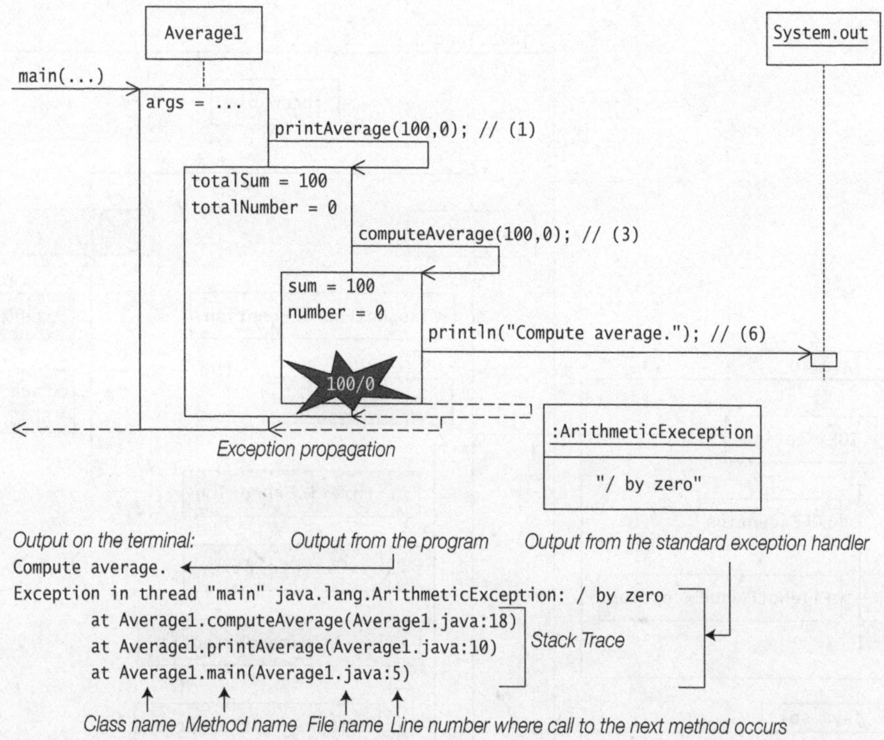

If an exception is thrown during the evaluation of the left-hand operand of a binary expression, then the right-hand operand is not evaluated. Similarly, if an exception is thrown during the evaluation of a list of expressions (e.g., a list of actual parameters in a method call), evaluation of the rest of the list is skipped.

If the line numbers in the stack trace are not printed in the output as shown previously, use the following command to run the program:

```
>java -Djava.compiler=NONE Average1
```

6.6 Exception Types

Exceptions in Java are objects. All exceptions are derived from the `java.lang.Throwable` class. Figure 6.9 shows a partial hierarchy of classes derived from the `Throwable` class. The two main subclasses `Exception` and `Error` constitute the main categories of *throwables*, the term used to refer to both exceptions and errors. Figure 6.9 also shows that not all exception classes are found in the `java.lang` package.

Figure 6.9 *Partial Exception Inheritance Hierarchy*

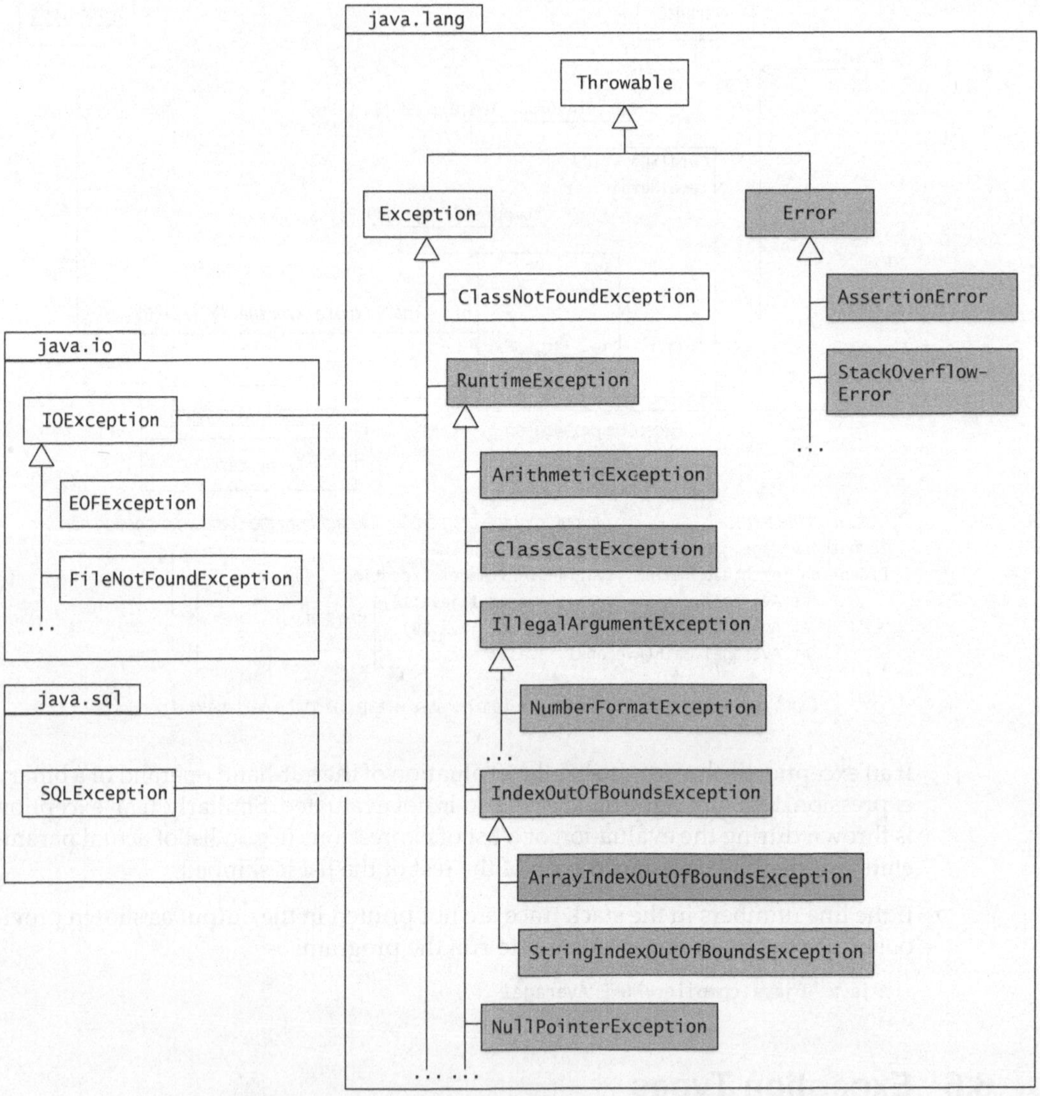

Classes that are shaded (and their subclasses) represent unchecked exceptions.

The `Throwable` class provides a `String` variable that can be set to provide a *detail message* when an exception is constructed. The purpose of the detail message is to provide more information about the actual exception. All classes of throwables define a one-parameter constructor that takes a string as the detail message.

The class `Throwable` provides the following common methods to query an exception:

`String getMessage()`

Returns the detail message.

`void printStackTrace()`

Prints the stack trace on the standard error stream. The stack trace comprises the method invocation sequence on the JVM stack when the exception was thrown. The stack trace can also be written to a `PrintStream` or a `PrintWriter` by supplying such a destination as an argument to one of the two overloaded `printStackTrace()` methods. Any suppressed exceptions associated with an exception on the stack trace are also printed. It will also print the cause of an exception (which is also an exception) if one is available.

`String toString()`

Returns a short description of the exception, which typically comprises the class name of the exception together with the string returned by the `getMessage()` method.

In dealing with throwables, it is important to recognize *situations* in which particular throwables can occur, and the *source* that is responsible for throwing them. By *source* we mean:

- The *JVM* that is responsible for throwing the throwable, or
- The throwable that is explicitly thrown *programmatically* by the code in the application or by any API used by the application.

In further discussion of exception types, we provide an overview of situations in which selected throwables can occur and the source responsible for throwing them.

The `Exception` Class

The class `Exception` represents exceptions that a program would normally want to catch. Its subclass `RuntimeException` represents many common programming errors that can manifest at runtime (see the next subsection). Other subclasses of the `Exception` class define other categories of exceptions, such as I/O-related exceptions in the `java.io` package (`IOException`, `FileNotFoundException`, `EOFException`) and database-related exceptions in the `java.sql` package (`SQLException`).

ClassNotFoundException

The subclass `ClassNotFoundException` signals that the JVM tried to load a class by its string name, but the class could not be found. A typical example of this situation is when the class name is misspelled while starting program execution with the `java` command. The source in this case is the JVM throwing the exception to signal that the class cannot be found and therefore execution cannot be started.

The `RuntimeException` Class

Runtime exceptions are all subclasses of the `java.lang.RuntimeException` class, which is a subclass of the `Exception` class. As these runtime exceptions are usually caused by program bugs that should not occur in the first place, it is usually more appropriate to treat them as faults in the program design and let them be handled by the default exception handler.

ArithmeticException

This exception represents situations where an illegal arithmetic operation is attempted, such as integer division by 0. It is typically thrown by the JVM. See Chapter 5 for details on illegal arithmetic operations.

ArrayIndexOutOfBoundsException

Java provides runtime checking of the array index value, meaning out-of-bounds array indices. The subclass `ArrayIndexOutOfBoundsException` represents exceptions thrown by the JVM that signal out-of-bound errors specifically for arrays—that is, an error in which an invalid index is used to access an element in the array. The index value must satisfy the relation 0 ≤ *index value* < *length of the array*. See §3.4, p. 58, covering arrays.

ClassCastException

This exception is thrown by the JVM to signal that an attempt was made to cast a reference value to a type that was not legal, such as casting the reference value of an `Integer` object to the `Long` type. Casting reference values is discussed in §7.11, p. 320.

IllegalArgumentException and NumberFormatException

The `IllegalArgumentException` is thrown programmatically to indicate that a method was called with an illegal or inappropriate argument. For example, the `ofPattern(String pattern)` method in the `java.time.format.DateTimeFormatter` class throws an `IllegalArgumentException` when the letter pattern passed as an argument is invalid (§11.4, p. 495).

The class `NumberFormatException` is a subclass of the `IllegalArgumentException` class, and is specialized to signal problems when converting a string to a numeric value if the format of the characters in the string is not appropriate for the conversion. This exception is also thrown programmatically. The numeric wrapper classes all have methods that throw this exception when conversion from a string to a numeric value is not possible (§8.3, p. 346).

NullPointerException

This exception is typically thrown by the JVM when an attempt is made to use the `null` value as a reference value to refer to an object. This might involve calling an instance method using a reference that has the `null` value, or accessing a field using a reference that has the `null` value. This programming error has made this exception one of the exceptions most often thrown by the JVM.

The `Error` Class

The class `Error` and its subclasses define errors that are invariably never explicitly caught and are usually irrecoverable. Not surprisingly, most such errors are signaled by the JVM. Apart from the subclasses mentioned in the following subsections, other subclasses of the `java.lang.Error` class define errors that indicate class linkage (`LinkageError`), thread (`ThreadDeath`), and virtual machine (`VirtualMachineError`) problems.

AssertionError

The subclass `AssertionError` of the `java.lang.Error` class is used by the Java assertion facility. This error is thrown by the JVM in response to the condition in the `assert` statement evaluating to `false`. The assertion facility is not discussed in this book.

StackOverflowError

This error occurs when the JVM stack has no more room for new method activation frames. In such a case, we say that the stack has *overflowed*. This situation can occur when method execution in an application recurses too deeply. Here is a *recursive method* to illustrate stack overflow:

```
public void callMe() {
  System.out.println("Don't do this at home!");
  callMe();
}
```

Once this method is called, it will keep on calling itself until the JVM stack is full, resulting in the `StackOverflowError` being thrown by the JVM.

Checked and Unchecked Exceptions

Except for `RuntimeException`, `Error`, and their subclasses, all exceptions are *checked* exceptions. That is, the compiler ensures that if a method can throw a checked exception, directly or indirectly, the method must explicitly deal with it. The method must either catch the exception and take the appropriate action, or pass on the exception to its caller (§6.9, p. 251).

Exceptions defined by the `Error` and `RuntimeException` classes and their subclasses are known as *unchecked* exceptions, meaning that a method is not obliged to deal with these kinds of exceptions (shown with gray color in Figure 6.9). They are either irrecoverable (exemplified by the `Error` class), in which case the program should not attempt to deal with them, or they are programming errors (exemplified by the RuntimeException class) and should usually be dealt with as such, and not as exceptions.

Defining Customized Exceptions

Customized exceptions are usually defined to provide fine-grained categorization of error situations, instead of using existing exception classes with descriptive detail messages to differentiate among the various situations. New customized exceptions are usually defined by either extending the Exception class or one of its checked subclasses, thereby making the new exceptions checked, or extending the RuntimeException subclass to create new unchecked exceptions.

As exceptions are defined by classes, they can declare fields and methods, thereby providing more information as to their cause and remedy when they are thrown and caught. The super() call can be used to set the detail message for the exception. Note that the exception class must be instantiated to create an exception object that can be thrown and subsequently caught and dealt with. The following code sketches a class declaration for an exception that can include all pertinent information about the exception. At a minimum, the new exception class should provide a constructor to set the detail message.

```
public class EvacuateException extends Exception {
  // Data
  Date date;
  Zone zone;
  TransportMode transport;

  // Constructor
  public EvacuateException(Date d, Zone z, TransportMode t) {
    // Call the constructor of the superclass
    super("Evacuation of zone " + z);
    // ...
  }
  // Methods
  // ...
}
```

Several examples in subsequent sections illustrate exception handling.

6.7 Exception Handling: try, catch, and finally

The mechanism for handling exceptions is embedded in the try-catch-finally construct, which has the following basic form:

```
try {                                            // try block
  statements
} catch (exception_type1 parameter1) {         // uni-catch clause
  statements
}
...
```

```
catch (exception_typen parametern) {        // uni-catch clause
  statements
} finally {                                  // finally clause
  statements
}
```

A few aspects about the syntax of this construct should be noted. For each `try` block, there can be zero or more `catch` clauses (i.e., it can have *multiple* `catch` clauses), but only one `finally` clause. The `catch` clauses and the `finally` clause must always appear in conjunction with a `try` block, and in the right order. A `try` block must be followed by at least one `catch` clause, or a `finally` clause must be specified. In addition to the `try` block, each `catch` clause and the `finally` clause specify a block, `{ }`. The block notation is mandatory.

Exceptions thrown during execution of the `try` block can be caught and handled in a `catch` clause. Each `catch` clause defines an exception handler. The header of the `catch` clause specifies exactly one exception parameter. The exception type must be of the `Throwable` class or one of its subclasses. The type of the exception parameter of a `catch` clause is specified by a *single* exception type in the syntax given earlier, and such a `catch` clause is called a *uni*-`catch` clause.

A `finally` clause is guaranteed to be executed, regardless of the cause of exit from the `try` block, or whether any `catch` clause was executed. Figure 6.10 shows three typical scenarios of control flow through the `try-catch-finally` construct.

Figure 6.10 *The* `try-catch-finally` *Construct*

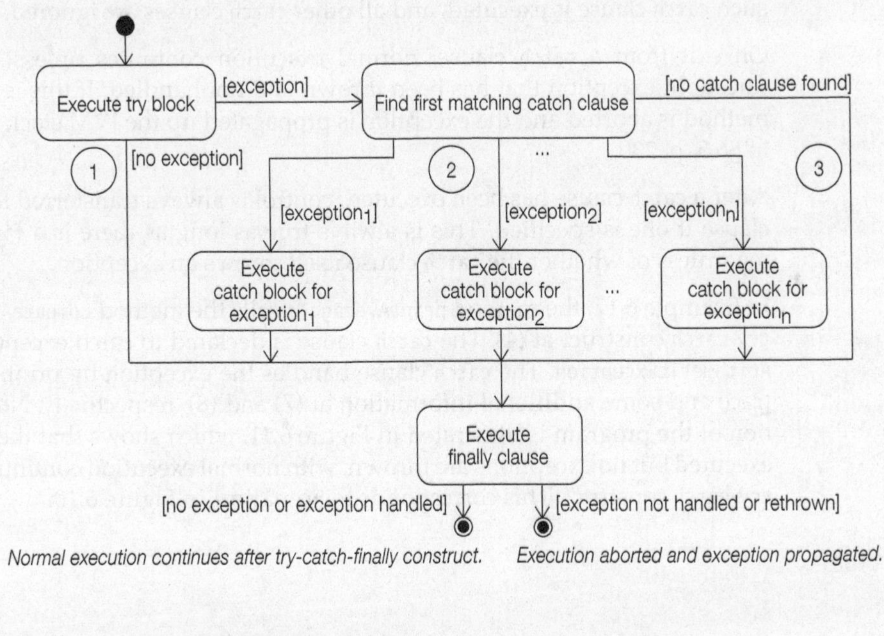

The try block, the catch clause, and the finally clause of a try-catch-finally construct can contain arbitrary code, which means that a try-catch-finally construct can be nested in any block of the try-catch-finally construct. However, such nesting can easily make the code difficult to read and is best avoided, if possible.

The try Block

The try block establishes a context for exception handling. Termination of a try block occurs as a result of encountering an exception, or from successful execution of the code in the try block.

The catch clauses are skipped for all normal exits from the try block when no exceptions are thrown, and control is transferred to the finally clause if one is specified ((1) in Figure 6.10).

For all exits from the try block resulting from exceptions, control is transferred to the catch clauses—if any such clauses are specified—to find a matching catch clause ((2) in Figure 6.10). If no catch clause matches the thrown exception, control is transferred to the finally clause if one is specified ((3) in Figure 6.10).

The catch Clause

Only an exit from a try block resulting from an exception can transfer control to a catch clause. A catch clause can catch the thrown exception only if the exception is assignable to the parameter in the catch clause (§7.8, p. 311). The code of the first such catch clause is executed, and all other catch clauses are ignored.

On exit from a catch clause, normal execution continues unless there is any uncaught exception that has been thrown and not handled. If this is the case, the method is aborted and the exception is propagated up the JVM stack as explained in §6.5, p. 230.

After a catch clause has been executed, control is always transferred to the finally clause if one is specified. This is always true as long as there is a finally clause, regardless of whether the catch clause itself throws an exception.

In Example 6.12, the method printAverage() calls the method computeAverage() in a try-catch construct at (4). The catch clause is declared to catch exceptions of type ArithmeticException. The catch clause handles the exception by printing the stack trace and some additional information at (7) and (8), respectively. Normal execution of the program is illustrated in Figure 6.11, which shows that the try block is executed but no exceptions are thrown, with normal execution continuing after the try-catch construct. This corresponds to Scenario 1 in Figure 6.10.

Figure 6.11 *Exception Handling (Scenario 1)*

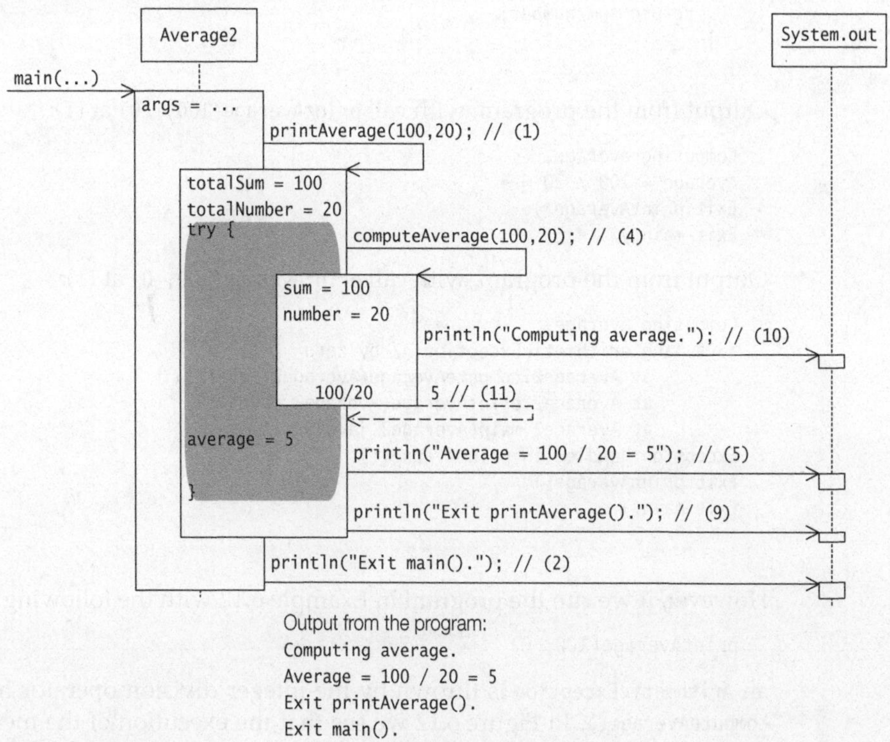

Example 6.12 *The* `try-catch` *Construct*

```
public class Average2 {

  public static void main(String[] args) {
    printAverage(100, 20);                                          // (1)
    System.out.println("Exit main().");                             // (2)
  }

  public static void printAverage(int totalSum, int totalNumber) {
    try {                                                           // (3)
      int average = computeAverage(totalSum, totalNumber);         // (4)
      System.out.println("Average = " +                             // (5)
          totalSum + " / " + totalNumber + " = " + average);
    } catch (ArithmeticException ae) {                              // (6)
      ae.printStackTrace();                                         // (7)
      System.out.println("Exception handled in printAverage().");  // (8)
    }
    System.out.println("Exit printAverage().");                     // (9)
  }
```

```
  public static int computeAverage(int sum, int number) {
    System.out.println("Computing average.");                    // (10)
    return sum/number;                                           // (11)
  }
}
```

Output from the program, with call `printAverage(100, 20)` at (1):

```
Computing average.
Average = 100 / 20 = 5
Exit printAverage().
Exit main().
```

Output from the program, with call `printAverage(100, 0)` at (1):

```
Computing average.
java.lang.ArithmeticException: / by zero
        at Average2.computeAverage(Average2.java:23)
        at Average2.printAverage(Average2.java:11)
        at Average2.main(Average2.java:5)
Exception handled in printAverage().
Exit printAverage().
Exit main().
```

However, if we run the program in Example 6.12 with the following call in (1):

```
printAverage(100, 0)
```

an `ArithmeticException` is thrown by the integer division operator in the method `computeAverage()`. In Figure 6.12 we see that the execution of the method `computeAverage()` is stopped and the exception propagated to method `printAverage()`, where it is handled by the `catch` clause at (6). Normal execution of the method continues at (9) after the `try-catch` construct, as witnessed by the output from the statements at (9) and (2). This corresponds to Scenario 2 in Figure 6.10.

In Example 6.13, the `main()` method calls the `printAverage()` method in a `try-catch` construct at (1). The `catch` clause at (3) is declared to catch exceptions of type `ArithmeticException`. The `printAverage()` method calls the `computeAverage()` method in a `try-catch` construct at (7), but here the `catch` clause is declared to catch exceptions of type `IllegalArgumentException`. Execution of the program is illustrated in Figure 6.13, which shows that the `ArithmeticException` is first propagated to the `catch` clause in the `printAverage()` method. Because this `catch` clause cannot handle this exception, it is propagated further to the `catch` clause in the `main()` method, where it is caught and handled. Normal execution continues at (6) after the exception is handled.

Note that the execution of the `try` block at (7) in the `printAverage()` method is never completed: The statement at (9) is never executed. The `catch` clause at (10) is skipped. The execution of the `printAverage()` method is aborted: The statement at (13) is never executed, and the exception is propagated. This corresponds to Scenario 3 in Figure 6.10.

Figure 6.12 *Exception Handling (Scenario 2)*

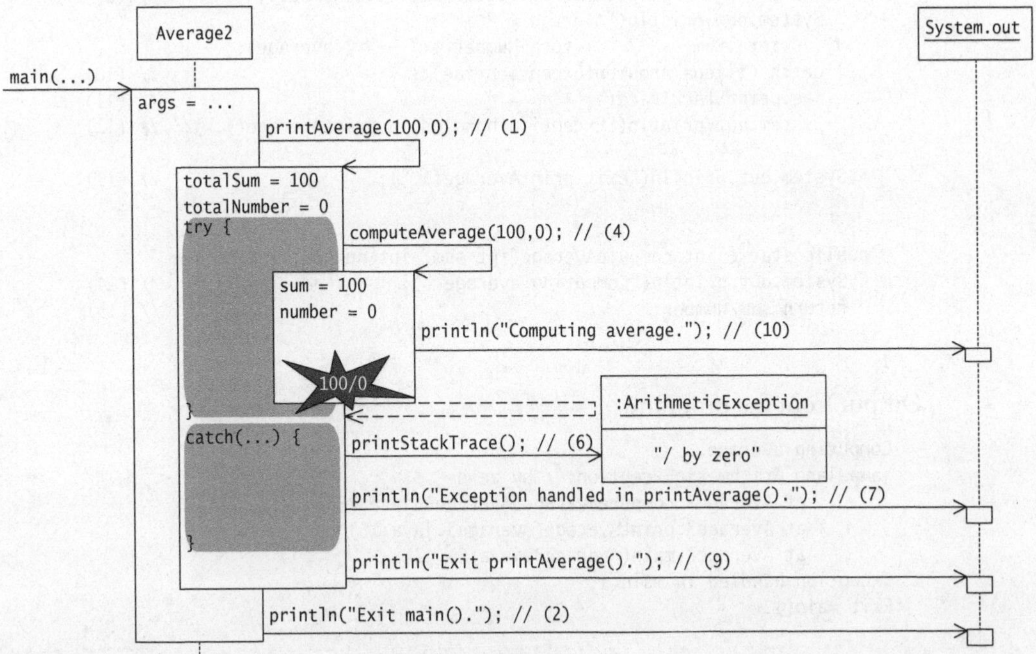

Output from the program:

```
Computing average.
java.lang.ArithmeticException: / by zero
        at Average2.computeAverage(Average2.java:23)
        at Average2.printAverage(Average2.java:11)
        at Average2.main(Average2.java:5)
Exception handled in printAverage().
Exit printAverage().
Exit main().
```

Example 6.13 *Exception Propagation*

```
public class Average3 {

  public static void main(String[] args) {
    try {                                                      // (1)
      printAverage(100, 0);                                    // (2)
    } catch (ArithmeticException ae) {                         // (3)
      ae.printStackTrace();                                    // (4)
      System.out.println("Exception handled in main().");      // (5)
    }
    System.out.println("Exit main().");                        // (6)
  }
```

```
  public static void printAverage(int totalSum, int totalNumber) {
    try {                                                         // (7)
      int average = computeAverage(totalSum, totalNumber);        // (8)
      System.out.println("Average = " +                           // (9)
          totalSum + " / " + totalNumber + " = " + average);
    } catch (IllegalArgumentException iae) {                      // (10)
      iae.printStackTrace();                                      // (11)
      System.out.println("Exception handled in printAverage()."); // (12)
    }
    System.out.println("Exit printAverage().");                   // (13)
  }

  public static int computeAverage(int sum, int number) {
    System.out.println("Computing average.");                    // (14)
    return sum/number;                                            // (15)
  }
}
```

Output from the program:

```
Computing average.
java.lang.ArithmeticException: / by zero
        at Average3.computeAverage(Average3.java:28)
        at Average3.printAverage(Average3.java:16)
        at Average3.main(Average3.java:6)
Exception handled in main().
Exit main().
```

The scope of the parameter name in the catch clause is the clause itself. As mentioned earlier, the type of the exception object must be *assignable* to the type of the argument in the catch clause (§7.8, p. 311). In the body of the catch clause, the exception object can be queried like any other object by using the parameter name. The javac compiler also complains if a catch clause for a superclass exception shadows the catch clause for a subclass exception, as the catch clause of the subclass exception will never be executed (a situation known as *unreachable code*). The following example shows incorrect order of the catch clauses at (1) and (2), which will result in a compile-time error: The superclass Exception will shadow the subclass ArithmeticException.

```
...
// Compiler-time error at (1).
catch (Exception e) {                    // (1) superclass
  System.out.println(e);
} catch (ArithmeticException e) {        // (2) subclass
  System.out.println(e);
}
...
```

Figure 6.13 *Exception Handling (Scenario 3)*

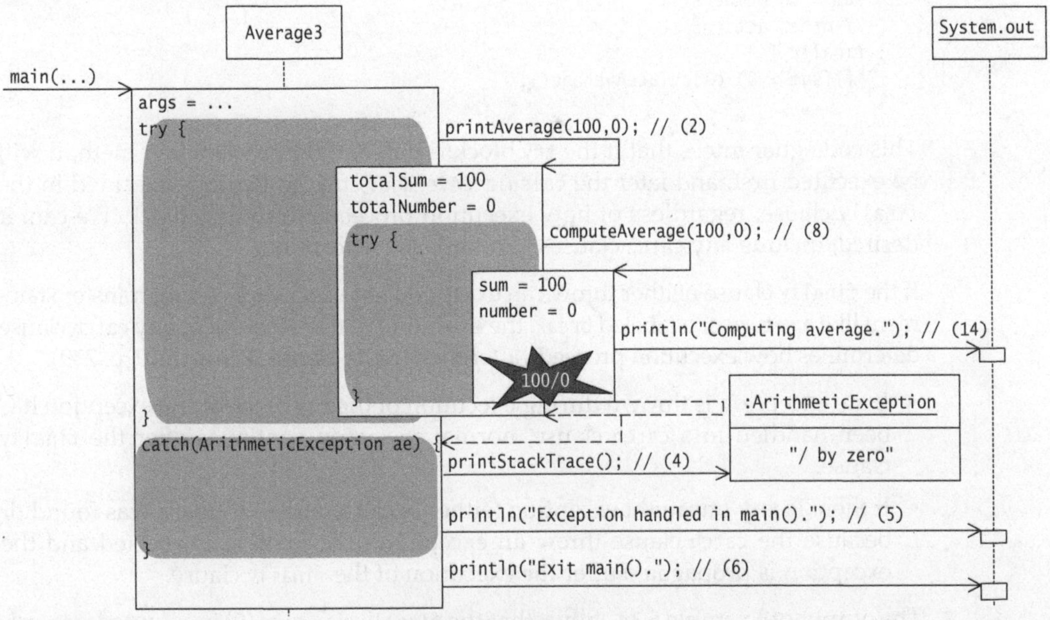

Output from the program:

```
Computing average.
java.lang.ArithmeticException: / by zero
        at Average3.computeAverage(Average3.java:28)
        at Average3.printAverage(Average3.java:16)
        at Average3.main(Average3.java:6)
Exception handled in main().
Exit main().
```

The `finally` Clause

If the `try` block is executed, then the `finally` clause is guaranteed to be executed, regardless of whether any `catch` clause was executed. Since the `finally` clause is always executed before control transfers to its final destination, the `finally` clause can be used to specify any clean-up code (e.g., to free resources such as files and net connections). However, the `try`-with-resources statement provides a better solution for handling resources, and eliminates use of the `finally` clause in many cases. But that is a story for another day, as this topic is not on the OCAJP8 exam.

A `try-finally` construct can be used to control the interplay between two actions that must be executed in the correct order, possibly with other intervening actions. In the following code, the operation in the `calculateAverage()` method is dependent on the success of the `sumNumbers()` method, which is checked by the value of the `sum` variable before calling the `calculateAverage()` method:

```
int sum = 0;
try {
  sum = sumNumbers();
  // other actions
} finally {
  if (sum > 0) calculateAverage();
}
```

This code guarantees that if the `try` block is entered, the `sumNumbers()` method will be executed first, and later the `calculateAverage()` method will be executed in the `finally` clause, regardless of how execution proceeds in the `try` block. We can, if desired, include any `catch` clauses to handle any exceptions.

If the `finally` clause neither throws an exception nor executes a control transfer statement like a `return` or a labeled `break`, the execution of the `try` block or any `catch` clause determines how execution proceeds after the `finally` clause (Figure 6.10, p. 239).

- If no exception is thrown during execution of the `try` block or the exception has been handled in a `catch` clause, normal execution continues after the `finally` clause.
- If there is any uncaught exception (either because no `catch` clause was found or because the `catch` clause threw an exception), the method is aborted and the exception is propagated after the execution of the `finally` clause.

The output of Example 6.14 shows that the `finally` clause at (9) is executed, regardless of whether an exception is thrown in the `try` block at (3). If an exception is thrown, it is caught and handled by the `catch` clause at (6). After the execution of the `finally` clause at (9), normal execution continues at (10).

Example 6.14 *The* `try-catch-finally` *Construct*

```
public class Average4 {

  public static void main(String[] args) {
    printAverage(100, 20);                                         // (1)
    System.out.println("Exit main().");                            // (2)
  }

  public static void printAverage(int totalSum, int totalNumber) {
    try {                                                          // (3)
      int average = computeAverage(totalSum, totalNumber);         // (4)
      System.out.println("Average = " +                            // (5)
          totalSum + " / " + totalNumber + " = " + average);
    } catch (ArithmeticException ae) {                             // (6)
      ae.printStackTrace();                                        // (7)
      System.out.println("Exception handled in printAverage()."); // (8)
    } finally {                                                    // (9)
      System.out.println("Finally done.");
    }
    System.out.println("Exit printAverage().");                    // (10)
  }
```

```
  public static int computeAverage(int sum, int number) {
    System.out.println("Computing average.");                // (11)
    return sum/number;                                        // (12)
  }
}
```

Output from the program, with the call `printAverage(100, 20)` at (1):

```
Computing average.
Average = 100 / 20 = 5
Finally done.
Exit printAverage().
Exit main().
```

Output from the program, with the call `printAverage(100, 0)` at (1):

```
Computing average.
java.lang.ArithmeticException: / by zero
        at Average4.computeAverage(Average4.java:25)
        at Average4.printAverage(Average4.java:11)
        at Average4.main(Average4.java:5)
Exception handled in printAverage().
Finally done.
Exit printAverage().
Exit main().
```

On exiting from the `finally` clause, if there is any uncaught exception, the method is aborted and the exception propagated as explained earlier. This is illustrated in Example 6.15. The method `printAverage()` is aborted after the `finally` clause at (6) has been executed, as the `ArithmeticException` thrown at (9) is not handled by any method. In this case, the exception is handled by the default exception handler. Notice the difference in the output from Example 6.14 and Example 6.15.

Example 6.15 *The* `try-finally` *Construct*

```
public class Average5 {

  public static void main(String[] args) {
    printAverage(100, 0);                                     // (1)
    System.out.println("Exit main().");                       // (2)
  }

  public static void printAverage(int totalSum, int totalNumber) {
    try {                                                     // (3)
      int average = computeAverage(totalSum, totalNumber);    // (4)
      System.out.println("Average = " +                       // (5)
          totalSum + " / " + totalNumber + " = " + average);
    } finally {                                               // (6)
      System.out.println("Finally done.");
    }
    System.out.println("Exit printAverage().");               // (7)
  }
```

```
  public static int computeAverage(int sum, int number) {
    System.out.println("Computing average.");                    // (8)
    return sum/number;                                           // (9)
  }
}
```

Output from the program:

```
Computing average.
Finally done.
Exception in thread "main" java.lang.ArithmeticException: / by zero
        at Average5.computeAverage(Average5.java:22)
        at Average5.printAverage(Average5.java:11)
        at Average5.main(Average5.java:4)
```

If the `finally` clause executes a control transfer statement, such as a `return` or a labeled `break`, this control transfer statement determines how the execution will proceed—regardless of how the `try` block or any `catch` clause was executed. In particular, a value returned by a `return` statement in the `finally` clause will supercede any value returned by a `return` statement in the `try` block or a `catch` clause.

Example 6.16 shows how the execution of a control transfer statement such as a `return` in the `finally` clause affects the program execution. The first output from the program shows that the average is computed but the value returned is from the `return` statement at (8) in the `finally` clause, not from the `return` statement at (6) in the `try` block. The second output shows that the `ArithmeticException` thrown in the `computeAverage()` method and propagated to the `printAverage()` method is nullified by the `return` statement in the `finally` clause. Normal execution continues after the `return` statement at (8), with the value 0 being returned from the `printAverage()` method.

If the `finally` clause throws an exception, this exception is propagated with all its ramifications—regardless of how the `try` block or any `catch` clause was executed. In particular, the new exception overrules any previously uncaught exception.

Example 6.16 *The `finally` Clause and the `return` Statement*

```
public class Average6 {

  public static void main(String[] args) {
    System.out.println("Average: " + printAverage(100, 20));     // (1)
    System.out.println("Exit main().");                          // (2)
  }

  public static int printAverage(int totalSum, int totalNumber) {
    int average = 0;
    try {                                                        // (3)
      average = computeAverage(totalSum, totalNumber);           // (4)
      System.out.println("Average = " +                          // (5)
          totalSum + " / " + totalNumber + " = " + average);
      return average;                                            // (6)
```

```
      } finally {                                              // (7)
        System.out.println("Finally done.");
        return average*2;                                      // (8)
      }
    }

    public static int computeAverage(int sum, int number) {
      System.out.println("Computing average.");                // (9)
      return sum/number;                                       // (10)
    }
  }
```

Output from the program, with call `printAverage(100, 20)` in (1):

```
Computing average.
Average = 100 / 20 = 5
Finally done.
Average: 10
Exit main().
```

Output from the program, with call `printAverage(100, 0)` in (1):

```
Computing average.
Finally done.
Average: 0
Exit main().
```

6.8 The `throw` Statement

Earlier examples in this chapter have shown how an exception can be thrown implicitly by the JVM during execution. Now we look at how an application can programmatically throw an exception using the `throw` statement. The general format of the `throw` statement is as follows:

`throw` *object_reference_expression*;

The compiler ensures that the *object reference expression* is of the type `Throwable` class or one of its subclasses. At runtime a `NullPointerException` is thrown by the JVM if the *object reference expression* is `null`. This ensures that a `Throwable` will always be propagated. A detail message is often passed to the constructor when the exception object is created.

```
throw new ArithmeticException("Integer division by 0");
```

When an exception is thrown, normal execution is suspended. The runtime system proceeds to find a `catch` clause that can handle the exception. The search starts in the context of the current `try` block, propagating to any enclosing `try` blocks and through the JVM stack to find a handler for the exception. Any associated `finally` clause of a `try` block encountered along the search path is executed. If no handler is found, then the exception is dealt with by the default exception handler at the top level. If a handler is found, normal execution resumes after the code in its `catch` clause has been executed, barring any rethrowing of an exception.

In Example 6.17, an exception is thrown using a `throw` statement at (17). This exception is propagated to the `main()` method, where it is caught and handled by the `catch` clause at (3). Note that the `finally` clauses at (6) and (14) are executed. Execution continues normally at (7).

Example 6.17 *Throwing Exceptions*

```
public class Average7 {

  public static void main(String[] args) {
    try {                                                         // (1)
      printAverage(100, 0);                                       // (2)
    } catch (ArithmeticException ae) {                            // (3)
      ae.printStackTrace();                                       // (4)
      System.out.println("Exception handled in main().");         // (5)
    } finally {
      System.out.println("Finally in main().");                   // (6)
    }
    System.out.println("Exit main().");                           // (7)
  }

  public static void printAverage(int totalSum, int totalNumber) {
    try {                                                         // (8)
      int average = computeAverage(totalSum, totalNumber);        // (9)
      System.out.println("Average = " +                           // (10)
          totalSum + " / " + totalNumber + " = " + average);
    } catch (IllegalArgumentException iae) {                      // (11)
      iae.printStackTrace();                                      // (12)
      System.out.println("Exception handled in printAverage()."); // (13)
    } finally {
      System.out.println("Finally in printAverage().");           // (14)
    }
    System.out.println("Exit printAverage().");                   // (15)
  }

  public static int computeAverage(int sum, int number) {
    System.out.println("Computing average.");
    if (number == 0)                                              // (16)
      throw new ArithmeticException("Integer division by 0");     // (17)
    return sum/number;                                            // (18)
  }
}
```

Output from the program:

```
Computing average.
Finally in printAverage().
java.lang.ArithmeticException: Integer division by 0
      at Average7.computeAverage(Average7.java:33)
      at Average7.printAverage(Average7.java:18)
      at Average7.main(Average7.java:6)
Exception handled in main().
Finally in main().
Exit main().
```

6.9 The `throws` Clause

A `throws` clause can be specified in a method or a constructor header to declare any checked exceptions that can be thrown by a statement in the body of a method or a constructor. It is declared immediately preceding the body of the method or the constructor.

... `throws` $ExceptionType_1$, $ExceptionType_2$, ..., $ExceptionType_n$ `{ ... }`

Each $ExceptionType_i$ is an exception type, although usually only checked exceptions are specified. The compiler enforces that if a checked exception can be the result of executing a method or a constructor, then either the exception type of this exception or a supertype of its exception type is specified in the `throws` clause of the method or the constructor. The `throws` clause can specify unchecked exceptions, but this is seldom done and the compiler does not enforce any restrictions on their usage.

The `throws` clause is part of the contract that a method or a constructor offers to its clients. The `throws` clause can specify any number of exception types, even those that are not thrown by the method or the constructor. The compiler simply ensures that any checked exception that can actually be thrown in the method or constructor body is covered by the `throws` clause. Of course, the clients cannot ignore the checked exceptions in the `throws` clause.

In a method or a constructor, a checked exception can be thrown directly by a `throw` statement, or indirectly by calling other methods or constructors that can throw a checked exception. If a checked exception is thrown, it must be handled in one of three ways:

- By using a `try` block and catching the exception in a handler and dealing with it
- By using a `try` block and catching the exception in a handler, but throwing another exception that is either unchecked or declared in its `throws` clause
- By explicitly allowing propagation of the exception to its caller by declaring it in the `throws` clause of its header

This mechanism (also known as *catch-or-declare*) ensures that a checked exception will be dealt with, regardless of the path of execution. This aids development of robust programs, as allowance can be made for many contingencies. Native methods can also declare checked exceptions in their `throws` clause, but the compiler is not able to check them for consistency.

In Example 6.18, a new checked exception is defined, where the checked exception class `IntegerDivisionByZero` extends the `Exception` class. The method `main()` calls the method `printAverage()` in a `try` block at (1). In the `if` statement at (9), the method `computeAverage()` throws the checked exception `IntegerDivisionByZero`. Neither the `computeAverage()` method nor the `printAverage()` method catches the exception, but instead throws it to the caller, as declared in the `throws` clauses in their headers at (6) and (8). The exception propagates to the `main()` method. Since the `printAverage()` method was called from the context of the `try` block at (1) in the `main()` method, the exception is successfully caught by its `catch` clause at (3). The exception is handled and the `finally` clause at (4) executed, with normal execution resuming from (5). If the method `main()` did not catch the exception, it would have to declare this exception in a `throws` clause. In that case, the exception would end up being handled by the default exception handler.

Example 6.18 *The* `throws` *Clause*

```
// File: IntegerDivisionByZero.java
public class IntegerDivisionByZero extends Exception {
  IntegerDivisionByZero(String str) { super(str); }
}
```

```
// File: Average8.java
public class Average8 {
  public static void main(String[] args) {
    try {                                                          // (1)
      printAverage(100, 0);                                        // (2)
    } catch (IntegerDivisionByZero idbz) {                         // (3)
      idbz.printStackTrace();
      System.out.println("Exception handled in main().");
    } finally {                                                    // (4)
      System.out.println("Finally done in main().");
    }
    System.out.println("Exit main().");                            // (5)
  }

  public static void printAverage(int totalSum, int totalNumber)
      throws IntegerDivisionByZero {                               // (6)
    int average = computeAverage(totalSum, totalNumber);
    System.out.println("Average = " +
        totalSum + " / " + totalNumber + " = " + average);
    System.out.println("Exit printAverage().");                    // (7)
  }

  public static int computeAverage(int sum, int number)
      throws IntegerDivisionByZero {                               // (8)
    System.out.println("Computing average.");
    if (number == 0)                                               // (9)
      throw new IntegerDivisionByZero("Integer Division By Zero");
    return sum/number;                                             // (10)
  }
}
```

Output from the program:

```
Computing average.
IntegerDivisionByZero: Integer Division By Zero
        at Average8.computeAverage(Average8.java:27)
        at Average8.printAverage(Average8.java:17)
        at Average8.main(Average8.java:5)
Exception handled in main().
Finally done in main().
Exit main().
```

As mentioned earlier, the exception type specified in the `throws` clause can be a superclass of the actual exceptions thrown; that is, the exceptions thrown must be assignable to the type of the exceptions specified in the `throws` clause. If a method or a constructor can throw a checked exception, then the `throws` clause must declare its exception type or a supertype of its exception type; otherwise, a compile-time error will occur. In the `printAverage()` method, the method header could specify the superclass `Exception` of the subclass `IntegerDivisionByZero` in the `throws` clause. This would also entail that the `main()` method either catch an `Exception` or declare it in a `throws` clause.

```
public static void main(String[] args) throws Exception {
  /* ... */
}
public static void printAverage(int totalSum, int totalNumber) throws Exception {
  /* ... */
}
```

It is generally considered bad programming style to specify exception superclasses in the `throws` clause of the header when the actual exceptions thrown are instances of their subclasses. It is also recommended to use the `@throws` tag in a Javadoc comment to document the checked exceptions that a method or a constructor can throw, together with any unchecked exceptions that might also be relevant to catch.

Overriding the `throws` Clause

A subclass can *override* a method defined in its superclass by providing a new implementation (§7.2, p. 268). What happens when a superclass method with a list of exceptions in its `throws` clause is overridden in a subclass? The method declaration in the subclass need not specify a `throws` clause if it does not throw any checked exceptions, and if it does, it can specify only *checked* exception classes that are already in the `throws` clause of the superclass method, or that are subclasses of the checked exceptions in the `throws` clause of the superclass method. As a consequence, an overriding method *cannot* allow more checked exceptions in its `throws` clause than the superclass method does. Allowing more checked exceptions in the overriding method would create problems for clients who already deal with the exceptions specified in the superclass method. Such clients would be ill prepared if an object of the subclass threw a checked exception they were not prepared for. However, there are no restrictions on specifying *unchecked* exceptions in the `throws` clause of the overriding method. The preceding discussion also applies to methods from an interface that a class implements, as these methods are overridden by any class implementing the interface.

In the following code, the method `superclassMethodX` in superclass `A` is overridden in subclass `B`. The `throws` clause of the method in subclass `B` at (2) specifies a subset of the checked exceptions specified in the throws clause at (1) and adds the more specific subclass exception, SubFirstException, of the superclass exception, FirstException, specified in the throws clause at (1).

```
// New exception classes:
class FirstException    extends Exception { }
class SecondException   extends Exception { }
class ThirdException    extends Exception { }
class SubFirstException extends FirstException { }

// Superclass
class A {
  // ...
  protected void superclassMethodX()
    throws FirstException, SecondException, ThirdException {/* ... */}     // (1)
  // ...
}
// Subclass
class B extends A {
  // ...
  @Override protected void superclassMethodX()
    throws FirstException, ThirdException, SubFirstException { /* ... */ } // (2)
  // ...
}
```

6.10 Advantages of Exception Handling

Robustness refers to the ability of a software system to respond to errors during execution. A system should respond to unexpected situations at runtime in a responsible way. Applications that provide the user with frequent cryptic messages with error codes or that repeatedly give the user the silent treatment when something goes wrong can hardly be considered robust.

The exception handling mechanism in Java offers the following advantages that facilitate developing robust applications in Java:

- Separation of Exception Handling Code

  The code for handling error situations can be separated from the code for the program logic by using the exception handling constructs provided by the language. Code that can result in error situations is confined in the try block, and their handling in the catch clause.

- Transparent Exception Propagation

  Propagation of a checked exception in the JVM stack cannot be ignored by an active method. The method must comply with the catch-or-declare requirement: either catch and handle the exception, or propagate it by declaring it in the method's throws clause. Error situations causing exception propagation are thus always detected, and can be caught and remedied.

- Exception Categorization and Specialization

  The exception and error classes in the Java SE platform API are organized in an inheritance hierarchy (Figure 6.9, p. 234). Classes higher up in this hierarchy represent *categories* of exceptions and errors (`Exception`, `RuntimeException`, `IOException`, `Error`), whereas classes lower in this hierarchy represent more *specific* exceptions and errors (`NullPointerException`, `FileNotFoundException`, `AssertionError`). The `try-catch` construct allows flexibility in catching and handling exceptions. A `catch` clause can specify an exception category for coarse-grained exception handling, as the exception category class will subsume its more specific exception subclasses, or it can specify a more specific exception class for fine-grained exception handling. Best practice dictates that fine-grained exception handling be used.

Review Questions

6.16 Which digits, and in which order, will be printed when the following program is run?

```
public class DemoClass {
  public static void main(String[] args) {
    int k=0;
    try {
      int i = 5/k;
    } catch (ArithmeticException e) {
      System.out.println("1");
    } catch (RuntimeException e) {
      System.out.println("2");
      return;
    } catch (Exception e) {
      System.out.println("3");
    } finally {
      System.out.println("4");
    }
    System.out.println("5");
  }
}
```

Select the one correct answer.

(a) The program will only print 5.
(b) The program will only print 1 and 4, in that order.
(c) The program will only print 1, 2, and 4, in that order.
(d) The program will only print 1, 4, and 5, in that order.
(e) The program will only print 1, 2, 4, and 5, in that order.
(f) The program will only print 3 and 5, in that order.

6.17 Given the following program, which statements are true?

```
public class Exceptions {
  public static void main(String[] args) {
    try {
      if (args.length == 0) return;
      System.out.println(args[0]);
    } finally {
      System.out.println("The end");
    }
  }
}
```

Select the two correct answers.

(a) If run with no arguments, the program will produce no output.
(b) If run with no arguments, the program will print `The end`.
(c) The program will throw an `ArrayIndexOutOfBoundsException`.
(d) If run with one argument, the program will simply print the given argument.
(e) If run with one argument, the program will print the given argument followed by `"The end"`.

6.18 Which of the following statements are true?

Select the two correct answers.

(a) If an exception is not caught in a method, the method will terminate and normal execution will resume.
(b) An overriding method must declare that it throws the same exception classes as the method it overrides.
(c) The `main()` method of a program can declare that it throws checked exceptions.
(d) A method declaring that it throws an exception of a certain class may throw instances of any subclass of that exception class.
(e) `finally` clauses are executed if, and only if, an exception gets thrown while inside the corresponding `try` block.

6.19 Which digits, and in which order, will be printed when the following program is run?

```
public class RQ6A19 {
  public static void main(String[] args) throws InterruptedException {
    try {
      throwIt();
      System.out.println("1");
    } finally {
      System.out.println("2");
    }
    System.out.println("3");
  }

  // InterruptedException is a direct subclass of Exception.
  static void throwIt() throws InterruptedException {
    throw new InterruptedException("Time to go home.");
  }
}
```

Select the one correct answer.

(a) The program will print 2 and throw InterruptedException.
(b) The program will print 1 and 2, in that order.
(c) The program will print 1, 2, and 3, in that order.
(d) The program will print 2 and 3, in that order.
(e) The program will print 3 and 2, in that order.
(f) The program will print 1 and 3, in that order.

6.20 What is wrong with the following code?

```
public class RQ6A20 {
  public static void main(String[] args) throws A {
    try {
      action();
    } finally {
      System.out.println("Done.");
    } catch (A e) {
      throw e;
    }
  }

  public static void action() throws B {
    throw new B();
  }
}

class A extends Throwable {}

class B extends A {}
```

Select the one correct answer.

(a) The main() method must declare that it throws B.
(b) The finally clause must follow the catch clause in the main() method.
(c) The catch clause in the main() method must declare that it catches B rather than A.
(d) A single try block cannot be followed by both catch and finally clauses.
(e) The declaration of class A is illegal.

6.21 Which throws clause should be inserted at (1) for the overriding method compute() in the following code so that the code will compile without errors?

```
class A {
  // InterruptedException is a direct subclass of Exception.
  void compute() throws ArithmeticException, InterruptedException {
    div(5, 5);
  }

  int div(int i, int j) throws ArithmeticException {
    return i/j;
  }
}
```

```
public class Client extends A {
  void compute() /* (1) INSERT throws CLAUSE HERE. */ {
    try {
      div(5, 0);
    } catch (ArithmeticException e) {
      return;
    }
    throw new RuntimeException("ArithmeticException was expected.");
  }
}
```

Select the one correct answer.

(a) No `throws` clause is necessary.
(b) `throws ArithmeticException`
(c) `throws InterruptedException`
(d) `throws RuntimeException`
(e) `throws ArithmeticException, InterruptedException`

Chapter Summary

The following information was covered in this chapter:

- The selection statements: `if`, `if-else`, `switch`
- The iteration statements: `for(;;)`, `for(:)`, `while`, `do-while`
- The transfer statements: `break`, `continue`, `return`
- Exception handling and exception classes in the core API
- Defining customized exception types
- The `try-catch-finally` construct and control flow paths through the construct
- Using multiple `catch` clauses with the `try` statement
- Throwing exceptions programmatically with the `throw` statement
- Using the `throws` clause to specify checked exceptions

Programming Exercises

6.1 Create different versions of a program that finds all the primes smaller than 100. Create one version that uses only the `for(;;)` loop (i.e., no `while` or `do-while`). Create another version that uses only the `while` loop.

6.2 Here is a skeleton of a system for simulating a nuclear power plant. Implement the methods in the class named `Control`. Modify the method declarations if necessary. The Javadoc comments for each method give a description of what the implementation should do. Some of the methods in the other classes have unspecified implementations. Assume that these methods have been properly implemented and provide hooks to the rest of the system.

```
package energy;
/** A PowerPlant with a reactor core. */
public class PowerPlant {
  /** Each power plant has a reactor core.
      This field has package accessibility so that the Control class,
      defined in the same package, can access it. */
  final Reactor core;

  /** Initializes the power plant, creates a reactor core. */
  public PowerPlant() {
    core = new Reactor();
  }

  /** Sounds the alarm to evacuate the power plant. */
  public void soundEvacuateAlarm() {
    // ... implementation unspecified ...
  }

  /** @return the level of reactor output that is most desirable at this time.
      (Units are unspecified.) */
  public int getOptimalThroughput() {
    // ... implementation unspecified ...
    return 0;
  }

  /** The main entry point of the program: sets up a PowerPlant object
      and a Control object and lets the Control object run the power plant. */
  public static void main(String[] args) {
    PowerPlant plant = new PowerPlant();
    Control ctrl = new Control(plant);
    ctrl.runSystem();
  }
}
//____________________________________________________________________

/** A reactor core that has a throughput that can be either decreased or
    increased. */
class Reactor {
  /** @return the current throughput of the reactor. (Units are unspecified.) */
  public int getThroughput() {
    // ... implementation unspecified ...
    return 0;
  }

  /** @return true if the reactor status is critical, false otherwise. */
  public boolean isCritical() {
    // ... implementation unspecified ...
    return false;
  }
```

```
  /** Asks the reactor to increase throughput. */
  void increaseThroughput() throws ReactorCritical {
    // ... implementation unspecified ...
  }

  /** Asks the reactor to decrease throughput. */
  void decreaseThroughput() {
    // ... implementation unspecified ...
  }
}

//_____________________________________________________________________

/** This exception class should be used to report that the reactor status is
    critical. */
class ReactorCritical extends Exception {}

//_____________________________________________________________________

/** A controller that will manage the power plant to make sure that the
    reactor runs with optimal throughput. */
class Control {

  private final PowerPlant thePlant;

  static final int TOLERANCE = 10;

  /** @param p the power plant to control */
  public Control(PowerPlant p) {
    thePlant = p;
  }

  /** Runs the power plant by continuously monitoring the
      optimal throughput and the actual throughput of the reactor.
      If the throughputs differ by more than 10 units (i.e. tolerance),
      adjust the reactor throughput.
      If the reactor goes critical, the evacuate alarm is
      sounded and the reactor is shut down.
      The runSystem() method calls the methods needAdjustment(),
      adjustThroughput(), and shutdown(). */
  public void runSystem() {
    // ... provide implementation here ...
  }

  /** Reports whether the throughput of the reactor needs adjusting.
      This method should also monitor and report if the reactor goes critical.
      @param target the desired throughput.
      @return true if the optimal and actual throughput values differ by
      more than 10 units. */
  public boolean needAdjustment(int target) {
    // ... provide implementation here ...
    return true;
  }
```

```
    /** Adjusts the throughput of the reactor by calling increaseThroughput()
        and decreaseThroughput() methods until the actual throughput is within
        10 units of the target throughput.
        @param target the desired throughput. */
    public void adjustThroughput(int target) {
      // ... provide implementation here ...
    }

    /** Shuts down the reactor by lowering the throughput to 0. */
    public void shutdown() {
      // ... provide implementation here ...
    }
  }
```

7 Object-Oriented Programming

Programmer I Exam Objectives	
[6.1] Create methods with arguments and return values; including overloaded methods o *For method declarations, see §3.2, p. 49.* o *For parameter passing, see §3.5, p. 72.* o *For return statement, see §6.4, p. 224.*	*§7.2, p. 273*
[6.5] Apply encapsulation principles to a class	*§7.14, p. 334*
[7.1] Describe inheritance and its benefits	*§7.1, p. 264* *§7.13, p. 331*
[7.2] Develop code that demonstrates the use of polymorphism; including overriding and object type versus reference type	*§7.2, p. 268* *§7.12, p. 329*
[7.3] Determine when casting is necessary	*§7.11, p. 320*
[7.4] Use super and this to access objects and constructors o *For the* `this` *reference, see §3.2, p. 50.*	*§7.4, p. 276* *§7.5, p. 282*
[7.5] Use abstract classes and interfaces o *For abstract classes, see §4.6, p. 120.*	*§7.6, p. 290*
Supplementary Objectives	
• Access hidden members when subtyping	*§7.3, p. 275*
• Understand array subtyping	*§7.7, p. 309*
• Understand the contexts in which widening and narrowing reference conversions are applied	*§7.8, p. 311* *§7.9, p. 312* *§7.10, p. 315*

7.1 Single Implementation Inheritance

Inheritance is one of the fundamental mechanisms for code reuse in object-oriented programming (OOP). It allows new classes to be derived from existing ones. The new class (also called a *subclass, subtype, derived class,* or *child class*) can inherit members from the old class (also called a *superclass, supertype, base class,* or *parent class*). The subclass can add new behavior and properties and, under certain circumstances, modify its inherited behavior.

In Java, *implementation inheritance* (also known as *class inheritance*) is achieved by extending classes (i.e., adding new fields and methods) and modifying inherited members (§7.2, p. 268). Inheritance of members is closely tied to their declared *accessibility*. If a superclass member is accessible by its simple name in the subclass (without the use of any extra syntax like `super`), that member is considered inherited. Conversely, private, overridden, and hidden members of the superclass are *not* inherited. Inheritance should not be confused with the *existence* of such members in the state of a subclass object (Example 7.1).

A subclass specifies the name of its superclass in the subclass header using the `extends` clause.

```
class TubeLight extends Light { ... }   // TubeLight is a subclass of Light.
```

The subclass specifies only the additional new and modified members in its class body. The rest of its declaration is made up of its inherited members. If no `extends` clause is specified in the header of a class declaration, the class implicitly inherits from the `java.lang.Object` class (§8.2, p. 342). This implicit inheritance is assumed in the declaration of the `Light` class at (1) in Example 7.1. Also in Example 7.1, the subclass `TubeLight` at (2) explicitly uses the `extends` clause and specifies only members other than those that it already inherits from the superclass `Light` (which, in turn, inherits from the `Object` class). Members of the superclass `Light`, which are accessible by their simple names in the subclass `TubeLight`, are inherited by the subclass, as evident from the output in Example 7.1.

Private members of the superclass are not inherited by the subclass and can be accessed only indirectly. The private field `indicator` of the superclass `Light` is not inherited, but exists in the subclass object and is indirectly accessible through public methods.

Using appropriate accessibility modifiers, the superclass can limit which members can be accessed directly and, therefore, inherited by its subclasses (§4.7, p. 123). As shown in Example 7.1, the subclass can use the inherited members as if they were declared in its own class body. This is not the case for members that are declared as `private` in the superclass. Members that have package accessibility in the superclass are also not inherited by subclasses in other packages, as these members are accessible by their simple names only in subclasses within the same package as the superclass.

Since constructors (§7.5, p. 282) are *not* members of a class, they are *not* inherited by a subclass.

Example 7.1 *Extending Classes: Inheritance and Accessibility*

```
// File: Utility.java
class Light {                                   // (1)
  // Instance fields:
            int     noOfWatts;                  // Wattage
  private   boolean indicator;                  // On or off
  protected String  location;                   // Placement

  // Static field:
  private static int counter;                   // Number of Light objects created

  // No-argument constructor:
  Light() {
    noOfWatts = 50;
    indicator = true;
    location  = "X";
    counter++;
  }

  // Instance methods:
  public  void    switchOn()  { indicator = true; }
  public  void    switchOff() { indicator = false; }
  public  boolean isOn()      { return indicator; }
  private void    printLocation() {
    System.out.println("Location: " + location);
  }

  // Static methods:
  public static void writeCount() {
    System.out.println("Number of lights: " + counter);
  }
  //...
}
//______________________________________________________________________
class TubeLight extends Light {                 // (2) Subclass uses the extends clause.
  // Instance fields:
  private int tubeLength = 54;
  private int colorNo    = 10;

  // Instance methods:
  public int getTubeLength() { return tubeLength; }

  public void printInfo() {
    System.out.println("From the subclass:");
    System.out.println("Tube length: "  + tubeLength);
    System.out.println("Color number: " + colorNo);
    System.out.println("Tube length: "  + getTubeLength());
    System.out.println();
    System.out.println("From the superclass:");
    System.out.println("Wattage: "      + noOfWatts);      // Inherited.
//  System.out.println("Indicator: "    + indicator);      // Not inherited.
    System.out.println("Location: "     + location);       // Inherited.
//  System.out.println("Counter: "    + counter);          // Not inherited.
```

```
      switchOn();                                           // Inherited
      switchOff();                                          // Inherited
      System.out.println("Indicator: "    + isOn());        // Inherited.
  //  printLocation();                                      // Not inherited.
      writeCount();                                         // Inherited.
    }
    // ...
  }
  //______________________________________________________________________
  public class Utility {                            // (3)
    public static void main(String[] args) {
      new TubeLight().printInfo();
    }
  }
```

Output from the program:

```
From the subclass:
Tube length: 54
Color number: 10
Tube length: 54

From the superclass:
Wattage: 50
Location: X
Indicator: false
Number of lights: 1
```

In Java, a class can extend only *one* class; that is, it can have only one immediate superclass. This kind of inheritance is sometimes called *single* or *linear implementation inheritance*. The name is appropriate, as the subclass inherits the *implementations* of its superclass members. The inheritance relationship can be depicted as an *inheritance hierarchy* (also called a *class hierarchy*). Classes higher up in the hierarchy are more *generalized* (often called *broader*), as they abstract the class behavior. Classes lower down in the hierarchy are more *specialized* (often called *narrower*), as they customize the inherited behavior by additional properties and behavior. Figure 7.1 illustrates the inheritance relationship between the class `Light`, which represents the more general abstraction, and its more specialized subclasses. The `java.lang.Object` class is always at the top (the *root*) of any Java inheritance hierarchy, as all classes, with the exception of the `Object` class itself, inherit (either directly or indirectly) from this class.

Relationships: is-a and has-a

Inheritance defines the relationship *is-a* (also called the *superclass–subclass* relationship) between a superclass and its subclasses. Thus, an object of a subclass *is-a* superclass object, and can be used wherever an object of the superclass can be used. This criterion is often employed as a litmus test for choosing inheritance in object-oriented design. It has particular consequences for how objects can be used. An object of the `TubeLight` class *is-an* object of the superclass `Light`. Referring to

Figure 7.1 *Inheritance Hierarchy*

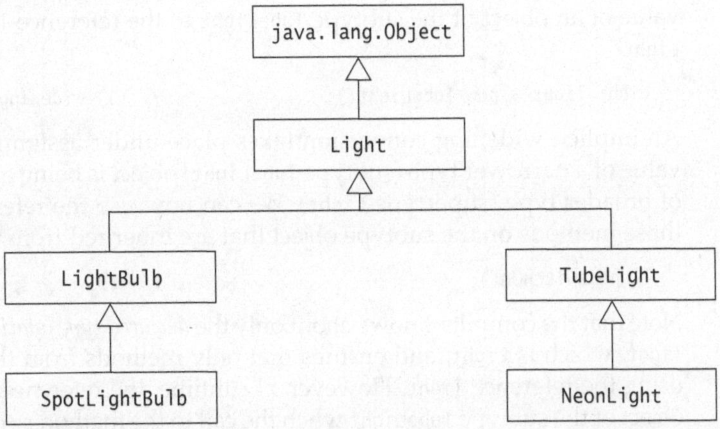

Figure 7.1, an object of the `TubeLight` class can be used wherever an object of the superclass `Light` can be used. The inheritance relationship is transitive: If class `B` extends class `A` and class `C` extends class `B`, then class `C` will also inherit from class `A` via class `B`. An object of the `SpotLightBulb` class *is-an* object of the class `Light`. The *is-a* relationship does not hold between peer classes: An object of the `LightBulb` class is not an object of the class `TubeLight`, and vice versa.

Whereas inheritance defines the relationship *is-a* between a superclass and its subclasses, *aggregation* defines the relationship *has-a* (also called the *whole–part* relationship) between an instance of a class and its constituents (also called *parts*). Aggregation comprises the *usage* of objects. An instance of class `Light` *has* (or *uses*) the following parts: a field to store its wattage (`noOfWatts`), a field to store whether it is on or off (`indicator`), and a `String` object to store its location (denoted by the field reference `location`). In Java, a composite object cannot contain other objects. It can store only *reference values* of its constituent objects in its fields. This relationship defines an *aggregation hierarchy* (also called *object hierarchy*) that embodies the *has-a* relationship. As explained in §1.7, p. 12, constituent objects can be shared between objects. If their lifetimes are dependent on the lifetime of the composite object, then this relationship is called *composition*, and implies strong ownership of the parts by the composite object. Inheritance and aggregation are compared in §7.13, p. 331.

The Supertype–Subtype Relationship

A class defines a *reference type*, a data type whose objects can be accessed only by references. Therefore the inheritance hierarchy can be regarded as a *type hierarchy*, embodying the *supertype–subtype relationship* between reference types. In the context of Java, the supertype–subtype relationship implies that the reference value of a subtype object can be assigned to a supertype reference, because a subtype object can be substituted for a supertype object. This assignment involves a *widening reference conversion* (§5.1, p. 145), as references are assigned *up* the inheritance hierarchy. Using the reference types in Example 7.1, the following code assigns the reference value of an object of the subtype `TubeLight` to the reference `light` of the supertype `Light`:

```
Light light = new TubeLight();                // (1) widening reference conversion
```

An implicit widening conversion takes place under assignment, as the reference value of a narrower type (subtype `TubeLight`) object is being assigned to a reference of broader type (supertype `Light`). We can now use the reference `light` to invoke those methods on the subtype object that are inherited from the supertype `Light`:

```
light.switchOn();                             // (2)
```

Note that the compiler knows about only the *declared type* (*static type*) of the reference `light`, which is `Light`, and ensures that only methods from this type can be called using the reference `light`. However, at runtime, the reference `light` will refer to an object of the subtype `TubeLight` when the call to the method `switchOn()` is executed. It is the *type of the object* that the reference refers to at runtime that determines which method is executed. The subtype object inherits the `switchOn()` method from its supertype `Light`, so this method is executed. The type of the object that the reference refers to at runtime is often called the *dynamic type* of the reference.

One might be tempted to invoke methods exclusive to the `TubeLight` subtype via the supertype reference `light`:

```
light.getTubeLength();                        // (3) Not OK.
```

This code will not work, as the compiler does not know which object the reference `light` will denote at runtime; it merely knows the declared type of the reference. As the declaration of the class `Light` does not have a method called `getTubeLength()`, this method call at (3) results in a compile-time error. As we shall see later in this chapter, eliciting subtype-specific behavior using a supertype reference requires a narrowing reference conversion with an explicit cast (§7.11, p. 320).

The rest of this chapter elaborates on various aspects of OOP. Understanding them is fundamental in understanding the consequences of the subtype–supertype relationship.

7.2 Overriding Methods

Instance Method Overriding

Under certain circumstances, a subclass can *override instance methods* that it inherits from its superclass. Overriding such a method allows the subclass to provide its *own* implementation of the method. The overridden method in the superclass is *not* inherited by the subclass. When the method is invoked on an object of the subclass, it is the method implementation in the subclass that is executed. The new method in the subclass must abide by the following rules of method overriding:

- The new method definition in the subclass must have the same *method signature*. In other words, the method name, and the types and the number of parameters, including their order, must be the same as in the overridden method of the superclass.

  Whether parameters in the overriding method should be `final` is at the discretion of the subclass (§3.7, p. 86). A method's signature does not comprise the `final` modifier of parameters, only their types and order.

- The return type of the overriding method can be a *subtype* of the return type of the overridden method (called *covariant return,* p. 273).

- The new method definition cannot *narrow* the accessibility of the method, but it can *widen* it (§4.7, p. 123).

- The new method definition can throw either all or none, or a subset of the checked exceptions (including their subclasses) that are specified in the `throws` clause of the overridden method in the superclass (§6.9, p. 253).

These requirements also apply to interfaces, where a subinterface can override abstract and default method declarations from its superinterfaces (§7.6, p. 290).

Example 7.2 illustrates overriding, overloading, and hiding of members in a class. Figure 7.2 gives an overview of the two main classes in Example 7.2. The new definition of the `energyCost()` method at (7) in the subclass `TubeLight` has the same signature and the same return type as the method at (2) in the superclass `Light`. The new definition specifies a subset of the exceptions (`ZeroHoursException`) thrown by the overridden method (the exception class `InvalidHoursException` is a superclass of `NegativeHoursException` and `ZeroHoursException`). The new definition also widens the accessibility (`public`) from what it was in the overridden definition (`protected`). The overriding method declares the parameter to be `final`, but this has no bearing in overriding the method.

Figure 7.2 *Inheritance Hierarchy for Example 7.2 and Example 7.3*

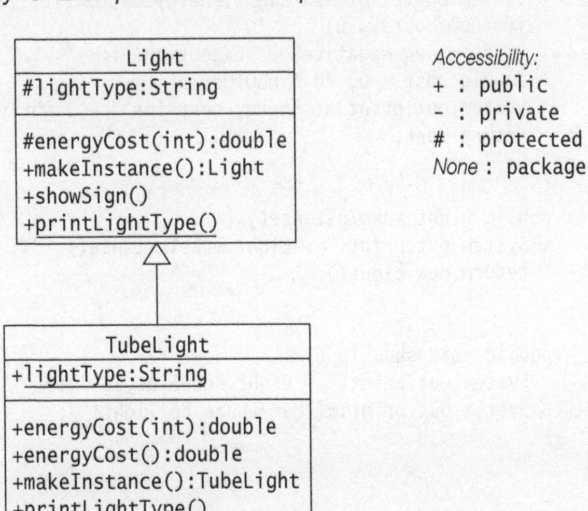

The astute reader will have noticed the `@Override` annotation preceding the method definition at (7). The compiler will now report an error if the method definition at (7) does *not* override an inherited method. The annotation helps to ensure that the method definition overrides the inherited method, rather than overloading another method silently.

Invocation of the method `energyCost()` on an object of subclass `TubeLight` using references of the subclass and the superclass at (15) and (16) results in the new definition at (7) being executed, since both references are aliases of the `TubeLight` object created at (12).

```
tubeLight.energyCost(50);                    // (15) Invokes method at (7).
light1.energyCost(50);                       // (16) Invokes method at (7).
```

Not surprisingly, the invocation of the method `energyCost()` on an object of superclass `Light`, using a reference of the superclass at (17), results in the overridden definition at (2) being executed:

```
light2.energyCost(50);                       // (17) Invokes method at (2).
```

Example 7.2 *Overriding, Overloading, and Hiding*

```
// File: Client2.java
// Exceptions
class InvalidHoursException extends Exception {}
class NegativeHoursException extends InvalidHoursException {}
class ZeroHoursException extends InvalidHoursException {}

class Light {

  protected String lightType = "Generic Light";   // (1) Instance field

  protected double energyCost(int noOfHours)      // (2) Instance method
      throws InvalidHoursException {
    System.out.print(">> Light.energyCost(int): ");
    if (noOfHours < 0)
      throw new NegativeHoursException();
    double cost = 00.20 * noOfHours;
    System.out.println("Energy cost for " + lightType + ": " + cost);
    return cost;
  }

  public Light makeInstance() {                   // (3) Instance method
    System.out.print(">> Light.makeInstance(): ");
    return new Light();
  }

  public void showSign() {                        // (4) Instance method
    System.out.print(">> Light.showSign(): ");
    System.out.println("Let there be light!");
  }
```

```
  public static void printLightType() {          // (5) Static method
    System.out.print(">> Static Light.printLightType(): ");
    System.out.println("Generic Light");
  }
}
//______________________________________________________________________
class TubeLight extends Light {

  public static String lightType = "Tube Light";  // (6) Hiding field at (1).

  @Override
  public double energyCost(final int noOfHours)   // (7) Overriding instance
      throws ZeroHoursException {                 //     method at (2).
    System.out.print(">> TubeLight.energyCost(int): ");
    if (noOfHours == 0)
      throw new ZeroHoursException();
    double cost = 00.10 * noOfHours;
    System.out.println("Energy cost for " + lightType + ": " + cost);
    return cost;
  }

  public double energyCost() {              // (8) Overloading method at (7).
    System.out.print(">> TubeLight.energyCost(): ");
    double flatrate = 20.00;
    System.out.println("Energy cost for " + lightType + ": " + flatrate);
    return flatrate;
  }

  @Override
  public TubeLight makeInstance() {      // (9) Overriding instance method at (3).
    System.out.print(">> TubeLight.makeInstance(): ");
    return new TubeLight();
  }

  public static void printLightType() { // (10) Hiding static method at (5).
    System.out.print(">> Static TubeLight.printLightType(): ");
    System.out.println(lightType);
  }
}
//______________________________________________________________________
public class Client2 {
  public static void main(String[] args)       // (11)
      throws InvalidHoursException {

    TubeLight tubeLight = new TubeLight();     // (12)
    Light     light1    = tubeLight;           // (13) Aliases.
    Light     light2    = new Light();         // (14)

    System.out.println("Invoke overridden instance method:");
    tubeLight.energyCost(50);                  // (15) Invokes method at (7).
    light1.energyCost(50);                     // (16) Invokes method at (7).
    light2.energyCost(50);                     // (17) Invokes method at (2).
```

```
        System.out.println(
            "\nInvoke overridden instance method with covariant return:");
        System.out.println(
            light2.makeInstance().getClass());    // (18) Invokes method at (3).
        System.out.println(
            tubeLight.makeInstance().getClass()); // (19) Invokes method at (9).

        System.out.println("\nAccess hidden field:");
        System.out.println(tubeLight.lightType); // (20) Accesses field at (6).
        System.out.println(light1.lightType);    // (21) Accesses field at (1).
        System.out.println(light2.lightType);    // (22) Accesses field at (1).

        System.out.println("\nInvoke hidden static method:");
        tubeLight.printLightType();               // (23) Invokes method at (10).
        light1.printLightType();                  // (24) Invokes method at (5).
        light2.printLightType();                  // (25) Invokes method at (5).

        System.out.println("\nInvoke overloaded method:");
        tubeLight.energyCost();                   // (26) Invokes method at (8).
    }
}
```

Output from the program:

```
Invoke overridden instance method:
>> TubeLight.energyCost(int): Energy cost for Tube Light: 5.0
>> TubeLight.energyCost(int): Energy cost for Tube Light: 5.0
>> Light.energyCost(int): Energy cost for Generic Light: 10.0

Invoke overridden instance method with covariant return:
>> Light.makeInstance(): class Light
>> TubeLight.makeInstance(): class TubeLight

Access hidden field:
Tube Light
Generic Light
Generic Light

Invoke hidden static method:
>> Static TubeLight.printLightType(): Tube Light
>> Static Light.printLightType(): Generic Light
>> Static Light.printLightType(): Generic Light

Invoke overloaded method:
>> TubeLight.energyCost(): Energy cost for Tube Light: 20.0
```

Here are a few more facts to note about overriding. First, a subclass must use the keyword `super` to invoke an overridden method in the superclass (p. 276).

Second, a `final` method cannot be overridden, because the modifier `final` prevents method overriding. An attempt to override a `final` method will result in a compile-time error. An `abstract` method, in contrast, requires the non-abstract subclasses to override the method, so as to provide an implementation.

Third, the accessibility modifier `private` for a method means that the method is not accessible outside the class in which it is defined; therefore, a subclass cannot override it. However, a subclass can give its own definition of such a method, which may have the same signature as the method in its superclass.

Fourth, a subclass within the same package as the superclass can override any non-`final` and non-`private` methods declared in the superclass. However, a subclass in a different package can override only the non-`final` methods that are declared as either `public` or `protected` in the superclass.

Fifth, an instance method in a subclass cannot override a `static` method in the superclass. The compiler will flag such an attempt as an error. A static method is class-specific and not part of any object, while overriding methods are invoked on behalf of objects of the subclass. However, a static method in a subclass can *hide* a `static` method in the superclass, as we shall see (p. 275). Constructors, since they are not methods, cannot be overridden.

Covariant `return` in Overriding Methods

In Example 7.2, the definition of the method `makeInstance()` at (9) overrides the method definition at (3). Note that the method signatures are the same, but the return type at (9) is a subtype of the return type at (3). The method at (9) returns an object of the subtype `TubeLight`, whereas the method at (3) returns an object of the supertype `Light`. This is an example of *covariant return*.

Depending on whether we call the method `makeInstance()` on an object of the subtype `TubeLight` or an object of the supertype `Light`, the respective method definition will be executed. The code at (18) and (19) illustrates which object is returned by the method, depending on which method definition is executed.

Note that covariant return applies only to *reference* types, not to primitive types. For example, changing the return type of the `energyCost()` method at (7) to `float` will result in a compile-time error. There is no supertype–subtype relationship between primitive types.

Overriding versus Overloading

Method overriding should not be confused with *method overloading* (§3.2, p. 52).

Method overriding always requires the same method signature (name and parameter types) and the same or covariant return types. Overloading occurs when the method names are the same, but the parameter lists differ. Therefore, to overload methods, the parameters must differ in either type, order, or number. As the return type is not a part of the method signature, just having different return types is not enough to overload methods.

Only non-`final` instance methods in the superclass that are directly accessible from the subclass using their simple name can be overridden. Both instance and static methods can be overloaded in the class they are defined in or in a subclass of their class.

Invoking an overridden method in the superclass from a subclass requires a special syntax (e.g., the keyword `super`). This is not necessary for invoking an overloaded method in the superclass from a subclass. If the right kinds of arguments are passed in the method call occurring in the subclass, the overloaded method in the superclass will be invoked. In Example 7.2, the method `energyCost()` at (2) in class `Light` is overridden in class `TubeLight` at (7) and overloaded at (8). When invoked at (26), the overloaded definition at (8) is executed.

For overloaded methods, which method implementation will be executed at runtime is determined at *compile time* (§7.10, p. 316). In contrast, for overridden methods, the method implementation to be executed is determined at *runtime* (§7.12, p. 329). Table 7.1 provides a comparison between overriding and overloading.

Table 7.1 *Overriding versus Overloading*

Comparison criteria	Overriding	Overloading
Method name	Must be the same.	Must be the same.
Argument list	Must be the same.	Must be different.
Return type	Can be the same type or a covariant type.	Can be different.
`throws` clause	Must not throw new checked exceptions. Can be restrictive about exceptions thrown.	Can be different.
Accessibility	Can make it less restrictive, but not more restrictive.	Can be different.
`final` modifier	Cannot be overridden.	Can be overloaded in the same class or in a subclass.
Declaration context	An instance method can only be overridden in a subclass.	An instance or static method can be overloaded in the same class or in a subclass.
Method call resolution	The *dynamic type* of the reference (i.e., the type of the object referenced at *runtime*) determines which method is selected for execution (§7.12, p. 329).	At compile time, the *declared type* of the reference is used to determine which method will be executed at runtime (§7.10, p. 316).

7.3 Hiding Members

Field Hiding

A subclass cannot override inherited fields of the superclass, but it can *hide* them. The subclass can define fields with the same name as in the superclass. If this is the case, the fields in the superclass cannot be accessed in the subclass by their simple names; therefore, they are not inherited by the subclass. A hidden static field can always be invoked by using the superclass name in the subclass declaration. Additionally, the keyword `super` can be used in non-static code in the subclass declaration to access hidden static fields (§7.4, p. 276).

The following distinction between invoking instance methods on an object and accessing fields of an object must be noted. When an instance method is invoked on an object using a reference, it is the *dynamic type* of the reference (i.e., *the type of the current object* denoted by the reference at runtime), not the declared type of the reference, that determines which method implementation will be executed. In Example 7.2 at (15), (16), and (17), this is evident from invoking the overridden method `energyCost()`: The method from the class corresponding to the current object is executed, regardless of the declared reference type. When a field of an object is accessed using a reference, it is the *declared type* of the reference, not the type of the current object denoted by the reference, that determines which field will actually be accessed. In Example 7.2 at (20), (21), and (22), this is evident from accessing the hidden field `lightType`: The field accessed is the one declared in the class corresponding to the declared reference type, regardless of the object denoted by the reference at runtime.

In contrast to method overriding, where an instance method cannot override a static method, there are no such restrictions on the hiding of fields. The field `lightType` is `static` in the subclass, but not in the superclass. The declared type of the fields need not be the same either—only the field name matters in the hiding of fields.

Static Method Hiding

A static method in a subclass *cannot* override an instance method from the superclass, but it can *hide* a *static* method from the superclass if the exact requirements for overriding instance methods are fulfilled (§7.2, p. 268). A hidden superclass static method is not inherited. The compiler will flag the code as containing an error if the signatures are the same, but the other requirements regarding return type, `throws` clause, and accessibility are not met. If the signatures are different, the method name is overloaded, not hidden.

A call to a `static` or `final` method is bound to a method implementation at compile time (`private` methods are implicitly `final`). Example 7.2 illustrates invocation of static methods. Analogous to accessing fields, the static method invoked in (23),

(24), and (25) is determined by the *declared type* of the reference. In (23), the declared reference type is `TubeLight`; therefore, the static method `printLightType()` at (10) in this class is invoked. In (24) and (25), the declared reference type is `Light`, and the hidden static method `printLightType()` at (5) in that class is invoked. This is borne out by the output from the program.

Analogous to hidden fields, a hidden static method can always be invoked by using the superclass name or by using the keyword `super` in non-static code in the subclass declaration (§7.4, p. 276).

Table 7.2 summarizes the consequences when a subclass method has the same signature as a method in the superclass.

Table 7.2 *Same Signature for Subclass and Superclass Method*

Subclass method has the same signature as the superclass method	Instance method in superclass	Static method in superclass
Instance method in subclass	Overriding	Compile-time error
Static method in subclass	Compile-time error	Hiding

7.4 The Object Reference `super`

The `this` reference can be used in non-static code to refer to the current object (§3.2, p. 50). The keyword `super`, in contrast, can be used in non-static code to access fields and invoke methods from the superclass (Table 4.1, p. 115). The keyword `super` provides a reference to the current object as an instance of its superclass. In method invocations with `super`, the method from the superclass is invoked regardless of what the actual type of the current object is or whether the current class overrides the method. This approach is typically used to invoke methods that are overridden, and to access members that are hidden in the subclass. Unlike the `this` keyword, the `super` keyword cannot be used as an ordinary reference. For example, it cannot be assigned to other references or cast to other reference types.

Example 7.3 uses the classes `Light` and `TubeLight` from Example 7.2, which are also shown in Figure 7.2. In Example 7.3, the class `NeonLight` extends the class `TubeLight`. The declaration of the method `demonstrate()` at (11) in the class `NeonLight` makes use of the `super` keyword to access members higher up in its inheritance hierarchy. This is the case when the `showSign()` method is invoked at (12). This method is defined at (4) in the class `Light`, rather than in the immediate superclass `TubeLight` of the subclass `NeonLight`. The overridden method `energyCost()` at (7) and its overloaded version at (8) in the class `TubeLight` are invoked, using the object reference `super` at (13) and (14), respectively.

The superclass `Light` has a field named `lightType` and a method named `energyCost` defined at (1) and (2), respectively. One might be tempted to use the syntax super.super.energyCost(20) in the subclass NeonLight to invoke this method, but this is not a valid construct. One might also be tempted to cast the this reference to the class Light and try again, as shown at (15). The output shows that the method energyCost() at (7) in the class TubeLight was executed, not the one from the class Light. The reason is that a cast simply changes the type of the reference (in this case to Light), not the class of the object (which is still NeonLight). Method invocation is determined by the class of the current object, resulting in the inherited method energyCost() in the class TubeLight being executed. There is no way to invoke the method energyCost() in the class Light from the subclass NeonLight, without declaring a reference of the type Light.

At (16), the keyword super is used to access the field lightType at (6) in the class TubeLight, but is redundant in this case. At (17), the field lightType from the class Light is accessed successfully by casting the this reference, because it is the type of the reference that determines which field is accessed. From non-static code in a subclass, it is possible to directly access fields in a class higher up in the inheritance hierarchy by casting the this reference. However, it is futile to cast the this reference to invoke instance methods in a class higher up in the inheritance hierarchy, as illustrated earlier for the overridden method energyCost().

Finally, the calls to the static methods at (18) and (19) using the super and this references, respectively, exhibit runtime behavior analogous to accessing fields, as discussed previously.

Example 7.3 *Using the* super *Keyword*

```
// File: Client3.java
//Exceptions
class InvalidHoursException extends Exception {}
class NegativeHoursException extends InvalidHoursException {}
class ZeroHoursException extends InvalidHoursException {}

class Light {

  protected String lightType = "Generic Light";   // (1) Instance field

  protected double energyCost(int noOfHours)      // (2) Instance method
      throws InvalidHoursException {
    System.out.print(">> Light.energyCost(int): ");
    if (noOfHours < 0)
      throw new NegativeHoursException();
    double cost = 00.20 * noOfHours;
    System.out.println("Energy cost for " + lightType + ": " + cost);
    return cost;
  }

  public Light makeInstance() {                   // (3) Instance method
    System.out.print(">> Light.makeInstance(): ");
    return new Light();
  }
```

```
  public void showSign() {                          // (4) Instance method
    System.out.print(">> Light.showSign(): ");
    System.out.println("Let there be light!");
  }

  public static void printLightType() {             // (5) Static method
    System.out.print(">> Static Light.printLightType(): ");
    System.out.println("Generic Light");
  }
}
//______________________________________________________________________
class TubeLight extends Light {

  public static String lightType = "Tube Light";  // (6) Hiding field at (1).

  @Override
  public double energyCost(final int noOfHours)   // (7) Overriding instance
      throws ZeroHoursException {                 //     method at (2).
    System.out.print(">> TubeLight.energyCost(int): ");
    if (noOfHours == 0)
      throw new ZeroHoursException();
    double cost = 00.10 * noOfHours;
    System.out.println("Energy cost for " + lightType + ": " + cost);
    return cost;
  }

  public double energyCost() {            // (8) Overloading method at (7).
    System.out.print(">> TubeLight.energyCost(): ");
    double flatrate = 20.00;
    System.out.println("Energy cost for " + lightType + ": " + flatrate);
    return flatrate;
  }

  @Override
  public TubeLight makeInstance() {  // (9) Overriding instance method at (3).
    System.out.print(">> TubeLight.makeInstance(): ");
    return new TubeLight();
  }

  public static void printLightType() { // (10) Hiding static method at (5).
    System.out.print(">> Static TubeLight.printLightType(): ");
    System.out.println(lightType);
  }
}
//______________________________________________________________________
class NeonLight extends TubeLight {
  // ...
  public void demonstrate()                             // (11)
      throws InvalidHoursException {
    super.showSign();                                   // (12) Invokes method at (4)
    super.energyCost(50);                               // (13) Invokes method at (7)
    super.energyCost();                                 // (14) Invokes method at (8)
```

```
        ((Light) this).energyCost(50);                // (15) Invokes method at (7)

        System.out.println(super.lightType);          // (16) Accesses field at (6)
        System.out.println(((Light) this).lightType); // (17) Accesses field at (1)

        super.printLightType();                       // (18) Invokes method at (10)
        ((Light) this).printLightType();              // (19) Invokes method at (5)
    }
}
//______________________________________________________________________________
public class Client3 {
    public static void main(String[] args)
        throws InvalidHoursException {
        NeonLight neonRef = new NeonLight();
        neonRef.demonstrate();
    }
}
```

Output from the program:

```
>> Light.showSign(): Let there be light!
>> TubeLight.energyCost(int): Energy cost for Tube Light: 5.0
>> TubeLight.energyCost(): Energy cost for Tube Light: 20.0
>> TubeLight.energyCost(int): Energy cost for Tube Light: 5.0
Tube Light
Generic Light
>> Static TubeLight.printLightType(): Tube Light
>> Static Light.printLightType(): Generic Light
```

Review Questions

7.1 Which of the following statements are true?

Select the two correct answers.

(a) In Java, the `extends` clause is used to specify the inheritance relationship.
(b) The subclass of a non-`abstract` class can be declared as `abstract`.
(c) All members of the superclass are inherited by the subclass.
(d) A `final` class can be `abstract`.
(e) A class in which all the members are declared `private` cannot be declared as `public`.

7.2 Which of the following statements are true?

Select the two correct answers.

(a) A class can be extended by only one class.
(b) Every Java object has a `public` method named `equals`.
(c) Every Java object has a `public` method named `length`.
(d) A class can extend any number of classes.
(e) A non-`final` class can be extended by any number of classes.

7.3 Given the following classes and declarations, which statements are true?

```
// Classes
class Foo {
  private int i;
  public void f() { /* ... */ }
  public void g() { /* ... */ }
}

class Bar extends Foo {
  public int j;
  public void g() { /* ... */ }
}

// Declarations:
  Foo a = new Bar();
  Bar b = new Bar();
```

Select the three correct answers.

(a) The `Bar` class is a subclass of `Foo`.
(b) The statement `b.f();` is legal.
(c) The statement `a.j = 5;` is legal.
(d) The statement `a.g();` is legal.
(e) The statement `b.i = 3;` is legal.

7.4 Given classes `A`, `B`, and `C`, where `B` extends `A`, and `C` extends `B`, and where all classes implement the instance method `void doIt()`, how can the `doIt()` method in `A` be called from an instance method in `C`?

Select the one correct answer.

(a) `doIt();`
(b) `super.doIt();`
(c) `super.super.doIt();`
(d) `this.super.doIt();`
(e) `A.this.doIt();`
(f) `((A) this).doIt();`
(g) It is not possible.

7.5 What would be the result of compiling and running the following program?

```
public class UserClass {
  public static void main(String[] args) {
    B b = new C();
    System.out.println(b.max(13, 29));
  }
}

class A {
  int max(int x, int y) { if (x>y) return x; else return y; }
}

class B extends A {
  int max(int x, int y) { return super.max(y, x) - 10; }
}
```

```
class C extends B {
  int max(int x, int y) { return super.max(x+10, y+10); }
}
```

Select the one correct answer.

(a) The code will fail to compile.
(b) The code will compile, but throw an exception at runtime.
(c) The code will compile, and print 13 at runtime.
(d) The code will compile, and print 23 at runtime.
(e) The code will compile, and print 29 at runtime.
(f) The code will compile, and print 39 at runtime.

7.6 Which is the simplest expression that can be inserted at (1), so that the program prints the value of the `text` field from the `Message` class?

```
// File: MyClass.java
class Message {
  // The message that should be printed:
  String text = "Hello, world!";
}
class MySuperclass {
  Message msg = new Message();
}

public class MyClass extends MySuperclass {
  public static void main(String[] args) {
    MyClass object = new MyClass();
    object.print();
  }

  public void print() {
    System.out.println( /* (1) INSERT THE SIMPLEST EXPRESSION HERE */ );
  }
}
```

Select the one correct answer.

(a) `text`
(b) `Message.text`
(c) `msg.text`
(d) `this.msg.text`
(e) `super.msg.text`
(f) `this.super.msg.text`

7.7 What would be the result of compiling and running the following program?

```
class Vehicle {
  static public String getModelName() { return "Volvo"; }
  public long getRegNo() { return 12345; }
}
```

```
class Car extends Vehicle {
  static public String getModelName() { return "Toyota"; }
  public long getRegNo() { return 54321; }
}

public class TakeARide {
  public static void main(String[] args) {
    Car c = new Car();
    Vehicle v = c;

    System.out.println("|" + v.getModelName() + "|" + c.getModelName() +
                       "|" + v.getRegNo()     + "|" + c.getRegNo() + "|");
  }
}
```

Select the one correct answer.

(a) The code will fail to compile.
(b) The code will compile, and print `|Toyota|Volvo|12345|54321|` at runtime.
(c) The code will compile, and print `|Volvo|Toyota|12345|54321|` at runtime.
(d) The code will compile, and print `|Toyota|Toyota|12345|12345|` at runtime.
(e) The code will compile, and print `|Volvo|Volvo|12345|54321|` at runtime.
(f) The code will compile, and print `|Toyota|Toyota|12345|12345|` at runtime.
(g) The code will compile, and print `|Volvo|Toyota|54321|54321|` at runtime.

7.5 Chaining Constructors Using `this()` and `super()`

Constructors are discussed in §3.3, p. 53. Other uses of the keywords `this` and `super` can be found in §7.2, p. 268.

The `this()` Constructor Call

Constructors cannot be inherited or overridden. They can be overloaded, but only in the same class. Since a constructor always has the same name as the class, each parameter list must be different when defining more than one constructor for a class. In Example 7.4, the class `Light` has three overloaded constructors. In the constructor at (3), the `this` reference is used to access the fields shadowed by the parameters. In the `main()` method at (4), the appropriate constructor is invoked depending on the arguments in the constructor call, as illustrated by the program output.

Example 7.4 *Constructor Overloading*

```
// File: DemoConstructorCall.java
class Light {
  // Fields:
  private int     noOfWatts;       // wattage
  private boolean indicator;       // on or off
  private String  location;        // placement
```

```
  // Constructors:
  Light() {                                    // (1) No-argument constructor
    noOfWatts = 0;
    indicator = false;
    location  = "X";
    System.out.println("Returning from no-argument constructor no. 1.");
  }
  Light(int watts, boolean onOffState) {                       // (2)
    noOfWatts = watts;
    indicator = onOffState;
    location  = "X";
    System.out.println("Returning from constructor no. 2.");
  }
  Light(int noOfWatts, boolean indicator, String location) {  // (3)
    this.noOfWatts = noOfWatts;
    this.indicator = indicator;
    this.location  = location;
    System.out.println("Returning from constructor no. 3.");
  }
}
//________________________________________________________________________
public class DemoConstructorCall {
  public static void main(String[] args) {                     // (4)
    System.out.println("Creating Light object no. 1.");
    Light light1 = new Light();
    System.out.println("Creating Light object no. 2.");
    Light light2 = new Light(250, true);
    System.out.println("Creating Light object no. 3.");
    Light light3 = new Light(250, true, "attic");
  }
}
```

Output from the program:

```
Creating Light object no. 1.
Returning from no-argument constructor no. 1.
Creating Light object no. 2.
Returning from constructor no. 2.
Creating Light object no. 3.
Returning from constructor no. 3.
```

Example 7.5 illustrates the use of the `this()` construct, which is used to implement *local chaining* of constructors in the class when an instance of the class is created. The first two constructors at (1) and (2) from Example 7.4 have been rewritten using the `this()` construct in Example 7.5 at (1) and (2), respectively. The `this()` construct can be regarded as being locally overloaded, since its parameters (and hence its signature) can vary, as shown in the body of the constructors at (1) and (2). The `this()` call invokes the local constructor with the corresponding parameter list. In the `main()` method at (4), the appropriate constructor is invoked depending on the arguments in the constructor call when each of the three `Light` objects are created. Calling the no-argument constructor at (1) to create a `Light` object results in the constructors at

(2) and (3) being executed as well. This is confirmed by the output from the program. In this case, the output shows that the constructor at (3) completed first, followed by the constructor at (2), and finally by the no-argument constructor at (1) that was called first. Bearing in mind the definition of the constructors, the constructors are invoked in the *reverse* order; that is, invocation of the no-argument constructor immediately leads to invocation of the constructor at (2) by the call `this(0, false)`, and its invocation leads to the constructor at (3) being called immediately by the call `this(watt, ind, "X")`, with the completion of the execution in the reverse order of their invocation. Similarly, calling the constructor at (2) to create an instance of the `Light` class results in the constructor at (3) being executed as well.

Java requires that any `this()` call must occur as the *first* statement in a constructor. The `this()` call can be followed by any other relevant code. This restriction is due to Java's handling of constructor invocation in the superclass when an object of the subclass is created. This mechanism is explained in the next subsection.

Example 7.5 *The* `this()` *Constructor Call*

```
// File: DemoThisCall.java
class Light {
  // Fields:
  private int     noOfWatts;
  private boolean indicator;
  private String  location;

  // Constructors:
  Light() {                                    // (1) No-argument constructor
    this(0, false);
    System.out.println("Returning from no-argument constructor no. 1.");
  }
  Light(int watt, boolean ind) {                                     // (2)
    this(watt, ind, "X");
    System.out.println("Returning from constructor no. 2.");
  }
  Light(int noOfWatts, boolean indicator, String location) { // (3)
    this.noOfWatts = noOfWatts;
    this.indicator = indicator;
    this.location  = location;
    System.out.println("Returning from constructor no. 3.");
  }
}
//______________________________________________________________________
public class DemoThisCall {
  public static void main(String[] args) {                           // (4)
    System.out.println("Creating Light object no. 1.");
    Light light1 = new Light();                                      // (5)
    System.out.println("Creating Light object no. 2.");
    Light light2 = new Light(250, true);                             // (6)
    System.out.println("Creating Light object no. 3.");
    Light light3 = new Light(250, true, "attic");                    // (7)
  }
}
```

Output from the program:

```
Creating Light object no. 1.
Returning from constructor no. 3.
Returning from constructor no. 2.
Returning from no-argument constructor no. 1.
Creating Light object no. 2.
Returning from constructor no. 3.
Returning from constructor no. 2.
Creating Light object no. 3.
Returning from constructor no. 3.
```

The `super()` Constructor Call

The `super()` construct is used in a subclass constructor to invoke a constructor in the *immediate* superclass. This allows the subclass to influence the initialization of its inherited state when an object of the subclass is created. A `super()` call in the constructor of a subclass will result in the execution of the relevant constructor from the superclass, based on the signature of the call. Since the superclass name is known in the subclass declaration, the compiler can determine the superclass constructor invoked from the signature of the parameter list.

A constructor in a subclass can access the class's inherited members by their simple names. The keyword `super` can also be used in a subclass constructor to access inherited members via its superclass. One might be tempted to use the `super` keyword in a constructor to specify initial values for inherited fields. However, the `super()` construct provides a better solution to initialize the inherited state.

In Example 7.6, the constructor at (3) of the class `Light` has a `super()` call (with no arguments) at (4). Although the constructor is not strictly necessary, as the compiler will insert one—as explained later—it is included here for expositional purposes. The constructor at (6) of the class `TubeLight` has a `super()` call (with three arguments) at (7). This `super()` call will match the constructor at (3) of the superclass `Light`. This is evident from the program output.

Example 7.6 *The* `super()` *Constructor Call*

```
// File: Chaining.java
class Light {
  // Fields:
  private int     noOfWatts;
  private boolean indicator;
  private String  location;

  // Constructors:
  Light() {                                 // (1) No-argument constructor
    this(0, false);
    System.out.println(
    "Returning from no-argument constructor no. 1 in class Light");
  }
```

```
  Light(int watt, boolean ind) {                            // (2)
    this(watt, ind, "X");
    System.out.println(
    "Returning from constructor no. 2 in class Light");
  }
  Light(int noOfWatts, boolean indicator, String location) { // (3)
    super();                                                  // (4)
    this.noOfWatts = noOfWatts;
    this.indicator = indicator;
    this.location  = location;
    System.out.println(
        "Returning from constructor no. 3 in class Light");
  }
}
//____________________________________________________________________
class TubeLight extends Light {
  // Instance variables:
  private int tubeLength;
  private int colorNo;

  // Constructors:
  TubeLight(int tubeLength, int colorNo) {                  // (5)
    this(tubeLength, colorNo, 100, true, "Unknown");
    System.out.println(
           "Returning from constructor no. 1 in class TubeLight");
  }
  TubeLight(int tubeLength, int colorNo, int noOfWatts,
            boolean indicator, String location) {           // (6)
    super(noOfWatts, indicator, location);                  // (7)
    this.tubeLength = tubeLength;
    this.colorNo    = colorNo;
    System.out.println(
           "Returning from constructor no. 2 in class TubeLight");
  }
}
//____________________________________________________________________
public class Chaining {
  public static void main(String[] args) {
    System.out.println("Creating a TubeLight object.");
    TubeLight tubeLightRef = new TubeLight(20, 5);          // (8)
  }
}
```

Output from the program:

```
Creating a TubeLight object.
Returning from constructor no. 3 in class Light
Returning from constructor no. 2 in class TubeLight
Returning from constructor no. 1 in class TubeLight
```

The super() construct has the same restrictions as the this() construct: If used, the super() call must occur as the *first* statement in a constructor, and it can only be used in a constructor declaration. This implies that this() and super() calls cannot both occur in the same constructor. The `this()` construct is used to *chain* constructors in the *same* class. The constructor at the end of such a chain can invoke a superclass constructor using the `super()` construct. Just as the `this()` construct leads to chaining of constructors in the same class, so the `super()` construct leads to chaining of subclass constructors to superclass constructors. This chaining behavior guarantees that all superclass constructors are called, starting with the constructor of the class being instantiated, all the way to the top of the inheritance hierarchy, which is always the `Object` class. Note that the body of the constructor is executed in the reverse order to the call order, as the `super()` call can occur only as the first statement in a constructor. This order of execution ensures that the constructor from the `Object` class is completed first, followed by the constructors in the other classes down to the class being instantiated in the inheritance hierarchy. It is called (subclass–superclass) *constructor chaining*. The output from Example 7.6 clearly illustrates this chain of events when an object of the class `TubeLight` is created.

If a constructor at the end of a `this()` chain (which may not be a chain at all if no `this()` call is invoked) does not have an explicit call to `super()`, the call `super()` (without the parameters) is implicitly inserted by the compiler to invoke the no-argument constructor of the superclass. In other words, if a constructor has neither a `this()` call nor a `super()` call as its first statement, the compiler inserts a `super()` call to the no-argument constructor in the superclass. The code

```
class A {
  A() {}                 // No-argument constructor.
  // ...
}
class B extends A {   // No constructors.
  // ...
}
```

is equivalent to

```
class A {
  A() { super(); }    // (1) Call to no-argument superclass constructor inserted.
  // ...
}
class B extends A {
  B() { super(); }    // (2) Default constructor inserted.
  // ...
}
```

where the compiler inserts a `super()` call in the no-argument constructor for class `A` at (1) and inserts the default constructor for class `B` at (2). The `super()` call at (2) will result in a call to the no-argument constructor in `B` at (1), and the `super()` call at (1) will result in a call to the no-argument constructor in the superclass of `A`—that is, the `Object` class.

If a superclass defines just non-zero argument constructors (i.e., only constructors with parameters), its subclasses cannot rely on the implicit `super()` call being inserted. This will be flagged as a compile-time error. The subclasses must then explicitly call a superclass constructor, using the `super()` construct with the right arguments.

```
class NeonLight extends TubeLight {
  // Field
  String sign;

  NeonLight() {                               // (1)
    super(10, 2, 100, true, "Roof-top");      // (2) Cannot be commented out.
    sign = "All will be revealed!";
  }
  // ...
}
```

The preceding declaration of the subclass `NeonLight` provides a no-argument constructor at (1). The call of the constructor at (2) in the superclass `TubeLight` cannot be omitted. If it is omitted, any insertion of a `super()` call (with no arguments) in this constructor will try to match a no-argument constructor in the superclass `TubeLight`, which provides only non-zero argument constructors. The class `NeonLight` will not compile unless an explicit valid `super()` call is inserted at (2).

If the superclass provides just non-zero argument constructors (i.e., it does not have a no-argument constructor), this has implications for its subclasses. A subclass that relies on its default constructor will fail to compile, because the default constructor of the subclass will attempt to call the (nonexistent) no-argument constructor in the superclass. A constructor in a subclass must explicitly use the `super()` call, with the appropriate arguments, to invoke a non-zero argument constructor in the superclass. This call is necessary because the constructor in the subclass cannot rely on an implicit `super()` call to the no-argument constructor in the superclass.

Review Questions

7.8 Which constructors can be inserted at (1) in `MySub` without causing a compile-time error?

```
class MySuper {
  int number;
  MySuper(int i) { number = i; }
}

class MySub extends MySuper {
  int count;
  MySub(int count, int num) {
    super(num);
    this.count = count;
  }

  // (1) INSERT CONSTRUCTOR HERE
}
```

Select the one correct answer.

(a) `MySub() {}`

(b) `MySub(int count) { this.count = count; }`

(c) `MySub(int count) { super(); this.count = count; }`
(d) `MySub(int count) { this.count = count; super(count); }`
(e) `MySub(int count) { this(count, count); }`
(f) `MySub(int count) { super(count); this(count, 0); }`

7.9 Which of the following statements is true?

Select the one correct answer.

(a) A `super()` or `this()` call must always be provided explicitly as the first statement in the body of a constructor.
(b) If both a subclass and its superclass do not have any declared constructors, the implicit default constructor of the subclass will call `super()` when run.
(c) If neither `super()` nor `this()` is specified as the first statement in the body of a constructor, `this()` will implicitly be inserted as the first statement.
(d) If `super()` is the first statement in the body of a constructor, `this()` can be declared as the second statement.
(e) Calling `super()` as the first statement in the body of a constructor of a subclass will always work, since all superclasses have a default constructor.

7.10 What will the following program print when run?

```
public class MyClass {
  public static void main(String[] args) {
    B b = new B("Test");
  }
}

class A {
  A() { this("1", "2"); }

  A(String s, String t) { this(s + t); }

  A(String s) { System.out.println(s); }
}

class B extends A {
  B(String s) { System.out.println(s); }

  B(String s, String t) { this(t + s + "3"); }

  B() { super("4"); };
}
```

Select the one correct answer.

(a) It will just print `Test`.
(b) It will print `Test` followed by `Test`.
(c) It will print `123` followed by `Test`.
(d) It will print `12` followed by `Test`.
(e) It will print `4` followed by `Test`.

7.6 Interfaces

Extending classes using *single implementation inheritance* creates new class types. A superclass reference can refer to objects of its own type and its subclasses strictly according to the inheritance hierarchy. Because this relationship is linear, it rules out *multiple implementation inheritance*, in which a subclass inherits from more than one superclass. Instead Java provides *interfaces*, which not only allow new named reference types to be introduced, but also permit *multiple interface inheritance*.

Defining Interfaces

A top-level interface has the following simplified syntax, which will suffice for the purposes of this book:

```
accessibility_modifier interface interface_name
                              extends_interface_clause // Interface header
{ // Interface body
  abstract_method_declarations
  default_method_declarations
  static_method_declarations
  constant_declarations
}
```

In the interface header, the name of the interface is preceded by the keyword `interface`. The interface name can also include a list of *formal type parameters* for declaring a generic interface. In addition, the interface header can specify the following information:

- The *accessibility modifier* must be `public`, and the lack of an accessibility modifier implies package accessibility, as one would expect (§4.5, p. 118).
- The *extends interface clause* specifies a comma-separated list of any superinterfaces that the interface extends (p. 294).

The interface body can contain *member declarations* that include any of the following:

- *Abstract method declarations* (p. 291)
- *Default method declarations* (p. 297)
- *Static method declarations* (p. 300)
- *Constant declarations* (p. 302)

An interface is `abstract` by definition, which means that it cannot be instantiated. Declaring an interface as `abstract` is superfluous and seldom done in practice. It is the only non-accessibility modifier that can be specified for a top-level interface (apart from the keyword `strictfp`).

The member declarations can appear in any order in the interface body, which can be empty. Since interfaces are meant to be implemented by classes, interface members implicitly have `public` accessibility and the `public` modifier can be omitted. The following declaration is an example of a bare-bones interface that has an empty body:

```
interface Playable { }
```

Interfaces with empty bodies can be used as *markers* to *tag* classes as having a certain property or behavior. Such interfaces are also called *ability* interfaces. The Java SE platform API provides several examples of such marker interfaces—namely, `java.lang.Cloneable`, `java.io.Serializable`, and `java.util.EventListener`.

Abstract Methods in Interfaces

An interface defines a *contract* by specifying a set of abstract and default method declarations, but provides implementations only for the default methods—not for the abstract methods. The abstract methods in an interface are all implicitly `abstract` and `public` by virtue of their definitions. Only the modifiers `abstract` and `public` are allowed, but these are invariably omitted. An abstract method declaration has the following simple form in a top-level interface:

return_type method_name (*formal_parameter_list*) *throws_clause*;

An abstract method declaration is essentially a method header terminated by a semicolon (`;`). Note that an abstract method is an *instance method* whose implementation will be provided by a class that implements the interface in which the abstract method is declared. The *throws clause* is discussed in §6.9, p. 251.

The interface `Playable` shown next declares an abstract method `startPlaying()`. That it is `public` and `abstract` is implicitly implied.

```
interface Playable {
  void startPlaying();        // Abstract method: no implementation
}
```

An interface that has no direct superinterfaces implicitly declares a public abstract method for each public instance method in the `java.lang.Object` class.

In contrast to the syntax of abstract methods in top-level interfaces, abstract methods in top-level classes must be explicitly specified with the keyword `abstract`, and can have `public`, `protected`, and package accessibility (§4.8, p. 136).

Functional interfaces, meaning interfaces with a single abstract method, are discussed together with lambda expressions in §10.2, p. 442.

The rest of this chapter provides numerous examples of using interfaces.

Implementing Interfaces

A class can implement, wholly or partially, zero or more interfaces. A class specifies the interfaces it implements as a comma-separated list of unique interface names in an `implements` clause in the class header. The interface methods must all have `public` accessibility when implemented in the class (or its subclasses). A class can neither narrow the accessibility of an interface method nor specify new exceptions in the method's `throws` clause, as attempting to do so would amount to altering the interface's contract, which is illegal. The criteria for overriding methods also apply when implementing abstract methods (§7.2, p. 268).

A class can provide implementations of methods declared in an interface. To reap the benefits of interfaces, however, the class must also specify the interface name in its `implements` clause.

In Example 7.7, the class `StackImpl` implements the interface `IStack`. It both specifies the interface name using the `implements` clause in its class header at (2) and provides the implementation for the abstract methods in the interface at (3) and (4). Changing the `public` accessibility of these methods in the class will result in a compile-time error, as this would narrow their accessibility.

Example 7.7 *Implementing Interfaces*

```
// File: RetailSeller.java
interface IStack {                                                    // (1)
  void   push(Object item);
  Object pop();
}
//________________________________________________________________________
class StackImpl implements IStack {                                   // (2)
  protected Object[] stackArray;
  protected int      tos;  // top of stack

  public StackImpl(int capacity) {
    stackArray = new Object[capacity];
    tos        = -1;
  }

  @Override
  public void push(Object item) { stackArray[++tos] = item; }         // (3)

  @Override
  public Object pop() {                                               // (4)
    Object objRef = stackArray[tos];
    stackArray[tos] = null;
    tos--;
    return objRef;
  }

  public Object peek() { return stackArray[tos]; }
}
//________________________________________________________________________
interface ISafeStack extends IStack {                                 // (5)
  boolean isEmpty();
  boolean isFull();
}
//________________________________________________________________________
```

```
class SafeStackImpl extends StackImpl implements ISafeStack {      // (6)

  public SafeStackImpl(int capacity) { super(capacity); }
  @Override public boolean isEmpty() { return tos < 0; }                   // (7)
  @Override public boolean isFull()  { return tos >= stackArray.length-1; }// (8)
}
//______________________________________________________________________________
public class StackUser {

  public static void main(String[] args) {                           // (9)
    SafeStackImpl safeStackRef  = new SafeStackImpl(10);
    StackImpl     stackRef      = safeStackRef;
    ISafeStack    isafeStackRef = safeStackRef;
    IStack        istackRef     = safeStackRef;
    Object        objRef        = safeStackRef;

    safeStackRef.push("Dollars");                                     // (10)
    stackRef.push("Kroner");
    System.out.println(isafeStackRef.pop());
    System.out.println(istackRef.pop());
    System.out.println(objRef.getClass());
  }
}
```

Output from the program:

```
Kroner
Dollars
class SafeStackImpl
```

A class can choose to implement only some of the abstract methods of its interfaces (i.e., give a partial implementation of its interfaces). The class must then be declared as `abstract` (§4.6, p. 120). Note that abstract methods cannot be declared as `static`, because they comprise the contract fulfilled by the *objects* of the class implementing the interface. Abstract methods are always implemented as instance methods.

The interfaces that a class implements and the classes that it extends (directly or indirectly) are called *supertypes* of the class. Conversely, the class is a *subtype* of its supertypes. Classes implementing interfaces introduce multiple interface inheritance into their implementation inheritance hierarchy. Even so, regardless of how many interfaces a class implements directly or indirectly, it provides just a single implementation of any abstract method declared in multiple interfaces.

Single implementation of an abstract method is illustrated by the following code, where the `Worker` class at (5) provides only one implementation of the `doIt()` method that is declared in both interfaces, at (1) and (2). The class `Worker` fulfills the contract for both interfaces, as the `doIt()` method declarations at (1) and (2) have the same method signature and return type. However, the class `Combined` at (3) declares that it implements the two interfaces, but does not provide any implementation of the `doIt()` method; consequently, it must be declared as `abstract`.

```
interface IA { int doIt(); }                          // (1)

interface IB { int doIt(); }                          // (2)

abstract class Combined implements IA, IB { }         // (3)

public class Worker implements IA, IB {               // (4)
  @Override
  public int doIt() { return 0; }                     // (5)
}
```

If the `doIt()` methods in the two interfaces at (1) and (2) had the same signatures but different return types, the `Worker` class would not be able to implement both interfaces. This is illustrated by the next code snippet. The `doIt()` methods at (1) and (2) have the same signature, but different return types. The `Worker` class provides two implementations of the `doIt()` method at (5) and (6), which results in compile-time errors, because a class cannot have two methods with the same signature but different return types. Removing either implementation from the `Worker` class will be flagged as a compile-time error, because the `Worker` class will not be implementing both interfaces. There is no way the `Worker` class can implement both interfaces, given the declarations shown in the code. In addition, the `abstract` class `Combined` at (3) will not compile, because it will be inheriting two methods with conflicting abstract method declarations. In fact, the compiler complains of duplicate methods.

```
interface IA { int doIt(); }                                // (1)

interface IB { double doIt(); }                             // (2)

abstract class Combined implements IA, IB { }               // (3) Compile-time error.

public class LameWorker implements IA, IB {                 // (4)
  @Override
  public int doIt() { return 0; }                           // (5) Compile-time error.
  @Override
  public double doIt() {                                    // (6) Compile-time error.
    System.out.println("Sorry!");
    return = 0.0;
  }
}
```

Extending Interfaces

An interface can extend other interfaces, using the `extends` clause. Unlike when extending classes, an interface can extend several interfaces. The interfaces extended by an interface (directly or indirectly) are called *superinterfaces*. Conversely, the interface is a *subinterface* of its superinterfaces. Since interfaces define new reference types, superinterfaces and subinterfaces are also supertypes and subtypes, respectively.

A subinterface inherits from its superinterfaces, all members of those superinterfaces, *except* for the following:

- Abstract or default methods that it overrides (p. 297)
- Any static methods declared in its superinterfaces (p. 300)
- Any constants that it hides (p. 302)

Barring any conflicts, a subinterface inherits abstract and default method declarations that are not overridden, as well as constants that it does not hide in its superinterfaces. Abstract, static, and default method declarations can also be overloaded, analogous to method overloading in classes.

Example 7.7 illustrates the relationships between classes and interfaces. In Example 7.7, the interface `ISafeStack` extends the interface `IStack` at (5). The class `SafeStackImpl` both extends the `StackImpl` class and implements the `ISafeStack` interface at (6). Both the implementation and the interface inheritance hierarchies for classes and interfaces defined in Example 7.7 are shown in Figure 7.3.

Figure 7.3 *Inheritance Hierarchies*

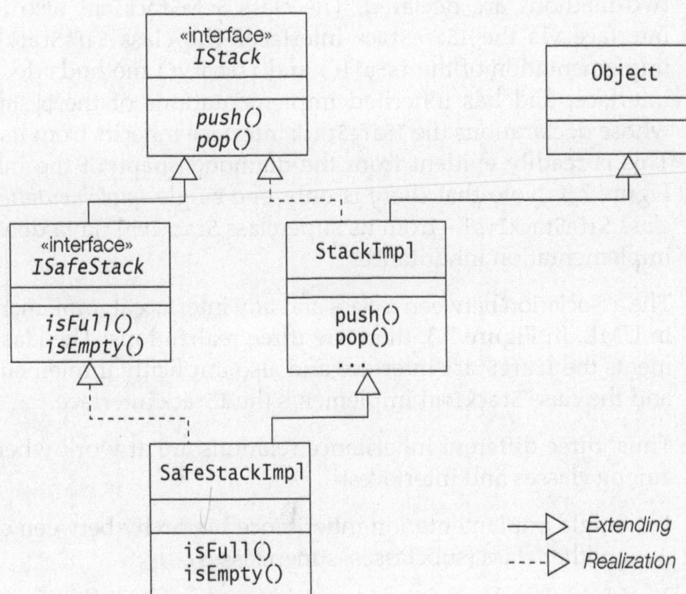

In UML, an interface resembles a class. One way to differentiate between them is to use an *«interface»* stereotype, as in Figure 7.3. Interface inheritance is depicted in a similar manner to implementation inheritance, but is indicated by an unbroken inheritance arrow.

Thinking in terms of types, every reference type in Java is a subtype of the `Object` class. In turn, any interface type is also a subtype of the `Object` class, but it does *not* inherit from the `Object` class. An interface that has *no direct superinterfaces implicitly declares* a `public abstract` method for *each* `public` instance method in the `Object` class. These abstract method declarations are inherited by all subinterfaces of such an interface. Note that this does not mean the *implementation* is inherited. The implicit public abstract method declarations in an interface allow public instance methods in the Object class to be invoked on objects referred to by an interface reference. All classes implement these methods, whether they are inherited or overridden from the Object class. Any interface can also provide *explicit* public abstract method declarations for *non-final* public instance methods in the Object class.

```
interface IStack {                                                    // (1)
  void   push(Object item);
  Object pop();
  @Override boolean equals(Object other);        // public method in Object class.
  @Override String toString();                   // public method in Object class.
//@Override Class getClass(); // Compile-time error! final method in Object class.
}
```

It is instructive to consider how the class SafeStackImpl implements the IStack interface: It inherits the implementations of the push() and pop() methods from its superclass StackImpl, which itself implements the IStack interface in which these two methods are declared. The class SafeStackImpl also implements the IStack interface via the ISafeStack interface. The class SafeStackImpl provides its own implementation of the isFull() and isEmpty() methods declared in the ISafeStack interface, and has inherited implementations of the push() and pop() methods whose declarations the ISafeStack interface inherits from its superinterface IStack. This is readily evident from the diamond shape of the inheritance hierarchy in Figure 7.3. Note that there is only one single *implementation* inheritance into the class SafeStackImpl—from its superclass StackImpl. Java does not support multiple implementation inheritance.

The association between a class and any interface it implements is called a *realization* in UML. In Figure 7.3, there are three realizations: The class SafeStackImpl implements the ISafeStack interface and also implicitly implements the IStack interface, and the class StackImpl implements the IStack interface.

Thus, three different inheritance relations are at work when defining inheritance among classes and interfaces:

1. Single implementation inheritance hierarchy between classes: a class extends another class (subclasses–superclasses).
2. Multiple inheritance hierarchy between interfaces: an interface extends other interfaces (subinterfaces–superinterfaces).
3. Multiple interface inheritance hierarchy between classes and interfaces: a class implements interfaces (realization).

Interface References

Although interfaces cannot be instantiated, references of an interface type can be declared. The reference value of an object can be assigned to references of the object's supertypes. In Example 7.7, an object of the class SafeStackImpl is created in the main() method of the class StackUser at (9). The reference value of the object is assigned to references of all the object's supertypes, which are used to manipulate the object. The references are aliases to the same SafeStackImpl object, but they can only be used to manipulate this object as an object of the reference type. For example, calling the method isFull() on this object using the stackRef reference will be flagged as a compile-time error, as the class StackImpl does not provide such a method. Polymorphic behavior of supertype references is discussed in §7.12, p. 329.

Default Methods in Interfaces

Only interfaces can define default methods. A default method is an *instance method* declared with the keyword default and whose implementation is provided by the interface. However, a default method in a top-level interface always has public accessibility, whether the keyword public is specified or not.

default *return_type method_name (formal_parameter_list) throws_clause*
{ *implementaion_of_method_body* }

A class implementing an interface can optionally decide to override any default method in the interface. If the class does not override a default method to provide a new implementation, the default implementation provided by the interface is inherited by the class.

No other non-accessibility modifiers , such as abstract, final, or static, are allowed in a default method declaration, except the keyword strictfp. A default method is not abstract because it provides an implementation; is not final because it can be overridden; and is not static because it can be invoked only on instances of a class that implements the interface in which the default method is declared.

Example 7.8 illustrates the use of default methods. The default method printSlogan() at (1) in the interface ISlogan is overridden at (2) in the class JavaGuru, and inherited by the class JavaGeek at (3). The output from the program shows that this is the case.

Example 7.8 *Default Methods in Interfaces*

```
// File: JavaParty.java
interface ISlogan {
  default void printSlogan() {                        // (1)
    System.out.println("Happiness is getting certified!");
  }
}
//____________________________________________________________
class JavaGuru implements ISlogan {
  @Override
  public void printSlogan() {                         // (2) overrides (1)
    System.out.println("Happiness is catching all the exceptions!");
  }
}
//____________________________________________________________
class JavaGeek implements ISlogan { }                 // (3) inherits (1)
```

```
//______________________________________________________________
public class JavaParty {
  public static void main(String[] args) {
    JavaGuru guru = new JavaGuru();
    guru.printSlogan();                                    // (4)
    JavaGeek geek = new JavaGeek();
    geek.printSlogan();                                    // (5)
  }
}
```

Output from the program:

```
Happiness is catching all the exceptions!
Happiness is getting certified!
```

The keyword `default` in the context of a default method should not be confused with default or package accessibility of a method in a class, which is implied in the absence of any accessibility modifier. The keyword `default` is also used only for default method declarations in interfaces that provide an implementation for such methods, and not by classes that override them.

Overriding a default method from an interface does not necessarily imply that a new implementation is being provided. The default method can also be overridden by providing an abstract method declaration, as illustrated by the next code snippet. The default method `printSlogan()` at (1) in the interface `ISlogan` is overridden by an abstract method declaration at (2) and (3) in the interface `INewSlogan` and the abstract class `JavaMaster`, respectively. This strategy effectively forces the subtypes of the interface `INewSlogan` and of the abstract class `JavaMaster` to provide a new concrete implementation for the method, as one would expect for an abstract method.

```
interface ISlogan {
  default void printSlogan() {            // (1) Default method.
    System.out.println("Happiness is getting certified!");
  }
}

interface INewSlogan extends ISlogan {
  @Override
  abstract void printSlogan();           // (2) overrides (1) with abstract method.
}

abstract class JavaMaster implements ISlogan {
  @Override
  public abstract void printSlogan();  // (3) overrides (1) with abstract method.
}
```

Problems with multiple inheritance can arise when default methods are inherited from multiple interfaces. Example 7.9 illustrates one such case. The default method `printSlogan()` is declared at (1) and (2) in the interfaces `ICheapSlogan` and `IFunnySlogan`, respectively. The two method declarations have the same signature. The interface `IAvailableSlogan` at (3) tries to extend the two interfaces `ICheapSlogan` and `IFunnySlogan`. If this was allowed, the interface `IAvailableSlogan` would inherit two implementations of methods that have the same signature, which of course is not allowed—so the compiler flags it as an error. By the same token, the compiler flags an error at (4), indicating that the abstract class `Wholesaler` cannot inherit two methods with the same signature.

The way out of this dilemma is to override the conflicting methods. The abstract class `RetailSeller` that implements the interfaces `ICheapSlogan` and `IFunnySlogan` overrides the conflicting methods by providing an abstract method declaration of the default method `printSlogan()` at (5). Similarly, the class `NetSeller` that implements the interfaces `ICheapSlogan` and `IFunnySlogan` overrides the conflicting methods by providing an implementation of the default method `printSlogan()` at (6).

The upshot of this solution is that clients of the classes `RetailSeller` and `NetSeller` now have to deal with the new declarations of the `printSlogan()` method provided by these classes. One such client is the class `MutlipleInheritance` at (10), which calls the method `printSlogan()` on an instance of class `NetSeller` at (11). Not surprisingly, the program output shows that the method in the `NetSeller` class was executed.

What if the class `NetSeller` wanted to invoke the default method `printSlogan()` in the interfaces it implements? The overridden default method can be called by the overriding subtype (in this case, `NetSeller`) using the keyword `super` in conjunction with the fully qualified name of the interface and the name of the method, as shown at (8) and (9). This syntax works for calling overridden default methods in the *direct* superinterface, but not at any higher level in the inheritance hierarchy. The class `NetSeller` can call only default methods in its direct superinterfaces `ICheapSlogan` and `IFunnySlogan`. It would not be possible for the class `NetSeller` to call any default methods inherited by these superinterfaces, even if they had any.

Example 7.9 *Default Methods and Multiple Inheritance*

```
// File: MultipleInheritance.java
interface ICheapSlogan {
  default void printSlogan() {            // (1)
    System.out.println("Override, don't overload.");
  }
}
//______________________________________________________________________
interface IFunnySlogan {
  default void printSlogan() {            // (2)
    System.out.println("Catch exceptions, not bugs.");
  }
}
//______________________________________________________________________
interface IAvailableSlogan                // (3) Compile-time error.
          extends ICheapSlogan, IFunnySlogan { }
//______________________________________________________________________
abstract class Wholesaler                 // (4) Compile-time error.
               implements ICheapSlogan, IFunnySlogan { }
```

```
//______________________________________________________________________________
abstract class RetailSeller implements ICheapSlogan, IFunnySlogan {
  @Override                              // Abstract method.
  public abstract void printSlogan();    // (5) overrides (1) and (2).
}
//______________________________________________________________________________
class NetSeller implements ICheapSlogan, IFunnySlogan {
  @Override                              // Concrete method.
  public void printSlogan() {            // (6) overrides (1) and (2).
    System.out.println("Think outside of the class.");
  }

  public void invokeDirect() {           // (7)
    ICheapSlogan.super.printSlogan();    // (8) calls ICheapSlogan.printSlogan()
    IFunnySlogan.super.printSlogan();    // (9) calls IFunnySlogan.printSlogan()
  }
}
//______________________________________________________________________________
public class MultipleInheritance {       // (10)
  public static void main(String[] args) {
    NetSeller seller = new NetSeller();
    seller.printSlogan();                // (11)
    seller.invokeDirect();
  }
}
```

Output from the program:

```
Think outside of the class.
Override, don't overload.
Catch exceptions, not bugs.
```

Static Methods in Interfaces

An interface can also declare static methods. Static method declarations in a top-level interface are analogous to static method declarations in a class (§4.8, p. 132). However, a static method in a top-level interface always has `public` accessibility, whether the keyword `public` is specified or not. As with static methods in a class, the keyword `static` is mandatory; otherwise, the code will not compile. Without the keyword `static`, the method declaration is identical to that of an instance method, but such instance methods cannot be declared in an interface.

`static` *return_type method_name (formal_parameter_list) throws_clause*
  { *implementaion_of_method_body* }

Static methods in an interface differ from those in a class in one important respect: Static methods in an interface *cannot* be inherited, unlike static methods in classes. This essentially means that such methods cannot be invoked directly by calling the method in subinterfaces or in classes that extend or implement interfaces containing such methods, respectively. A static method can be invoked only by using its qualified name—that is, the name of the interface in which it is declared—together with its simple name, using the dot notation (.).

Example 7.10 illustrates the use of static methods in interfaces. The static method getNumOfCylinders() at (1) is declared in the IMaxEngineSize interface. There are two implementations of the method getEngineSize(), at (2) and (3), in the interface IMaxEngineSize and its subinterface INewEngineSize, respectively. The class CarRace implements the subinterface INewEngineSize.

It is not possible to invoke the method getNumOfCylinders() directly, as shown at (4). It is also not possible to invoke directly the method getEngineSize() from either interface, as shown at (6). The respective implementations of the static methods can be invoked only by using their qualified names, as shown at (5), (7) and (8). It does not matter that a static method is redeclared in a subinterface; the static method is not inherited. Each static method declaration in Example 7.10 is a new method.

Example 7.10 *Static Methods in Interfaces*

```
// File: CarRace.java
import static java.lang.System.out;

interface IMaxEngineSize {
  static int getNumOfCylinders() { return 6; }          // (1) Static method
  static double getEngineSize() { return 1.6; }         // (2) Static method
}
//______________________________________________________________________
interface INewEngineSize extends IMaxEngineSize {
  static double getEngineSize() { return 2.4; }         // (3) Static method
}
//______________________________________________________________________
public class CarRace implements INewEngineSize {
  public static void main(String[] args) {
//  out.println("No. of cylinders: " +
//              getNumOfCylinders());                   // (4) Compile-time error.
    out.println("No. of cylinders: " +
        IMaxEngineSize.getNumOfCylinders());            // (5)
//  out.println("Engine size: " + getEngineSize());     // (6) Compile-time error.
    out.println("Max engine size: " + IMaxEngineSize.getEngineSize()); // (7)
    out.println("New engine size: " + INewEngineSize.getEngineSize()); // (8)
  }
}
```

Output from the program:

```
No. of cylinders: 6
Max engine size: 1.6
New engine size: 2.4
```

Constants in Interfaces

An interface can also define named constants. Naming conventions recommend using uppercase letters for their names, with multiple words in the name being separated by underscores. Such constants are defined by field declarations and are considered to be `public`, `static`, and `final`. These modifiers can be omitted from the declaration. Such a constant must be initialized with an initializer expression.

An interface constant can be accessed by any client (a class or interface) using its qualified name, regardless of whether the client extends or implements its interface. However, if the client is a class that implements this interface or is an interface that extends this interface, then the client can also access such constants directly by their simple names. Such a client inherits the interface constants. Typical usage of constants in interfaces is illustrated in Example 7.11, showing access both by the constant's simple name and its qualified name in the print statements at (1) and (2), respectively.

Example 7.11 *Constants in Interfaces*

```
// File: Client.java
interface Constants {
  double PI_APPROXIMATION = 3.14;
  String AREA_UNITS       = "sq.cm.";
  String LENGTH_UNITS     = "cm.";
}
//______________________________________________________________________________
public class Client implements Constants {
  public static void main(String[] args) {
    double radius = 1.5;

    // (1) Using simple name:
    System.out.printf("Area of circle is %.2f %s%n",
               PI_APPROXIMATION * radius*radius, AREA_UNITS);

    // (2) Using qualified name:
    System.out.printf("Circumference of circle is %.2f %s%n",
             2.0 * Constants.PI_APPROXIMATION * radius, Constants.LENGTH_UNITS);
  }
}
```

Output from the program:

```
Area of circle is 7.06 sq.cm.
Circumference of circle is 9.42 cm.
```

Extending an interface that has constants is analogous to extending a class having static variables. This is illustrated by Figure 7.4 and Example 7.12. Note the diamond shape of the inheritance hierarchy, indicating the presence of multiple inheritance paths through which constants can be inherited. The constants IDLE and BUSY at (1) and (2) in the interface IBaseStates are inherited by the subinterface IAllStates via both the interface IExtStatesA and the interface IExtStatesB. In such cases, the constant is considered to be inherited only once, and can be accessed by its simple name, as shown at (12) in Example 7.12.

Constants can be *hidden* by the subinterfaces. The declaration of the constant BLOCKED at (6) in the interface IAllStates hides the declaration of the constant at (2) in the interface IBaseStates. The new declaration can be accessed by its simple name in a class implementing the interface IAllStates, as shown at (10) in Example 7.12. The hidden constant declaration can always be accessed by using its qualified name as shown at (11) in Example 7.12.

In the case of multiple inheritance of interface constants, any name conflicts can be resolved by using the qualified name to access the constants. This is illustrated by the constant DISMANTLED, which is declared in both the IExtStatesA and IExtStatesB interfaces. Both declarations are inherited by the subinterface IAllStates. Such declarations are said to be *ambiguous*. The compiler will report an error only if such constants are accessed by their simple names, as shown at (7) and (8) for the constant DISMANTLE. Only the qualified name can be used to disambiguate such constants and resolve the conflict, as shown at (7a) and (8a) for the constant DISMANTLE.

When defining a *set of related constants*, the recommended practice is to use an enumerated type, rather than named constants in an interface.

Figure 7.4 *Inheritance Relationships for Interface Constants*

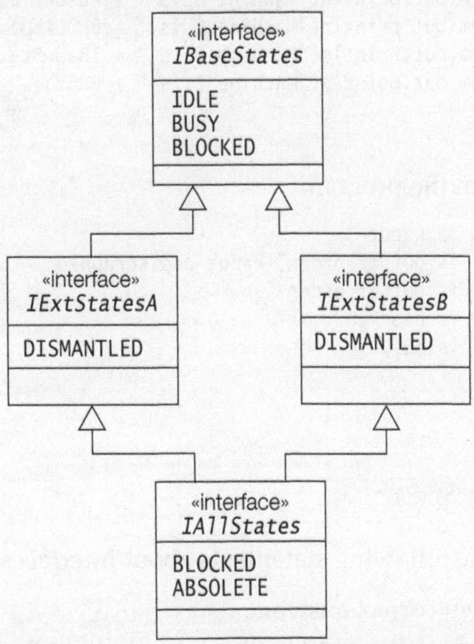

Example 7.12 *Inheriting Constants in Interfaces*

```
// File: Factory.java
interface IBaseStates {
  String IDLE = "idle";                                    // (1)
  String BUSY = "busy";                                    // (2)
  String BLOCKED = "blocked";                              // (3)
}
//_______________________________________________________________
interface IExtStatesA extends IBaseStates {
  String DISMANTLED = "dismantled";                        // (4)
}
//_______________________________________________________________
interface IExtStatesB extends IBaseStates {
  String DISMANTLED = "kaput";                             // (5)
}
//_______________________________________________________________
interface IAllStates extends IExtStatesB, IExtStatesA {
  String BLOCKED = "out of order";                         // (6) hides (3)
//String ABSOLETE = BLOCKED + ", " +
//                  DISMANTLED + " and scrapped.";         // (7) Ambiguous
  String ABSOLETE = BLOCKED + ", " +
              IExtStatesB.DISMANTLED + " and scrapped";    // (7a)
}
//_______________________________________________________________
public class Factory implements IAllStates {
  public static void main(String[] args) {
//  System.out.println("Machine A is " + DISMANTLED);              // (8) Ambiguous.
    System.out.println("Machine A is " + IExtStatesB.DISMANTLED);// (8a)
    System.out.println("Machine B is " + ABSOLETE);   // (9)  IAllStates.ABSOLETE
    System.out.println("Machine C is " + BLOCKED);    // (10) IAllStates.BLOCKED
    System.out.println("Machine D is " + IBaseStates.BLOCKED); // (11)
    System.out.println("Machine E is " + BUSY);       // (12) Simple name
  }
}
```

Output from the program:

```
Machine A is kaput
Machine B is out of order, kaput and scrapped
Machine C is out of order
Machine D is blocked
Machine E is busy
```

Review Questions

7.11 Which of the following statements about interfaces are true?

Select the two correct answers.

(a) Interfaces allow multiple implementation inheritance.
(b) Interfaces can be extended by any number of interfaces.

(c) Interfaces can extend any number of interfaces.
(d) Members of an interface are never static.
(e) Members of an interface can always be declared `static`.

7.12 Which modifiers can methods declared in a top-level interface specify?

Select the four correct answers.

(a) `public`
(b) `protected`
(c) `private`
(d) `default`
(e) `abstract`
(f) `static`
(g) `final`

7.13 Which modifiers are implicitly implied for interface variables?

Select the three correct answers.

(a) `public`
(b) `protected`
(c) `private`
(d) `default`
(e) `abstract`
(f) `static`
(g) `final`

7.14 How many errors will the compiler report for the following code?

```
public interface Vehicle {
  final static int NUMBER_OF_HEADLIGHTS;  // (1)
  void increaseSpeed(int increment) {     // (2)
    System.out.println("Increasing speed by " + increment);
  }
  static void reduceSpeed(int decrement); // (3)

  final default void stop() {             // (4)
    System.out.println("Slamming the brakes!");
  }
}
```

Select the one correct answer.

(a) No errors
(b) 1 error
(c) 2 errors
(d) 3 errors
(e) More than 3 errors

7.15 Which method calls can be inserted at both (1) and (2), so that the following code will still compile?

```
// File: Company.java
interface ISlogan {
  String SLOGAN = "Happiness shared is happiness doubled!";
  default void printSlogan() { System.out.println(SLOGAN); }
}
//_______________________________________________________________
public class Company implements ISlogan {
  public static void main(String[] args) {
    Company co = new Company();
    ISlogan sl = co;
    // (1) INSERT THE METHOD CALL HERE.
  }

  public void testSlogan() {
    Company co = new Company();
    ISlogan sl = co;
    // (2) INSERT THE METHOD CALL HERE.
  }
}
```

Select the two correct answers.

(a) `printSlogan();`
(b) `co.printSlogan();`
(c) `sl.printSlogan();`
(d) `Company.printSlogan();`
(e) `ISlogan.printSlogan();`

7.16 Which method call can be inserted at both (1) and (2), so that the following code will still compile?

```
// File: Firm.java
interface INewSlogan {
  String SLOGAN = "Trouble shared is trouble halved!";
  static void printSlogan() { System.out.println(SLOGAN); }
}
//_______________________________________________________________
public class Firm implements INewSlogan {
  public static void main(String[] args) {
    Firm co = new Firm();
    INewSlogan sl = co;
    // (1) INSERT THE STATEMENT EXPRESSION HERE.
  }

  void testSlogan() {
    Firm co = new Firm();
    INewSlogan sl = co;
    // (2) INSERT THE STATEMENT EXPRESSION HERE.
  }
}
```

Select the one correct answer.

(a) `printSlogan();`
(b) `co.printSlogan();`
(c) `sl.printSlogan();`
(d) `Firm.printSlogan();`
(e) `INewSlogan.printSlogan();`

7.17 What will the following program print when compiled and run?

```
// File: RaceA.java
interface IJogger {
  default boolean justDoIt(String msg) { return false; }  // (1)
  static  boolean justDoIt(int i)      { return true; }   // (2)
}

class Athlete implements IJogger {
  public boolean justDoIt(String msg)  { return true; }   // (3)
  public boolean justDoIt(int i)       { return false; }  // (4)
}

public class RaceA {
  public static void main(String[] args) {
    Athlete athlete = new Athlete();
    IJogger jogger = athlete;
    System.out.print(jogger.justDoIt("Run"));              // (5)
    System.out.println("|" + athlete.justDoIt(10));        // (6)
  }
}
```

Select the one correct answer.

(a) The program will not compile.
(b) `true|true`
(c) `true|false`
(d) `false|true`
(e) `false|false`

7.18 What will the following program print when compiled and run?

```
// File: HouseC
interface ISwitch {
  default boolean isOn() { return false; }  // (1)
}

class Light implements ISwitch {
  boolean isOn() { return true; }           // (2)
}

public class HouseC {
  public static void main(String[] args) {
    ISwitch lightswitch = new Light();
    System.out.println(lightswitch.isOn());
  }
}
```

Select the one correct answer.

(a) The program will not compile.
(b) The program will compile, and print `true` when run.
(c) The program will compile, and print `false` when run.
(d) The program will compile, and throw an exception when run.

7.19 Which of these field declarations are legal within the body of an interface?

Select the three correct answers.

(a) `public static int ANSWER = 42;`
(b) `int ANSWER;`
(c) `static final int ANSWER = 42;`
(d) `public int ANSWER = 42;`
(e) `private static final int ANSWER = 42;`

7.20 Which statements about the keywords `extends` and `implements` are true?

Select the two correct answers.

(a) The keyword `extends` is used to specify that an interface inherits from another interface.
(b) The keyword `extends` is used to specify that a class implements an interface.
(c) The keyword `implements` is used to specify that an interface inherits from another interface.
(d) The keyword `implements` is used to specify that a class inherits from an interface.
(e) The keyword `implements` is used to specify that a class inherits from another class.

7.21 Which statement is true about the following code?

```
// File: MyClass.java
abstract class MyClass implements Interface1, Interface2 {
  public void f() { }
  public void g() { }
}

interface Interface1 {
  int VAL_A = 1;
  int VAL_B = 2;

  void f();
  void g();
}

interface Interface2 {
  int VAL_B = 3;
  int VAL_C = 4;

  void g();
  void h();
}
```

Select the one correct answer.

(a) `MyClass` implements only `Interface1`; the implementation for `void h()` from `Interface2` is missing.
(b) The declarations of `void g()` in the two interfaces are in conflict, so the code will not compile.
(c) The declarations of `int VAL_B` in the two interfaces are in conflict, so the code will not compile.
(d) Nothing is wrong with the code; it will compile without errors.

7.22 Which declaration can be inserted at (1) without resulting in a compile-time error?

```
interface MyConstants {
  int R = 42;
  int S = 69;
  // (1) INSERT CODE HERE
}
```

Select the two correct answers.

(a) `final double CIRCUMFERENCE = 2 * Math.PI * R;`
(b) `int TOTAL = TOTAL + R + S;`
(c) `int AREA = R * S;`
(d) `public static MAIN = 15;`
(e) `protected int CODE = 13082009;`

7.7 Arrays and Subtyping

Table 7.3 summarizes the types found in Java. Only primitive data and reference values can be stored in variables. Only class and array types can be explicitly instantiated to create objects.

Table 7.3 *Types and Values*

Types	Values
Primitive data types	Primitive data values
Class, interface, enum, and array types (*reference types*)	Reference values

Arrays and Subtype Covariance

Arrays are objects in Java. Array types (`boolean[]`, `Object[]`, `StackImpl[]`) implicitly augment the inheritance hierarchy. The inheritance hierarchy depicted in Figure 7.3, for example, can be augmented by the corresponding array types to produce the *type hierarchy* shown in Figure 7.5. An array type is shown as a "class" with the `[]` notation appended to the name of the element type. The class `SafeStackImpl` is a subclass of the class `StackImpl`. The corresponding array types, `SafeStackImpl[]` and

StackImpl[], are shown as the subtype and the supertype, respectively, in the type hierarchy. Figure 7.5 also shows array types corresponding to some of the primitive data types.

Figure 7.5 *Reference Type Hierarchy: Arrays and Subtype Covariance*

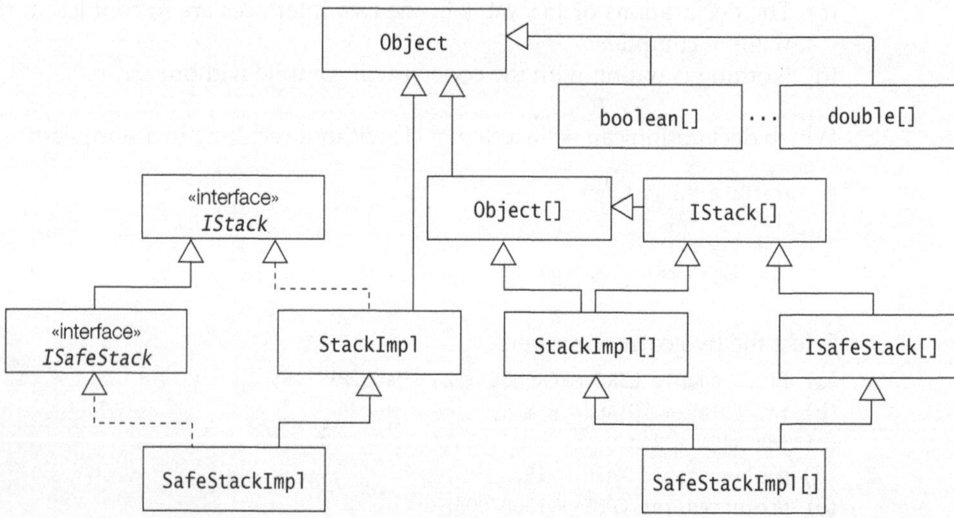

From the type hierarchy in Figure 7.5, the following facts are apparent:

- *All* reference types are subtypes of the Object type. This applies to classes, interfaces, enums, and array types, as these are all reference types.
- All arrays of reference types are also subtypes of the array type Object[], but arrays of primitive data types are not. Note that the array type Object[] is also a subtype of the Object type.
- If a non-generic reference type is a subtype of another non-generic reference type, the corresponding array types also have an analogous subtype–supertype relationship. This is called the *subtype covariance relationship*.
- There is no subtype–supertype relationship between a type and its corresponding array type.

We can create an array of an interface type, but we cannot instantiate an interface (as is the case with abstract classes). In the following declaration statement, the reference iSafeStackArray has type ISafeStack[] (i.e., an array of the interface type ISafeStack):

```
ISafeStack[] iSafeStackArray = new ISafeStack[5];
```

The array creation expression creates an array whose element type is ISafeStack. The array object can accommodate five references of the type ISafeStack. The declaration statement does not initialize these references to refer to any objects; instead, they are initialized to the default value null.

Array Store Check

An array reference exhibits polymorphic behavior like any other reference, subject to its location in the type hierarchy (§7.12, p. 329). However, a runtime check is necessary when objects are inserted in an array, as the next example illustrates.

The following assignment is valid, as a supertype reference (`StackImpl[]`) can refer to objects of its subtype (`SafeStackImpl[]`):

```
StackImpl[] stackImplArray = new SafeStackImpl[2];        // (1)
```

Since `StackImpl` is a supertype of `SafeStackImpl`, the following assignment is also valid:

```
stackImplArray[0] = new SafeStackImpl(10);                // (2)
```

The assignment at (2) assigns the reference value of a new `SafeStackImpl` object to the reference at index `0` in the `SafeStackImpl[]` object (i.e., the array of `SafeStackImpl`) created at (1).

Since the type of `stackImplArray[i]`, (`0 ≤ i < 2`), is `StackImpl`, it should be possible to make the following assignment as well:

```
stackImplArray[1] = new StackImpl(20);                    // (3) ArrayStoreException
```

At compile time there are no problems, as the compiler cannot deduce that the array variable `stackImplArray` will actually denote a `SafeStackImpl[]` object at runtime. However, the assignment at (3) results in an `ArrayStoreException` being thrown at runtime, because an array of `SafeStackImpl` objects cannot possibly contain objects of its supertype `StackImpl`.

The array store check at runtime ensures that an object being stored in the array is assignment compatible (p. 314) with the element type of the array. To make the array store check feasible at runtime, the array retains information about its declared element type at runtime.

7.8 Reference Values and Conversions

A review of conversions (§5.1, p. 144) is recommended before proceeding with this section.

Reference values, like primitive values, can be assigned, cast, and passed as arguments. Conversions can occur in the following contexts:

- Assignment
- Method invocation
- Casting

The rule of thumb for the primitive data types is that widening conversions are permitted, but narrowing conversions require an explicit cast. The rule of thumb for reference values is that widening conversions up the type hierarchy are permitted, but narrowing conversions down the hierarchy require an explicit cast. In other words, conversions that are from a subtype to its supertypes are allowed, but other conversions require an explicit cast or are otherwise illegal. There is no notion of promotion for reference values.

7.9 Reference Value Assignment Conversions

In the context of assignments, the following conversions are permitted (Table 5.1, p. 147):

- Widening primitive and reference conversions (`long` ← `int`, `Object` ← `String`)
- Boxing conversion of primitive values, followed by optional widening reference conversion (`Integer` ← `int`, `Number` ← `Integer` ← `int`)
- Unboxing conversion of a primitive value wrapper object, followed by optional widening primitive conversion (`long` ← `int` ← `Integer`)

For assignment conversions only, the following conversions are also possible:

- Narrowing conversion for constant expressions of non-`long` integer types, with optional boxing (`Byte` ← `byte` ← `int`)

Note that these rules imply that a widening conversion *cannot* be followed by any boxing conversion, but the converse is permitted.

Widening reference conversions typically occur during assignment *up* the type hierarchy, with implicit conversion of the source reference value to that of the destination reference type:

```
Object obj = "Up the tree";     // Widening reference conversion: Object <-- String
String str1 = obj;         // Not OK. Narrowing reference conversion requires a cast.
String str2 = new Integer(10); // Illegal. No relation between String and Integer.
```

The source value can be a primitive value, in which case the value is boxed in a wrapper object corresponding to the primitive type. If the destination reference type is a supertype of the wrapper type, a widening reference conversion can occur:

```
Integer iRef = 10;  // Only boxing
Number num = 10L;   // Boxing, followed by widening: Number <--- Long <--- long
Object obj = 100;   // Boxing, followed by widening: Object <--- Integer <--- int
```

More examples of boxing during assignment can be found in §5.1, p. 145.

Example 7.13 *Assigning and Passing Reference Values*

```
interface IStack                        { /* From Example 7.7 */ }
interface ISafeStack extends IStack     { /* From Example 7.7 */ }
class StackImpl implements IStack       { /* From Example 7.7 */ }
class SafeStackImpl extends StackImpl
                implements ISafeStack   { /* From Example 7.7 */ }
```

```
public class ReferenceConversion {

  public static void main(String[] args) {
    // Reference declarations:
    Object        objRef;
    StackImpl     stackRef;
    SafeStackImpl safeStackRef;
    IStack        iStackRef;
    ISafeStack    iSafeStackRef;

    // SourceType is a class type:
    safeStackRef  = new SafeStackImpl(10);
    objRef        = safeStackRef;    // (1) Always possible
    stackRef      = safeStackRef;    // (2) Subclass to superclass assignment
    iStackRef     = stackRef;        // (3) StackImpl implements IStack
    iSafeStackRef = safeStackRef;    // (4) SafeStackImpl implements ISafeStack

    // SourceType is an interface type:
    objRef    = iStackRef;           // (5) Always possible
    iStackRef = iSafeStackRef;       // (6) Sub- to super-interface assignment

    // SourceType is an array type:
    Object[]        objArray        = new Object[3];
    StackImpl[]     stackArray      = new StackImpl[3];
    SafeStackImpl[] safeStackArray  = new SafeStackImpl[5];
    ISafeStack[]    iSafeStackArray = new ISafeStack[5];
    int[]           intArray        = new int[10];

    // Reference value assignments:
    objRef     = objArray;           // (7) Always possible
    objRef     = stackArray;         // (8) Always possible
    objArray   = stackArray;         // (9) Always possible
    objArray   = iSafeStackArray;    // (10) Always possible
    objRef     = intArray;           // (11) Always possible
    //  objArray   = intArray;       // (12) Compile-time error:
                                     //      int[] not subtype of Object[]
    stackArray = safeStackArray;     // (13) Subclass array to superclass array
    iSafeStackArray = safeStackArray;// (14) SafeStackImpl implements ISafeStack

    // Method invocation conversions:
    System.out.println("First call:");
    sendParams(stackRef, safeStackRef, iStackRef,
               safeStackArray, iSafeStackArray);                      // (15)
    //  Call Signature: sendParams(StackImpl, SafeStackImpl, IStack,
    //                             SafeStackImpl[], ISafeStack[]);

    System.out.println("Second call:");
    sendParams(iSafeStackArray, stackRef, iSafeStackRef,
               stackArray, safeStackArray);                           // (16)
    //  Call Signature: sendParams(ISafeStack[], StackImpl, ISafeStack,
    //                             StackImpl[], SafeStackImpl[]);
  }
```

```
  public static void sendParams(Object objRefParam, StackImpl stackRefParam,
      IStack iStackRefParam, StackImpl[] stackArrayParam,
      IStack[] iStackArrayParam) {                                   // (17)
    //  Signature: sendParams(Object, StackImpl, IStack, StackImpl[], IStack[])
    //  Print class name of object denoted by the reference at runtime.
    System.out.println(objRefParam.getClass());
    System.out.println(stackRefParam.getClass());
    System.out.println(iStackRefParam.getClass());
    System.out.println(stackArrayParam.getClass());
    System.out.println(iStackArrayParam.getClass());
  }
}
```

Output from the program:

```
First call:
class SafeStackImpl
class SafeStackImpl
class SafeStackImpl
class [LSafeStackImpl;
class [LSafeStackImpl;
Second call:
class [LSafeStackImpl;
class SafeStackImpl
class SafeStackImpl
class [LSafeStackImpl;
class [LSafeStackImpl;
```

The rules for reference value assignment are stated in this section, based on the following code:

```
SourceType srcRef;
// srcRef is appropriately initialized.
DestinationType destRef = srcRef;
```

If an assignment is legal, the reference value of `srcRef` is said to be *assignable* (or *assignment compatible*) to the reference of `DestinationType`. The rules are illustrated by concrete cases from Example 7.13. Note that the code in Example 7.13 uses reference types from Example 7.7, p. 292.

- If the `SourceType` is a *class type*, the reference value in `srcRef` may be assigned to the `destRef` reference, provided the `DestinationType` is one of the following:
  - `DestinationType` is a superclass of the subclass `SourceType`.
  - `DestinationType` is an interface type that is implemented by the class `SourceType`.

```
objRef        = safeStackRef;    // (1) Always possible
stackRef      = safeStackRef;    // (2) Subclass to superclass assignment
iStackRef     = stackRef;        // (3) StackImpl implements IStack
iSafeStackRef = safeStackRef;    // (4) SafeStackImpl implements ISafeStack
```

- If the SourceType is an *interface type*, the reference value in srcRef may be assigned to the destRef reference, provided the DestinationType is one of the following:
  - DestinationType is the Object class.
  - DestinationType is a superinterface of the subinterface SourceType.

```
objRef    = iStackRef;     // (5) Always possible
iStackRef = iSafeStackRef; // (6) Subinterface to superinterface assignment
```

- If the SourceType is an *array type*, the reference value in srcRef may be assigned to the destRef reference, provided the DestinationType is one of the following:
  - DestinationType is the Object class.
  - DestinationType is an array type, where the element type of the SourceType is assignable to the element type of the DestinationType.

```
objRef      = objArray;            // (7) Always possible
objRef      = stackArray;          // (8) Always possible
objArray    = stackArray;          // (9) Always possible
objArray    = iSafeStackArray;     // (10) Always possible
objRef      = intArray;            // (11) Always possible
// objArray   = intArray;          // (12) Compile-time error:
                                   //      int[] not subtype of Object[]
stackArray = safeStackArray;       // (13) Subclass array to superclass array
iSafeStackArray = safeStackArray;// (14) SafeStackImpl implements ISafeStack
```

The rules for assignment are enforced at compile time, guaranteeing that no type conversion error will occur during assignment at runtime. Such conversions are *type-safe*. The reason the rules can be enforced at compile time is that they concern the *declared type* of the reference (which is always known at compile time) rather than the actual type of the object being referenced (which is known at runtime).

7.10 Method Invocation Conversions Involving References

The conversions for reference value assignment are also applicable to *method invocation conversions*, except for the narrowing conversion for constant expressions of non-long integer type (Table 5.1, p. 147). This is reasonable, as parameters in Java are passed by value (§3.5, p. 72), requiring that values of the actual parameters must be assignable to formal parameters of the compatible types.

In Example 7.13, the method sendParams() at (17) has the following signature, showing the types of the formal parameters:

```
sendParams(Object, StackImpl, IStack, StackImpl[], IStack[])
```

The method call at (15) has the following signature, showing the types of the actual parameters:

```
sendParams(StackImpl, SafeStackImpl, IStack, SafeStackImpl[], ISafeStack[]);
```

Note that the assignment of the values of the actual parameters to the corresponding formal parameters is legal, according to the rules for assignment discussed earlier.

The method call at (16) provides another example of the parameter passing conversion. It has the following signature:

```
sendParams(ISafeStack[], StackImpl, ISafeStack, StackImpl[], SafeStackImpl[]);
```

Analogous to assignment, the rules for parameter passing conversions are based on the reference type of the parameters and are enforced at compile time. The output in Example 7.13 shows the class of the actual objects referenced by the formal parameters at runtime, which in this case turns out to be either `SafeStackImpl` or `SafeStackImpl[]`. The characters `[L` in the output indicate a one-dimensional array of a class or interface type (see the `Class.getName()` method in the Java SE platform API documentation).

Overloaded Method Resolution

In this subsection, we take a look at some aspects regarding *overloaded method resolution*—namely, how the compiler determines which overloaded method will be invoked by a given method call at runtime.

Resolution of overloaded methods selects the *most specific* method for execution. One method is considered more specific than another method if all actual parameters that can be accepted by the one method can be accepted by the other method. If more than one such method is present, the call is described as *ambiguous*. The following overloaded methods illustrate this situation:

```
private static void flipFlop(String str, int i, Integer iRef) { // (1)
    out.println(str + " ==> (String, int, Integer)");
}
private static void flipFlop(String str, int i, int j) {        // (2)
    out.println(str + " ==> (String, int, int)");
}
```

Their method signatures follow:

```
flipFlop(String, int, Integer)                                 // See (1)
flipFlop(String, int, int)                                     // See (2)
```

The following method call is ambiguous:

```
flipFlop("(String, Integer, int)", new Integer(4), 2004);  // (3) Ambiguous call
```

It has the call signature:

```
flipFlop(String, Integer, int)                                 // See (3)
```

The method at (1) can be called with the second argument unboxed and the third argument boxed, as can the method at (2) with only the second argument unboxed. In other words, for the call at (3), none of the methods is more specific than the others.

Example 7.14 illustrates a simple case of how method resolution is done to choose the most specific overloaded method. The method `testIfOn()` is overloaded at (1) and (2) in the class `Overload`. The call `client.testIfOn(tubeLight)` at (3) *satisfies* the parameter lists in both implementations given at (1) and (2), as the reference `tubeLight` can also be assigned to a reference of its superclass `Light`. The *most specific* method, (2), is chosen, resulting in `false` being written on the terminal. The call `client.testIfOn(light)` at (4) satisfies only the parameter list in the implementation given at (1), resulting in `true` being written on the terminal. This is also the case at (5). The object referred to by the argument in the call is irrelevant; rather, it is the *type* of the argument that is important for overloaded method resolution.

Example 7.14 *Choosing the Most Specific Method (Simple Case)*

```
class Light { /* ... */ }

class TubeLight extends Light { /* ... */ }

public class Overload {
  boolean testIfOn(Light aLight)         { return true; }    // (1)
  boolean testIfOn(TubeLight aTubeLight) { return false; }   // (2)

  public static void main(String[] args) {

    TubeLight tubeLight = new TubeLight();
    Light     light     = new Light();
    Light     light2    = new TubeLight();

    Overload client = new Overload();
    System.out.println(client.testIfOn(tubeLight)); // (3) ==> method at (2)
    System.out.println(client.testIfOn(light));     // (4) ==> method at (1)
    System.out.println(client.testIfOn(light2));    // (5) ==> method at (2)
  }
}
```

Output from the program:

```
false
true
true
```

The algorithm used by the compiler for the resolution of overloaded methods incorporates the following phases:

1. The compiler performs overload resolution without permitting boxing, unboxing, or the use of a variable arity call.
2. If phase (1) fails, the compiler performs overload resolution allowing boxing and unboxing, but excluding the use of a variable arity call.
3. If phase (2) fails, the compiler performs overload resolution combining a variable arity call, boxing, and unboxing.

Example 7.15 provides some insight into how the compiler determines the most specific overloaded method using these three phases. The example has six overloaded declarations of the method `action()`. The signature of each method is given by the local variable `signature` in each method. The first formal parameter of each method is the *signature of the call* that invoked the method. The printout from each method allows us to see which method call resolved to which method. The `main()` method contains 10 calls, (8) to (17), of the `action()` method. In each call, the first argument is the signature of that method call.

An important point to note is that the compiler chooses a *fixed arity* call over a variable arity call, as seen in the calls from (8) to (12):

`(String) => (String)`	(8) calls (1)
`(String, int) => (String, int)`	(9) calls (2)
`(String, Integer) => (String, int)`	(10) calls (2)
`(String, int, byte) => (String, int, int)`	(11) calls (3)
`(String, int, int) => (String, int, int)`	(12) calls (3)

An unboxing conversion (`Integer` to `int`) takes place for the call at (10). A widening primitive conversion (`byte` to `int`) takes place for the call at (11).

Variable arity calls are chosen from (13) to (17):

`(String, int, long) => (String, Number[])`	(13) calls (5)
`(String, int, int, int) => (String, Integer[])`	(14) calls (4)
`(String, int, double) => (String, Number[])`	(15) calls (5)
`(String, int, String) => (String, Object[])`	(16) calls (6)
`(String, boolean) => (String, Object[])`	(17) calls (6)

When a variable arity call is chosen, the method determined has the most specific variable arity parameter that is applicable for the actual argument. For example, in the method call at (14), the type `Integer[]` is more specific than either `Number[]` or `Object[]`. Note also the boxing of the elements of the implicitly created array in the calls from (13) to (17).

Example 7.15 *Overloaded Method Resolution*

```
import static java.lang.System.out;

class OverloadResolution {

  public void action(String str) {                  // (1)
    String signature = "(String)";
    out.println(str + " => " + signature);
  }

  public void action(String str, int m) {           // (2)
    String signature = "(String, int)";
    out.println(str + " => " + signature);
  }
```

```
  public void action(String str, int m, int n) {   // (3)
    String signature = "(String, int, int)";
    out.println(str + " => " + signature);
  }

  public void action(String str, Integer... data) { // (4)
    String signature = "(String, Integer[])";
    out.println(str + " => " + signature);
  }

  public void action(String str, Number... data) {  // (5)
    String signature = "(String, Number[])";
    out.println(str + " => " + signature);
  }

  public void action(String str, Object... data) {  // (6)
    String signature = "(String, Object[])";
    out.println(str + " => " + signature);
  }

  public static void main(String[] args) {
    OverloadResolution ref = new OverloadResolution();
    ref.action("(String)");                                           // (8)  calls (1)
    ref.action("(String, int)",            10);                      // (9)  calls (2)
    ref.action("(String, Integer)",        new Integer(10));         // (10) calls (2)
    ref.action("(String, int, byte)",      10, (byte)20);            // (11) calls (3)
    ref.action("(String, int, int)",       10,  20);                 // (12) calls (3)
    ref.action("(String, int, long)",      10,  20L);                // (13) calls (5)
    ref.action("(String, int, int, int)",  10,  20,  30);            // (14) calls (4)
    ref.action("(String, int, double)",    10,  20.0);               // (15) calls (5)
    ref.action("(String, int, String)",    10,  "what?");            // (16) calls (6)
    ref.action("(String, boolean)",        false);                   // (17) calls (6)
  }
}
```

Output from the program (with remarks to the output on the right):

```
(String) => (String)                            (8) calls (1)
(String, int) => (String, int)                  (9) calls (2)
(String, Integer) => (String, int)              (10) calls (2)
(String, int, byte) => (String, int, int)       (11) calls (3)
(String, int, int) => (String, int, int)        (12) calls (3)
(String, int, long) => (String, Number[])       (13) calls (5)
(String, int, int, int) => (String, Integer[])  (14) calls (4)
(String, int, double) => (String, Number[])     (15) calls (5)
(String, int, String) => (String, Object[])     (16) calls (6)
(String, boolean) => (String, Object[])         (17) calls (6)
```

7.11 Reference Casting and the `instanceof` Operator

The Cast Operator

The type cast expression for reference types has the following syntax:

(*destination_type*) *reference_expression*

where the *reference expression* evaluates to a reference value of an object of some reference type. A type cast expression checks that the reference value refers to an object whose type is compatible with the *destination type*, meaning that its type is a subtype of the *destination type*. The construct (*destination_type*) is usually called the *cast operator*. The result of a type cast expression for references is always a reference value of an object. The literal `null` can be cast to any reference type.

The next code snippet illustrates the various scenarios that arise when using the cast operator. In this discussion, it is the type cast expression that is important, not the evaluation of the assignment operator in the declaration statements. In (1), the cast is from the superclass `Object` to the subclass `String`; the code compiles and at runtime this cast is permitted, as the reference `obj` will denote an object of class `String`. In (2), the cast is from the superclass `Object` to the subclass `Integer`; the code compiles, but at runtime this cast results in a `ClassCastException`, since the reference `obj` will denote an object of class `String`, which cannot be converted to an `Integer`. In (3), the cast is from the class `String` to the class `Integer`. As these two classes are unrelated, the compiler flags an error for the cast.

```
Object  obj = new String("Cast me!");
String  str = (String) obj;           // (1) Cast from Object to String.
Integer iRef1 = (Integer) obj;        // (2) Cast from Object to Integer, but
                                      //     ClassCastException at runtime.
Integer iRef2 = (Integer) str;        // (3) Compile-time error!
                                      //     Cast between unrelated types.
```

The following conversions can be applied to the operand of a cast operator:

- Both widening and narrowing reference conversions, followed optionally by an unchecked conversion
- Both boxing and unboxing conversions

Boxing and unboxing conversions that can occur during casting are illustrated by the following code. Again, it is the type cast expression that is important in this discussion, rather than whether the assignment operator requires one in the declaration statements.

```
// (1) Boxing and casting: Number <-- Integer <-- int:
Number num = (Number) 100;
// (2) Casting, boxing, casting: Object <-- Integer <-- int <-- double:
Object obj = (Object) (int) 10.5;
// (3) Casting, unboxing, casting: double <--- int <-- Integer <-- Object:
double d = (double) (Integer) obj;
```

Note that the resulting object in (1) and (2) is an `Integer`, but the resulting value in (3) is a `double`. The boxing conversions from `int` to `Integer` in (1) and (2) are implicit, and the unboxing conversion from `Integer` to `int` in (3) is also implicit.

The `instanceof` Operator

The binary `instanceof` operator can be used for comparing *types*. It has the following syntax (note that the keyword is composed of lowercase letters only):

reference_expression `instanceof` *destination_type*

The `instanceof` operator returns `true` if the left-hand operand (i.e., the reference value that results from the evaluation of *reference expression*) can be a *subtype* of the right-hand operand (*destination_type*). It always returns `false` if the left-hand operand is `null`. If the `instanceof` operator returns `true`, the corresponding type cast expression will always be valid. Both the type cast expression and the `instanceof` operators require a compile-time check and a runtime check, as explained later in this section.

The compile-time check determines whether there is a subtype–supertype relationship between the source and destination types. Given that the type of the *reference expression* is *source type*, the compiler determines whether a reference of *source type* and a reference of *destination type* can refer to objects of a reference type that are a common subtype of both *source type* and *destination type* in the type hierarchy. If this is not the case, then obviously there is no relationship between the types, and neither the cast nor the `instanceof` operator application would be valid. At runtime, the *reference expression* evaluates to a reference value of an object. It is the type of the actual object that determines the outcome of the operation, as explained earlier.

With the classes `Light` and `String` as *source type* and *destination type*, respectively, there is no subtype–supertype relationship between *source type* and *destination type*. The compiler would reject casting a reference of type `Light` to type `String` or applying the `instanceof` operator, as shown at (2) and (3) in Example 7.16. References of the classes `Light` and `TubeLight` can refer to objects of the class `TubeLight` (or its subclasses) in the inheritance hierarchy depicted in Figure 7.1. Therefore, it makes sense to apply the `instanceof` operator or cast a reference of the type `Light` to the type `TubeLight` as shown at (4) and (5), respectively, in Example 7.16.

At runtime, the result of applying the `instanceof` operator at (4) is `false`, because the reference `light1` of the class `Light` will actually denote an object of the subclass `LightBulb`, and this object cannot be denoted by a reference of the peer class `TubeLight`. Applying the cast at (5) results in a `ClassCastException` for the same reason. This is the reason why cast conversions are said to be *unsafe*, as they may throw a `ClassCastException` at runtime. Note that if the result of the `instanceof` operator is `false`, the cast involving the operands will throw a `ClassCastException`.

In Example 7.16, the result of applying the `instanceof` operator at (6) is also `false`, because the reference `light1` will still denote an object of the class `LightBulb`, whose objects cannot be denoted by a reference of its subclass `SpotLightBulb`. Thus applying the cast at (7) causes a `ClassCastException` to be thrown at runtime.

The situation shown at (8), (9), and (10) illustrates typical usage of the `instanceof` operator to determine which object a reference is denoting, so that it can be cast for the purpose of carrying out some specific action. The reference `light1` of the class `Light` is initialized to an object of the subclass `NeonLight` at (8). The result of the `instanceof` operator at (9) is `true`, because the reference `light1` will denote an object of the subclass `NeonLight`, whose objects can also be denoted by a reference of its superclass `TubeLight`. By the same token, the cast at (10) is valid. If the result of the `instanceof` operator is `true`, the cast involving the operands will be valid as well.

Example 7.16 *The `instanceof` and Cast Operators*

```
// See Figure 7.1, p. 267, for inheritance hierarchy.
class Light { /* ... */ }
class LightBulb extends Light { /* ... */ }
class SpotLightBulb extends LightBulb { /* ... */ }
class TubeLight extends Light { /* ... */ }
class NeonLight extends TubeLight { /* ... */ }

public class WhoAmI {
  public static void main(String[] args) {
    boolean result1, result2, result3;
    Light light1 = new LightBulb();                   // (1)
    // String str = (String) light1;                  // (2) Compile-time error!
    // result1 = light1 instanceof String;            // (3) Compile-time error!

    result2 = light1 instanceof TubeLight;            // (4) false: peer class.
    // TubeLight tubeLight1 = (TubeLight) light1;     // (5) ClassCastException!

    result3 = light1 instanceof SpotLightBulb;        // (6) false: superclass.
    // SpotLightBulb spotRef = (SpotLightBulb) light1;// (7) ClassCastException!

    light1 = new NeonLight();                         // (8)
    if (light1 instanceof TubeLight) {                // (9) true.
      TubeLight tubeLight2 = (TubeLight) light1;      // (10) OK.
      // Can now use tubeLight2 to access an object of the class NeonLight,
      // but only those members that the object inherits or overrides
      // from the class TubeLight.
    }
  }
}
```

As we have seen, the `instanceof` operator effectively determines whether the reference value in the reference on the left-hand side refers to an object whose class is a subtype of the type of the reference specified on the right-hand side. At runtime, it is the type of the actual object denoted by the reference on the left-hand side that is compared with the type specified on the right-hand side. In other words, what matters at runtime is the type of the actual object denoted by the reference, not the declared type of the reference.

Example 7.17 provides more examples of the `instanceof` operator. It is instructive to go through the print statements and understand why those results printed out. The literal `null` is not an instance of any reference type, as shown in the print statements at (1), (2), and (16). An instance of a superclass is not an instance of its subclass, as shown in the print statement at (4). An instance of a class is not an instance of a totally unrelated class, as shown in the print statement at (10). An instance of a class is not an instance of an interface type that the class does not implement, as shown in the print statement at (6). Any array of non-primitive type is an instance of both `Object` and `Object[]` types, as shown in the print statements at (14) and (15), respectively.

Example 7.17 *Using the* `instanceof` *Operator*

```
// See Figure 7.3, p. 295, for inheritance hierarchy.
interface IStack                       { /* From Example 7.7 */ }
interface ISafeStack extends IStack    { /* From Example 7.7 */ }
class StackImpl implements IStack      { /* From Example 7.7 */ }
class SafeStackImpl extends StackImpl
              implements ISafeStack    { /* From Example 7.7 */ }
```

```
public class Identification {
  public static void main(String[] args) {
    Object obj = new Object();
    StackImpl stack = new StackImpl(10);
    SafeStackImpl safeStack = new SafeStackImpl(5);
    IStack iStack;

    String strFormat = "(%d)  %-25s instance of %-25s: %s%n";
    System.out.printf(strFormat, 1,
        null, Object.class,
        null instanceof Object);      // Always false.
    System.out.printf(strFormat, 2,
        null, IStack.class,
        null instanceof IStack);      // Always false.

    System.out.printf(strFormat, 3,
        stack.getClass(), Object.class,
        stack instanceof Object);     // true: instance of subclass of Object.
    System.out.printf(strFormat, 4,
        obj.getClass(), StackImpl.class,
        obj instanceof StackImpl);    // false: Object not subtype of StackImpl.
    System.out.printf(strFormat, 5,
        stack.getClass(), StackImpl.class,
        stack instanceof StackImpl);  // true: instance of StackImpl.
    System.out.printf(strFormat, 6,
        obj.getClass(), IStack.class,
        obj instanceof IStack);       // false: Object does not implement IStack.
    System.out.printf(strFormat, 7,
        safeStack.getClass(), IStack.class,
        safeStack instanceof IStack); // true: SafeStackImpl implements IStack.
```

```
        obj = stack;              // No cast required: assigning subclass to superclass.
        System.out.printf(strFormat, 8,
            obj.getClass(), StackImpl.class,
            obj instanceof StackImpl);    // true: instance of StackImpl.
        System.out.printf(strFormat, 9,
            obj.getClass(), IStack.class,
            obj instanceof IStack);       // true: StackImpl implements IStack.
        System.out.printf(strFormat, 10,
            obj.getClass(), String.class,
            obj instanceof String);       // false: no relationship.

        iStack = (IStack) obj; // Cast required: assigning superclass to subclass.
        System.out.printf(strFormat, 11,
            iStack.getClass(), Object.class,
            iStack instanceof Object);    // true: instance of subclass of Object.
        System.out.printf(strFormat, 12,
            iStack.getClass(), StackImpl.class,
            iStack instanceof StackImpl); // true: instance of StackImpl.

        String[] strArray = new String[10];
//      System.out.printf(strFormat, 13,
//          strArray.getClass(), String.class,
//          strArray instanceof String);     // Compile-time error: no relationship.
        System.out.printf(strFormat, 14,
            strArray.getClass(), Object.class,
            strArray instanceof Object);     // true: array subclass of Object.
        System.out.printf(strFormat, 15,
            strArray.getClass(), Object[].class,
            strArray instanceof Object[]);   // true: array subclass of Object[].
        System.out.printf(strFormat, 16,
            strArray[0], Object.class,
            strArray[0] instanceof Object);  // false: strArray[0] is null.
        System.out.printf(strFormat, 17,
            strArray.getClass(), String[].class,
            strArray instanceof String[]);   // true: array of String.

        strArray[0] = "Amoeba strip";
        System.out.printf(strFormat, 18,
            strArray[0].getClass(), String.class,
            strArray[0] instanceof String);  // true: strArray[0] instance of String.
    }
}
```

Output from the program:

```
(1)  null                     instance of class java.lang.Object   : false
(2)  null                     instance of interface IStack         : false
(3)  class StackImpl          instance of class java.lang.Object   : true
(4)  class java.lang.Object   instance of class StackImpl          : false
(5)  class StackImpl          instance of class StackImpl          : true
(6)  class java.lang.Object   instance of interface IStack         : false
(7)  class SafeStackImpl      instance of interface IStack         : true
(8)  class StackImpl          instance of class StackImpl          : true
(9)  class StackImpl          instance of interface IStack         : true
(10) class StackImpl          instance of class java.lang.String   : false
```

```
(11)  class StackImpl            instance of class java.lang.Object   : true
(12)  class StackImpl            instance of class StackImpl          : true
(14)  class [Ljava.lang.String;  instance of class java.lang.Object   : true
(15)  class [Ljava.lang.String;  instance of class [Ljava.lang.Object;: true
(16)  null                       instance of class java.lang.Object   : false
(17)  class [Ljava.lang.String;  instance of class [Ljava.lang.String;: true
(18)  class java.lang.String     instance of class java.lang.String   : true
```

Review Questions

7.23 Which statement about the following program is true?

```
public class MyClass {
  public static void main(String[] args) {
    A[] arrA;
    B[] arrB;

    arrA = new A[10];
    arrB = new B[20];
    arrA = arrB;        // (1)
    arrB = (B[]) arrA; // (2)
    arrA = new A[10];
    arrB = (B[]) arrA; // (3)
  }
}

class A {}

class B extends A {}
```

Select the one correct answer.

(a) The program will fail to compile because of the assignment at (1).
(b) When run, the program will throw a `java.lang.ClassCastException` in the assignment at (2).
(c) When run, the program will throw a `java.lang.ClassCastException` in the assignment at (3).
(d) The program will compile and run without errors, even if the cast operator `(B[])` in the statements at (2) and (3) is removed.
(e) The program will compile and run without errors, but will not do so if the cast operator `(B[])` in statements at (2) and (3) is removed.

7.24 Which statements will cause a compile-time error in the following code?

```
public class MyClass {
  public static void main(String[] args) {
    MyClass a;
    MySubclass b;

    a = new MyClass();             // (1)
    b = new MySubclass();          // (2)

    a = b;                         // (3)
    b = a;                         // (4)
```

```
        a = new MySubclass();                  // (5)
        b = new MyClass();                     // (6)
    }
}

class MySubclass extends MyClass {}
```

Select the two correct answers.

(a) (1)
(b) (2)
(c) (3)
(d) (4)
(e) (5)
(f) (6)

7.25 Given the following type and reference declarations, which assignment is legal?

```
// Type declarations:
interface I1 {}
interface I2 {}
class C1 implements I1 {}
class C2 implements I2 {}
class C3 extends C1 implements I2 {}

// Reference declarations:
  C1 obj1 = null;
  C2 obj2 = null;
  C3 obj3 = null;
```

Select the one correct answer.

(a) `obj2 = obj1;`
(b) `obj3 = obj1;`
(c) `obj3 = obj2;`
(d) `I1 a = obj2;`
(e) `I1 b = obj3;`
(f) `I2 c = obj1;`

7.26 Given the following class and reference declarations, what can be said about the statement `y = (Sub) x`?

```
// Class declarations:
class Super {}
class Sub extends Super {}

// Reference declarations:
  Super x = null;
  Sub y = null;
```

Select the one correct answer.

(a) It is illegal at compile time.
(b) It is legal at compile time, but might be illegal at runtime.
(c) It is definitely legal at runtime, but the cast operator `(Sub)` is not strictly needed.
(d) It is definitely legal at runtime, and the cast operator `(Sub)` is needed.

7.27 Given three classes A, B, and C, where B is a subclass of A, and C is a subclass of B, which one of these boolean expressions is true only when the reference o refers to an object of class B, and not to an object of class A or class C?

Select the one correct answer.

(a) `(o instanceof B) && (!(o instanceof A))`
(b) `(o instanceof B) && (!(o instanceof C))`
(c) `!((o instanceof A) || (o instanceof B))`
(d) `(o instanceof B)`
(e) `(o instanceof B) && !((o instanceof A) || (o instanceof C))`

7.28 What will the following program print when run?

```
public class RQ07A100 {
  public static void main(String[] args) {
    I x = new D();
    if (x instanceof I) System.out.print("I");
    if (x instanceof J) System.out.print("J");
    if (x instanceof C) System.out.print("C");
    if (x instanceof D) System.out.print("D");
    System.out.println();
  }
}
interface I{}
interface J{}
class C implements I {}
class D extends C implements J {}
```

Select the one correct answer.

(a) The program will not print any letters.
(b) `ICD`
(c) `IJD`
(d) `IJCD`
(e) `ID`

7.29 What is the result of compiling and running the following program?

```
class YingYang {
  void yingyang(Integer i) {
    System.out.println("Integer: " + i);
  }

  void yingyang(Integer[] ints) {
    System.out.println("Integer[]: " + ints[0]);
  }

  void yingyang(Integer... ints) {
    System.out.println("Integer...: " + ints[0]);
  }
}
```

```
public class RQ800A50 {
  public static void main(String[] args) {
    YingYang yy = new YingYang();
    yy.yingyang(10);
    yy.yingyang(10,12);
    yy.yingyang(new Integer[] {10, 20});
    yy.yingyang(new Integer(10), new Integer(20));
  }
}
```

Select the one correct answer.

(a) The program will not compile because of errors.

(b) The program will compile, but throw an exception at runtime.

(c) The program will compile and print:

```
Integer: 10
Integer...: 10
Integer...: 10
Integer...: 10
```

(d) The program will compile and print:

```
Integer: 10
Integer...: 10
Integer[]: 10
Integer...: 10
```

7.30 What will be the result of compiling and running the following program?

```
public class RQ800A20 {
  static void compute(int... ia) {                              // (1)
    System.out.print("|");
    for(int i : ia) {
      System.out.print(i + "|");
    }
    System.out.println();
  }
  static void compute(int[] ia1, int... ia2) {                  // (2)
    compute(ia1);
    compute(ia2);
  }
  static void compute(int[] ia1, int[]... ia2d) {                // (3)
    for(int[] ia : ia2d) {
      compute(ia);
    }
  }
  public static void main(String[] args) {
    compute(new int[] {10, 11}, new int[] {12, 13, 14});        // (4)
    compute(15, 16);                                            // (5)
    compute(new int[] {17, 18}, new int[][] {{19}, {20}});      // (6)
    compute(null, new int[][] {{21}, {22}});                    // (7)
  }
}
```

Select the one correct answer.

(a) The program does not compile because of errors in one or more calls to the `compute()` method.

(b) The program compiles, but throws a `NullPointerException` when run.

(c) The program compiles and prints:
```
|10|11|
|12|13|14|
|15|16|
|19|
|20|
|21|
|22|
```

(d) The program compiles and prints:
```
|12|13|14|
|15|16|
|10|11|
|19|
|20|
|21|
|22|
```

7.12 Polymorphism and Dynamic Method Lookup

Which object a reference will actually denote during runtime cannot always be determined at compile time. Polymorphism allows a reference to denote objects of different types at different times during execution. A supertype reference exhibits polymorphic behavior since it can denote objects of its subtypes.

When a non-`private` instance method is invoked on an object, the method definition actually executed is determined both by the type of the object at runtime and by the method signature. *Dynamic method lookup* (also known as *late binding, dynamic binding,* and *virtual method invocation*) is the process of determining which method definition a method signature denotes during runtime, based on the type of the object. However, a call to a `private` instance method is not polymorphic. Such a call can occur only within the class and gets bound to the `private` method implementation at compile time.

The inheritance hierarchy depicted in Figure 7.6 is implemented in Example 7.18. The implementation of the method `draw()` is overridden in all subclasses of the class `Shape`. The invocation of the `draw()` method in the two loops at (3) and (4) in Example 7.18 relies on the polymorphic behavior of references and dynamic method lookup. The array `shapes` holds `Shape` references denoting a `Circle`, a `Rectangle`, and a `Square`, as shown at (1). At runtime, dynamic lookup determines the `draw()` implementation that will execute, based on the type of the object denoted by each element in the array. This is also the case for the elements of the array `drawables` at (2), which holds `IDrawable` references that can be assigned the reference value of any object of a class that implements the `IDrawable` interface. The first loop will still work without any change if objects of new subclasses of the class `Shape` are added

Figure 7.6 *Type Hierarchy That Illustrates Polymorphism*

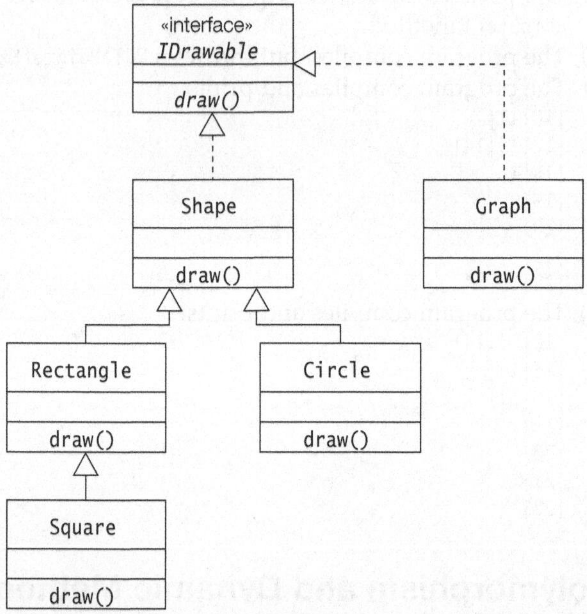

to the array `shapes`. If they did not override the `draw()` method, an inherited version of the method would be executed. This polymorphic behavior applies to the array `drawables`, where the subtype objects are guaranteed to have implemented the `IDrawable` interface.

Polymorphism and dynamic method lookup form a powerful programming paradigm that simplifies client definitions, encourages object decoupling, and supports dynamically changing relationships between objects at runtime.

Example 7.18 *Polymorphism and Dynamic Method Lookup*

```
// File: PolymorphRefs.java
interface IDrawable {
  void draw();
}
//______________________________________________________________
class Shape implements IDrawable {
  @Override public void draw() { System.out.println("Drawing a Shape."); }
}
//______________________________________________________________
class Circle extends Shape {
  @Override public void draw() { System.out.println("Drawing a Circle."); }
}
//______________________________________________________________
class Rectangle extends Shape {
  @Override public void draw() { System.out.println("Drawing a Rectangle."); }
}
```

```
//______________________________________________________________________
class Square extends Rectangle {
  @Override public void draw() { System.out.println("Drawing a Square."); }
}
//______________________________________________________________________
class Graph implements IDrawable {
  @Override public void draw() { System.out.println("Drawing a Graph."); }
}
//______________________________________________________________________
public class PolymorphRefs {
  public static void main(String[] args) {
    Shape[] shapes = {new Circle(), new Rectangle(), new Square()};         // (1)
    IDrawable[] drawables = {new Shape(), new Rectangle(), new Graph()};  // (2)

    System.out.println("Draw shapes:");
    for (Shape shape : shapes)                                              // (3)
      shape.draw();

    System.out.println("Draw drawables:");
    for (IDrawable drawable : drawables)                                    // (4)
      drawable.draw();
  }
}
```

Output from the program:

```
Draw shapes:
Drawing a Circle.
Drawing a Rectangle.
Drawing a Square.
Draw drawables:
Drawing a Shape.
Drawing a Rectangle.
Drawing a Graph.
```

7.13 Inheritance versus Aggregation

Figure 7.7 is a UML class diagram showing several aggregation relationships and one inheritance relationship. This class diagram shows a queue defined by aggregation and a stack defined by inheritance, both of which are based on linked lists. A linked list, in turn, is defined by aggregation. Example 7.19 shows a non-generic implementation of these data structures. The purpose of the example is to illustrate inheritance and aggregation, not industrial-strength implementation of queues and stacks. The class `Node` at (1) is straightforward, defining two fields: one denoting the data and the other denoting the next node in the list. The class `LinkedList` at (2) keeps track of the list by managing head and tail references. Nodes can be inserted in the front or back, but deleted only from the front of the list.

Figure 7.7 *Implementing Data Structures by Inheritance and Aggregation*

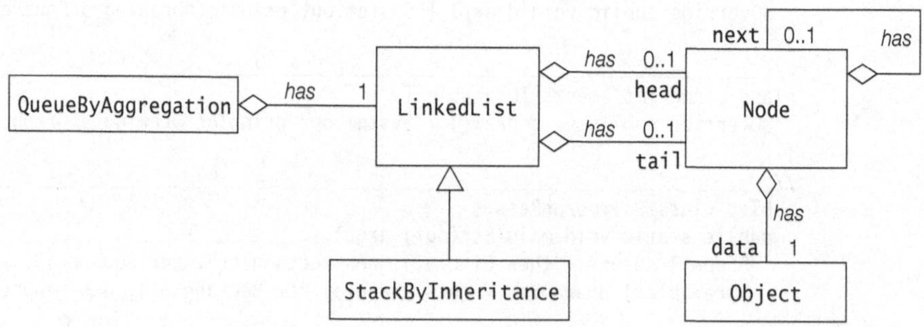

Example 7.19 *Implementing Data Structures by Inheritance and Aggregation*

```
class Node {                                                              // (1)
  private Object data;     // Data
  private Node   next;     // Next node

  // Constructor for initializing data and reference to the next node.
  Node(Object data, Node next) {
    this.data = data;
    this.next = next;
  }

  // Methods:
  public void   setData(Object obj) { data = obj; }
  public Object getData()           { return data; }
  public void   setNext(Node node)  { next = node; }
  public Node   getNext()           { return next; }
}
//______________________________________________________________________
class LinkedList {                                                        // (2)
  protected Node head = null;
  protected Node tail = null;

  // Methods:
  public boolean isEmpty() { return head == null; }
  public void insertInFront(Object dataObj) {
    if (isEmpty()) head = tail = new Node(dataObj, null);
    else head = new Node(dataObj, head);
  }
  public void insertAtBack(Object dataObj) {
    if (isEmpty())
      head = tail = new Node(dataObj, null);
    else {
      tail.setNext(new Node(dataObj, null));
      tail = tail.getNext();
    }
  }
```

```
    public Object deleteFromFront() {
      if (isEmpty()) return null;
      Node removed = head;
      if (head == tail) head = tail = null;
      else head = head.getNext();
      return removed.getData();
    }
  }
  //______________________________________________________________________
  class QueueByAggregation {                                        // (3)
    private LinkedList qList;

    // Constructor
    QueueByAggregation() {
      qList = new LinkedList();
    }

    // Methods:
    public boolean isEmpty() { return qList.isEmpty(); }
    public void enqueue(Object item) { qList.insertAtBack(item); }
    public Object dequeue() {
      if (qList.isEmpty()) return null;
      return qList.deleteFromFront();
    }
    public Object peek() {
      return (qList.isEmpty() ? null : qList.head.getData());
    }
  }
  //______________________________________________________________________
  class StackByInheritance extends LinkedList {                     // (4)
    public void push(Object item) { insertInFront(item); }
    public Object pop() {
      if (isEmpty()) return null;
      return deleteFromFront();
    }
    public Object peek() {
      return (isEmpty() ? null : head.getData());
    }
  }
  //______________________________________________________________________
  public class Client {                                             // (5)
    public static void main(String[] args) {
      String string1 = "Queues are boring to stand in!";
      int length1 = string1.length();
      QueueByAggregation queue = new QueueByAggregation();
      for (int i = 0; i<length1; i++)
        queue.enqueue(new Character(string1.charAt(i)));
      while (!queue.isEmpty())
        System.out.print(queue.dequeue());
      System.out.println();

      String string2 = "!no tis ot nuf era skcatS";
      int length2 = string2.length();
      StackByInheritance stack = new StackByInheritance();
      for (int i = 0; i<length2; i++)
        stack.push(new Character(string2.charAt(i)));
```

```
    stack.insertAtBack(new Character('!'));                    // (6)
    while (!stack.isEmpty())
      System.out.print(stack.pop());
    System.out.println();
  }
}
```

Output from the program:

```
Queues are boring to stand in!
Stacks are fun to sit on!!
```

Choosing between inheritance and aggregation to model relationships can be a crucial design decision. A good design strategy advocates that inheritance should be used only if the relationship *is-a* is unequivocally maintained throughout the lifetime of the objects involved; otherwise, aggregation is the best choice. A *role* is often confused with an *is-a* relationship. For example, given the class `Employee`, it would not be a good idea to model the roles that an employee can play (such as manager or cashier) by inheritance, if these roles change intermittently. Changing roles would involve a new object to represent the new role every time this happens.

Code reuse is also best achieved by aggregation when there is no *is-a* relationship. Enforcing an artificial *is-a* relationship that is not naturally present is usually not a good idea. Since the class `StackByInheritance` at (4) in Example 7.19 is a subclass of the class `LinkedList` at (2), any inherited method from the superclass can be invoked on an instance of the subclass. Also, methods that contradict the abstraction represented by the subclass can be invoked, as shown at (6). Using aggregation in such a case results in a better solution, as demonstrated by the class `QueueByAggregation` at (3). The class defines the operations of a queue by *delegating* such requests to the underlying class `LinkedList`. Clients implementing a queue in this manner do not have access to the underlying class and, therefore, cannot break the abstraction.

Both inheritance and aggregation promote encapsulation of *implementation*, as changes to the implementation are localized to the class. Changing the *contract* of a superclass can have consequences for the subclasses (called the *ripple effect*) as well as for clients that are dependent on a particular behavior of the subclasses.

Polymorphism is achieved through inheritance and interface implementation. Code relying on polymorphic behavior will still work without any change if new subclasses or new classes implementing the interface are added. If no obvious *is-a* relationship is present, polymorphism is best achieved by using aggregation with interface implementation.

7.14 Basic Concepts in Object-Oriented Design

In this section, we provide a brief explanation of some basic concepts in object-oriented (OO) design. For more details, the reader is encouraged to consult the vast body of literature that is readily available on this subject.

Encapsulation

An object has properties and behaviors that are *encapsulated* inside the object. The services that the object offers to its clients make up its *contract*, or public interface. Only the contract defined by the object is available to the clients. The *implementation* of its properties and behavior is not a concern of the clients. Encapsulation helps to make clear the distinction between an object's contract and implementation. This demarcation has major consequences for program development, as the implementation of an object can change without affecting the clients. Encapsulation also reduces complexity, as the internals of an object are hidden from the clients, which cannot alter its implementation.

Encapsulation is achieved through *information hiding*, by making judicious use of language features provided for this purpose. Information hiding in Java can be achieved at different levels of granularity:

- Method or block level

  Localizing information in a method hides it from the outside.

- Class level

  The accessibility of members declared in a class can be controlled through member accessibility modifiers. One much-advocated information-hiding technique is to prevent direct access by clients to data maintained by an object. The fields of the object are private, and its contract defines public methods for the services provided by the object. Such tight encapsulation helps to separate the use from the implementation of a class.

- Package level

  Classes that belong together can be grouped into relevant packages by using the `package` statement. Interpackage accessibility of classes can be controlled by class accessibility modifiers.

Cohesion

Cohesion is an *interclass* measure of how well structured and closely related the functionality is in a class. The objective is to design classes with *high* cohesion, that perform well-defined and related tasks (also called *functional cohesion*). The public methods of a highly cohesive class typically implement a single specific task that is related to the purpose of the class. For example, in an MVC-based application, the respective classes for the Model, the View, and the Controller should focus on providing functionality that relates to their individual purpose. In other words, a method in one class should not perform a task that should actually be implemented by one of the other two classes.

Lack of cohesion in a class means that the purpose of the class is not focused, and unrelated functionality is ending up in the class (also called *coincidental cohesion*)—which will eventually impact the maintainability of the application.

Coupling

Coupling is a measure of *intraclass dependencies*. Because objects need to interact with one another, dependencies between classes are inherent in OO design. However, these dependencies should be minimized to achieve *loose* coupling, which facilitates the creation of extensible applications.

One major source of intraclass dependencies is the exposure of implementation details of an object. Such details can be utilized by other objects, and this dependency can impede changes in the implementation, resulting in less extensible applications.

High cohesion and loose coupling help to achieve the main goals of OO design: maintainability, reusability, extensibility, and reliability.

Review Questions

7.31 What will be the result of compiling and running the following program?

```
public class Polymorphism {
  public static void main(String[] args) {
    A ref1 = new C();
    B ref2 = (B) ref1;
    System.out.println(ref2.f());
  }
}

class A           { int f() { return 0; } }
class B extends A { int f() { return 1; } }
class C extends B { int f() { return 2; } }
```

Select the one correct answer.

(a) The program will fail to compile.
(b) The program will compile, but will throw a `ClassCastException` at runtime.
(c) The program will compile, and print `0` when run.
(d) The program will compile, and print `1` when run.
(e) The program will compile, and print `2` when run.

7.32 What will be the result of compiling and running the following program?

```
public class Polymorphism2 {
  public static void main(String[] args) {
    A ref1 = new C();
    B ref2 = (B) ref1;
    System.out.println(ref2.g());
  }
}

class A {
  private int f() { return 0; }
  public int g() { return 3; }
}
```

```
class B extends A {
  private int f() { return 1; }
  public int g() { return f(); }
}
class C extends B {
  public int f() { return 2; }
}
```

Select the one correct answer.

(a) The program will fail to compile.
(b) The program will compile, and print 0 when run.
(c) The program will compile, and print 1 when run.
(d) The program will compile, and print 2 when run.
(e) The program will compile, and print 3 when run.

7.33 Which statements about the following program are true?

```
public interface HeavenlyBody { String describe(); }

class Star {
  String starName;
  public String describe() { return "star " + starName; }
}

class Planet extends Star {
  String name;
  public String describe() {
    return "planet " + name + " orbiting star " + starName;
  }
}
```

Select the three correct answers:

(a) The code will fail to compile.
(b) The code defines a `Planet` *is-a* `Star` relationship.
(c) The code will fail to compile if the name `starName` is replaced with the name `bodyName` throughout the declaration of the `Star` class.
(d) The code will fail to compile if the name `starName` is replaced with the name `name` throughout the declaration of the `Star` class.
(e) An instance of `Planet` is a valid instance of `HeavenlyBody`.
(f) The code defines a `Planet` *has-a* `Star` relationship.

7.34 Given the following code, which statement is true?

```
public interface HeavenlyBody { String describe(); }

class Star implements HeavenlyBody {
  String starName;
  public String describe() { return "star " + starName; }
}

class Planet {
  String name;
  Star orbiting;
```

```
    public String describe() {
      return "planet " + name + " orbiting " + orbiting.describe();
    }
  }
```

Select the one correct answer:

(a) The code will fail to compile.
(b) The code defines a `Planet` *has-a* `Star` relationship.
(c) The code will fail to compile if the name `starName` is replaced with the name `bodyName` throughout the declaration of the `Star` class.
(d) The code will fail to compile if the name `starName` is replaced with the name `name` throughout the declaration of the `Star` class.
(e) An instance of `Planet` is a valid instance of a `HeavenlyBody`.
(f) The code defines a `Planet` *is-a* `Star` relationship.

7.35 Which of the following statements is not true?

Select the one correct answer.

(a) Maximizing cohesion and minimizing coupling are the hallmarks of a well-designed application.
(b) Coupling is an inherent property of any nontrivial OO design.
(c) Dependencies between classes can be minimized by hiding implementation details.
(d) Each method implementing a single task that is related to the purpose of the class will result in a class that has high cohesion.
(e) None of the above.

Chapter Summary

The following topics were covered in this chapter:

- Inheritance and its implications in object-oriented programming
- Overriding and hiding of superclass members
- Method overriding versus method overloading
- Use of the `super` reference to access superclass members
- Use of `this()` and `super()` calls, including constructor chaining
- Interfaces and multiple interface inheritance
- Subtype–supertype relationships
- Conversions when assigning, casting, and passing reference values
- Resolution of overloaded methods
- Identifying the type of objects using the `instanceof` operator

- Polymorphism and dynamic method lookup
- Inheritance (*is-a*) versus aggregation (*has-a*)
- Best practices for object-oriented design: tight encapsulation, loose coupling, and high cohesion in classes

Programming Exercises

7.1 Declare an interface called `Function` that has a method named `evaluate` that takes an `int` parameter and returns an `int` value.

Create a class called `Half` that implements the `Function` interface. The implementation of the method `evaluate()` should return the value obtained by dividing the `int` argument by 2.

In a client, create a method that takes an arbitrary number of `int` values as a varargs parameter, and returns an array that has length equal to the number of values passed in the varargs parameter, but with the value of an element in the new array being half that of the corresponding value in the varargs parameter. Let the implementation of this method create an instance of `Half`, and use this instance to calculate values for the array that is returned.

7.2 Rewrite the method that operated on `int` values from the previous exercise: The method should now also accept a `Function` reference as an argument, and use this argument instead of an instance of the `Half` class.

Create a class called `Print` that implements the method `evaluate()` in the `Function` interface. This method simply prints the `int` value passed as an argument, and returns this value.

Now write a program that does the following:

- Prints an arbitrary number of int values using an instance of the `Print` class and the method described earlier.
- Halves the values in the array and prints the values again, using the `Half` and `Print` classes, and the method described earlier.

Fundamental Classes

8

Programmer I Exam Objectives	
[2.5] Develop code that uses wrapper classes such as Boolean, Double, and Integer	§8.3, p. 346
[3.2] Test equality between Strings and other objects using == and equals() ○ *For equality operator (==), see §5.12, p. 181.*	§8.4, p. 357 §8.4, p. 363
[9.1] Manipulate data using the StringBuilder class and its methods	§8.5, p. 374
[9.2] Creating and manipulating Strings	§8.4, p. 357
Supplementary Objectives	
• Understand the functionality inherited by all classes from the `Object` class	§8.2, p. 342
• Understand the significance of immutability of `String` objects	§8.4, p. 357
• Discuss the differences among the `String`, `StringBuilder`, and `StringBuffer` classes	§8.5, p. 376

8.1 Overview of the `java.lang` Package

The `java.lang` package is indispensable when programming in Java. It is automatically imported into every source file at compile time. The package contains the `Object` class that is the superclass of all classes, and the wrapper classes (`Boolean`, `Character`, `Byte`, `Short`, `Integer`, `Long`, `Float`, `Double`) that are used to handle primitive values as objects. It provides classes essential for interacting with the JVM (`Runtime`), for security (`SecurityManager`), for loading classes (`ClassLoader`), for dealing with threads (`Thread`), and for exceptions (`Throwable`, `Error`, `Exception`, `RuntimeException`). The `java.lang` package also contains classes that provide the standard input, output, and error streams (`System`), string handling (`String`, `StringBuilder`, `StringBuffer`), and mathematical functions (`Math`).

Figure 8.1 shows the important classes that are discussed in detail in this chapter.

Figure 8.1 *Partial Inheritance Hierarchy in the* `java.lang` *Package*

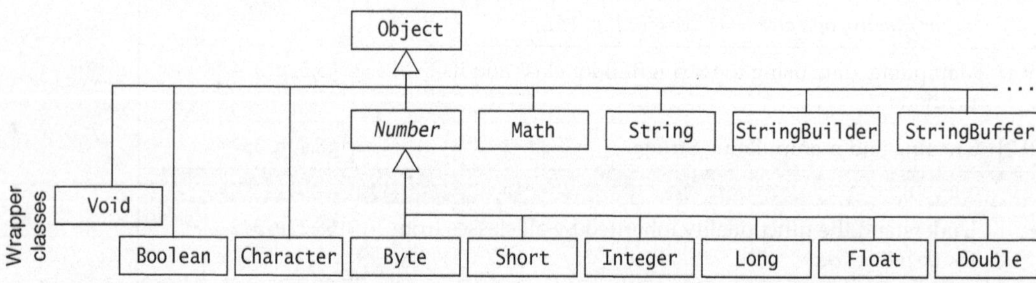

8.2 The `Object` Class

All classes extend the `Object` class, either directly or indirectly. A class declaration, without the `extends` clause, implicitly extends the `Object` class (§7.1, p. 264). Thus, the `Object` class is always at the root of any inheritance hierarchy. The `Object` class defines the basic functionality that all objects exhibit and all classes inherit. This relationship also applies to arrays, since these are genuine objects in Java.

The `Object` class provides the following general utility methods (see Example 8.1 for usage of some of these methods):

```
boolean equals(Object obj)
```

Object reference and value equality are discussed together with the `==` and `!=` operators (§5.12, p. 181). The `equals()` method in the `Object` class returns `true` only if the two references compared denote the same object. The `equals()` method is usually overridden to provide the semantics of object value equality, as is the case for the wrapper classes (§8.3, p. 350) and the `String` class (§8.4, p. 363).

`int hashCode()`

When storing objects in hash tables, this method can be used to get a hash value for an object. This value is guaranteed to be consistent during the execution of the program, provided the information used in the `equals()` comparisons on the object does not change. This method tries to return distinct integers for distinct objects as their default hash value. The `hashCode()` method is usually overridden by a class, as is the case for the wrapper classes and the `String` class.

`final Class<?> getClass()`

Returns the *runtime class* of the object, which is represented by an object of the class `java.lang.Class` at runtime.

`protected Object clone() throws CloneNotSupportedException`

New objects that are exactly the same (i.e., have identical states) as the current object can be created by using the `clone()` method; that is, primitive values and reference values are copied. This is called *shallow copying*. A class can override this method to provide its own notion of cloning. For example, cloning a composite object by recursively cloning the constituent objects is called *deep copying*. When overridden, the method in the subclass is usually declared as `public` to allow any client to clone objects of the class. If the overriding `clone()` method in the subclass relies on the `clone()` method in the `Object` class (i.e., a shallow copy), the subclass must implement the `Cloneable` marker interface to indicate that its objects can be safely cloned. Otherwise, the `clone()` method in the `Object` class will throw a checked `CloneNotSupportedException`.

`String toString()`

If a subclass does not override this method, it returns a textual representation of the object, which has the following format:

"<*name of the class*>@<*hash code value of object*>"

Since the default hash value of an object is an `int` value, this value is printed as a hexadecimal number (e.g., `3e25a5`). This method is usually overridden. The method call `System.out.println(objRef)` will implicitly convert its argument to a textual representation by calling the `toString()` method on the argument. See also the binary string concatenation operator +, discussed in §5.7 on page 169.

`protected void finalize() throws Throwable`

This method is discussed in connection with garbage collection (§9.4, p. 390). It is called on an object just before it is garbage collected, so that any cleaning up can be done. However, the default `finalize()` method in the `Object` class does not do anything useful.

In addition, the `Object` class provides support for thread communication in synchronized code, through the following methods. This important topic is beyond the scope of this book.

```
final void wait(long timeout) throws InterruptedException
final void wait(long timeout, int nanos) throws InterruptedException
final void wait() throws InterruptedException
final void notify()
final void notifyAll()
```

A thread invokes these methods on the object whose lock it holds. A thread waits for notification by another thread.

Example 8.1 *Methods in the* `Object` *Class*

```
// File: ObjectMethods.java
class MyClass implements Cloneable {
  @Override
  public MyClass clone() {
    MyClass obj = null;
    try { obj = (MyClass) super.clone(); } // Calls overridden method.
    catch (CloneNotSupportedException e) { System.out.println(e);}
    return obj;
  }
}
//______________________________________________________________________
public class ObjectMethods {
  public static void main(String[] args) {
    // Two objects of MyClass.
    MyClass obj1 = new MyClass();
    MyClass obj2 = new MyClass();

    // Two strings.
    String str1 = new String("WhoAmI");
    String str2 = new String("WhoAmI");

    // Method hashCode() overridden in String class.
    // Strings that are equal have the same hash code.
    System.out.println("hash code for str1: " + str1.hashCode());
    System.out.println("hash code for str2: " + str2.hashCode() + "\n");

    // Hash codes are different for different MyClass objects.
    System.out.println("hash code for MyClass obj1: " + obj1.hashCode());
    System.out.println("hash code for MyClass obj2: " + obj2.hashCode()+"\n");

    // Method equals() overridden in the String class.
    System.out.println("str1.equals(str2): " + str1.equals(str2));
    System.out.println("str1 == str2:      " + (str1 == str2) + "\n");

    // Method equals() from the Object class called.
    System.out.println("obj1.equals(obj2): " + obj1.equals(obj2));
    System.out.println("obj1 == obj2:      " + (obj1 == obj2) + "\n");

    // The runtime object that represents the class of an object.
    Class rtStringClass  = str1.getClass();
```

```
    Class rtMyClassClass = obj1.getClass();
    // The name of the class represented by the runtime object.
    System.out.println("Class for str1: " + rtStringClass);
    System.out.println("Class for obj1: " + rtMyClassClass + "\n");

    // The toString() method is overridden in the String class.
    String textRepStr = str1.toString();
    String textRepObj = obj1.toString();
    System.out.println("Text representation of str1: " + textRepStr);
    System.out.println("Text representation of obj1: " + textRepObj + "\n");

    // Shallow copying of arrays.
    MyClass[] array1 = {new MyClass(), new MyClass(), new MyClass()};
    MyClass[] array2 = array1.clone();
    // Array objects are different, but share the element objects.
    System.out.println("array1 == array2:          " + (array1 == array2));
    for(int i = 0; i < array1.length; i++) {
      System.out.println("array1[" + i + "] == array2[" + i + "] : " +
                         (array1[i] == array2[i]));
    }
    System.out.println();

    // Clone an object of MyClass.
    MyClass obj3 = obj1.clone();
    System.out.println("hash code for MyClass obj3: " + obj3.hashCode());
    System.out.println("obj1 == obj3: " + (obj1 == obj3));
  }
}
```

Probable output from the program:

```
hash code for str1: -1704812257
hash code for str2: -1704812257

hash code for MyClass obj1: 25669322
hash code for MyClass obj2: 14978587

str1.equals(str2): true
str1 == str2:      false

obj1.equals(obj2): false
obj1 == obj2:      false

Class for str1: class java.lang.String
Class for obj1: class MyClass

Text representation of str1: WhoAmI
Text representation of obj1: MyClass@187aeca

array1 == array2:         false
array1[0] == array2[0] : true
array1[1] == array2[1] : true
array1[2] == array2[2] : true

hash code for MyClass obj3: 19770577
obj1 == obj3: false
```

Review Questions

8.1 What is the return type of the `hashCode()` method in the `Object` class?

Select the one correct answer.

(a) `String`
(b) `int`
(c) `long`
(d) `Object`
(e) `Class`

8.2 Which of the following statements is true?

Select the one correct answer.

(a) If the references `x` and `y` denote two different objects, the expression `x.equals(y)` is always `false`.
(b) If the references `x` and `y` denote two different objects, the expression `(x.hashCode() == y.hashCode())` is always `false`.
(c) The `hashCode()` method in the `Object` class is declared as `final`.
(d) The `equals()` method in the `Object` class is declared as `final`.
(e) All arrays have a method named `clone`.

8.3 Which exception can the `clone()` method of the `Object` class throw?

Select the one correct answer.

(a) `CloneNotSupportedException`
(b) `NotCloneableException`
(c) `IllegalCloneException`
(d) `NoClonesAllowedException`

8.3 The Wrapper Classes

Wrapper classes were introduced with the discussion of the primitive data types (§2.2, p. 37), and also in connection with boxing and unboxing of primitive values (§5.1, p. 145). Primitive values in Java are not objects. To manipulate these values as objects, the `java.lang` package provides a *wrapper* class for each of the primitive data types (shown in the bottom left of Figure 8.2). The name of the wrapper class is the name of the primitive data type with a uppercase letter, except for `int` (`Integer`) and `char` (`Character`). All wrapper classes are `final`. The objects of all wrapper classes that can be instantiated are *immutable*; in other words, the value in the wrapper object cannot be changed.

Although the `Void` class is considered a wrapper class, it does not wrap any primitive value and is not instantiable (i.e., has no `public` constructors). It just denotes the `Class` object representing the keyword `void`. The `Void` class will not be discussed further in this section.

In addition to the methods defined for constructing and manipulating objects of primitive values, the wrapper classes define useful constants, fields, and conversion methods.

Figure 8.2 *Converting Values among Primitive, Wrapper, and* `String` *Types*

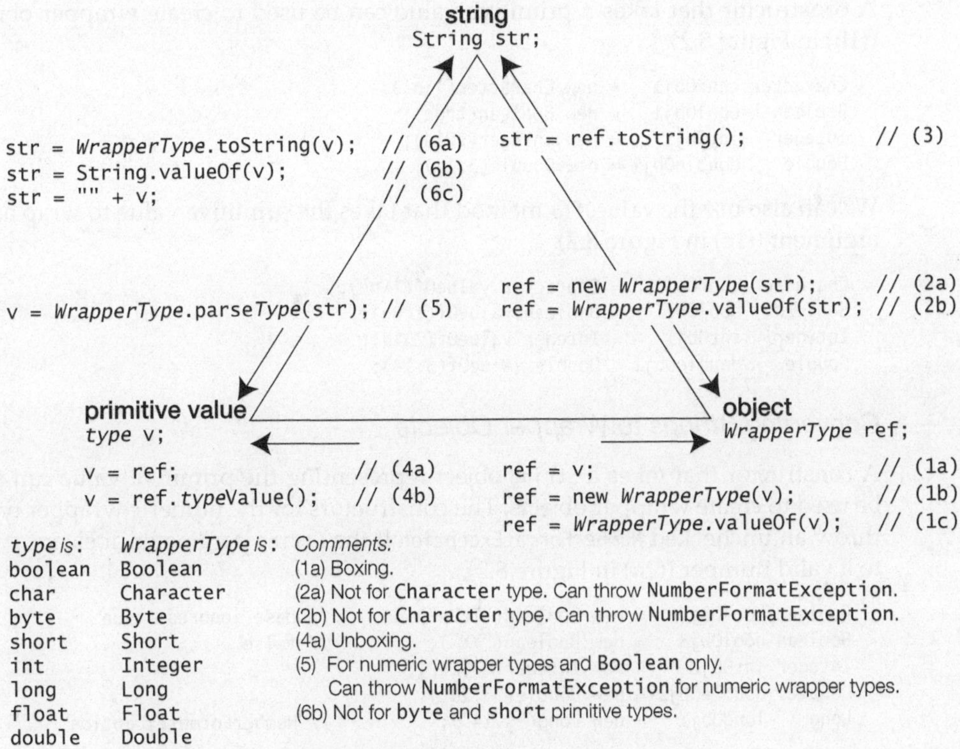

Common Wrapper Class Constructors

The `Character` class has only one `public` constructor, taking a `char` value as its parameter. The other wrapper classes all have two `public` one-argument constructors: one takes a primitive value and the other takes a string.

```
WrapperType(type v)
WrapperType(String str)
```

The *type* is a primitive data type. The string argument is converted to a primitive value that corresponds to the *WrapperType*. An unchecked `NumberFormatException` is thrown if the string cannot be converted to a primitive value that corresponds to a numeric *WrapperType*.

Wrapping Primitive Values in Objects

Boxing is a convenient way to wrap a primitive value in an object ((1a) in Figure 8.2 and §5.1, p. 145).

```
Character charObj1   = '\n';
Boolean   boolObj1   = true;
Integer   intObj1    = 2014;
Double    doubleObj1 = 3.14;
```

A constructor that takes a primitive value can be used to create wrapper objects ((1b) in Figure 8.2).

```
Character charObj1   = new Character('\n');
Boolean   boolObj1   = new Boolean(true);
Integer   intObj1    = new Integer(2014);
Double    doubleObj1 = new Double(3.14);
```

We can also use the `valueOf()` method that takes the primitive value to wrap as an argument ((1c) in Figure 8.2).

```
Character charObj1   = Character.valueOf('\n');
Boolean   boolObj1   = Boolean.valueOf(true);
Integer   intObj1    = Integer.valueOf(2014);
Double    doubleObj1 = Double.valueOf(3.14);
```

Converting Strings to Wrapper Objects

A constructor that takes a `String` object representing the primitive value can also be used to create wrapper objects. The constructors for the numeric wrapper types throw an unchecked `NumberFormatException` if the `String` parameter does not parse to a valid number ((2a) in Figure 8.2).

```
Boolean boolObj2   = new Boolean("TrUe");        // case ignored: true
Boolean boolObj3   = new Boolean("XX");          // false
Integer intObj2    = new Integer("2014");
Double  doubleObj2 = new Double("3.14");
Long    longObj1   = new Long("3.14");           // NumberFormatException
```

Common Wrapper Class Utility Methods

Converting Strings to Wrapper Objects

Each wrapper class (except `Character`) defines the static method `valueOf(String str)` that returns the wrapper object corresponding to the primitive value represented by the `String` object passed as an argument ((6b) in Figure 8.2). This method for the numeric wrapper types also throws a `NumberFormatException` if the `String` parameter is not a valid number.

```
static WrapperType valueOf(String str)
```

```
Boolean boolObj4   = Boolean.valueOf("false");
Integer intObj3    = Integer.valueOf("1949");
Double  doubleObj3 = Double.valueOf("-3.0");
```

In addition to the one-argument `valueOf()` method, the integer wrapper classes define an overloaded static `valueOf()` method that can take a second argument. This argument specifies the base (or *radix*) in which to interpret the string representing the signed integer in the first argument.

```
static IntegerWrapperType valueOf(String str, int base)
                          throws NumberFormatException
```

```
Byte    byteObj1  = Byte.valueOf("1010", 2);    // Decimal value 10
Short   shortObj2 = Short.valueOf("12", 8);     // Not "\012". Decimal value 10.
Integer intObj4   = Integer.valueOf("-a", 16); // Not "-0xa". Decimal value -10.
Long    longObj2  = Long.valueOf("-a", 16);    // Not "-0xa". Decimal value -10L.
```

Converting Wrapper Objects to Strings

Each wrapper class overrides the `toString()` method from the `Object` class. The overriding method returns a `String` object containing the string representation of the primitive value in the wrapper object ((3) in Figure 8.2).

```
String toString()
```

```
String charStr   = charObj1.toString();    // "\n"
String boolStr   = boolObj2.toString();    // "true"
String intStr    = intObj1.toString();     // "2014"
String doubleStr = doubleObj1.toString();  // "3.14"
```

Converting Primitive Values to Strings

Each wrapper class defines a static method `toString(type v)` that returns the string corresponding to the primitive value of *type*, which is passed as an argument ((6a) in Figure 8.2).

```
static String toString(type v)
```

```
String charStr2   = Character.toString('\n');  // "\n"
String boolStr2   = Boolean.toString(true);    // "true"
String intStr2    = Integer.toString(2014);    // Base 10. "2014"
String doubleStr2 = Double.toString(3.14);     // "3.14"
```

For integer primitive types, the base is assumed to be 10. For floating-point numbers, the textual representation (decimal form or scientific notation) depends on the sign and the magnitude (absolute value) of the number. The NaN value, positive infinity, and negative infinity will result in the strings `"NaN"`, `"Infinity"`, and `"-Infinity"`, respectively.

In addition, the wrapper classes `Integer` and `Long` define methods for converting integers to string representations in decimal, binary, octal, and hexadecimal notation (p. 353).

Converting Wrapper Objects to Primitive Values

Unboxing is a convenient way to unwrap the primitive value in a wrapper object ((4a) in Figure 8.2 and §5.1, p. 145).

```
char    c = charObj1;                // '\n'
boolean b = boolObj2;                // true
int     i = intObj1;                 // 2014
double  d = doubleObj1;              // 3.14
```

Each wrapper class defines a *type*`Value()` method that returns the primitive value in the wrapper object ((4b) in Figure 8.2).

```
type typeValue()
```

```
char    c = charObj1.charValue();             // '\n'
boolean b = boolObj2.booleanValue();          // true
int     i = intObj1.intValue();               // 2014
double  d = doubleObj1.doubleValue();         // 3.14
```

In addition, each numeric wrapper class defines *type*`Value()` methods for converting the primitive value in the wrapper object to a value of any numeric primitive data type. These methods are discussed later.

Wrapper Comparison, Equality, and Hash Code

Each wrapper class implements the `Comparable<Type>` interface, which defines the following method:

```
int compareTo(Type obj2)
```

This method returns a value that is less than, equal to, or greater than zero, depending on whether the primitive value in the current wrapper *Type* object is less than, equal to, or greater than the primitive value in the wrapper *Type* object denoted by argument `obj2`.

```
// Comparisons based on objects created earlier
Character charObj2    = 'a';
int result1 = charObj1.compareTo(charObj2);       //  result1 < 0
int result2 = intObj1.compareTo(intObj3);         //  result2 > 0
int result3 = doubleObj1.compareTo(doubleObj2);   // result == 0
int result4 = doubleObj1.compareTo(intObj1);      // Compile-time error!
```

Each wrapper class overrides the `equals()` method from the `Object` class. The overriding method compares two wrapper objects for object value equality.

```
boolean equals(Object obj2)
```

```
// Comparisons based on objects created earlier
boolean charTest   = charObj1.equals(charObj2);        // false
boolean boolTest   = boolObj2.equals(Boolean.FALSE);   // false
boolean intTest    = intObj1.equals(intObj2);          // true
boolean doubleTest = doubleObj1.equals(doubleObj2);    // true
boolean test       = intObj1.equals(new Long(2014));   // false. Not same type.
```

The following values are *interned* when they are wrapped during boxing. That is, only *one* wrapper object exists in the program for these primitive values when boxing is applied:

- The `boolean` values `true` or `false`
- A `byte`
- A `char` with a Unicode value in the interval `[\u0000, \u007f]` (i.e., decimal interval [0, 127])
- An `int` or `short` value in the interval `[-128, 127]`

If references `w1` and `w2` refer to two wrapper objects that box the *same* value, which is among the ones mentioned here, then `w1 == w2` is always `true`. In other words, for the values listed previously, object equality and reference equality give the same result.

```
// Reference and object equality
Byte bRef1 = 10;
Byte bRef2 = 10;
System.out.println(bRef1 == bRef2);                // true
System.out.println(bRef1.equals(bRef2));           // true

Integer iRef1 = 1000;
Integer iRef2 = 1000;
System.out.println(iRef1 == iRef2);                // false
System.out.println(iRef1.equals(iRef2));           // true
```

Each wrapper class also overrides the `hashCode()` method in the `Object` class. The overriding method returns a hash value based on the primitive value in the wrapper object.

```
int hashCode()
```

```
int index = charObj1.hashCode();                   // 10 ('\n')
```

Numeric Wrapper Classes

The numeric wrapper classes `Byte`, `Short`, `Integer`, `Long`, `Float`, and `Double` are all subclasses of the `abstract` class `Number` (Figure 8.1).

Each numeric wrapper class defines an assortment of constants, including the minimum and maximum values of the corresponding primitive data type:

```
NumericWrapperType.MIN_VALUE
NumericWrapperType.MAX_VALUE
```

The following code retrieves the minimum and maximum values of various numeric types:

```
byte   minByte   = Byte.MIN_VALUE;     // -128
int    maxInt    = Integer.MAX_VALUE;  // 2147483647
double maxDouble = Double.MAX_VALUE;   // 1.7976931348623157e+308
```

Converting Numeric Wrapper Objects to Numeric Primitive Types

Each numeric wrapper class defines the following set of *type*`Value()` methods for converting the primitive value in the wrapper object to a value of any numeric primitive type:

```
byte   byteValue()
short  shortValue()
int    intValue()
long   longValue()
float  floatValue()
double doubleValue()
```

See also (4b) in Figure 8.2.

The following code shows conversion of values in numeric wrapper objects to any numeric primitive type:

```
Byte    byteObj2   = new Byte((byte) 16);        // Cast mandatory
Integer intObj5    = new Integer(42030);
Double  doubleObj4 = new Double(Math.PI);

short  shortVal  = intObj5.shortValue();        // (1)
long   longVal   = byteObj2.longValue();
int    intVal    = doubleObj4.intValue();       // (2) Truncation
double doubleVal = intObj5.doubleValue();
```

Notice the potential for loss of information at (1) and (2), when the primitive value in a wrapper object is converted to a narrower primitive data type.

Converting Strings to Numeric Values

Each numeric wrapper class defines a static method `parse`*Type*`(String str)`, which returns the primitive numeric value represented by the `String` object passed as an argument. The *Type* in the method name `parse`*Type* stands for the name of a numeric wrapper class, except for the name of the `Integer` class, which is abbreviated to `Int`. These methods throw a `NumberFormatException` if the `String` parameter is not a valid argument ((5) in Figure 8.2.)

```
static type parseType(String str) throws NumberFormatException
```

```
byte   value1 = Byte.parseByte("16");
int    value2 = Integer.parseInt("2010");       // parseInt, not parseInteger
int    value3 = Integer.parseInt("7UP");        // NumberFormatException
double value4 = Double.parseDouble("3.14");
```

For the integer wrapper types, the overloaded static method `parse`*Type*`()` can additionally take a second argument, which can specify the base in which to interpret the string representing the signed integer in the first argument:

```
type parseType(String str, int base) throws NumberFormatException
```

```
byte  value6 = Byte.parseByte("1010", 2); // Decimal value 10.
short value7 = Short.parseShort("12", 8); // "012", not "\012". Decimal value 10.
int   value8 = Integer.parseInt("-a", 16);// Not "-0xa". Decimal value -10.
long  value9 = Long.parseLong("-a", 16);  // Not "-0xa". Decimal value -10L.
```

Converting Integer Values to Strings in Different Notations

The wrapper classes `Integer` and `Long` provide static methods for converting integers to string representations in decimal, binary, octal, and hexadecimal notation. Some of these methods from the `Integer` class are listed here, but analogous methods are also defined in the `Long` class. Example 8.2 demonstrates the use of these methods.

```
static String toBinaryString(int i)
static String toHexString(int i)
static String toOctalString(int i)
```

These three methods return a string representation of the integer argument as an *unsigned* integer in base 2, 16, and 8, respectively, with no extra leading zeroes.

```
static String toString(int i, int base)
static String toString(int i)
```

The first method returns the minus sign `'-'` as the first character if the integer `i` is negative. In all cases, it returns the string representation of the *magnitude* of the integer `i` in the specified base.

The last method is equivalent to the method `toString(int i, int base)`, where the base has the value 10, and which returns the string representation as a signed decimal ((6a) in Figure 8.2).

Example 8.2 *String Representation of Integers*

```
public class IntegerRepresentation {
  public static void main(String[] args) {
    int positiveInt = +41;    // 0b101001, 051, 0x29
    int negativeInt = -41;    // 0b11111111111111111111111111010111, -0b101001,
                              // 037777777727, -051, 0xffffffd7, -0x29
    System.out.println("String representation for decimal value: " + positiveInt);
    integerStringRepresentation(positiveInt);
    System.out.println("String representation for decimal value: " + negativeInt);
    integerStringRepresentation(negativeInt);
  }

  public static void integerStringRepresentation(int i) {
    System.out.println("    Binary:     " + Integer.toBinaryString(i));
    System.out.println("    Octal:      " + Integer.toOctalString(i));
    System.out.println("    Hex:        " + Integer.toHexString(i));
    System.out.println("    Decimal:    " + Integer.toString(i));

    System.out.println("    Using toString(int i, int base) method:");
    System.out.println("    Base 2:     " + Integer.toString(i, 2));
    System.out.println("    Base 8:     " + Integer.toString(i, 8));
    System.out.println("    Base 16:    " + Integer.toString(i, 16));
    System.out.println("    Base 10:    " + Integer.toString(i, 10));
  }
}
```

Output from the program:

```
String representation for decimal value: 41
    Binary:     101001
    Octal:      51
    Hex:        29
    Decimal:    41
    Using toString(int i, int base) method:
    Base 2:     101001
    Base 8:     51
    Base 16:    29
    Base 10:    41
String representation for decimal value: -41
    Binary:     11111111111111111111111111010111
    Octal:      37777777727
    Hex:        ffffffd7
    Decimal:    -41
    Using toString(int i, int base) method:
    Base 2:     -101001
    Base 8:     -51
    Base 16:    -29
    Base 10:    -41
```

The Character Class

The Character class defines a myriad of constants, including the following, which represent the minimum and the maximum values of the char type (§2.2, p. 38):

```
Character.MIN_VALUE
Character.MAX_VALUE
```

The Character class also defines a plethora of static methods for handling various attributes of a character, and case issues relating to characters, as defined by the Unicode standard:

```
static int     getNumericValue(char ch)
static boolean isLowerCase(char ch)
static boolean isUpperCase(char ch)
static boolean isTitleCase(char ch)
static boolean isDigit(char ch)
static boolean isLetter(char ch)
static boolean isLetterOrDigit(char ch)
static char    toUpperCase(char ch)
static char    toLowerCase(char ch)
static char    toTitleCase(char ch)
```

The following code converts a lowercase character to an uppercase character:

```
char ch = 'a';
if (Character.isLowerCase(ch)) ch = Character.toUpperCase(ch);
```

The `Boolean` Class

In addition to the common utility methods for wrapper classes discussed earlier in this section, the `Boolean` class defines the following wrapper objects to represent the primitive values `true` and `false`, respectively:

```
Boolean.TRUE
Boolean.FALSE
```

Converting Strings to Boolean Values

The wrapper class `Boolean` defines the following static method, which returns the `boolean` value `true` only if the `String` argument is equal to the string `"true"`, ignoring the case; otherwise, it returns the `boolean` value `false`. Note that this method does not throw any exceptions, as its numeric counterparts do.

```
static boolean parseBoolean(String str)
```

```
boolean b1 = Boolean.parseBoolean("TRUE");       // true.
boolean b2 = Boolean.parseBoolean("true");       // true.
boolean b3 = Boolean.parseBoolean("false");      // false.
boolean b4 = Boolean.parseBoolean("FALSE");      // false.
boolean b5 = Boolean.parseBoolean("not true");  // false.
```

Review Questions

8.4 Which of the following are wrapper classes?

Select the three correct answers.

(a) `java.lang.Void`
(b) `java.lang.Int`
(c) `java.lang.Boolean`
(d) `java.lang.Long`
(e) `java.lang.String`

8.5 Which of the following classes do not extend the `java.lang.Number` class?

Select the two correct answers.

(a) `java.lang.Float`
(b) `java.lang.Byte`
(c) `java.lang.Character`
(d) `java.lang.Boolean`
(e) `java.lang.Short`

8.6 Which of these classes define immutable objects?

Select the three correct answers.

(a) `Character`
(b) `Byte`
(c) `Number`
(d) `Short`
(e) `Object`

8.7 Which of these classes have a single-parameter constructor taking a string?

Select the two correct answers.

(a) `Void`
(b) `Integer`
(c) `Boolean`
(d) `Character`
(e) `Object`

8.8 Which of the wrapper classes have a `booleanValue()` method?

Select the one correct answer

(a) All wrapper classes
(b) All wrapper classes except `Void`
(c) All wrapper classes that also implement the `compareTo()` method
(d) All wrapper classes extending `Number`
(e) Only the class `Boolean`

8.9 Which statements are true about wrapper classes?

Select the two correct answers.

(a) `String` is a wrapper class.
(b) `Double` has a `compareTo()` method.
(c) `Character` has a `intValue()` method.
(d) `Byte` extends `Number`.

8.10 What will the following program print when compiled and run?

```
public class RQ200A70 {
  public static void main(String[] args) {
    Integer i = new Integer(-10);
    Integer j = new Integer(-10);
    Integer k = -10;
    System.out.print((i==j) + "|");
    System.out.print(i.equals(j) + "|");
    System.out.print((i==k) + "|");
    System.out.print(i.equals(k));
  }
}
```

Select the one correct answer.

(a) `false|true|false|true`
(b) `true|true|true|true`
(c) `false|true|true|true`
(d) `true|true|false|true`
(e) None of the above.

8.4 The `String` Class

Handling character sequences is supported through three `final` classes: `String`, `StringBuilder`, and `StringBuffer`. The Java platform uses the variable-length UTF-16 encoding to store characters in `char` arrays and in the string handling classes. The UTF-16 encoding allows characters whose Unicode values are in the range 0000 to 10FFFF. The `char` type represents Unicode values in the range 0000 to FFFF—that is, characters that can be represented in a single 16-bit word. As a consequence, the *supplementary characters* are represented by multiple `char` values, or multiple 16-bit words, when these are stored in a string or a `char` array. The string handling classes provide methods to handle the full range of characters in the UTF-16 encoding, but we will not dwell on the subject in this book.

Immutability

The `String` class implements immutable character strings, which are read-only once the string has been created and initialized. Operations on a `String` object that modify the characters return a new `String` object. The `StringBuilder` class implements dynamic character strings. The `StringBuffer` class is a *thread-safe* version of the `StringBuilder` class.

This section discusses the class `String` that provides facilities for creating, initializing, and manipulating character strings. The next section discusses the `StringBuilder` and `StringBuffer` classes.

Creating and Initializing Strings

String Literals Revisited

The easiest way to create a `String` object is to use a string literal:

```
String str1 = "You cannot change me!";
```

A string literal is a *reference* to a `String` object. The value in the `String` object is the character sequence enclosed in the double quotes of the string literal. Since a string literal is a reference, it can be manipulated like any other `String` reference. The reference value of a string literal can be assigned to another `String` reference: The reference `str1` will denote the `String` object with the value `"You cannot change me!"`

after the preceding assignment. A string literal can be used to invoke methods on its `String` object:

```
int strLength = "You cannot change me!".length(); // 21
```

The compiler optimizes handling of string literals (and compile-time constant expressions that evaluate to strings): Only one `String` object is shared by all string-valued constant expressions with the same character sequence. Such strings are said to be *interned*, meaning that they share a unique `String` object if they have the same content. The `String` class maintains a *string literal pool* where such strings are interned.

```
String str2 = "You cannot change me!";       // Already interned.
```

Both `String` references `str1` and `str2` denote the same interned `String` object initialized with the character string: `"You cannot change me!"` So does the reference `str3` in the following code. The compile-time evaluation of the constant expression involving the two string literals results in a string that is already interned:

```
String str3 = "You cannot" + " change me!"; // Compile-time constant expression
```

In the following code, both the references `can1` and `can2` denote the same interned `String` object, which contains the string `"7Up"`:

```
String can1 = 7 + "Up";  // Value of compile-time constant expression: "7Up"
String can2 = "7Up";     // "7Up"
```

However, in the following code, the reference `can4` denotes a *new* `String` object that will have the value `"7Up"` at runtime:

```
String word = "Up";
String can4 = 7 + word;  // Not a compile-time constant expression.
```

The sharing of `String` objects between string-valued constant expressions poses no problem, since the `String` objects are immutable. Any operation performed on one `String` reference will never have any effect on the usage of other references denoting the same object. The `String` class is also declared as `final`, so that no subclass can override this behavior.

String Constructors

The `String` class has numerous constructors to create and initialize `String` objects based on various types of arguments. Here we present a few selected constructors:

`String()`

This constructor creates a new `String` object, whose content is the *empty string*, `""`.

`String(String str)`

This constructor creates a new `String` object, whose contents are the same as those of the `String` object passed as argument.

```
String(char[] value)
String(char[] value, int offset, int count)
```

These constructors create a new `String` object, whose contents are copied from a `char` array. The second constructor allows extraction of a certain number of characters (`count`) from a given `offset` in the array.

```
String(StringBuilder builder)
String(StringBuffer buffer)
```

These constructors allow interoperability with the `StringBuilder` and `StringBuffer` classes, respectively.

Note that using a constructor creates a brand-new `String` object; using a constructor does not intern the string. A reference to an interned string can be obtained by calling the `intern()` method in the `String` class—although in practice, there is usually no reason to do so.

In the following code, the `String` object denoted by `str4` is different from the interned `String` object passed as an argument:

```
String str4 = new String("You cannot change me!");
```

Constructing `String` objects can also be done from arrays of bytes, arrays of characters, or string builders:

```
byte[] bytes = {97, 98, 98, 97};
char[] characters = {'a', 'b', 'b', 'a'};
StringBuilder strBuilder = new StringBuilder("abba");
//...
String byteStr  = new String(bytes);      // Using array of bytes: "abba"
String charStr  = new String(characters); // Using array of chars: "abba"
String buildStr = new String(strBuilder); // Using string builder: "abba"
```

In Example 8.3, note that the reference `str1` does not denote the same `String` object as the references `str4` and `str5`. Using the `new` operator with a `String` constructor always creates a new `String` object. The expression `"You cannot" + words` is not a constant expression and, therefore, results in the creation of a new `String` object. The local references `str2` and `str3` in the `main()` method and the static reference `str1` in the `Auxiliary` class all denote the same interned string. Object value equality is hardly surprising between these references. Indeed, it might be tempting to use the operator `==` for object value equality of string literals, but this is not advisable.

Example 8.3 *String Construction and Equality*

```
// File: StringConstruction.java
class Auxiliary {
  static String str1 = "You cannot change me!";          // Interned
}
//______________________________________________________________________
public class StringConstruction {

  static String str1 = "You cannot change me!";          // Interned
```

```
  public static void main(String[] args) {
    String emptyStr = new String();                          // ""
    System.out.println("emptyStr: \"" + emptyStr + "\"");

    String str2 = "You cannot change me!";                   // Interned
    String str3 = "You cannot" + " change me!";              // Interned
    String str4 = new String("You cannot change me!");       // New String object

    String words = " change me!";
    String str5 = "You cannot" + words;                      // New String object

    System.out.println("str1 == str2:        " +  (str1 == str2));      // (1) true
    System.out.println("str1.equals(str2): " +  str1.equals(str2));   // (2) true

    System.out.println("str1 == str3:        " + (str1 == str3));       // (3) true
    System.out.println("str1.equals(str3): " + str1.equals(str3));    // (4) true

    System.out.println("str1 == str4:        " + (str1 == str4));       // (5) false
    System.out.println("str1.equals(str4): " + str1.equals(str4));    // (6) true

    System.out.println("str1 == str5:        " + (str1 == str5));       // (7) false
    System.out.println("str1.equals(str5): " + str1.equals(str5));    // (8) true

    System.out.println("str1 == Auxiliary.str1:        " +
                       (str1 == Auxiliary.str1));          // (9) true
    System.out.println("str1.equals(Auxiliary.str1): " +
                        str1.equals(Auxiliary.str1));      // (10) true

    System.out.println("\"You cannot change me!\".length(): " +
                       "You cannot change me!".length());// (11) 21
  }
}
```

Output from the program:

```
emptyStr: ""
str1 == str2:        true
str1.equals(str2): true
str1 == str3:        true
str1.equals(str3): true
str1 == str4:        false
str1.equals(str4): true
str1 == str5:        false
str1.equals(str5): true
str1 == Auxiliary.str1:        true
str1.equals(Auxiliary.str1): true
"You cannot change me!".length(): 21
```

The CharSequence Interface

This interface defines a readable sequence of `char` values. It is implemented by all three classes: `String`, `StringBuilder`, and `StringBuffer`. Many methods in these classes accept arguments of this interface type, and specify it as their return type.

This interface facilitates interoperability between these classes. It defines the following methods:

`char charAt(int index)`

A character at a particular index in a sequence can be read using the `charAt()` method. The first character is at index `0` and the last one at index 1 less than the number of characters in the string. If the index value is not valid, an `IndexOutOfBoundsException` is thrown.

`int length()`

This method returns the number of `char` values in this sequence.

`CharSequence subSequence(int start, int end)`

This method returns a new `CharSequence` that is a subsequence of this sequence. Characters from the current sequence are read from index `start` to the index `end-1`, inclusive.

`String toString()`

This method returns a string containing the characters in this sequence in the same order as this sequence.

Reading Characters from a String

The following methods can be used for character-related operations on a string:

`char charAt(int index)`

This method is defined in the `CharSequence` interface, which the `String` class implements (p. 360).

`char[] toCharArray()`

This method returns a new character array, with length equal to the length of this string, that contains the characters in this string.

`void getChars(int srcBegin, int srcEnd, char[] dst, int dstBegin)`

This method copies characters from the current string into the destination character array. Characters from the current string are read from index `srcBegin` to the index `srcEnd-1`, inclusive. They are copied into the destination array (`dst`), starting at index `dstBegin` and ending at index `dstbegin+(srcEnd-srcBegin)-1`. The number of characters copied is `(srcEnd-srcBegin)`. An `IndexOutOfBoundsException` is thrown if the indices do not meet the criteria for the operation.

`int length()`

This method is defined in the `CharSequence` interface, which the `String` class implements (p. 360).

`boolean isEmpty()`

This method returns `true` if the length of the string is `0`, and `false otherwise`.

Example 8.4 uses some of these methods at (3), (4), (5), and (6). The program prints the frequency of a character in a string and illustrates copying from a string into a character array.

Example 8.4 *Reading Characters from a String*

```
public class ReadingCharsFromString {
  public static void main(String[] args) {
    int[] frequencyData = new int [Character.MAX_VALUE];     // (1)
    String str = "You cannot change me!";                    // (2)

    // Count the frequency of each character in the string.
    for (int i = 0; i < str.length(); i++) {                 // (3)
      try {
        frequencyData[str.charAt(i)]++;                      // (4)
      } catch(StringIndexOutOfBoundsException e) {
        System.out.println("Index error detected: "+ i +" not in range.");
      }
    }

    // Print the character frequency.
    System.out.println("Character frequency for string: \"" + str + "\"");
    for (int i = 0; i < frequencyData.length; i++) {
      if (frequencyData[i] != 0)
        System.out.println((char)i + " (code "+ i +"): " + frequencyData[i]);
    }

    System.out.println("Copying into a char array:");
    char[] destination = new char [str.length() - 3];        // 3 characters less.
    str.getChars( 0,            7, destination, 0);          // (5) "You can"
    str.getChars(10, str.length(), destination, 7);          // (6) " change me!"
                                                             // "not" not copied.
    // Print the character array.
    for (int i = 0; i < destination.length; i++) {
      System.out.print(destination[i]);
    }
    System.out.println();
  }
}
```

Output from the program:

```
Character Frequency for string: "You cannot change me!"
  (code 32): 3
! (code 33): 1
Y (code 89): 1
a (code 97): 2
c (code 99): 2
e (code 101): 2
g (code 103): 1
h (code 104): 1
m (code 109): 1
n (code 110): 3
```

```
o (code 111): 2
t (code 116): 1
u (code 117): 1
Copying into a char array:
You can change me!
```

In Example 8.4, the `frequencyData` array at (1) stores the frequency of each character that can occur in a string. The string in question is declared at (2). Since a `char` value is promoted to an `int` value in arithmetic expressions, it can be used as an index in an array. Each element in the `frequencyData` array functions as a frequency counter for the character corresponding to the index value of the element:

```
frequencyData[str.charAt(i)]++;                    // (4)
```

The calls to the `getChars()` method at (5) and (6) copy particular substrings from the string into designated places in the `destination` array, before printing the whole character array.

Comparing Strings

Characters are compared based on their Unicode values.

```
boolean test = 'a' < 'b';    // true since 0x61 < 0x62
```

Two strings are compared *lexicographically*, as in a dictionary or telephone directory, by successively comparing their corresponding characters at each position in the two strings, starting with the characters in the first position. The string `"abba"` is less than `"aha"`, since the second character `'b'` in the string `"abba"` is less than the second character `'h'` in the string `"aha"`. The characters in the first position in each of these strings are equal.

The following public methods can be used for comparing strings:

```
boolean equals(Object obj)
boolean equalsIgnoreCase(String str2)
```

The `String` class overrides the `equals()` method from the `Object` class. The `String` class `equals()` method implements `String` object value equality as two `String` objects having the same sequence of characters. The `equalsIgnoreCase()` method does the same, but ignores the case of the characters.

```
int compareTo(String str2)
```

The `String` class implements the `Comparable<String>` interface. The `compareTo()` method compares the two strings, and returns a value based on the outcome of the comparison:

- The value `0`, if this string is equal to the string argument
- A value less than `0`, if this string is lexicographically less than the string argument
- A value greater than `0`, if this string is lexicographically greater than the string argument

Here are some examples of string comparisons:

```
String strA = new String("The Case was thrown out of Court");
String strB = new String("the case was thrown out of court");

boolean b1 = strA.equals(strB);              // false
boolean b2 = strA.equalsIgnoreCase(strB);    // true

String str1 = new String("abba");
String str2 = new String("aha");

int compVal1 = str1.compareTo(str2);          // negative value => str1 < str2
```

Character Case in a String

```
String toUpperCase()
String toUpperCase(Locale locale)
String toLowerCase()
String toLowerCase(Locale locale)
```

Note that the original string is returned if none of the characters needs its case changed, but a new `String` object is returned if any of the characters needs its case changed. These methods delegate the character-by-character case conversion to corresponding methods from the `Character` class.

These methods use the rules of the (default) *locale* (returned by the method `Locale.getDefault()`), which embodies the idiosyncrasies of a specific geographical, political, or cultural region regarding number/date/currency formats, character classification, alphabet (including case idiosyncrasies), and other localizations.

Example of case in strings:

```
String strA = new String("The Case was thrown out of Court");
String strB = new String("the case was thrown out of court");

String strC = strA.toLowerCase();  // Case conversion => New String object:
                                   // "the case was thrown out of court"
String strD = strB.toLowerCase();  // No case conversion => Same String object
String strE = strA.toUpperCase();  // Case conversion => New String object:
                                   // "THE CASE WAS THROWN OUT OF COURT"

boolean test1 = strC == strA;      // false
boolean test2 = strD == strB;      // true
boolean test3 = strE == strA;      // false
```

Concatenation of Strings

Concatenation of two strings results in a new string that consists of the characters of the first string followed by the characters of the second string. The overloaded operator + for string concatenation is discussed in §5.7, p. 169. In addition, the following method can be used to concatenate two strings:

```
String concat(String str)
```

The concat() method does not modify the String object on which it is invoked, as String objects are immutable. Instead, the concat() method returns a reference to a brand-new String object:

```
String billboard = "Just";
billboard.concat(" lost in space."); // (1) Returned reference value not stored.
System.out.println(billboard);        // (2) "Just"
billboard = billboard.concat(" advertise").concat(" here.");  // (3) Chaining.
System.out.println(billboard);        // (4) "Just advertise here."
```

At (1), the reference value of the String object returned by the method concat() is not stored. This String object becomes inaccessible after (1). We see that the reference billboard still denotes the string literal "Just" at (2).

At (3), two method calls to the concat() method are *chained*. The first call returns a reference value to a new String object, whose content is "Just advertise". The second method call is invoked on this String object using the reference value that was returned in the first method call. The second call results in yet another new String object, whose content is "Just advertise here.". The reference value of this String object is assigned to the reference billboard. Because String objects are immutable, the creation of the temporary String object with the content "Just advertise" is inevitable at (3).

Some more examples of string concatenation follow:

```
String motto = new String("Program once");       // (1)
motto += ", execute everywhere.";                // (2)
motto = motto.concat(" Don't bet on it!");       // (3)
```

Note that a new String object is assigned to the reference motto each time in the assignments at (1), (2), and (3). The String object with the contents "Program once" becomes inaccessible after the assignment at (2). The String object with the contents "Program once, execute everywhere." becomes inaccessible after (3). The reference motto denotes the String object with the following contents after execution of the assignment at (3):

```
"Program once, execute everywhere. Don't bet on it!"
```

Joining of CharSequence Objects

One operation commonly performed on a sequence of strings is to format them so that each string is separated from the next one by a delimiter. For example, given the following sequence of strings:

```
"2014"
"January"
"11"
```

we wish to format them so that individual strings are separated by the delimiter "/":

```
"2014/January/11"
```

The following static methods in the `String` class can be used for this purpose:

```
static String join(CharSequence delimiter, CharSequence... elements)
static String join(CharSequence delimiter,
                   Iterable<? extends CharSequence> elements)
```

Both static methods return a new `String` composed of copies of the `CharSequence` elements joined together with a copy of the specified `CharSequence` delimiter. Thus, the resulting string is composed of textual representations of the elements separated by the textual representation of the specified delimiter.

If an element is `null`, the string `"null"` is added as its textual representation. If the delimiter is `null`, a `NullPointerException` is thrown.

Note that both the individual strings and the delimiter string are `CharSequence` objects. The examples in this section use `String` and `StringBuilder` objects that implement the `CharSequence` interface (p. 360).

An `Iterable` provides an iterator to traverse over its elements. The following examples use an `ArrayList` (§10.1, p. 423) that implements the `Iterable` interface. The second `join()` method is then able to traverse the `Iterable` using the iterator. This method will accept only an `Iterable` whose elements are either of type `CharSequence` or subtypes of `CharSequence`.

The first example shows joining of `String` objects. The first `join()` method is called in this case.

```
// (1) Joining individual String objects:
String dateStr = String.join("/", "2014", "January", "11");
System.out.println(dateStr);                          // 2014/January/11
```

The second example shows joining of elements in a `StringBuilder` array. Again the first `join()` method is called, with the array being passed as the second parameter.

```
// (2) Joining elements in a StringBuilder array:
StringBuilder left = new StringBuilder("Left");
StringBuilder right = new StringBuilder("Right");
StringBuilder[] strBuilders = { left, right, left };
String march = String.join("-->", strBuilders);
System.out.println(march);                            // Left-->Right-->Left
```

The third example shows joining of elements in an `ArrayList` of `StringBuilder`. The second `join()` method is called, with the `ArrayList` being passed as the second parameter. Note that some of the elements of the `ArrayList` are `null`.

```
// (3) Joining elements in a StringBuilder list:
ArrayList<StringBuilder> sbList = new ArrayList<>();
sbList.add(right); sbList.add(null); sbList.add(left); sbList.add(null);
String resultStr = "[" + String.join(", ", sbList) + "]";
System.out.println(resultStr);                        // [Right, null, Left, null]
```

The last example shows joining of elements in an `ArrayList` of `CharSequence`. Again the second `join()` method is called, with the `ArrayList` being passed as the second parameter. Note that elements of the `ArrayList` are `String` and `StringBuilder` objects that are also of type `CharSequence`.

```
// (4) Joining elements in a CharSequence list:
ArrayList<CharSequence> charSeqList = new ArrayList<>();
charSeqList.add(right); charSeqList.add(left);      // Add StringBuilder objects.
charSeqList.add("Right"); charSeqList.add("Left"); // Add String objects.
String resultStr2 = "<" + String.join("; ", charSeqList) + ">";
System.out.println(resultStr2);                    // <Right; Left; Right; Left>
```

Searching for Characters and Substrings

The following overloaded methods can be used to find the index of a character or the start index of a substring in a string. These methods search *forward* toward the end of the string. In other words, the index of the *first* occurrence of the character or substring is found. If the search is unsuccessful, the value –1 is returned.

```
int indexOf(int ch)
int indexOf(int ch, int fromIndex)
```

The first method finds the index of the first occurrence of the argument character in a string. The second method finds the index of the first occurrence of the argument character in a string, starting at the index specified in the second argument. If the index argument is negative, the index is assumed to be 0. If the index argument is greater than the length of the string, it is effectively considered to be equal to the length of the string, resulting in the value -1 being returned.

```
int indexOf(String str)
int indexOf(String str, int fromIndex)
```

The first method finds the start index of the first occurrence of the substring argument in a string. The second method finds the start index of the first occurrence of the substring argument in a string, starting at the index specified in the second argument.

The `String` class also defines a set of methods that search for a character or a substring, but the search is *backward* toward the start of the string. In other words, the index of the *last* occurrence of the character or substring is found.

```
int lastIndexOf(int ch)
int lastIndexOf(int ch, int fromIndex)
int lastIndexOf(String str)
int lastIndexOf(String str, int fromIndex)
```

The following methods can be used to create a string in which all occurrences of a character or a subsequence in a string have been replaced with another character or subsequence:

```
String replace(char oldChar, char newChar)
String replace(CharSequence target, CharSequence replacement)
```

The first method returns a new `String` object that is the result of replacing all occurrences of the `oldChar` in the current string with the `newChar`. The current string is returned if no occurrences of the `oldChar` can be found.

The second method returns a new `String` object that is the result of replacing all occurrences of the character sequence `target` in the current string with the character sequence `replacement`. The current string is returned if no occurrences of the `target` can be found.

The following methods can be used to test whether a string satisfies a given criterion:

`boolean contains(CharSequence cs)`

This method returns `true` if the current string contains the specified character sequence, and `false` otherwise.

`boolean startsWith(String prefix)`

This method returns `true` if the current string starts with the character sequence specified by parameter `prefix`, and `false` otherwise.

`boolean startsWith(String prefix, int index)`

This method returns `true` if the substring of the current string at the specified `index` starts with the character sequence specified by parameter `prefix`, and `false` otherwise.

`boolean endsWith(String suffix)`

This method returns `true` if the current string ends with the character sequence specified by parameter `suffix`, and `false` otherwise.

Examples of search and replace methods:

```
String funStr = "Java Jives";
//               0123456789
int jInd1a = funStr.indexOf('J');             // 0
int jInd1b = funStr.indexOf('J', 1);          // 5
int jInd2a = funStr.lastIndexOf('J');         // 5
int jInd2b = funStr.lastIndexOf('J', 4);      // 0

String banner = "One man, One vote";
//               01234567890123456
int subInd1a = banner.indexOf("One");         // 0
int subInd1b = banner.indexOf("One", 3);      // 9
int subInd2a = banner.lastIndexOf("One");     // 9
int subInd2b = banner.lastIndexOf("One", 10); // 9
int subInd2c = banner.lastIndexOf("One", 8);  // 0
int subInd2d = banner.lastIndexOf("One", 2);  // 0

String newStr = funStr.replace('J', 'W');           // "Wava Wives"
String newBanner = banner.replace("One", "No");     // "No man, No vote"
boolean found1 = banner.contains("One");            // true
boolean found2 = newBanner.contains("One");         // false

String song = "Start me up!";
//             012345677890
boolean found3    = song.startsWith("Start");       // true
boolean notFound1 = song.startsWith("start");       // false
```

```
boolean found4    = song.startsWith("me", 6);      // true
boolean found5    = song.endsWith("up!");          // true
boolean notFound2 = song.endsWith("up");           // false
```

Extracting Substrings

```
String trim()
```

This method can be used to create a string where whitespace (in fact, all characters with values less than or equal to the space character '\u0020') has been removed from the front (leading) and the end (trailing) of a string.

```
String substring(int startIndex)
String substring(int startIndex, int endIndex)
```

The `String` class provides these overloaded methods to extract substrings from a string. A new `String` object containing the substring is created and returned. The first method extracts the string that starts at the given index `startIndex` and extends to the end of the string. The end of the substring can be specified by using a second argument `endIndex` that is the index of the first character *after* the substring—that is, the last character in the substring is at index `endIndex-1`. If the index value is not valid, an `IndexOutOfBoundsException` is thrown.

Examples of extracting substrings:

```
String utopia = "\t\n  Java Nation \n\t  ";
utopia = utopia.trim();                          // "Java Nation"
utopia = utopia.substring(5);                    // "Nation"
String radioactive = utopia.substring(3,6);      // "ion"
```

Converting Primitive Values and Objects to Strings

The `String` class overrides the `toString()` method in the `Object` class and returns the `String` object itself:

```
String toString()
```

This method is defined in the `CharSequence` interface, which the `String` class implements (p. 360).

The `String` class also defines a set of static overloaded `valueOf()` methods to convert objects and primitive values into strings:

```
static String valueOf(Object obj)
static String valueOf(char[] charArray)
static String valueOf(boolean b)
static String valueOf(char c)
```

All of these methods return a string representing the given parameter value. A call to the method with the parameter `obj` is equivalent to `obj.toString()` when `obj` is not `null`; otherwise, the `"null"` string is returned. The `boolean` values `true` and `false` are converted into the strings `"true"` and `"false"`. The `char` parameter is converted to a string consisting of a single character.

```
static String valueOf(int i)
static String valueOf(long l)
static String valueOf(float f)
static String valueOf(double d)
```

The static `valueOf()` method, which accepts a primitive value as an argument, is equivalent to the static `toString()` method in the corresponding wrapper class for each of the primitive data types ((6a) and (6b) in §8.3, p. 347). Note that there are no `valueOf()` methods that accept a `byte` or a `short`.

Examples of string conversions:

```
String anonStr   = String.valueOf("Make me a string.");      // "Make me a string."
String charStr   = String.valueOf(new char[] {'a', 'h', 'a'});// "aha"
String boolTrue  = String.valueOf(true);                      // "true"
String doubleStr = String.valueOf(Math.PI);                   // "3.141592653589793"
```

Formatted Strings

We have used the `System.out.printf()` method to format values and print them to the terminal window (§1.9, p. 15). To just create the string with the formatted values, but not print the formatted result, we can use the following static method from the `String` class. It accepts the same arguments as the `printf()` method, and uses the same format specifications (Table 1.2, p. 20).

```
static String format(String format, Object... args)
```

The method returns a string with the result of formatting the values in the var-args parameter `args` according to the `String` parameter `format`. The format string contains format specifications that determine how each subsequent value in the var-args parameter `args` will be formatted.

Any error in the format string will result in a runtime exception.

The following call to the `format()` method creates a formatted string with the three values formatted according to the specified format string:

```
String formattedStr = String.format("Formatted values|%5d|%8.3f|%5s|",
                                    2016, Math.PI, "Hi");
System.out.println(formattedStr); // Formatted values| 2016|   3.142|   Hi|
formattedStr = formattedStr.toUpperCase();
System.out.println(formattedStr); // FORMATTED VALUES| 2016|   3.142|   HI|
```

Other miscellaneous methods exist in the `String` class for pattern matching (`matches()`), splitting strings (`split()`), and converting a string to an array of bytes (`getBytes()`). The method `hashCode()` can be used to compute a hash value based on the characters in the string. Consult the Java SE platform API documentation for more details.

Review Questions

8.11 Which of the following operators cannot have an operand of type `String`?

Select the two correct answers.

(a) `+`
(b) `-`
(c) `+=`
(d) `.`
(e) `&`

8.12 Which expression will extract the substring `"kap"`, given the following declaration:

```
String str = "kakapo";
```

Select the one correct answer.

(a) `str.substring(2, 2)`
(b) `str.substring(2, 3)`
(c) `str.substring(2, 4)`
(d) `str.substring(2, 5)`
(e) `str.substring(3, 3)`

8.13 What will be the result of attempting to compile and run the following code?

```
class MyClass {
  public static void main(String[] args) {
    String str1 = "str1";
    String str2 = "str2";
    String str3 = "str3";

    str1.concat(str2);
    System.out.println(str3.concat(str1));
  }
}
```

Select the one correct answer.

(a) The code will fail to compile because the expression `str3.concat(str1)` will not result in a valid argument for the `println()` method.
(b) The program will print `str3str1str2` at runtime.
(c) The program will print `str3` at runtime.
(d) The program will print `str3str1` at runtime.
(e) The program will print `str3str2` at runtime.

8.14 Which statement about the `trim()` method of the `String` class is true?

Select the one correct answer.

(a) It returns a string where the leading whitespace of the original string has been removed.
(b) It returns a string where the trailing whitespace of the original string has been removed.

(c) It returns a string where both the leading and trailing whitespace of the original string has been removed.
(d) It returns a string where all the whitespace of the original string has been removed.
(e) None of the above.

8.15 Which of the following statements are true?

Select the two correct answers.

(a) `String` objects are immutable.
(b) Subclasses of the `String` class can be mutable.
(c) All wrapper classes are declared as `final`.
(d) All objects have a `public` method named `clone`.
(e) The expression `((new char[] {'o', 'k'}) instanceof String)` is always `true`.

8.16 What will be the result of attempting to compile and run the following program?

```
public class RefEq {
  public static void main(String[] args) {
    String s = "ab" + "12";
    String t = "ab" + 12;
    String u = new String("ab12");
    System.out.println((s==t) + " " + (s==u));
  }
}
```

Select the one correct answer.

(a) The program will fail to compile.
(b) The program will print `false false` at runtime.
(c) The program will print `false true` at runtime.
(d) The program will print `true false` at runtime.
(e) The program will print `true true` at runtime.

8.17 Which of these parameter lists can be found in a constructor of the `String` class?

Select the five correct answers.

(a) `()`
(b) `(int capacity)`
(c) `(char[] data)`
(d) `(String str)`
(e) `(CharSequence cs)`
(f) `(StringBuilder sb)`
(g) `(char c)`
(h) `(Object o)`
(i) `(String str, int beginIndex, int endIndex)`
(j) `(char[] data, int offset, int count)`

8.18 Which of the following methods is not defined in the `String` class?

Select the one correct answer.

(a) `trim()`
(b) `length()`
(c) `concat(String)`
(d) `hashCode()`
(e) `reverse()`

8.19 What will the following program print when run?

```
public class Uppity {
  public static void main(String[] args) {
    String str1 = "lower", str2 = "LOWER", str3 = "UPPER";
    str1.toUpperCase();
    str1.replace("LOWER","UPPER");
    System.out.println((str1.equals(str2)) + " " + (str1.equals(str3)));
  }
}
```

Select the one correct answer.

(a) The program will print `false true`.
(b) The program will print `false false`.
(c) The program will print `true false`.
(d) The program will print `true true`.
(e) The program will fail to compile.
(f) The program will compile, but throw an exception at runtime.

8.20 What will the following program print when run?

```
public class FunCharSeq {
  private static void putO(String s1) {
    s1 = s1.trim();
    s1 += "O";
  }

  public static void main(String[] args) {
    String s1 = " W ";
    putO(s1);
    s1.concat("W");
    System.out.println("|" + s1 + "|");
  }
}
```

Select the one correct answer.

(a) `|WOW|`
(b) `| W W|`
(c) `|WO|`
(d) `| W |`
(e) The program will fail to compile.
(f) The program will compile, but throw an exception at runtime.

8.5 The `StringBuilder` and `StringBuffer` Classes

Thread-Safety

The classes `StringBuilder` and `StringBuffer` implement *mutable* sequences of characters. Both classes support the same operations, but the `StringBuffer` class is the *thread-safe* analog of the `StringBuilder` class. Certain operations on a string buffer are synchronized, so that when used by multiple threads, these operations are performed in an orderly manner. Note that a `String` object is also thread-safe—because it is immutable, a thread cannot change its state. String builders are preferred when heavy modification of character sequences is involved and synchronization of operations is not important.

Although the rest of this section focuses on string builders, it is equally applicable to string buffers.

Mutability

In contrast to the `String` class, which implements immutable character sequences, the `StringBuilder` class implements mutable character sequences. Not only can the character sequences in a string builder be changed, but the capacity of the string builder can also change dynamically. The *capacity* of a string builder is the maximum number of characters that a string builder can accommodate before its size is automatically augmented.

Although there is a close relationship between objects of the `String` and `StringBuilder` classes, these are two independent `final` classes, both directly extending the `Object` class. Hence, `String` references cannot be stored (or cast) to `StringBuilder` references, and vice versa. However, both classes implement the `CharSequence` interface (p. 360).

The `StringBuilder` class provides various facilities for manipulating string builders:

- Constructing string builders
- Changing, deleting, and reading characters in string builders
- Constructing strings from string builders
- Appending, inserting, and deleting in string builders
- Controlling string builder capacity

Constructing String Builders

The `final` class `StringBuilder` provides four constructors that create and initialize `StringBuilder` objects and set their initial capacity.

```
StringBuilder(String str)
StringBuilder(CharSequence charSeq)
```

The contents of the new `StringBuilder` object are the same as the contents of the `String` object or the character sequence passed as an argument. The initial capacity of the string builder is set to the length of the argument sequence, plus room for 16 more characters.

```
StringBuilder(int initialCapacity)
```

The new `StringBuilder` object has no content. The initial capacity of the string builder is set to the value of the argument, which cannot be less than 0.

```
StringBuilder()
```

This constructor also creates a new `StringBuilder` object with no content. The initial capacity of the string builder is set to 16 characters.

Examples of `StringBuilder` object creation and initialization:

```
StringBuilder strBuilder1 = new StringBuilder("Phew!");  // "Phew!", capacity 21
StringBuilder strBuilder2 = new StringBuilder(10);       // "", capacity 10
StringBuilder strBuilder3 = new StringBuilder();         // "", capacity 16
```

Reading and Changing Characters in String Builders

`int length()` — From the `CharSequence` interface (p. 360).

Returns the number of characters in the string builder.

`char charAt(int index)` — From the `CharSequence` interface (p. 360).
`void setCharAt(int index, char ch)`

These methods read and change the character at a specified index in the string builder, respectively. The first character is at index 0, and the last one is at index 1 less than the number of characters in the string builder. A `IndexOutOfBoundsException` is thrown if the index is not valid.

```
CharSequence subSequence(int start, int end)
```

This method is implemented as part of the `CharSequence` interface (p. 360).

The following is an example of reading and changing string builder contents:

```
StringBuilder strBuilder = new StringBuilder("Javv");          // "Javv", capacity 20
strBuilder.setCharAt(strBuilder.length()-1, strBuilder.charAt(1)); // "Java"
```

Constructing Strings from String Builders

The `StringBuilder` class overrides the `toString()` method from the `Object` class (see also the `CharSequence` interface, p. 360). It returns the contents of a string builder in a `String` object.

```
String fromBuilder = strBuilder.toString();                     // "Java"
```

Differences between the String and StringBuilder Classes

Since the `StringBuilder` class does not override the `equals()` method from the `Object` class, nor does it implement the `Comparable` interface, the contents of string builders should be converted to `String` objects for string comparison.

The `StringBuilder` class also does not override the `hashCode()` method from the `Object` class. Again, a string builder can be converted to a `String` object to obtain a hash value.

Appending, Inserting, and Deleting Characters in String Builders

Appending, inserting, and deleting characters automatically results in adjustment of the string builder's structure and capacity, if necessary. The indices passed as arguments in the methods must be equal to or greater than 0. An `IndexOutOfBoundsException` is thrown if an index is not valid.

Note that the methods in this subsection return the reference value of the modified string builder, making it convenient to chain calls to these methods.

Appending Characters to a String Builder

The overloaded method `append()` can be used to *append* characters at the *end* of a string builder.

```
StringBuilder append(Object obj)
```

The `obj` argument is converted to a string as if by the static method call `String.valueOf(obj)`, and this string is appended to the current string builder.

```
StringBuilder append(String str)
StringBuilder append(CharSequence charSeq)
StringBuilder append(CharSequence charSeq, int start, int end)
StringBuilder append(char[] charArray)
StringBuilder append(char[] charArray, int offset, int length)
StringBuilder append(char c)
```

These methods allow characters from various sources to be appended to the end of the current string builder.

```
StringBuilder append(boolean b)
StringBuilder append(int i)
StringBuilder append(long l)
StringBuilder append(float f)
StringBuilder append(double d)
```

These methods convert the primitive value of the argument to a string by applying the static method `String.valueOf()` to the argument, before appending the result to the string builder.

Inserting Characters in a String Builder

The overloaded method `insert()` can be used to *insert* characters at a *given position* in a string builder.

```
StringBuilder insert(int offset, Object obj)
StringBuilder insert(int dstOffset, CharSequence seq)
StringBuilder insert(int dstOffset, CharSequence seq, int start, int end)
StringBuilder insert(int offset, String str)
StringBuilder insert(int offset, char[] charArray)
StringBuilder insert(int offset, char c)
StringBuilder insert(int offset, boolean b)
StringBuilder insert(int offset, int i)
StringBuilder insert(int offset, long l)
StringBuilder insert(int offset, float f)
StringBuilder insert(int offset, double d)
```

The argument is converted, if necessary, by applying the static method `String.valueOf()`. The `offset` argument specifies where the characters are to be inserted in the string builder, and must be greater than or equal to 0.

Deleting Characters in a String Builder

The following methods can be used to delete characters from *specific positions* in a string builder:

```
StringBuilder deleteCharAt(int index)
StringBuilder delete(int start, int end)
```

The first method deletes a character at a specified index in the string builder, contracting the string builder by one character. The second method deletes a substring, which is specified by the `start` index (inclusive) and the `end` index (exclusive), contracting the string builder accordingly.

Among other miscellaneous methods included in the class `StringBuilder` is the following method, which reverses the contents of a string builder:

```
StringBuilder reverse()
```

Examples of appending, inserting, and deleting in string builders:

```
StringBuilder builder = new StringBuilder("banana split");   // "banana split"
builder.delete(4,12);                                         // "bana"
builder.append(42);                                           // "bana42"
builder.insert(4,"na");                                       // "banana42"
builder.reverse();                                            // "24ananab"
builder.deleteCharAt(builder.length()-1);                     // "24anana"
builder.append('s');                                          // "24ananas"
```

All of the previously mentioned methods modify the contents of the string builder and return a reference value denoting the current string builder. This allows *chaining* of method calls. The method calls invoked on the string builder denoted by the reference builder can be chained as follows, giving the same result:

```
builder.delete(4,12).append(42).insert(4,"na").reverse().
       deleteCharAt(builder.length()-1).append('s');          // "24ananas"
```

The method calls in the chain are evaluated from left to right, so that the previous chain of calls is interpreted as follows:

```
(((((builder.delete(4,12)).append(42)).insert(4,"na")).reverse()).
     deleteCharAt(builder.length()-1)).append('s');           // "24ananas"
```

Each method call returns the reference value of the modified string builder, which is then used to invoke the next method. The string builder remains denoted by the reference builder.

The compiler uses string builders to implement string concatenation with the + operator in String-valued non-constant expressions. The following code illustrates this optimization:

```
String theChosen = "U";
String str1 = 4 + theChosen + "Only";          // (1) Non-constant expression.
```

The assignment statement at (1) is equivalent to the following code using one string builder:

```
String str2 = new StringBuilder().
                 append(4).append(theChosen).append("Only").toString(); // (2)
```

The code at (2) does not create any temporary String objects when concatenating several strings, since a single StringBuilder object is modified and finally converted to a String object having the string content "4UOnly".

Controlling String Builder Capacity

The following methods can be used to control various capacity-related aspects of a string builder:

`int capacity()`

Returns the current capacity of the string builder, meaning the number of characters the current builder can accommodate without allocating a new, larger array to hold characters.

`void ensureCapacity(int minCapacity)`

Ensures that there is room for at least a minCapacity number of characters. It expands the string builder, depending on the current capacity of the builder.

`void trimToSize()`

Attempts to reduce the storage used for the character sequence. It may affect the capacity of the string builder.

`void setLength(int newLength)`

Ensures that the actual number of characters—that is, the length of the string builder—is exactly equal to the value of the `newLength` argument, which must be greater than or equal to 0. This operation can result in the string being truncated or padded with null characters (`'\u0000'`).

This method affects the capacity of the string builder only if the value of the parameter `newLength` is greater than the current capacity.

One use of this method is to clear the string builder:

```
builder.setLength(0);      // Empty the builder.
```

Review Questions

8.21 What will be the result of attempting to compile and run the following program?

```
public class MyClass {
  public static void main(String[] args) {
    String s = "hello";
    StringBuilder sb = new StringBuilder(s);
    sb.reverse();
    if (s == sb) System.out.println("a");
    if (s.equals(sb)) System.out.println("b");
    if (sb.equals(s)) System.out.println("c");
  }
}
```

Select the one correct answer.

(a) The program will fail to compile.
(b) The program will compile, but throw an exception at runtime.
(c) The program will compile, but will not print anything.
(d) The program will compile, and will print `abc`.
(e) The program will compile, and will print `bc`.
(f) The program will compile, and will print `a`.
(g) The program will compile, and will print `b`.
(h) The program will compile, and will print `c`.

8.22 What will be the result of attempting to compile and run the following program?

```
public class MyClass {
  public static void main(String[] args) {
    StringBuilder sb = new StringBuilder("have a nice day");
    sb.setLength(6);
    System.out.println(sb);
  }
}
```

Select the one correct answer.

(a) The code will fail to compile, because there is no method named `setLength` in the `StringBuilder` class.
(b) The code will fail to compile, because the `StringBuilder` reference `sb` is not a legal argument to the `println()` method.
(c) The program will throw a `StringIndexOutOfBoundsException` at runtime.
(d) The program will print `have a nice day` at runtime.
(e) The program will print `have a` at runtime.
(f) The program will print `ce day` at runtime.

8.23 Which of these parameter lists can be found in a constructor of the `StringBuilder` class?

Select the four correct answers.

(a) `()`
(b) `(int capacity)`
(c) `(char[] data)`
(d) `(String str)`
(e) `(CharSequence cs)`
(f) `(StringBuilder sb)`
(g) `(char c)`
(h) `(Object o)`
(i) `(String str, int beginIndex, int endIndex)`
(j) `(char[] data, int offset, int count)`

8.24 Which of the following methods is not defined in the `StringBuilder` class?

Select the one correct answer.

(a) `trim()`
(b) `length()`
(c) `append(String)`
(d) `reverse()`
(e) `setLength(int)`

8.25 What will the following program print when run?

```
public class PeskyCharSeq {
  public static void main (String[] args) {
    StringBuilder sb1 = new StringBuilder("WOW");
    StringBuilder sb2 = new StringBuilder(sb1);
    System.out.println((sb1==sb2) + " " + sb1.equals(sb2));
  }
}
```

Select the one correct answer.

(a) The program will print `false true`.
(b) The program will print `false false`.

(c) The program will print `true false`.
(d) The program will print `true true`.
(e) The program will fail to compile.
(f) The program will compile, but throws an exception at runtime.

8.26 What will the following program print when run?

```
public class MoreCharSeq {
  public static void main (String[] args) {
    String s1 = "WOW";
    StringBuilder s2 = new StringBuilder(s1);
    String s3 = new String(s2);
    System.out.println((s1.hashCode() == s2.hashCode()) + " " +
                       (s1.hashCode() == s3.hashCode()));
  }
}
```

Select the one correct answer.

(a) The program will print `false true`.
(b) The program will print `false false`.
(c) The program will print `true false`.
(d) The program will print `true true`.
(e) The program will fail to compile.
(f) The program will compile, but throw an exception at runtime.

8.27 What will the following program print when run?

```
public class Appendage {
  private static void put0(StringBuilder s1) {
    s1.append("0");
  }

  public static void main(String[] args) {
    StringBuilder s1 = new StringBuilder("W");
    put0(s1);
    s1.append("W!");
    System.out.println(s1);
  }
}
```

Select the one correct answer.

(a) The program will print `WW!`.
(b) The program will print `WOW!`.
(c) The program will print `W`.
(d) The program will print `WO`.
(e) The program will fail to compile.
(f) The program will compile, but throw an exception at runtime.

Chapter Summary

The following topics were covered in this chapter:

- The `Object` class, which is the most fundamental class in Java
- Wrapper classes, which not only allow primitive values to be treated as objects, but also contain useful methods for converting values
- The `String` class, including how immutable strings are created and used
- The `StringBuilder` class, including how dynamic strings are created and manipulated
- Comparison of the `String`, `StringBuilder`, and `StringBuffer` classes

Programming Exercises

8.1 Create a class named `Pair`, which aggregates two arbitrary objects. Implement the `equals()` and `hashCode()` methods in such a way that a `Pair` object is identical to another `Pair` object if, and only if, the pair of constituent objects are identical. Make the `toString()` implementation return the textual representation of both the constituent objects in a `Pair` object. Objects of the `Pair` class should be immutable.

8.2 A palindrome is a text phrase that is spelled the same way backward and forward. The word *redivider* is a palindrome, since the word would be spelled the same even if the character sequence were reversed. Write a program that takes a string as an argument and reports whether the string is a *case-sensitive* palindrome. For example, the word *Redivider* would not be a palindrome in this case, since we distinguish between uppercase and lowercase letters.

Object Lifetime

9

Programmer I Exam Objectives	
[2.4] Explain an Object's Lifecycle (creation, "dereference by reassignment" and garbage collection)	§9.1, p. 384 §9.2, p. 384 §9.3, p. 386
Supplementary Objectives	
• Recognize the point at which an object becomes eligible for garbage collection in the code	§9.3, p. 386
• Understand the behavior of the `Object.finalize()` method	§9.4, p. 390 §9.5, p. 391
• Understand how garbage collection can be requested programmatically	§9.6, p. 393
• Understand forward references in initializers	§9.8, p. 400 §9.9, p. 402 §9.10, p. 404
• Understand the declaration order of initializers	§9.8, p. 400 §9.9, p. 402 §9.10, p. 404
• Understand the procedure involved in initializing the object state when an object is created using the `new` operator	§9.11, p. 406

9.1 Garbage Collection

Efficient memory management is essential in a runtime system. Storage for objects is allocated in a designated part of the memory called the *heap*, which has a finite size. Garbage collection is a process of managing the heap efficiently, by reclaiming memory occupied by objects that are no longer needed and making it available for new objects. Java provides automatic garbage collection, meaning that the runtime environment can take care of memory management without the program having to take any special action. Objects allocated on the heap (through the `new` operator) are administered by the automatic garbage collector. The automatic garbage collection scheme guarantees that a reference to an object is always valid while the object is needed by the program. Specifically, the object will not be reclaimed, leaving the reference dangling.

Having an automatic garbage collector frees the programmer from the responsibility of writing code for deleting objects. By relying on the automatic garbage collector, a Java program also forfeits any significant influence on the garbage collection of its objects (p. 393). However, this price is insignificant when compared to the cost of putting the code for object management in place and plugging all the memory leaks. Time-critical applications should recognize that the automatic garbage collector runs as a background task and may have a negative impact on their performance.

9.2 Reachable Objects

An automatic garbage collector essentially performs two tasks:

- Decides if and when memory needs to be reclaimed
- Finds objects that are no longer needed by the program and reclaims their storage

A program has no guarantees that the automatic garbage collector will be run during its execution. Consequently, a program should not rely on the scheduling of the automatic garbage collector for its behavior (p. 393).

To understand how the automatic garbage collector finds objects whose storage should be reclaimed, we need to look at the activity happening in the JVM. Java provides thread-based multitasking, meaning that several threads can be executing concurrently in the JVM, each doing its own task. A thread is an independent path of execution through the program code. A thread is alive if it has not completed its execution. Each live thread has its own JVM stack, as explained in §6.5, p. 230. The JVM stack contains activation frames of methods that are currently active. Local references declared in a method can always be found in the method's activation frame, stored on the JVM stack associated with the thread in which the method is called. Objects, in contrast, are always created on the heap. If an object has a field reference, the field will be found inside the object in the heap, and the object denoted by the field reference will also be found in the heap.

An example of how memory is organized during execution is depicted in Figure 9.1, which shows two live threads (t_1 and t_2) and their respective JVM stacks with the activation frames. The diagram indicates which objects in the heap are referenced by local references in the method activation frames. It also identifies field references in objects, which refer to other objects in the heap. Some objects have several aliases.

An object in the heap is said to be *reachable* if it is referenced by any *local* reference in a JVM stack. Likewise, any object that is denoted by a reference in a reachable object is said to be reachable. Reachability is a transitive relationship. Thus, a reachable object has at least one chain of reachable references from the JVM stack. Any reference that makes an object reachable is called a *reachable reference*. An object that is not reachable is said to be *unreachable*.

A reachable object is *alive*, and is *accessible* by a live thread. Note that an object can be accessible by more than one thread. Any object that is *not* accessible by a live thread is a candidate for garbage collection. When an object becomes unreachable and is waiting for its memory to be reclaimed, it is said to be *eligible* for garbage collection. An object is eligible for garbage collection if all references denoting it are in eligible objects. Eligible objects do not affect the future course of program execution. When the garbage collector runs, it finds and reclaims the storage of eligible objects, although garbage collection does not necessarily occur as soon as an object becomes unreachable.

In Figure 9.1, the objects `o4`, `o5`, `o11`, `o12`, `o14`, and `o15` all have reachable references. Objects `o13` and `o16` have no reachable references and, therefore, are eligible for garbage collection.

From the preceding discussion we can conclude that if a composite object becomes unreachable, its constituent objects also become unreachable, barring any reachable references to the constituent objects. Although the objects `o1`, `o2`, and `o3` in Figure 9.1 form a circular list, they do not have any reachable references. Thus, these objects are all eligible for garbage collection. Conversely, the objects `o5`, `o6`, and `o7` form a linear list, but they are all reachable, as the first object in the list, `o5`, is reachable. The objects `o8`, `o10`, `o11`, and `o9` also form a linear list (in that order), but not all objects in the list are reachable. Only the objects `o9` and `o11` are reachable, as object `o11` has a reachable reference. The objects `o8` and `o10` are eligible for garbage collection.

The *lifetime* of an object is the time from its creation to the time it is garbage collected. Under normal circumstances, an object is accessible from the time when it is created to the time when it becomes unreachable. The lifetime of an object can also include a period when it is eligible for garbage collection, waiting for its storage to be reclaimed. The finalization mechanism (p. 390) in Java does provide a means for *resurrecting* an object after it is eligible for garbage collection, but the finalization mechanism is rarely used for this purpose.

Figure 9.1 *Memory Organization at Runtime*

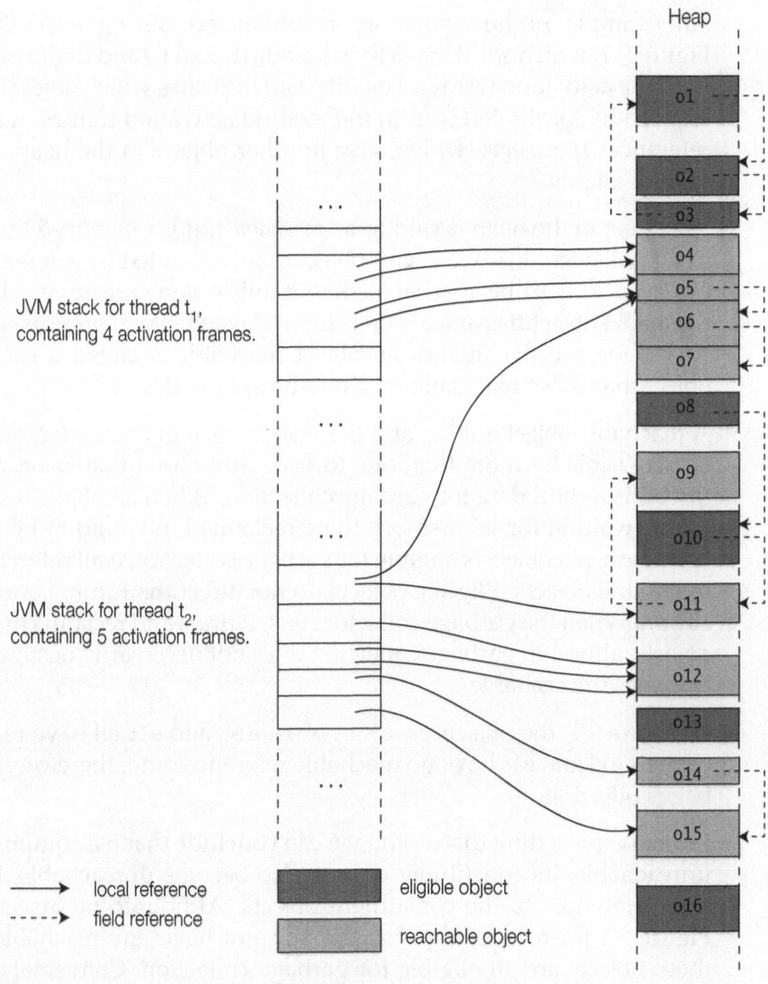

9.3 Facilitating Garbage Collection

The automatic garbage collector determines which objects are not reachable and, therefore, eligible for garbage collection. It will certainly go to work if there is an imminent memory shortage. Even so, automatic garbage collection should not be perceived as a license for creating a plethora of objects and then forgetting about them. Nevertheless, certain programming practices can help in minimizing the overhead associated with garbage collection during program execution.

Certain objects, such as files and network connections, can tie up resources and should be disposed of properly when they are no longer needed. In most cases, the `try`-with-resources statement (not in the scope of this book) provides a convenient facility for such purposes, as it will always ensure proper closing of the `AutoCloseable` resources.

To optimize its memory footprint, a live thread should retain access to an object as long for only as the object is needed for its execution. The program can allow objects to become eligible for garbage collection as early as possible by removing all references to an object when it is no longer needed.

Objects that are created and accessed by local references in a method are eligible for garbage collection when the method terminates, unless reference values to these objects are exported out of the method. This can occur if a reference value is returned from the method, passed as argument to another method that records the reference value, or thrown as an exception. However, a method need not always leave objects to be garbage collected after its termination. It can facilitate garbage collection by taking suitable action—for example, by nulling references.

```
import java.io.*;

class WellBehavedClass {
  // ...
  void wellBehavedMethod() {
    File aFile;
    long[] bigArray = new long[20000];
    // ... uses local variables ...
    // Does clean-up (before starting something extensive)
    aFile = null;                           // (1)
    bigArray = null;                        // (2)

    // Start some other extensive activity
    // ...
  }
  // ...
}
```

In this code, the local variables are set to `null` after use at (1) and (2), before starting some other extensive activity. This makes the objects denoted by the local variables eligible for garbage collection from this point onward, rather than after the method terminates. This optimization technique of nulling references should be used only as a last resort when resources are scarce.

Here are some other techniques to facilitate garbage collection:

- When a method returns a reference value and the object denoted by the value is not needed, not assigning this value to a reference facilitates garbage collection.
- If a reference is assigned a new value, the object that was previously denoted by the reference can become eligible for garbage collection.
- Removing reachable references to a composite object can make the constituent objects become eligible for garbage collection, as explained earlier.

Example 9.1 illustrates how a program can influence garbage collection eligibility. The class HeavyItem represents objects with a large memory footprint, for which we want to monitor garbage collection. Each composite HeavyItem object has a reference to a large array. The class overrides the finalize() method from the Object class to print out an ID when the object is finalized. This method is always called on an eligible object before it is destroyed (p. 390). We use it to indicate in the output if and when a HeavyItem is reclaimed. To illustrate the effect of garbage collection on object hierarchies, each HeavyItem object may also have a reference to another HeavyItem.

In Example 9.1, the class RecyclingBin defines a method createHeavyItem() at (4). In this method, the HeavyItem created at (5) is eligible for garbage collection after the reassignment of reference itemA at (6), as this object will then have no references. The HeavyItem created at (6) is accessible on return from the method. Its fate depends on the code that calls this method.

In Example 9.1, the class RecyclingBin also defines a method createList() at (8). It returns the reference value in the reference item1, which denotes the first item in a list of three HeavyItem objects. Because of the list structure, none of the HeavyItem objects in the list is eligible for garbage collection on return from the method. Again, the fate of the objects in the list is decided by the code that calls this method. It is enough for the first item in the list to become unreachable, so that all objects in the list become eligible for garbage collection (barring any reachable references).

Example 9.1 *Garbage Collection Eligibility*

```
// File: RecyclingBin.java
class HeavyItem {                                      // (1)
  int[]     itemBody;
  String    itemID;
  HeavyItem nextItem;

  HeavyItem(String ID, HeavyItem itemRef) {            // (2)
    itemBody = new int[1_000_000];
    itemID   = ID;
    nextItem = itemRef;
  }

  @Override
  protected void finalize() throws Throwable {         // (3)
    System.out.println(itemID + ": recycled.");
    super.finalize();
  }
}
//________________________________________________________________________
public class RecyclingBin {

  public static HeavyItem createHeavyItem(String itemID) {           // (4)
    HeavyItem itemA = new HeavyItem(itemID + ": local item", null);// (5)
    itemA = new HeavyItem(itemID, null);                             // (6)
```

```
    System.out.println("Return from creating HeavyItem " + itemID);
    return itemA;                                                    // (7)
  }

  public static HeavyItem createList(String listID) {                // (8)
    HeavyItem item3 = new HeavyItem(listID + ": item3", null);      // (9)
    HeavyItem item2 = new HeavyItem(listID + ": item2", item3);     // (10)
    HeavyItem item1 = new HeavyItem(listID + ": item1", item2);     // (11)
    System.out.println("Return from creating list " + listID);
    return item1;                                                    // (12)
  }

  public static void main(String[] args) {                           // (13)
    HeavyItem list = createList("X");                                // (14)
    list = createList("Y");                                          // (15)

    HeavyItem itemOne = createHeavyItem("One");                      // (16)
    HeavyItem itemTwo = createHeavyItem("Two");                      // (17)
    itemOne = null;                                                  // (18)
    createHeavyItem("Three");                                        // (19)
    createHeavyItem("Four");                                         // (20)
    System.out.println("Return from main().");
  }
}
```

Probable output from the program:

```
Return from creating list X
Return from creating list Y
X: item3: recycled.
X: item2: recycled.
X: item1: recycled.
Return from creating HeavyItem One
Return from creating HeavyItem Two
Return from creating HeavyItem Three
Three: local item: recycled.
Three: recycled.
Two: local item: recycled.
Return from creating HeavyItem Four
One: local item: recycled.
One: recycled.
Return from main().
```

In Example 9.1, the `main()` method at (13) in the class `RecyclingBin` uses the methods `createHeavyItem()` and `createList()`. It creates a list `X` at (14), but the reference to its first item is reassigned at (15), making objects in list `X` eligible for garbage collection after (15). The first item of list `Y` is stored in the reference `list`, making this list non-eligible for garbage collection during the execution of the `main()` method.

The `main()` method creates two items at (16) and (17), storing their reference values in the references `itemOne` and `itemTwo`, respectively. The reference `itemOne` is nulled at (18), making the `HeavyItem` object with identity `One` eligible for garbage collection. The two calls to the `createHeavyItem()` method at (19) and (20) return reference values to `HeavyItem` objects, which are not stored, making each object eligible for garbage collection immediately after their respective method calls return.

The output from the program bears out the observations made earlier. Objects in list `Y` (accessible through the reference `list`) and the `HeavyItem` object with identity `Two` (accessible through the reference `itemTwo`) remain non-eligible while the `main()` method executes. Although the output shows that the `HeavyItem` object with identity `Four` was never garbage collected, it is not accessible once it becomes eligible for garbage collection at (20). Any objects in the heap after the program terminates are reclaimed by the operating system.

9.4 Object Finalization

Object finalization provides an object with a last resort to undertake any action before its storage is reclaimed. The automatic garbage collector calls the `finalize()` method in an object that is eligible for garbage collection before actually destroying the object. The `finalize()` method is defined in the `Object` class:

```
protected void finalize() throws Throwable
```

An implementation of the `finalize()` method is called a *finalizer*. A subclass can override the finalizer from the `Object` class so as to take more specific and appropriate action before an object of the subclass is destroyed. Note that the overriding method cannot narrow the visibility of the overridden method and must be declared as either `protected` or `public`.

A finalizer, like any other method, can catch and throw exceptions (§6.7, p. 238). When a finalizer is called explicitly by the program code, exception handling is no different during execution of a finalizer than during execution of any other method. However, any exception thrown but not caught by a finalizer that is called by the garbage collector is ignored, and the finalization of this object is terminated. The finalizer is called only once on an object, regardless of whether any exception is thrown during its execution. In case of finalization failure, the object remains eligible for disposal at the discretion of the garbage collector (unless it has been resurrected, as explained later in this section). Since there is no guarantee that the garbage collector will ever run, there is also no guarantee that the finalizer will ever be called.

In the following code, the finalizer at (1) will take appropriate action if and when called on objects of the class before they are garbage collected, ensuring that the resource is freed. Since it is not guaranteed that the finalizer will ever be called at all, a program should not rely on the finalization to do any critical operations.

```
public class AnotherWellBehavedClass {
  SomeResource objRef;
  // ...
```

```
    @Override
    protected void finalize() throws Throwable {             // (1)
      try {                                                  // (2)
        if (objRef != null) objRef.close();
      } finally {                                            // (3)
        super.finalize();                                    // (4)
      }
    }
  }
```

The finalizer in a subclass should explicitly call the finalizer in its superclass as its last action, as shown at (4). The call to the finalizer of the superclass is in a `finally` block at (3), which is guaranteed to execute regardless of any exceptions thrown by the code in the `try` block at (2). (Another example of finalizer chaining is provided in Example 9.2 in the next section.)

The finalizer of an object can make the object non-eligible again (i.e., *resurrect* it), thereby avoiding garbage collection of the object. One simple technique is to assign the object's `this` reference to a static field, which then becomes a reachable reference for the object. Since a finalizer is called only once on an object before it is garbage collected, an object can be resurrected only once. In other words, if the object again becomes eligible for garbage collection and the garbage collector runs, the finalizer will not be called. Such object resurrections are not recommended, as they undermine the purpose of the finalization mechanism.

Note that an *enum type* cannot declare a finalizer. Therefore, an enum constant may never be finalized.

9.5 Finalizer Chaining

Unlike subclass constructors, overridden finalizers are not implicitly chained (§7.5, p. 282). Chaining of finalizers requires an explicit call to the overridden finalizer. Example 9.2 illustrates the process of programmatically chaining finalizers. It creates a user-specified number of large objects of a user-specified size; the number and size are provided through command-line program arguments. The loop at (7) in the `main()` method creates `Blob` objects, but does not store any references to them. Objects created are instances of the class `Blob` defined at (3). The `Blob` constructor at (4) initializes the field `size` by constructing a large array of integers. The `Blob` class extends the `BasicBlob` class, which assigns each blob a unique number (`blobId`) and keeps track of the number of blobs (`population`) not yet garbage collected.

Creation of each `Blob` object by the constructor at (4) prints the ID number of the object and the message `"Hello"`. The `finalize()` method at (5) is called before a `Blob` object is garbage collected. It prints the inherited field `blobId` of the `Blob` object and the message `"Bye"`, before calling the `finalize()` method in the superclass `BasicBlob` at (2), which decrements the population count. The program output shows that two blobs were not garbage collected at the time the print statement at (8) was executed. It is evident from the number of `"Bye"` messages that three blobs were garbage collected before all five blobs were created in the loop at (7).

Example 9.2 *Using Finalizers*

```
// File: Finalizers.java
class BasicBlob {                                                   // (1)
  private static int idCounter;
  private static int population;

  protected int blobId;

  BasicBlob() {
    blobId = idCounter++;
    ++population;
  }

  @Override
  protected void finalize() throws Throwable {                      // (2)
    --population;
    super.finalize();
  }

  public static int getPopulation() {
    return population;
  }
}
//______________________________________________________________________
class Blob extends BasicBlob {                                      // (3)
  private int[] size;

  Blob(int bloatedness) {                                           // (4)
    size = new int[bloatedness];
    System.out.println(blobId + ": Hello");
  }

  @Override
  protected void finalize() throws Throwable {                      // (5)
    System.out.println(blobId + ": Bye");
    super.finalize();
  }
}
//______________________________________________________________________
public class Finalizers {
  public static void main(String[] args) {                          // (6)
    int blobsRequired, blobSize;
    try {
      blobsRequired = Integer.parseInt(args[0]);
      blobSize      = Integer.parseInt(args[1]);
    } catch(IndexOutOfBoundsException e) {
      System.out.println("Too few program arguments.");
      System.out.println("Usage: Finalizers <number of blobs> <blob size>");
      return;
    } catch(NumberFormatException e) {
      System.out.println("Illegal program argument.");
      System.out.println("Usage: Finalizers <number of blobs> <blob size>");
      return;
    }
```

```
      for (int i = 0; i < blobsRequired; ++i) {                    // (7)
        new Blob(blobSize);
      }
      System.out.println(BasicBlob.getPopulation() + " blobs alive");  // (8)
    }
  }
```

Probable output from running the program with the following command:

```
>java Finalizers 5 500000
0: Hello
1: Hello
2: Hello
0: Bye
1: Bye
2: Bye
3: Hello
4: Hello
2 blobs alive
```

9.6 Invoking Garbage Collection Programmatically

Although Java provides facilities to invoke the garbage collection explicitly, there are no guarantees that it will be run. The program can request that garbage collection be performed, but there is no way to force garbage collection to be activated.

The `System.gc()` method can be used to request garbage collection, and the `System.runFinalization()` method can be called to suggest that any pending finalizers be run for objects eligible for garbage collection.

`static void gc()`

Requests that garbage collection be run.

`static void runFinalization()`

Requests that any pending finalizers be run for objects eligible for garbage collection.

Alternatively, corresponding methods in the `Runtime` class can be used. A Java application has a unique `Runtime` object that can be used by the application to interact with the JVM. An application can obtain this object by calling the method `Runtime.getRuntime()`. The `Runtime` class provides several methods related to memory issues:

`static Runtime getRuntime()`

Returns the `Runtime` object associated with the current application.

`void gc()`

Requests that garbage collection be run. However, it is recommended to use the more convenient static method `System.gc()`.

`void runFinalization()`

Requests that any pending finalizers be run for objects eligible for garbage collection. Again, it is more convenient to use the static method `System.runFinalization()`.

`long freeMemory()`

Returns the amount of free memory (bytes) in the JVM that is available for new objects.

`long totalMemory()`

Returns the total amount of memory (bytes) available in the JVM, including both memory occupied by current objects and memory available for new objects.

Example 9.3 illustrates the process of invoking garbage collection. The class `MemoryCheck` is an adaptation of the class `Finalizers` from Example 9.2. The `RunTime` object for the application is obtained at (7). This object is used to get information regarding total memory and free memory in the JVM at (8) and (9), respectively. Blobs are created in the loop at (10). The amount of free memory after blob creation is printed at (11). From the program output, it is apparent that some blobs were already garbage collected before the execution reached (11). A request for garbage collection is made at (12). Checking free memory after this request shows that more memory has become available, indicating that the request was honored. It is instructive to run the program without the method call `System.gc()` at (12) to compare the results with and without this call.

Example 9.3 *Invoking Garbage Collection*

```
class BasicBlob              { /* See Example 9.2. */ }
class Blob extends BasicBlob { /* See Example 9.2. */ }
//____________________________________________________________________
public class MemoryCheck {
  public static void main(String[] args) {                      // (6)
    int blobsRequired, blobSize;
    try {
      blobsRequired = Integer.parseInt(args[0]);
      blobSize      = Integer.parseInt(args[1]);
    } catch(IndexOutOfBoundsException e) {
      System.out.println("Too few program arguments.");
      System.out.println("Usage: MemoryCheck <number of blobs> <blob size>");
      return;
    } catch(NumberFormatException e) {
      System.out.println("Illegal program argument.");
      System.out.println("Usage: MemoryCheck <number of blobs> <blob size>");
      return;
    }
```

```
        Runtime environment = Runtime.getRuntime();                       // (7)
        System.out.println("Total memory: " + environment.totalMemory());// (8)
        System.out.println("Free memory before blob creation: " +
                           environment.freeMemory());                     // (9)
        for (int i = 0; i < blobsRequired; ++i) {                         // (10)
          new Blob(blobSize);
        }
        System.out.println("Free memory after blob creation: " +
                           environment.freeMemory());                     // (11)
        System.gc();                                                      // (12)
        System.out.println("Free memory after requesting GC: " +
                           environment.freeMemory());                     // (13)
        System.out.println(BasicBlob.getPopulation() + " blobs alive");  // (14)
      }
    }
```

Probable output from running the program with the following command:

```
>java MemoryCheck 5 100000
Total memory: 2031616
Free memory before blob creation: 1773192
0: Hello
1: Hello
2: Hello
1: Bye
2: Bye
3: Hello
0: Bye
3: Bye
4: Hello
Free memory after blob creation: 818760
4: Bye
Free memory after requesting GC: 1619656
0 blobs alive
```

The following points regarding automatic garbage collection should be noted:

- There are no guarantees that the finalizers of objects eligible for garbage collection will be executed. Garbage collection might not even be run if the program execution does not warrant it. Thus, any memory allocated during program execution might remain allocated after program termination, but will eventually be reclaimed by the operating system.
- There are also no guarantees about the order in which the objects will be garbage collected, or the order in which their finalizers will be executed. Therefore, the program should not make any assumptions based on these criteria.
- Garbage collection does not guarantee that there will be enough memory for the program to run. A program can rely on the garbage collector to run when memory gets very low, and it can expect an `OutOfMemoryException` to be thrown if its memory demands cannot be met.

Review Questions

9.1 Which of the following statements is true?

Select the one correct answer.

(a) Objects can be explicitly destroyed using the keyword `delete`.
(b) An object will be garbage collected immediately after it becomes unreachable.
(c) If object `obj1` is accessible from object `obj2`, and object `obj2` is accessible from `obj1`, then `obj1` and `obj2` are not eligible for garbage collection.
(d) Once an object has become eligible for garbage collection, it will remain eligible until it is destroyed.
(e) If object `obj1` can access object `obj2` that is eligible for garbage collection, then `obj1` is also eligible for garbage collection.

9.2 Identify the location in the following program where the object, initially referenced by `arg1`, is eligible for garbage collection.

```
public class MyClass {
  public static void main(String[] args) {
    String msg;
    String pre = "This program was called with ";
    String post = " as first argument.";
    String arg1 = new String((args.length > 0) ? "'" + args[0] + "'" :
                              "<no argument>");
    msg = arg1;
    arg1 = null;              // (1)
    msg = pre + msg + post;   // (2)
    pre = null;               // (3)
    System.out.println(msg);
    msg = null;               // (4)
    post = null;              // (5)
    args = null;              // (6)
  }
}
```

Select the one correct answer.

(a) After the line labeled (1)
(b) After the line labeled (2)
(c) After the line labeled (3)
(d) After the line labeled (4)
(e) After the line labeled (5)
(f) After the line labeled (6)

9.3 How many objects are eligible for garbage collection when control reaches (1)?

```
public class Eligible {
  public static void main(String[] args) {
    for (int i = 0; i < 5; i++) {
      Eligible obj = new Eligible();
      new Eligible();
    }
    System.gc();     // (1)
  }
}
```

Select the one correct answer.

(a) 0
(b) 5
(c) 10
(d) Hard to say

9.4 How many objects are eligible for garbage collection when control reaches (1)?

```
public class Link {
  private Link next;
  Link(Link next) { this.next = next; }
  public void finialize() { System.out.print("X"); }

  public static void main(String[] args) {
    Link p = null;
    for (int i = 0; i < 5; i++) {
      p = new Link(p);
    }
    System.gc();                          // (1);
  }
}
```

Select the one correct answer.

(a) 0
(b) 5
(c) 10
(d) Hard to say

9.5 Which of the following statements is true?

Select the one correct answer.

(a) If an exception is thrown during execution of the `finalize()` method of an eligible object, the exception is ignored and the object is destroyed.
(b) All objects have a `finalize()` method.
(c) Objects can be destroyed by explicitly calling the `finalize()` method.
(d) The `finalize()` method can be declared with any accessibility.
(e) The compiler will fail to compile code that defines an overriding `finalize()` method that does not explicitly call the overridden `finalize()` method from the superclass.

9.6 Which of the following statements is true?

Select the one correct answer.

(a) The compiler will fail to compile code that explicitly tries to call the `finalize()` method.
(b) The `finalize()` method can be overridden, but it must be declared with `protected` accessibility.
(c) An overriding `finalize()` method in any class can always throw checked exceptions.

(d) The `finalize()` method can be overloaded.
(e) The body of the `finalize()` method can access only other objects that are eligible for garbage collection.

9.7 Which method headers will result in a correct implementation of a finalizer for the following class?

```
public class Curtain {
  // (1) INSERT METHOD HEADER HERE ...
  {
    System.out.println("Final curtain");
    super.finalize();
  }
}
```

Select the two correct answers.

(a) `void finalize() throws Throwable`
(b) `void finalize() throws Exception`
(c) `void finalize()`
(d) `protected void finalize() throws Throwable`
(e) `protected void finalize() throws Exception`
(f) `protected void finalize()`
(g) `public void finalize() throws Throwable`
(h) `public void finalize() throws Exception`
(i) `public void finalize()`
(j) `private void finalize() throws Throwable`
(k) `private void finalize() throws Exception`
(l) `private void finalize()`

9.8 Which scenario can definitely *not* be the result of compiling and running the following program?

```
public class Grade {
  private char grade;
  Grade(char grade) { this.grade = grade; }

  public void finalize() throws Throwable {
    System.out.print(grade);
    super.finalize();
  }
  public static void main(String[] args) {
    new Grade('A'); new Grade('F');
    System.gc();
  }
}
```

Select the one correct answer.

(a) The program may print `AF`.
(b) The program may print `FA`.

(c) The program may print A.
(d) The program may print F.
(e) The program may print AFA.
(f) The program may not print anything.

9.9 Which scenarios can be the result of compiling and running the following program?

```
public class MyString {
  private String str;
  MyString(String str) { this.str = str; }

  public void finalize() throws Throwable {
    System.out.print(str);
    super.finalize();
  }

  public void concat(String str2) {
    this.str.concat(str2);
  }

  public static void main(String[] args) {
    new MyString("A").concat("B");
    System.gc();
  }
}
```

Select the two correct answers.
(a) The program may print AB.
(b) The program may print BA.
(c) The program may print A.
(d) The program may print B.
(e) The program may not print anything.

9.7 Initializers

Initializers can be used to set initial values for fields in objects and classes. There are three kinds of initializers:

- *Field initializer expressions*
- *Static initializer blocks*
- *Instance initializer blocks*

Subsequent sections in this chapter provide details on these initializers, concluding with a discussion of the procedure involved in constructing the state of an object when the object is created by using the new operator.

9.8 Field Initializer Expressions

Initialization of fields can be specified in field declaration statements using initializer expressions. The value of the initializer expression must be assignment compatible with the declared field (see §5.6, p. 158 and §7.9, p. 312). We distinguish between static and non-static field initializers.

```
class ConstantInitializers {
         int minAge = 12;                // (1) Non-static
  static double pensionPoints = 10.5; // (2) Static
  // ...
}
```

The fields of an object are initialized with the values of initializer expressions when the object is created by using the `new` operator. In the previous example, the declaration at (1) will result in the field `minAge` being initialized to `12` in every object of the class `ConstantInitializers` created with the `new` operator. If no explicit initializer expressions are specified, default values (§2.4, p. 42) are assigned to the fields.

When a class is loaded, it is initialized, meaning its static fields are initialized with the values of the initializer expressions. The declaration at (2) will result in the static field `pensionPoints` being initialized to `10.5` when the class is loaded by the JVM. Again, if no explicit initializers are specified, default values are assigned to the static fields.

An initializer expression for a static field cannot refer to non-static members by their simple names. The keywords `this` and `super` cannot occur in a static initializer expression.

Since a class is always initialized before it can be instantiated, an instance initializer expression can always refer to any static member of a class, regardless of the member declaration order. In the following code, the instance initializer expression at (1) refers to the static field `NO_OF_WEEKS` declared and initialized at (2). Such a *forward reference* is legal. More examples of forward references are given in the next subsection.

```
class MoreInitializers {
         int noOfDays    = 7 * NO_OF_WEEKS;    // (1) Non-static
  static int NO_OF_WEEKS = 52;                 // (2) Static
  // ...
}
```

Initializer expressions can also be used to define constants in interfaces (§7.6, p. 302). Such initializer expressions are implicitly static, as they define values of `static final` fields.

Initializer expressions are used to initialize local variables as well (§2.3, p. 40). A local variable is initialized with the value of the initializer expression every time the local variable declaration is executed.

Declaration Order of Initializer Expressions

When an object is created using the `new` operator, instance initializer expressions are executed in the order in which the instance fields are declared in the class.

Java requires that the declaration of a field must occur before its usage in any initializer expression if the field is *used on the right-hand side of an assignment* in the initializer expression. This essentially means that the declaration of a field must occur before the value of the field is *read* in an initializer expression. Using the field on the left-hand side of an assignment in the initializer expression does not violate the declaration-before-reading rule, as this constitutes a write operation. This rule applies when the usage of the field is by its simple name.

There is one caveat to the declaration-before-reading rule: It does not apply if the initializer expression defines an anonymous class, as the usage then occurs in a different class that has its own accessibility rules in the enclosing context. The restrictions outlined earlier help to detect initialization anomalies at compile time.

In the next code example, the initialization at (2) generates a compile-time error, because the field `width` in the initializer expression violates the declaration-before-reading rule. Because the usage of the field `width` in the initializer expression at (2) does not occur on the left-hand side of the assignment, this is an illegal forward reference. To remedy the error, the declaration of the field `width` at (4) can be moved in front of the declaration at (2). In any case, we can use the keyword `this` as shown at (3), but it will read the default value `0` in the field `width`.

```
class NonStaticInitializers {
  int length  = 10;                   // (1)
//double area = length * width;       // (2) Not OK. Illegal forward reference.
  double area = length * this.width;  // (3) OK, but width has default value 0.
  int width   = 10;                   // (4)

  int sqSide = height = 20;           // (5) OK. Legal forward reference.
  int height;                         // (6)
}
```

The forward reference at (5) is legal. The usage of the field `height` in the initializer expression at (5) occurs on the left-hand side of the assignment. The initializer expression at (5) is evaluated as `(sqSide = (height = 20))`. Every object of the class `NonStaticInitializers` will have the fields `height` and `sqSide` set to the value `20`.

The declaration-before-reading rule is equally applicable to static initializer expressions when static fields are referenced by their simple names.

Example 9.4 shows why the order of field initializer expressions can be important. The initializer expressions in this example are calls to methods defined in the class, and methods are not subject to the same access rules as initializer expressions. The call at (2) to the method `initMaxGuests()` defined at (4) is expected to return the maximum number of guests, but the field `occupancyPerRoom` at (3) will not have been explicitly initialized at this point; therefore, its default value `0` will be used in the method `initMaxGuests()`, which will return an incorrect value. The program output shows that after object creation, the occupancy per room is correct, but the maximum number of guests is wrong.

Example 9.4 *Initializer Expression Order and Method Calls*

```
// File: TestOrder.java
class Hotel {
  private int noOfRooms          = 12;                              // (1)
  private int maxNoOfGuests      = initMaxGuests();                 // (2) Bug
  private int occupancyPerRoom = 2;                                 // (3)

  public int initMaxGuests() {                                      // (4)
    System.out.println("occupancyPerRoom: " + occupancyPerRoom);
    System.out.println("maxNoOfGuests:    " + noOfRooms * occupancyPerRoom);
    return noOfRooms * occupancyPerRoom;
  }

  public int getMaxGuests() { return maxNoOfGuests; }              // (5)

  public int getOccupancy() { return occupancyPerRoom; }           // (6)
}
//______________________________________________________________________
public class TestOrder {
  public static void main(String[] args) {
    Hotel hotel = new Hotel();                                      // (7)
    System.out.println("After object creation: ");
    System.out.println("occupancyPerRoom: " + hotel.getOccupancy()); // (8)
    System.out.println("maxNoOfGuests:    " + hotel.getMaxGuests()); // (9)
  }
}
```

Output from the program:

```
occupancyPerRoom: 0
maxNoOfGuests:    0
After object creation:
occupancyPerRoom: 2
maxNoOfGuests:    0
```

9.9 Static Initializer Blocks

Java allows static initializer blocks to be defined in a class. Although such blocks can include arbitrary code, they are primarily used for initializing static fields. The code in a static initializer block is executed only once, when the class is loaded and initialized.

The syntax of a static initializer block comprises the keyword `static` followed by a local block that can contain arbitrary code, as shown at (3).

```
class StaticInitializers {

  static final int ROWS = 12, COLUMNS = 10;         // (1)
  static long[][] matrix = new long[ROWS][COLUMNS];  // (2)
```

```
  // ...
  static {                                        // (3) Static initializer
    for (int i = 0; i < matrix.length; i++)
      for (int j = 0; j < matrix[i].length; j++)
        matrix[i][j] = 2*i + j;
  }
  // ...
}
```

When the class `StaticInitializers` is first loaded in the previous example, the `static final` fields at (1) are initialized. Then the array of arrays `matrix` of specified size is created at (2), followed by the execution of the static block at (3).

If a class relies on native method implementations, a static initializer can be used to load any external libraries that the class needs (§4.8, p. 137).

Note that the static initializer block is not contained in any method. A class can have more than one static initializer block. Initializer blocks are *not* members of a class, and they cannot have a `return` statement because they cannot be called directly.

When a class is initialized, the initializer expressions in static field declarations and static initializer blocks are executed in the order in which they are specified in the class. In the previous example, the initializer expressions at (1) and (2) are executed before the static initializer block at (3).

Similar restrictions apply to static initializer blocks as for static initializer expressions: The keywords `this` and `super` cannot occur in a static initializer block, because such a block defines a static context.

Declaration Order of Static Initializers

When making forward references using simple names, code in a static initializer block is also subject to the declaration-before-reading rule discussed in the previous subsection. Example 9.5 illustrates forward references and the order of execution for static initializer expressions and static initializer blocks. An illegal forward reference occurs at (4), where an attempt is made to read the value of the field `sf1` before its declaration. At (11), the read operation occurs after the declaration, so it is allowed. Forward reference made on the left-hand side of the assignment is always allowed, as shown at (2), (5), and (7). The initializers are executed in their declaration order. A static field has the value that it was last assigned in an initializer. If there is no explicit assignment, the field has the default value of its type.

Example 9.5 *Static Initializers and Forward References*

```
public class StaticForwardReferences {

  static {                    // (1) Static initializer block.
    sf1 = 10;                 // (2) OK. Assignment to sf1 allowed.
```

```
  //  sf1 = if1;         // (3) Not OK. Non-static field access in static context.
  //  int a = 2 * sf1; // (4) Not OK. Read operation before declaration.
    int b = sf1 = 20;    // (5) OK. Assignment to sf1 allowed.
    int c = StaticForwardReferences.sf1;    // (6) OK. Not accessed by simple name.
  }

  static int sf1 = sf2 = 30;  // (7) Static field. Assignment to sf2 allowed.
  static int sf2;             // (8) Static field.
  int if1 = 5;                // (9) Non-static field.

  static {                    // (10) Static initializer block.
    int d = 2 * sf1;          // (11) OK. Read operation after declaration.
    int e = sf1 = 50;         // (12) OK. Assignment to sf1 allowed.
  }

  public static void main(String[] args) {
    System.out.println("sf1: " + StaticForwardReferences.sf1);
    System.out.println("sf2: " + StaticForwardReferences.sf2);
  }
}
```

Output from the program:

```
sf1: 50
sf2: 30
```

9.10 Instance Initializer Blocks

Just as static initializer blocks can be used to initialize static fields in a named class, so Java provides the ability to initialize fields during object creation using instance initializer blocks. In this respect, such blocks serve the same purpose as constructors during object creation. The syntax of an instance initializer block is the same as that of a local block, as shown at (2) in the following code. The code in the local block is executed every time an instance of the class is created.

```
class InstanceInitializers {
  long[] squares = new long[10];    // (1)
  // ...
  {                                 // (2) Instance Initializer
    for (int i = 0; i < squares.length; i++)
      squares[i] = i*i;
  }
  // ...
}
```

The array squares of specified length is first created at (1); its creation is followed by the execution of the instance initializer block at (2) every time an instance of the class InstanceInitializers is created. Note that the instance initializer block is not contained in any method. A class can have more than one instance initializer block, and these (and any instance initializer expressions in instance field declarations) are executed in the order they are specified in the class.

Declaration Order of Instance Initializers

Analogous to the other initializers discussed earlier, an instance initializer block cannot make a forward reference to a field that violates the declaration-before-reading rule. In Example 9.6, an illegal forward reference occurs in the code at (4), which attempts to read the value of the field `nsf1` before it is declared. The read operation at (11) occurs after the declaration and, therefore, is allowed. Forward reference made on the left-hand side of the assignment is always allowed, as shown at (2), (3), (5), and (7).

As in an instance initializer expression, the keywords `this` and `super` can be used to refer to the current object in an instance initializer block. As in a static initializer block, the `return` statement is not allowed in instance initializer blocks.

An instance initializer block can be used to factor out common initialization code that will be executed regardless of which constructor is invoked.

Example 9.6 *Instance Initializers and Forward References*

```
public class NonStaticForwardReferences {

  {                         // (1) Instance initializer block.
    nsf1 = 10;              // (2) OK. Assignment to nsf1 allowed.
    nsf1 = sf1;             // (3) OK. Static field access in non-static context.
    // int a = 2 * nsf1;    // (4) Not OK. Read operation before declaration.
    int b = nsf1 = 20;      // (5) OK. Assignment to nsf1 allowed.
    int c = this.nsf1;      // (6) OK. Not accessed by simple name.
  }

  int nsf1 = nsf2 = 30;     // (7) Non-static field. Assignment to nsf2 allowed.
  int nsf2;                 // (8) Non-static field.
  static int sf1 = 5;       // (9) Static field.

  {                         // (10) Instance initializer block.
    int d = 2 * nsf1;       // (11) OK. Read operation after declaration.
    int e = nsf1 = 50;      // (12) OK. Assignment to nsf1 allowed.
  }

  public static void main(String[] args) {
    NonStaticForwardReferences objRef = new NonStaticForwardReferences();
    System.out.println("nsf1: " + objRef.nsf1);
    System.out.println("nsf2: " + objRef.nsf2);
  }
}
```

Output from the program:

```
nsf1: 50
nsf2: 30
```

9.11 Constructing Initial Object State

Object initialization involves constructing the initial state of an object when it is created by the `new` operator. First the fields are initialized to their default values (§2.4, p. 42)—whether they are subsequently given non-default initial values or not—and then the constructor is invoked. This can lead to *local* chaining of constructors. The invocation of the constructor at the end of the local chain of constructor invocations results in the following actions, before the constructor's execution resumes:

- Implicit or explicit invocation of the superclass constructor. Constructor chaining ensures that the inherited state of the object is constructed first (§7.5, p. 282).
- Initialization of the instance fields by executing their instance initializer expressions and any instance initializer blocks, in the order they are specified in the class declaration.

Example 9.7 illustrates object initialization. The `new` operator is used at (8) to create an object of `SubclassB`. The no-argument constructor `SubclassB()` at (2) uses the `this()` construct to locally chain to the non-zero argument constructor at (3). This constructor then leads to an implicit call of the superclass constructor. As can be seen from the program output, the execution of the superclass's constructor at (1) reaches completion first. This is followed by the execution of the instance initializer block at (4) and the instance initializer expression at (6). Then the execution of the body of the non-zero argument constructor at (3) resumes. Finally, the no-argument constructor completes its execution, thereby completing the construction of the object state.

Note that the instance initializers are executed in the order they are specified in the class declaration. The forward reference to the field `value` at (5) is legal, because the usage of the field `value` is on the left-hand side of the assignment (it does not violate the declaration-before-reading rule). The default value of the field `value` is overwritten by the instance initializer block at (5). The field `value` is again overwritten by the instance initializer expression at (6), and finally by the non-zero argument constructor at (3).

Example 9.7 *Object State Construction*

```
// File: ObjectConstruction.java
class SuperclassA {
  public SuperclassA() {                         // (1)
    System.out.println("Constructor in SuperclassA");
  }
}
//_______________________________________________________________________
class SubclassB extends SuperclassA {

  SubclassB() {                                  // (2) No-argument constructor
    this(3);
    System.out.println("No-argument constructor in SubclassB");
  }
```

```
  SubclassB(int i) {                          // (3) Non-zero argument constructor
    System.out.println("Non-zero argument constructor in SubclassB");
    value = i;
  }

  {                                           // (4) Instance initializer block
    System.out.println("Instance initializer block in SubclassB");
    value = 2;                                // (5)
  }

  int value = initializerExpression();        // (6)

  private int initializerExpression() {       // (7)
    System.out.println("Instance initializer expression in SubclassB");
    return 1;
  }
}
//______________________________________________________________________________
public class ObjectConstruction {
  public static void main(String[] args) {
    SubclassB objRef = new SubclassB();         // (8)
    System.out.println("value: " + objRef.value);
  }
}
```

Output from the program:

```
Constructor in SuperclassA
Instance initializer block in SubclassB
Instance initializer expression in SubclassB
Non-zero argument constructor in SubclassB
No-argument constructor in SubclassB
value: 3
```

Some care should be exercised when writing constructors for non-`final` classes, since the object that is constructed might be a subclass instance. Example 9.8 shows a situation where use of overridden methods in *superclass* initializers and constructors can give unexpected results. The example intentionally uses the `this` reference to underline that the instance methods and constructors are invoked on the current object, and that the constructor call results in the initialization of the object state, as expected.

The program output from Example 9.8 shows that the field `superValue` at (1) in `SuperclassA` never gets initialized explicitly when an object of `SubclassB` is created at (8). The `SuperclassA` constructor at (2) does have a call to a method that has the name `doValue` at (3). A method with such a name is defined in `SuperclassA` at (4), but is also overridden in `SubclassB` at (7). The program output indicates that the method `doValue()` from `SubclassB` is called at (3) in the `SuperclassA` constructor. The implementation of the method `doValue()` at (4) never gets executed when an object of `SubclassB` is created. Method invocation always determines the implementation of the method to be executed, based on the *actual* type of the object. Keeping in mind that it is an object of `SubclassB` that is being initialized, the call to the method named `doValue` at (3) results in the method from `SubclassB` being executed. This can lead to unintended results. The overriding method `doValue()` at (7) in `SubclassB` can access the field `value` declared at (5) before its initializer expression has been executed; thus, the method invoked can access the state of the object *before* this has been completely initialized. The value `0` is then printed, as the field `value` has not yet been initialized with the value `800` when the superclass constructor is executed.

Example 9.8 *Initialization Anomaly under Object State Construction*

```
// File: ObjectInitialization.java
class SuperclassA {
  protected int superValue;                                   // (1)
  SuperclassA() {                                             // (2)
    System.out.println("Constructor in SuperclassA");
    this.doValue();                                           // (3)
  }
  void doValue() {                                            // (4)
    this.superValue = 911;
    System.out.println("superValue: " + this.superValue);
  }
}
//____________________________________________________________________
class SubclassB extends SuperclassA {
  private int value = 800;                                    // (5)
  SubclassB() {                                               // (6)
    System.out.println("Constructor in SubclassB");
    this.doValue();
    System.out.println("superValue: " + this.superValue);
  }
  @Override
  void doValue() {                                            // (7)
    System.out.println("value: " + this.value);
  }
}
//____________________________________________________________________
public class ObjectInitialization {
  public static void main(String[] args) {
    System.out.println("Creating an object of SubclassB.");
    new SubclassB();                                          // (8)
  }
}
```

Output from the program:

```
Creating an object of SubclassB.
Constructor in SuperclassA
value: 0
Constructor in SubclassB
value: 800
superValue: 0
```

Class initialization takes place before any instance of the class can be created or a static method of the class can be invoked. A superclass is initialized before its subclasses are initialized. Initializing a class involves initialization of the static fields by executing their static initializer expressions and any static initializer blocks.

Initialization of an interface involves execution of any static initializer expressions for the static fields declared in the interface. An interface cannot specify instance initializer expressions, because it has no instance fields, nor can it specify any initializer blocks, because it cannot be instantiated.

Review Questions

9.10 Given the following class, which of these static initializer blocks can be independently inserted at (1)?

```
public class MyClass {
  private static int count = 5;
  static final int STEP = 10;
  boolean alive;

  // (1) INSERT STATIC INITIALIZER BLOCK HERE
}
```

Select the three correct answers.

(a) `static { alive = true; count = 0; }`
(b) `static { STEP = count; }`
(c) `static { count += STEP; }`
(d) `static ;`
(e) `static {;}`
(f) `static { count = 1; }`

9.11 What will be the result of compiling and running the following program?

```
public class MyClass {
  public static void main(String[] args) {
    MyClass obj = new MyClass(n);
  }

  static int i = 5;
  static int n;
  int j = 7;
  int k;

  public MyClass(int m) {
    System.out.println(i + ", " + j + ", " + k + ", " + n + ", " + m);
  }

  { j = 70; n = 20; } // Instance initializer block

  static { i = 50; }  // Static initializer block
}
```

Select the one correct answer.

(a) The code will fail to compile, because of the instance initializer block.
(b) The code will fail to compile, because of the static initializer block.
(c) The code will compile, and print `50, 70, 0, 20, 0` at runtime.
(d) The code will compile, and print `50, 70, 0, 20, 20` at runtime.
(e) The code will compile, and print `5, 70, 0, 20, 0` at runtime.
(f) The code will compile, and print `5, 70, 0, 20, 20` at runtime.
(g) The code will compile, and print `5, 7, 0, 20, 0` at runtime.
(h) The code will compile, and print `5, 7, 0, 20, 20` at runtime.

9.12 Given the following class, which instance initializer block inserted independently at (1) will allow the class to be compiled?

```
public class FirstClass {
  static int gap = 10;
  double length;
  final boolean active;

  // (1) INSERT CODE HERE
}
```

Select the one correct answer.

(a) `instance { active = true; }`
(b) `FirstClass { gap += 5; }`
(c) `{ gap = 5; length = (active ? 100 : 200) + gap; }`
(d) `{ ; }`
(e) `{ length = 4.2; }`
(f) `{ active = (gap > 5); length = 5.5 + gap;}`

9.13 What will be the result of compiling and running the following program?

```
public class Initialization {
  private static String msg(String msg) {
    System.out.println(msg);
    return msg;
  }

  public Initialization() { m = msg("1"); }

  { m = msg("2"); }

  String m = msg("3");

  public static void main(String[] args) {
    Object obj = new Initialization();
  }
}
```

Select the one correct answer.

(a) The program will fail to compile.
(b) The program will compile, and print 1, 2, and 3 at runtime.
(c) The program will compile, and print 2, 3, and 1 at runtime.
(d) The program will compile, and print 3, 1, and 2 at runtime.
(e) The program will compile, and print 1, 3, and 2 at runtime.

9.14 Which of the labeled lines in the following code can be independently *uncommented* by removing the // characters, such that the code will still compile?

```
class GeomInit {
//int width = 14;                /* Line A */
  {
//  area = width * height;       /* Line B */
  }
  int width = 37;
  {
//  height = 11;                 /* Line C */
  }
  int height, area;
//area = width * height;         /* Line D */
  {
//  int width = 15;              /* Line E */
    area = 100;
  }
}
```

Select the two correct answers.

(a) Line A
(b) Line B
(c) Line C
(d) Line D
(e) Line E

Chapter Summary

The following topics were covered in this chapter:

- Automatic garbage collection, including the workings of the garbage collector and guidelines for facilitating garbage collection
- Object finalization and chaining as part of garbage collection
- Static and instance initializers, both as initializer expressions and as initializer blocks
- The role played by initializers in initializing objects, classes, and interfaces

The ArrayList<E> Class and Lambda Expressions

10

Programmer I Exam Objectives	
[9.4] Declare and use an ArrayList of a given type	*§10.1, p. 414*
[9.5] Write a simple Lambda expression that consumes a Lambda Predicate expression	*§10.2, p. 433*
Supplementary Objectives	
• Understand the concept of a list	*§10.1, p. 414*
• Understand the inheritance hierarchy of the `ArrayList<E>` class	*§10.1, p. 414*
• Use the diamond operator (<>) when creating objects of generic classes	*§10.1, p. 416*
• Compare arrays and `ArrayList`s	*§10.1, p. 425*
• Understand behavior parameterization in functional-style programming	*§10.2, p. 434*
• Provide an overview of the general-purpose functional interfaces in the `java.util.function` package	*§10.2, p. 443*
• Implement lambda expressions in the context of a functional interface	*§10.2, p. 442* *§10.2, p. 444*
• Understand the implications of a lambda expression in the context where it is defined	*§10.2, p. 446* *§10.2, p. 448*
• Understand type checking and deferred execution of a lambda expression	*§10.2, p. 450*
• Define selection criteria as predicates for filtering `ArrayList`s	*§10.2, p. 434* *§10.2, p. 451*

10.1 The `ArrayList<E>` Class

A program manipulates data, so organizing and using data efficiently are naturally important in a program. *Data structures* are ways to organize data. Java uses the term *collection* to mean a data structure that can maintain a group of objects so that the objects can be manipulated as a *single entity* or *unit*. Objects can be stored, retrieved, and manipulated as *elements* of a collection. The term *container* is also used in the literature for such data structures. Arrays are an example of one kind of collection. Other examples include lists, sets, queues, and stacks, among many others.

Lists

Once an array is created, its length cannot be changed. This inflexibility can be a significant drawback when the amount of data to be stored in an array is not known a priori. In Java, the structures known as lists alleviate this shortcoming. Lists are collections that maintain their elements *in order* and can contain duplicates. The order of elements in a list is *positional order*, and individual elements can be accessed according to their position in the list. Each element, therefore, has a position in the list. A zero-based index can be used to access the element at the position designated by the index value, analogous to accessing elements in an array. However, unlike in an array, the position of an element in a list can change as elements are inserted or deleted from the list—that is, as the list is changed structurally.

Sorting implies ordering the elements in a collection according to some *ranking criteria*, usually based on the *values* of the elements. However, elements is an `ArrayList` are maintained in the order they are inserted in the list, known as the *insertion order*. The elements in such a list are therefore *ordered*, but they are *not* sorted, as it is not the values of the elements that determine their ranking in the list. Thus, ordering does *not* necessarily imply sorting.

The Java Collections Framework

The `Collection` interface in the `java.util` package (also known as the Java Collections Framework) defines the general operations that a collection should provide. Other subinterfaces in the Java Collections Framework augment this interface to provide specific operations for particular kinds of collections. The `java.util.List` interface extends the `java.util.Collection` interface with the necessary operations to maintain the collection as a list (see Figure 10.1). In addition to the operations inherited from the `java.util.Collection` interface, the `java.util.List` interface defines operations that work specifically on lists: position-based access of the list elements, searching in a list, operations on parts of a list (called *open range-view* operations), and creation of customized iterators to traverse a list.

The concrete class `java.util.ArrayList` implements the `java.util.List` interface. In Figure 10.1, the *type parameter* `E` in angular brackets (<>) after a reference type name indicates that the reference type is a *generic type*. The type parameter `E` represents the type of the element in the collection. Use of a generic type requires a *concrete*

Figure 10.1 *Partial* `ArrayList` *Inheritance Hierarchy*

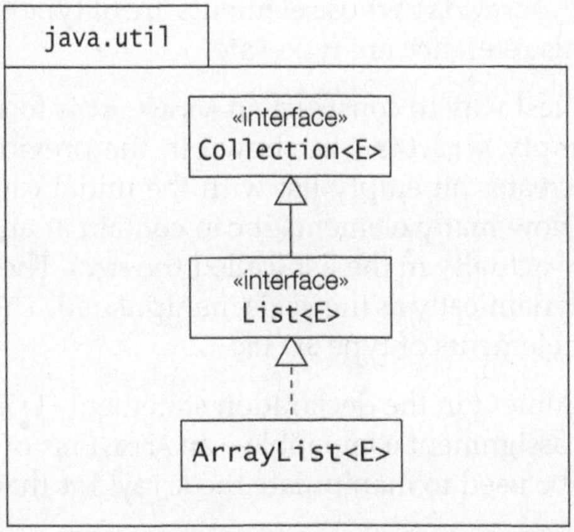

reference type to be substituted for the type parameter `E`. Examples in this section will make amply clear how to use a generic type, and in particular, the class `ArrayList`.

The `ArrayList` class is a dynamically resizable implementation of the `List` interface using arrays (also known as *dynamic arrays*), providing fast random access (i.e., position-based access in constant time) and fast list traversal—very much like using an ordinary array. The `ArrayList` class is not *thread-safe*; that is, its integrity can be jeopardized by concurrent access. The Java Collections Framework provides other implementations of the `List` interface, but in most cases the `ArrayList` implementation is the overall best choice for implementing lists.

This section covers the basics of using an `ArrayList`. The Java Collections Framework is an extensive topic, far beyond the scope of this book. However, diving deep into the Java Collections Framework is a beneficial exercise that is highly recommended for all Java programmers.

Declaring References and Constructing `ArrayLists`

In the discussion that follows, we assume that any class or interface used from the `java.util` package has been imported with an appropriate `import` statement.

The following declaration statement shows how we can declare a reference that can refer to an `ArrayList` of a specific element type. It also illustrates how we can create an empty `ArrayList` of a specific element type, and assign its reference value to a reference:

```
ArrayList<String> palindromes = new ArrayList<String>(); // (1)
```

As this code indicates, the element type is specified using angular brackets (<>). The reference `palindromes` can refer to any `ArrayList` whose element type is `String`.

The type parameter `E` of the class `ArrayList` in Figure 10.1 is replaced by the concrete class `String`. The compiler ensures that the reference `palindromes` can only refer to an `ArrayList` whose elements are of type `String`, and any operations on this list via this reference are type-safe.

The simplest way to construct an `ArrayList` is to use the default constructor to create an empty `ArrayList`, as shown in the previous declaration. The default constructor creates an empty list with the initial capacity of 10. The *capacity* of a list refers to how many elements it can contain at any given time, not how many elements are actually in the list (called the *size*). The capacity of a list and its size can change dynamically as the list is manipulated. The `ArrayList` created in (1) can contain only elements of type `String`.

The assignment in the declaration statement (1) is valid because the types on both sides are assignment compatible—an `ArrayList` of `String`. The reference `palindromes` can now be used to manipulate the `ArrayList` that was created.

The Diamond Operator: <>

The element type within the angular brackets (<>) can be omitted in the `ArrayList` creation expression on the right-hand side of the declaration statement. In this particular context, the compiler can infer the element type of the `ArrayList` from the declaration of the reference type on the left-hand side.

```
ArrayList<String> palindromes = new ArrayList<>(); // Using the diamond operator
```

The empty angular brackets, <>, are commonly referred to as the *diamond operator*. This operator must be used with the `new` operator when constructing an object of a generic type, like `ArrayList`, where the type information for its usage can be inferred by the compiler from the context, as in the preceding declaration statement.

However, if the diamond operator is omitted, the compiler will issue an *unchecked conversion warning*, as shown at (2) in the next code snippet. A new `ArrayList` is created based on an `ArrayList` of `Integer` that is passed as an argument to the constructor. The `ArrayList` of `Integer` is created at (1). The reference `newList1` of type `ArrayList<String>` refers to an `ArrayList` whose element type is `Integer`, not `String`. The code at (2) compiles, but we get a `ClassCastException` at runtime at (3) when we retrieve an element from this list. The `get()` method call at (3) expects a `String` in the `ArrayList`, but gets an `Integer`. If the diamond operator is used, as shown at (4), the compiler reports a compile-time error, and the problem described at (3) cannot occur at runtime. By issuing an unchecked conversion warning at (2), the compiler alerts us to the fact that it cannot guarantee type-safety of the list created at (2).

```
ArrayList<Integer> intList = new ArrayList<>();           // (1) ArrayList of Integer
intList.add(10); intList.add(100); intList.add(1000);

ArrayList<String> newList1 = new ArrayList(intList);      // (2) Unchecked conversion
                                                          //     warning
System.out.println(newList1.get(0));                      // (3) ClassCastException!

ArrayList<String> newList2 = new ArrayList<>(intList);    // (4) Compile-time error!
```

Best practices advocate *programming to an interface*. In practical terms, this means using references of an interface type to manipulate objects of a concrete class that implement this interface. Since the class `java.util.ArrayList` implements the `java.util.List` interface, the declaration (1) can be written as shown in the next code snippet. This declaration is valid, since the reference value of a subtype object (`ArrayList<String>`) can be assigned to a reference of its supertype (`List<String>`).

```
List<String> palindromes = new ArrayList<>();      // (2) List reference
```

This best practice provides great flexibility in substituting other objects for a task when necessary. The current concrete class can easily be replaced by another concrete class that implements the same interface. Only code creating objects needs to be changed. As it happens, the Java Collections Framework provides another implementation of lists: the `java.util.LinkedList` class, which also implements the `List` interface. If this class is found to be more conducive for maintaining palindromes in a list, we need simply change the name of the class in declaration (2), and continue using the reference `palindromes` in the program:

```
List<String> palindromes = new LinkedList<>(); // Changing implementation.
```

The `ArrayList` class also provides a constructor that allows an empty `ArrayList` to be created with a specific initial capacity.

```
List<String> palindromes = new ArrayList<>(20); // Initial capacity is 20.
```

The `ArrayList` class provides the `add(E)` method to append an element to the list. This object is added after the last element in the list, thereby increasing the list size by 1.

```
palindromes.add("level"); palindromes.add("Ada"); palindromes.add("kayak");
System.out.println(palindromes);
```

The print statement calls the `toString()` method in the `ArrayList` class to print the elements in the list. This `toString()` method applies the `toString()` method of the individual elements to create a textual representation in the following default format:

```
[level, Ada, kayak]
```

A third constructor allows an `ArrayList` to be constructed from another collection. The following code creates a list of words from a list of palindromes. The order of the elements in the new `ArrayList` is the same as that in the `ArrayList` that was passed as an argument in the constructor.

```
List<String> wordList = new ArrayList<>(palindromes);
System.out.println(wordList); // [level, Ada, kayak]
wordList.add("Naan");
System.out.println(wordList); // [level, Ada, kayak, Naan]
```

The next examples illustrate the creation of empty lists of different types of elements. The compiler ensures that operations on the `ArrayList` are type-safe with respect to the element type. Declaration (3) shows how we can create nested list structures (i.e., list of lists), analogous to an array of arrays. Note that the diamond operator is not nested in (3). Declaration (4) shows that the element type cannot be a primitive type; rather, it must be a reference type.

```
List<StringBuilder> synonyms   = new ArrayList<>(); // List of StringBuilder
List<Integer> attendance       = new ArrayList<>(); // List of Integer
List<List<String>> listOfLists = new ArrayList<>(); // (3) List of List of String
List<int> frequencies          = new ArrayList<>(); // (4) Compile-time error!
```

When comparing arrays and `ArrayList`s, there is one other significant difference that concerns the subtype relationship.

```
Object[] objArray = new String[10];                  // (5) OK!
```

In declaration (5), since `String` is a subtype of `Object`, `String[]` is a subtype of `Object[]`. Thus we can manipulate the array of `String` using the `objArray` reference.

```
objArray[2] = "Green";                               // (6) OK!
objArray[1] = new Integer(2016);                     // ArrayStoreException!
```

The preceding assignment requires a runtime check to guarantee that the assignment is type compatible. Otherwise, an `ArrayStoreException` is thrown at runtime.

For the `ArrayList`, the following declarations will not compile:

```
ArrayList<Object> objList1 = new ArrayList<String>();// (7) Compile-time error!
List<Object> objList2 = new ArrayList<String>();     // (8) Compile-time error!
```

Although `String` is a subtype of `Object`, it is not the case that an `ArrayList<String>` is a subtype of `ArrayList<Object>`. If this was the case, we could use the `objList1` reference to add other types of objects to the `ArrayList` of `String`, thereby jeopardizing its type-safety. Since there is no information about the element type `E` available at runtime to carry out a type compatibility check, as in the case of arrays, the subtype relationship is not allowed in (7). For the same reason, (8) will not compile: `ArrayList<String>` is not a subtype of `List<Object>`. In general, the subtype relationship does not hold for generic types. The Java language provides ways to overcome this restriction, but we will not pursue this matter further.

The `ArrayList` constructors are summarized here:

```
ArrayList()
ArrayList(int initialCapacity)
ArrayList(Collection<? extends E> c)
```

The default constructor creates a new, empty `ArrayList` with an initial capacity of 10.

The second constructor creates a new, empty `ArrayList` with the specified initial capacity.

The third constructor creates a new `ArrayList` containing the elements in the specified collection. The declaration of the parameter `c` essentially means that parameter `c` can refer to any collection whose element type is `E` or whose element type is a subtype of `E`. The new `ArrayList` will retain any duplicates. The ordering in the `ArrayList` will be determined by the traversal order of the iterator for the collection passed as an argument.

Modifying an `ArrayList`

A summary of selected methods that can modify the contents of a list is given here:

```
boolean add(E element)
void add(int index, E element)
```

The first method will append the specified element to the *end* of the list. It returns `true` if the collection was modified as a result of the operation.

The second method inserts the specified element at the specified index. If necessary, it shifts the element previously at this index and any subsequent elements one position toward the end of the list. The method will throw an `IndexOutOfBoundsException` if the index is out of range (`index < 0 || index > size()`).

The type parameter `E` represents the element type of the list.

```
boolean addAll(Collection<? extends E> c)
boolean addAll(int index, Collection<? extends E> c)
```

The first method inserts the elements from the specified collection at the end of the list. The second method inserts the elements from the specified collection at the specified index; that is, the method splices the elements of the specified collection into the list at the specified index. The methods return `true` if any elements were added. Elements are inserted using an iterator of the specified collection. The second method will throw an `IndexOutOfBoundsException` if the index is out of range (`index < 0 || index > size()`).

The declaration of the parameter `c` essentially means that parameter `c` can refer to any collection whose element type is `E` or whose element type is a subtype of `E`.

```
E set(int index, E element)
```

This method replaces the element at the specified index with the specified element. It returns the previous element at the specified index. The method throws an `IndexOutOfBoundsException` if the index is out of range (`index < 0 || index >= size()`).

```
E remove(int index)
boolean remove(Object element)
```

The first method deletes and returns the element at the specified index. The method throws an `IndexOutOfBoundsException` if the index is out of range (`index < 0 || index >= size()`).

The second method removes the *first* occurrence of the element from the list, using object value equality. The method returns `true` if the call was successful.

Both methods will contract the list accordingly if any elements are removed.

```
boolean removeAll(Collection<?> c)
boolean removeIf(Predicate<? super E> filter)
```

The `removeAll()` method removes from this list all elements that are contained in the specified collection.

The `removeIf()` method removes from this list all elements that satisfy the filtering criteria defined by a lambda expression that implements the `Predicate<T>` functional interface (p. 452).

Both methods return `true` if the call was successful. The list is contracted accordingly if any elements are removed.

```
void trimToSize()
```

This method trims the capacity of this list to its current size.

```
void clear()
```

This method deletes all elements from the list. The list is empty after the call, so it has size 0.

All the code snippets is this section can be found in Example 10.1, p. 427. The method `printListWithIndex()` at (16) in Example 10.1 prints the elements prefixed with their index in the list, making it easier to see how the list changes structurally:

```
[0:level, 1:Ada, 2:Java, 3:kayak, 4:Bob, 5:Rotator, 6:Bob]
```

We have seen that the `add(E)` method appends an element to the end of the list. The following code adds the strings from an array of `String` to an `ArrayList` of `String`. The output from Example 10.1 at (2) shows how the elements are added at the end of the list.

```
System.out.println("\n(2) Add elements to list:");
for (String str : wordArray) {
  strList.add(str);
  printListWithIndex(strList);
}
```

We can insert a new element at a specific index using the overloaded method `add(int, E)`. The output from the following code shows how inserting an element at index 2 shifted the elements structurally in the list.

```
                                // [0:level, 1:Ada, 2:kayak, 3:Bob, 4:Rotator, 5:Bob]
strList.add(2, "Java");         // Insert an element at index 2 in the list.
printListWithIndex(strList); // [0:level, 1:Ada, 2:Java, 3:kayak, 4:Bob,
                                //   5:Rotator, 6:Bob]
```

Note that an index value equal to 0 or the size of the list is always allowed for the method `add(int, E)`.

```
List<String> list1 = new ArrayList<>();   // []
list1.add(0, "First");                     // [First]
list1.add(list1.size(), "Last");           // [First, Last]
```

We can replace an element at a specified index using the `set(int, E)` method. The method returns the element that was replaced.

```
System.out.println("(3) Replace the element at index 1:");
String oldElement = strList.set(1, "Naan");
System.out.println("Element that was replaced: " + oldElement);   // "Ada"
printListWithIndex(strList); // [0:level, 1:Naan, 2:Java, 3:kayak, 4:Bob,
                             //  5:Rotator, 6:Bob]
```

We can also remove elements from a list, with the list being contracted accordingly.

```
System.out.println("(4) Remove the element at index 0:");
System.out.println("Element removed: " + strList.remove(0));        // "level"
printListWithIndex(strList); // [0:Naan, 1:Java, 2:kayak, 3:Bob, 4:Rotator, 5:Bob]

System.out.println("(5) Remove the first occurrence of \"Java\":");
System.out.println("Element removed: " + strList.remove("Java")); // true
printListWithIndex(strList); // [0:Naan, 1:kayak, 2:Bob, 3:Rotator, 4:Bob]
```

The `remove(int)` removes the element at the specified index. The method `remove(Object)` needs to search the list and compare the argument object with elements in the list for object value equality. This test requires that the argument object override the `equals()` method from the `Object` class, which merely determines reference value equality. The `String` class provides the appropriate `equals()` method. However, the following code will not give the expected result, because the `StringBuilder` class does not provide its own `equals()` method.

```
List<StringBuilder> sbList = new ArrayList<>();
for (String str : wordArray)
  strList.add(str);
System.out.println(sbList); // [level, Ada, kayak, Bob, Rotator, Bob]
StringBuilder element = new StringBuilder("Ada");
System.out.println("Element to be removed: " + element);          // Ada
System.out.println("Element removed: " + sbList.remove(element)); // false
System.out.println(sbList); // [level, Ada, kayak, Bob, Rotator, Bob]
```

Primitive Values and ArrayLists

Since primitive values cannot be stored in an `ArrayList`, we can use the wrapper classes to box such values first. In the following code, we create a list of `Integer` in which the `int` values are autoboxed in `Integer` objects and then added to the list. We try to delete the element with value `1`, but end up deleting the element at index 1 instead (i.e, the value `20`).

```
List<Integer> intList = new ArrayList<>();
intList.add(10); intList.add(20); intList.add(1);
System.out.println(intList);                                // [10, 20, 1]
System.out.println("Element to be removed: " + 1);          // 1
System.out.println("Element removed: " + intList.remove(1)); // 20
System.out.println(intList);                                // [10, 1]
```

The method call

```
intList.remove(1)
```

has the signature

```
intList.remove(int)
```

This signature matches the overloaded method that removes the element at a specified index, so it is this method that is called at runtime. We say that this method is the *most specific* in this case. For the code to work as intended, the primitive value must be explicitly boxed.

```
System.out.println(intList);                                        // [10, 20, 1]
System.out.println("Element to be removed: " + 1);                              // 1
System.out.println("Element removed: " + intList.remove(new Integer(1))); // true
System.out.println(intList);                                        // [10, 20]
```

The method call

```
intList.remove(new Integer(1))
```

has the signature

```
intList.remove(Integer)
```

This call matches the overloaded `remove(Object)` method, since an `Integer` object can be passed to an `Object` parameter. This method is the most specific in this case, and is executed.

Querying an `ArrayList`

A summary of useful methods that can be used to query a list is provided here:

`int size()`

Returns the number of elements currently in the list. In a non-empty list, the first element is at index 0 and the last element is at `size()-1`.

`boolean isEmpty()`

Determines whether the list is empty (i.e., whether its size is 0).

`E get(int index)`

Returns the element at the specified *positional index*. The method throws an `IndexOutOfBoundsException` if the index is out of range (`index < 0 || index >= size()`).

`boolean equals(Object o)`

Compares the specified object with this list for object value equality. It returns `true` if and only if the specified object is also a list, both lists have the same size, and all corresponding pairs of elements in the two lists are equal according to object value equality.

`boolean contains(Object element)`

Determines whether the argument object is contained in the collection, using object value equality. This is called the *membership test*.

```
int indexOf(Object o)
int lastIndexOf(Object o)
```

Return the indexes of the first and last occurrences of the element that are equal (using object value equality) to the specified argument, respectively, if such an element exists in the list; otherwise, the value –1 is returned. These methods provide *element search* in the list.

The method `get(int)` retrieves the element at the specified index.

```
System.out.println("First element: " + strList.get(0);                // Naan
System.out.println("Last element: " + strList.get(strList.size()-1));  // Bob
```

The `equals()` method of the `ArrayList` class can be used to compare two lists for equality with regard to size and corresponding elements being equal in each list.

```
List<String> strList2 = new ArrayList<>(strList);
boolean trueOrFalse = strList.equals(strList2); // true
```

The membership test is carried out by the `contains(Object)` method. We can find the index of a specified element in the list by using the `indexOf()` and `lastIndexOf()` methods.

```
boolean found = strList.contains("Naan");    // true
int pos = strList.indexOf("Bob");            // 2
pos = strList.indexOf("BOB");                // -1 (Not found)
pos = strList.lastIndexOf("Bob");            // 4 (Last occurrence)
```

Again, these methods require that the element type provide a meaningful `equals()` method for object value equality testing.

Traversing an `ArrayList`

A very common task is to traverse a list so as to perform some operation on each element of the list. We can use positional access to traverse a list with the `for(;;)` loop. The generic method `printListWithIndex()` in Example 10.1 uses the `for(;;)` loop to create a new `ArrayList` of `String` that contains each element of the argument list prefixed with the index of the element.

```
public static <E> void printListWithIndex(List<E> list) {
  List<String> newList = new ArrayList<>();
  for (int i = 0; i < list.size(); i++) {
    newList.add(i + ":" + list.get(i));
  }
  System.out.println(newList);
}
```

Sample output from the method call `printWithIndex(strList)` is shown here:

```
[0:level, 1:Ada, 2:kayak, 3:Bob, 4:Rotator, 5:Bob]
```

The method `printListWithIndex()` in Example 10.1 can print *any* list in this format. Its header declaration says that it accepts a list of element type `E`. The element type

E is determined from the method call. In the preceding example, E is determined to be String, as a List of String is passed in the method call.

Since the ArrayList class implements the Iterable interface (i.e., the class provides an iterator), we can use the for(:) loop to traverse a list.

```
for (String str : strList) {
  System.out.print(str + " ");
}
```

The ArrayList also provides specialized iterators to traverse a list, and the diligent reader is encouraged to make their acquaintance at his or her own leisure.

One pertinent question to ask is how to remove elements from the list when traversing the list. The for(:) loop does not allow the list structure to be modified:

```
for (String str : strList) {
  if (str.length() <= 3) {
    strList.remove(str);                  // Throws ConcurrentModificationException
  }
}
```

We can use positional access in a loop to traverse the list, but must be careful in updating the loop variable, as the list contracts when an element is removed. A better solution is to use the ArrayList method removeIf(), passing the criteria for selection as an argument (p. 452). An iterator can also be used explicitly for this purpose, but we leave that as an exercise.

Converting an ArrayList to an Array

The two following methods can be used to convert an ArrayList to an array:

```
Object[] toArray()
<T> T[] toArray(T[] a)
```

The first method returns an array of type Object filled with all the elements of a collection.

The second method is a generic method that stores the elements of a collection in an array of type T. If the specified array is big enough, the elements are stored in this array. If there is room to spare in the array—that is, if the length of the array is greater than the number of elements in the collection—the element found immediately after storing the elements of the collection is set to the null value before the array is returned. If the array is too small, a new array of type T and appropriate size is created. If T is not a supertype of the runtime type of every element in the collection, an ArrayStoreException is thrown.

The actual element type of the elements in the Object array returned by the first toArray() method can be any subtype of Object. It may be necessary to cast the Object reference of an element to the appropriate type, as in the following code:

```
System.out.println("(14) Convert list to array:");
Object[] objArray = strList.toArray();                       // Object[]
System.out.println("Object[] length: " + objArray.length); // 5
System.out.print("Length of each string in the Object array: ");
for (Object obj : objArray) {
  String str = (String) obj;                                 // Cast required.
  System.out.print(str.length() + " ");
}
System.out.println();
```

The second toArray() method returns an array of type T, when it is passed an array of type T as argument. In the following code, the array of String returned has the same length as the size of the list of String, even though a String array of length 0 was passed as argument:

```
String[] strArray = strList.toArray(new String[0]);          // String[]
System.out.println("String[] length: " + strArray.length);  // 5
System.out.print("Length of each string in the String array: ");
for (String str : strArray) {
  System.out.print(str.length() + " ");
}
System.out.println();
```

Sorting an ArrayList

The following static method of the java.util.Collections class can be used to sort elements of a list. Note the name of the class. It also provides many useful utility methods for collections.

```
static <T extends Comparable<? super T>> void sort(List<T> list)
```

This generic method sorts the specified list into ascending order, according to the *natural ordering* of its elements. The declaration essentially says that elements of the list have to be *comparable*; in other words, they can be compared with the compareTo() method of the Comparable interface.

Here is an example of sorting a list:

```
System.out.println("Unsorted list: " + strList);//[Naan, kayak, Bob, Rotator, Bob]
Collections.sort(strList);
System.out.println("Sorted list: " + strList);  //[Bob, Bob, Naan, Rotator, kayak]
```

The String class implements the Comparable interface, and its natural ordering is lexicographical ordering, based on the Unicode values of the characters in the string.

Arrays versus ArrayList

Table 10.1 summarizes the differences between arrays and ArrayLists.

Table 10.1 *Summary of Arrays versus* `ArrayLists`

	Arrays	`ArrayLists`
Construct support	Built into the language.	Provided by a generic class.
Initial length/size specification	Length is specified in the array construction expression directly or indirectly by the initialization block.	Cannot specify the size at construction time. However, initial capacity can be specified.
Length/size	The length of an array is static (fixed) once it is created. Each array has a `public final int` field called `length`. (The `String` and the `StringBuilder` class provide the method `length()` for this purpose.)	Both size and capacity can change dynamically. `ArrayList` provides the method `size()` to obtain the current size of the list.
Element type	Primitive and reference types.	Only reference types.
Operations on elements	An element in the array is designated by the array name and an index using the `[]` operator, and can be used as a simple variable.	The `ArrayList` class provides various methods to add, insert, retrieve, replace, and remove elements from a list.
Iterator	Arrays do not provide an iterator, apart from using the `for(:)` loop for traversal.	The `ArrayList` class provides customized iterators for lists, in addition to the `for(:)` loop for traversal.
Generics	Cannot create arrays of generic types using the `new` operator. Runtime check required for storage at runtime.	`ArrayList` is a generic type. Can create `ArrayList` of reference types using the `new` operator. No runtime check required for storage at runtime, as type-safety is checked at compile time.
Subtype relationship	Subtype relationship between two reference types implies subtype relationship between arrays of the two types.	Subtype relationship between two reference types does not imply subtype relationship between `ArrayLists` of the two types.
Sorting	`java.util.Arrays.sort(array)`	`java.util.Collections.sort(list)`
Textual representation	`java.util.Arrays.toString(array)`	`list.toString()`

Example 10.1 *Using an* `ArrayList`

```
import java.util.ArrayList;
import java.util.Collections;
import java.util.List;

public class UsingArrayList {

  public static void main(String[] args) {

    String[] wordArray = { "level", "Ada", "kayak", "Bob", "Rotator", "Bob" };

    System.out.println("(1) Create an empty list of strings:");
    List<String> strList = new ArrayList<>();
    printListWithIndex(strList);

    System.out.println("\n(2) Add elements to list:");
    for (String str : wordArray) {
      strList.add(str);
      printListWithIndex(strList);
    }
    System.out.println("Insert an element at index 2 in the list:");
    strList.add(2, "Java");
    printListWithIndex(strList);

    System.out.println("\n(3) Replace the element at index 1:");
    String oldElement = strList.set(1, "Naan");
    System.out.println("Element that was replaced: " + oldElement);
    printListWithIndex(strList);

    System.out.println("\n(4) Remove the element at index 0:");
    System.out.println("Element removed: " + strList.remove(0));
    printListWithIndex(strList);

    System.out.println("\n(5) Remove the first occurrence of \"Java\":");
    System.out.println("Element removed: " + strList.remove("Java"));
    printListWithIndex(strList);

    System.out.println("\n(6) Determine the size of the list:");
    System.out.println("The size of the list is " + strList.size());

    System.out.println("\n(7) Determine if the list is empty:");
    boolean result = strList.isEmpty();
    System.out.println("The list " + (result ? "is" : "is not") + " empty.");

    System.out.println("\n(8) Get the element at specific index:");
    System.out.println("First element: " + strList.get(0));
    System.out.println("Last element: " + strList.get(strList.size() - 1));

    System.out.println("\n(9) Compare two lists:");
    List<String> strList2 = new ArrayList<>(strList);
    boolean trueOrFalse = strList.equals(strList2);
    System.out.println("The lists strList and strList2 are"
        + (trueOrFalse ? "" : " not") + " equal.");
```

```
    strList2.add(null);
    printListWithIndex(strList2);
    trueOrFalse = strList.equals(strList2);
    System.out.println("The lists strList and strList2 are"
        + (trueOrFalse ? "" : " not") + " equal.");

    System.out.println("\n(10) Membership test:");
    boolean found = strList.contains("Naan");
    String msg = found ? "contains" : "does not contain";
    System.out.println("The list " + msg + " the string \"Naan\".");

    System.out.println("\n(11) Find the index of an element:");
    int pos = strList.indexOf("Bob");
    System.out.println("The index of string \"Bob\" is: " + pos);
    pos = strList.indexOf("BOB");
    System.out.println("The index of string \"BOB\" is: " + pos);
    pos = strList.lastIndexOf("Bob");
    System.out.println("The last index of string \"Bob\" is: " + pos);
    printListWithIndex(strList);

    System.out.println("\n(12) Traversing the list using the for(;;) loop:");
    for (int i = 0; i < strList.size(); i++) {
      System.out.print(i + ":" + strList.get(i) + " ");
    }
    System.out.println();

    System.out.println("\n(13) Traversing the list using the for(:) loop:");
    for (String str : strList) {
      System.out.print(str + " ");
      // strList.remove(str);          // Throws ConcurrentModificationException.
    }
    System.out.println();

    System.out.println("\n(14) Convert list to array:");
    Object[] objArray = strList.toArray();
    System.out.println("Object[] length: " + objArray.length);
    System.out.print("Length of each string in the Object array: ");
    for (Object obj : objArray) {
      String str = (String) obj; // Cast required.
      System.out.print(str.length() + " ");
    }
    System.out.println();
    String[] strArray = strList.toArray(new String[0]);
    System.out.println("String[] length: " + strArray.length);
    System.out.print("Length of each string in the String array: ");
    for (String str : strArray) {
      System.out.print(str.length() + " ");
    }
    System.out.println();

    System.out.println("\n(15) Sorting a list:");
    List<StringBuilder> sbList = new ArrayList<>();
    for (String str : strArray) {
      sbList.add(new StringBuilder(str));
    }
```

```
    // Collections.sort(sbList);                        // Compile-time error!
    System.out.println("Unsorted list: " + strList);
    Collections.sort(strList);
    System.out.println("Sorted list: " + strList);
  }

  /**
   * Print the elements of a list, together with their index:
   * [0:value0, 1:value1, ...]
   * @param list   List to print with index
   */
  public static <E> void printListWithIndex(List<E> list) {          // (16)
    List<String> newList = new ArrayList<>();
    for (int i = 0; i < list.size(); i++) {
      newList.add(i + ":" + list.get(i));
    }
    System.out.println(newList);
  }
}
```

Output from the program:

```
(1) Create an empty list of strings:
[]

(2) Add elements to list:
[0:level]
[0:level, 1:Ada]
[0:level, 1:Ada, 2:kayak]
[0:level, 1:Ada, 2:kayak, 3:Bob]
[0:level, 1:Ada, 2:kayak, 3:Bob, 4:Rotator]
[0:level, 1:Ada, 2:kayak, 3:Bob, 4:Rotator, 5:Bob]
Insert an element at index 2 in the list:
[0:level, 1:Ada, 2:Java, 3:kayak, 4:Bob, 5:Rotator, 6:Bob]

(3) Replace the element at index 1:
Element that was replaced: Ada
[0:level, 1:Naan, 2:Java, 3:kayak, 4:Bob, 5:Rotator, 6:Bob]

(4) Remove the element at index 0:
Element removed: level
[0:Naan, 1:Java, 2:kayak, 3:Bob, 4:Rotator, 5:Bob]

(5) Remove the first occurrence of "Java":
Element removed: true
[0:Naan, 1:kayak, 2:Bob, 3:Rotator, 4:Bob]

(6) Determine the size of the list:
The size of the list is 5

(7) Determine if the list is empty:
The list is not empty.

(8) Get the element at specific index:
First element: Naan
Last element: Bob
```

```
(9) Compare two lists:
The lists strList and strList2 are equal.
[0:Naan, 1:kayak, 2:Bob, 3:Rotator, 4:Bob, 5:null]
The lists strList and strList2 are not equal.

(10) Membership test:
The list contains the string "Naan".

(11) Find the index of an element:
The index of string "Bob" is: 2
The index of string "BOB" is: -1
The last index of string "Bob" is: 4
[0:Naan, 1:kayak, 2:Bob, 3:Rotator, 4:Bob]

(12) Traversing the list using the for(;;) loop:
0:Naan 1:kayak 2:Bob 3:Rotator 4:Bob

(13) Traversing the list using the for(:) loop:
Naan kayak Bob Rotator Bob

(14) Convert list to array:
Object[] length: 5
Length of each string in the Object array: 4 5 3 7 3
String[] length: 5
Length of each string in the String array: 4 5 3 7 3

(15) Sorting a list:
Unsorted list: [Naan, kayak, Bob, Rotator, Bob]
Sorted list: [Bob, Bob, Naan, Rotator, kayak]
```

Review Questions

10.1 Which statement is true about the `java.util.ArrayList` class?

Select the one correct answer.

(a) The method `delete()` can be used to delete an element at a specific index in an `ArrayList`.

(b) The method `deleteAll()` can be used to delete all elements in an `ArrayList`.

(c) The method `insert()` can be used to insert an element at a specific index in an `ArrayList`.

(d) The method `append()` can be used to append an element at the end of an `ArrayList`.

(e) The method `replace()` can be used to replace the element at a specific index with another element in an `ArrayList`.

(f) The method `find()` can be used to determine whether an element is in an `ArrayList`.

(g) The method `capacity()` can be used to determine the current capacity of an `ArrayList`.

(h) None of the above.

10.2 What will the following program print when compiled and run?

```
import java.util.ArrayList;
import java.util.List;

public class RQ12A10 {
  public static void main(String[] args) {
    List<String> strList = new ArrayList<>();
    strList.add("Anna"); strList.add("Ada"); strList.add("Ada");
    strList.add("Bob"); strList.add("Bob"); strList.add("Adda");
    for (int i = 0; i < strList.size(); /* empty */) {
      if (strList.get(i).length() <= 3) {
        strList.remove(i);
      } else {
        ++i;
      }
    }
    System.out.println(strList);
  }
}
```

Select the one correct answer.

(a) The program will not compile.
(b) The program will throw an `IndexOutOfBoundsException` at runtime.
(c) The program will throw a `ConcurrentModificationException` at runtime.
(d) The program will not terminate when run.
(e) The program will print: `[Anna, Adda]`.
(f) The program will print: `[Anna, Ada, Bob, Adda]`.

10.3 What will the following program print when compiled and run?

```
import java.util.ArrayList;
import java.util.List;

public class RQ12A15 {
  public static void main(String[] args) {
    doIt1(); doIt2();
  }

  public static void doIt1() {
    List<StringBuilder> sbListOne = new ArrayList<>();
    sbListOne.add(new StringBuilder("Anna"));
    sbListOne.add(new StringBuilder("Ada"));
    sbListOne.add(new StringBuilder("Bob"));
    List<StringBuilder> sbListTwo = new ArrayList<>(sbListOne);
    sbListOne.add(null);
    sbListTwo.get(1).reverse();
    System.out.println(sbListOne);                                     // (1)
  }

  public static void doIt2() {
    List<String> listOne = new ArrayList<>();
    listOne.add("Anna"); listOne.add("Ada"); listOne.add("Bob");
    List<String> listTwo = new ArrayList<>(listOne);
    String strTemp = listOne.get(0);
    listOne.set(0, listOne.get(listOne.size()-1));
```

```
    listOne.set(listOne.size()-1, strTemp);
    System.out.println(listTwo);                                   // (2)
  }
}
```

Select the two correct answers.

(a) (1) will print `[Anna, Ada, Bob, null]`.
(b) (1) will print `[Anna, adA, Bob, null]`.
(c) (2) will print `[Anna, Ada, Bob]`.
(d) (2) will print `[Bob, Ada, Anna]`.
(e) The program will throw an `IndexOutOfBoundsException` at runtime.

10.4 What will the following program print when compiled and run?

```
import java.util.ArrayList;
import java.util.List;

public class RQ12A20 {
  public static void main(String[] args) {
    List<String> strList = new ArrayList<>();
    strList.add("Anna"); strList.add("Ada"); strList.add(null);
    strList.add("Bob"); strList.add("Bob"); strList.add("Adda");
    for (int i = 0; i < strList.size(); ++i) {
      if (strList.get(i).equals("Bob")) {
        System.out.print(i);
      }
    }
    System.out.println();
  }
}
```

Select the one correct answer.

(a) The program will not compile.
(b) The program will throw an `IndexOutOfBoundsException` at runtime.
(c) The program will throw a `NullPointerException` at runtime.
(d) The program will print: `34`.

10.5 What will the following program print when compiled and run?

```
import java.util.ArrayList;
import java.util.List;

public class RQ12A30 {
  public static void main(String[] args) {
    List<String> strList = new ArrayList<>();
    strList.add("Anna"); strList.add("Ada");
    strList.add("Bob"); strList.add("Bob");
    for (int i = 0; i < strList.size(); ++i) {
      if (strList.get(i).equals("Bob")) {
        strList.remove(i);
      }
    }
    System.out.println(strList);
  }
}
```

Select the one correct answer.

(a) The program will not compile.
(b) The program will throw an `IndexOutOfBoundsException` at runtime.
(c) The program will throw a `NullPointerException` at runtime.
(d) The program will throw a `ConcurrentModificationException` at runtime.
(e) The program will not terminate when run.
(f) The program will print `[Anna, Ada, Bob]`.
(g) The program will print `[Anna, Ada]`.

10.6 What will the following program print when compiled and run?

```
import java.util.ArrayList;
import java.util.List;

public class RQ12A40 {
  public static void main(String[] args) {
    List<String> strList = new ArrayList<>();
    strList.add("Anna"); strList.add("Ada"); strList.add(null);
    strList.add("Bob"); strList.add("Bob"); strList.add("Adda");
    while(strList.remove("Bob"));
    System.out.println(strList);
  }
}
```

Select the one correct answer.

(a) The program will not compile.
(b) The program will throw a `NullPointerException` at runtime.
(c) The program will not terminate when run.
(d) The program will print: `[Anna, Ada, Adda]`.
(e) The program will print: `[Anna, Ada, Bob, Adda]`.
(f) The program will print: `[Anna, Ada, null, Adda]`.
(g) The program will print:
`[Anna, Ada, null, Bob, Adda]`
`[Anna, Ada, null, Adda]`

10.2 Lambda Expressions

In many ways, Java 8 represents a watershed in the history of the language. Before Java 8, the language supported only object-oriented programming. Packing state and behavior into objects that communicate in a procedural manner was the order of the day. Java 8 brings *functional-style programming* into the language, where code representing *functionality* can be passed as values to tailor the *behavior* of methods.

This section gives a taste of what functional-style programming brings to Java. It provides an introduction to two language features (functional interfaces and lambda expressions) that are the basis for this programming style in Java. That suffices for the purposes of this book. However, functional-style programming is a powerful paradigm worth exploring further, and any Java programmer who ignores it does so at his or her own peril.

Behavior Parameterization

To demonstrate how functional-style programming can be useful, we will use a running example that we will gradually refine to implement an efficient and concise solution using lambda expressions and functional interfaces.

A common operation on elements in a collection is to select those elements that satisfy a certain criterion. This operation is called *filtering*. Example 10.2 creates a list of strings at (1). We would like to filter this list for one-word *palindromes*, words that are spelled the same way forward and backward. For example, "anana" is a palindrome, but "banana" is not.

Filtering Using Customized Methods

A straightforward and naive solution is to implement a customized method that takes a list of words and returns a list of the words that fulfill the criteria for being a palindrome. The method filterPalindromes() at (4) in Example 10.2 does exactly that. It traverses the list and selects elements with the following code:

```
if (word.equals(new StringBuilder(word).reverse().toString())) {   // (5)
  result.add(word);
}
```

The argument to the equals() method creates a StringBuilder based on the current word in the list. The contents of the StringBuilder are reversed and converted back to a String. The original word is compared for object value equality with the reversed word to determine whether it is a palindrome. Because the equality test is based on the Unicode values of the characters, this criterion takes into account the case of the letters, as can be seen from the output.

What if we wanted to create a filter that was case insensitive? We need to implement a new method, as shown in (6). We see that the method equalsIgnoreCase() used for equality comparison at (7) ignores the case, and the output bears this out.

```
if (word.equalsIgnoreCase(
               new StringBuilder(word).reverse().toString())) {      // (7)
  result.add(word);
}
```

Creating a new method every time we want to filter on a new criterion is certainly not viable. There is lot of code duplication, and the most significant change occurs only in the condition of the if statement at (5) and (7).

Example 10.2 *Implementing Customized Methods for Filtering an* ArrayList

```
import java.util.ArrayList;
import java.util.List;
```

```
public class FunWithPalindromesV0 {

  public static void main(String[] args) {
    // Create a list of words:                                           (1)
    List<String> words = new ArrayList<>();
    words.add("Otto"); words.add("ADA"); words.add("Alyla");
    words.add("Bob"); words.add("HannaH"); words.add("Java");
    System.out.println("List of words:                  " + words);

    // Call a method to filter the list for palindromes (case sensitive).  (2)
    List<String> palindromes = filterPalindromes(words);
    System.out.println("Case-sensitive palindromes:   " + palindromes);

    // Call a method to filter the list for palindromes (case insensitive). (3)
    List<String> palindromesIgnoreCase = filterPalindromesIgnorecase(words);
    System.out.println("Case-insensitive palindromes: " + palindromesIgnoreCase);
  }

  /**                                                                    (4)
   * Finds palindromes in a list of words. Uses case-sensitive filtering.
   * @param words List of strings
   * @return      List of palindromes found
   */
  public static List<String> filterPalindromes(List<String> words) {
    List<String> result = new ArrayList<>();
    for (String word : words) {
      if (word.equals(new StringBuilder(word).reverse().toString())) {  // (5)
        result.add(word);
      }
    }
    return result;
  }

  /**                                                                    (6)
   * Finds palindromes in a list of words. Uses case-insensitive filtering.
   * @param words List of strings
   * @return      List of palindromes found
   */
  public static List<String> filterPalindromesIgnorecase(List<String> words) {
    List<String> result = new ArrayList<>();
    for (String word : words) {
      if (word.equalsIgnoreCase(
                    new StringBuilder(word).reverse().toString())) {     // (7)
        result.add(word);
      }
    }
    return result;
  }
}
```

Output from the program:

```
List of words:                [Otto, ADA, Alyla, Bob, HannaH, Java]
Case-sensitive palindromes:   [ADA, HannaH]
Case-insensitive palindromes: [Otto, ADA, Alyla, Bob, HannaH]
```

Filtering Using an Interface

In Example 10.3, we have generalized the method that applies the criteria and selects the elements. The method `filterStrings()` at (9) takes as input a list and a selection criteria object that implements an interface, and returns a list with elements that satisfy the selection criteria.

The best practice of programming to an interface certainly makes sense here. That way the `filterStrings()` method can be used for filtering on any criteria. An appropriate object for filtering can be passed to the method as long as it implements the interface. This object must implement the `StrPredicate` interface, declared at (1), supplying the `boolean` method `test()` that actually determines whether an element is selected. The `test()` method is an example of a *predicate*, a function that takes an argument and returns a `boolean` value.

Examples 10.3 shows two approaches to how the criteria object can be created. We can define *concrete* classes that implement the `StrPredicate` interface. The classes `PalindromeCaseSensitive` and `PalindromeCaseInsensitive` at (2) and (3) in Example 10.3, respectively, implement the `StrPredicate` interface and provide an implementation of the `test()` method. Objects of these classes are passed as arguments to the `filterStrings()` method at (5) and (6) to filter the list. Again note that any new selection criterion implemented by this approach requires a new concrete class, resulting in proliferation of classes, when all that needs changing is the code in the body of the `test()` method.

Instead of concrete classes, we can use *anonymous classes* to instantiate the criteria object, as shown at (7) and (8) in Example 10.3. We will not go into details of explaining the syntax of an anonymous class. The basic idea is that we can declare and instantiate the class at the same time, where it is needed in the code—in our case, as an argument in the call to the `filterStrings()` method. The `new` operator creates an object of the anonymous class whose body resembles that of a concrete class. The name of the interface in the declaration ensures that this class will implement the methods of the interface. In our case, the anonymous classes provide implementation of the `test()` method. By using anonymous classes we avoid creating concrete classes, but the verbosity of declaring anonymous classes to encapsulate a single method is inescapable. Also, we still have to declare a new anonymous class for each selection criterion, duplicating a lot of boilerplate code.

Example 10.3 *Implementing an Interface for Filtering an* `ArrayList`

```
/** Interface to test two strings according to a criterion. */
public interface StrPredicate {                                        // (1)
  boolean test(String str);
}
```

```
/** Tests whether a string is a palindrome (case sensitive). */
public class PalindromeCaseSensitive implements StrPredicate {          // (2)
```

```
  @Override public boolean test(String str) {
    return str.equals(new StringBuilder(str).reverse().toString());
  }
}
```

```
/** Tests whether a string is a palindrome (case insensitive). */
public class PalindromeCaseInsensitive implements StrPredicate {          // (3)
  @Override public boolean test(String str) {
    return str.equalsIgnoreCase(new StringBuilder(str).reverse().toString());
  }
}
```

```
import java.util.ArrayList;
import java.util.List;

public class FunWithPalindromesV1 {

  public static void main(String[] args) {
    // Create a list of words:                                              (4)
    List<String> words = new ArrayList<>();
    words.add("Otto"); words.add("ADA"); words.add("Alyla");
    words.add("Bob"); words.add("HannaH"); words.add("Java");
    System.out.println("List of words:                " + words);

    // Use a class to filter for palindromes (case sensitive).              (5)
    List<String> palindromes1 = filterStrings(words,
                                   new PalindromeCaseSensitive());
    System.out.println("Case-sensitive palindromes:   " + palindromes1);

    // Use a class to filter for palindromes (case insensitive).            (6)
    List<String> palindromes2 = filterStrings(words,
                                   new PalindromeCaseInsensitive());
    System.out.println("Case-insensitive palindromes: " + palindromes2);

    // Use an anonymous class to filter for palindromes (case sensitive).  (7)
    List<String> palindromes3 = filterStrings(words,
        new StrPredicate() {
          @Override
          public boolean test(String str) {
            return str.equals(new StringBuilder(str).reverse().toString());
          }
        }
    );
    System.out.println("Case-sensitive palindromes:   " + palindromes3);

    // Use an anonymous class to filter for palindromes (case insensitive). (8)
    List<String> palindromes4 = filterStrings(words,
        new StrPredicate() {
          @Override
          public boolean test(String str) {
            return str.equalsIgnoreCase(
                          new StringBuilder(str).reverse().toString());
          }
        }
    );
```

```
    System.out.println("Case-insensitive palindromes: " + palindromes4);
  }

  /**
   * Filters a list of strings according to the criteria of the predicate.
   * @param strList    List of strings to filter
   * @param predicate  Provides the criteria for filtering the strings
   * @return           List of strings that match the criteria
   */
  public static List<String> filterStrings(List<String> strList,          // (9)
                                           StrPredicate predicate) {
    List<String> result = new ArrayList<>();
    for (String str : strList) {
      if (predicate.test(str)) {                                           // (10)
        result.add(str);
      }
    }
    return result;
  }
}
```

Output from the program:

```
List of words:                 [Otto, ADA, Alyla, Bob, HannaH, Java]
Case-sensitive palindromes:    [ADA, HannaH]
Case-insensitive palindromes: [Otto, ADA, Alyla, Bob, HannaH]
Case-sensitive palindromes:    [ADA, HannaH]
Case-insensitive palindromes: [Otto, ADA, Alyla, Bob, HannaH]
```

Filtering Using Lambda Expressions

Ideally we would like to pass the code for the selection criteria as an argument to the `filterStrings()` method so that the method can apply the criteria to the elements in the list; that is, we would like to be able to change the behavior of the `filterStrings()` method depending on the selection criteria. Example 10.4 is a step in that direction.

The `StrPredicate` interface and the `filterStrings()` method are still the same as in Example 10.3, but the implementation of the `StrPredicate` interface at (2) and (4) in Example 10.4 is specified by lambda expressions.

The `StrPredicate` interface is an example of a *functional interface* (p. 442). Such an interface has exactly one abstract method. In the case of the `StrPredicate` method, this method is the `test()` method, which takes a `String` object as an argument and returns a `boolean` value. Knowing that something is a `StrPredicate`, all the information about its sole abstract method can be inferred, as it is the only abstract method in the interface; in other words, we know its name, its parameters, any value it returns, and whether it throws any exceptions.

Implementation of the sole abstract method of a functional interface can be provided by a *lambda expression* (p. 444), in contrast to a conventional method implementation in concrete and anonymous classes, as seen in Example 10.3. The assignment at (2) in Example 10.4 uses a lambda expression to provide an implementation for the `StrPredicate` functional interface:

```
StrPredicate predicate1 = (String str) ->
    str.equals(new StringBuilder(str).reverse().toString());        // (2)
```

The reference `predicate1` on the left-hand side is of type `StrPredicate`, and it is assigned the value of the lambda expression on the right-hand side. A lambda expression has three parts:

- A *parameter list* that is analogous to the parameter list of a method. In (2), the parameter list has only one parameter:

  ```
  (String str)
  ```

- The -> operator (the *arrow*) that separates the parameter list from the lambda body.
- A *lambda body* that is either a *single expression* or a *statement block*. In (2), the lambda body is a single expression, whose value is returned when the lambda expression is evaluated. The lambda body expression evaluates to a `boolean` value, since the call to the `equals()` method returns a `boolean` value.

  ```
  str.equals(new StringBuilder(str).reverse().toString()); // Lambda body expression
  ```

The lambda expression at (2) defines a nameless function that takes a `String` as the only parameter, and returns a `boolean` value. Recall that the `test()` method of the `StrPredicate` functional interface does exactly that.

Lambda expressions are also called *anonymous functions*, as they do not have names. They can be stored as *values* in references, as in the reference `predicate1` in (2). The compiler can type check that the lambda expression is assignable to the reference on the left-hand side, since the expression represents an anonymous function that is compatible with the sole abstract method `test()` of the `StrPredicate` interface.

The lambda expression at (2) is passed as an argument to the `filterStrings()` method via the reference `predicate1` at (3). It is executed only when the `test()` method is called with a `String` argument in the `filterStrings()` method at (7).

Now we just need to pass a new lambda expression to the `filterStrings()` method to filter a list of strings based on a selection criterion. Example 10.4 is more precise, concise, and readable than the previous versions, especially as you become comfortable with lambda expressions.

Example 10.4 *User-Defined Functional Interface for Filtering an* `ArrayList`

```
/** Interface to test two strings according to a criterion. */
public interface StrPredicate {                                       // (1)
  boolean test(String str);
}
```

```
import java.util.ArrayList;
import java.util.List;

public class FunWithPalindromesV2 {

  public static void main(String[] args) {

    // Create a list of words:
    List<String> words = new ArrayList<>();
    words.add("Otto"); words.add("ADA"); words.add("Alyla");
    words.add("Bob"); words.add("HannaH"); words.add("Java");
    System.out.println("List of words:              " + words);

    StrPredicate predicate1 = (String str) ->
        str.equals(new StringBuilder(str).reverse().toString());         // (2)
    List<String> palindromes1 = filterStrings(words, predicate1);          // (3)
    System.out.println("Case-sensitive palindromes:   " + palindromes1);

    StrPredicate predicate2 = (String str) ->
        str.equalsIgnoreCase(new StringBuilder(str).reverse().toString());// (4)
    List<String> palindromes2 = filterStrings(words, predicate2);          // (5)
    System.out.println("Case-insensitive palindromes: " + palindromes2);
  }

  /**                                                                      // (6)
   * Filters a list of strings according to the criteria of the predicate.
   * @param strList    List of strings to filter
   * @param predicate  Provides the criteria for filtering the strings
   * @return           List of strings that match the criteria
   */
  public static List<String> filterStrings(List<String> strList,
                                           StrPredicate predicate) {
    List<String> result = new ArrayList<>();
    for (String str : strList) {
      if (predicate.test(str)) {                                           // (7)
        result.add(str);
      }
    }
    return result;
  }
}
```

Output from the program:

```
List of words:               [Otto, ADA, Alyla, Bob, HannaH, Java]
Case-sensitive palindromes:   [ADA, HannaH]
Case-insensitive palindromes: [Otto, ADA, Alyla, Bob, HannaH]
```

Filtering Using the `Predicate<T>` *Functional Interface*

Example 10.4 used a user-defined functional interface `StrPredicate`. The Java SE platform API provides functional interfaces for many tasks (such as testing an object and creating objects). For implementing predicates, we can use the generic java.util.function.Predicate<T> functional interface, which specifies the single-parameter boolean method test(T t). It is a more generalized version of the StrPredicate functional interface that we have used earlier.

Example 10.5 uses the generic Predicate<T> functional interface, where the *type parameter* T represents the concrete type String. In Example 10.4, we simply need to replace the name StrPredicate with the name Predicate<String> in (2), (4), and (6), and import the Predicate<T> functional interface from the java.util.function package ((1) in Example 10.5). The discussion of type checking and evaluation of lambda expressions in Example 10.4 also applies to Example 10.5.

Functional interfaces and lambda expressions together allow *behavior parameterization*, a powerful programming paradigm that allows code representing behavior to be passed around as values, and executed when the abstract method of the functional interface is invoked. This approach is scalable, requiring only a lambda expression to represent the filtering criteria.

Functional-style programming is also beneficial in developing parallel code. In the multicore world in which we live, we can use all the help we can get to utilize the computing power that new hardware architectures are putting at our disposal.

The rest of this section provides more insight into these two features of the language: functional interfaces and lambda expressions.

Example 10.5 *Using the* Predicate<T> *Functional Interface for Filtering an* ArrayList

```
import java.util.ArrayList;
import java.util.List;
import java.util.function.Predicate;                                    // (1)

public class FunWithPalindromesV3 {

  public static void main(String[] args) {

    List<String> words = new ArrayList<>();
    words.add("Otto"); words.add("ADA"); words.add("Alyla");
    words.add("Bob"); words.add("HannaH"); words.add("Java");
    System.out.println("List of words:                " + words);

    Predicate<String> predicate1 = (String str) ->
        str.equals(new StringBuilder(str).reverse().toString());        // (2)
    List<String> palindromes1 = filterStrings(words, predicate1);       // (3)
    System.out.println("Case-sensitive palindromes:   " + palindromes1);

    Predicate<String> predicate2 = (String str) ->
        str.equalsIgnoreCase(new StringBuilder(str).reverse().toString());// (4)
    List<String> palindromes2 = filterStrings(words, predicate2);       // (5)
    System.out.println("Case-insensitive palindromes: " + palindromes2);
  }
```

```
  /**                                                                // (6)
   * Filters a list of strings according to the criteria of the predicate.
   * @param strList    List of strings to filter
   * @param predicate  Provides the criteria for filtering the strings
   * @return           List of strings that match the criteria
   */
  public static List<String> filterStrings(List<String> strList,
                                           Predicate<String> predicate) {
    List<String> result = new ArrayList<>();
    for (String str : strList) {
      if (predicate.test(str)) {                                     // (7)
        result.add(str);
      }
    }
    return result;
  }
}
```

Output from the program:

```
List of words:                 [Otto, ADA, Alyla, Bob, HannaH, Java]
Case-sensitive palindromes:    [ADA, HannaH]
Case-insensitive palindromes:  [Otto, ADA, Alyla, Bob, HannaH]
```

Functional Interfaces

A functional interface can have only one abstract method. This abstract method is called the *functional method* for that interface. Like any other interface, a functional interface can have any number of static and default methods. Such an interface can also provide *explicit* `public abstract` method declarations for *non-final* `public` instance methods in the `Object` class, but these are excluded from the definition of a functional interface. Note that abstract methods declared in an interface are implicitly `abstract` and `public`. Interfaces are discussed in §7.6, p. 290.

We defined and used the `StrPredicate` interface earlier. It has exactly one abstract method.

```
@FunctionalInterface
interface StrPredicate {
  boolean test(String str);                  // Sole public abstract method.
}
```

The annotation `@FunctionalInterface` is useful when defining functional interfaces. The compiler will issue an error if the declaration violates the definition of a functional interface, as illustrated by the following `XStrPredicate` interface. Its declaration has two abstract methods.

```
@FunctionalInterface
interface XStrPredicate {                                  // Compile-time error!
  boolean test(String str);                                // Abstract method.
  String  reverse(String str);                             // Abstract method.
}
```

The next functional interface `NewStrPredicate` declares only one abstract method at (1). In addition, it provides the implementations of one default method and one static method at (2) and (3), respectively. The abstract method declaration at (4) is that of a non-`final` `public` method from the `Object` class, but such declarations are excluded from the definition of a functional interface.

```
@FunctionalInterface
interface NewStrPredicate  {
  boolean test(String str);                                    // (1) Abstract method
  default void msg(String str) { System.out.println(str); } // (2) Default method
  static void info() { System.out.println("Testing!"); }    // (3) Static method
  @Override boolean equals(Object obj);                      // (4) From Object class
}
```

The interface `StrFormat` provides the abstract method declaration of the non-`final` `public` method `toString()` from the `Object` class, but such declarations are excluded from the definition of a functional interface. Effectively, there is no abstract method declared in the `StrFormat` interface. The code would compile as an interface without the annotation `@FunctionalInterface`, but it is not a functional interface.

```
@FunctionalInterface
interface StrFormat {                                          // Compile-time error!
  @Override String toString();                                // From Object class
}
```

Earlier in this section, we used the generic functional interface `java.util.function.Predicate<T>`, which provides the abstract method `test()` to implement predicates. This functional interface also has one static method (`isEqual()`) and three default methods (`and()`, `or()`, `negate()`). The default methods implement short-circuit logical operators that can be used for composing predicates on `Predicate` objects.

The functional subinterface `IStrPredicate` that follows is customized to the `String` type by extending the `java.util.function.Predicate<T>` functional interface, where the type parameter `T` is `String`. It can readily be used for implementing predicates on strings.

```
@FunctionalInterface
interface IStrPredicate extends Predicate<String> { }
```

Functional Interfaces in Java SE Platform API

The Java SE platform API has many functional and nonfunctional interfaces, all of which support the practice of programming to interfaces. For example, the `java.lang` package includes five functional interfaces: `Runnable`, `Comparable<T>`, `AutoCloseable`, `Iterable<T>`, and `Readable`. However, the main support for functional interfaces is found in the `java.util.function` package. It includes general-purpose functional interfaces that implement basic concepts in functional-style programming (Table 10.2). In addition, the package provides a wide range of functional interfaces for various purposes, so that implementing new extensions should hardly be necessary.

Table 10.2 *Selected Functional Interfaces from the* `java.util.function` *Package*

Functional interface (`T` and `R` are type parameters)	Abstract method signature	Function
`Predicate<T>`	`test: T -> boolean`	Evaluate a predicate on a `T`
`Consumer<T>`	`accept: T -> void`	Perform action on a `T`
`Function<T, R>`	`apply: T -> R`	Transform a `T` to an `R`
`UnaryOperator<T>`	`apply: T -> T`	Operator on a unary argument
`BinaryOperator<T>`	`apply: (T, T) -> T`	Operator on binary arguments
`Supplier<T>`	`get: () -> T`	Provide an instance of a `T`

The `java.util.function` package includes functional interfaces that are specialized for primitive values. Their use enables programmers to avoid excessive boxing and unboxing of primitive values when such values are used as objects. The functional interfaces `IntPredicate`, `LongPredicate`, and `DoublePredicate` provide an abstract `test()` method to evaluate predicates with `int`, `long`, and `double` arguments, respectively.

```
Predicate<Integer> integerPred = (Integer i) -> i%2 == 0;// i as operand unboxed.
System.out.println(integerPred.test(2015));              // Argument boxed. false

IntPredicate intPred = (int i) -> i%2 == 0;
System.out.println(intPred.test(2016));                  // true
```

Defining Lambda Expressions

Lambda expressions implement functional interfaces by defining anonymous functions that facilitate behavior parameterization. They can be passed and used as values in a program, without the excess baggage of first being packaged into objects in the source code. The compiler takes care of whatever that needs to be done internally to make their usage feasible.

A lambda expression has the following syntax:

formal_parameter_list -> lambda_body

The parameter list and the body are separated by the -> operator. The lambda expression syntax resembles a simplified declaration of a method, without many of the bells and whistles of a method declaration. That streamlining is important, as it avoids verbosity and provides a simple and succinct notation with which to write lambda expressions on the fly.

In the rest of this section, we take a closer look at the parameter list, the lambda body, and the type checking and evaluation of lambda expressions.

Lambda Parameters

The parameter list of a lambda expression is a comma-separated list of formal parameters that is enclosed in parentheses, (), analogous to the parameter list in a method declaration. There are other shorthand forms as well, as we shall see shortly.

If the types of the parameters are specified, they are known as *declared-type parameters*. If the types of the parameters are not specified, they are known as *inferred-type parameters*. Types of the inferred-type parameters are derived from the functional interface type that is the target type of the lambda expression.

Parameters are either all declared-type or all inferred-type. Parentheses are mandatory with multiple parameters, whether they are declared-type or inferred-type. For a parameter list with a single inferred-type parameter, the parentheses can be omitted. Also, only declared-type parameters can have modifiers.

```
() -> ..                                   // Empty parameter list
(Integer x, Integer y, Integer z) -> ..    // Multiple declared-type parameters
(x, y, z)      -> ..                       // Multiple inferred-type parameters
(String str) -> ..                         // Single declared-type parameter
(str)          -> ..                       // Single inferred-type parameter
str            -> ..                       // Single inferred-type parameter
String str     -> ..                       // Illegal: Missing parentheses
Integer x, Integer y, Integer z -> ..      // Illegal: Missing parentheses
i, j, k        -> ..                       // Illegal: Missing parentheses
(String str, j)        -> ..  // Illegal: Cannot mix inferred and declared type
(final int i, int j) -> ..    // OK: Modifier with declared-type parameter
(final i, j)           -> ..  // Illegal: No modifier with inferred-type parameter
```

Lambda Body

A lambda body is either a single expression or a statement block. Execution of a lambda body has either a non-void return (i.e., returns a value) or a void return (i.e., does not return a value), or its evaluation throws an exception.

A single-expression lambda body is used for short and succinct lambda expressions. A single-expression lambda body with a void return type is commonly used to achieve side effects. The return keyword is not allowed in a single-expression lambda body.

In the examples that follow, the body of the lambda expressions is an *expression* whose execution returns a value (i.e., has a non-void return):

```
() -> 2015                             // Expression body, non-void return
() -> null                             // Expression body, non-void return
(i, j) -> i + j                        // Expression body, non-void return
(i, j) -> i <= j ? i : j               // Expression body, non-void return
str -> str.length() > 3                // Expression body, non-void return
str -> str != null                     // Expression body, non-void return
       && !str.equals("") && str.length() > 3
       && str.equals(new StringBuilder(str).reverse().toString())
```

In the next set of examples, the lambda body is an *expression statement* that can have a `void` or a non-`void` return. However, if the abstract method of the functional interface returns `void`, the non-`void` return of a lambda expression with an expression statement as body can be interpreted as a `void` return (i.e., the return value is ignored).

```
val -> System.out.println(val)     // Method invocation statement, void return
sb -> sb.trimToSize()              // Method invocation statement, void return
sb -> sb.append("!")               // Method invocation statement, non-void return
() -> new StringBuilder("?")       // Object creation statement, non-void return
value -> value++                   // Increment statement, non-void return
value -> value *= 2                // Assignment statement, non-void return
```

The following examples are not legal lambda expressions:

```
(int i) -> while (i < 10) ++i  // Illegal: not an expression but a statement
(x, y) -> return x + y         // Illegal: return not allowed in expression
```

The statement block comprises declarations and statements enclosed in braces (`{}`). The `return` statement is allowed only in a block lambda body.

```
() -> {}                                           // Block body, void return
() -> { return 2015; }                             // Block body, non-void return
() -> { return 2015 }        // Illegal: statement terminator (;) in block missing
() -> { new StringBuilder("Go nuts."); }           // Block body, void return
() -> { return new StringBuilder("Go nuts!"); }    // Block body, non-void return
(int i) -> { while (i < 10) ++i; }                 // Block body, void return
(i, j) -> { if (i <= j) return i; else return j; } // Block body, non-void return
(done) -> {                      // Multiple statements in block body, void return
  if (done) {
    System.out.println("You deserve a break!");
    return;
  }
  System.out.println("Stay right here!");
}
```

Accessing Members in the Enclosing Class

Since a lambda expression is not associated with any class, there is no notion of a `this` reference associated with it. If it is used in a lambda expression, the `this` reference refers to the enclosing object, and can be used to access members of this object. The name of a member in the enclosing object has the same meaning when used in a lambda expression. In other words, there are no restrictions on accessing members in the enclosing object. In the case of shadowing member names, the keyword `this` can be explicitly used, and the keyword `super` can be used to access any members inherited by the enclosing object.

In Example 10.6, the `getPredicate()` method at (7) defines a lambda expression at (8). This lambda expression accesses the `static` field `strList` and the instance field `banner` in the enclosing class at (1) and (2), respectively.

In the main() method in Example 10.6, an ArrayList is assigned to the static field strList at (3) and is initialized. The ArrayList referred to by the static field strList has the following content:

```
[Otto, ADA, Alyla, Bob, HannaH, Java]
```

A MembersOnly object is created at (4). Its StringBuilder field banner is initialized with the string "love ", and the local variable obj refers to this MembersOnly object. At (5), a Predicate object is created by calling the getPredicate() method on the MembersOnly object referred to by the local variable obj. This predicate is first evaluated when the test() method is called at (6) on the Predicate object, with the argument string "never dies!". Calling the test() method results in the lambda expression created at (5) by the getPredicate() method being evaluated in the enclosing MembersOnly object referred to by the local variable obj.

The parameter str of the lambda expression is initialized with the string "never dies!", the argument to the test() method. In the body of the lambda expression, the ArrayList referred to by the static field strList is first printed at (9):

```
List: [Otto, ADA, Alyla, Bob, HannaH, Java]
```

At (10), the parameter str (with contents "never dies!") is appended to the StringBuilder (with contents "love ") referred to by the instance field banner in the enclosing object, resulting in the following contents in this StringBuilder:

```
"love never dies!"
```

Since the length of the string "never dies!", referred to by the parameter str, is greater than 5, the lambda expression returns true at (11). This is the value returned by the test() method call in (6).

In the call to the println() method at (6), the argument

```
p.test("never dies!") + " " + obj.banner
```

now evaluates as

```
true + " " + "love never dies!"
```

Example 10.6 *Accessing Members in an Enclosing Object*

```
import java.util.ArrayList;
import java.util.List;
import java.util.function.Predicate;

public class MembersOnly {

  // Instance variable
  private StringBuilder banner;                                  // (1)

  // Static variable
  private static List<String> strList;                           // (2)
```

```
  // Constructor
  public MembersOnly(String str) {
    banner = new StringBuilder(str);
  }

  // Static method
  public static void main(String[] args) {
    strList = new ArrayList<>();                                   // (3)
    strList.add("Otto"); strList.add("ADA"); strList.add("Alyla");
    strList.add("Bob"); strList.add("HannaH"); strList.add("Java");

    MembersOnly obj = new MembersOnly("love ");                    // (4)
    Predicate<String> p = obj.getPredicate();                      // (5)
    System.out.println(p.test("never dies!") + " " + obj.banner);  // (6)
  }

  // Instance method
  public Predicate<String> getPredicate() {          // (7)
    return str -> {                                  // (8)  Lambda expression
      System.out.println("List: " + strList);        // (9)  MembersOnly.strList
      banner.append(str);                            // (10) this.banner
      return str.length() > 5;                       // (11) boolean value
    };
  }
}
```

Output from the program:

```
List: [Otto, ADA, Alyla, Bob, HannaH, Java]
true love never dies!
```

Accessing Local Variables in the Enclosing Context

As mentioned earlier, a lambda expression is not associated with a class or any of its members. Apart from not having a `this` reference, a lambda expression also does not create its own scope. Instead, it is part of the scope of the enclosing context—it has *lexical or block scope* (§4.4, p. 117). All variable declarations in a lambda expression follow the rules of block scoping. They are not accessible outside of the lambda expression. In addition, we cannot *redeclare* local variables already declared in the enclosing scope. In Example 10.7, redeclaring the local variables `banner` and `words` at (6) and (7), respectively, results in a compile-time error.

Local variables declared in the enclosing method, including its formal parameters, can be accessed in a lambda expression provided they are *effectively final*. This means that once a local variable has been assigned a value, its value does not change in the method. Using the `final` modifier in the declaration of a local variable explicitly instructs the compiler to ensure that this is the case. The `final` modifier implies effectively final. If the `final` modifier is omitted and a local variable is used in a lambda expression, the compiler effectively performs the same analysis as if the `final` modifier had been specified. A lambda expression might be executed at a later time, after the method has finished execution. At that point, the local variables used in the lambda expression are no longer accessible. To ensure their availability, *copies of their values* are maintained with the lambda expression. This is called *variable capture*, although in essence it is the values that are captured. Note that it is not the object that is copied in the case of a local reference variable, but rather the reference value. Objects reside on the heap and are accessible via a copy of the reference value. Correct execution of the lambda expression is guaranteed, since these effectively final values cannot change. Note that the state of an object referred to by a `final` or an effectively final reference can change, but not the reference value in the reference; thus, such a reference will continue refer to the same object once it is initialized.

In Example 10.7, the method `getPredicate()` at (1) has one formal parameter (`banner`), and a local variable (`words`) declared at (2). Although the state of the `ArrayList` object, referred to by the reference `words`, is changed in the method (we add elements to it), the reference value in the reference does not change; that is, it continues to refer to the same object whose reference value it was assigned at (2). The parameter `banner` is assigned the reference value of the argument object when the method is invoked, and continues to refer to this object throughout the method. Both local variables are effectively final. Their values are captured by the lambda expression, and used when the lambda expression is executed after the call to the `getPredicate()` method in the `main()` method.

If we uncomment (3) and (4) in Example 10.7, then both local variables are *not* effectively final. Their reference values are changed at (3) and (4), respectively. The compiler now flags errors in (8) and (9), respectively, because these non-final local variables are used in the lambda expression.

Example 10.7 *Accessing Local Variables in an Enclosing Method*

```
import java.util.ArrayList;
import java.util.List;
import java.util.function.Predicate;

public class LocalsOnly {

  public static void main(String[] args) {
    StringBuilder banner = new StringBuilder("love ");
    LocalsOnly instance = new LocalsOnly();
    Predicate<String> p = instance.getPredicate(banner);
    System.out.println(p.test("never dies!") + " " + banner);
  }

  public Predicate<String> getPredicate(StringBuilder banner) {   // (1)
    List<String> words = new ArrayList<>();                        // (2)
    words.add("Otto"); words.add("ADA"); words.add("Alyla");
    words.add("Bob"); words.add("HannaH"); words.add("Java");

//  banner = new StringBuilder();              // (3) Illegal: Not effectively final
//  words = new ArrayList<>();                 // (4) Illegal: Not effectively final
```

```
      return str -> {                                    // (5) Lambda expression
  //      String banner = "Don't redeclare me!";         // (6) Illegal: Redeclared
  //      String[] words = new String[6];                // (7) Illegal: Redeclared
          System.out.println("List: " + words);          // (8)
          banner.append(str);                            // (9)
          return str.length() > 5;
      };
    }
  }
```

Output from the program:

```
List: [Otto, ADA, Alyla, Bob, HannaH, Java]
true love never dies!
```

Type Checking and Execution of Lambda Expressions

The use of lambda expressions is tightly coupled with functional interfaces. A lambda expression can be defined in a context where a functional interface can be used—for example, in an assignment context, a method call context, or a cast context. The compiler determines the *target type* that is required in the context where the lambda expression is defined. This target type is always a functional interface type. In the assignment context that follows, the target type is `Predicate<Integer>`, as it is the target of the assignment statement. Note that the type parameter `T` of the functional interface is `Integer`.

```
Predicate<Integer> p1 = i -> i%2 == 0;  // (1) Target type: Predicate<Integer>
```

The *method type* of a method declaration comprises its type parameters, formal parameter types, return type, and any exceptions the method throws.

The *function type* of a functional interface is the method type of its single abstract method. The target type `Predicate<Integer>` has the following method, where type parameter `T` is `Integer`:

```
public boolean test(Integer t);           // Method type: Integer -> boolean
```

The function type of the target type `Predicate<Integer>` is the method type of the this `test()` method:

```
Integer -> boolean
```

The type of the lambda expression defined in a given context must be compatible with the function type of the target type. If the lambda expression has inferred-type parameters, their type is inferred from the function type, and if necessary from the context. From the function type of the target type `Predicate<Integer>`, the compiler can infer that the parameter `i` in the lambda expression at (1) should be of type `Integer`. The lambda body returns a `boolean` value. The type of the lambda expression in (1) is

```
Integer -> boolean
```

The type of the lambda expression is compatible with the function type of the target type `Predicate<Integer>`.

In the following assignment, the target type is `java.util.function.IntPredicate`:

```
IntPredicate p2 = i -> i%2 == 0;          // (2) Target type: IntPredicate
```

The `IntPredicate` functional interface has the following abstract method:

```
public boolean test(int i);              // Method type: int -> boolean
```

The function type of the target type `IntPredicate` is the method type of its abstract method:

```
int -> boolean
```

The compiler infers that the type of the inferred-type parameter `i` in the lambda expression at (2) should be `int`. As the lambda body returns a `boolean` value, the type of the lambda expression in (2) is

```
int -> boolean
```

The type of the lambda expression is compatible with the function type of the target type `IntPredicate`.

Note that in both examples, the lambda expression is the same, but their types are different in the two contexts: They represent two different values. The type of a lambda expression is determined by the context in which it is defined.

```
System.out.println(p1 == p2);                         // false
```

The process of type checking a lambda expression in a given context is called *target typing*. The presentation here is simplified, but suffices for our purposes to give an idea of what is involved.

The compiler does the type checking necessary to use lambda expressions, and the runtime environment provides the rest of the magic to make it all work. At runtime, the lambda expression is executed when the sole abstract method of the functional interface is invoked. As mentioned earlier, this is an example of deferred execution. Lambda execution is similar to invoking a method on an object. We define a lambda expression as a *function* and use it like a *method*, letting the compiler and the runtime environment put it all together.

```
boolean result1 = p1.test(2015);                       // false
boolean result2 = p2.test(2016);                       // true
```

Filtering Revisited: The `Predicate<T>` Functional Interface

Example 10.8 includes the two previous examples of filtering a list for palindromes at (2) and (3). In addition, it presents several examples of filtering a list using different criteria defined on properties of a string. Determining whether a string is a case-sensitive or case-insensitive palindrome is now done by the two `static` methods `isCaseSensitivePalindrome()` and `isCaseInsensitivePalindrome()`, respectively.

Also note that the `filterStrings()` method , which we used earlier, is now a generic method to filter *any* list, not just a list of strings, (14).

The examples in Example 10.8 have intentionally been written to illustrate the syntax of lambda expressions. We draw attention to the predicate at (11) that takes into account whether the string element has a `null` value, whether it is an empty string, and whether its length is greater than 3, before testing it for a palindrome:

```
Predicate<String> predicateE = str ->                                    // (11)
    str != null &&  !str.equals("") &&  str.length() > 3
    &&  isCaseSensitivePalindrome(str);
```

This lambda expression avoids throwing a `NullPointerException`. There are other, more sophisticated ways of dealing with a `NullPointerException`, but they are beyond the scope of this book. The `Predicate<T>` interface also provides methods to compose compound predicates.

The filtering examples in this chapter make heavy use of traversal over a list using a loop. Functional-style programming frees us from the tyranny of explicit traversal over collections, but we have merely scratched the surface here. Earlier in this chapter (p. 424), we discussed the removal of elements from a list. The `removeIf()` method of the `ArrayList` class provides a safe and convenient way of deleting all elements that satisfy any criteria expressed as a `Predicate<T>`. Thus, the traversal process is now internal. The lambda expression in (11) tests whether the string contains the character a. All strings satisfying this criterion are removed from the list, as confirmed by the output from the program.

```
words.removeIf(str -> str.indexOf('a') > 0);                           // (12)
```

Another example of the use of this method is given in (13), where it is used to remove all strings with length greater than 3:

```
words.removeIf(str -> str.length() > 3);                               // (13)
```

It is instructive to walk through the code in Example 10.8, and compare it to the solution we initially wrote in Example 10.2, p. 434.

Example 10.8 *Filtering an* `ArrayList`

```
import java.util.ArrayList;
import java.util.List;
import java.util.function.Predicate;

public class FunWithPalindromesV4 {

  private static boolean isCaseSensitivePalindrome(String str) {
    return str.equals(new StringBuilder(str).reverse().toString());
  }

  private static boolean isCaseInsensitivePalindrome(String str) {
    return str.equalsIgnoreCase(new StringBuilder(str).reverse().toString());
  }
```

```
  public static void main(String[] args) {

    // Create a list of words:                                    // (1)
    List<String> words = new ArrayList<>();
    words.add("Otto"); words.add("ADA"); words.add("Alyla");
    words.add("Bob"); words.add("HannaH"); words.add("Java");
    System.out.println("List of words:                 " + words);

    List<String> palindromes1 = filterStrings(words,              // (2)
        str -> isCaseSensitivePalindrome(str));
    System.out.println("Case-sensitive palindromes:      " + palindromes1);

    List<String> palindromes2 = filterStrings(words, str ->       // (3)
        isCaseInsensitivePalindrome(str));
    System.out.println("Case-insensitive palindromes:    " + palindromes2);

    Predicate<String> predicate3 = str -> !isCaseSensitivePalindrome(str); // (4)
    List<String> nonPalindromes = filterStrings(words, predicate3);
    System.out.println("Non-palindromes, case sensitive: " + nonPalindromes);

    Predicate<String> predicate4 = str -> str.length() > 3;      // (5)
    List<String> strGT3 = filterStrings(words, predicate4);
    System.out.println("Words with length > 3:           " + strGT3);

    Predicate<String> predicate5 = str ->                         // (6)
        str.length() > 3 && isCaseSensitivePalindrome(str);
    List<String> palindromesGT3 = filterStrings(words, predicate5);
    System.out.println("Case-sensitive palindromes, length > 3: "
                       + palindromesGT3);

    Predicate<String> predicateA = str -> {                       // (7)
      return str.length() > 3 && isCaseSensitivePalindrome(str);
    };
    System.out.println("Case-sensitive palindromes, length > 3: "
                        + filterStrings(words, predicateA));

    Predicate<String> predicateB = str -> {                       // (8)
      boolean result1 = str.length() > 3;
      boolean result2 = isCaseSensitivePalindrome(str);
      return  result1 && result2;
    };
    System.out.println("Case-sensitive palindromes, length > 3: "
                        + filterStrings(words, predicateB));

    Predicate<String> predicateC = str -> {                       // (9)
      if (str == null || str.equals("") || str.length() <= 3) {
        return false;
      }
      StringBuilder sb = new StringBuilder(str);
      boolean result = str.equals(sb.reverse().toString());
      return result;
    };
    System.out.println("Case-sensitive palindromes, length > 3: "
                        + filterStrings(words, predicateC));
```

```
    Predicate<String> predicateD = str ->                                 // (10)
        (str == null || str.equals("") || str.length() <= 3)
        ? false: isCaseSensitivePalindrome(str);
    System.out.println("Case-sensitive palindromes, length > 3: "
                       + filterStrings(words, predicateD));

    Predicate<String> predicateE = str ->                                 // (11)
        str != null &&  !str.equals("") &&  str.length() > 3
        &&  isCaseSensitivePalindrome(str);
    System.out.println("Case-sensitive palindromes, length > 3: "
                     + filterStrings(words, predicateE));

    // Removing elements from a list:
    words.removeIf(str -> str.indexOf('a') > 0);                          // (12)
    System.out.println("List of words, no 'a':      " + words);

    words.removeIf(str -> str.length() > 3);                              // (13)
    System.out.println("List of words, length <= 3: " + words);
  }

  /**
   * Filters a list according to the criteria of the predicate.
   * @param list        List to filter
   * @param predicate   Provides the criteria for filtering the list
   * @return            List of elements that match the criteria
   */
  public static <E> List<E> filterStrings(List<E> list,                   // (14)
                                          Predicate<E> predicate) {
    List<E> result = new ArrayList<>();
    for (E element : list)
      if (predicate.test(element))
        result.add(element);
    return result;
  }
}
```

Output from the program:

```
List of words:                     [Otto, ADA, Alyla, Bob, HannaH, Java]
Case-sensitive palindromes:        [ADA, HannaH]
Case-insensitive palindromes:      [Otto, ADA, Alyla, Bob, HannaH]
Non-palindromes, case sensitive: [Otto, Alyla, Bob, Java]
Words with length > 3:             [Otto, Alyla, HannaH, Java]
Case-sensitive palindromes, length > 3: [HannaH]
Case-sensitive palindromes, length > 3: [HannaH]
Case-sensitive palindromes, length > 3: [HannaH]
Case-sensitive palindromes, length > 3: [HannaH]
Case-sensitive palindromes, length > 3: [HannaH]
Case-sensitive palindromes, length > 3: [HannaH]
List of words, no 'a':      [Otto, ADA, Bob]
List of words, length <= 3: [ADA, Bob]
```

Review Questions

10.7 Which statement is true about functional interfaces and lambda expressions?

Select the one correct answer.

(a) A functional interface can be implemented only by lambda expressions.
(b) A functional interface declaration can have only one method declaration.
(c) In the body of a lambda expression, only `public` members in the enclosing class can be accessed.
(d) In the body of a lambda expression, all local variables in the enclosing scope can be accessed.
(e) A lambda expression in a program can implement only one functional interface.
(f) None of the above.

10.8 Which statements are true about the following code?

```
import java.util.function.Predicate;

public class RQ12A98 {
  public static final String lock1 = "Brinks";
  private static String lock2 = "Yale";

  public static void main(String[] args) {
    Predicate<Object> p;
    p = lock -> { boolean p = lock.equals("Master"); return p; };          // (1)
    p = lock -> { return lock.toString().equals("YALE"); };                // (2)
    p = lock -> { (args.length > 0) ? lock.equals(args[0]) : false; };    // (3)
    p = lock -> { return lock.equals(lock1); };                            // (4)
    p = lock -> { return lock.equals(lock2); };                            // (5)
    p = lock2 -> { return lock2.equals(RQ12A98.lock2); };                  // (6)
  }
}
```

Select the two correct answers.

(a) (1) will not compile.
(b) (2) will not compile.
(c) (3) will not compile.
(d) (4) will not compile.
(e) (5) will not compile.
(f) (6) will not compile.

10.9 Which statements are true about the following code?

```
interface Funky1    { void    absMethod1(String s); }
interface Funky2    { String  absMethod2(String s); }

public class RQ12A99 {
  public static void main(String[] args) {
```

```
    Funky1 p1;
    p1 = s -> System.out.println(s);              // (1)
    p1 = s -> s.length();                         // (2)
    p1 = s -> s.toUpperCase();                    // (3)
    p1 = s -> { s.toUpperCase(); };               // (4)
    p1 = s -> { return s.toUpperCase(); };        // (5)

    Funky2 p2;
    p2 = s -> System.out.println(s);              // (6)
    p2 = s -> s.length();                         // (7)
    p2 = s -> s.toUpperCase();                    // (8)
    p2 = s -> { s.toUpperCase(); };               // (9)
    p2 = s -> { return s.toUpperCase(); };        // (10)
  }
}
```

Select the four correct answers.

(a) (1) will not compile.
(b) (2) will not compile.
(c) (3) will not compile.
(d) (4) will not compile.
(e) (5) will not compile.
(f) (6) will not compile.
(g) (7) will not compile.
(h) (8) will not compile.
(i) (9) will not compile.
(j) (10) will not compile.

10.10 Which statement is true about the following program?

```
import java.util.Arrays;
import java.util.function.IntPredicate;

public class RQ12A96 {

  public static void main(String[] args) {
    int[] intArray = {0, -1, -2, -3, -4, -5, -6, -7, -8, -9};
    filterInt(intArray, val -> val < 0 && val % 2 == 0);
    System.out.println(Arrays.toString(intArray));
  }

  public static void filterInt(int[] intArr,
                               IntPredicate predicate) {
    for (int i = 0; i < intArr.length; ++i) {
      if (predicate.test(intArr[i])) {
        intArr[i] = Math.abs(intArr[i]);
      }
    }
  }
}
```

Select the one correct answer.

(a) The program will not compile.
(b) The program will compile, but will throw an exception when run.
(c) The program will compile and print the following when run:
`[0, 1, -2, 3, -4, 5, -6, 7, -8, 9]`
(d) The program will compile and print the following when run:
`[0, -1, 2, -3, 4, -5, 6, -7, 8, -9]`
(e) The program will compile and print the following when run:
`[0, 1, 2, 3, 4, 5, 6, 7, 8, 9]`

10.11 Which statement is true about the following code?

```
interface InterfaceA { void doIt(); }
interface InterfaceB extends InterfaceA {}
interface InterfaceC extends InterfaceB {
  void doIt();
  boolean equals(Object obj);
}

class Beta implements InterfaceB {
  public void doIt() {
    System.out.print("Jazz|");
  }
}

public class RQ12A999 {
  public static void main(String[] args) {
    InterfaceA a = () -> System.out.print("Java|");     // (1)
    InterfaceB b = () -> System.out.print("Jive|");     // (2)
    InterfaceC c = () -> System.out.print("Jingle|");   // (3)
    Object o = a = c;                                   // (4)
    b = new Beta();                                     // (5)
    a.doIt();                                           // (6)
    b.doIt();                                           // (7)
    c.doIt();                                           // (8)
    ((InterfaceA) o).doIt();                            // (9)
  }
}
```

Select the one correct answer.

(a) The program will not compile.
(b) The program will throw a `ClassCastException`.
(c) The program will print: `Jingle|Jingle|Jazz|Jingle|`
(d) The program will print: `Jingle|Jazz|Jingle|Jingle|`
(e) The program will print: `Jingle|Jingle|Jingle|Jazz|`

Chapter Summary

The following topics were covered in this chapter:

- The concept of a list as a collection
- The inheritance relationship between the `ArrayList<E>` class, the `List<E>` interface, and the `Collection<E>` interface in the Java Collections Framework
- Use of the diamond operator (<>) when creating objects of generic classes
- Declaring and using references of the `ArrayList` type
- Creating, querying, traversing, converting, and sorting `ArrayLists`
- Comparison of arrays and `ArrayLists`
- Behavior parameterization in functional-style programing
- The role of lambda expressions and functional interfaces in implementing behavior parameterization
- Referencing the general-purpose functional interfaces in the `java.util.function` package
- Implementing the `Predicate<T>` functional interface using lambda expressions
- Defining selection criteria as predicates for filtering `ArrayLists`
- Defining and type checking lambda expressions in the context of a functional interface
- The deferred execution of a lambda expression
- The implications of using class members from the enclosing class, and of using local variables from the enclosing method
- Passing and assigning lambda values using functional interface references

Programming Exercise

10.1 Find all elements in a list that satisfy all given predicates.

Skeleton code for this problem is provided in this exercise. The `main()` method at (1) creates a list of strings from an array of strings. It also creates a list of predicates. The following predicates should be included in this list:

- A string is not `null`.
- A string contains the substring `"up"` by first converting the string to lowercase.
- The first character of a string is a letter.

The `main()` method calls the methods at (2), (4), and (5). The output from the program is shown here. The textual representation of the lambda expressions might vary.

```
[Cheer up!, 7Up coming up!, null, Bottoms up!, Get down!, What's up?]
[FilterFun$$Lambda$1/12251916@192e0f4, FilterFun$$Lambda$2/18340259@a418fc,
FilterFun$$Lambda$3/19888781@105068a]
[Cheer up!, Bottoms up!, What's up?]
[Cheer up!, Bottoms up!, What's up?]
[Cheer up!, Bottoms up!, What's up?]
```

Complete the implementation of the `main()` method, and at least implement the methods at (2) and (3).

To implement the methods at (4) and(5), see the methods `and()` and `negate()` provided by the `java.util.function.Predicate<T>` interface.

The methods at (4) and(5) also make use of the `ArrayList.removeIf()` method.

The method at (5) is a straightforward generic version of the method at (4), so that any list can be filtered this way.

```
import java.util.ArrayList;
import java.util.List;
import java.util.function.Predicate;

public class FilterFun {

  public static void main(String[] args) {                                   // (1)
    // Create a list of strings:
    String[] strings = { "Cheer up!", "7Up coming up!", null,
                         "Bottoms up!","Get down!", "What's up?" };
    List<String> strList = new ArrayList<>();
    /* WRITE CODE TO POPULATE THE LIST OF STRINGS HERE. */
    System.out.println(strList);

    // Create a list of predicates.
    List<Predicate<String>> predList = new ArrayList<>();
    /* WRITE CODE TO POPULATE THE LIST OF PREDICATES HERE. */
    System.out.println(predList);

    // Apply filtering.
    applyAllPredicates(strList, predList);
    applyAllPredicatesAlt(strList, predList);
    applyAllPredicatesGenAlt(strList, predList);
  }

  /**
   * Prints all the strings in the specified list that satisfy all the
   * predicates in the list of predicates.
   * It uses the andPredicates() method at (3).
   * @param list        List of strings to apply the predicates on
   * @param predicates  List of predicates to apply
   */
  public static void applyAllPredicates(List<String> list,                   // (2)
                                        List<Predicate<String>> predicates) {
    /* IMPLEMENT THIS METHOD */
  }
```

```
  /**
   * Determines whether a string satisfies all the predicates.
   * @param str          String to apply the predicates on
   * @param predicates   List of predicates to apply
   * @return             true only if the string satisfies all the predicates
   */
  public static boolean andPredicates(String str,                      // (3)
                                     List<Predicate<String>> predicates) {
    /* IMPLEMENT THIS METHOD */
  }

  /**
   * Removes all the elements in the specified list that do not satisfy all the
   * predicates in the list of predicates, and prints the remaining elements
   * that do.
   * Uses Predicate.and(), Predicate.negate(), and List.removeIf() methods.
   * @param list         List of strings to apply the predicates on
   * @param predicates   List of predicates to apply
   */
  public static void applyAllPredicatesAlt(List<String> list,          // (4)
                                         List<Predicate<String>> predicates) {
    /* IMPLEMENT THIS METHOD */
  }

  /** Generic version.
   * Removes all the elements in the specified list that do not satisfy all the
   * predicates in the list of predicates, and prints the remaining elements
   * that do.
   * Uses Predicate.and(), Predicate.negate(), and List.removeIf() methods.
   * @param list         List of elements to apply the predicates on
   * @param predicates   List of predicates to apply
   */
  public static <T> void applyAllPredicatesGenAlt(List<T> list,          // (5)
                                            List<Predicate<T>> predicates) {
    /* IMPLEMENT THIS METHOD */
  }
}
```

Date and Time

11

Programmer I Exam Objectives		
[9.3]	Create and manipulate calendar data using classes from java.time.LocalDateTime, java.time.LocalDate, java.time.LocalTime, java.time.format.DateTimeFormatter, java.time.Period	*§11.1, p. 462* *§11.2, p. 462* *§11.3, p. 476* *§11.4, p. 486*
Supplementary Objectives		
•	Understand the consequences of immutability for objects that represent temporal concepts	*Chapter 11*
•	Understand the naming conventions used for methods in the temporal classes	*§11.2, p. 463*
•	Use temporal arithmetic	*§11.2, p. 474* *§11.3, p. 479*
•	Use predefined formatters for formatting and parsing	*§11.4, p. 488*
•	Use localized formatters based on the predefined format styles defined by the `java.time.format.FormatStyle` enum type	*§11.4, p. 490*
•	Use letter patterns to create customized formatters for formatting and parsing	*§11.4, p. 495*

11.1 Basic Date and Time Concepts

Java 8 introduced a new comprehensive API for handling temporal concepts. In this chapter, we primarily concentrate on classes that represent the date, time, and period. The Java 8 API also provides support for formatting and parsing temporal objects. These classes are all based on the ISO calendar system, which is the *de facto* world calendar. The Date and Time API is fairly comprehensive, and includes support for other temporal concepts such as instants, durations, offsets, time zones, and different calendars—topics that are beyond the scope of this book.

We will use the term *temporal objects* to mean objects of classes that represent temporal concepts. Two packages provide the main support for handling, formatting, and parsing temporal objects:

- The `java.time` package provides the classes `LocalDate`, `LocalTime`, `LocalDateTime`, and `Period` that represent a date, a (clock) time, a combined date-time, and a period, respectively.

  `LocalDate`: This class represents a date in terms of *date-based values* (year, month, day). Date objects have no time-based values or a time zone.

  `LocalTime`: This class represents time in a 24-hour day in terms of *time-based values* (hours, minutes, seconds, nanoseconds). Time objects have no date-based values or a time zone.

  `LocalDateTime`: This class represents the concept of date and time combined, in terms of *both* date-based and time-based values. Date-time objects have no time zone.

  `Period`: This class represents a *directed* amount or quantity of time in terms of number of days, months, and years, which can be negative. Period objects have no notion of a clock time, a date, or a time zone.

- The `java.time.format` package provides the class `DateTimeFormatter` for formatting and parsing temporal objects.

  `DateTimeFormatter`: This class provides implementation of formatters: predefined formatters (e.g., `DateTimeFormatter.ISO_LOCAL_TIME`), and localized formatters that use predefined format styles (e.g., `FormatStyle.SHORT`), and customized formatters that use letter patterns (e.g., `"MM/dd/uuuu"`). A formatter can be used to obtain a string representation of a temporal object (called *formatting*), and conversely to obtain a temporal object from a string (called *parsing*).

This chapter provides examples demonstrating how to create, combine, convert, query, compare, format, and parse temporal objects, including the use of temporal arithmetic.

11.2 Working with Temporal Classes

The temporal classes implement *immutable* and *thread-safe* temporal objects. The state of an immutable object cannot be changed. Any method that is supposed to modify such an object returns a modified copy of the temporal object. It is a common mistake to ignore the new object, thinking that the current object has been modified, which can lead to incorrect results. Thread-safety guarantees that the state of such an object is not affected by concurrent access.

Another common mistake is to access, format, or parse a temporal object that does not have the required temporal values. For example, a `LocalTime` object has only time-based values, so trying to format it with a formatter for date-based values will result in a `java.time.DateTimeException`. Many methods will also throw an exception if an invalid or an out-of-range argument is passed in the method call. It is important to keep in mind which temporal values constitute the state of a temporal object.

Here we ignore the implications of a time zone, since the temporal objects discussed in this chapter are time zone agnostic. However, the coverage here will facilitate the inquisitive reader to further explore the features of the Date and Time API.

Before diving into the Date and Time API, we provide an overview of the method naming conventions used in the temporal classes (Table 11.1). This method naming convention makes it easy to use the API, as it ensures method naming is standardized across all temporal classes.

The temporal classes `LocalTime`, `LocalDate`, and `LocalDateTime` are all found in the `java.time` package. An appropriate `import` statement should be included in the source file to use any of these classes.

Table 11.1 *Selected Common Method Prefix of the Temporal Classes*

Prefix	Usage
`of`	Static factory methods for constructing temporal objects from constituent temporal values.
`at`	Create a new temporal object by combining this temporal object with another temporal object.
`get`	Access specific values in this temporal object.
`is`	Check specific properties of this temporal object.
`to`	Convert this temporal object to another type.
`with`	Create a copy of a temporal object with one temporal value modified.
`minus`	Return a copy of this temporal object after subtracting an amount of time.
`plus`	Return a copy of this temporal object after adding an amount of time.
`until`	Return the amount of time from this temporal object to the specified temporal object.
`format`	Use a formatter to create a textual representation of this temporal object.
`parse`	Static method for parsing a string to create an object of the target temporal class.

Creating Temporal Objects

The temporal classes do not provide any `public` constructors to create temporal objects. Instead, they provide overloaded static factory methods named `of` with which to create temporal objects from constituent temporal values. We use the term *temporal values* to mean both time-based and date-based values. The `of()` methods check that the values of the arguments are in range. Any invalid argument results in a `java.time.DateTimeException`.

All code snippets in this subsection can be found in Example 11.1, p. 467, ready for running and experimenting.

The declaration statements that follow show examples of creating instances of the `LocalTime` class to represent time on a 24-hour clock in terms of hours, minutes, seconds, and nanoseconds. The ranges of values for the hours (0–23), minutes (0–59), seconds (0–59), and nanoseconds (0–999,999,999) are defined by the ISO standard. The `toString()` method of the class will format the time-based values according to the ISO standard as `HH:mm:ss.SSSSSSSSS`. Omitting the seconds (`ss`) and fractions of seconds (`SSSSSSSSS`) implies that their value is zero. (More on formatting in §11.4, p. 495.) In the second declaration statement, the seconds and the nanoseconds are not specified in the method call, resulting in their values being set to zero. In the third statement, the hour value (25) is out of range, and if uncommented, will result in a `DateTimeException`.

```
LocalTime time1 = LocalTime.of(8, 15, 35, 900);   // 08:15:35.000000900
LocalTime time2 = LocalTime.of(16, 45);           // 16:45
// LocalTime time3 = LocalTime.of(25, 13, 30);    // DateTimeException
```

Creating instances of the `LocalDate` class is analogous to creating instances of the `LocalTime` class. The `of()` method of the `LocalDate` class is passed date-based values: the year, month of the year, and day of the month. The ranges of the values for the year, the month, and the day are (–999,999,999 to +999,999,999), (1–12), and (1–31), respectively. The month can also be specified using the enum constants of the `java.time.Month` class, as in the second declaration statement in the next set of examples. A `DateTimeException` is thrown if the value of any parameter is out of range, or if the day is invalid for the specified month of the year. In the third declaration, the month value 13 is out of range. In the last declaration, the month of February cannot have 29 days, since the year 2015 is not a leap year.

```
LocalDate date1 = LocalDate.of(1969, 7, 20);                 // 1969-07-20
LocalDate date2 = LocalDate.of(-3113, Month.AUGUST, 11);// -3113-08-11
//  LocalDate date3 = LocalDate.of(2015, 13, 11);            // DateTimeException
//  LocalDate date4 = LocalDate.of(2015, 2, 29);             // DateTimeException
```

The year is represented as a *proleptic year* in the ISO standard, which can be negative. A year in CE (Current Era, or AD) has the same value as a proleptic year; for example, 2015 CE is same as the proleptic year 2015. However, for a year in BCE (Before Current Era, or BC), the proleptic year 0 corresponds to 1 BCE, the proleptic year –1 corresponds to 2 BCE, and so on. The `toString()` method of the class will format the date-based values according to the ISO standard as uuuu-MM-dd (see also §11.4, p. 495). In the second declaration in the preceding set of examples, the date -3113-08-11 corresponds to 11 August 3114 BCE.

```
// LocalTime
static LocalTime of(int hour, int minute)
static LocalTime of(int hour, int minute, int second)
static LocalTime of(int hour, int minute, int second, int nanoOfSecond)
```

This overloaded static factory method in the LocalTime class returns an instance of LocalTime from the specified time-based values. The second and nanosecond values are set to zero, if not specified.

```
// LocalDate
static LocalDate of(int year, int month, int dayOfMonth)
static LocalDate of(int year, Month month, int dayOfMonth)
```

This overloaded static factory method in the LocalDate class returns an instance of LocalDate from the specified date-based values. The java.time.Month enum type allows months to be referred by name—for example, Month.MARCH. Note that month numbering starts with 1 (Month.JANUARY).

```
// LocalDateTime
static LocalDateTime of(int year, int month, int dayOfMonth,
                        int hour, int minute)
static LocalDateTime of(int year, int month, int dayOfMonth,
                        int hour, int minute, int second)
static LocalDateTime of(int year, int month, int dayOfMonth, int hour,
                        int minute, int second, int nanoOfSecond)
static LocalDateTime of(int year, Month month, int dayOfMonth,
                        int hour, int minute, int second)
static LocalDateTime of(int year, Month month, int dayOfMonth,
                        int hour, int minute)
static LocalDateTime of(int year, Month month, int dayOfMonth,
                        int hour, int minute, int second, int nanoOfSecond)
static LocalDateTime of(LocalDate date, LocalTime time)
```

This overloaded static factory method in the LocalDateTime class returns an instance of LocalDateTime from the specified time and date-based values. The second and nanosecond values are set to zero, if not specified. The java.time.Month enum type allows months to be referred by name—for example, Month.MARCH (i.e., month 3 in the year).

The class LocalDateTime allows the date and the time to be combined into one entity, which is useful for representing such concepts as appointments. The of() methods in the LocalDateTime class are combinations of the of() methods from the LocalTime and LocalDate classes, taking both time-based and date-based values as arguments. The toString() method of this class will format the temporal values according to the ISO standard as uuuu-MM-dd'T'HH:mm:ss.SSSSSSSSS. The letter T separates the date-based values from the time-based values (§11.4, p. 495).

```
// 2015-04-28T12:15
LocalDateTime dt1 = LocalDateTime.of(2015, 4, 28, 12, 15);
// 2015-08-19T14:00
LocalDateTime dt2 = LocalDateTime.of(2015, Month.AUGUST, 19, 14, 0);
```

The `LocalDateTime` class also provides an `of()` method that combines a `LocalDate` object and a `LocalTime` object. The first declaration in the next code snippet combines a date and a time. The static field `LocalTime.NOON` defines the time at noon. In addition, the `LocalTime` class provides the instance method `atDate()`, which takes a specified date as an argument and returns a `LocalDateTime` object. The second declaration combines the time at noon with the date referred to by the reference `date1`. Conversely, the `LocalDate` class provides the overloaded instance method `atTime()` to combine a date with a specified time. In the last two declarations, the `atTime()` method is passed a `LocalTime` object and specific time-based values, respectively.

```
// 1969-07-20T12:00
LocalDateTime dt3 = LocalDateTime.of(date1, LocalTime.NOON);
LocalDateTime dt4 = LocalTime.of(12, 0).atDate(date1);
LocalDateTime dt5 = date1.atTime(LocalTime.NOON);
LocalDateTime dt6 = date1.atTime(12, 0);
```

As a convenience, each temporal class provides a static method `now()` that reads the system clock and returns the relevant temporal values in an instance of the target class.

```
LocalTime currentTime = LocalTime.now();
LocalDate currentDate = LocalDate.now();
LocalDateTime currentDateTime = LocalDateTime.now();
```

Example 11.1 includes the different ways to create temporal objects that we have discussed so far.

```
// LocalTime
LocalDateTime atDate(LocalDate date)
```

Returns a `LocalDateTime` that combines this time with the specified date.

```
// LocalDate
LocalDateTime atTime(int hour, int minute)
LocalDateTime atTime(int hour, int minute, int second)
LocalDateTime atTime(int hour, int minute, int second, int nanoOfSecond)
LocalDateTime atTime(LocalTime time)
```

Returns a `LocalDateTime` that combines this date with the specified time-based values. The second and nanosecond values are set to zero, if not specified.

```
// LocalTime, LocalDate, LocalDateTime
static TemporalType now()
```

Each temporal class has this static factory method, which returns either the current time, date, or date-time from the system clock in the default time zone, where *TemporalType* is either `LocalTime`, `LocalDate`, or `LocalDateTime`, respectively.

Example 11.1 *Creating Temporal Objects*

```
import java.time.LocalDate;
import java.time.LocalDateTime;
import java.time.LocalTime;
import java.time.Month;

public class CreatingTemporals {

  public static void main(String[] args) {

    // Creating a specific time from time-based values:
    LocalTime time1 = LocalTime.of(8, 15, 35, 900);// 08:15:35.000000900
    LocalTime time2 = LocalTime.of(16, 45);         // 16:45
//  LocalTime time3 = LocalTime.of(25, 13, 30);     // DateTimeException
    System.out.println("Surveillance start time: " + time1);
    System.out.println("Closing time: " + time2);

    // Creating a specific date from date-based values:
    LocalDate date1 = LocalDate.of(1969, 7, 20);               // 1969-07-20
    LocalDate date2 = LocalDate.of(-3113, Month.AUGUST, 11);// -3113-08-11
//  LocalDate date3 = LocalDate.of(2015, 13, 11);              // DateTimeException
//  LocalDate date4 = LocalDate.of(2015, 2, 29);               // DateTimeException
    System.out.println("Date of lunar landing:         " + date1);
    System.out.println("Start Date of Mayan Calendar: " + date2);

    // Creating a specific date-time from date- and time-based values.
    // 2015-04-28T12:15
    LocalDateTime dt1 = LocalDateTime.of(2015, 4, 28, 12, 15);
    // 2015-08-17T14:00
    LocalDateTime dt2 = LocalDateTime.of(2015, Month.AUGUST, 17, 14, 0);
    System.out.println("Car service appointment: " + dt1);
    System.out.println("Hospital appointment:    " + dt2);

    // Combining date and time objects.
    // 1969-07-20T12:00
    LocalDateTime dt3 = LocalDateTime.of(date1, LocalTime.NOON);
    LocalDateTime dt4 = LocalTime.of(12, 0).atDate(date1);
    LocalDateTime dt5 = date1.atTime(LocalTime.NOON);
    LocalDateTime dt6 = date1.atTime(12, 0);
    System.out.println("Factory date-time combo: " + dt3);
    System.out.println("Time with date combo:    " + dt4);
    System.out.println("Date with time combo:    " + dt5);
    System.out.println("Date with explicit time combo: " + dt6);

    // Current time:
    LocalTime currentTime = LocalTime.now();
    System.out.println("Current time:       " + currentTime);

    // Current date:
    LocalDate currentDate = LocalDate.now();
    System.out.println("Current date:       " + currentDate);
```

```
    // Current date and time:
    LocalDateTime currentDateTime = LocalDateTime.now();
    System.out.println("Current date-time: " + currentDateTime);
  }
}
```

Possible output from the program:

```
Surveillance start time: 08:15:35.000000900
Closing time: 16:45
Date of lunar landing:          1969-07-20
Start Date of Mayan Calendar: -3113-08-11
Car service appointment: 2015-04-28T12:15
Hospital appointment:    2015-08-17T14:00
Factory date-time combo: 1969-07-20T12:00
Time with date combo:    1969-07-20T12:00
Date with time combo:    1969-07-20T12:00
Date with explicit time combo: 1969-07-20T12:00
Current time:      10:32:03.069
Current date:      2015-08-21
Current date-time: 2015-08-21T10:32:03.083
```

Querying Temporal Objects

A temporal object provides *get* methods that are tailored to access the specific temporal values that constitute its state. The `LocalTime` class provides get methods for the time-based values, and the `LocalDate` class provides get methods for the date-based values. Not surprisingly, the `LocalDateTime` class provides get methods for both time- and date-based values. Usage of the get methods is straightforward, as shown in Example 11.2.

```
// LocalTime, LocalDateTime
int getHour()
int getMinute()
int getSecond()
int getNano()
```

Gets the appropriate time-based value from the current `LocalTime` or `LocalDateTime` object.

```
// LocalDate, LocalDateTime
int       getDayOfMonth()
DayOfWeek getDayOfWeek()
int       getDayOfYear()
Month     getMonth()
int       getMonthValue()
int       getYear()
```

Gets the appropriate date-based value from the current `LocalDate` or `LocalDateTime` object. The enum type `DayOfWeek` allows days of the week to be referred to by name—for example, `DayOfWeek.MONDAY` is day 1 of the week. The enum type `Month` allows months of the year to be referred by name—for example, `Month.JANUARY`. The month value is from 1 (`Month.JANUARY`) to 12 (`Month.DECEMBER`).

The temporal class `LocalDateTime` also provides two methods to obtain the date and the time as temporal objects, in contrast to accessing individual date- and time-based values.

```
LocalDateTime doomsday = LocalDateTime.of(1945, 8, 6, 8, 15);
LocalDate date = doomsday.toLocalDate();                    // 1945-08-06
LocalTime time = doomsday.toLocalTime();                    // 08:15
```

```
// LocalDateTime
LocalDate toLocalDate()
LocalTime toLocalTime()
```

These methods can be used to get the `LocalDate` and `LocalTime` part of this date-time, respectively.

It is also possible to check whether a temporal object represents a point in time before or after another temporal object of the same type. In addition, the `LocalDate` and `LocalDateTime` classes provide an `isEqual()` method that determines whether a temporal object is equal to another temporal object of the same type. In contrast, the `equals()` method allows equality comparison with an arbitrary object.

```
LocalDate d1 = LocalDate.of(-1004, 3, 1);                   // -1004-03-01
LocalDate d2 = LocalDate.of(1004, 3, 1);                    // 1004-03-01
boolean result1 = d1.isBefore(d2);                          // true
boolean result2 = d2.isAfter(d1);                           // true
boolean result3 = d1.isAfter(d1);                           // false
boolean result4 = d1.isEqual(d2);                           // false
boolean result5 = d1.isEqual(d1);                           // true
boolean result6 = d2.isLeapYear();                          // true
```

The `isLeapYear()` method of the `LocalDate` class checks whether a year in a date is a leap year.

```
// LocalTime
boolean isAfter(LocalTime other)
boolean isBefore(LocalTime other)
```

These methods determine whether this `LocalTime` represents a point on the local time-line after or before the other time, respectively.

```
// LocalDate
boolean isAfter(ChronoLocalDate other)
boolean isBefore(ChronoLocalDate other)
boolean isEqual(ChronoLocalDate other)
boolean isLeapYear()
```

The first two methods determine whether this `LocalDate` represents a point on the local timeline after or before the other date, respectively. The `LocalDate` class implements the `ChronoLocalDate` interface.

The third method determines whether this date is equal to the specified date.

The last method checks for a leap year according to the ISO proleptic calendar system rules.

```
// LocalDateTime
boolean isAfter(ChronoLocalDateTime<?> other)
boolean isBefore(ChronoLocalDateTime<?> other)
boolean isEqual(ChronoLocalDateTime<?> other)
```

The first two methods determine whether this `LocalDateTime` represents a point on the local timeline after or before the specified date-time, respectively. The `LocalDateTime` class implements the `ChronoLocalDateTime` interface.

The third method determines whether this date-time represents the same point on the local timeline as the other date-time.

Comparing Temporal Objects

The temporal classes implement the `Comparable` interface, providing the `compareTo()` method so that temporal objects can be compared in a meaningful way. The temporal classes also override the `equals()` method of the `Object` class. These methods make it possible to both search for and sort temporal objects.

```
int compareTo(LocalTime other)                 // LocalTime
int compareTo(ChronoLocalDate other)           // LocalDate
int compareTo(ChronoLocalDateTime<?> other)    // LocalDateTime
```

These methods compare this temporal object to another temporal object. The three temporal classes implement the `Comparable` functional interface. The `compareTo()` method returns `0` if the two temporal objects are equal, a negative value if this temporal object is less than the other temporal object, and a positive value if this temporal object is greater than the other temporal object.

```
boolean equals(Object obj)        // LocalTime, LocalDate, LocalDateTime
```

The three temporal classes override the `equals()` method of the `Object` class. The method checks whether this temporal object is equal to another object. The specified object must be of the same type as this temporal object; otherwise, the result is `false`.

Creating Modified Copies of Temporal Objects

An immutable object does not provide any *set* methods that can change its state. Instead, it usually provides what are known as `with` methods (or "*withers*") that return a copy of the original object where exactly one property has been set to a new value. The `LocalTime` and `LocalDate` classes provide `with` methods to set a time- or date-based value, respectively. Not surprisingly, the `LocalDateTime` class provides `with` methods to set both time- and date-based values individually. A `with` method changes a specific property in an absolute way, which is reflected in the state of the new temporal object; the original object, however, is not affected. Such `with` methods are also called *absolute adjusters*, in contrast to the *relative adjusters* that we will meet later (p. 474).

```
LocalDate date2 = LocalDate.of(2015, 3, 1);                          // 2015-03-01
date2 = date2.withYear(2016).withMonth(2).withDayOfMonth(28); // 2016-02-28
```

The preceding code lines are from Example 11.2. In the second assignment statement, the method calls are chained. Three instances of the `LocalDate` class are created consecutively, as each `with` method is called to set a specific date-based value.

```
date2 = date2.withYear(2016);                          // 2016-03-01
date2.withMonth(2).withDayOfMonth(28);                 // date2 is still 2016-03-01.
```

This code contains a logical error, such that the last two `LocalDate` instances returned by the `with` methods are ignored, and the reference `date2` never gets updated.

In the next code examples, each call to a `with` method throws a `DateTimeException`. The minute and hour values are out of range for a `LocalTime` object. Certainly the month value 13 is out of range for a `LocalDate` object. The day of the month value 31 is not valid for the April month, which has 30 days. The day of the year value 366 is out of range as well, since the year 2015 is not a leap year.

```
LocalTime time = LocalTime.of(14, 45);       // 14:45
time = time.withMinute(100);             // Out of range. DateTimeException.
time = time.withHour(25);                // Out of range. DateTimeException.

LocalDate date = LocalDate.of(2015, 4, 30);  // 2015-04-30
date = date.withMonth(13);               // Out of range. DateTimeException.
date = date.withDayOfMonth(31);          // Out of range for month. DateTimeException.
date = date.withDayOfYear(366);          // Out of range for year. DateTimeException.
```

The next code snippet illustrates how the `withYear()` and the `withMonth()` methods adjust the day of the month, if necessary, when the year or the month is changed, respectively. The year in the date 2016-02-29 is changed to 2017, resulting in the following date: 2017-02-29. Since the year 2017 is not a leap year, the month of February cannot have 29 days. The `withYear()` method adjusts the day of the month to the last valid day of the month, 28. Similarly, the month in the date 2015-03-31 is changed to 4 (i.e., April), resulting in the following date: 2015-04-31. Since the month April has 30 days, the `withMonth()` method adjusts the day of the month to the last valid day of the month, 30.

```
LocalDate date3 = LocalDate.of(2016, 2, 29);  // Original: 2016-02-29
date3 = date3.withYear(2017);                 // Expected: 2017-02-29
System.out.println("Date3: " + date3);        // Adjusted: 2017-02-28

LocalDate date4 = LocalDate.of(2015, 3, 31);  // Original: 2015-03-31
date4 = date4.withMonth(4);                   // Expected: 2015-04-31
System.out.println("Date4: " + date4);        // Adjusted: 2015-04-30
```

```
// LocalTime, LocalDateTime
LocalTime/LocalDateTime withHour(int hour)
LocalTime/LocalDateTime withMinute(int minute)
LocalTime/LocalDateTime withSecond(int second)
LocalTime/LocalDateTime withNano(int nanoOfSecond)
```

Returns a copy of this `LocalTime` or `LocalDateTime` with the appropriate time-based value changed to the specified value. A `DateTimeException` is thrown if the argument value is out of range.

```
// LocalDate, LocalDateTime
LocalDate/LocalDateTime withYear(int year)
LocalDate/LocalDateTime withMonth(int month)
LocalDate/LocalDateTime withDayOfMonth(int dayOfMonth)
LocalDate/LocalDateTime withDayOfYear(int dayOfYear)
```

Returns a copy of this `LocalDate` or `LocalDateTime` with the appropriate date-based value changed to the specified value. A `DateTimeException` is thrown, if the specified value is out of range or is invalid in combination with other time- or date-based values in the temporal object.

The first and second methods will adjust the day of the month to the *last valid day* of the month, if the day of month becomes invalid when the year or the month is changed (e.g., the month value 2 will change the date 2016-03-31 to 2016-02-29).

In contrast, the third method will throw a `DateTimeException` if the specified day of the month is invalid for the month-year combination (e.g., the day of month 29 is invalid for February 2015), as will the last method if the day of the year is invalid for the year (e.g., the day of year 366 is invalid for the year 2015).

Example 11.2 *Using Temporal Objects*

```
import java.time.DayOfWeek;
import java.time.LocalDate;
import java.time.LocalDateTime;
import java.time.LocalTime;
import java.time.Month;

public class UsingTemporals {

  public static void main(String[] args) {
    // Date-Time: 1945-08-06T08:15
    LocalDateTime doomsday = LocalDateTime.of(1945, 8, 6, 8, 15);
    LocalDate date = doomsday.toLocalDate();                    // 1945-08-06
    LocalTime time = doomsday.toLocalTime();                    // 08:15
    System.out.println("Date-Time: " + doomsday);

    // Time: 08:15
    int hour       = time.getHour();                            // 8
    int minute     = time.getMinute();                          // 15
    int second     = time.getSecond();                          // 0
    System.out.println("Time: " + time);
    System.out.println("Hour: " + hour);
    System.out.println("Min:  " + minute);
    System.out.println("Sec:  " + second);

    // Date: 1945-08-06
    int year       = date.getYear();                            // 1945
    int monthValue = date.getMonthValue();                      // 8
    Month month    = date.getMonth();                           // AUGUST
    DayOfWeek dow  = date.getDayOfWeek();                       // MONDAY
    int day        = date.getDayOfMonth();                      // 6
```

```
    System.out.println("Date:  " + date);
    System.out.println("Year:  " + year);
    System.out.println("Month value: " + monthValue);
    System.out.println("Month: " + month);
    System.out.println("DoW:   " + dow);
    System.out.println("DoM:   " + day);

    // Ordering
    LocalDate d1 = LocalDate.of(-1004, 3, 1);              // -1004-03-01
    LocalDate d2 = LocalDate.of(1004, 3, 1);               // 1004-03-01
    boolean result1 = d1.isBefore(d2);                     // true
    boolean result2 = d2.isAfter(d1);                      // true
    boolean result3 = d1.isAfter(d1);                      // false
    boolean result4 = d1.isEqual(d2);                      // false
    boolean result5 = d1.isEqual(d1);                      // true
    boolean result6 = d2.isLeapYear();                     // true

    System.out.println(d1 + " is before "   + d2 + ": " + result1);
    System.out.println(d2 + " is after "    + d1 + ": " + result2);
    System.out.println(d1 + " is after "    + d1 + ": " + result3);
    System.out.println(d1 + " is equal to " + d2 + ": " + result4);
    System.out.println(d1 + " is equal to " + d1 + ": " + result5);
    System.out.println(d2.getYear() + " is a leap year: " + result6);

    // Absolute adjusters:
    LocalDate date2 = LocalDate.of(2015, 3, 1);
    System.out.println("Date before adjusting: " + date2);   // 2015-03-01
    date2 = date2.withYear(2016).withMonth(2).withDayOfMonth(28);
    System.out.println("Date after adjusting:  " + date2);   // 2016-02-28
  }
}
```

Output from the program:

```
Date-Time: 1945-08-06T08:15
Time: 08:15
Hour: 8
Min:  15
Sec:  0
Date:  1945-08-06
Year:  1945
Month value: 8
Month: AUGUST
DoW:   MONDAY
DoM:   6
-1004-03-01 is before 1004-03-01: true
1004-03-01 is after -1004-03-01: true
-1004-03-01 is after -1004-03-01: false
-1004-03-01 is equal to 1004-03-01: false
-1004-03-01 is equal to -1004-03-01: true
1004 is a leap year: true
Date before adjusting: 2015-03-01
Date after adjusting:  2016-02-28
```

Temporal Arithmetic

The temporal classes provide *plus* and *minus* methods that return a copy of the original object that has been *incremented or decremented by a specific amount of time*—for example, by number of hours or by number of months.

The `LocalTime` and `LocalDate` classes provide `plus/minus` methods to increment/decrement a time or a date by a specific amount in terms of a *time unit* (for example, hours, minutes, and seconds) or a *date unit* (for example, years, months, and days), respectively. The `LocalDateTime` class provides `plus/minus` methods to increment/decrement a date-time by an amount that is specified in terms of either a time unit or a date unit. For example, the `plusMonths()` method in the `LocalDate` class returns a new `LocalDate` object after adding the specified number of months passed as an argument to the method. Similarly, the `minusMinutes()` method in the `LocalTime` class returns a new `LocalTime` object after subtracting the specified number of minutes passed as an argument to the method. The change is relative, and reflected in the new temporal object that is returned. Such `plus/minus` methods are also called *relative adjusters*, in contrast to *absolute adjusters* (p. 470).

Example 11.3 demonstrates what we can call *temporal arithmetic*, where a `LocalDate` object is modified by adding or subtracting an amount specified as days, weeks, or months. Note how the date-based values are adjusted after each operation. The date `2015-10-23` is created at (1), and 10 months, 3 weeks, and 40 days are successively added to the new date object returned by each `plus` method call at (2), (3), and (4), respectively, resulting in the date `2016-10-23`. We then subtract 2 days, 4 weeks, and 11 months successively from the new date object returned by each `minus` method call at (5), (6), and (7), respectively, resulting in the date `2015-10-23`. In Example 11.3, several assignment statements are used to print the intermediate dates, but the code can be made more compact by method chaining.

```
LocalDate date = LocalDate.of(2015, 10, 23);                    // 2015-10-23
date = date.plusMonths(10).plusWeeks(3).plusDays(40);           // Method chaining
System.out.println(date);                                       // 2016-10-23
date = date.minusDays(2).minusWeeks(4).minusMonths(11);         // Method chaining
System.out.println(date);                                       // 2015-10-23
```

The following code snippet illustrates the wrapping of time around midnight, as one would expect on a 24-hour clock. Each method call returns a new `LocalTime` object.

```
LocalTime witchingHour = LocalTime.MIDNIGHT                     // 00:00
    .plusHours(14)                                              // 14:00
    .plusMinutes(45)                                            // 14:45
    .plusMinutes(30)                                            // 15:15
    .minusHours(15)                                             // 00:15
    .minusMinutes(15);                                          // 00:00
```

The next code snippet illustrates how the `plusYears()` method adjusts the day of the month, if necessary, when the year value is changed. The year in the date 2016-02-29 is changed to 2017 by adding 1 year, resulting in the following date: 2017-02-29. The `plusYears()` method adjusts the day of the month to the last valid day of the month, 28; as the year 2017 is not a leap year, the month of February cannot have 29 days.

```
LocalDate date5 = LocalDate.of(2016, 2, 29);  // Original: 2016-02-29
date5 = date5.plusYears(1);                   // Expected: 2017-02-29
System.out.println("Date5: " + date5);        // Adjusted: 2017-02-28
```

```
// LocalTime, LocalDateTime
LocalTime/LocalDateTime minusHours/plusHours(long hours)
LocalTime/LocalDateTime minusMinutes/plusMinutes(long minutes)
LocalTime/LocalDateTime minusSeconds/plusSeconds(long seconds)
LocalTime/LocalDateTime minusNanos/plusNanos(long nanos)
```

These methods return a copy of this `LocalTime` or `LocalDateTime` object with the specified amount either subtracted or added to a specific time-based value. The calculation always wraps around midnight.

For the methods of the `LocalDateTime` class, a `DateTimeException` is thrown if the result exceeds the date range.

```
// LocalDate, LocalDateTime
LocalDate/LocalDateTime minusYears/plusYears(long years)
LocalDate/LocalDateTime minusMonths/plusMonths(long months)
LocalDate/LocalDateTime minusWeeks/plusWeeks(long weeks)
LocalDate/LocalDateTime minusDays/plusDays(long days)
```

These methods return a copy of this `LocalDate` or `LocalDateTime` with the specified amount either subtracted or added to a specific date-based value.

All methods throw a `DateTimeException` if the result exceeds the date range.

The first and second methods will change the day of the month to the *last valid day* of the month if necessary, when the day of month becomes invalid as a result of the operation.

The third and last methods will adjust the month and year fields as necessary to ensure a valid result.

Example 11.3 *Temporal Arithmetic*

```
import java.time.LocalDate;

public class TemporalArithmetic {

  public static void main(String[] args) {

    LocalDate date = LocalDate.of(2015, 10, 23);          // (1)
    System.out.println("Date:             " + date);       // 2015-10-23
    date = date.plusMonths(10);                            // (2)
    System.out.println("10 months after:  " + date);       // 2016-08-23
    date = date.plusWeeks(3);                              // (3)
    System.out.println("3 weeks after:    " + date);       // 2016-09-13
    date = date.plusDays(40);                              // (4)
    System.out.println("40 days after:    "+ date);        // 2016-10-23
```

```
        date = date.minusDays(2);                                    // (5)
        System.out.println("2 days before:     " + date);           // 2016-10-21
        date = date.minusWeeks(4);                                   // (6)
        System.out.println("4 weeks before:    " + date);           // 2016-09-23
        date = date.minusMonths(11);                                 // (7)
        System.out.println("11 months before: " + date);            // 2015-10-23
    }
}
```

Output from the program:

```
Date:             2015-10-23
10 months after:  2016-08-23
3 weeks after:    2016-09-13
40 days after:    2016-10-23
2 days before:    2016-10-21
4 weeks before:   2016-09-23
11 months before: 2015-10-23
```

11.3 Working with Periods

For representing *an amount of time*, the Date and Time API provides the two classes `Period` and `Duration`. We will briefly mention the `Duration` class, and concentrate on the `Period` class.

The `Duration` class models an amount of time in terms of seconds and nanoseconds, but a `Duration` object can also be accessed in terms of days, hours, and minutes. It essentially represents a *time-based amount of time*, whereas the `Period` class represents a *date-based amount of time* in terms of years, months, and days. The time-based `Duration` class can be used with the `LocalTime` class, and not surprisingly, the date-based `Period` class can be used with the `LocalDate` class. Of course, the `LocalDateTime` class can use both classes.

The `Period` class is in the same package (`java.time`) as the temporal classes, and its repertoire of methods should also look familiar, as it shares many of the method prefixes with the temporal classes (Table 11.1, p. 463).

The mantra of immutable and thread-safe objects also applies to the `Period` class.

Creating Periods

Like the temporal classes, the `Period` class does not provide any `public` constructors, but rather provides an overloaded static factory method `of()` to construct periods of different lengths, based on a date unit.

```
Period p = Period.of(2, 4, 8);              // (1)
System.out.println(p);                      // (2) P2Y4M8D (2 Years, 4 Months, 8 Days)
Period p1 = Period.ofYears(10);             // P10Y, period of 10 years.
Period p2 = Period.ofMonths(14);            // P14M, period of 14 months.
```

```
Period p3 = Period.ofDays(40);          // P40D, period of 40 days.
Period p4 = Period.ofWeeks(2);          // P14D, period of 14 days (2 weeks).
```

The most versatile of() method requires the amount of time for all date units: years, months, and days, as in (1). The toString() method of the Period class returns a textual representation of a Period object in the ISO standard. The output from (2), P2Y4M8D, indicates a period of 2 years, 4 months, and 8 days. Other of() methods create a period based on a particular date unit, as shown in the previous examples.

The next code snippet does *not* create a period of 3 years, 4 months, and 5 days. The first method call uses the class name, and the subsequent method calls use the Period object returned as a consequence of the previous call. The of() method creates a new Period object based on its argument.

```
Period period = Period.ofYears(3).ofMonths(4).ofDays(5);   // P5D. Logical error.
```

As we would expect, we can create a period that represents the amount of time between two dates by calling the static method between() of the Period class.

```
LocalDate d1 = LocalDate.of(2015, 3, 1); // 2015-03-01
LocalDate d2 = LocalDate.of(2016, 3, 1); // 2016-03-01
Period period12 = Period.between(d1, d2); // P1Y
Period period21 = Period.between(d2, d1); // P-1Y
```

The Period class also provides the static method parse() to create a period from a string that contains a textual representation of a period in the ISO standard. If the format is not correct, a java.time.format.DateTimeParseException is thrown.

```
Period period2 = Period.parse("P1Y15M20D"); // 1 year, 15 months, 20 days
Period period3 = Period.parse("P20D");      // 20 days
Period period4 = Period.parse("P5W");       // 35 days (5 weeks)
//  Period pX = Period.parse("P24H"); // java.time.format.DateTimeParseException
```

```
static Period of(int years, int months, int days)
static Period ofYears(int years)
static Period ofMonths(int months)
static Period ofWeeks(int weeks)
static Period ofDays(int days)
```

These static factory methods return a Period representing an amount of time equal to the specified value of a date unit. Date-based values implicitly implied are set to zero. A week is equal to 7 days. The argument value can be negative.

```
static Period between(LocalDate startDateInclusive,
                      LocalDate endDateExclusive)
```

This static method returns a Period consisting of the number of years, months, and days between two dates. The calculation excludes the end date.

```
static Period parse(CharSequence text)
```

This static method returns a Period parsed from a character sequence—for example, "P3Y10M2D" (3 years, 10 months, 2 days). A java.time.format.DateTimeParseException is thrown if the text cannot be parsed to a period.

Querying Periods

The Period class provides the obvious *get* methods to read the date-based parts of a Period object. The class also has methods to check if *any* date-based part of a period is negative or if *all* date-based parts of a period are zero.

```
Period period5 = Period.of(2, 4, -10);
System.out.println("Period: " + period5);                // Period: P2Y4M-10D
System.out.println("Years:  " + period5.getYears());     // Years:  2
System.out.println("Months: " + period5.getMonths());    // Months: 4
System.out.println("Days:   " + period5.getDays());      // Days:   -10
System.out.println("Total months: " + period5.toTotalMonths()); // 28 months
System.out.println(period5.isNegative());                // true
System.out.println(period5.isZero());                    // false
```

The class Period provides the method toTotalMonths() to derive the *total* number of months in a period. However, this calculation is solely based on the number of years and months in the period; the number of days is not considered. A Period just represents an amount of time, so it has no notion of a date. Conversion between months and years is not a problem, as 1 year is 12 months. However, conversion between the numbers of days and the other date units is problematic. The number of days in a year and in a month are very much dependent on whether the year is a leap year and on a particular month in the year, respectively. A Period is oblivious about both the year and the month in the year.

The Period class overrides the equals() method of the Object class. Each date-based part is compared individually, and must have the same value to be considered equal. A period of 1 year and 14 months is not equal to a period of 2 years and 2 months, or to a period of 26 months.

```
Period px = Period.of(1, 14, 0);
Period py = Period.of(2, 2, 0);
Period pz = Period.ofMonths(26);
System.out.println(px.equals(py));           // false
System.out.println(px.equals(pz));           // false
System.out.println(px.equals(Period.ZERO));  // false
```

```
int getYears()
int getMonths()
int getDays()
```

Returns the value of a specific date unit of this period.

```
boolean isNegative()
```

Determines whether any of the date-based values of this period are negative.

```
boolean isZero()
```

Determines whether all date-based values of this period are zero.

```
long toTotalMonths()
```

Returns the total number of months in this period, based on the years and the months value. The days value is not considered.

`boolean equals(Object obj)`

Determines whether this period is equal to another period, meaning that each date unit has the same value.

Creating Modified Copies of Periods

The `Period` class provides `with` methods to set a new value for each date unit individually, while the values of the other date units remain unchanged. Note that each method call returns a new `Period` object, and chaining method calls works as expected.

```
Period p5 = Period.of(2, 1, 30) // P2Y1M30D
    .withYears(3)               // P3Y1M30D, sets the number of years
    .withMonths(16)             // P3Y16M30D, sets the number of months
    .withDays(1);               // P3Y16M1D, sets the number of days
```

```
Period withYears(int years)
Period withMonths(int months)
Period withDays(int days)
```

Returns a copy of this period where a specific date unit is set to the value of the argument. The values of the other date units are not affected.

More Temporal Arithmetic

The `Period` class provides *plus* and *minus* methods that return a copy of the original object that has been *incremented or decremented by a specific amount* specified in terms of a date unit—for example, as a number of years, months, or days. As the next code snippet shows, only the value of a specific date unit is changed; the other date-based values are unaffected. There is no implicit normalization performed, unless the `normalized()` method is called. This method normalizes only the months, adjusting the values of the months and years as necessary.

```
Period p6 = Period.of(2, 10, 30)  // P2Y10M30D
    .plusDays(10)                 // P2Y10M40D
    .plusMonths(8)                // P2Y18M40D
    .plusYears(1)                 // P3Y18M40D
    .normalized();                // P4Y6M40D
```

We can do simple arithmetic with periods. The next code examples use the `plus()` and `minus()` methods of the `Period` class that take a `TemporalAmount` as an argument. Both the `Period` and the `Duration` classes implement the `TemporalAmount` interface. In the last assignment statement, we have shown the state of both new `Period` objects that are created.

```
Period p7 = Period.of(1, 1, 1);            // P1Y1M1D
Period p8 = Period.of(2, 12, 30);          // P2Y12M30D
Period p9 = p8.minus(p7);                  // P1Y11M29D
p8 = p8.plus(p7).plus(p8);                 // P3Y13M31D, P5Y25M61D
```

```
Period minusYears/plusYears(long years)
Period minusMonths/plusMonths(long months)
Period minusDays/plusDays(long days)
```

Returns a copy of this period, with the specified date-based value subtracted or added. The other date-based values are unaffected.

```
Period minus/plus(TemporalAmount amount)
```

Returns a copy of this period, with the specified amount subtracted or added. The amount is of the interface type `TemporalAmount` that is implemented by the classes `Period` and `Duration`. There is no normalization performed. A `DateTimeException` is thrown if the operation cannot be performed.

```
Period normalized()
```

Returns a copy of this period where the years and months are normalized. The number of days is not affected.

```
Period negated()
```

Returns a new instance of `Period` where each date-based value in this period is individually negated.

```
Period multipliedBy(int scalar)
```

Returns a new instance where each date-based value in this period is individually multiplied by the specified scalar.

We can also do simple arithmetic with dates and periods. The following code uses the `plus()` and `minus()` methods of the `LocalDate` class that take a `TemporalAmount` as an argument:

```
Period p10 = Period.of(1, 1, 1);                // P1Y1M1D
LocalDate date1 = LocalDate.of(2015, 4, 1);     // 2015-04-01
LocalDate date2 = date1.plus(p10);              // 2016-05-02
date1 = date1.minus(p10);                       // 2014-02-28
```

We can add and subtract periods from `LocalDate` and `LocalDateTime` objects, but not from `LocalTime` objects, as a `LocalTime` object has only time-based values.

```
LocalTime time = LocalTime.NOON;
time = time.plus(p10);      // java.time.temporal.UnsupportedTemporalTypeException
```

```
// LocalTime, LocalDate, LocalDateTime
TemporalType minus(TemporalAmount amount)
TemporalType plus(TemporalAmount amount)
```

Each temporal class provides these two methods, which return a copy of this temporal object with the specified amount either subtracted or added, where *TemporalType* is either `LocalTime`, `LocalDate`, or `LocalDateTime`.

The amount is of the interface type `TemporalAmount`, which is implemented by the classes `Period` and `Duration`.

Both methods throw a `DateTimeException` if the operation cannot be performed.

```
// LocalDate
Period until(ChronoLocalDate endDateExclusive)
```

This method calculates the amount of time between this date and another date as a `Period`. The calculation excludes the end date.

Example 11.4 is a simple example to illustrate implementing period-based loops. The method `reserveDates()` at (1) is a stub for reserving certain dates, depending on the period passed as an argument. The `for(;;)` loop at (2) uses the `LocalDate.isBefore()` method to terminate the loop, and the `LocalDate.plus()` method to increment the current date with the specified period.

Example 11.4 *Period-Based Loop*

```
import java.time.LocalDate;
import java.time.Period;

public class PeriodBasedLoop {
  public static void main(String[] args) {
    reserveDates(Period.ofDays(7),
                 LocalDate.of(2015, 10, 20), LocalDate.of(2015, 11, 20));
    System.out.println();
    reserveDates(Period.ofMonths(1),
                 LocalDate.of(2015, 10, 20), LocalDate.of(2016, 1, 20));
    System.out.println();
    reserveDates(Period.of(0, 1, 7),
                 LocalDate.of(2015, 10, 20), LocalDate.of(2016, 1, 21));
  }

  public static void reserveDates(Period period,                 // (1)
                                  LocalDate fromDate,
                                  LocalDate toDateExclusive) {
    System.out.println("Start date: " + fromDate);
    for (LocalDate date = fromDate.plus(period);                 // (2)
         date.isBefore(toDateExclusive);
         date = date.plus(period)) {
      System.out.println("Reserved (" + period + "): " + date);
    }
    System.out.println("End date: " + toDateExclusive);
  }
}
```

Output from the program:

```
Start date: 2015-10-20
Reserved (P7D): 2015-10-27
Reserved (P7D): 2015-11-03
Reserved (P7D): 2015-11-10
Reserved (P7D): 2015-11-17
End date: 2015-11-20

Start date: 2015-10-20
Reserved (P1M): 2015-11-20
Reserved (P1M): 2015-12-20
End date: 2016-01-20
```

```
Start date: 2015-10-20
Reserved (P1M7D): 2015-11-27
Reserved (P1M7D): 2016-01-03
End date: 2016-01-21
```

We conclude this section with Example 11.5, which brings together some of the methods of the Date and Time API. Given a date of birth, the method `birthdayInfo()` at (1) calculates the age and the time to next birthday. The age is calculated at (2) using the `Period.between()` method, which computes the period between two dates. The date for next birthday is set at (3) as the birth date with the current year. The `if` statement at (4) adjusts the next birthday date by 1 year at (5), if the birthday has already passed. The statement at (6) calculates the time until next birthday by calling the `LocalDate.until()` method. We could also have used the `Period.between()` method at (6). The choice between these methods really depends on which method makes the code more readable in a given context.

Example 11.5 *More Temporal Arithmetic*

```
import java.time.LocalDate;
import java.time.Month;
import java.time.Period;

public class ActYourAge {

  public static void main(String[] args) {
    birthdayInfo(LocalDate.of(1981, Month.AUGUST, 19));
    birthdayInfo(LocalDate.of(1935, Month.JANUARY, 8));
  }

  public static void birthdayInfo(LocalDate dateOfBirth) {          // (1)
    LocalDate today = LocalDate.now();
    System.out.println("Today:         " + today);

    System.out.println("Date of Birth: " + dateOfBirth);
    Period p1 = Period.between(dateOfBirth, today);                 // (2)
    System.out.println("Age:           " +
                                 p1.getYears()  + " years, " +
                                 p1.getMonths() + " months, and " +
                                 p1.getDays()   + " days");

    LocalDate nextBirthday =  dateOfBirth.withYear(today.getYear()); // (3)
    if (nextBirthday.isBefore(today) ||                              // (4)
        nextBirthday.isEqual(today)) {
      nextBirthday = nextBirthday.plusYears(1);                      // (5)
    }
    Period p2 = today.until(nextBirthday);                           // (6)
    System.out.println("Birthday in " + p2.getMonths() + " months and " +
                                        p2.getDays()   + " days");
  }
}
```

Possible output from the program:

```
Today:          2015-11-20
Date of Birth: 1981-08-19
Age:            34 years, 3 months, and 1 days
Birthday in 8 months and 30 days
Today:          2015-11-20
Date of Birth: 1935-01-08
Age:            80 years, 10 months, and 12 days
Birthday in 1 months and 19 days
```

Review Questions

11.1 Which statement is true about the Date and Time API?

Select the one correct answer.

(a) The classes LocalDate and LocalDateTime provide the isLeapYear() method to check for a leap year.
(b) The classes LocalTime, LocalDate, and LocalDateTime provide the isEqual() method to test whether two temporal objects of the same type are equal.
(c) The class Period provides the withWeeks() method, which returns a copy of this period, where the number of days is set according to the number of weeks specified.
(d) The classes LocalTime, LocalDate, and Period provide the plusWeeks() method, which returns a new object, where the number of days corresponding to the specified number of weeks has been added.
(e) None of the above.

11.2 What will the following program print when compiled and run?

```
import java.time.LocalDate;

public class RQ11A05 {
  public static void main(String[] args) {
    LocalDate date = LocalDate.of(2016, 3, 1);
    date.withMonth(4);
    System.out.println(date.getYear() + "|" +
                       date.getMonth() + "|" + date.getDayOfMonth());
  }
}
```

Select the one correct answer.

(a) The program will not compile.
(b) The program will throw a runtime exception when run.
(c) The program will print 2016|APRIL|1.
(d) The program will print 2016|4|1.
(e) The program will print 2016|MARCH|1.
(f) The program will print 2016|3|1.
(g) The program will print 2016|JULY|1.
(h) The program will print 2016|7|1.

11.3 Which declarations will correctly create the date 13 August 2009?

Select the four correct answers.

(a) `LocalDate date0 = LocalDate.of(2009, 7, 13);`
(b) `LocalDate date1 = LocalDate.of(2009, 8, 13);`
(c) `LocalDate date2 = LocalDate.of(2009, Month.AUGUST, 13);`
(d) `LocalDate date3 = LocalDate.of(0, 0, 0).withYear(2009).withMonth(8). withDayOfMonth(13);`
(e) `LocalDate date4 = LocalDate.of(2008, 7, 12).plusYears(1).plusMonths(1). plusDays(1);`
(f) `LocalDate date5 = new LocalDate(2009, 8, 13);`
(g) `LocalDate date6 = LocalDate.of(1, 1, 1).plus(Period.of(2008, 7, 12));`

11.4 Which declarations will correctly assign an instance of the `LocalTime` class to the declared reference?

Select the three correct answers.

(a) `LocalTime time1 = LocalTime.of(12, 60);`
(b) `LocalTime time2 = new LocalTime(12, 60);`
(c) `LocalTime time3 = LocalTime.NOON.plusHours(-3);`
(d) `LocalTime time4 = LocalTime.NOON.minusHours(12);`
(e) `LocalTime time5 = LocalTime.MIDNIGHT.withHours(12);`
(f) `LocalTime time6 = LocalTime.of(12,00).plusMinutes(-15);`

11.5 What will the following program print when compiled and run?

```
import java.time.LocalTime;

public class RQ11A20 {
  public static void main(String[] args) {
    LocalTime time = LocalTime.NOON;
    time = time.plusHours(10).plusMinutes(120);
    System.out.println(time);
  }
}
```

Select the one correct answer.

(a) The program will not compile.
(b) The program will throw a runtime exception when run.
(c) The program will print `00:00`.
(d) The program will print `24:00`.
(e) None of the above.

11.6 What will the following program print when compiled and run?

```
import java.time.Period;

public class RQ11A55 {
  public static void main(String[] args) {
    Period p1 = Period.of(1, 1, 1);
```

```
      Period p2 = Period.of(2, 12, 30);
      p1 = p1.plus(p2).plus(p1);
      System.out.println(p1);
    }
  }
```

Select the one correct answer.

(a) The program will not compile.
(b) The program will throw a runtime exception when run.
(c) The program will print P6Y26M62D.
(d) The program will print P4Y14M32D.
(e) None of the above.

11.7 What will the following program print when compiled and run?

```
import java.time.LocalDate;

public class RQ11A30 {
  public static void main(String[] args) {
    LocalDate date = LocalDate.of(2015, 1, 1);
    date = date.withYear(5).plusMonths(14);
    System.out.println(date);
  }
}
```

Select the one correct answer.

(a) The program will not compile.
(b) The program will throw a runtime exception when run.
(c) The program will print 0006-03-01.
(d) The program will print 2021-03-01.
(e) The program will print 0005-15-01.
(f) None of the above.

11.8 Which expressions, when inserted at (1), will result in the following output: date2 is after date1?

```
import java.time.LocalDate;
import java.time.Period;

public class RQ11A45 {
  public static void main(String[] args) {
    LocalDate date1 = LocalDate.of(2015, 8, 19);
    LocalDate date2 = LocalDate.of(2015, 10, 23);
    if ( /*(1) INSERT CODE HERE */ ) {
      System.out.println("date2 is after date1");
    }
  }
}
```

Select the five correct answers.

(a) `date2.isAfter(date1)`
(b) `date1.isAfter(date2)`
(c) `date2.isBefore(date1)`
(d) `date1.isBefore(date2)`
(e) `Period.between(date2, date1).isNegative()`
(f) `Period.between(date1, date2).isNegative()`
(g) `date2.until(date1).isNegative()`
(h) `date1.until(date2).isNegative()`
(i) `date1.compareTo(date2) < 0`
(j) `date2.compareTo(date1) < 0`

11.4 Formatting and Parsing

A *formatter* has two primary functions. The first is to create a human-readable textual representation of an object, a process called *formatting* an object. The second is to create an object from a string containing a textual representation of an object, which is the inverse of formatting. This process is called *parsing* a string.

In this section we take a closer look at formatting and parsing of temporal objects. In particular, we consider the following formatters, which provide increasing flexibility in customizing formatting and parsing of temporal objects:

- *Default formatters* are implicitly used by such methods as the `toString()` method of the temporal classes.
- *Predefined formatters* are ready-made formatters provided as constants by the `java.time.format.DateTimeFormatter` class, such as those that adhere to the ISO standard (Table 11.2, p. 489).
- *Localized formatters* are locale-sensitive formatters that use the format styles defined by the constants of the `java.time.format.FormatStyle` enum type (Table 11.3, p. 490). These formatters are created by the static factory methods `ofLocalized`*`Type`*`()` of the `DateTimeFormatter` class, where *`Type`* is either `Time`, `Date`, or `DateTime` (Table 11.4, p. 491).
- *Customized formatters* use customized format styles defined by *pattern letters* (Table 11.5, p. 496). These formatters are created by the static factory method `ofPattern()` of the `DateTimeFormatter` class.

The idiom for using a formatter is to obtain a formatter first, and then pass it to the methods responsible for formatting and parsing. The `DateTimeFormatter` class provides factory methods for obtaining a formatter. Each of the temporal classes `LocalTime`, `LocalDate`, and `LocalDateTime` provides the following methods: an instance method `format()` and a static method `parse()`. These two methods do the formatting and the parsing according to the rules of the formatter that is passed as argument, respectively. Analogous methods for formatting and parsing are also provided by the `DateTimeFormatter` class, but are not considered here.

It is again time to chant the mantra of immutability and thread-safety. Formatters supplied by the `DateTimeFormatter` class also subscribe to this creed. From the method headers of the `format()` and the `parse()` methods of the temporal classes, we can see that these methods will readily compile with *any* `DateTimeFormatter`. The validity of the formatter for a given temporal object is resolved at runtime, resulting in a resounding exception if it is not valid.

```
// LocalTime, LocalDate, LocalDateTime
String format(DateTimeFormatter formatter)
```

This method formats the temporal object using the specified formatter, and returns the resulting string. Each temporal class provides this method. The temporal object is formatted according to the rules of the formatter. The method throws a `java.time.DateTimeException` if formatting is unsuccessful.

```
// LocalTime, LocalDate, LocalDateTime
static TemporalType parse(CharSequence text)
static TemporalType parse(CharSequence text, DateTimeFormatter formatter)
```

Each temporal class provides these two static methods, where *`TemporalType`* can be any of the temporal classes `LocalTime`, `LocalDate`, or `LocalDateTime`.

The first method returns an instance of the *`TemporalType`* from a character sequence, using the default parsing rules for the *`TemporalType`*.

The second method obtains an instance of the *`TemporalType`* from a character sequence, using the specified formatter.

Both methods return an object of a specific temporal class, and both throw a `java.time.format.DateTimeParseException` if parsing is unsuccessful.

Default Formatters

So far in this chapter we have relied on the `toString()` method of the individual temporal classes for creating a textual representation of a temporal object. The default formatter used by the `toString()` method applies the formatting rules defined by the ISO standard. In the following code, the result of formatting a `LocalTime` object is shown at (1):

```
LocalTime time = LocalTime.of(12, 30, 15, 99);
String strTime = time.toString();                 // (1) 12:30:15.000000099
LocalTime parsedTime = LocalTime.parse(strTime);  // (2)
System.out.println(time.toString().equals(parsedTime.toString())); // true
```

Each temporal class provides a static method `parse(CharSequence text)` that parses a character sequence using a default formatter that complies with the ISO standard. In the preceding code, the textual representation created in (1) is parsed in (2) to obtain a new `LocalTime` object. Not surprisingly, the textual representations of the two `LocalTime` objects referred to by the references `time` and `parsedTime` are equal.

The next line of code shows that the argument string passed to the `parse()` method is not in accordance with the ISO standard, resulting in a runtime exception:

```
LocalTime badTime = LocalTime.parse("12.30.15");  // DateTimeParseException
```

Example 11.6 shows examples of formatting and parsing objects of the three temporal classes `LocalTime`, `LocalDate`, and `LocalDateTime`. It is worth studying the output from this example to familiarize yourself with the ISO standard for formatting temporal objects. To summarize, this standard is employed by the `toString()` and `parse(CharSequence text)` methods when formatting and parsing temporal objects, respectively.

Example 11.6 *Using Default Date and Time Formatters*

```
import java.time.LocalDate;
import java.time.LocalDateTime;
import java.time.LocalTime;

public class DefaultFormattingParsing {
  public static void main(String[] args) {

    System.out.printf("%70s%n", "Default formatting|Default parsing");
    // LocalTime
    LocalTime time = LocalTime.of(12, 30, 15, 99);
    String strTime = time.toString();                   // (1) 12:30:15.000000099
    LocalTime parsedTime = LocalTime.parse(strTime);  // (2)
    System.out.printf("LocalTime: %33s|%s%n", strTime, parsedTime);

    // LocalDate
    LocalDate date = LocalDate.of(2015, 4, 28);
    String strDate = date.toString();                        // 2015-04-28
    LocalDate parsedDate = LocalDate.parse(strDate);
    System.out.printf("LocalDate: %33s|%s%n", strDate, parsedDate);

    // LocalDateTime
    LocalDateTime dateTime = LocalDateTime.of(date, time);
    String strDateTime = dateTime.toString();   // 2015-04-28T12:30:15.000000099
    LocalDateTime parsedDateTime = LocalDateTime.parse(strDateTime);
    System.out.printf("LocalDateTime: %23s|%s%n", strDateTime, parsedDateTime);
  }
}
```

Output from the program:

```
                               Default formatting|Default parsing
LocalTime:                    12:30:15.000000099|12:30:15.000000099
LocalDate:                            2015-04-28|2015-04-28
LocalDateTime: 2015-04-28T12:30:15.000000099|2015-04-28T12:30:15.000000099
```

Predefined Formatters

The `DateTimeFormatter` class provides a myriad of predefined formatters for temporal objects, the majority of which comply with the ISO standard. Table 11.2 shows four ISO-based predefined formatters from this class. We have also indicated which temporal classes they can be used with for formatting and parsing; with certain classes, however, they can be used only for either formatting or parsing.

Table 11.2 *Selected ISO-Based Predefined Formatters for Date and Time*

DateTimeFormatter	Description	Examples	Used with: (*format time part, †format date part, ‡parse time part, §parse date part)
ISO_LOCAL_TIME	ISO local time	12:30:15	LocalTime LocalDateTime*
BASIC_ISO_DATE	Basic ISO date	20150428	LocalDate LocalDateTime†
ISO_LOCAL_DATE	ISO local date	2015-04-28	LocalDate LocalDateTime†
ISO_LOCAL_DATE_TIME	ISO local date-time	2015-04-28T12:30:15	LocalTime‡ LocalDate§ LocalDateTime

An example of using an ISO-based predefined formatter is given next. Note that the formatter obtained at (1) is a formatter for date-based values. It can be used only with temporal objects that have date-based values—in other words, the `LocalDate` and `LocalDateTime` classes. This formatter is passed at (2) to the `format()` method, to create a textual representation of a date. The resulting string is parsed at (3) by the `parse()` method that uses the same formatter. The resulting date is also formatted using the same formatter at (4). It is hardly surprising that the textual representations of both dates are equal.

```
DateTimeFormatter df = DateTimeFormatter.ISO_LOCAL_DATE;        // (1)
LocalDate date = LocalDate.of(1935, 1, 8);
String strDate = date.format(df);                               // (2) 1935-01-08
LocalDate parsedDate = LocalDate.parse(strDate, df);            // (3)
System.out.println(strDate + "|" +
                   parsedDate.format(df));              // (4) 1935-01-08|1935-01-08
```

As this code shows, a formatter can be reused, both for formatting and for parsing. The code at (4) in the next example applies the formatter from (1) in the preceding code snippet to format a `LocalDateTime` object. It should not come as a surprise that the resulting textual representation of the `LocalDateTime` object pertains to only date-based values in the object; the time-based values of the `LocalDateTime` object are ignored. Parsing this textual representation back with the same formatter at (5) will yield only a `LocalDate` object.

```
LocalDateTime dateTime = LocalDateTime.of(1935, 1, 8, 12, 45);
String strDate2 = dateTime.format(df);                          // (4) 1935-01-08
LocalDate parsedDate2 = LocalDate.parse(strDate2, df);          // (5) LocalDate
```

To summarize, the `DateTimeFormatter.ISO_LOCAL_DATE` can be used to format and parse a `LocalDate`, but can only format the date part of a `LocalDateTime` object.

Using this date-based formatter with a `LocalTime` object is courting disaster, as shown by the following code. Formatting with this formatter results in a java.time.temporal.UnsupportedTemporalTypeException, and parsing results in a java.time.format.DateTimeParseException.

```
String timeStr2 = LocalTime.NOON.format(df);   // UnsupportedTemporalTypeException
LocalTime time2 = LocalTime.parse("12:00", df);// DateTimeParseException
```

Localized Formatters

For more flexible formatters than the predefined ISO-based formatters, the DateTimeFormatter class provides the static factory methods ofLocalized*Type*(), where *Type* is either Time, Date, or DateTime. These methods create formatters that use a locale-specific format style. However, the format style cannot be changed after the formatter is created. Format styles are defined by the enum type java.time.format.FormatStyle, and are shown in Table 11.3. The styles define locale-specific format patterns that vary in their degree of verbosity.

```
static DateTimeFormatter ofLocalizedTime(FormatStyle timeStyle)
static DateTimeFormatter ofLocalizedDate(FormatStyle dateStyle)
static DateTimeFormatter ofLocalizedDateTime(FormatStyle dateTimeStyle)
static DateTimeFormatter ofLocalizedDateTime(FormatStyle dateStyle,
                                             FormatStyle timeStyle)
```

These static factory methods of the DateTimeFormatter create a locale-specific formatter that will format or parse a time, a date, or a date-time, respectively, using the specified format style.

Table 11.3 *Format Styles for Date and Time*

Styles for date/time	Verbosity	Examplel formatting a date (Default locale: United States)
FormatStyle.SHORT	Short-style pattern	1/11/14
FormatStyle.MEDIUM	Medium-style pattern	Jan 11, 2014
FormatStyle.LONG	Long-style pattern	January 11, 2014
FormatStyle.FULL	Full-style pattern	Saturday, January 11, 2014

In the code that follows, the date formatter created at (1) is used at (3) to parse the input string from (2).

```
DateTimeFormatter df = DateTimeFormatter.ofLocalizedDate(FormatStyle.SHORT);// (1)
String inputStr = "2/29/15";                                       // (2)
LocalDate date = LocalDate.parse(inputStr, df);                    // (3)
System.out.println(date.format(df));                               // (4) 2/28/15
System.out.println(date);                                          // (5) 2015-02-28
```

In this code, the input string "2/29/15" is specified in the short style of the default locale (which in our case is the United States). The input string is parsed by the date formatter (using the short format style) to create a new LocalDate object. Although the value 29 is invalid for the number of days in February for the year 2015, the output shows that it was adjusted correctly. The format style in the date formatter (in this case,

FormatStyle.SHORT) and the contents of the input string (in this case, "2/29/15") must be compatible. If this is not the case, a DateTimeParseException is thrown. The LocalDate object parsed from the input string is formatted at (4) using the same formatter. Note that in the print statement at (5), the LocalDate object from the parsing is converted to a string by the LocalDate.toString() method using the implicit ISO-based formatter.

Table 11.4 shows which temporal classes can be formatted and parsed by a combination of a format style from Table 11.3 and an ofLocalized*Type*() method of the DateTimeFormatter class, where *Type* is either Time, Date, or DateTime. The table also indicates that certain classes can only be either formatted or parsed, depending on the formatter returned by the method. For example, in Table 11.4 we can see that the method call DateTimeFormatter.ofLocalizedDate(FormatStyle.SHORT) will return a formatter that can be used to both format and parse instances of the LocalDate class, but it will only format the date part of a LocalDateTime object. This formatter will use the specified format style, FormatStyle.SHORT.

Example 11.7, Example 11.8, and Example 11.9 illustrate the use of the formatters supplied by the DateTimeFormatter class. It is recommended to study the output from these examples, together with Table 11.2, Table 11.3, and Table 11.4.

Table 11.4 *Combination of Format Styles and Localized Formatters*

Format-Style.	Factory methods of the DateTimeFormatter class for localized formatters		
	Example 11.7 ofLocalizedTime(style) **(*format time part)**	**Example 11.8** ofLocalizedDate(style) **(†format date part)**	**Example 11.9** ofLocalizedDateTime(style) **(‡parse time part, §parse date part)**
SHORT	LocalTime LocalDateTime*	LocalDate LocalDateTime†	LocalTime‡ LocalDate§ LocalDateTime
MEDIUM	LocalTime LocalDateTime*	LocalDate LocalDateTime†	LocalTime‡ LocalDate§ LocalDateTime
LONG	Requires time zone	LocalDate LocalDateTime†	Requires time zone
FULL	Requires time zone	LocalDate LocalDateTime†	Requires time zone

Example 11.7 illustrates formatters returned by the ofLocalizedTime() method (the second column in Table 11.4). Combinations of this method and valid format styles are created in a DateTimeFormatter array at (1). These formatters can be used to format and parse temporal objects comprising only time-based values (i.e., LocalTime objects), as shown at (4) and (5), respectively. In addition, these formatters can be used to format only the time part of a LocalDateTime object, as shown at (6). These formatters cannot be used for LocalDate objects, as they do not deal with date-based values.

Example 11.7 *Using Predefined Format Styles with Time-Based Values*

```
import java.time.DateTimeException;
import java.time.LocalDateTime;
import java.time.LocalTime;
import java.time.format.DateTimeFormatter;
import java.time.format.DateTimeParseException;
import java.time.format.FormatStyle;

public class FormattingParsingTime {
  public static void main(String[] args) {
    // Create some time formatters:
    DateTimeFormatter[] timeFormatters = {                               // (1)
        DateTimeFormatter.ISO_LOCAL_TIME,
        DateTimeFormatter.ofLocalizedTime(FormatStyle.SHORT),
        DateTimeFormatter.ofLocalizedTime(FormatStyle.MEDIUM),
//      The following two combinations result in a DateTimeException at runtime:
//      DateTimeFormatter.ofLocalizedTime(FormatStyle.LONG),
//      DateTimeFormatter.ofLocalizedTime(FormatStyle.FULL)
    };
    String[] formatStyles = {"ISO", "SHORT", "MEDIUM", "LONG", "FULL"};

    // Formatting and parsing a time:
    LocalTime time = LocalTime.of(14, 15, 30);                          // (2)
    LocalDateTime dateTime = LocalDateTime.of(2015, 12, 1, 14, 15, 30);  // (3)
    int i = 0;
    System.out.println("Style  Formatting of time, date-time | Parsing of time");
    for(DateTimeFormatter tf : timeFormatters)
      try {
        String strTime = time.format(tf);                             // (4)
        LocalTime parsedTime = LocalTime.parse(strTime, tf);          // (5)
        String strTime2 = dateTime.format(tf);                        // (6)
        System.out.printf("%-7s", formatStyles[i++]);
        System.out.printf("%14s| %14s| %14s%n",
                          strTime, strTime2, parsedTime.format(tf));
      } catch (DateTimeParseException pe) {
        System.out.println(pe);
        return;
      } catch (DateTimeException dte) {
        System.out.println(dte);
        return;
      }
  }
}
```

Output from the program (default locale is the United States):

```
Style  Formatting of time, date-time | Parsing of time
ISO          14:15:30|       14:15:30|       14:15:30
SHORT         2:15 PM|        2:15 PM|        2:15 PM
MEDIUM     2:15:30 PM|     2:15:30 PM|     2:15:30 PM
```

Example 11.8 illustrates formatters returned by the `ofLocalizedDate()` method (the third column in Table 11.4, p. 491). Combinations of this method and a valid format style are created in a `DateTimeFormatter` array at (1). These formatters can be used to format and parse temporal objects comprising only date-based values (i.e., `LocalDate` objects), as shown at (4) and (5), respectively. In addition, these formatters can be used to format only the date part of a `LocalDateTime` object, as shown at (6). These formatters cannot be used for `LocalTime` objects, as they do not deal with time-based values.

Example 11.8 *Using Predefined Format Styles with Date-Based Values*

```
import java.time.DateTimeException;
import java.time.LocalDate;
import java.time.LocalDateTime;
import java.time.format.DateTimeFormatter;
import java.time.format.DateTimeParseException;
import java.time.format.FormatStyle;

public class FormattingParsingDate {
  public static void main(String[] args) {
    // Create some date formatters:
    DateTimeFormatter[] dateFormatters =                        { // (1)
        DateTimeFormatter.BASIC_ISO_DATE,
        DateTimeFormatter.ISO_LOCAL_DATE,
        DateTimeFormatter.ofLocalizedDate(FormatStyle.SHORT),
        DateTimeFormatter.ofLocalizedDate(FormatStyle.MEDIUM),
        DateTimeFormatter.ofLocalizedDate(FormatStyle.LONG),
        DateTimeFormatter.ofLocalizedDate(FormatStyle.FULL)
    };
    String[] formatStyles = {"BASIC", "ISO", "SHORT", "MEDIUM", "LONG", "FULL"};

    // Formatting and parsing a date:
    LocalDate date = LocalDate.of(2015, 12, 1);                           // (2)
    LocalDateTime dateTime = LocalDateTime.of(2015, 12, 1, 14, 15, 30);   // (3)
    int i = 0;
    System.out.printf("%s%39s%30s%n", "Style", "Formatting of date, date-time",
                      "| Parsing of date");
    for(DateTimeFormatter df : dateFormatters)
      try {
        String strDate = date.format(df);                               // (4)
        LocalDate parsedDate = LocalDate.parse(strDate, df);            // (5)
        String strDate2 = dateTime.format(df);                          // (6)
        System.out.printf("%-6s", formatStyles[i++]);
        System.out.printf("%25s|%25s|%s%n",
                          strDate, strDate2, parsedDate.format(df));
      } catch (DateTimeParseException pe) {
        System.out.println(pe);
        return;
      } catch (DateTimeException dte) {
        System.out.println(dte);
        return;
      }
  }
}
```

Output from the program (default locale is the United States, output edited to fit on page):

```
Style      Formatting of date, date-time                  | Parsing of date
BASIC           20151201|                        20151201|20151201
ISO           2015-12-01|                      2015-12-01|2015-12-01
SHORT            12/1/15|                         12/1/15|12/1/15
MEDIUM       Dec 1, 2015|                     Dec 1, 2015|Dec 1, 2015
LONG    December 1, 2015|                December 1, 2015|December 1, 2015
FULL Tuesday, December 1, 2015|Tuesday, December 1, 2015|Tuesday, December 1, 2015
```

Example 11.9 illustrates formatters returned by the `ofLocalizedDateTime()` method (the fourth column in Table 11.4, p. 491). Combinations of this method and valid format styles are created in a `DateTimeFormatter` array at (1). These formatters can be used to format and parse temporal objects comprising both time-based and date-based values (i.e., `LocalDateTime` objects), as shown at (3) and (4), respectively. In addition, these formatters can be used to parse the time part or the date part of a date-time textual representation to obtain a `LocalTime` object or a `LocalDate` object, as shown at (5) and (6), respectively. These formatters cannot be used to format either a `LocalTime` object or a `LocalDate` object, as they require both time-based and date-based values when used for formatting.

Example 11.9 *Using Predefined Format Styles with Date and Time-Based Values*

```
import java.time.DateTimeException;
import java.time.LocalDate;
import java.time.LocalDateTime;
import java.time.LocalTime;
import java.time.format.DateTimeFormatter;
import java.time.format.DateTimeParseException;
import java.time.format.FormatStyle;

public class FormattingParsingDateTime {
  public static void main(String[] args) {
    // Create some date-time formatters:
    DateTimeFormatter[] dtFormatters =                          {        // (1)
        DateTimeFormatter.ISO_LOCAL_DATE_TIME,
        DateTimeFormatter.ofLocalizedDateTime(FormatStyle.SHORT),
        DateTimeFormatter.ofLocalizedDateTime(FormatStyle.MEDIUM),
        DateTimeFormatter.ofLocalizedDateTime(FormatStyle.MEDIUM,
                                              FormatStyle.SHORT),
        DateTimeFormatter.ofLocalizedDateTime(FormatStyle.SHORT,
                                              FormatStyle.MEDIUM),
//      The following two combinations result in a DateTimeException at runtime:
//      DateTimeFormatter.ofLocalizedDateTime(FormatStyle.LONG),
//      DateTimeFormatter.ofLocalizedDateTime(FormatStyle.FULL)
    };
    String[] formatStyles = {"ISO", "SHORT", "MEDIUM",
                             "MEDIUM,SHORT", "SHORT,MEDIUM"};
```

```
    // Formatting and parsing a date-time:
    LocalDateTime dateTime = LocalDateTime.of(2015, 12, 1, 14, 15, 30);   // (2)
    int i = 0;
    System.out.printf("%s%31s%38s%n", "Style", "Formatting of date-time|",
                      "Parsing of date-time, date, time");
    for(DateTimeFormatter dtf : dtFormatters)
      try {
        String strDateTime = dateTime.format(dtf);                        // (3)
        LocalDateTime parsedDateTime
                         = LocalDateTime.parse(strDateTime, dtf);  // (4)
        LocalTime parsedTime = LocalTime.parse(strDateTime, dtf);         // (5)
        LocalDate parsedDate = LocalDate.parse(strDateTime, dtf);         // (6)
        System.out.printf("%-12s", formatStyles[i++]);
        System.out.printf("%23s|%22s|%s|%8s%n", strDateTime,
                         parsedDateTime.format(dtf), parsedDate, parsedTime);
      } catch (DateTimeParseException pe) {
        System.out.println(pe);
        return;
      } catch (DateTimeException dte) {
        System.out.println(dte);
        return;
      }
  }
}
```

Output from the program (default locale is the United States):

```
Style        Formatting of date-time|      Parsing of date-time, date, time
ISO              2015-12-01T14:15:30|   2015-12-01T14:15:30|2015-12-01|14:15:30
SHORT                12/1/15 2:15 PM|         12/1/15 2:15 PM|2015-12-01|   14:15
MEDIUM         Dec 1, 2015 2:15:30 PM|Dec 1, 2015 2:15:30 PM|2015-12-01|14:15:30
MEDIUM,SHORT      Dec 1, 2015 2:15 PM|   Dec 1, 2015 2:15 PM|2015-12-01|   14:15
SHORT,MEDIUM       12/1/15 2:15:30 PM|      12/1/15 2:15:30 PM|2015-12-01|14:15:30
```

Customized Formatters

For more fine-grained formatting and parsing capabilities for date/time-based values, we can use the `ofPattern()` method of the `DateTimeFormatter` class. This method creates formatters that interpret date/time-based values according to a string pattern that is defined using the *pattern letters* shown in Table 11.5.

`static DateTimeFormatter ofPattern(String pattern)`

This static method creates a formatter using the specified pattern. The set of temporal objects it can be used with depends on the pattern letters used in the specification of the pattern. The letter pattern defines the rules used by the formatter. The method throws an `IllegalArgumentException` if the pattern is invalid.

Table 11.5 provides an overview of selected pattern letters. All letters are reserved when used in a letter pattern. A sequence of characters can be escaped by enclosing it in single quotes (e.g., `"EEEE 'at' HH:mm"`). Non-letter characters in the string are interpreted verbatim and need not be escaped using single quotes (e.g., `"uuuu.MM.dd @ HH:mm:ss"`). The number of times a pattern letter is repeated can have a bearing on the interpretation of the corresponding date/time-based value. The uppercase letter `M` (Month of the year) should not be confused with the lowercase letter `m` (minutes in the hour).

Table 11.5 *Selected Date/Time Pattern Letters*

Date or time component	Pattern letter	Examples

Year
(2: Two rightmost digits)
Proleptic year: use `u`
Year of era (AD/BC): use `y`
	`u`
	`uu`
	`uuu`
	`uuuu`
	`uuuuu`
		
		`2015; -2000 (2001 BC)`
		`15;    0` (i.e., 1 BC); `-1` (i.e., 2 BC)
		`2015; -2015` (i.e., 2016 BC)
		`02015 (padding)`

Month in year
(1–2: Number)
(3: Abbreviated text form)
(4: Full text form)
	`M`
	`MM`
	`MMM`
	`MMMM`
		`8`
		`08`
		`Aug`
		`August`

Day in month	`d` `dd`	`6` `06`

Day name in week
(1–3: Abbreviated text form)
(4: Full text form)
	`E`
	`EE`
	`EEE`
	`EEEE`
		`Tue`
		`Tue`
		`Tue`
		`Tuesday`

Hour in day (0–23)
Hour in am/pm (1–12)
(Does not include the AM/PM marker, but required for parsing)
	`H`
	`HH`
	`h`
	`hh`
		`9`
		`09`
		`7`
		`07`

Minute in hour (0–59)	`m` `mm`	`6` `06`
Second in minute (0–59)	`s` `ss`	`2` `02`

Fraction of a second (`S`)	`SSS`
	`SSSSSS`
	`SSSSSSSSS`
		`123`
		`123456`
		`123456789`

Era designator (AD/BC)	`G`	`AD`
AM/PM marker	`a`	`AM`
Escape for text	`'`	`'T'` prints as `T`
Single quote	`''`	`'`

A letter pattern can be used to format a temporal object if the temporal object has the temporal values required by the pattern. The pattern `"'Hour': HH"` can be used to format the hour part of any `LocalTime` object or a `LocalDateTime` object, but not a `LocalDate`.

A letter pattern can be used to parse a string if the string matches the pattern *and* the letter pattern specifies the mandatory parts needed to construct a temporal object. The pattern `"MM/dd/uuuu"` can be used to parse the string `"08/13/2009"` to obtain a `LocalDate` object, but not a `LocalDateTime` object. The latter requires the time part as well.

Example 11.10 demonstrates both formatting and parsing of temporal objects using letter patterns.

- The code at (1) and (2) demonstrates using a letter pattern for the time part to both format and parse a `LocalTime` object, respectively. The same pattern is used at (3) to format only the time part of a `LocalDateTime` object.
- The code at (4) and (5) demonstrates using a letter pattern for the date part to both format and parse a `LocalDate` object, respectively. The same pattern is used at (6) to format only the date part of a `LocalDateTime` object.
- The code at (7) and (8) demonstrates using a letter pattern for the date and time parts to both format and parse a `LocalDateTime` object, respectively. The same pattern is used at (9) and (10) to parse the textual representation of a `LocalDateTime` to obtain a `LocalDate` and a `LocalTime` object, respectively.

The usage of letter patterns with the `ofPattern()` method in Example 11.10 is analogous to the usage of the predefined format styles with the `ofLocalized`*`Type`*`()` methods (Table 11.4, p. 491). The main difference is that letter patterns provide great flexibility in creating customized format styles.

Example 11.10 *Formatting and Parsing with Letter Patterns*

```
import java.time.LocalDate;
import java.time.LocalDateTime;
import java.time.LocalTime;
import java.time.format.DateTimeFormatter;

public class FormattingParsingWithPatterns {
  public static void main(String[] args) {

    LocalTime time = LocalTime.of(12, 30, 15, 99);
    LocalDate date = LocalDate.of(2015, 4, 28);
    LocalDateTime dateTime = LocalDateTime.of(date, time);
    System.out.printf("Time : %s%n", time);
    System.out.printf("Date : %s%n", date);
    System.out.printf("DateTime : %s%n%n", dateTime);

    // Time part
    String timePattern = "HH::mm::ss:SSS";
    DateTimeFormatter timeFormatter = DateTimeFormatter.ofPattern(timePattern);
```

```
        String strTime = time.format(timeFormatter);                      // (1)
        LocalTime parsedTime = LocalTime.parse(strTime, timeFormatter);   // (2)
        String strTime2 = dateTime.format(timeFormatter);                 // (3)
        System.out.printf("Time pattern: %s%n", timePattern);
        System.out.printf("LocalTime: %s|%s%n",
                          strTime, parsedTime.format(timeFormatter));
        System.out.printf("LocalDateTime (formatted time part): %s%n%n", strTime2);

        // Date part
        String datePattern = "EEEE, uuuu/MMMM/dd";
        DateTimeFormatter dateFormatter = DateTimeFormatter.ofPattern(datePattern);
        String strDate = date.format(dateFormatter);                      // (4)
        LocalDate parsedDate = LocalDate.parse(strDate, dateFormatter);   // (5)
        String strDate2 = dateTime.format(dateFormatter);                 // (6)
        System.out.printf("Date pattern: %s%n", datePattern);
        System.out.printf("LocalDate: %s|%s%n",
                          strDate, parsedDate.format(dateFormatter));
        System.out.printf("LocalDateTime (formatted date part): %s%n%n", strDate2);

        // Date and time parts
        String dtPattern = "EE, HH::mm::ss 'on' uuuu/MM/dd";
        DateTimeFormatter dtFormatter = DateTimeFormatter.ofPattern(dtPattern);
        String strDateTime = dateTime.format(dtFormatter);                  // (7)
        LocalDateTime parsedDateTime = LocalDateTime.parse(strDateTime,     // (8)
                                                           dtFormatter);
        LocalDate parsedDate3 = LocalDate.parse(strDateTime, dtFormatter);  // (9)
        LocalTime parsedTime3 = LocalTime.parse(strDateTime, dtFormatter);  // (10)
        System.out.printf("DateTime pattern: %s%n", dtPattern);
        System.out.printf("LocalDateTime: %s|%s%n",
                          strDateTime, parsedDateTime.format(dtFormatter));
        System.out.printf("LocalDate (parsed date part): %s%n",
                          parsedDate3.format(dateFormatter));
        System.out.printf("LocalTime (parsed time part): %s%n",
                          parsedTime3.format(timeFormatter));
    }
}
```

Probable output from the program:

```
Time : 12:30:15.000000099
Date : 2015-04-28
DateTime : 2015-04-28T12:30:15.000000099

Time pattern: HH::mm::ss:SSS
LocalTime: 12::30::15:000|12::30::15:000
LocalDateTime (formatted time part): 12::30::15:000

Date pattern: EEEE, uuuu/MMMM/dd
LocalDate: Tuesday, 2015/April/28|Tuesday, 2015/April/28
LocalDateTime (formatted date part): Tuesday, 2015/April/28

DateTime pattern: EE, HH::mm::ss 'on' uuuu/MM/dd
LocalDateTime: Tue, 12::30::15 on 2015/04/28|Tue, 12::30::15 on 2015/04/28
LocalDate (parsed date part): Tuesday, 2015/April/28
LocalTime (parsed time part): 12::30::15:000
```

Example 11.11 demonstrates the versatility of letter patterns for formatting temporal objects. Note how a pattern can be used to format specific parts of a date-time, and how the interpretation of a pattern letter changes with the number of times it is repeated.

Example 11.11 *Formatting with Date/Time Letter Patterns*

```
import java.time.LocalDateTime;
import java.time.format.DateTimeFormatter;

public class DateTimeFormattingPatterns {
  static public void main(String[] args) {
    // DateTime to format.
    LocalDateTime dateTime = LocalDateTime.of(1972, 12, 2, 14, 45, 30);

    // Formatting patterns.
    String[] patterns = {
        "dd/MM/uu",
        "u/M/d",
        "d MMMM uuuu",
        "'Anniversary': d MMMM",
        "uuuu.MM.dd",
        "uuuu.MM.dd@hh:mm:ss",
        "uuuu.MMMM.dd hh:mm a",
        "EEE, MMM d'th', ''uu",
        "EEEE d MMMM uuuu",
        "EEE d MMM uuu",
        "EE d MM uu",
        "E d M u",
        "h:m a",
        "hh:mm",
        "HH:mm",
        "HH:mm:ss",
        "'Hour': HH",
        "EEE at hh:mm", // IllegalArgumentException - Unknown pattern letter: t
        "hh::mmm",      // IllegalArgumentException - Too many pattern letters: m
    };

    System.out.println("Formatting date/time (" + dateTime + ")" +
                       " according to different patterns:");
    for (String pattern : patterns) {
      String output;
      try {
        DateTimeFormatter formatter = DateTimeFormatter.ofPattern(pattern);
        output = dateTime.format(formatter);
      } catch (IllegalArgumentException e) {
        output = String.format("%s - %s", e.getClass().getSimpleName(),
                               e.getMessage());
      }
      System.out.printf("%25s  %s%n", pattern, output);
    }
  }
}
```

Probable output from the program (default locale is the United States):

```
Formatting date/time (1972-12-02T14:45:30) according to different patterns:
                   dd/MM/uu  02/12/72
                      u/M/d  1972/12/2
                d MMMM uuuu  2 December 1972
    'Anniversary': d MMMM  Anniversary: 2 December
                 uuuu.MM.dd  1972.12.02
       uuuu.MM.dd@hh:mm:ss  1972.12.02@02:45:30
       uuuu.MMMM.dd hh:mm a  1972.December.02 02:45 PM
      EEE, MMM d'th', ''uu  Sat, Dec 2th, '72
          EEEE d MMMM uuuu  Saturday 2 December 1972
             EEE d MMM uuu  Sat 2 Dec 1972
                EE d MM uu  Sat 2 12 72
                   E d M u  Sat 2 12 1972
                     h:m a  2:45 PM
                     hh:mm  02:45
                     HH:mm  14:45
                  HH:mm:ss  14:45:30
               'Hour': HH  Hour: 14
              EEE at hh:mm  IllegalArgumentException - Unknown pattern letter: t
                  hh::mmm  IllegalArgumentException - Too many pattern letters: m
```

Review Questions

11.9 Which statement is true about formatting and parsing of temporal objects?

Select the one correct answer.

(a) The `DateTimeFormatter` class provides only factory methods to obtain predefined formatters.

(b) The styles defined by the `java.time.format.FormatStyle` enum type are based on the ISO standard.

(c) The `ofLocalizedDate()` method of the `DateTimeFormatter` class returns a formatter that is based on a letter pattern passed as argument to the method.

(d) The pattern `"yy-mm-dd"` can be used to create a formatter that can format a `LocalDate` object.

(e) None of the above.

11.10 Which code, when inserted at (1), will make the program compile and execute normally?

```
import java.time.LocalDate;
import java.time.LocalDateTime;
import java.time.LocalTime;
import java.time.format.DateTimeFormatter;

public class RQ11A75 {
  public static void main(String[] args) {
    String pattern  = "MM/dd/yyyy 'at' HH:mm:ss";
    String inputStr = "02/29/2015 at 00:15:30";
    DateTimeFormatter dtf = DateTimeFormatter.ofPattern(pattern);
    // (1) INSERT CODE HERE.
  }
}
```

Select the four correct answers.

(a) `LocalTime time = LocalTime.parse(inputStr, dtf);`
(b) `LocalDate date = LocalDate.parse(inputStr, dtf);`
(c) `LocalDateTime dateTime = LocalDateTime.parse(inputStr, dtf);`
(d) `String timeStr = LocalTime.MIDNIGHT.format(dtf);`
(e) `String dateStr = LocalDate.of(2015, 12, 24).format(dtf);`
(f) `String dateTimeStr = LocalDateTime.of(2015, 12, 24, 0, 0).format(dtf);`

11.11 Which code, when inserted at (1), will make the program compile and execute normally?

```
import java.time.LocalDate;
import java.time.LocalDateTime;
import java.time.LocalTime;
import java.time.format.DateTimeFormatter;

public class RQ11A85 {
  public static void main(String[] args) {
    String pattern = "'Date:' dd|MM|yyyy";
    String inputStr = "Date: 02|12|2015";
    DateTimeFormatter dtf = DateTimeFormatter.ofPattern(pattern);
    // (1) INSERT CODE HERE.
  }
}
```

Select the three correct answers.

(a) `LocalTime time = LocalTime.parse(inputStr, dtf);`
(b) `LocalDate date = LocalDate.parse(inputStr, dtf);`
(c) `LocalDateTime dateTime = LocalDateTime.parse(inputStr, dtf);`
(d) `String timeStr = LocalTime.MIDNIGHT.format(dtf);`
(e) `String dateStr = LocalDate.of(2015, 12, 24).format(dtf);`
(f) `String dateTimeStr = LocalDateTime.of(2015, 12, 24, 0, 0).format(dtf);`

11.12 Which code, when inserted at (1), will result in the following output:

```
5 minutes past 9
import java.time.LocalTime;
import java.time.format.DateTimeFormatter;

public class RQ11A96 {
  public static void main(String[] args) {
    // (1) INSERT CODE HERE.

    String inputStr = "5 minutes past 9";
    DateTimeFormatter formatter = DateTimeFormatter.ofPattern(pattern);
    LocalTime time = LocalTime.parse(inputStr, formatter);
    System.out.println(time.format(formatter));
  }
}
```

Select the one correct answer.

(a) `String pattern = "m' minutes past 'h";`
(b) `String pattern = "M' minutes past 'h";`
(c) `String pattern = "m' minutes past 'ha";`
(d) `String pattern = "m' minutes past 'Ha";`
(e) `String pattern = "m' minutes past 'H";`
(f) `String pattern = "mm' minutes past 'H";`
(g) `String pattern = "M' minutes past 'H";`

11.13 Which code, when inserted at (1), will make the program compile and execute normally?

```
import java.time.LocalDate;
import java.time.LocalDateTime;
import java.time.LocalTime;
import java.time.format.DateTimeFormatter;
import java.time.format.FormatStyle;

public class RQ11A90 {
  public static void main(String[] args) {
    // (1) INSERT CODE HERE.

    String timeStr = LocalTime.NOON.format(dtf);
    String dateStr = LocalDate.of(2015, 12, 24).format(dtf);
    String dateTimeStr = LocalDateTime.of(2015, 12, 24, 12, 0).format(dtf);
  }
}
```

Select the one correct answer.

(a) `DateTimeFormatter dtf =`
`DateTimeFormatter.ofLocalizedTime(FormatStyle.SHORT);`
(b) `DateTimeFormatter dtf =`
`DateTimeFormatter.ofLocalizedDate(FormatStyle.SHORT);`
(c) `DateTimeFormatter dtf =`
`DateTimeFormatter.ofLocalizedDateTime(FormatStyle.SHORT);`
(d) None of the above.

Chapter Summary

The following topics were covered in this chapter:

- An overview of classes in the `java.time` package that represent a point in time: a (clock) time (`LocalTime`), a date (`LocalDate`), a date-time combination (`LocalDateTime`), and a class that represents an amount of time in years, months, and days (`Period`).
- The consequences of immutability for objects that represent temporal concepts
- The naming conventions used for methods in the temporal classes that facilitate their usage
- Creating, querying, converting, and comparing temporal objects

- Writing code to do temporal arithmetic
- Formatting and parsing using default formatters
- Formatting and parsing using ISO-based predefined formatters of the `DateTimeFormatter` class
- Formatting and parsing using localized formatters that are based on the predefined format styles defined by the `java.time.format.FormatStyle` enum type
- Formatting and parsing using customized formatters that are based on letter patterns
- The exceptions thrown when formatting and parsing temporal objects

Programming Exercise

11.1 Print statistics about astronauts who have stayed on a space station.

Skeleton code for the problem is provided in this exercise. The class `Astronaut` represents statistics about an astronaut:

- The name of the astronaut (`astronautName`)
- The date and time when the astronaut arrived at the space station (`arrivalDateTime`)
- The scheduled date of return to Earth for the astronaut (`scheduledReturnDate`)
- The actual period of stay at the space station (`actualPeriodOfStay`), which can be longer or shorter than the scheduled length of stay

The program should print the following report:

```
Name              Arr.Date   Sched.Return Act.Return  Status Act.Stay Sched.Stay Diff
Astro Ali        2010/03/01  2010/05/01  2010/06/01 Delayed    P3M        P2M     P1M
Laila Lightyear  2015/02/01  2015/06/30  2015/08/30 Delayed  P210D     P4M29D     P2M
Orbit Orwell     2014/03/01  2014/09/01  2014/09/01 On time    P6M        P6M     P0D
Rocket Rogers    2013/07/31  2013/09/30  2013/09/29   Early   P60D     P1M30D    P-1D
Sam Spacey       2009/01/01  2009/11/01  2009/04/01   Early   P90D       P10M    P-7M
```

Each row contains the name (`Name` column), the arrival date at the space station (`Arr.Date` column), and the scheduled return date (`Sched.Return` column) for each astronaut. In addition, each row contains the actual date of return (`Act.Return` column) determined by the actual length of stay (`Act.Stay` column); whether the astronaut was `Delayed`, `On time`, or `Early` in returning to Earth (`Status` column); the scheduled length of stay that was originally planned (`Sched.Stay` column); and the difference between the scheduled return date and the actual return date (`Diff` column).

Further information is provided in the documentation included in the code. Implement the four methods (`getActualReturnDate()`, `getReturnStatus()`, `getPlannedPeriodOfStay()`, `getDiffPeriodOfStay()`) of the `Astronaut` class, and complete the implementation of the `printReport()` method in the `SpaceStationStats` class.

```
import java.time.LocalDate;
import java.time.LocalDateTime;
import java.time.Period;

/** Class represents statistics about an astronaut. */
public class Astronaut {

  private final String        astronautName;
  private final LocalDateTime arrivalDateTime;
  private final LocalDate     scheduledReturnDate;
  private final Period        actualPeriodOfStay;

  public Astronaut(String name, LocalDateTime arrival, Period period,
                   LocalDate returnDate) {
    astronautName = name;
    arrivalDateTime = arrival;
    actualPeriodOfStay = period;
    scheduledReturnDate = returnDate;
  }

  public String getAstronautName()            { return astronautName; }
  public LocalDateTime getArrivalDateTime() { return arrivalDateTime; }
  public Period getActualPeriodOfStay()      { return actualPeriodOfStay; }
  public LocalDate getScheduledReturnDate() { return scheduledReturnDate; }

  /** @return LocalDate The actual date of return. */
  public LocalDate getActualReturnDate() {
    /* IMPLEMENT THIS METHOD. */
  }

  /**
   * Returns status of the actual return compared to the scheduled return,
   * whether it was on time, delayed, or early.
   * @return String Indicating "On time", "Delayed", or "Early".
   */
  public String getReturnStatus() {
    /* IMPLEMENT THIS METHOD. */
  }

  /** @return Period The planned stay according to the scheduled return.*/
  public Period getPlannedPeriodOfStay() {
    /* IMPLEMENT THIS METHOD. */
  }

  /**
   * @return Period The difference between the actual return date and
   *                the scheduled return date. */
  public Period getDiffPeriodOfStay() {
    /* IMPLEMENT THIS METHOD. */
  }
}
```

```
import java.time.LocalDate;
import java.time.LocalDateTime;
import java.time.Period;
import java.time.format.DateTimeFormatter;

public class SpaceStationStats {

  public static void main(String[] args) {
    // Astronaut data
    Astronaut[] astronauts = {
        new Astronaut("Astro Ali",
            LocalDateTime.of(2010, 3, 1, 10, 45), Period.ofMonths(3),
            LocalDate.of(2010, 5, 1)),
        new Astronaut("Laila Lightyear",
            LocalDateTime.of(2015, 2, 1, 17, 0),  Period.ofWeeks(30),
            LocalDate.of(2015, 6, 30)),
        new Astronaut("Orbit Orwell",
            LocalDateTime.of(2014, 3, 1, 20, 20), Period.ofMonths(6),
            LocalDate.of(2014, 9, 1)),
        new Astronaut("Rocket Rogers",
            LocalDateTime.of(2013, 7, 31, 15, 30), Period.ofDays(60),
            LocalDate.of(2013, 9, 30)),
        new Astronaut("Sam Spacey",
            LocalDateTime.of(2009, 1, 1, 12, 15), Period.ofDays(90),
            LocalDate.of(2009, 11, 1)),
    };
    printReport(astronauts);
  }

  /**
   * Method prints statistics about stay on a space station.
   * See the exercise text for the format of the report.
   * @param astronauts The array with astronaut data
   */
  private static void printReport(Astronaut[] astronauts) {
    System.out.println("Name            Arr.Date  Sched.Return"
                     + " Act.Return  Status Act.Stay Sched.Stay Diff");
    String reportFormatStr = "%-16s%10s%12s%12s%8s%6s%10s%9s%n";
    /* IMPLEMENT THE REST OF THE METHOD. */
  }
}
```

Appendix A

Taking the Java SE 8 Programmer I Exam

Please note that all information presented in this appendix was valid as of January 2016. It is imperative to visit the websites mentioned in this appendix regularly, as Oracle is known to change the practical information about the exam and the exam objectives intermittently.

The primary focus of this book is the *Java SE 8 Programmer I Exam* (*1Z0-808*) required to qualify as an *Oracle Certified Associate (OCA), Java SE 8 Programmer* (OCAJP8). Pertinent information about this exam can be found here:

```
http://education.oracle.com/pls/web_prod-plq-dad/db_pages.get-
page?page_id=5001&get_params=p_exam_id:1Z0-808
```

This exam is the first of two required to obtain *Oracle Certified Professional (OCP), Java SE 8 Programmer Certification* (OCPJP8). The second exam required for this professional certification is the *Java SE 8 Programmer II Exam* (*1Z0-809*). We will not go into the details about the second exam in this appendix, but more information about the second exam can be found here:

```
https://education.oracle.com/pls/web_prod-plq-dad/db_pages.get-
page?page_id=5001&get_params=p_exam_id:1Z0-809
```

For authoritative information about the certification path for Java SE, consult the following web page:

```
https://education.oracle.com/pls/web_prod-plq-dad/db_pages.get-
page?page_id=653&get_params=p_id:357#tabs-1-1
```

Appendix B contains specific information about the exam objectives for the *Java SE 8 Programmer I* exam.

A.1 Preparing for the Exam

The goal of the exam is to test practical knowledge and usage of the Java programming language. The exam requires thorough understanding of both the syntax and the semantics of the language. The exam covers a wide variety of topics, as defined in the objectives for the exam (Appendix B). Central to the exam is language constructs, usage of the core API, and specific topics, with heavy emphasis on interpreting code scenarios.

The need for real-world experience prior to taking the exam cannot be stressed enough. It requires very thorough preparation to pass the exam without having some actual experience programming in Java. Simply reading straight through this book is not recommended. Readers should take time to try out what they have learned along every step of the way. Readers are encouraged to test their newly acquired knowledge using the review questions provided after every major topic.

Experimenting with the examples and working through the programming exercises in this book will serve to give the reader a much better chance of passing the exam. Numbered examples in the book are complete Java programs, the source code for which is available from the book website. Whether one uses the tools in the JDK or an IDE (integrated development environment), it is the hands-on programming that is important. Tools in the JDK are to be preferred as preparation for the exam, as there is less reliance on programming support provided by an IDE.

When the reader feels ready, she should test her skills on the mock exam provided in Appendix E. This will give an indication of how well the reader is prepared for the exam, and which topics need further study. The structure of the book should make it easy for the reader to focus on single topics, if necessary.

The exam is considered to be difficult, and requires a fair amount of studying on the part of the candidate. Even seasoned Java programmers should invest some time in preparing for the exam. Simply having real-world experience is also not enough to pass the exam.

Devising a study plan is highly recommended, incorporating the activities we mentioned previously. Disruptions in the study plan should be avoid, as this can result in revising the material already covered when you pick up the thread. The exam should be scheduled immediately after the study period, when the momentum from the preparation is at its maximum.

We also highly recommend joining an online Java certification community, such as CodeRanch (`www.coderanch.com`), which has dedicated active forums for the different Java certifications. All things Java are discussed in a friendly manner around the bonfire at this ranch, where greenhorns are specially welcome. The forum for OCAJP can be found here:

```
www.coderanch.com/forums/f-117/ocajp
```

A.2 Registering for the Exam

The website for the exam provides all the relevant information on the procedure for registering, paying, and scheduling the exam.

It is a good idea to have an Oracle web account and authenticate the account in the CertView certification portal, where the exam results will be made available. These steps can be accomplished at `certview.oracle.com`.

Contact Information

Both Oracle and Pearson VUE have offices and associates around the world that can provide information about the exam. They can be contacted to purchase a voucher for the exam before signing up for the test at a local testing center.

The best way to find contact information and local testing centers is to visit their websites.

Oracle University

`http://education.oracle.com/`

Pearson VUE

`http://pearsonvue.com/oracle/`

Obtaining an Exam Voucher

Exam vouchers are sold by Oracle and Pearson VUE. Be sure to obtain the correct voucher for the exam. Credit card information is required to arrange payment. The cost of the voucher may vary depending on the country you live in. For U.S. residents, it cost $245 at the time of this book's writing.

Note that the voucher has an expiration date, usually 6 months after it is acquired. Neither Oracle nor Pearson VUE will replace lost or expired vouchers, nor will they offer refunds for unused vouchers.

Signing Up for the Test

After obtaining the exam voucher, Pearson VUE can be contacted to sign up for the test by making an appointment at one of the local testing centers. The exam can be rescheduled without penalty up to 24 hours before the appointment time.

After Taking the Exam

The candidate will immediately receive an email from Oracle informing her that the exam results are available in CertView. On passing the exam, the candidate will receive an email informing her that an eCertificate is available in CertView. Instructions for requesting a printed copy of the certificate are included in this email.

A candidate who fails the exam can register to retake the exam after a 14-day waiting period.

A.3 How the Exam Is Conducted

The Testing Locations

To be on the safe side, a candidate should bring two forms of ID on the day of the exam. When a candidate shows up at the local testing center at the appointed time, she will be escorted to her own little cubicle with a desktop computer. The test will be conducted in this cubicle, using a testing program on the computer. The program will ask questions, record answers, and tabulate scores.

Candidates will not be allowed to bring any personal belongings or food with them to the cubicle. A candidate will be provided with either erasable or nonerasable boards. During the exam, candidates can use the board to make notes, but they will not be allowed to take anything with them after the exam. Quite often the exam area is fitted with security cameras.

Utilizing the Allotted Time

The exam consists of a fixed number of questions that must be answered within the allocated time. Some of these questions may be unscored, meaning they do not contribute to the final score, whether they are answered correctly or not. There is also no way to distinguish whether a question is scored or unscored on the exam.

The questions vary in difficulty. Some are easy and some are difficult. With limited time to answer each question, the candidate cannot afford to get stuck on the hard questions. If the answer does not become apparent within a reasonable time, it is advisable to move on to the next question. Time permitting, it is possible to return to the unanswered questions later. It is important to answer *all* question. A wrong answer and a blank answer carry the same penalty: loss of points. Therefore it is better to guess an answer than to leave it blank, and hope that the guess is right. The process of elimination can sometimes be useful in narrowing down the answer to a question. Eliminating obvious incorrect choices increases the chances of arriving at the right answer.

An experienced Java programmer used to taking exams should be able to complete the exam within the allotted time. Any remaining time is best used in reviewing the answers.

The Exam Program

The computer program used to conduct the exam will select a set of questions at random, and present them through a graphical user interface. The interface is designed in such a way that candidates are able to move back and forth through the questions for reviewing purposes. Questions can be temporarily left unanswered, and the candidate can return to them later. Questions can also be marked for review at the end of the exam.

Before the exam starts, the candidate is allowed a test run with the computer program. A demo test that has nothing to do with the Java exam is used. Its sole purpose is to acquaint the candidate with the program being used to conduct the exam.

The Exam Result

After taking the exam, the candidate should log on to the CertView certification portal to see the result. The candidate will be presented with the following information:

- An indication of whether the candidate passed or failed.
- The total score. Only the scored questions on the exam contribute to the final score. All the scored questions are weighted equally, and the score is calculated based on the percentage of correct answers. No credit is given for partially correct answers for the scored questions.
- Indications on how well the candidate did on each of the categories of the objectives. Candidates who fail the exam should pay close attention to this information. If the candidate is planning to retake the exam, it may give a good indication of which topics need closer attention.

The result will not divulge which questions were answered correctly.

A.4 The Questions

Assumptions about the Exam Questions

The website for the *Java SE 8 Programmer I Exam* lists certain assumptions about the exam questions. In the following list, we provide a short explanation of these assumptions.

- *Missing package and import statements*

  Unless explicitly provided, stated, or referred to in the question, assume that the code is in the same package and all necessary import statements are given.

- *No file or directory path names for classes*

  In this case, assume that either all classes are in the same file or each class is in a separate file and these files are in the same directory.

- *Unintended line breaks*

  Line breaks that make the code lines appear to be wrapped unintentionally should be ignored, and the code assumed to compile without errors.

- *Code fragments*

  Assume that the necessary context exists to compile and execute the code, if such context is not explicitly specified by the question.

- *Descriptive comments*

  Such comments should be taken at their face value, providing the intent described in the comment.

Types of Questions Asked

Most of the questions follow a common format that requires candidates to apply their knowledge in a special way.

- Analyzing program code. The question provides a source code snippet, and asks a specific question pertaining to the snippet. Will running the program provide the expected result? What will be written to the standard output when the program is run? Will the code compile?
- Identifying true or false statements.

When analyzing program code, it is useful to try to apply the same rules as the compiler: examining the exact syntax used, rather than making assumptions on what the code tries to accomplish.

The wording of the questions is precise, and the responses selected in multiple-choice questions are likewise expected to be precise. This often causes the test to be perceived as fastidious. Close attention should be paid to the wording of the responses in a multiple-choice question.

None of the questions is intentionally meant to be a trick question. Exam questions have been reviewed by both Java experts and language experts to remove as much ambiguity from their wording as possible.

Since the program used in the exam will select and present the questions in a random fashion, there is no point in trying to guess the form of the questions. The order of the answers in multiple-choice questions has been randomized and, therefore, has no significance.

Types of Answers Expected

All exam questions are multiple choice. The correct number of alternatives to select is designated in the question, and all must be selected for the question as a whole to be considered correctly answered.

There should be no problem identifying which form of answer each question requires. The wording of the questions will indicate this, and the software used will present the candidate with an input method corresponding to the form of answer expected.

For multiple-choice questions, the program will ask the candidate to select a specific number of answers from a list. Where a single correct answer is expected, radio buttons will allow the selection of only one answer. The most appropriate response should be selected.

In questions where all appropriate responses should be selected, check boxes will allow the selection of each response individually. In this case, all choices should be considered on their own merits; that is, responses should not be weighed against each other. It can be helpful to think of each of the choices as an individual true–false question.

Topics Covered by the Questions

Topics covered by the exam are basically derived from the set of exam objectives defined by Oracle. The objectives for the *Java SE 8 Programmer I* exam are included in Appendix B, with references to where the topics are covered in the book.

The ultimate goal of an exam is to distinguish experienced Java programmers from the rest. To this end, some of the questions are aimed at topics that new Java programmers usually find difficult. Such topics include:

- Casting and conversion
- Polymorphism, overriding, and overloading
- Exception handling with `try-catch-finally` blocks

Knowledge obtained from studying other languages such as C++ should be used with care. Some of the questions often seem to lead astray C++ programmers who have not grasped the many differences between C++ and Java. Those with a C++ background should pay special attention to the following Java topics:

- Using `null`, not `NULL`
- Using `true` and `false`, not `1` and `0`
- Widening conversions
- Conditional and boolean logic operators
- Accessibility rules
- Polymorphism

Some of the questions may require intimate knowledge of the core Java API. This book covers the most important classes and methods of the Java SE platform API, but it does not go as far as listing every member of every class. The Java SE platform API documentation should be consulted. It is essential that readers familiarize themselves with the relevant parts of the API documentation.

Appendix B

Exam Topics: Java SE 8 Programmer I

Please note that all information presented in this appendix was valid as of January 2016. It is imperative to visit the exam website mentioned in this appendix regularly while you are preparing for the exam, as Oracle is known to change the exam objectives intermittently.

Exam Name: *Java SE 8 Programmer I*	Duration: *150 minutes*
Exam Number: *1Z0-808*	Number of Questions: *77*
Associated Certification: *Oracle Certified Associate, Java SE 8 Programmer*	Passing Score: *65%*
	Exam Price: *$245*

The *Java SE 8 Programmer I* exam is required to qualify as *Oracle Certified Associate, Java SE 8 Programmer* (OCAJP8). Pertinent information about this exam can be found at:

```
http://education.oracle.com/pls/web_prod-plq-dad/
db_pages.getpage?page_id=5001&get_params=p_exam_id:1Z0-808
```

The web page also provides links to the exam topics defined by Oracle. The topics are organized in *sections*, and each section is *reproduced verbatim* in this appendix. For each section, we have provided references to where in the book the exam topics in the section are covered. In addition, the extensive index at the end of the book can be used to look up specific topics.

General information about taking the exam can be found in Appendix A. Oracle has also specified certain important assumptions about the exam questions, which can found in Appendix A, p. 511.

Section 1: Java Basics	
[1.1] Define the scope of variables	*§2.4, p. 44* *§4.4, p. 114*
[1.2] Define the structure of a Java class	*§1.2, p. 2* *§3.1, p. 48*
[1.3] Create executable Java applications with a main method; run a Java program from the command line; including console output	*§1.10, p. 16* *§4.3, p. 107*
[1.4] Import other Java packages to make them accessible in your code	*§4.2, p. 97*
[1.5] Compare and contrast the features and components of Java such as: platform independence, object orientation, encapsulation, etc.	*§1.12, p. 21*
Section 2: Working with Java Data Types	
[2.1] Declare and initialize variables (including casting of primitive data types)	*§2.3, p. 40* *§2.4, p. 42* *§5.6, p. 158*
[2.2] Differentiate between object reference variables and primitive variables	*§2.3, p. 40*
[2.3] Know how to read or write to object fields	*§1.3, p. 4*
[2.4] Explain an Object's Lifecycle (creation, "dereference by reassignment" and garbage collection)	*§9.1, p. 384* *§9.2, p. 384* *§9.3, p. 386*
[2.5] Develop code that uses wrapper classes such as Boolean, Double, and Integer	*§8.3, p. 346*
Section 3: Using Operators and Decision Constructs	
[3.1] Use Java operators; including parentheses to override operator precedence	*§5.3, p. 150* *§5.4, p. 152* *§5.6–§5.17, p. 158*
[3.2] Test equality between Strings and other objects using == and equals()	*§5.12, p. 181* *§8.4, p. 357* *§8.4, p. 363*
[3.3] Create if and if/else and ternary constructs	*§5.16, p. 194* *§6.2, p. 200*
[3.4] Use a switch statement	*§6.2, p. 203*

Section 4: Creating and Using Arrays	
[4.1] Declare, instantiate, initialize, and use a one-dimensional array	§3.4, p. 58
[4.2] Declare, instantiate, initialize, and use multi-dimensional array	§3.4, p. 64

Section 5: Using Loop Constructs	
[5.1] Create and use while loops	§6.3, p. 213
[5.2] Create and use for loops including the enhanced for loop	§6.3, p. 215 §6.3, p. 217
[5.3] Create and use do/while loops	§6.3, p. 214
[5.4] Compare loop constructs	§6.3, p. 213
[5.5] Use break and continue	§6.4, p. 219

Section 6: Working with Methods and Encapsulation	
[6.1] Create methods with arguments and return values; including overloaded methods	§3.2, p. 49 §3.5, p. 72 §6.4, p. 224 §7.2, p. 273
[6.2] Apply the static keyword to methods and fields	§4.8, p. 132
[6.3] Create and overload constructors; including impact on default constructors	§3.3, p. 53
[6.4] Apply access modifiers	§4.5, p. 118 §4.7, p. 123
[6.5] Apply encapsulation principles to a class	§7.14, p. 334
[6.6] Determine the effect upon object references and primitive values when they are passed into methods that change the values	§3.5, p. 72 §5.2, p. 147

Section 7: Working with Inheritance		
[7.1]	Describe inheritance and its benefits	*§7.1, p. 264* *§7.13, p. 331*
[7.2]	Develop code that demonstrates the use of polymorphism; including overriding and object type versus reference type	*§7.2, p. 268* *§7.12, p. 329*
[7.3]	Determine when casting is necessary	*§7.11, p. 320*
[7.4]	Use super and this to access objects and constructors	*§3.2, p. 50* *§7.4, p. 276* *§7.5, p. 282*
[7.5]	Use abstract classes and interfaces	*§4.6, p. 120* *§7.6, p. 290*
Section 8: Handling Exceptions		
[8.1]	Differentiate among checked exceptions, unchecked exceptions, and Errors	*§6.6, p. 237*
[8.2]	Create a try-catch block and determine how exceptions alter normal program flow	*§6.7, p. 238*
[8.3]	Describe the advantages of exception handling	*§6.10, p. 254*
[8.4]	Create and invoke a method that throws an exception	*§6.8, p. 249* *§6.9, p. 251*
[8.5]	Recognize common exception classes (such as NullPointerException, ArithmeticException, ArrayIndexOutOfBoundsException, ClassCastException)	*§6.6, p. 233*
Section 9: Working with Selected Classes from the Java API		
[9.1]	Manipulate data using the StringBuilder class and its methods	*§8.5, p. 374*
[9.2]	Creating and manipulating Strings	*§8.4, p. 357*
[9.3]	Create and manipulate calendar data using classes from java.time.LocalDateTime, java.time.LocalDate, java.time.LocalTime, java.time.format.DateTimeFormatter, java.time.Period	*§11.1, p. 462* *§11.2, p. 462* *§11.3, p. 476* *§11.4, p. 486*
[9.4]	Declare and use an ArrayList of a given type	*§10.1, p. 414*
[9.5]	Write a simple Lambda expression that consumes a Lambda Predicate expression	*§10.2, p. 433*

Appendix C

Annotated Answers to Review Questions

1 Basics of Java Programming

1.1 *(d)*

A method is an operation defining the behavior for a particular abstraction. Java implements abstractions using classes that have properties and behavior. Behavior is defined by the operations of the abstraction.

1.2 *(b)*

An object is an instance of a class. Objects are created from classes that implement abstractions. The objects that are created are concrete realizations of those abstractions. An object is neither a reference nor a variable.

1.3 *(b)*

(2) is the first line of a constructor declaration. A constructor in Java is declared like a method, but does not specify a return value. (1) is the header of a class declaration, (3) is the first statement in the constructor body, and (4), (5) and (6) are instance method declarations.

1.4 *(b) and (f)*

Two objects and three references are created by the code. Objects are normally created by using the `new` operator. The declaration of a reference creates a variable regardless of whether a reference value is assigned to it.

1.5 *(d)*

An instance member is a field or an instance method. These members belong to an instance of the class rather than to the class as a whole. Members that are not explicitly declared as `static` in a class declaration are instance members.

1.6 *(c)*

An object communicates with another object by calling an instance method of the other object.

1.7 *(d) and (f)*

Given the declaration `class B extends A {...}`, we can conclude that class `B` extends class `A`, class `A` is the superclass of class `B`, class `B` is a subclass of class `A`, and class `B` inherits from class `A`, which means that objects of class `B` will inherit the field `value1` from class `A`.

1.8 *(b), (d), and (g)*

A `Train` object can share both the `TrainDriver` and its `Carriage` objects with other `Train` objects, when it is not using them. In other words, they can outlive the `Train` object. This is an example of aggregation. However, a `Train` object owns the array object used for handling its carriages. The lifetime of an array object is nested in the lifetime of its `Train` object. This is an example of composition.

1.9 *(d)*

The compiler supplied with the JDK is named `javac`. The names of the source files to be compiled are listed on the command line after the command `javac`.

1.10 *(a)*

Java programs are executed by the Java Virtual Machine (JVM). In the JDK, the command `java` is used to start the execution by the JVM. The `java` command requires the name of a class that has a valid `main()` method. The JVM starts the program execution by calling the `main()` method of the given class. The exact name of the class should be specified, rather than the name of the class file; that is, the `.class` extension in the class file name should not be specified.

1.11 *(e)*

(a): The JVM must be compatible with the Java Platform on which the program was developed.

(b): The JIT feature of the JVM translates bytecode to machine code.

(c): Other languages, such as Scala, also compile to bytecode and can be executed by a JVM.

(d): A Java program can only create objects; destroying objects occurs at the discretion of the automatic garbage collector.

2 Language Fundamentals

2.1 *(c)*

`52pickup` is not a legal identifier. The first character of an identifier cannot be a digit. An underscore is treated as a letter in identifier names.

2.2 *(b), (c), (d), and (f)*

In (b), the underscore is not between digits. In (c), digit 9 is not valid in an octal literal. In (d), the underscore is not between digits. In (f), there is no such escape sequence.

2.3 (e)

In Java, the identifiers `delete`, `thrown`, `exit`, `unsigned`, and `next` are not keywords. Java has a `goto` keyword, but it is reserved and not currently used.

2.4 (e)

Everything from the start sequence (/*) of a multiple-line comment to the first occurrence of the end sequence (*/) of a multiple-line comment is ignored by the compiler. Everything from the start sequence (//) of a single-line comment to the end of the line is ignored by the compiler. In (e), the multiple-line comment ends with the first occurrence of the end sequence (*/), leaving the second occurrence of the end sequence (*/) unmatched.

2.5 *(a) and (d)*

`String` is a class, and `"hello"` and `"t"` denote `String` objects. Java has the following primitive data types: `boolean`, `byte`, `short`, `char`, `int`, `long`, `float`, and `double`.

2.6 *(a), (c), and (e)*

(a) is a `boolean` data type, while (c) and (e) are floating-point data types.

2.7 (c)

The bit representation of `int` is 32 bits wide and can hold values in the range -2^{31} through $2^{31} - 1$.

2.8 *(a), (c), and (d)*

The `\u`*xxxx* notation can be used anywhere in the source to represent Unicode characters.

2.9 (c)

Local variable `i` is declared but not initialized. The first line of code declares the local variables `i` and `j`. The second line of code initializes the local variable `j`. Local variable `i` remains uninitialized.

2.10 (c)

The local variable of type `float` will remain uninitialized. Fields and static variables are initialized with a default value. An instance variable of type `int[]` is a reference variable that will be initialized with the `null` value. Local variables remain uninitialized unless explicitly initialized. The type of the variable does not affect whether a variable is initialized.

2.11 (e)

The program will compile. The compiler can figure out that the local variable `price` will always be initialized, since the value of the condition in the `if` statement is `true`. The two instance variables and the two static variables are all initialized to the respective default value of their type.

3 Declarations

3.1 *(b)*

Only (b) is a valid method declaration. Methods must specify a return type or must be declared as `void`. This makes (d) and (e) invalid. Methods must specify a list of zero or more comma-separated parameters enclosed by parentheses, `()`. The keyword `void` cannot be used to specify an empty parameter list. This makes (a) and (c) invalid.

3.2 *(a), (b), and (e)*

Non-static methods have an implicit `this` object reference. The `this` reference cannot be changed, as in (c). The `this` reference can be used in a non-static context to refer to both instance and static members. However, it cannot be used to refer to local variables, as in (d).

3.3 *(a) and (e)*

The first and third pairs of methods will compile. The second pair of methods will not compile, since their method signatures do not differ. The compiler has no way of differentiating between the two methods. Note that the return type and the names of the parameters are not a part of the method signature. Both methods in the first pair are named `fly` and have different numbers of parameters, thus overloading this method name. The methods in the last pair do not overload the method name `glide`, since only one method has that name. The method named `Glide` is distinct from the method named `glide`, as identifiers are case sensitive in Java.

3.4 *(a)*

A constructor cannot specify any return type, not even `void`. A constructor cannot be `final`, `static`, or `abstract`.

3.5 *(b) and (e)*

A constructor can be declared as `private`, but this means that this constructor can be used only within the class. Constructors need not initialize all the fields when a class is instantiated. A field will be assigned a default value if not explicitly initialized. A constructor is non-static and, as such, it can directly access both the static and non-static members of the class.

3.6 *(c)*

A compile-time error will occur at (3), since the class does not have a constructor accepting a single argument of type `int`. The declaration at (1) declares a method, not a constructor, since it is declared as `void`. The method happens to have the same name as the class, but that is irrelevant. The class has a default constructor, since the class contains no constructor declarations. This constructor will be invoked to create a `MyClass` object at (2).

3.7 *(d)*

In Java, arrays are objects. Each array object has a `public final` field named `length` that stores the size of the array.

3.8 *(a)*

Java allows arrays of length zero. Such an array is passed as an argument to the `main()` method when a Java program is run without any program arguments.

3.9 *(c)*

The `[]` notation can be placed both after the type name and after the variable name in an array declaration. Multidimensional arrays are created by constructing arrays that can contain references to other arrays. The expression `new int[4][]` will create an array of length 4, which can contain references to arrays of `int` values. The expression `new int[4][4]` will also create a two-dimensional array, but will in addition create four more one-dimensional arrays, each of length 4 and of the type `int[]`. References to each of these arrays are stored in the two-dimensional array. The expression `int[][4]` will not work, because the arrays for the dimensions must be created from left to right.

3.10 *(b) and (e)*

The size of the array cannot be specified, as in (b) and (e). The size of the array is given implicitly by the initialization code. The size of the array is never specified in the declaration of an array reference. The size of an array is always associated with the array instance (on the right-hand side), not the array reference (on the left-hand side).

3.11 *(e)*

The array declaration is valid, and will declare and initialize an array of length 20 containing `int` values. All the values of the array are initialized to their default value of 0. The `for(;;)` loop will print all the values in the array; that is, it will print `0` twenty times.

3.12 *(d)*

The program will print `0 false 0 null` at runtime. All the instance variables, and the array element, will be initialized to their default values. When concatenated with a string, the values are converted to their string representation. Notice that the `null` pointer is converted to the string `"null"`, rather than throwing a `NullPointerException`.

3.13 *(b)*

Evaluation of the actual parameter `i++` yields 0, and increments `i` to 1 in the process. The value 0 is copied into the formal parameter `i` of the method `addTwo()` during method invocation. However, the formal parameter is local to the method, and changing its value does not affect the value in the actual parameter. The value of the variable `i` in the `main()` method remains 1.

3.14 *(d)*

The variables `a` and `b` are local variables that contain primitive values. When these variables are passed as arguments to another method, the method receives copies of the primitive values in the variables. The actual variables are unaffected by operations performed on the copies of the primitive values within the called method. The variable `bArr` contains a reference value that denotes an array object containing primitive values. When the variable is passed as a parameter to another method, the method receives a copy of the reference value. Using this reference value, the method can manipulate the object that the reference value denotes. This allows the elements in the array object referenced by `bArr` to be accessed and modified in the method `inc2()`.

3.15 *(a) and (f)*

A value can be assigned to a `final` variable only once. A `final` formal parameter is assigned the value of the actual parameter at method invocation. Within the method body, it is illegal to reassign or modify the value stored in a `final` parameter. This causes `a++` and `c = d` to fail. Whether the actual parameter is `final` does not constrain the client that invoked the method, since the actual parameter values are assigned to the formal parameters.

3.16 *(a), (d), and (f)*

The ellipses (`...`) must be specified before the parameter name. Only one variable arity parameter is permitted, and it must be the last parameter in the formal parameter list.

3.17 *(c)*

In (a) and (b), the arguments are encapsulated as elements in the implicitly created array that is passed to the method. In (c), the `int` array object itself is encapsulated as an element in the implicitly created array that is passed to the method. (a), (b) and (c) are fixed arity calls. Note that `int[]` is not a subtype of `Object[]`. In (d), (e), and (f), the argument is a subtype of `Object[]`, and the argument itself is passed without the need of an implicitly created array; that is, these are fixed arity method calls. However, in (d) and (e), the compiler issues a warning that both fixed arity and variable arity method calls are feasible, but chooses fixed arity method calls.

4 Access Control

4.1 *(a) and (c)*

Bytecode of all reference type declarations in the file is placed in the designated package, and all reference type declarations in the file can access the imported types.

4.2 *(e)*

Both classes are in the same package `app`, so the first two import statements are unnecessary. The package `java.lang` is always imported in all compilation units, so the next two import statements are unnecessary. The last static import statement is necessary to access the static variable `frame` in the `Window` class by its simple name.

4.3 *(b), (c), (d), and (e)*

(a): The import statement imports types from the `mainpkg` package, but `Window` is not one of them.

(b): The import statement imports types from the `mainpkg.subpkg1` package, and `Window` is one of them.

(c): The import statement imports types from the `mainpkg.subpkg2` package, and `Window` is one of them.

(d): The first import statement is type-import-on-demand and the second import statement is single-type-import. Both import the type `Window`. The second overrides the first one.

(e): The first import statement is single-type-import and the second import statement is type-import-on-demand. Both import the type `Window`. The first overrides the second one.

(f): Both import statements import the type `Window`, making the import ambiguous.

(g): Both single-type-import statements import the type `Window`. The second import statement causes a conflict with the first.

4.4 *(c) and (e)*

The name of the class must be fully qualified. A parameter list after the method name is not permitted. (c) illustrates single static import and (e) illustrates static import on demand.

4.5 *(b), (d), and (f)*

In (a), the file `A.class` will be placed in the same directory as the file `A.java`. There is no `-D` option for the `javac` command, as in (c). The compiler maps the package structure to the file system, creating the necessary (sub)directories.

4.6 *(b) and (d)*

In (a) and (c), class `A` cannot be found. In (e) and (f), class `B` cannot be found—there is no package under the current directory `/top/wrk/pkg` to search for class `B`. Note that specifying `pkg` in the classpath in (d) is superfluous. The *parent* directory of the package must be specified, meaning the *location* of the package.

4.7 *(d) and (f)*

The *parent* directory (or *location*) of the package must be specified. Only (d) and (f) do that. (d) specifies the current directory first, but there is no file `top/sub/A.class` under the current directory. Searching under `../bin` (i.e., `/proj/bin`) finds the file `top/sub/A.class`.

4.8 *(c) and (d)*

A class or interface name can be referred to by using either its fully qualified name or its simple name. Using the fully qualified name will always work, but to use the simple name it has to be imported. When `net.basemaster.*` is imported, all the type names from the package `net.basemaster` will be imported and can now be referred to using simple names. Importing `net.*` will not import the subpackage `basemaster`.

4.9 *(c)*

Any non-final class can be declared as `abstract`. A class cannot be instantiated if the class is declared as `abstract`. The declaration of an `abstract` method cannot provide an implementation. The declaration of a non-`abstract` method must provide an implementation. If any method in a class is declared as `abstract`, then the class must be declared as `abstract`, so (a) is invalid. The declaration in (b) is not valid, since it omits the keyword `abstract` in the method declaration. The declaration in

(d) is not valid, since it omits the keyword `class`. In (e), the return type of the method is missing.

4.10 *(e)*

Only a `final` class cannot be extended, as in (d). (c) and (e) will also not compile. The keyword `native` can be used only for methods, not for classes and fields. A class cannot be declared as both `final` and `abstract`.

4.11 *(b)*

Outside the package, the member `j` is accessible to any class, whereas the member `k` is accessible only to subclasses of `MyClass`.

The field `i` has package accessibility, and is accessible to only classes inside the package. The field `j` has public accessibility, and is accessible from anywhere. The field `k` has protected accessibility, and is accessible from any class inside the package and from subclasses anywhere. The field `l` has private accessibility, and is accessible only within its own class.

4.12 *(c)*

The default accessibility for members is more restrictive than protected accessibility, but less restrictive than private accessibility. Members with default accessibility are accessible only within the class itself and from classes in the same package. Protected members are, in addition, accessible from subclasses anywhere. Members with private accessibility are accessible only within the class itself.

4.13 *(b)*

A private member is accessible only within the class of the member. If no accessibility modifier has been specified for a member, the member has default accessibility, also known as package accessibility. The keyword `default` is not an accessibility modifier. A member with package accessibility is accessible only from classes in the same package. Subclasses in other packages cannot access a member with default accessibility.

4.14 *(a), (c), (d), (e), and (h)*

The lines (1), (3), (4), (5), and (8) will compile. A `protected` member of a superclass is always inherited by a subclass. Direct access to the `protected` field `pf` is permitted in subclasses `B` and `C` at (1) and (5), respectively.

A subclass in another package can access protected members in the superclass only via references of its own type or its subtypes. In `packageB`, the subclass `B` can access the protected field `pf` in the superclass `packageA.A` via references of type `B` (i.e., parameter `obj2`) and references of its subclass `C` (i.e., parameter `obj3`). However, the subclass `C` can access the protected field `pf` in the superclass `packageA.A` only via references of type `C` (i.e., parameter `obj3`). This is the case at (3), (4), and (8).

The class `D` does not have any inheritance relationship with any of the other classes, and therefore the `protected` field `pf` is not accessible in the class `D`. This rules out the lines from (9) to (12).

4.15 *(b) and (e)*

If no accessibility modifier (`public`, `protected`, or `private`) is given in the member declaration of a class, the member is accessible only to classes in the same package. A subclass does not have access to members with default accessibility declared in a superclass, unless they are in the same package.

Local variables cannot be declared as `static` or have an accessibility modifier.

4.16 *(c)*

Line (3) `void k() { i++; }` can be reinserted without introducing errors. Reinserting line (1) will cause the compilation to fail, since `MyOtherClass` will try to override a `final` method. Reinserting line (2) will fail, since `MyOtherClass` will no longer have the (no-argument) default constructor. The `main()` method needs to call the no-argument constructor. Reinserting line (3) will work without any problems, but reinserting line (4) will fail, since the method will try to access a `private` member of the superclass.

4.17 *(b)*

The keyword `this` can be used only in non-static code, as in non-static methods, constructors, and instance initializer blocks. Only one occurrence of each static variable of a class is created, when the class is loaded by the JVM. This occurrence is shared among all the objects of the class (and for that matter, by other clients). Local variables are accessible only within the block scope, regardless of whether the block scope is defined within a static context.

4.18 *(c)*

The declaration in (c) is not legal, as variables cannot be declared as `abstract`. The keywords `static` and `final` are valid modifiers for both field and method declarations. The modifiers `abstract` and `native` are valid for methods, but not together. They cannot be specified for fields.

4.19 *(a) and (c)*

Abstract classes can declare both `final` methods and non-`abstract` methods. Non-`abstract` classes cannot, however, contain `abstract` methods. Nor can `abstract` classes be `final`. Only methods can be declared `native`.

4.20 *(a)*

The keyword `transient` signifies that the fields should not be stored when objects are serialized. Constructors cannot be declared as `abstract`. When an array object is created, as in (c), the elements in the array object are assigned the default value corresponding to the type of the elements. Whether the reference variable denoting the array object is a local variable or a member variable is irrelevant. Abstract methods from a superclass need not be implemented by a subclass, but the subclass must then be declared as `abstract`. Static methods can also be accessed in a non-static context—for example, in instance methods, constructors, and instance initializer blocks.

5 Operators and Expressions

5.1 *(a)*

A value of type `char` can be assigned to a variable of type `int`. A widening conversion will convert the value to an `int`.

5.2 *(d)*

An assignment statement is an expression statement. The value of the expression statement is the value of the expression on the right-hand side. Since the assignment operator is right associative, the statement `a = b = c = 20` is evaluated as follows: `(a = (b = (c = 20)))`. This results in the value 20 being assigned to `c`, then the same value being assigned to `b` and finally to `a`. The program will compile, and print `20` at runtime.

5.3 *(c)*

Strings are objects. The variables `a`, `b`, and `c` are references that can denote such objects. Assigning to a reference only changes the reference value; it does not create a copy of the source object or change the object denoted by the old reference value in the target reference. In other words, assignment to references affects only which object the target reference denotes. The reference value of the `"cat"` object is first assigned to `a`, then to `b`, and later to `c`. The program prints the string denoted by `c`, `"cat"`. The local `final String` variable `b` is initialized only once in the code.

5.4 *(a), (d), and (e)*

A binary expression with any floating-point operand will be evaluated using floating-point arithmetic. Expressions such as `2/3`, where both operands are integers, will use integer arithmetic and evaluate to an integer value. In (e), the result of `(0x10 * 1L)` is promoted to a floating-point value.

5.5 *(b)*

The / operator has higher precedence than the + operator. This means that the expression is evaluated as `((1/2) + (3/2) + 0.1)`. The associativity of the binary operators is from left to right, giving `(((1/2) + (3/2)) + 0.1)`. Integer division results in `((0 + 1) + 0.1)`, which evaluates to 1.1.

5.6 *(e)*

`0x10` is a hexadecimal literal equivalent to the decimal value 16. `10` is a decimal literal. `010` is an octal literal equivalent to the decimal value 8. `0b10` is a binary literal equivalent to the decimal value 2. The `println()` method will print the sum of these values, which is 36, in decimal form.

5.7 *(b), (c), and (f)*

The unary + and - operators with right associativity are used in the valid expressions (b), (c), and (f). Expression (a) tries to use a nonexistent unary - operator with left associativity, expression (d) tries to use a decrement operator (--) on an expression that does not resolve to a variable, and expression (e) tries to use a nonexistent unary * operator. (c) compiles because the unary operators cannot be interpreted as increment (++) or decrement (--) operators: `(+(-(+(-(+(-1))))))`.

5.8 *(b)*

The expression evaluates to –6. The whole expression is evaluated as `(((-(-1)) - ((3 * 10) / 5)) - 1)` according to the precedence and associativity rules.

5.9 *(a), (b), (d), and (e)*

In (a), the conditions for implicit narrowing conversion are fulfilled: The source is a constant expression of type `int`, the destination type is of type `short`, and the value of the source (12) is in the range of the destination type. The assignments in (b), (d), and (e) are valid, since the source type is narrower than the target type and an implicit widening conversion will be applied. The expression (c) is not valid. Values of type `boolean` cannot be converted to other types.

5.10 *(a), (c), and (d)*

The left associativity of the `+` operator makes the evaluation of `(1 + 2 + "3")` proceed as follows: `(1 + 2) + "3"` → `3 + "3"` → `"33"`. Evaluation of the expression `("1" + 2 + 3)`, however, will proceed as follows: `("1" + 2) + 3` → `"12" + 3` → `"123"`. `(4 + 1.0f)` evaluates as `4.0f + 1.0f` → `5.0f` and `(10/9)` performs integer division, resulting in the value 1. The operand `'a'` in the expression `('a' + 1)` will be promoted to `int`, and the resulting value will be of type `int`.

5.11 *(d)*

The expression `++k + k++ + + k` is evaluated as `((++k) + (k++)) + (+k)` → `((2) + (2) + (3))`, resulting in the value `7`.

5.12 *(d)*

The types `char` and `int` are both integral. A `char` value can be assigned to an `int` variable since the `int` type is wider than the `char` type and an implicit widening conversion will be done. An `int` type cannot be assigned to a `char` variable because the `char` type is narrower than the `int` type. The compiler will report an error about a possible loss of precision in (4).

5.13 *(c)*

Variables of the type `byte` can store values in the range –128 to 127. The expression on the right-hand side of the first assignment is the `int` literal 128. Had this literal been in the range of the `byte` type, an implicit narrowing conversion would have been applied to convert it to a `byte` value during assignment. Since 128 is outside the range of the type `byte`, the program will not compile.

5.14 *(a)*

First, the expression `++i` is evaluated, resulting in the value 2. Now the variable `i` also has the value 2. The target of the assignment is now determined to be the element `array[2]`. Evaluation of the right-hand expression, `--i`, results in the value 1. The variable `i` now has the value 1. The value of the right-hand expression, 1, is then assigned to the array element `array[2]`, causing the array contents to become `{4, 8, 1}`. The program computes and prints the sum of these values, `13`.

5.15 *(a) and (c)*

In (a) and (e), both operands are evaluated, with (a) yielding `true`, but (e) yielding `false`. The `null` literal can be compared, so `(null != null)` yields `false`. The expression `(4 <= 4)` is `true`. `(!true)` is `false`.

5.16 *(c) and (e)*

The remainder operator `%` is not limited to integral values, but can also be applied to floating-point operands. Short-circuit evaluation occurs only with the conditional operators (`&&`, `||`). The operators `*`, `/`, and `%` have the same level of precedence. The data type `short` is a 16-bit signed two's complement integer, so the range of values is from `-32768` to `+32767`, inclusive. `(+15)` is a legal expression using the unary `+` operator.

5.17 *(a), (c), and (e)*

The `!=` and `^` operators, when used on boolean operands, will return `true` if and only if one operand is `true`, and `false` otherwise. This means that `d` and `e` in the program will always be assigned the same value, given any combination of truth values in `a` and `b`. The program will, therefore, print `true` four times.

5.18 *(b)*

The element referenced by `a[i]` is determined based on the current value of `i`, which is 0—that is, the element `a[0]`. The expression `i = 9` will evaluate to the value 9, which will be assigned to the variable `i`. The value 9 is also assigned to the array element `a[0]`. After the execution of the statement, the variable `i` will contain the value 9, and the array `a` will contain the values 9 and 6. The program will print `9 9 6` at runtime.

5.19 *(c) and (d)*

Note that the logical and conditional operators have lower precedence than the relational operators. Unlike the `&` and `|` operators, the `&&` and `||` operators short-circuit the evaluation of their operands if the result of the operation can be determined from the value of the first operand. The second operand of the `||` operator in the program is never evaluated because of short-circuiting. All the operands of the other operators are evaluated. Variable `i` ends up with the value 3, which is the first digit printed, and `j` ends up with the value 1, which is the second digit printed.

5.20 *(d) and (f)*

`&&=` and `%%` are not operators in Java. The operators `%`, `&&`, `%=`, `<=`, and `->` are called remainder, conditional AND, remainder compound assignment, relational less than or equal, and arrow operator, respectively.

5.21 *(c), (e), and (f)*

In (a), the third operand has the type `double`, which is not assignment compatible with the type `int` of the variable `result1`. Blocks are not legal operands in the conditional operator, as in (b). In (c), the last two operands result in wrapper objects with type `Integer` and `Double`, respectively, which are assignment compatible with the type `Number` of the variable `number`. The evaluation of the conditional expression results in the reference value of an `Integer` object, with value `20` being assigned to the number variable. All three operands of the operator are mandatory, which is not the case in (d). In (e), the last two operands are of type int, and the evaluation of the conditional expression results in an int value (21), whose string representation is printed. In (f), the value of the second operand is boxed into a Boolean. The evaluation of the conditional expression results in a string literal ("i not equal to j"), which is printed. The println() method creates and prints a string representation of any object whose reference value is passed as parameter.

5.22 *(d)*

The condition in the outer conditional expression is false. The condition in the nested conditional expression is true, resulting in the value of m1 (i.e., 20) being printed.

6 Control Flow

6.1 *(d)*

The program will display the letter b when run. The second if statement is evaluated since the boolean expression of the first if statement is true. The else clause belongs to the second if statement. Since the boolean expression of the second if statement is false, the if block is skipped and the else clause is executed.

6.2 *(a), (b), and (e)*

The condition of an if statement can be any expression, including method calls, as long as it evaluates or can be unboxed to a value of type boolean. The expression (a = b) does not compare the variables a and b, but assigns the value of b to the variable a. The result of the expression is the value being assigned. Since a and b are either boolean or Boolean variables, the value returned by the expression is also either boolean or Boolean. This allows the expression to be used as the condition for an if statement. An if statement must always have an if block, but the else clause is optional. The expression if (false) ; else ; is legal. In this case, both the if block and the else block are simply the empty statement.

6.3 *(f)*

There is nothing wrong with the code. The case and default labels do not have to be specified in any specific order. The use of the break statement is not mandatory, and without it the control flow will simply fall through the labels of the switch statement.

6.4 *(c)*

The case label value 2 * iLoc is a constant expression whose value is 6, the same as the switch expression. Fall-through results in the program output shown in (c).

6.5 *(b)*

The switch expression, when unboxed, has the value 5. The statement associated with the default label is executed, and the fall-through continues until the break statement.

6.6 *(a), (b), (f), and (j)*

In (a), (b), (f), and (j), the string expression involves constant values and evaluates to `"TomTom"`. Program output is `"Hi, TomTom!"` In (i), the constant string expression evaluates to `"304Tom"` (`84+111+109+"Tom"`). The first three literals are of type `char`, and their `int` values are added before being concatenated with last `String` operand. Program output is `"Whatever!"` In (c), (d), (e), (g), and (h), the `case` label is not a constant string expression, and the program will not compile.

6.7 *(e)*

The loop body is executed twice and the program will print `3`. The first time the loop is executed, the variable `i` changes from 1 to 2 and the variable `b` changes from `false` to `true`. Then the loop condition is evaluated. Since `b` is `true`, the loop body is executed again. This time the variable `i` changes from 2 to 3 and the variable `b` changes from `true` to `false`. The loop condition is then evaluated again. Since `b` is now `false`, the loop terminates and the current value of `i` is printed.

6.8 *(b) and (e)*

Both the first and second numbers printed will be `10`. Both the loop body and the update expression will be executed exactly 10 times. Each execution of the loop body will be directly followed by an execution of the update expression. Afterward, the condition `j < 10` is evaluated to see whether the loop body should be executed again.

6.9 *(c)*

Only (c) contains a valid `for` loop. The initialization in a `for(;;)` statement can contain either declarations or a list of expression statements, but not both as attempted in (a). The loop condition must be of type `boolean`. (b) tries to use an assignment of an `int` value (notice the use of `=` rather than `==`) as a loop condition and, therefore, is not valid. The loop condition in the `for` loop (d) tries to use the uninitialized variable `i`, and the `for(;;)` loop in (e) is syntactically invalid, as there is only one semicolon.

6.10 *(f)*

The code will compile without error, but will never terminate when run. All the sections in the `for` header are optional and can be omitted (but not the semicolons). An omitted loop condition is interpreted as being `true`. Thus, a `for(;;)` loop with an omitted loop condition will never terminate, unless an appropriate control transfer statement is encountered in the loop body. The program will enter an infinite loop at (4).

6.11 *(b), (d), and (e)*

The loop condition in a `while` statement is not optional. It is missing in (a). It is not possible to break out of the `if` statement in (c). Notice that if this `if` statement had been placed within a `switch` statement or a loop, the usage of `break` would be valid. Inside a labeled block, a labeled `break` statement would be required.

6.12 *(a) and (d)*

"`i=1, j=0`" and "`i=2, j=1`" are part of the output. The variable `i` iterates through the values 0, 1, and 2 in the outer loop, while `j` toggles between the values 0 and 1 in the inner loop. If the values of `i` and `j` are equal, the printing of the values is skipped and the execution continues with the next iteration of the outer loop. The following can be deduced when the program is run: Variables `i` and `j` are both 0 and the execution continues with the update expression of the outer loop. "`i=1, j=0`" is printed and the next iteration of the inner loop starts. Variables `i` and `j` are both 1 and the execution continues with the update expression of the outer loop. "`i=2, j=0`" is printed and the next iteration of the inner loop starts. "`i=2, j=1`" is printed, `j` is incremented, `j < 2` is `false`, and the inner loop ends. Variable `i` is incremented, `i < 3` is `false`, and the outer loop ends.

6.13 *(b)*

The code will fail to compile, since the condition of the `if` statement is not of type `boolean`. The variable `i` is of type `int`. There is no conversion between `boolean` and other primitive types.

6.14 *(c) and (d)*

The element type of the array `nums` must be assignment compatible with the type of the loop variable, `int`. Only the element type in (c), `Integer`, can be automatically unboxed to an `int`. The element type in (d) is `int`.

6.15 *(d) and (e)*

In the header of a `for(:)` loop, we can declare only one local variable. This rules out (a) and (b), as they specify two local variables. Also the array expression in (a), (b), and (c) is not valid. Only (d) and (e) specify a legal `for(:)` header.

6.16 *(d)*

The program will print `1`, `4`, and `5`, in that order. The expression `5/k` will throw an `ArithmeticException`, since `k` equals 0. Control is transferred to the first `catch` clause, since it is the first clause that can handle the arithmetic exceptions. This exception handler simply prints `1`. The exception has now been caught and normal execution can resume. Before leaving the `try` statement, the `finally` clause is executed. This clause prints `4`. The last statement of the `main()` method prints `5`.

6.17 *(b) and (e)*

If run with no arguments, the program will print `The end`. If run with one argument, the program will print the given argument followed by "`The end`". The `finally` clause will always be executed, no matter how control leaves the `try` block.

6.18 *(c) and (d)*

Normal execution will resume only if the exception is caught by the method. The uncaught exception will propagate up the JVM stack until some method handles it. An overriding method need simply declare that it can throw a subset of the checked exceptions that the overridden method can throw. The `main()` method can declare that it throws checked exceptions just like any other method. The `finally` clause will always be executed, no matter how control leaves the `try` block.

6.19 *(a)*

The program will print `2` and throw an `InterruptedException`. An `InterruptedException` is thrown in the `try` block. There is no `catch` clause to handle the exception, so it will be sent to the caller of the `main()` method—that is, to the default exception handler. Before this happens, the `finally` clause is executed. The code to print `3` is never reached.

6.20 *(b)*

The only thing that is wrong with the code is the ordering of the `catch` and `finally` clauses. If present, the `finally` clause must always appear last in a `try-catch-finally` construct.

6.21 *(a)*

Overriding methods can specify all, none, or a subset of the checked exceptions that the overridden method declares in its `throws` clause. The `InterruptedException` is the only checked exception specified in the `throws` clause of the overridden method. The overriding method `compute()` need not specify the `Interrupted-Exception` from the `throws` clause of the overridden method, because the exception is not thrown here.

7 Object-Oriented Programming

7.1 *(a) and (b)*

The `extends` clause is used to specify that a class extends another class. A subclass can be declared as `abstract` regardless of whether the superclass was declared as `abstract`. Private, overridden, and hidden members from the superclass are not inherited by the subclass. A class cannot be declared as both `abstract` and `final`, since an `abstract` class needs to be extended to be useful, and a `final` class cannot be extended. The accessibility of the class is not limited by the accessibility of its members. A class with all the members declared `private` can still be declared as `public`.

7.2 *(b) and (e)*

The `Object` class has a `public` method named `equals`, but it does not have any method named `length`. Since all classes are subclasses of the `Object` class, they all inherit the `equals()` method. Thus, all Java objects have a `public` method named `equals`. In Java, a class can extend only a single superclass, but there is no limit on how many subclasses can extend a superclass.

7.3 *(a), (b), and (d)*

`Bar` is a subclass of `Foo` that overrides the method `g()`. The statement `a.j = 5` is not legal, since the member `j` in the class `Bar` cannot be accessed through a `Foo` reference. The statement `b.i = 3` is not legal either, since the `private` member `i` cannot be accessed from outside of the class `Foo`.

7.4 *(g)*

It is not possible to invoke the `doIt()` method in `A` from an instance method in class `C`. The method in `C` needs to call a method in a superclass two levels up in the inheritance hierarchy. The `super.super.doIt()` strategy will not work, since `super` is a keyword and cannot be used as an ordinary reference, nor can it be accessed like a field. If the member to be accessed had been a field, the solution would be to cast the `this` reference to the class of the field and use the resulting reference to access the field. Field access is determined by the declared type of the reference, whereas the instance method to execute is determined by the actual type of the object denoted by the reference at runtime.

7.5 (e)

The code will compile without errors. None of the calls to a `max()` method are ambiguous. When the program is run, the `main()` method will call the `max()` method on the `C` object referred to by the reference `b` with the parameters `13` and `29`. This method will call the `max()` method in `B` with the parameters `23` and `39`. The `max()` method in `B` will in turn call the `max()` method in `A` with the parameters `39` and `23`. The `max()` method in `A` will return `39` to the `max()` method in `B`. The `max()` method in `B` will return `29` to the `max()` method in `C`. The `max()` method in `C` will return `29` to the `main()` method.

7.6 (c)

The simplest way to print the message in the class `Message` would be to use `msg.text`. The `main()` method creates an instance of `MyClass`, which results in the creation of a `Message` instance. The field `msg` denotes this `Message` object in `MySuperclass` and is inherited by the `MyClass` object, as this field has default accessibility. Thus, the message in the `Message` object can be accessed directly by `msg.text` in the `print()` method of `MyClass`, and also by `this.msg.text` and `super.msg.text`.

7.7 (g)

In the class `Car`, the static method `getModelName()` hides the static method of the same name in the superclass `Vehicle`. In the class `Car`, the instance method `getRegNo()` overrides the instance method of the same name in the superclass `Vehicle`. The declared type of the reference determines the method to execute when a static method is called, but the actual type of the object at runtime determines the method to execute when an overridden method is called.

7.8 (e)

The class `MySuper` does not have a no-argument constructor. This means that constructors in subclasses must explicitly call the superclass constructor and provide the required parameters. The supplied constructor accomplishes this by calling `super(num)` in its first statement. Additional constructors can accomplish this either by calling the superclass constructor directly using the `super()` call, or by calling another constructor in the same class using the `this()` call, which in turn calls the superclass constructor. (a) and (b) are not valid, since they do not call the superclass constructor explicitly. (d) fails, since the `super()` call must always be the first statement in the constructor body. (f) fails, since the `super()` and `this()` calls cannot be combined.

7.9 *(b)*

In a subclass without any declared constructors, the default constructor will call `super()`. The use of the `super()` and `this()` statements are not mandatory as long as the superclass has a default constructor. If neither `super()` nor `this()` is declared as the first statement in the body of a constructor, then the default `super()` will implicitly be the first statement. A constructor body cannot have both a `super()` and a `this()` statement. Calling `super()` will not always work, since a superclass might not have a default constructor.

7.10 *(d)*

The program will print `12` followed by `Test`. When the `main()` method is executed, it will create a new instance of `B` by passing `"Test"` as an argument. This results in a call to the constructor of `B`, which has one `String` parameter. The constructor does not explicitly call any superclass constructor or any overloaded constructor in `B` using a `this()` call; instead, the no-argument constructor of the superclass `A` is called implicitly. The no-argument constructor of `A` calls the constructor in `A` that has two `String` parameters, passing it the argument list `("1", "2")`. This constructor calls the constructor with one `String` parameter, passing the argument `"12"`. This constructor prints the argument, after implicitly invoking the no-argument constructor of the superclass `Object`. Now the execution of all the constructors in `A` is completed, and execution continues in the constructor of `B`. This constructor now prints the original argument `"Test"` and returns to the `main()` method.

7.11 *(b) and (c)*

Interface declarations do not provide any method implementations and permit only multiple interface inheritance. An interface can extend any number of interfaces and can be extended by any number of interfaces. Fields in interfaces are always `static`, and can be declared as `static` explicitly. Abstract method declarations in interfaces are always non-`static`, and cannot be declared static.
Interfaces allow only multiple interface inheritance. An interface can extend any number of interfaces, and can be extended by any number of interfaces. Fields in interfaces are always `static`, and can be declared as `static` explicitly. Static methods, of course, can be declared as `static`. Abstract method declarations in interfaces are always non-`static`, and cannot be declared as `static`.

7.12 *(a), (d), (e), and (f)*

The keywords `protected`, `private`, and `final` cannot be applied to interface methods. The keyword `public` is implied, but can be specified for all interface methods. The keywords `default`, `abstract`, and `static` can be specified for default, abstract, and static methods, respectively. The keywords `default` and `static` are required for default and static methods, respectively, but the keyword `abstract` is optional and is implicitly implied for abstract methods.

7.13 *(a), (f), and (g)*

Only the keywords `public`, `static`, and `final` are implicitly implied for interface variables.

7.14 *(e)*

(1): The final static constant is not initialized.

(2): The abstract method cannot have an implementation.

(3): The static method is missing the implementation.

(4): The default method cannot be final.

7.15 *(b) and (c)*

The default instance method `printSlogan()` is inherited by the class `Company`.

(a): It can be called from a non-static context (instance method `testSlogan()`) by its simple name, but not from a static context (static method `main()`).

(b), (c): An instance method can be invoked on an instance via a reference, regardless of whether it is in a static or non-static context.

(d), (e): An instance method cannot be invoked via a reference type, but only on an instance via a reference; that is, you cannot make a static reference to a non-static method.

7.16 *(e)*

The `static` method `printSlogan()` is *not* inherited by the class `Firm`. It can be invoked by using a static reference, the name of the interface in which it is declared, regardless of whether the call is in a static or a non-static context.

7.17 *(c)*

The instance method at (3) overrides the default method at (1). The static method at (2) is not inherited by the class `RaceA`. The instance method at (4) does not override the static method at (2).

The method to be invoked by the call at (5) is determined at runtime by the object type of the reference, which in this case is `Athlete`, resulting in the method at (3) being invoked. Similarly, the call at (6) will invoke the instance method at (4).

7.18 *(a)*

The program will not compile, because the overriding method at (2) cannot have narrower accessibility than the overridden method at (1). The method at (1) has `public` accessibility, whereas the method at (2) has package accessibility.

7.19 *(a), (c), and (d)*

Fields in interfaces declare named constants, and are always `public`, `static`, and `final`. None of these modifiers is mandatory in a constant declaration. All named constants must be explicitly initialized in the declaration.

7.20 *(a) and (d)*

The keyword `implements` is used when a class implements an interface. The keyword `extends` is used when an interface inherits from another interface or a class inherits from another class.

7.21 *(d)*

The code will compile without errors. The class `MyClass` declares that it implements the interfaces `Interface1` and `Interface2`. Since the class is declared as `abstract`, it does not need to implement all abstract method declarations defined in these interfaces. Any non-`abstract` subclasses of `MyClass` must provide the missing method implementations. The two interfaces share a common abstract method declaration `void g()`. `MyClass` provides an implementation for this abstract method declaration that satisfies both `Interface1` and `Interface2`. Both interfaces provide declarations of constants named `VAL_B`. This can lead to ambiguity when referring to `VAL_B` by its simple name from `MyClass`. The ambiguity can be resolved by using the qualified names: `Interface1.VAL_B` and `Interface2.VAL_B`. However, there are no problems with the code as it stands.

7.22 *(a) and (c)*

Declaration (b) fails, since it contains an illegal forward reference to its own named constant. The type of the constant is missing in declaration (d). Declaration (e) tries (illegally) to use the `protected` modifier, even though named constants always have `public` accessibility. Such constants are implicitly `public`, `static`, and `final`.

7.23 *(c)*

The program will throw a `java.lang.ClassCastException` in the assignment at (3) at runtime. The statement at (1) will compile, since the assignment is done from a subclass reference to a superclass reference. The cast at (2) assures the compiler that `arrA` refers to an object that can be cast to type `B[]`. This will work when run, since `arrA` will refer to an object of type `B[]`. The cast at (3) assures the compiler that `arrA` refers to an object that can be cast to type `B[]`. This will not work when run, since `arrA` will refer to an object of type `A[]`.

7.24 *(d) and (f)*

(4) and (6) will cause a compile-time error, since an attempt is made to assign a reference value of a supertype object to a reference of a subtype. The type of the source reference value is `MyClass` and the type of the destination reference is `MySubclass`. (1) and (2) will compile, since the reference is assigned a reference value of the same type. (3) will also compile, since the reference is assigned a reference value of a subtype.

7.25 *(e)*

Only the assignment `I1 b = obj3` is valid. The assignment is allowed, since `C3` extends `C1`, which implements `I1`. The assignment `obj2 = obj1` is not legal, since `C1` is not a subclass of `C2`. The assignments `obj3 = obj1` and `obj3 = obj2` are not legal, since neither `C1` nor `C2` is a subclass of `C3`. The assignment `I1 a = obj2` is not legal, since `C2` does not implement `I1`. Assignment `I2 c = obj1` is not legal, since `C1` does not implement `I2`.

7.26 *(b)*

The compiler will allow the statement, as the cast is from the supertype (`Super`) to the subtype (`Sub`). However, if at runtime the reference `x` does not denote an object of the type `Sub`, a `ClassCastException` will be thrown.

7.27 *(b)*

The expression `(o instanceof B)` will return `true` if the object referred to by `o` is of type `B` or a subtype of `B`. The expression `(!(o instanceof C))` will return `true` unless the object referred to by `o` is of type `C` or a subtype of `C`. Thus, the expression `(o instanceof B) && (!(o instanceof C))` will return `true` only if the object is of type `B` or a subtype of `B` that is not `C` or a subtype of `C`. Given objects of the classes `A`, `B`, and `C`, this expression will return `true` only for objects of class `B`.

7.28 *(d)*

The program will print all the letters `I`, `J`, `C`, and `D` at runtime. The object referred to by the reference `x` is of class `D`. Class `D` extends class `C` and implements `J`, and class `C` implements interface `I`. This makes `I`, `J`, and `C` supertypes of class `D`. The reference value of an object of class `D` can be assigned to any reference of its supertypes and, therefore, is an `instanceof` these types.

7.29 *(a)*

The signatures `yingyang(Integer[])` and `yingyang(Integer...)` are equivalent and, therefore, are not permitted in the same class.

7.30 *(c)*

The calls to the `compute()` method in the method declarations at (2) and at (3) are to the `compute()` method declaration at (1), as the argument is always an `int[]`.

The method call at (4) calls the method at (2). The signature of the call at (4) is

```
compute(int[], int[])
```

which matches the signature of the method at (2). No implicit array is created.

The method call in (5) calls the method at (1). An implicit array of int is created to store the argument values.

The method calls in (6) and (7) call the method in (3). Note the type of the variable arity parameter in (3): an `int[][]`. The signature of the calls at (6) and (7) is

```
compute(int[], int[][])
```

which matches the signature of the method at (3). No implicit array is created.

7.31 *(e)*

The program will print `2` when `System.out.println(ref2.f())` is executed. The object referenced by `ref2` is of class `C`, but the reference is of type `B`. Since `B` contains a method `f()`, the method call will be allowed at compile time. During execution it is determined that the object is of class `C`, and dynamic method lookup will cause the overriding method in `C` to be executed.

7.32 *(c)*

The program will print `1` when run. The `f()` methods in `A` and `B` are `private`, and are not accessible by the subclasses. Because of this, the subclasses cannot overload or override these methods, but simply define new methods with the same signature. The object being called is of class `C`. The reference used to access the object is of type `B`. Since `B` contains a method `g()`, the method call will be allowed at compile time. During execution it is determined that the object is of class `C`, and dynamic method lookup will cause the overriding method `g()` in `B` to be executed. This method calls a method named `f`. It can be determined during compilation that this can refer to only the `f()` method in `B`, since the method is `private` and cannot be overridden. This method returns the value `1`, which is printed.

7.33 *(b), (c), and (d)*

The code as it stands will compile. The use of inheritance in this code defines a `Planet` *is-a* `Star` relationship. The code will fail if the name of the field `starName` is changed in the `Star` class, since the subclass `Planet` tries to access it using the name `starName`. An instance of `Planet` is not an instance of `HeavenlyBody`. Neither `Planet` nor `Star` implements `HeavenlyBody`.

7.34 *(b)*

The code will compile. The code will not fail to compile if the name of the field `starName` is changed in the `Star` class, since the `Planet` class does not try to access the field by name, but instead uses the `public` method `describe()` in the `Star` class for that purpose. An instance of `Planet` is not an instance of `HeavenlyBody`, since it neither implements `HeavenlyBody` nor extends a class that implements `HeavenlyBody`.

7.35 *(e)*

(a) to (f) are all true; therefore (e) is not.

8 Fundamental Classes

8.1 *(b)*

The method `hashCode()` in the `Object` class returns a hash code value of type `int`.

8.2 *(e)*

All arrays are genuine objects and inherit all the methods defined in the `Object` class, including the `clone()` method. Neither the `hashCode()` method nor the `equals()` method is declared as `final` in the `Object` class, and it cannot be guaranteed that implementations of these methods will differentiate among all objects.

8.3 *(a)*

The `clone()` method of the `Object` class will throw a `CloneNotSupportedException` if the class of the object does not implement the `Cloneable` interface.

8.4 *(a), (c), and (d)*

The class `java.lang.Void` is considered a wrapper class, although it does not wrap any value. There is no class named `java.lang.Int`, but there is a wrapper class named `java.lang.Integer`. A class named `java.lang.String` also exists, but it is not a wrapper class since all strings in Java are objects.

8.5 *(c) and (d)*

The classes `Character` and `Boolean` are non-numeric wrapper classes and do not extend the `Number` class. The classes `Byte`, `Short`, `Integer`, `Long`, `Float`, and `Double` are numeric wrapper classes that extend the abstract `Number` class.

8.6 *(a), (b), and (d)*

All instances of concrete wrapper classes are immutable. The `Number` class is an `abstract` class.

8.7 *(b) and (c)*

All instances of wrapper classes except `Void` and `Character` have a constructor that accepts a single `String` parameter. The class `Object` has only a no-argument constructor.

8.8 *(e)*

While all numeric wrapper classes have the methods `byteValue()`, `doubleValue()`, `floatValue()`, `intValue()`, `longValue()`, and `shortValue()`, only the `Boolean` class has the `booleanValue()` method. Likewise, only the `Character` class has the `charValue()` method.

8.9 *(b) and (d)*

`String` is not a wrapper class. All wrapper classes except `Void` have a `compareTo()` method. Only the numeric wrapper classes have an `intValue()` method. The `Byte` class, like all other numeric wrapper classes, extends the `Number` class.

8.10 *(a)*

Using the `new` operator creates a new object. Boxing also creates a new object if one is not already interned from before.

8.11 *(b) and (e)*

The operators `-` and `&` cannot be used in conjunction with a `String` object. The operators `+` and `+=` perform concatenation on strings, and the dot operator accesses members of the `String` object.

8.12 *(d)*

The expression `str.substring(2,5)` will extract the substring `"kap"`. The method extracts the characters from index 2 to index 4, inclusive.

8.13 *(d)*

The program will print `str3str1` when run. The `concat()` method will create and return a new `String` object, which is the concatenation of the current `String` object and the `String` object given as an argument. The expression statement `str1.concat(str2)` creates a new `String` object, but its reference value is not stored after the expression is evaluated. Therefore this `String` object gets discarded.

8.14 *(c)*

The `trim()` method of the `String` class returns a string where both the leading and trailing whitespace of the original string have been removed.

8.15 *(a) and (c)*

The `String` class and all wrapper classes are declared as `final` and, therefore, cannot be extended. The `clone()` method is declared as `protected` in the `Object` class. `String` objects and wrapper class objects are immutable and, therefore, cannot be modified. The class String and char array types are unrelated, resulting in a compile-time error.

8.16 *(d)*

The constant expressions "ab" + "12" and "ab" + 12 will, at compile time, be evaluated to the string-valued constant "ab12". Both variables s and t are assigned a reference to the same interned String object containing "ab12". The variable u is assigned a new String object, created by using the new operator.

8.17 *(a), (c), (d), (f), and (j)*

The String class has constructors with the parameter lists given in (a), (c), (d), (f), and (j).

8.18 *(e)*

The String class has no reverse() method.

8.19 *(b)*

The reference value in the reference str1 never changes; it always refers to the string literal "lower". The calls to toUpperCase() and replace() return a new String object whose reference value is ignored.

8.20 *(d)*

The call to the put0() method does not change the String object referred to by the s1 reference in the main() method. The reference value returned by the call to the concat() method is ignored.

8.21 *(a)*

The code will fail to compile, since the expression (s == sb) is illegal. It compares references of two classes that are not related.

8.22 *(e)*

The program will compile without errors and will print have a when run. The contents of the string buffer are truncated to 6 characters by the method call sb.setLength(6).

8.23 *(a), (b), (d), and (e)*

The StringBuilder class has only constructors with the parameter lists given in (a), (b), (d), and (e).

8.24 *(a)*

The StringBuilder class does not define a trim() method.

8.25 *(b)*

The references sb1 and sb2 are not aliases. The StringBuilder class does not override the equals() method; hence the answer is (b).

8.26 *(a)*

The StringBuilder class does not override the hashCode() method, but the String class does. The references s1 and s2 refer to a String object and a StringBuilder object, respectively. The hash values of these objects are computed by the hashCode()

method in the `String` and the `Object` class, respectively—giving different results. The references `s1` and `s3` refer to two different `String` objects that are equal; hence they have the same hash value.

8.27 *(b)*

The call to the `put0()` method changes the `StringBuilder` object referred to by the `s1` reference in the `main()` method. So does the call to the `append()` method.

9 Object Lifetime

9.1 *(e)*

An object is eligible for garbage collection only if all remaining references to the object are from other objects that are also eligible for garbage collection. Therefore, if an object `obj2` is eligible for garbage collection and object `obj1` contains a reference to it, then object `obj1` must also be eligible for garbage collection. Java does not have a keyword `delete`. An object will not necessarily be garbage collected immediately after it becomes unreachable, but the object will be eligible for garbage collection. Circular references do not prevent objects from being garbage collected; only reachable references do. An object is not eligible for garbage collection as long as the object can be accessed by any live thread. An object that is eligible for garbage collection can be made non-eligible if the `finalize()` method of the object creates a reachable reference to the object.

9.2 *(b)*

Before (1), the `String` object initially referenced by `arg1` is denoted by both `msg` and `arg1`. After (1), the `String` object is denoted by only `msg`. At (2), reference `msg` is assigned a new reference value. This reference value denotes a new `String` object created by concatenating the contents of several other `String` objects. After (2), there are no references to the `String` object initially referenced by `arg1`. The `String` object is now eligible for garbage collection.

9.3 *(d)*

It is difficult to say how many objects are eligible for garbage collection when control reaches (1), because some of the eligible objects may have already been finalized.

9.4 *(a)*

All the objects created in the loop are reachable via `p`, when control reaches (1).

9.5 *(b)*

The `Object` class defines a `protected finalize()` method. All classes inherit from `Object`; thus, all objects have a `finalize()` method. Classes can override the `finalize()` method and, as with all overriding, the new method must not reduce the accessibility. The `finalize()` method of an eligible object is called by the garbage collector to allow the object to do any cleaning up before the object is destroyed. When the garbage collector calls the `finalize()` method, it will ignore any exceptions thrown by the `finalize()` method. If the `finalize()` method is called explicitly, normal exception handling occurs when an exception is thrown during the execution of the `finalize()` method; that is, exceptions are not simply ignored. Calling the `finalize()` method does not in itself destroy the object. Chaining of the `finalize()` method is not enforced by the compiler, and it is not mandatory to call the overridden `finalize()` method.

9.6 *(d)*

The `finalize()` method is like any other method: It can be called explicitly if it is accessible. However, such a method is intended to be called by the garbage collector to clean up before an object is destroyed. Overloading the `finalize()` method is allowed, but only the method with the original signature will be called by the garbage collector. The `finalize()` method in the `Object` class is `protected`. This means that any overriding method must be declared as either `protected` or `public`. The `finalize()` method in the `Object` class specifies a `Throwable` object in its `throws` clause. An overriding definition of this method can throw any type of `Throwable`. Overriding methods can limit the range of throwables to *unchecked* exceptions or specify no exceptions at all. Further overriding definitions of this method in subclasses will then *not* be able to throw *checked* exceptions.

9.7 *(d) and (g)*

(a), (b), (c), (j), (k), and (l) reduce the visibility of the inherited method. In (e), (f), (h), and (i), the call to the `finalize()` method of the superclass can throw a `Throwable`, which is not handled by the method. The `Throwable` superclass is not assignable to the `Exception` subclass.

9.8 *(e)*

It is not guaranteed if and when garbage collection will occur, nor in which order the objects will be finalized. However, it is guaranteed that the finalization of an object will be run only once. Hence, (e) cannot possibly be a result from running the program.

9.9 *(c) and (e)*

It is not guaranteed if and when garbage collection will occur, nor in which order the objects will be finalized. Thus, the program may not print anything. If garbage collection does take place, the `MyString` object created in the program may get finalized before the program terminates. In that case, the `finalize()` method will print `A`, as the string in the field `str` is not changed by the `concat()` method. Keep in mind that a `String` object is immutable.

9.10 *(c), (e), and (f)*

The static initializer blocks (a) and (b) are not legal, since the fields `alive` and `STEP` are non-`static` and `final`, respectively. (d) is not a syntactically legal static initializer block. The static block in (e) will have no effect, as it executes the empty statement. The static block in (f) will change the value of the static field `count` from 5 to 1.

9.11 *(c)*

The program will compile, and print `50, 70, 0, 20, 0` at runtime. All fields are given default values unless they are explicitly initialized. Field `i` is assigned the value 50 in the static initializer block that is executed when the class is initialized. This assignment will override the explicit initialization of field `i` in its declaration statement. When the `main()` method is executed, the static field `i` is 50 and the static field `n` is 0. When an instance of the class is created using the `new` operator, the value of static field `n` (i.e., 0) is passed to the constructor. Before the body of the constructor is executed, the instance initializer block is executed, which assigns the values 70 and 20 to the fields `j` and `n`, respectively. When the body of the constructor is executed, the fields `i`, `j`, `k`, and `n` and the parameter `m` have the values 50, 70, 0, 20, and 0, respectively.

9.12 *(f)*

This class has a blank final `boolean` instance variable `active`. This variable must be initialized when an instance is constructed, or else the code will not compile. This also applies to blank `final static` variables. The keyword `static` is used to signify that a block is a static initializer block. No keyword is used to signify that a block is an instance initializer block. (a) and (b) are not instance initializers blocks, and (c), (d), and (e) fail to initialize the blank final variable `active`.

9.13 *(c)*

The program will compile, and print `2`, `3`, and `1` at runtime. When the object is created and initialized, the instance initializer block is executed first, printing `2`. Then the instance initializer expression is executed, printing `3`. Finally, the constructor body is executed, printing `1`. The forward reference in the instance initializer block is legal, as the use of the field `m` is on the left-hand side of the assignment.

9.14 *(c) and (e)*

Line A will cause an illegal redefinition of the field `width`. Line B uses an illegal forward reference to the fields `width` and `height`. The assignment in Line C is legal. Line D is an assignment statement, so it is illegal in this context. Line E declares a local variable inside an initializer block, with the same name as the instance variable `width`, which is allowed. The simple name in this block will refer to the local variable. To access the instance variable `width`, the `this` reference must be used in this block.

10 The ArrayList<E> Class and Lambda Expressions

10.1 *(h)*

The method `remove()` can be used to delete an element at a specific index in an `ArrayList`.

The method `clear()` can be used to delete all elements in an `ArrayList`.

The method `add(int, E)` can be used to insert an element at a specific index in an `ArrayList`.

The method `add()` can be used to append an element at the end of an `ArrayList`.

The method `set()` can be used to replace the element at a specific index with another element in an `ArrayList`.

The method `contains()` can be used to determine whether an element is in an `ArrayList`.

There is no method to determine the current capacity of an `ArrayList`.

10.2 *(e)*

The `for(;;)` loop correctly increments the loop variable so that all the elements in the list are traversed. Removing elements using the `for(;;)` loop does not throw a `ConcurrentModificationException` at runtime.

10.3 *(b) and (c)*

In the method `doIt1()`, one of the common elements (`"Ada"`) between the two lists is reversed. The value `null` is added to only one of the lists but not the other.

In the method `doIt2()`, the two lists have common elements. Swapping the elements in one list does not change their positions in the other list.

10.4 *(c)*

The element at index 2 has the value `null`. Calling the `equals()` method on this element throws a `NullPointerException`.

10.5 *(f)*

Deleting elements when traversing a list requires care, as the size changes and any elements to the right of the deleted element are shifted left. Incrementing the loop variable after deleting an element will miss the next element, as is the case with the last occurrence of `"Bob"`. Removing elements using the `for(;;)` loop does not throw a `ConcurrentModificationException` at runtime.

10.6 *(f)*

The `while` loop will execute as long as the `remove()` methods returns `true`—that is, as long as there is an element with the value `"Bob"` in the list. The `while` loop body is the empty statement. The `remove()` method does not throw an exception if an element value is `null`, or if it is passed a `null` value.

10.7 *(f)*

A functional interface can be implemented by lambda expressions and classes.

A functional interface declaration can have only one abstract method declaration.

In the body of a lambda expression, all members in the enclosing class can be accessed.

In the body of a lambda expression, only effectively final local variables in the enclosing scope can be accessed.

A lambda expression in a program can implement more than one functional interface. For example, the lambda expression `(i -> i%2 == 0)` can be the target type of both the functional interfaces `IntPredicate` and `Predicate<Integer>`.

10.8 *(a) and (c)*

(1) redeclares the local variable `p` from the enclosing scope, which is not legal.

In (2), the `equals()` method of the `String` class is called, because it is invoked on the textual representation of the parameter. In the other statements, the `equals()` method of the object referred to by the parameter is called.

The lambda body in (3) is a statement block with an expression whose value must be returned by the `return` statement.

(4) and (5) access static members in the class, which is legal.

In (6), the parameter name `lock2` shadows the static variable by the same name, but is a local variable in the lambda expression. The static variable is referred to using the class name.

10.9 *(e), (f), (g), and (i)*

Assignments in (5), (6), (7), and (9) will not compile. We must check whether the function type of the target type and the type of the lambda expression are compatible. The function type of the target type `p1` in the assignment statements from (1) to (5) is `String -> void`, or a `void` return. The function type of the target type `p2` in the assignment statements from (6) to (10) is `String -> String`, or a non-`void` return. In the following code, the functional type of the target type is shown in a comment with the prefix `LHS` (left-hand side), and the type of the lambda expression for each assignment from (1) to (10) is shown in a comment with the prefix `RHS` (right-hand side).

```
   Funky1 p1;                                  //     LHS: String -> void
   p1 = s -> System.out.println(s);            // (1) RHS: String -> void
   p1 = s -> s.length();                       // (2) RHS: String -> int
   p1 = s -> s.toUpperCase();                  // (3) RHS: String -> String
   p1 = s -> { s.toUpperCase(); };             // (4) RHS: String -> void
// p1 = s -> { return s.toUpperCase(); };      // (5) RHS: String -> String

   Funky2 p2;                                  //     LHS: String -> String
// p2 = s -> System.out.println(s);            // (6) RHS: String -> void
// p2 = s -> s.length();                       // (7) RHS: String -> int
   p2 = s -> s.toUpperCase();                  // (8) RHS: String -> String
// p2 = s -> { s.toUpperCase(); };             // (9) RHS: String -> void
   p2 = s -> { return s.toUpperCase(); };      // (10)RHS: String -> String
```

The non-`void` return of a lambda expression with an *expression statement* as the body can be interpreted as a `void` return, if the function type of the target type returns `void`. This is the case in (2) and (3). The return value is ignored. The type `String -> String` of the lambda expression in (5) is not compatible with the function type `String -> void` of the target type `p1`.

The type of the lambda expression in (6), (7), and (9) is not compatible with the function type `String -> String` of the target type `p2`.

10.10 *(d)*

The lambda expression filters all integer values that are both negative and even numbers. These values are replaced with their absolute values in the integer array. The functional interface `java.util.function.IntPredicate` has the abstract method: `boolean test(int i)`.

10.11 *(d)*

The three interfaces are functional interfaces. InterfaceB explicitly provides an abstract method declaration of the public method equals() from the Object class, but such declarations are excluded from the definition of a functional interface. Thus InterfaceB effectively has only one abstract method. A functional interface can be implemented by a concrete class, such as Beta. The function type of the target type in the assignments (1) to (3) is void -> void. The type of the lambda expression in (1) to (3) is also void -> void. The assignments (1) to (3) are legal.

The assignment in (4) is legal. Subtype references are assigned to supertype references. References o, a, and c refer to the lambda expression in (3).

The assignment in (5) is legal. The reference b has the type InterfaceB, and class Beta implements this interface.

(6), (7), and (8) invoke the method doIt(). (6) evaluates the lambda expression in (3), printing Jingle|. (7) invokes the doIt() method on an object of class Beta, printing Jazz|. (8) also evaluates the lambda expression in (3), printing Jingle|.

In (9), the reference o is cast down to InterfaceA. The reference o actually refers to the lambda expression in (3), which has target type InterfaceC. This interface is a subtype of InterfaceA. The subtype is cast to a supertype, which is allowed, so no ClassCastException is thrown at runtime. Invoking the doIt() method again results in evaluation of the lambda expression in (3), printing Jingle|.

Apart from the declarations of the lambda expressions, the rest of the code is plain-vanilla Java. Note also that the following assignment that defines a lambda expression would not be valid, since the Object class is not a functional interface and therefore cannot provide a target type for the lambda expression:

```
Object obj = () -> System.out.println("Jingle");      // Compile-time error!
```

11 Date and Time

11.1 *(e)*

The LocalDateTime class does not provide the isLeapYear() method.

The LocalTime class does not provide the isEqual() method.

The Period class does not provide the withWeeks() method, but does provide the ofWeeks() static method.

Both the Period and LocalTime classes do not provide the plusWeeks() method.

11.2 *(e)*

The date reference never gets updated, as the return value is ignored. If it had been updated, the correct answer would have been (c). The LocalDate.getMonth() method returns a Month enum constant—in this case, Month.MARCH. The LocalDate.getMonthValue() method returns the month as a value between 1 and 12—in this case, 3.

11.3 *(b), (c), (e), and (g)*

(a): The month numbers start with 1. August has month value 8.

(d): Invalid month (0) and day (0) arguments in the call to the `of()` method result in a `DateTimeException` being thrown at runtime.

(f): The `LocalDate` class does not provide a `public` constructor.

11.4 *(c), (d), and (f)*

(a): Invalid argument for the minutes (0–59).

(b): The `LocalTime` class does not provide a `public` constructor.

(c): The time assigned is 09:00.

(d): The time assigned is 00:00.

(e): There is no `withHours()` method, but there is a `withHour()` method in the `LocalTime` class.

(f): The time assigned is 11:45.

11.5 *(c)*

Both the hour and minutes are normalized by the `plus` methods, and the time of day wraps around midnight. The calculation of `time.plusHours(10).plusMinutes(120)` proceeds as follows:

```
12:00 + 10 hours ==> 22:00 + 120 min (i.e., 2 hrs.) ==> 00:00
```

11.6 *(d)*

The calculation of `p1.plus(p2).plus(p1)` proceeds as follows:

```
P1Y1M1D + P2Y12M30D ==> P3Y13M31D + P1Y1M1D ==> P4Y14M32D
```

11.7 *(c)*

The calculation of `date.withYear(5).plusMonths(14)` proceeds as follows:

```
2015-01-01 with year 5 ==> 0005-01-01 + 14 months (i.e., 1 year 2 months) ==>
0006-03-01
```

11.8 *(a), (d), (e), (g), and (i)*

The `between()` and `until()` methods return a `Period`, which can be negative. The `isAfter()`, `isBefore()`, `between()`, and `until()` methods are strict in the sense that the end date is excluded. The `compareTo()` method returns `0` if the two dates are equal, a negative value if `date1` is less than `date2`, and a positive value if `date1` is greater than `date2`.

11.9 *(e)*

(a): The `DateTimeFormatter` class provides factory methods to obtain both predefined and customized formatters.

(b): The styles defined by the `java.time.format.FormatStyle` enum type are locale sensitive.

(c): The `ofLocalizedDate()` method of the `DateTimeFormatter` class returns a formatter that is based on a format style (a constant of the `FormatStyle` enum type) passed as an argument to the method.

(d): The pattern `"yy-mm-dd"` cannot be used to create a formatter that can format a `LocalDate` object. The letter `m` stands for minutes of the hour, which is not a part of a date.

11.10 *(a), (b), (c), and (f)*

(a), (b), (c): The input string matches the pattern. The input string specifies the mandatory parts of both a date and a time, needed by the respective method to construct either a `LocalTime`, a `LocalDate`, or a `LocalDateTime`.

To use the pattern for formatting, the temporal object must provide the parts corresponding to the pattern letters in the pattern. The `LocalTime` object in (d) does not have the date part required by the pattern. The `LocalDate` object in (e) does not have the time part required by the pattern. Both (d) and (e) will throw an `Unsupported-TemporalTypeException`. Only the `LocalDateTime` object in (f) has both the date and time parts required by the pattern.

11.11 *(b), (e), and (f)*

The input string matches the pattern. It specifies the date-based values that can be used to construct a `LocalDate` object in (b), based on the date-related pattern letters in the pattern. No time-based values can be interpreted from the input string, as this pattern has only date-related pattern letters. (a) and (c), which require a time part, will throw a `DateTimeParseException`.

To use the pattern for formatting, the temporal object must provide values for the parts corresponding to the pattern letters in the pattern. The `LocalTime` object in (d) does not have the date part required by the pattern. (d) will throw an `Unsupported-TemporalTypeException`. The `LocalDate` object in (e) has the date part required by the pattern, as does the `LocalDateTime` object in (f). In (f), only the date part of the `Local-DateTime` object is formatted.

11.12 *(e)*

(a), (b), (c), (d), and (f) result in a `DateTimeParseException` when parsing.

(a): The pattern letter `h` represents hour in the day, but requires AM/PM information to resolve the hour in a 24-hour clock (i.e., pattern letter `a`), which is missing.

(b): The pattern letter `M` is interpreted correctly as month of the year (value 5). Matching the pattern letter `h` is the problem, as explained for (a).

(c), (d): The pattern letter `a` cannot be resolved from the input string, as an AM/PM marker is missing in the input string.

(e): The parse succeeds, with the `LocalTime` object having the value 09:05. Formatting this object with the formatter results in the output string: `5 minutes past 9`.

(f): The letter pattern `mm` cannot be resolved, as the minutes value has only one digit (i.e., 5) in the input string.

(g): The parse succeeds, with the resulting `LocalTime` object having the value 09:00. The month value 5 is ignored. Formatting this object with the formatter results in an `UnsupportedTemporalTypeException`, because now the pattern letter `M` requires a month value, which is not part of a `LocalTime` object.

11.13 *(d)*

(a): The formatter will format a `LocalTime` object, or the time part of a `LocalDateTime` object, but not a `LocalDate` object, as it knows nothing about formatting the date part.

(b): The formatter will format a `LocalDate` object, or the date part of a `LocalDateTime` object, but not a `LocalTime` object, as it knows nothing about formatting the time part.
(c): The formatter will format a `LocalDateTime` object, but not a `LocalDate` object or a `LocalTime` object, as it will format only temporal objects with both date and time parts.

The program throws a `java.time.temporal.UnsupportedTemporalTypeException` in all cases.

Appendix D

Solutions to Programming Exercises

1 Basics of Java Programming

1.1 The printStackElements() method of the PrintableCharStack class does not pop the elements.

```
// File: CharStack.java
public class CharStack {
  // Instance variables:
  protected char[] stackArray;   // The array implementing the stack.
  protected int    topOfStack;   // The top of the stack.

  // Static variable
  private static int counter;                                       // (1)

  // Constructor now increments the counter for each object created.
  public CharStack(int capacity) {                                  // (2)
    stackArray = new char[capacity];
    topOfStack = -1;
    counter++;
  }

  // Instance methods:
  public void push(char element) { stackArray[++topOfStack] = element; }
  public char pop()              { return stackArray[topOfStack--]; }
  public char peek()             { return stackArray[topOfStack]; }
  public boolean isEmpty()       { return topOfStack == -1; }
  public boolean isFull()        { return topOfStack == stackArray.length - 1; }

  // Static method                                                     (3)
  public static int getInstanceCount() { return counter; }
}
```

```
// File: PrintableCharStack.java
public class PrintableCharStack extends CharStack {                    // (1)

  // Instance method
  public void printStackElements() {                                   // (2)
    for (int i = 0; i <= topOfStack; i++)
      System.out.print(stackArray[i]); // print each char on terminal
    System.out.println();
  }

  // Constructor calls the constructor of the superclass explicitly.
  PrintableCharStack(int capacity) { super(capacity); }                // (3)
}
```

```
// File: Client.java
public class Client {

  public static void main(String[] args) {

    // Create a printable character stack.
    PrintableCharStack stack = new PrintableCharStack(40);

    // Create a string to push on the stack:
    String str = "!no tis ot nuf era skcatS";
    System.out.println("Original string: " + str);
    int length = str.length();

    // Push the string char by char onto the stack:
    for (int i = 0; i < length; i++) {
      stack.push(str.charAt(i));
    }

    System.out.print("Stack contents: ");
    stack.printStackElements();

    System.out.print("Reversed string: ");
    // Pop and print each char from the stack:
    while (!stack.isEmpty()) {
      System.out.print(stack.pop());
    }
    System.out.println();

    System.out.print("Stack contents: ");
    stack.printStackElements();
  }
}
```

2 Language Fundamentals

2.1 The following program compiles and runs without errors:

```
// File: Temperature.java
/* Identifiers and keywords in Java are case sensitive. Therefore, the
   the name of the public class must match the name of the file, and keywords must
   all be written in lowercase. The name of the String class has an
   uppercase S. The main method must be static and takes an array of
   String objects as an argument. */
public class Temperature {
  public static void main(String[] args) {  // Correct method signature
    double fahrenheit = 62.5;
    // A multiple-line comment, which can span several lines, starts with
    // the character sequence /* and ends with the character sequence */.
    /* Convert */
    double celsius = f2c(fahrenheit);
    // Character literals are enclosed in single quotes;
    // string literals are enclosed in double quotes.
    // Only the first character literal is quoted as a string to avoid addition.
    // The second char literal is implicitly converted to its string
    // representation, as string concatenation is performed by
    // the last + operator.
    // Java is case sensitive. The name Celsius should be changed to
    // the variable name celsius.
    System.out.println(fahrenheit + "F" + " = " + celsius + 'C');
  }
  /* Method should be declared static. */
  static double f2c(double fahr) {  // Note parameter type should be double.
    return (fahr - 32.0) * 5.0 / 9.0;
  }
}
```

3 Declarations

3.1

```
public class QuizGrader {

  /** Enum type to represent the result of answering a question. */
  enum Result { CORRECT, WRONG, UNANSWERED }

  private static final int PASS_MARK = 5;
  private static String[] correctAnswers = { "C", "A", "B", "D",
                                             "B", "C", "C", "A" };

  public static void main(String[] args) {

    System.out.println("Question  Submitted Ans. Correct Ans.  Result");

    // Counters for miscellaneous statistics:
    int numOfCorrectAnswers = 0;
    int numOfWrongAnswers = 0;
    int numOfUnanswered = 0;
```

```
    // Loop through submitted answers and correct answers:
    for (int i = 0; i < args.length; i++) {
      String submittedAnswer = args[i];
      String correctAnswer = correctAnswers[i];
      Result result = determineResult(submittedAnswer, correctAnswer);

      // Print report for current question.
      System.out.printf("%5d%10s%15s%15s%n",
                        i+1, submittedAnswer, correctAnswer, result);
      // Accumulate statistics:
      switch(result) {
        case CORRECT:    numOfCorrectAnswers++; break;
        case WRONG:      numOfWrongAnswers++;   break;
        case UNANSWERED: numOfUnanswered++;     break;
      }
    }
    // Print summary of statistics:
    System.out.println("No. of correct answers:      " + numOfCorrectAnswers);
    System.out.println("No. of wrong answers:        " + numOfWrongAnswers);
    System.out.println("No. of questions unanswered: " + numOfUnanswered);
    System.out.println("The candidate " +
                 (numOfCorrectAnswers >= PASS_MARK ? "PASSED." : "FAILED."));
  }

  /** Determines the result of answer to a question. */
  public static Result determineResult(String submittedAnswer,
                                       String correctAnswer) {
    Result result = null;
    if (submittedAnswer.equals(correctAnswer))
      result = Result.CORRECT;
    else if (submittedAnswer.equals("X"))
      result = Result.UNANSWERED;
    else
      result = Result.WRONG;
    return result;
  }
}
```

4 Access Control

4.1

```
// File: Account.java
package com.megabankcorp.records;

public class Account { }

// File: Database.java
// Specify package.
package com.megabankcorp.system;

// Refer to the Account class by using its simple name.
import com.megabankcorp.records.Account;
```

```
// Class must be abstract since it has abstract methods.
public abstract class Database {

  // Abstract and accessible to all classes in any package.
  public abstract void deposit(Account acc, double amount);

  // Abstract and accessible to all classes in any package.
  public abstract void withdraw(Account acc, double amount);

  // Abstract and accessible to all classes within its own package
  // and to subclasses in other packages.
  protected abstract double balance(Account acc);

  // Cannot be overridden by a subclass and accessible only
  // to classes within its own package.
  final void transfer(Account from, Account to, double amount) {
    withdraw(from, amount);
    deposit(to, amount);
  }
}
```

5 Operators and Expressions

5.1

```
// File: SunlightSolution.java
public class SunlightSolution {
  public static void main(String[] args) {
    // Distance from sun (150 million kilometers)
    /* The max value for int is 2_147_483_647, so using int here will
       work. */
    int kmFromSun = 150_000_000;

    // Again, using int for this value is OK.
    int lightSpeed = 299_792_458; // Meters per second

    // Convert distance to meters.
    /* The result of this equation will not fit in an int,
       so we use a long instead. We need to ensure that the values that
       are multiplied are actually multiplied using long
       data types, and not multiplied as int data types and later
       converted to long. The L suffix on the 1000L integer
       literal ensures this. The value of the variable kmFromSun will
       implicitly be converted from int to long to match the
       data type of the other factor. The conversion can be done
       implicitly by the compiler since the conversion represents
       a widening of the data type. */
    long mFromSun = kmFromSun * 1000L;

    /* We know that the result value will fit in an int.
       However, the narrowing conversion on assignment from long to int
       in this case requires a cast.*/
    int seconds = (int) (mFromSun / lightSpeed);
```

```
    System.out.print("Light will use ");
    printTime(seconds);
    System.out.println(" to travel from the sun to the earth.");
  }

  /* No changes necessary in this method. */
  public static void printTime(int sec) {
    int min = sec / 60;
    sec = sec - (min * 60);
    System.out.print(min + " minute(s) and " + sec + " second(s)");
  }
}
```

6 Control Flow

6.1 Finding primes using `for` loops.

```
// File: ForPrimes.java
public class ForPrimes {
  private static final int MAX = 100;
  public static void main(String[] args) {
    numbers:
      for (int num = 1; num < MAX; num++) {
        int divLim = (int) Math.sqrt( num );
        for (int div = 2; div <= divLim; div++) {
          if ((num % div) == 0) {
            continue numbers;
          }
        }
        System.out.println( num );
      }
  }
}
```

Finding primes using `while` loops.

```
// File: WhilePrimes.java
public class WhilePrimes {
  private static final int MAX = 100;
  public static void main(String[] args) {
    int num = 1;
    numbers:
      while (num < MAX) {
        int number = num++;
        int divLim = (int) Math.sqrt( number );
        int div = 2;
        while (div <= divLim) {
          if ((number % div++) == 0) {
            continue numbers;
          }
        }
        System.out.println( number );
      }
  }
}
```

6.2

```
package energy;
/** A PowerPlant with a reactor core.
    The solution presented here is provided by Jennie Yip. */
public class PowerPlant {
  /** Each power plant has a reactor core.
      This field has package accessibility so that the Control class,
      defined in the same package, can access it. */
  final Reactor core;

  /** Initializes the power plant, creates a reactor core. */
  PowerPlant() {
    core = new Reactor();
  }

  /** Sounds the alarm to evacuate the power plant. */
  public void soundEvacuateAlarm() {
    // ... implementation unspecified ...
  }

  /** @return the level of reactor output that is most desirable at this time.
      (Units are unspecified.) */
  public int getOptimalThroughput() {
    // ... implementation unspecified ...
    return 0;
  }

  /** The main entry point of the program: sets up a PowerPlant object
      and a Control object and lets the Control object run the power plant. */
  public static void main(String[] args) {
    PowerPlant plant = new PowerPlant();
    Control ctrl = new Control(plant);
    ctrl.runSystem();
  }
}

//_______________________________________________________________________

/** A reactor core that has a throughput that can be either decreased or
    increased. */
class Reactor {
  /** @return the current throughput of the reactor. (Units are unspecified.) */
  public int getThroughput() {
    // ... implementation unspecified ...
    return 0;
  }

  /** @return true if the reactor status is critical, false otherwise. */
  public boolean isCritical() {
    // ... implementation unspecified ...
    return false;
  }
```

```
  /** Asks the reactor to increase throughput. */
  void increaseThroughput() throws ReactorCritical {
    // ... implementation unspecified ...
  }

  /** Asks the reactor to decrease throughput. */
  void decreaseThroughput() {
    // ... implementation unspecified ...
  }
}

//______________________________________________________________________

/** This exception class should be used to report that the reactor status is
    critical. */
class ReactorCritical extends Exception {}

//______________________________________________________________________

/** A controller that will manage the power plant to make sure that the
    reactor runs with optimal throughput. */
class Control {
  private final PowerPlant thePlant;

  static final int TOLERANCE = 10;

  /** @param p the power plant to control */
  public Control(PowerPlant p) {
    thePlant = p;
  }

  /** Run the power plant by continuously monitoring the
      optimal throughput and the actual throughput of the reactor.
      If the throughputs differ by more than 10 units (i.e. tolerance),
      adjust the reactor throughput.
      If the reactor goes critical, the evacuate alarm is
      sounded and the reactor is shut down.
      The runSystem() method calls the methods needAdjustment(),
      adjustThroughput(), and shutdown(). */
  public void runSystem() {
    try {
      while (true) { // infinite loop
        int optimalThroughput = thePlant.getOptimalThroughput();
        if (needAdjustment(optimalThroughput)) {
          adjustThroughput(optimalThroughput);
        }
      }
    } catch (ReactorCritical rc) {
      thePlant.soundEvacuateAlarm();
    } finally {
      shutdown();
    }
  }
```

```
  /** Reports whether the throughput of the reactor needs adjusting.
      This method should also monitor and report if the reactor goes critical.
      @param target the desired throughput.
      @return true if the optimal and actual throughput values differ by
      more than 10 units.
      @throws ReactorCritical if the reactor goes critical */
  public boolean needAdjustment(int target) throws ReactorCritical {
    /* We added the throws clause to the method declaration so that
       the method can throw a ReactorCritical exception if the reactor
       goes critical. */
    if (thePlant.core.isCritical()) {
      throw new ReactorCritical();
    }
    return Math.abs(thePlant.core.getThroughput() - target) > TOLERANCE;
  }

  /** Adjusts the throughput of the reactor by calling increaseThroughput()
      and decreaseThroughput() methods until the actual throughput is within
      10 units of the target throughput.
      @param target the desired throughput.
      @throws ReactorCritical if the reactor goes critical. */
  public void adjustThroughput(int target) throws ReactorCritical {
    /* We added the throws clause to the method declaration because
       this method does not want to handle any ReactorCritical exception
       thrown by the increaseThroughput() method. */
    while (needAdjustment(target)) {
      if ((thePlant.core.getThroughput() - target) > TOLERANCE) {
        thePlant.core.increaseThroughput();
      } else {
        thePlant.core.decreaseThroughput();
      }
    }
  }

  /** Shuts down the reactor by lowering the throughput to 0. */
  public void shutdown() {
    while (thePlant.core.getThroughput() > 0) {
      thePlant.core.decreaseThroughput();
    }
  }
}
```

7 Object-Oriented Programming

7.1

```
// File: Exercise1.java
package chap07pe1;

interface Function {
  int evaluate(int arg);
}
```

```
class Half implements Function {
  @Override public int evaluate(int arg) {
    return arg/2;
  }
}

public class Exercise1 {

  public static int[] applyFunction(int... arrIn) {
    int length = arrIn.length;
    int[] arrOut = new int[length];
    Function func = new Half();
    for (int i = 0; i < length; i++) {
      arrOut[i] = func.evaluate(arrIn[i]);
    }
    return arrOut;
  }

  public static void main(String[] args) {

    // Halve the values.
    int[] myArr = applyFunction(2, 4, 6, 8);

    System.out.println("Array with values halved by integer division:");
    for (int value : myArr) {
      System.out.println(value);
    }
  }
}
```

7.2

```
// File: Exercise2.java
package chap07pe2;

interface Function {
  int evaluate(int arg);
}

class Half implements Function {
  @Override public int evaluate(int arg) {
    return arg/2;
  }
}

class Print implements Function {
  @Override public int evaluate(int arg) {
    System.out.println(arg);
    return arg;
  }
}
```

```
public class Exercise2 {
  public static int[] applyFunction(Function func, int... arrIn) {
    int length = arrIn.length;
    int[] arrOut = new int[length];
    for (int i = 0; i < length; i++) {
      arrOut[i] = func.evaluate(arrIn[i]);
    }
    return arrOut;
  }

  public static void main(String[] args) {
    // Create a print function.
    Function print = new Print();

    System.out.println("Original values:");
    int[] myArr = applyFunction(print, 2, 4, 6, 8);

    // Halve the array values.
    myArr = applyFunction(new Half(), myArr);

    System.out.println("Halved values:");
    applyFunction(print, myArr);
  }
}
```

8 Fundamental Classes

8.1

```
/**
 * Aggregate (non-generic) pairs of arbitrary objects.
 */
public final class Pair {
  private final Object first, second;

  /** Construct a Pair object. */
  public Pair(Object one, Object two) {
    first = one;
    second = two;
  }

  /** @return the first constituent object. */
  public Object getFirst() { return first; }

  /** @return the second constituent object. */
  public Object getSecond() { return second; }

  /** @return true if the pair of objects are identical. */
  @Override
  public boolean equals(Object other) {
    if (this == other) return true;
    if (! (other instanceof Pair)) return false;
    Pair otherPair = (Pair) other;
    return first.equals(otherPair.first) && second.equals(otherPair.second);
  }
```

```
  /** @return a hash code for the aggregate pair. */
  @Override
  public int hashCode() {
    // XORing the hash codes to create a hash code for the pair.
    return first.hashCode() ^ second.hashCode();
  }

  /** @return a textual representation of the aggregated object. */
  @Override
  public String toString() {
    return "[" + first + "," + second + "]";
  }
}
```

8.2

```
/** Determine whether a string is a case-sensitive palindrome. */
public class Palindrome {
  public static void main(String[] args) {
    if (args.length != 1) {
      System.out.println("Usage: java Palindrome <word>");
      return;
    }
    String word = args[0];
    StringBuilder reverseWord = new StringBuilder(word).reverse();
    boolean isPalindrome = word.equals(reverseWord.toString());
    System.out.println("The word " + word + " is " +
                       (isPalindrome ? "" : "not ") + "a palindrome");
  }
}
```

9 Object Lifetime

No programming exercises.

10 The ArrayList<E> Class and Lambda Expressions

10.1

```
/* Find all elements in a list that satisfy all predicates. */
import java.util.ArrayList;
import java.util.List;
import java.util.function.Predicate;

public class FilterFunSolution {

  public static void main(String[] args) {                          // (1)
    // Create a list of strings:
    String[] strings = { "Cheer up!", "7Up coming up!", null,
                         "Bottoms up!","Get down!", "What's up?" };
```

```
    List<String> strList = new ArrayList<>();
    /* WRITE CODE TO POPULATE THE LIST OF STRINGS HERE. */
    for (String str : strings)
      strList.add(str);
    System.out.println(strList);

    // Create a list of predicates.
    List<Predicate<String>> predList = new ArrayList<>();
    /* WRITE CODE TO POPULATE THE LIST OF PREDICATES HERE. */
    predList.add(str -> str != null);
    predList.add(str -> str.toLowerCase().contains("up"));
    predList.add(str -> Character.isLetter(str.charAt(0)));
    System.out.println(predList);

    // Apply filtering.
    applyAllPredicates(strList, predList);
    applyAllPredicatesAlt(strList, predList);
    applyAllPredicatesGenAlt(strList, predList);
  }

  /**
   * Prints all the strings in the specified list that satisfy all the
   * predicates in the list of predicates.
   * It uses the andPredicates() method at (3).
   * @param list          List of strings to apply the predicates on
   * @param predicates    List of predicates to apply
   */
  public static void applyAllPredicates(List<String> list,              // (2)
                                        List<Predicate<String>> predicates) {
    /* IMPLEMENT THIS METHOD */
    List<String> resultList = new ArrayList<>();
    for (String str : list) {
      if (andPredicates(str, predicates)) {
        resultList.add(str);
      }
    }
    System.out.println(resultList);
  }

  /**
   * Determines whether a string satisfies all the predicates.
   * @param str           String to apply the predicates on
   * @param predicates    List of predicates to apply
   * @return              true only if the string satisfies all the predicates
   */
  public static boolean andPredicates(String str,                       // (3)
                                      List<Predicate<String>> predicates) {
    /* IMPLEMENT THIS METHOD */
    boolean proceed = true;
    for (Predicate<String> p : predicates) {
      proceed = proceed && p.test(str);
      if (!proceed) break;
    }
    return proceed;
  }
```

```
  /**
   * Removes all the elements in the specified list that do not satisfy all the
   * predicates in the list of predicates, and prints the remaining elements
   * that do.
   * Uses Predicate.and(), Predicate.negate(), and List.removeIf() methods.
   * @param list          List of strings to apply the predicates on
   * @param predicates    List of predicates to apply
   */
  public static void applyAllPredicatesAlt(List<String> list,               // (4)
                                           List<Predicate<String>> predicates) {
    /* IMPLEMENT THIS METHOD */
    Predicate<String> compPred = s -> true;
    for (Predicate<String> p : predicates) {
      compPred = compPred.and(p);
    }
    list.removeIf(compPred.negate());
    System.out.println(list);
  }

  /** Generic version.
   * Removes all the elements in the specified list that do not satisfy all the
   * predicates in the list of predicates, and prints the remaining elements
   * that do.
   * Uses Predicate.and(), Predicate.negate(), and List.removeIf() methods.
   * @param list          List of elements to apply the predicates on
   * @param predicates    List of predicates to apply
   */
  public static <T> void applyAllPredicatesGenAlt(List<T> list,            // (5)
                                                  List<Predicate<T>> predicates) {
    /* IMPLEMENT THIS METHOD */
    Predicate<T> compPred = s -> true;
    for (Predicate<T> p : predicates) {
      compPred = compPred.and(p);
    }
    list.removeIf(compPred.negate());
    System.out.println(list);
  }
}
```

11 Date and Time

11.1

```
import java.time.LocalDate;
import java.time.LocalDateTime;
import java.time.Period;

/** Class represents statistics about an astronaut. */
public class Astronaut {

  private final String        astronautName;
  private final LocalDateTime arrivalDateTime;
  private final LocalDate     scheduledReturnDate;
  private final Period        actualPeriodOfStay;
```

```
  public Astronaut(String name, LocalDateTime arrival, Period period,
                   LocalDate returnDate) {
    astronautName = name;
    arrivalDateTime = arrival;
    actualPeriodOfStay = period;
    scheduledReturnDate = returnDate;
  }

  public String getAstronautName()          { return astronautName; }
  public LocalDateTime getArrivalDateTime() { return arrivalDateTime; }
  public Period getActualPeriodOfStay()     { return actualPeriodOfStay; }
  public LocalDate getScheduledReturnDate() { return scheduledReturnDate; }

  /** @return LocalDate The actual date of return. */
  public LocalDate getActualReturnDate() {
    /* IMPLEMENT THIS METHOD. */
    return arrivalDateTime.toLocalDate().plus(actualPeriodOfStay);
  }

  /**
   * Returns status of the actual return compared to the scheduled return,
   * whether it was on time, delayed, or early.
   * @return String Indicating "On time", "Delayed", or "Early".
   */
  public String getReturnStatus() {
    /* IMPLEMENT THIS METHOD. */
    String status = "On time";
    LocalDate actualReturnDate = getActualReturnDate();
    if (scheduledReturnDate.isBefore(actualReturnDate)) {
      status = "Delayed";
    } else if (scheduledReturnDate.isAfter(actualReturnDate)) {
      status = "Early";
    }
    return status;
  }

  /** @return Period The planned stay according to the scheduled return.*/
  public Period getPlannedPeriodOfStay() {
    /* IMPLEMENT THIS METHOD. */
    return Period.between(arrivalDateTime.toLocalDate(), scheduledReturnDate);
  }

  /**
   * @return Period The difference between the actual return date and
   *                the scheduled return date. */
  public Period getDiffPeriodOfStay() {
    /* IMPLEMENT THIS METHOD. */
    return scheduledReturnDate.until(getActualReturnDate());
    // Following code has logical error, as a period has no notion of a date.
    // return actualPeriodOfStay.minus(getPlannedPeriodOfStay());
  }
}
```

```
import java.time.LocalDate;
import java.time.LocalDateTime;
import java.time.Period;
import java.time.format.DateTimeFormatter;

public class SpaceStationStats {

  public static void main(String[] args) {
    // Astronaut data
    Astronaut[] astronauts = {
        new Astronaut("Astro Ali",
            LocalDateTime.of(2010, 3, 1, 10, 45), Period.ofMonths(3),
            LocalDate.of(2010, 5, 1)),
        new Astronaut("Laila Lightyear",
            LocalDateTime.of(2015, 2, 1, 17, 0),  Period.ofWeeks(30),
            LocalDate.of(2015, 6, 30)),
        new Astronaut("Orbit Orwell",
            LocalDateTime.of(2014, 3, 1, 20, 20), Period.ofMonths(6),
            LocalDate.of(2014, 9, 1)),
        new Astronaut("Rocket Rogers",
            LocalDateTime.of(2013, 7, 31, 15, 30), Period.ofDays(60),
            LocalDate.of(2013, 9, 30)),
        new Astronaut("Sam Spacey",
            LocalDateTime.of(2009, 1, 1, 12, 15), Period.ofDays(90),
            LocalDate.of(2009, 11, 1)),
    };
    printReport(astronauts);
  }

  /**
   * Method prints statistics about stay on a space station.
   * See the exercise text for the format of the report.
   * @param astronauts The array with astronaut data
   */
  private static void printReport(Astronaut[] astronauts) {
    System.out.println("Name               Arr.Date  Sched.Return"
                + " Act.Return  Status Act.Stay Sched.Stay Diff");
    String reportFormatStr = "%-16s%10s%12s%12s%8s%6s%10s%9s%n";
    /* IMPLEMENT THE REST OF THE METHOD. */
    DateTimeFormatter df = DateTimeFormatter.ofPattern("uuuu/MM/dd");
     for (Astronaut astro : astronauts) {
       String astronautName = astro.getAstronautName();
       LocalDate arrivalDate = astro.getArrivalDateTime().toLocalDate();
       LocalDate scheduledReturnDate = astro.getScheduledReturnDate();
       LocalDate actualReturnDate = astro.getActualReturnDate();
       String status = astro.getReturnStatus();
       Period periodOfStay = astro.getActualPeriodOfStay();
       Period plannedPeriodOfStay = astro.getPlannedPeriodOfStay();
       Period diffPeriodOfStay = astro.getDiffPeriodOfStay();
```

```
            System.out.printf(reportFormatStr, astronautName,
                              arrivalDate.format(df), scheduledReturnDate.format(df),
                              actualReturnDate.format(df), status,
                              periodOfStay, plannedPeriodOfStay, diffPeriodOfStay);
        }
    }
}
```

Appendix E

Mock Exam: Java SE 8 Programmer I

This is a mock exam for the *Java SE 8 Programmer I* exam. It comprises brand-new questions, which are similar to the questions that can be expected on the real exam. Working through this exam will give you a good indication of how well you are prepared for the real exam, and whether any topics need further study. Annotated answers to the questions can be found in Appendix F.

Questions

Q1 Which expression statements, when inserted at (1), will cause the following class to compile without errors?

```
public class Q6db8 {
  private int a;
  private int b = 0;
  private static int c;

  public void m() {
    int d;
    int e = 0;

    // (1) INSERT CODE HERE.
  }
}
```

Select the four correct answers.

(a) `a++;`
(b) `b++;`
(c) `c++;`
(d) `d++;`
(e) `e++;`

Q2 What will be printed when the following program is run?

```
public class Qd803 {
  public static void main(String[] args) {
    String word = "restructure";
    System.out.println(word.substring(2, 3));
  }
}
```

Select the one correct answer.

(a) `est`
(b) `es`
(c) `str`
(d) `st`
(e) `s`

Q3 What will be printed when the following program is run?

```
public class Q8929 {
  public static void main(String[] args) {
    for (int i = 12; i > 0; i -= 3)
      System.out.print(i);
    System.out.println("");
  }
}
```

Select the one correct answer.

(a) `12`
(b) `129630`
(c) `12963`
(d) `36912`
(e) None of the above.

Q4 What will be the result of compiling and running the following program?

```
public class Q275d {
  private static int a;
  private int b;

  public Q275d() {
    int c;
    c = a;          // (1)
    a++;            // (2)
    b += c;         // (3)
    a -= b;         // (4)
  }

  public static void main(String[] args) {
    new Q275d();
  }
}
```

Select the one correct answer.

(a) The program will fail to compile because of the line marked (1).
(b) The program will fail to compile because of the line marked (2).
(c) The program will fail to compile because of the line marked (3).
(d) The program will fail to compile because of the line marked (4).
(e) The program will compile and run without any problems.

Q5 What will be printed when the following program is run?

```
class Base {
  protected int i;
  Base() { add(1); }
  void add(int v) { i += v; }
  void print() { System.out.println(i); }
}

class Extension extends Base {
  Extension() { add(2); }
  void add(int v) { i += v*2; }
}

public class Qd073 {
  public static void main(String[] args) {
    bogo(new Extension());
  }

  static void bogo(Base b) {
    b.add(8);
    b.print();
  }
}
```

Select the one correct answer.

(a) 9
(b) 11
(c) 13
(d) 21
(e) 22

Q6 Which is the first line in the following code after which the object created in the line marked (0) will be a candidate for garbage collection, assuming no compiler optimizations are done?

```
class Widget {
  private String message;

  Widget(String message) {
    this.message = message;
  }

  public String toString() {
    return this.message;
  }
}
```

```
public class Q76a9 {
  static Widget fiddle() {
    Widget a = new Widget("hello");
    Widget b = new Widget("bye");      // (0)
    Widget c = new Widget(b + "!");   // (1)
    Widget d = b;                      // (2)
    b = a;                             // (3)
    d = a;                             // (4)
    return c;                          // (5)
  }
  public static void main(String[] args) {
    Widget giz = fiddle();
    System.out.println(giz);           // (6)
  }
}
```

Select the one correct answer.

(a) The line marked (1)
(b) The line marked (2)
(c) The line marked (3)
(d) The line marked (4)
(e) The line marked (5)
(f) The line marked (6)

Q7 Which methods from the `String` or the `StringBuilder` class modify the object on which they are invoked?

Select the two correct answers.

(a) The `charAt()` method of the `String` class
(b) The `toUpperCase()` method of the `String` class
(c) The `replace()` method of the `String` class
(d) The `replace()` method of the `StringBuilder` class
(e) The `reverse()` method of the `StringBuilder` class
(f) The `charAt()` method of the `StringBuilder` class

Q8 Which of the following statements, when inserted independently at (1), will throw a runtime exception?

```
class A {}

class B extends A {}

class C extends A {}

public class Q3ae4 {
  public static void main(String[] args) {
    A x = new A();
    B y = new B();
    C z = new C();

    // (1) INSERT CODE HERE.

  }
}
```

Select the one correct answer.

(a) `x = y;`
(b) `z = x;`
(c) `y = (B) x;`
(d) `z = (C) y;`
(e) `y = (A) y;`

Q9 Given the following program:

```
public class Q400A60 {
  public static void main(String[] args) {
    String str = "loop or not to loop";
    String[] strs = {"loop", "or", "not", "to", "loop"};
    // (1) INSERT LOOP HERE.
  }
}
```

Which code, when inserted independently at (1), will compile without errors?

Select the four correct answers.

(a)
```
for (char ch : str)
  System.out.print(ch);
```
(b)
```
for (char ch : str.toCharArray())
  System.out.print(ch);
```
(c)
```
for (Character ch : str.toCharArray())
  System.out.print(ch);
```
(d)
```
for (Character ch : str.toCharArray())
  System.out.print(ch.charValue());
```
(e)
```
for (String str : strs)
  System.out.print(str);
```
(f)
```
for (String elt : strs[])
  System.out.print(elt);
```
(g)
```
for (String elt : strs)
  System.out.print(elt);
```
(h)
```
for (Character ch : strs[strs.length-1].toArray())
  System.out.print(ch);
```

Q10 Which code initializes the two-dimensional array `matrix` so that `matrix[3][2]` is a valid element?

Select the two correct answers.

(a)
```
int[][] matrix = {
    { 0, 0, 0 },
    { 0, 0, 0 }
};
```
(b)
```
int matrix[][] = new int[4][];
for (int i = 0; i < matrix.length; i++) matrix[i] = new int[3];
```
(c)
```
int matrix[][] = {
    0, 0, 0, 0,
    0, 0, 0, 0,
    0, 0, 0, 0,
    0, 0, 0, 0
};
```
(d)
```
int matrix[3][2];
```
(e)
```
int[] matrix[] = { {0, 0, 0}, {0, 0, 0}, {0, 0, 0}, {0, 0, 0} };
```

Q11 What will be the result of attempting to run the following program?

```
public class Qaa75 {
  public static void main(String[] args) {
    String[][][] arr = {
        { {}, null },
        { { "1", "2" }, { "1", null, "3" } },
        {},
        { { "1", null } }
    };
        System.out.println(arr.length + arr[1][2].length);
  }
}
```

Select the one correct answer.

(a) The program will throw an `ArrayIndexOutOfBoundsException` and terminate.
(b) The program will throw a `NullPointerException` and terminate.
(c) The program will print `4`.
(d) The program will print `6`.
(e) The program will print `7`.

Q12 Which expressions will evaluate to `true` if preceded by the following code?

```
String a = "hello";
String b = new String(a);
String c = a;
char[] d = { 'h', 'e', 'l', 'l', 'o' };
```

Select the two correct answers.

(a) `(a == "Hello")`
(b) `(a == b)`
(c) `(a == c)`
(d) `a.equals(b)`
(e) `a.equals(d)`

Q13 Which statements are true about the value of a field, when no explicit initial value has been assigned?

Select the two correct answers.

(a) The value of a field of type `int` is undetermined.
(b) The value of a field of any numeric type is 0.
(c) The compiler may issue an error if the field is used in a method before it is initialized.
(d) A field of type `String` will denote the empty string ("").
(e) The value of all fields that are references is `null`.

Q14 Which `main()` method will succeed in printing the last program argument and terminate normally with no output, if no program arguments are specified?

Select the one correct answer.

(a)
```
public static void main(String[] args) {
  if (args.length != 0)
    System.out.println(args[args.length-1]);
}
```
(b)
```
public static void main(String[] args) {
  try { System.out.println(args[args.length]); }
  catch (ArrayIndexOutOfBoundsException e) {}
}
```
(c)
```
public static void main(String[] args) {
  int ix = args.length;
  String last = args[ix];
  if (ix != 0) System.out.println(last);
}
```
(d)
```
public static void main(String[] args) {
  int ix = args.length-1;
  if (ix > 0) System.out.println(args[ix]);
}
```
(e)
```
public static void main(String[] args) {
  try { System.out.println(args[args.length-1]); }
  catch (NullPointerException e) {}
}
```

Q15 What will be printed when the following program is executed?

```
public class Qcb90 {
  private int a;
  private int b;
  public void f() {
    a = 0;
    b = 0;
    int[] c = { 0 };
    g(b, c);
    System.out.println(a + " " + b + " " + c[0] + " ");
  }

  public void g(int b, int[] c) {
    a = 1;
    b = 1;
    c[0] = 1;
  }

  public static void main(String[] args) {
    Qcb90 obj = new Qcb90();

    obj.f();
  }
}
```

Select the one correct answer.

(a) 0 0 0
(b) 0 0 1
(c) 0 1 0
(d) 1 0 0
(e) 1 0 1

Q16 What will be the result of attempting to compile and run the following program?

```
public class Q28fd {
  public static void main(String[] args) {
    int counter = 0;
    l1:
    for (int i = 0; i < 10; i++) {
      l2:
      int j = 0;
      while (j++ < 10) {
        if (j > i) break l2;
        if (j == i) {
          counter++;
          continue l1;
        }
      }
    }
    System.out.println(counter);
  }
}
```

Select the one correct answer.

(a) The program will fail to compile.
(b) The program will not terminate normally.
(c) The program will print 10 and terminate normally.
(d) The program will print 0 and terminate normally.
(e) The program will print 9 and terminate normally.

Q17 Given the following interface declaration, which declaration is valid?

```
interface I {
  void setValue(int val);
  int getValue();
}
```

Select the one correct answer.

(a)
```
class A extends I {
  int value;
  void setValue(int val) { value = val; }
  int getValue() { return value; }
}
```
(b)
```
interface B extends I {
  void increment();
}
```
(c)
```
abstract class C implements I {
  int getValue() { return 0; }
  abstract void increment();
}
```
(d)
```
interface D implements I {
  void increment();
}
```
(e)
```
class E implements I {
  int value;
  public void setValue(int val) { value = val; }
}
```

Q18 What will be the result of attempting to compile and run the following code?

```
public class Q6b0c {
  public static void main(String[] args) {
    int i = 4;
    float f = 4.3;
    double d = 1.8;
    int c = 0;
    if (i == f) c++;
    if (((int) (f + d)) == ((int) f + (int) d)) c += 2;
    System.out.println(c);
  }
}
```

Select the one correct answer.

(a) The program will fail to compile.
(b) The program will print 0.
(c) The program will print 1.
(d) The program will print 2.
(e) The program will print 3.

Q19 Which operators will always evaluate all the operands?

Select the two correct answers.

(a) `||`
(b) `+`
(c) `&&`
(d) `? :`
(e) `%`

Q20 Which statement about the `switch` construct is true?

Select the one correct answer.

(a) All `switch` statements must have a `default` label.
(b) A statement within a `switch` statement can have only one case label.
(c) The keyword `continue` can never occur within the body of a `switch` statement.
(d) No `case` label may follow a `default` label in a single `switch` statement.
(e) A character literal can be used as a value for a `case` label.

Q21 What will be printed when the following program is run?

```
public class Q03e4 {
  public static void main(String[] args) {
    String space = " ";

    String composite = space + "hello" + space + space;
    composite.concat("world");

    String trimmed = composite.trim();

    System.out.println(trimmed.length());
  }
}
```

Select the one correct answer.

(a) 5
(b) 6
(c) 7
(d) 12
(e) 13

Q22 Which method declarations, when inserted at (1), will correctly overload the method `sum()`?

```
public class Qdd1f {
  public long sum(long a, long b) { return a + b; }

  // (1) INSERT CODE HERE.

}
```

Select the two correct answers.

(a) `public int sum(int a, int b) { return a + b; }`
(b) `public int sum(long a, long b) { return 0; }`
(c) `abstract int sum();`
(d) `private long sum(long a, long b) { return a + b; }`
(e) `public long sum(long a, int b) { return a + b; }`

Q23 What will the following program print when compiled and run?

```
public class Q200A80 {
  public static void main(String[] args) {
    callType(10);
  }

  private static void callType(Number num){
    System.out.println("Number passed");
  }

  private static void callType(Object obj){
    System.out.println("Object passed");
  }
}
```

Select the one correct answer.

(a) The program compiles and prints: `Object passed`.
(b) The program compiles and prints: `Number passed`.
(c) The program fails to compile, because the call to the `callType()` method is ambiguous.
(d) None of the above.

Q24 Which of these method declarations are valid declarations of the `main()` method that would be called by the JVM to start the execution of a Java application?

Select the three correct answers.

(a) `static void main(String[] args) { /* ... */ }`
(b) `public static int main(String[] args) { /* ... */ }`

(c) `public static void main(String args) { /* ... */ }`
(d) `final public static void main(String[] arguments) { /* ... */ }`
(e) `public int main(Strings[] args, int argc) { /* ... */ }`
(f) `static public void main(String args[]) { /* ... */ }`
(g) `static public void main(String... args) { /* ... */ }`

Q25 Given the class

```
public class Args {
  public static void main(String[] args) {
    System.out.println(args[0] + " " + args[args.length-1]);
  }
}
```

what would be the result of executing the following command line?

```
>java Args In politics stupidity is not a handicap
```

Select the one correct answer.

(a) The program will throw an `ArrayIndexOutOfBoundsException`.
(b) The program will print `java handicap`.
(c) The program will print `Args handicap`.
(d) The program will print `In handicap`.
(e) The program will print `Args a`.
(f) The program will print `In a`.

Q26 Which statement about the following program is true?

```
class MyClass {
  public static void main(String[] args) {
    String[] numbers = { "one", "two", "three", "four" };

    if (args.length == 0) {
      System.out.println("no arguments");
    } else {
      System.out.println(numbers[ args.length ] + " arguments");
    }
  }
}
```

Select the one correct answer.

(a) The program will fail to compile.
(b) The program will throw a `NullPointerException` when run with no program arguments.
(c) The program will print `no arguments` and `two arguments` when called with zero and three program arguments, respectively.
(d) The program will print `no arguments` and `three arguments` when called with zero and three program arguments, respectively.
(e) The program will print `no arguments` and `four arguments` when called with zero and three program arguments, respectively.
(f) The program will print `one arguments` and `four arguments` when called with zero and three program arguments, respectively.

Q27 Which statements are true about the import statement?

Select the two correct answers.

(a) Static import from a class automatically imports the names of static members of any nested types declared in that class.
(b) Static members of the default package cannot be imported.
(c) Static import statements must be specified after any type import statements.
(d) In the case of a name conflict, the name in the last static import statement is chosen.
(e) A declaration of a name in a compilation unit can shadow a name that is imported.

Q28 What would be the result of compiling and running the following program?

```
class MyClass {
  static MyClass ref;
  String[] arguments;

  public static void main(String[] args) {
    ref = new MyClass();
    ref.func(args);
  }

  public void func(String[] args) {
    ref.arguments = args;
  }
}
```

Select the one correct answer.

(a) The program will fail to compile, since the static method `main()` cannot have a call to the non-static method `func()`.
(b) The program will fail to compile, since the non-static method `func()` cannot access the static variable `ref`.
(c) The program will fail to compile, since the argument `args` passed to the static method `main()` cannot be passed to the non-static method `func()`.
(d) The program will compile, but will throw an exception when run.
(e) The program will compile and run successfully.

Q29 Given the following member declarations, which statement is true?

```
int a;                              // (1)
static int a;                       // (2)
int f() { return a; }               // (3)
static int f() { return a; }        // (4)
```

Select the one correct answer.

(a) Declarations (1) and (3) cannot occur in the same class declaration.
(b) Declarations (2) and (4) cannot occur in the same class declaration.
(c) Declarations (1) and (4) cannot occur in the same class declaration.
(d) Declarations (2) and (3) cannot occur in the same class declaration.

Q30 Which of these combinations of `switch` expression types and `case` label value types are legal within a `switch` statement?

Select the three correct answers.

(a) `switch` expression of type `int` and `case` label value of type `char`
(b) `switch` expression of type `float` and `case` label value of type `int`
(c) `switch` expression of type `byte` and `case` label value of type `float`
(d) `switch` expression of type `char` and `case` label value of type `long`
(e) `switch` expression of type `boolean` and `case` label value of type `boolean`
(f) `switch` expression of type `Byte` and `case` label value of type `byte`
(g) `switch` expression of type `byte` and `case` label value of type `Byte`
(h) `switch` expression of type `String` and `case` label value of type `String`

Q31 What will be the result of attempting to compile and run the following program?

```
public class Switcheroo {
  public static void main(String[] args) {
    final int iLoc = 3;
    final Integer iFour = 4;
    Integer iRef = 4;
    switch (iRef) {
      case iFour:
        System.out.println("It's OK.");
      case 1:
      case iLoc:
      case 2 * iLoc:
        System.out.println("I am not OK.");
      default:
        System.out.println("You are OK.");
    }
  }
}
```

Select the one correct answer.

(a) The program will fail to compile.
(b) The program will compile, but will throw a runtime exception.
(c) The program will compile correctly and will print the following at runtime:
```
It's OK.
I am not OK.
You are OK.
```
(d) The program will compile correctly and will print the following at runtime:
```
It's OK.
I am not OK.
```
(e) The program will compile correctly and will print the following at runtime:
```
It's OK.
```

Q32 Which of the following implementations of a `max()` method will correctly return the largest value?

```
// (1)
int max(int x, int y) {
  return (if (x > y) { x; } else { y; });
}

// (2)
int max(int x, int y) {
  return (if (x > y) { return x; } else { return y; });
}

// (3)
int max(int x, int y) {
  switch (x < y) {
    case true:
      return y;
    default:
      return x;
  };
}

// (4)
int max(int x, int y) {
  if (x > y) return x;
  return y;
}
```

Select the one correct answer.

(a) Implementation labeled (1)
(b) Implementation labeled (2)
(c) Implementation labeled (3)
(d) Implementation labeled (4)

Q33 Given the following code, which statement is true?

```
class MyClass {
  public static void main(String[] args) {
    int k = 0;
    int l = 0;
    for (int i = 0; i <= 3; i++) {
      k++;
      if (i == 2) break;
      l++;
    }
    System.out.println(k + ", " + l);
  }
}
```

Select the one correct answer.

(a) The program will fail to compile.
(b) The program will print `3, 3` at runtime.
(c) The program will print `4, 3` at runtime, if the `break` statement is replaced by the `continue` statement.

(d) The program will fail to compile if the `break` statement is replaced by the `return` statement.
(e) The program will fail to compile if the `break` statement is replaced by an empty statement.

Q34 Which statements are true?

Select the two correct answers.
(a) `{{}}` is a valid block statement.
(b) `{ continue; }` is a valid block statement.
(c) `block: { break block; }` is a valid block statement.
(d) `block: { continue block; }` is a valid block statement.
(e) The `break` statement can be used only in a loop (`while`, `do-while` or `for`) or a `switch` statement.

Q35 Given the declaration:

```
int[][] nums = {{20}, {30}, {40}};
```

Which code will compile and print `90` at runtime?

Select the one correct answer.

(a)
```
{
    int sum = 0;
    for (int[] row : nums[])
      for (int val : nums[row])
        sum += val;
    System.out.println(sum);
}
```
(b)
```
{
    int sum = 0;
    for (int[] row : nums[][])
      for (int val : nums[row])
        sum += val;
    System.out.println(sum);
}
```
(c)
```
{
    int sum = 0;
    for (int[] row : nums)
      for (int val : nums[row])
        sum += val;
    System.out.println(sum);
}
```
(d)
```
{
    int sum = 0;
    for (int[] row : nums)
      for (int val : row)
        sum += val;
    System.out.println(sum);
}
```

(e)
```
{
  int sum = 0;
  for (Integer[] row : nums)
    for (int val : row)
      sum += val;
  System.out.println(sum);
}
```

Q36 Which digits, and in what order, will be printed when the following program is compiled and run?

```
public class MyClass {
  public static void main(String[] args) {
    try {
      interruptForLunch();
    } catch (InterruptedException e) {
      System.out.println("1");
      throw new RuntimeException();
    } catch (RuntimeException e) {
      System.out.println("2");
      return;
    } catch (Exception e) {
      System.out.println("3");
    } finally {
      System.out.println("4");
    }
    System.out.println("5");
  }

  // InterruptedException is a direct subclass of Exception.
  static void interruptForLunch() throws InterruptedException {
    throw new InterruptedException("Time for lunch.");
  }
}
```

Select the one correct answer.

(a) The program will print 5.
(b) The program will print 1 and 4, in that order.
(c) The program will print 1, 2, and 4, in that order.
(d) The program will print 1, 4, and 5, in that order.
(e) The program will print 1, 2, 4, and 5, in that order.
(f) The program will print 3 and 5, in that order.

Q37 How many objects are reachable when control reaches (1)?

```
public class Nullify {

  private static void nullify(Object[] array) { array = null; }

  public static void main(String[] args) {
    args = null;
    Object[] array = new Object[4];
    for (int i = 0; i < 4; i++) {
      array[i] = new Object();
    }
```

```
        nullify(array);
        System.gc();                    // (1);
    }
}
```

Select the one correct answer.

(a) 0
(b) 1
(c) 4
(d) 5
(e) It is difficult to say.

Q38 Which statement describes the guaranteed behavior of the garbage collection and finalization mechanisms?

Select the one correct answer.

(a) Objects will not be destroyed until they have no references to them.
(b) An object eligible for garbage collection will eventually be destroyed by the garbage collector.
(c) If object `A` became eligible for garbage collection before object `B`, then object `A` will be destroyed before object `B`.
(d) An object, once eligible for garbage collection, can never become accessible by a live thread.
(e) None of the above.

Q39 Which of these expressions are legal?

Select the four correct answers.

(a) `"co".concat("ol")`
(b) `("co" + "ol")`
(c) `('c' + 'o' + 'o' + 'l')`
(d) `("co" + new String('o' + 'l'))`
(e) `("co" + new String("co"))`

Q40 Which statement about the `charAt()` method of the `String` class is true?

Select the one correct answer.

(a) The `charAt()` method takes a `char` value as an argument.
(b) The `charAt()` method returns a `Character` object.
(c) The expression `("abcdef").charAt(3)` is illegal.
(d) The expression `"abcdef".charAt(3)` evaluates to the character `'d'`.
(e) The index of the first character is 1.

Q41 Which expression will evaluate to `true`?

Select the one correct answer.

(a) `"hello: there!".equals("hello there")`
(b) `"HELLO THERE".equals("hello there")`
(c) `("hello".concat("there")).equals("hello there")`
(d) `"Hello There".compareTo("hello there") == 0`
(e) `"Hello there".toLowerCase().equals("hello there")`

Q42 What will the following program print when run?

```
public class Search {
  public static void main(String[] args) {
    String s = "Contentment!";
    int middle = s.length()/2;
    String nt = s.substring(middle-1, middle+1);
    System.out.println(s.lastIndexOf(nt, middle));
  }
}
```

Select the one correct answer.

(a) 2
(b) 4
(c) 5
(d) 7
(e) 9
(f) 11
(g) None of the above.

Q43 What will be the result of attempting to compile and run the following program?

```
public class StringMethods {
  public static void main(String[] args) {
    String str = new String("eeny");
    str.concat(" meeny");
    StringBuilder strBuilder = new StringBuilder(" miny");
    strBuilder.append(" mo");
    System.out.println(str + strBuilder);
  }
}
```

Select the one correct answer.

(a) The program will fail to compile.
(b) The program will print `eeny meeny miny mo` at runtime.
(c) The program will print `meeny miny mo` at runtime.
(d) The program will print `eeny miny mo` at runtime.
(e) The program will print `eeny meeny miny` at runtime.

Q44 What will be the result of attempting to compile this code, contained in a source file named `AClass.java`?

```
import java.util.*;

package com.acme.toolkit;

public class AClass {
  public Other anInstance;
}

class Other {
  int value;
}
```

Select the one correct answer.

(a) The code will fail to compile, since the class `Other` has not yet been declared when referenced in the class `AClass`.
(b) The code will fail to compile, since an `import` statement cannot occur as the first statement in a source file.
(c) The code will fail to compile, since the `package` declaration cannot occur after an `import` statement.
(d) The code will fail to compile, since the class `Other` must be defined in a file called `Other.java`.
(e) The code will fail to compile, since the class `Other` must be declared as `public`.
(f) The class will compile without errors.

Q45 Which code can be inserted at (1) so that the exception thrown by the program is caught by the `catch` clause?

```
public class Q1408a {
  public static void main(String[] args) {
    try {
      String[][] trio = {null, {null}, {"Tom"}, {}, {"Dick", "Harry"}};
      String substr = trio[3][0].substring(1, 2);
    } catch (/* (1) INSERT CODE HERE */) {
      System.out.println("Mind the index!");
    }
  }
}
```

Select the two correct answers.

(a) `ArrayIndexOutOfBoundsException e`
(b) `IndexOutOfBoundsException e`
(c) `StringIndexOutOfBoundsException e`
(d) `IllegalIndexFoundException e`
(e) `NullPointerException e`

Q46 What is the output from running the following program?

```
public class Q1408b {
  public static void main(String[] args) {
    int i = 0;
    while (++i == i) {
      System.out.println(i++);
    }
  }
}
```

Select the one correct answer.

(a) The program will execute and terminate normally, but will not print anything.
(b) The program will execute indefinitely, printing all numbers from 1 and upward.
(c) The program will execute indefinitely, printing all numbers from 2 and upward.
(d) The program will execute indefinitely, printing all even numbers from 2 and upward.

(e) The program will execute indefinitely, printing all odd numbers from 1 and upward.
(f) The program will execute indefinitely, printing all odd numbers from 3 and upward.

Q47 What is the output from running the following program?

```
public class RemainderFun {
  public static void main(String[] args) {
    int i = 24, k = 7;
    System.out.print( i %  k + "|");
    System.out.print( i % -k + "|");
    System.out.print(-i %  k + "|");
    System.out.println(-i % -k);
  }
}
```

Select the one correct answer.

(a) The program will fail to compile.
(b) The program will compile, but will throw a runtime exception.
(c) `3|-3|-3|3`
(d) `3|3|-3|-3`
(e) `3|-3|-3|-3`
(f) `3|-3|3|-3`

Q48 What is the output from running the following program?

```
public class Thingy {
  private String name;
  public Thingy(String name) {
    this.name = name;
  }

  public static void main(String[] args) {
    Thingy thing1 = new Thingy("thing1");
    Thingy thing2 = new Thingy("thing2");
    System.out.print(thing1.equals(thing2) + ",");

    thing2.name = "thing1";
    System.out.print(thing1.equals(thing2) + ",");

    thing2 = thing1;
    System.out.println(thing1.equals(thing2));
  }
}
```

Select the one correct answer.

(a) The program will fail to compile.
(b) The program will compile, but will throw a runtime exception.
(c) `false,true,true`
(d) `false,false,false`
(e) `false,false,true`
(f) `false,true,false`

Q49 Which statement is true about the following program?

```
public class Switchy {
  public static void main(String[] args) {
    final String s1 = "January";
    final String yr = " 2014";
    s1.concat(yr);
    switch (s1) {
      default:
        System.out.println("Sorry.");
      case "January" + yr: case s1 + " 2015":
        System.out.println("OK.");
    }
  }
}
```

Select the one correct answer.

(a) The program will not compile.
(b) The program will compile. When run, it will print:
`Sorry.`
`OK.`
(c) The program will compile. When run, it will print:
`Sorry.`
(d) The program will compile. When run, it will print:
`OK.`

Q50 Which statements will compile without errors?

Select the three correct answers.

(a) `Integer iRef = 0b111_000;`
(b) `byte b       = 0B1111_1111;`
(c) `double d     = 0B1111_1111D;`
(d) `Double dRef  = 3_____141.592_653_589_793e-3;`
(e) `int date1    = Integer.parseInt("_2014_01_11");`
(f) `int date2    = _2014_01_11;`
(g) `long date3   = 2014_01_11_L;`

Q51 Which array declarations will not compile?

Select the three correct answers.

(a) `int[]   array1   = new int[0];`
(b) `int[]   array2   = {};`
(c) `int[]   array3   = new int[] {};`
(d) `int[]   array4   = new int[4] {};`
(e) `int[]   array5   = new int[4] {0,1,2,3};`
(f) `int[]   array6   = new int[ ] {0,1,2,3};`
(g) `int[]   arr2d1[] = new int[4][ ];`
(h) `int[][] arr2d2   = new int[4][ ];`
(i) `int[][] arr2d3   = new int[ ][4];`
(j) `int[][] arr2d4   = new int[4][0];`

Q52 Which statements, when considered individually, are true about the following code?

```
public class Overloading {
  private String  xqt(int i) { return null; }  // (1)
  public  void    xqt()      {}                // (2)
  public  Integer xqt(int j) { return 1; }     // (3)
}
```

Select the two correct answers.

(a) The methods at (1) and (2) are correctly overloaded.
(b) The methods at (1) and (3) are correctly overloaded.
(c) The methods at (2) and (3) are correctly overloaded.
(d) All methods are correctly overloaded.

Q53 What is the output from the following program?

```
public class Gizmo {
  private StringBuilder name;
  private double weight;

  public Gizmo() {
    name = new StringBuilder("MyGizmo");
    weight = 10.0;
  }

  public String toString() { return "Name: " + name + ", Weight: " + weight; }

  private static void changeName(StringBuilder sb) { sb.append("2014"); }
  private static void changeWeight(double weight) { weight = 2 * weight; }

  public static void main(String[] arguments) {
    Gizmo giz = new Gizmo();
    changeName(giz.name);
    changeWeight(giz.weight);
    System.out.println(giz);
  }
}
```

Select the one correct answer.

(a) The program will fail to compile.
(b) The program will compile, but will throw a runtime exception.
(c) `Name: MyGizmo, Weight: 10.0`
(d) `Name: MyGizmo2014, Weight: 10.0`
(e) `Name: MyGizmo, Weight: 20.0`
(f) `Name: MyGizmo2014, Weight: 20.0`

Q54 Which code can be inserted independently at (1) so that the program prints the following: `Free Meal|Free Meal|Free Meal|`.

```
public class LoopDeLoop {
  public static void main(String[] args) {
    StringBuilder meals[] = {
        new StringBuilder(), new StringBuilder(), new StringBuilder()
    };
```

```
      // (1) INSERT CODE HERE
      for (StringBuilder meal : meals) System.out.print(meal + "|");
    }
  }
```

Select the four correct answers.

(a) `for (StringBuilder meal : meals) meal.insert(0, "Free Meal");`
(b) `for (StringBuilder meal : meals) meal = meal.insert(0, "Free Meal");`
(c) `StringBuilder freeMeal = new StringBuilder("Free Meal");`
    `for (StringBuilder meal : meals) meal = freeMeal;`
(d) `for (StringBuilder meal : meals) meal = new StringBuilder("Free Meal");`
(e) `for (StringBuilder meal : meals) meal.append("Free Meal");`
(f) `for (StringBuilder meal : meals) meal = meal.append("Free Meal");`

Q55 What is the output from the following program?

```
import java.util.ArrayList;
public class Weekend {
  public static void main(String[] args) {
    ArrayList<String> longWeekend = new ArrayList<>();
    longWeekend.add("Friday");
    longWeekend.add(2, "Saturday");
    longWeekend.add("Sunday");
    longWeekend.remove(0);
    System.out.println(longWeekend);
  }
}
```

Select the one correct answer.

(a) The program will not compile.
(b) The program will compile. When run, it will print `[Saturday, Sunday]`.
(c) The program will compile. When run, it will print `[Sunday, Saturday]`.
(d) The program will compile. When run, it will throw a `java.lang.IndexOutOf-BoundsException`.

Q56 What is the output from the following program?

```
class Room {
  static int numOfGuests;
}

public class Hotel {
  public static void main(String[] args) {
    Room r1 = new Room();
    Room r2 = new Room();
    r1.numOfGuests = 2;
    r2.numOfGuests = 3;
    System.out.println("Number of guests: " + r1.numOfGuests + r2.numOfGuests);
  }
}
```

Select the one correct answer.

(a) The program will fail to compile.
(b) The program will compile, but will throw a runtime exception.
(c) `Number of guests: 4`
(d) `Number of guests: 5`
(e) `Number of guests: 6`
(f) `Number of guests: 22`
(g) `Number of guests: 33`

Q57 In which scenarios would a `do-while` loop be preferable to a `while` loop?

Select the three correct answers.

(a) Admit one ticket-holder at a time into a movie theater until there are no more ticket-holders to admit.
(b) Guess an answer until the answer is correct.
(c) Add a little salt to the food until the food tastes right. Assume the food has too little salt to start with.
(d) Add candles to a birthday cake until there are the right number of candles.
(e) Let the mice play a little while the cat is away.

Q58 What is the output from the following program?

```
public class CodeMe {
  public static void main(String[] args) {
    boolean flag = false;
    if (false)          // (1)
      flag = !flag;
    System.out.println(flag);
  }
}
```

Select the two correct answers.

(a) The program, as it stands, does not compile.
(b) The program compiles without errors. When run, it will print `false`.
(c) The program compiles without errors. When run, it will print `true`.
(d) If the keyword `if` at (1) is replaced with the keyword `while`, the program compiles without errors. When run, it will print `false`.
(e) If the keyword `if` at (1) is replaced with the keyword `while`, the program compiles without errors. When run, it will print `true`.
(f) If the keyword `if` at (1) is replaced with the keyword `while`, the program will not compile.

Q59 What code can be inserted independently at (1) so that the program prints the value 2014?

```
public class CastMe {
  public static void main(String[] args) {
    Number num = 2014;
    // (1) INSERT CODE HERE.
    System.out.println(iRef);
  }
}
```

Select the one correct answer.

(a) `Integer iRef = ((Integer)num).intValue();`
(b) `Integer iRef = (Integer)num.intValue();`
(c) `Integer iRef = (Integer)(num.intValue());`
(d) `Integer iRef = num.intValue();`
(e) Any one of the above statements can be inserted at (1).
(f) None of the above.

Q60 What is the output from the following program?

```
class Person {
  public void compare(Person p) {
    System.out.print("Persons are equal.");
  }
}

class Student extends Person {
  public void compare(Student s) {
    System.out.print("Students are equal.");
  }
}

public class Calling {
  public static void main(String[] args) {
    Person p1 = new Person();
    Student s1 = new Student();
    Student s2 = new Student();
    Person p2 = s2;

    p1.compare(s1); p1.compare(p2); System.out.println();
    p2.compare(s1); p2.compare(p1); System.out.println();
    s1.compare(p1); s1.compare(p2); s1.compare(s2); System.out.println();
  }
}
```

Select the one correct answer.

(a)
```
Persons are equal.Persons are equal.
Students are equal.Persons are equal.
Persons are equal.Persons are equal.Students are equal.
```
(b)
```
Persons are equal.Persons are equal.
Persons are equal.Persons are equal.
Persons are equal.Persons are equal.Students are equal.
```
(c)
```
Persons are equal.Persons are equal.
Students are equal.Persons are equal.
Persons are equal.Students are equal.Students are equal.
```
(d)
```
Persons are equal.Persons are equal.
Persons are equal.Persons are equal.
Persons are equal.Students are equal.Students are equal.
```

Q61 What will the following program print when compiled and run?

```
import java.util.ArrayList;
import java.util.List;

public class MEQ12A56 {
  public static void main(String[] args) {
    List<String> strList = new ArrayList<>();
    strList.add(0, "Ada");
    strList.add("Alyla");
    strList.set(strList.size()-1, "Otto");
    strList.add(strList.size()-1, "Anna");
    System.out.println(strList);                    // (1)
    int size = strList.size();
    for (int i = 0; i < size; ++i) {
      strList.add(strList.get(size-1-i));
    }
    System.out.println(strList);                    // (2)
  }
}
```

Select the two correct answers.

(a) (1) will print `[Ada, Alyla, Anna]`.
(b) (1) will print `[Ada, Anna, Otto]`.
(c) (1) will print `[Ada, Otto, Alyla]`.
(d) (2) will print `[Ada, Alyla, Anna, Anna, Alyla, Ada]`.
(e) (2) will print `[Ada, Anna, Otto, Otto, Anna, Ada]`.
(f) (2) will print `[Ada, Otto, Alyla, Alyla, Otto, Ada]`.

Q62 What will the following program print when compiled and run?

```
import java.util.ArrayList;
import java.util.List;

public class MEQ12A70 {
  public static void main(String[] args) {
    List<String> list1 = new ArrayList<>(20);
    list1.add("Ada");
    List<String> list2 = new ArrayList<>(list1);
    list2.add(null);
    System.out.print(list1.size() == list2.size());
    System.out.print("-" + (list1 == list2));
    System.out.println("-" + list1.equals(list2));
  }
}
```

Select the one correct answer.

(a) The program will not compile.
(b) The program will throw an exception.
(c) The program will print `false-true-true`.
(d) The program will print `true-false-true`.
(e) The program will print `false-false-false`.

Q63 Which lines will be in the output when the following program is compiled and run?

```
import java.util.ArrayList;
import java.util.List;

public class MEQ12A99 {
  public static void main(String[] args) {
    List<Integer> numList = new ArrayList<>();
    numList.add(3); numList.add(1); numList.add(1, 4);
    numList.add(null); numList.add(0);
    System.out.println("(1) prints " + numList.get(3));
    System.out.println("(2) prints " + numList.set(1, 3));
    System.out.println("(3) prints " + numList.lastIndexOf(3));
    System.out.println("(4) prints " + numList.contains(3));
    System.out.println("(5) prints " + numList.remove(3));
    System.out.println("(6) prints " + numList.indexOf(3));
    System.out.println("(7) prints " + numList.remove(new Integer(4)));
  }
}
```

Select the six correct answers.

(a) `(1) prints null`
(b) `(2) prints 3`
(c) `(2) prints 4`
(d) `(3) prints 2`
(e) `(3) prints 1`
(f) `(4) prints true`
(g) `(5) prints null`
(h) `(5) prints 1`
(i) `(6) prints 1`
(j) `(7) prints true`
(k) `(7) prints false`

Q64 Which lines will result in a compile-time error?

```
import java.util.ArrayList;
import java.util.List;

public class MEQ12A80 {
  public static void main(String[] args) {
    List<String> strList = new ArrayList<>(0);                      // (1)
    List<Object> objList = strList;                                 // (2)
    List<Number> numList = new ArrayList<>();                       // (3)
    numList.add(1);                                                 // (4)
    numList.add(1.5);                                               // (5)
    List<> intList = new ArrayList<Integer>();                      // (6)
    ArrayList<ArrayList<Integer>> loList1 = new ArrayList<Integer>(); // (7)
    ArrayList<ArrayList<Integer>> loList2 = new ArrayList();        // (8)
  }
}
```

Select the three correct answers.

(a) Compile-time error in (1)
(b) Compile-time error in (2)
(c) Compile-time error in (3)
(d) Compile-time error in (4)
(e) Compile-time error in (5)
(f) Compile-time error in (6)
(g) Compile-time error in (7)
(h) Compile-time error in (8)

Q65 What will the following program print when compiled and run?

```
import java.util.ArrayList;
import java.util.List;

public class MEQ12A85 {
  public static void main(String[] args) {
    List<String> list = new ArrayList<>(20);
    list.add("Taco");
    for (int i = 0; i < 3; ++i) {
      list.add("" + list);
    }
    System.out.println(list);                    // (1)
    System.out.println(list.size());             // (2)
  }
}
```

Select the two correct answers.

(a) (1) will print:
`[Taco, Taco, Taco, Taco, Taco, Taco, Taco, Taco]`
(b) (1) will print:
`[Taco, [Taco, Taco], [Taco, Taco, Taco], [Taco, Taco, Taco, Taco]]`
(c) (1) will print:
`[Taco, [Taco], Taco, [Taco], Taco, [Taco], Taco, [Taco]]`
(d) (1) will print:
`[Taco, [Taco], [Taco, [Taco]], [Taco, [Taco], [Taco, [Taco]]]]`
(e) (2) will print 4.
(f) (2) will print 8.

Q66 What will the following program print when compiled and run?

```
import java.util.ArrayList;
import java.util.List;

public class MEQ12A55 {
  public static void main(String[] args) {
    List<String> strList = new ArrayList<>();
```

```
      strList.add(strList.size(), "Anna");
      strList.add(strList.size()-1, "Ada");
      strList.add(strList.size()-1, "Otto");
      strList.add(0, "Alyla");
      System.out.println(strList);
      int size = strList.size();
      for (int i = 0; i < size/2; ++i) {
        String strTemp = strList.get(i);
        strList.set(i, strList.get(size-1-i));
        strList.set(size-1-i, strTemp);
      }
      System.out.println(strList);
    }
  }
```

Select the one correct answer.

(a) The program will not compile.
(b) The program will throw an `IndexOutOfBoundsException`.
(c) The program will throw a `NullPointerException`.
(d) The program will print:
```
[Alyla, Ada, Otto, Anna]
[Anna, Otto, Ada, Alyla]
```
(e) The program will print:
```
[Ada, Otto, Alyla, Anna]
[Anna, Alyla, Otto, Ada]
```

Q67 Which statements are true about lambda expressions?

Select the two correct answers.

(a) A `return` statement is mandatory in a lambda expression if the lambda body is a statement block.
(b) A `return` statement is mandatory in a lambda expression if the lambda body is a single expression that returns a value.
(c) The formal parameters of a lambda expression are local variables in the block scope of the lambda expression.
(d) A local variable declaration in the block scope of a lambda expression can shadow a class member with the same name in the enclosing class.
(e) A local variable declaration in the block scope of a lambda expression can shadow a local variable with the same name in the enclosing method.

Q68 Which statements are true about the following code?

```
import java.util.function.Predicate;

public class MEQ12A92 {
  public static void main(String[] args) {
    Predicate<String> p1 = String obj -> obj.equals("Java");               // (1)
    Predicate<String> p2 = (final String obj) -> obj.equals("Java");       // (2)
    Predicate<String> p3 = (final obj) -> obj.equals("Java");              // (3)
    Predicate<String> p4 = (String obj) -> obj.equals("Java");             // (4)
    Predicate<String> p5 = (obj) -> obj.equals("Java");                    // (5)
    Predicate<String> p6 = obj -> obj.equals("Java");                      // (6)
    Predicate<String> p7 = obj -> return obj.equals("Java");               // (7)
    Predicate<String> p8 = obj -> { obj.equals("Java") };                  // (8)
    Predicate<String> p9 = obj -> { obj.equals("Java"); };                 // (9)
    Predicate<String> p10 = obj -> { return obj.equals("Java"); };         // (10)
    Predicate<Object> p11 = obj -> obj.equals("Java");                     // (11)
  }
}
```

Select the five correct answers.

(a) (1) will not compile.
(b) (2) will not compile.
(c) (3) will not compile.
(d) (4) will not compile.
(e) (5) will not compile.
(f) (6) will not compile.
(g) (7) will not compile.
(h) (8) will not compile.
(i) (9) will not compile.
(j) (10) will not compile.
(k) (11) will not compile.

Q69 Which statements are true about the following code?

```
import java.util.function.Predicate;

public class MEQ12A95 {

  public static void main(String[] args) {
    final String lock3 = "Trio";
    String lock4 = "Chubb";

    Predicate<Object> p;
    p = lock -> { lock = lock.toString(); return lock.equals("TRIO"); };     // (1)
    p = lock -> { if (args.length > 0) return lock.equals(args[0]); };       // (2)
    p = lock -> { String lock3 = "CHUBB"; return lock.equals(lock3); };      // (3)
    p = lock -> { return lock.equals(lock3); };                              // (4)
    p = lock -> { return lock.equals(lock4); };                              // (5)
    p = lock4 -> { return lock4.equals("Chubb"); };                          // (6)
  }
}
```

Select the three correct answers.

(a) (1) will compile.
(b) (2) will compile.
(c) (3) will compile.
(d) (4) will compile.
(e) (5) will compile.
(f) (6) will compile.

Q70 Given the following program:

```
import java.util.function.Predicate;

public class MEQ12A97 {
  public static void main(String[] args) {
    int[] intArray = {-12, 12, -123, 123, -1234, 1234 };
    filterInt(intArray, /* (1) INSERT CODE HERE */);
  }

  private static void filterInt(int[] intArr, Predicate<Integer> predicate) {
    for (int i = 0; i < intArr.length; ++i) {
      int intValue = intArr[i];
      if (predicate.test(intValue)) {
        System.out.print(intValue + " ");
      }
    }
    System.out.println();
  }
}
```

Which lambda expressions can be inserted at (1) so that the program prints all odd numbers that have three digits (i.e., `-123` and `123`)?

Select the four correct answers.

(a) `val -> val % 2 != 0 && String.valueOf(Math.abs(val)).length() == 3`
(b) `val -> return val % 2 != 0 && String.valueOf(Math.abs(val)).length() == 3`
(c) `val -> val % 2 != 0 && ("" + Math.abs(val)).length() == 3`
(d) `val -> { val % 2 != 0 && ("" + Math.abs(val)).length() == 3; }`
(e) `val -> val % 2 != 0 && new String(Math.abs(val)).length() == 3`
(f) `val -> { return val % 2 != 0 && new String(Math.abs(val)).length() == 3; }`
(g) `val -> val % 2 != 0 && Integer.toString(Math.abs(val)).length() == 3`
(h) `val -> val % 2 != 0 && new Integer(Math.abs(val)).toString().length() == 3`

Q71 Which statement is true about the following interfaces?

```
interface IA              { boolean equals(Object obj); }
interface IB extends IA { boolean doIt(String str); }
interface IC extends IB { boolean doIt(String str); }
interface ID extends IC { boolean equals(Object obj);}
```

Select the one correct answer.

(a) `IA` is a functional interface.
(b) `IB` is a functional interface.
(c) `IC` is not a functional interface.
(d) `ID` is not a functional interface.
(e) None of the above.

Q72 Which statement is true about the Date and Time API?

Select the one correct answer.

(a) The `isBefore()` and `isAfter()` methods of the `LocalTime`, `LocalDate`, and `LocalDateTime` classes always return `true` when this object is the same as the object passed as an argument.
(b) The `with` methods of the `LocalDate` and `LocalDateTime` classes will adjust the day of the month to the last valid day of the month, if the day of month becomes invalid when their date-based values are changed.
(c) The `toTotalDays()` method of the `Period` class returns the length of the period as the total number of days.
(d) The classes `LocalTime`, `LocalDate`, `LocalDateTime`, and `Period` implement the `Comparable` interface, providing an implementation of the `compareTo()` method so that two temporal objects of the same type can be compared.
(e) None of the above.

Q73 What will the following program print when compiled and run?

```
import java.time.LocalTime;

public class MEQ11A25 {
  public static void main(String[] args) {
    LocalTime time = LocalTime.NOON;
    time = time.withHour(10).plusMinutes(120);
    System.out.println(time);
  }
}
```

Select the one correct answer.

(a) The program will not compile.
(b) The program will throw a runtime exception.
(c) The program will print `00:00`.
(d) The program will print `12:00`.
(e) The program will print `24:00`.
(f) None of the above.

Q74 What will the following program print when compiled and run?

```
import java.time.LocalDate;

public class MEQ11A35 {
  public static void main(String[] args) {
    LocalDate date = LocalDate.of(2015, 1, 1);
    date.withYear(5);
    System.out.println(date.plusMonths(12));
  }
}
```

Select the one correct answer.

(a) The program will not compile.
(b) The program will throw a runtime exception.
(c) The program will print 0006-01-01.
(d) The program will print 2021-01-01.
(e) The program will print 2015-01-01.
(f) The program will print 2016-01-01.
(g) None of the above.

Q75 What will the following program print when compiled and run?

```
import java.time.Period;

public class MEQ11A40 {
  public static void main(String[] args) {
   Period period = Period.ofYears(10).ofMonths(16);
   System.out.println(period);
  }
}
```

Select the one correct answer.

(a) The program will not compile.
(b) The program will throw a runtime exception.
(c) The program will print P16M.
(d) The program will print P1Y4M.
(e) The program will print P11Y4M.
(f) The program will print P10Y16M.
(g) None of the above.

Q76 Which code, when inserted at (1), will make the program compile and execute normally?

```
import java.time.LocalDate;
import java.time.LocalDateTime;
import java.time.LocalTime;
import java.time.format.DateTimeFormatter;

public class MEQ11A90 {
  public static void main(String[] args) {
    // (1) INSERT CODE HERE.

    String timeStr = LocalTime.of(12, 5).format(dtf);
    String dateStr = LocalDate.of(2016, 4, 1).format(dtf);
    String dateTimeStr = LocalDateTime.of(2016, 4, 1, 12, 5).format(dtf);
  }
}
```

Select the one correct answer.

(a) `DateTimeFormatter dtf = DateTimeFormatter.ISO_LOCAL_TIME;`
(b) `DateTimeFormatter dtf = DateTimeFormatter.ISO_LOCAL_DATE;`
(c) `DateTimeFormatter dtf = DateTimeFormatter.ISO_LOCAL_DATE_TIME;`
(d) None of the above.

Q77 Which code, when inserted at (1), will make the program compile and execute normally?

```
import java.time.LocalDate;
import java.time.LocalDateTime;
import java.time.LocalTime;
import java.time.format.DateTimeFormatter;

public class MEQ11A95 {
  public static void main(String[] args) {
    String inputStr = "The time is 15 minutes past 10PM.";
    String pattern = "'The time is 'm' minutes past 'ha.";
    DateTimeFormatter dtf = DateTimeFormatter.ofPattern(pattern);
    // (1) INSERT CODE HERE.
  }
}
```

Select the three correct answers.

(a) `LocalTime time = LocalTime.parse(inputStr, dtf);`
(b) `LocalDate date = LocalDate.parse(inputStr, dtf);`
(c) `LocalDateTime dateTime = LocalDateTime.parse(inputStr, dtf);`
(d) `String timeStr = LocalTime.of(9, 20).format(dtf);`
(e) `String dateStr = LocalDate.of(2015, 12, 24).format(dtf);`
(f) `String dateTimeStr = LocalDateTime.of(2015, 12, 24, 22, 15).format(dtf);`

Appendix F

Annotated Answers to Mock Exam I

This appendix provides annotated answers to the questions in the mock exam for the *Java SE 8 Programmer I* certification found in Appendix E.

Annotated Answers

Q1 *(a), (b), (c), and (e)*
Only local variables need to be explicitly initialized before use. Fields are assigned a default value if not explicitly initialized.

Q2 *(e)*
Giving parameters `(2, 3)` to the method `substring()` constructs a string consisting of the characters from index 2 (inclusive) to index 3 (exclusive) of the original string; that is, the string returned contains the character at index 2. The first character is at index 0 and the last character is at index 1 less than the number of characters in the string.

Q3 *(c)*
The loop prints out the values `12`, `9`, `6`, and `3` before terminating. The loop terminates when the value in the loop variable `i` becomes less than or equal to 0. This happens after the value `3` has been printed.

Q4 *(e)*
The fact that a field is static does not mean that it is not accessible from non-static methods and constructors. All fields are assigned a default value if no initializer is specified. Static fields are initialized when the class is loaded, and instance fields are initialized when the class is instantiated. Only local variables must be explicitly initialized before use.

Q5 *(e)*
An object of the class `Extension` is created. The first thing the constructor of `Extension` does is invoke the constructor of `Base`, using an implicit `super()` call. All calls to the

method `void add(int)` are dynamically bound to the `add()` method in the `Extension` class, since the actual object is of type `Extension`. Therefore, this method is called by the constructor of `Base`, the constructor of `Extension`, and the `bogo()` method with the parameters `1`, `2`, and `8`, respectively. The instance field `i` changes value accordingly: `2`, `6`, and `22`. The final value of `22` is printed.

Q6 *(d)*

At (1), a new `Widget` object is constructed with the message that is a concatenation of the message `"bye"` in the `Widget` object denoted by `b` and the string `"!"`. After line (2), `d` and `b` are aliases. After line (3), `b` and `a` are aliases, but `d` still denotes the `Widget` object with the message `"bye"` from line (0). After line (4), `d` and `a` are aliases. Reference `d` no longer denotes the `Widget` object created in line (0). This `Widget` object has no references that refer to it and, therefore, is a candidate for garbage collection.

Q7 *(d) and (e)*

`String` objects are immutable. None of the methods of the `String` class modifies a `String` object. Methods `toUpperCase()` and `replace()` in the `String` class will return a new `String` object that contains the modified string. However, `StringBuilder` objects are mutable. The `charAt()` method of the `StringBuilder` class is a get method, returning the character at a specific index, without modifying the contents of the `StringBuilder` object.

Q8 *(c)*

Statement (a) will execute without problem, but (b), (d), and (e) will cause compile-time errors. Statements (b) and (e) will cause compile-time errors because it is not possible to convert from the superclass `A` to the subclasses `C` and `B`, respectively. Statement (d) will cause compile-time errors because a cast from `B` to `C` is invalid. Being an instance of `B` excludes the possibility of being an instance of `C`. Statement (c) will compile, but will throw a runtime exception because the object that is cast to `B` is not an instance of `B`.

Q9 *(b), (c), (d), and (g)*

In (a), a `String` is neither an array nor an `Iterable`. The method `toCharArray()` of the `String` class returns an array of type `char`. A `char` value is assignable to the local variable of type `char` in (b), and after autoboxing, assignable to the local variable of type `Character` in (c) and (d). In (e), the local variable `str` is redeclared. In (f), the occurrence of the array operator `[]` is not permitted. In (g), the array `strs` is permissible in the `for(:)` loop. In (h), the `String` class does not have a method named `toArray`, but it has a method named `toCharArray`.

Q10 *(b) and (e)*

For the expression `matrix[3][2]` to access a valid element of a two-dimensional array, the array must have at least four rows and the fourth row must have at least three elements. (a) produces a 2×3 array. (c) tries to initialize a two-dimensional array as a one-dimensional array. (d) tries to specify array dimensions in the type of the array reference declaration.

Q11 *(a)*

The expression `arr.length` will evaluate to 4. The expression `arr[1]` will access the array `{ { "1", "2" }, { "1", null, "3" } }`, and `arr[1][2]` will try to access the third element of this array. This results in an `ArrayIndexOutOfBoundsException`, since this array has only two elements.

Q12 *(c) and (d)*

`String` objects can have identical sequences of characters. The `==` operator, when used on `String` object references, will return `true` if and only if both references denote the same object (i.e., are aliases). The `equals()` method will return `true` whenever the contents of the `String` objects are identical. An array of `char` and a `String` are two totally different types, and when compared using the `equals()` method of the `String` class, the value returned will be `false`.

Q13 *(b) and (e)*

Unlike local variables, all fields are initialized with default initial values. All numeric fields are initialized to zero, `boolean` fields to `false`, `char` fields to `'\u0000'`, and *all* reference fields to `null`.

Q14 *(a)*

The `main()` method in (b) will always throw and catch an `ArrayIndexOutOfBoundsException`, since `args.length` is an illegal index in the `args` array. The `main()` method in (c) will always throw an `ArrayIndexOutOfBoundsException` since it also uses `args.length` as an index, but this exception is never caught. The `main()` method in (d) will fail to print the argument if only one program argument is supplied. The `main()` method in (e) will throw an uncaught `ArrayIndexOutOfBoundsException` if no program arguments are specified.

Q15 *(e)*

Method `g()` modifies the field `a`. Method `g()` modifies the parameter `b`, not the field `b`, since the parameter declaration shadows the field. Variables are passed by value, so the change of value in parameter `b` is confined to the method `g()`. Method `g()` modifies the array whose reference value is passed as a parameter. Change to the first element is visible after return from the method `g()`.

Q16 *(a)*

The program will fail to compile since the label `l2` cannot precede the declaration `int j = 0`. For a label to be associated with a loop, it must immediately precede the loop construct. If label `l2` preceded the `while` loop (instead of the declaration of `j`), the program would compile and print 9.

Q17 *(b)*

Classes cannot extend interfaces; they must implement them. Interfaces can extend other interfaces, but cannot implement them. A class must be declared as `abstract` if it does not provide an implementation for all abstract methods of the interfaces that it implements. Methods declared in interfaces are implicitly `public` and `abstract`. Classes that implement these methods must explicitly declare these methods to be `public`.

Q18 *(a)*

The code will fail to compile because the literal `4.3` has the type `double`. Assignment of a `double` value to a `float` variable without an explicit cast is not allowed. The code would compile and print `0` at runtime, if the literal `4.3` was replaced with `4.3F`.

Q19 *(b) and (e)*

The && and || operators exhibit short-circuit behavior. The first operand of the ternary operator (? :) is always evaluated. Based on the result of this evaluation, either the second or third operand is evaluated.

Q20 *(e)*

No labels are mandatory (including the `default` label), and labels can be placed in any order within the `switch` body. The keyword `continue` may occur within the body of a `switch` statement as long as it pertains to a loop. An enum constant, a non-`long` integral constant expression, or a string constant expression can be used for `case` labels as long as the type is compatible with the expression in the `switch` expression.

Q21 *(a)*

Strings are immutable, so the `concat()` method has no effect on the original `String` object. The string on which the `trim()` method is called consists of eight characters, where the first and two last characters are spaces (`" hello  "`). The `trim()` method returns a new `String` object in which the whitespace characters at each end have been removed. This leaves the five characters of the word `"hello"`.

Q22 *(a) and (e)*

Method overloading requires that the method signatures are different, but the method name is the same. The return type is irrelevant in this regard. The signature of the existing method is `sum(long, long)`.

The signature of the method in (a) is `sum(int, int)`. The signature of the method in (e) is `sum(long, int)`. Both signatures are different from the signature of the existing method.

Declarations (b) and (d) fail, since the method signature is identical to the existing method. Declaration (c) fails, since it declares an `abstract` method in a non-`abstract` class.

Q23 *(b)*

The method with the most specific signature is chosen. In this case the `int` argument `10` is boxed to an `Integer`, which is passed to the `Number` formal parameter, as type `Number` is more specific than `Object`.

Q24 *(d), (f), and (g)*

The `main()` method must be declared as `public` and `static`, with return type `void`, and takes a single array of `String` objects as argument. The order of the `static` and `public` keywords is irrelevant. Also, declaring the method `final` is irrelevant in this respect.

Q25 *(d)*

The length of the array passed to the `main()` method is equal to the number of program arguments specified in the command line. Unlike some other programming languages, the element at index 0 does not contain the name of the program. The first program argument specified is retrieved using `args[0]`, and the last program argument specified is retrieved using `args[args.length-1]`, when `args.length` is greater than `0`. A program argument is a string, and several arguments are separated by spaces on the command line. To pass several arguments as one argument, these must be enclosed in double quotes.

Q26 *(e)*
When the program is called with no program arguments, the `args` array will be of length 0. The program will in this case print `no arguments`. When the program is called with three arguments, the `args` array will have length 3. Using the index 3 in the `numbers` array will retrieve the string `"four"`, because the start index is 0.

Q27 *(b) and (e)*
Static import from a class does not automatically import static members of any nested types declared in that class. The order of the import statements is arbitrary as long as they are declared after any package statement and before any type declaration. Name conflicts must be disambiguated explicitly.

Q28 *(e)*
An object reference is needed to access non-static members. Static methods do not have the implicit object reference `this`, and must always supply an explicit object reference when referring to non-static members. The static method `main()` legally refers to the non-static method `func()`, using the reference variable `ref`. Static members are accessible from both static and non-static methods, using their simple names. No `NullPointerException` is thrown, as `ref` refers to an instance of `MyClass`.

Q29 *(c)*
Declaration (4) defines a static method that tries to access a variable named `a`, which is not locally declared. Since the method is `static`, this access will be valid only if variable `a` is declared as `static` within the class. Therefore, declarations (1) and (4) cannot occur in the same class declaration, while declarations (2) and (4) can.

Q30 *(a), (f), and (h)*
The type of the `switch` expression must be either an `enum` type or `String` type or one of the following: `byte`, `char`, `short`, `int`, or the corresponding wrapper type for these primitive types. This excludes (b) and (e). The type of the `case` labels must be assignable to the type of the `switch` expression. This excludes (c) and (d). The `case` label value must be a constant expression, which is not true in (g), where the `case` label value is of type `Byte`.

Q31 *(a)*
The value of the `case` label `iFour` is *not* a constant expression and, therefore, the code will not compile.

Q32 *(d)*
Implementation (4) will correctly return the largest value. The `if` statement does not return any value and, therefore, cannot be used as an expression statement in implementations (1) and (2). Implementation (3) is invalid since neither the `switch` expression nor the `case` label values can be of type `boolean`.

Q33 *(c)*

As it stands, the program will compile correctly and will print `3, 2` at runtime. If the `break` statement is replaced with a `continue` statement, the loop will perform all four iterations and will print `4, 3`. If the `break` statement is replaced with a `return` statement, the whole method will end when `i` equals 2, before anything is printed. If the `break` statement is simply removed, leaving the empty statement (`;`), the loop will complete all four iterations and will print `4, 4`.

Q34 *(a) and (c)*

The block statement `{}` is a compound statement. The compound statement can contain zero or more arbitrary statements. Thus, `{{}}` is a legal compound statement, containing one statement that is also a compound statement. This inner compound statement has no statements. The block `{ continue; }` by itself is not valid, since the `continue` statement cannot be used outside the context of a loop. (c) is a valid example of breaking out of a labeled block. (d) is not valid for the same reasons that (b) was not valid. The statement at (e) is not true, since the `break` statement can also be used to break out of labeled blocks, as illustrated by (c).

Q35 *(d)*

The type of `nums` is `int[][]`. The outer loop iterates over the rows, so the type of the loop variable in the outer loop must be `int[]`, and the loop expression is `nums`. The inner loop iterates over each row, `int[]`. The loop variable in the inner loop must be `int`, and the loop expression in the inner loop is a row given by the loop variable of the outer loop. Only in the loop headers in (d) are both element types compatible.

Q36 *(b)*

The program will print `1` and `4`, in that order. An `InterruptedException` is handled in the first `catch` clause. Inside this clause, a new `RuntimeException` is thrown. This exception was not thrown inside the `try` block and will not be handled by the `catch` clauses, but will be sent to the caller of the `main()` method. Before this happens, the `finally` clause is executed. The code to print `5` is never reached, since the `RuntimeException` remains uncaught after the execution of the `finally` clause.

Q37 *(d)*

The method `nullify()` does not affect the array reference in the `main()` method. The array referenced by `args` is no longer reachable when control reaches (1). Only the array object and its four `Object` elements (i.e., five objects) are reachable when control reaches (1).

Q38 *(e)*

An object can be eligible for garbage collection even if there are references denoting the object, as long as the objects owning these references are also eligible for garbage collection. There is no guarantee that the garbage collector will destroy an eligible object before the program terminates. The order in which the objects are destroyed is not guaranteed. A thread cannot access an object once it becomes eligible for garbage collection.

Q39 *(a), (b), (c), and (e)*

The expressions `('c' + 'o' + 'o' + 'l')` and `('o' + 'l')` are of type `int` due to numeric promotion. Their evaluation would result in the values 429 and 219, respectively. Expression (d) is illegal, since the `String` class has no constructor taking a single `int` parameter. Expression (a) is legal, since string literals are references that denote `String` objects.

Q40 *(d)*

The expression `"abcdef".charAt(3)` evaluates to the character `'d'`. The `charAt()` method takes an `int` value as an argument and returns a `char` value. The expression `("abcdef").charAt(3)` is legal; it also evaluates to the character `'d'`. The index of the first character in a string is 0.

Q41 *(e)*

The expression `"Hello there".toLowerCase().equals("hello there")` will evaluate to `true`. The `equals()` method in the `String` class will return `true` only if the two strings have the same sequence of characters. The `compareTo()` method in the `String` class will return `0` only if the two strings have the same sequence of characters. The string comparison by these two methods is case sensitive, being based on the Unicode value of the characters in the strings.

Q42 *(c)*

The variable `middle` is assigned the value 6. The variable `nt` is assigned the string `"nt"`. The substring `"nt"` occurs three times in the string `"Contentment!"`, starting at indices 2, 5, and 9. The call `s.lastIndexOf(nt, middle)` returns the start index of the last occurrence of `"nt"`, searching backward from position 6.

Q43 *(d)*

The program will construct an immutable `String` object containing `"eeny"` and a mutable `StringBuilder` object containing `" miny"`. The `concat()` method returns a reference value to a new immutable `String` object containing `"eeny meeny"`, but the reference value is not stored; consequently, this `String` object cannot be referenced. The `append()` method appends the string `" mo"` to the string builder.

Q44 *(c)*

The code will fail to compile, since the package declaration cannot occur after an `import` statement. The `package` and `import` statements, if present, must always precede any type declarations. If a file contains both `import` statements and a `package` statement, the `package` statement must occur before the `import` statements.

Q45 *(a) and (b)*

Note that `ArrayIndexOutOfBoundsException` and `StringIndexOutOfBoundsException` are subclasses of `IndexOutOfBoundsException`. The elements of the array are initialized as follows:

```
trio[0] = null;
trio[1][0] = null;
trio[2][0] = "Tom";
trio[3] = new String[0]; // {}, i.e., zero-length array
trio[4][0] = "Dick";
trio[4][1] = "Harry";
```

Element `trio[3][0]` does not exist because the array `trio[3]` is of zero length, resulting in an `ArrayIndexOutOfBoundsException` being thrown; this exception is also a subtype of `IndexOutOfBoundsException`. `IllegalIndexFoundException` is not defined.

Q46 *(e)*

The loop condition `++i == i` is always true, as we are comparing the value of `i` to itself, and the loop will execute indefinitely. The evaluation of the loop condition proceeds as follows: `((++i) == i)`, with the operands having the same value. For each iteration, the loop variable `i` is incremented twice: once in the loop condition and a second time in the parameter expression `i++`. However, the value of `i` is printed before it is incremented the second time, resulting in odd numbers from 1 and upward being printed. If the prefix operator is also used in the `println` statement, all even numbers from 2 and upward would be printed.

Q47 *(d)*

The expression `i % k` evaluates to the remainder value `3`. The expression `i % -k` also evaluates to the remainder value `3`. We ignore the sign of the operands, and negate the remainder only if the dividend (`j` in this case) is negative.

Q48 *(e)*

The class `Thingy` does not override the `equals()` method, so the `equals()` method from the `Object` class is executed each time. The method in the `Object` class compares the reference value for equality with the `==` operator. Having the same name in the second call to the `equals()` method does not make the `Thingy` objects equal. In the last call to the `equals()` method, the two references are aliases; that is, they have the same reference value.

Q49 *(b)*

Strings are immutable, so the method `concat()` does not change the state of the `s1` string. The `default` case is executed in the `switch` statement. Because of the fall-through in the `switch` statement, the last print statement is also executed.

Q50 *(a), (d), and (e)*

In (b), the right-hand side `int` value `255` requires a cast to convert to a `byte`. In (c), only integer literals can be specified in binary notation, not floating-point values. (e) will compile, but will throw a `NumberFormatException` at runtime. In (f), an underscore cannot occur at the start of an integer value. The compiler will interpret it as an identifier. In (g), an underscore cannot occur before or after any type designator (`L`).

Q51 *(d), (e), and (i)*

In (d) and (e), either the array length or the initializer block can be specified, as in (a), (c), and (f). In (i), the length of the leftmost dimension must be specified; the other dimensions are optional, as in (g) and (h).

Q52 *(a) and (c)*

The methods at (1) and (3) differ only in the return type, which is not sufficient for correct overloading. Method overloading requires that the method signatures are different, but the method name is the same. The return type is irrelevant in this regard. The code will not compile.

Q53 *(d)*

`StringBuilder` is mutable. The reference value in `giz.name` is copied to the formal parameter `sb` when the method is called. References `giz.name` and `sb` are aliases to the same string builder. Changes made to the string builder in the method are apparent when the call returns. In contrast, the `double` value in `giz.weight` is copied to the formal parameter `weight`, whose value is changed in the method, but this does not affect the value in the actual parameter, which remains unchanged.

Q54 *(a), (b), (e), and (f)*

`StringBuilder` is mutable. The methods `insert()` and `append()` of the `StringBuilder` return the reference value of the string builder, in addition to modifying it. The assignment in (b) and (f) is superfluous. In (c) and (d), only the local variable `meal` is assigned a reference value of a string builder, but it does it not change the string builder in the array `meals`.

Q55 *(d)*

After the first call to the overloaded `add()` method, the size of the array list is 1. Trying to insert an element at index 2 in the second call to the `add()` method results in a `java.lang.IndexOutOfBoundsException`, because index 2 is strictly greater than the current size of the array list.

Q56 *(g)*

The field `numOfGuests` is `static`, meaning the field belongs to the class `Room` and not to any object of the class. Such a field can be referenced by a reference whose type is the same as the class. The two references `r1` and `r2` refer to the same static field `numOfGuests`, which has the value 3. Because of string concatenation, the expression `"Number of guests: " + r1.numOfGuests + r2.numOfGuests` evaluates to `"Number of guests: 33"`.

Q57 *(b), (c), and (d)*

In (a), the theater cannot admit anyone unless there is a ticket-holder, so the test to see whether there is a ticket-holder comes first.

In (b), at least one guess has to be made, so the test can be done after making the guess.

In (c), some salt has to be added, as the food has too little salt initially. The test to see if the food tastes right can be done after some salt has been added.

In (d), at least one candle has to be added, so the test for the right number of candles can be done after adding a candle.

In (e), it a good idea to check first whether the cat is away before letting the mice play a little.

Q58 *(b) and (f)*

In both cases, the code in the `if` statement and the `while` loop is unreachable, so it can never be executed. In case of the `while` loop, the compiler flags an error. The `if` statement is treated as a special case by the compiler to simulate conditional compilation, allowing code that should not be executed.

Q59 *(e)*

The value `2014` is boxed into an `Integer`. The subclass `Integer` overrides the abstract method `intValue()` from the superclass `Number`, so that no cast or explicit parentheses are necessary. However, if this was not the case, only the syntax with the cast in (a) would be correct.

Q60 *(b)*

The thing to note is that the method `compare()` is overloaded in the subclass `Student`, and not overridden. Thus objects of the class `Student` have two methods with the same name `compare`. For overloaded methods, the method to be executed is determined at compile time, depending on the type of the reference used to invoke the method, and the type of the actual parameters. When the type of the reference is `Person` (as is the case for `p1` and `p2`), the method `compare()` in `Person` will always be executed. The method defined in the subclass `Student` is executed only by the last call `s1.compare(s2)` in the `main()` method.

Q61 *(b) and (e)*

The `add(element)` method adds an element at the end of the list. The `add(index, element)` method adds the element at the specified index in the list, shifting elements to the right from the specified index. The index satisfies `(index >= 0 && index <= size())`. The `set(index, element)` method replaces the element at the specified index in the list with the specified element. The index satisfies `(index >= 0 && index < size())`. The `for(;;)` loop adds the elements currently in the list at the end of the list. The list changes as follows:

```
[Ada]
[Ada, Alyla]
[Ada, Otto]
[Ada, Anna, Otto]
[Ada, Anna, Otto, Otto, Anna, Ada]
```

Q62 *(e)*

Elements with the `null` value count toward the size of the list. The lists have different sizes. The lists are two distinct lists, having unique reference values. The `equals()` test fails because the lists have different sizes.

Q63 *(a), (c), (e), (f), (g), and (k)*

The program prints the following, where the list contents are shown before and after each print statement. Note the return value from the `ArrayList` methods.

```
[3, 4, 1, null, 0]
(1) prints null
[3, 4, 1, null, 0]
(2) prints 4
[3, 3, 1, null, 0]
(3) prints 1
[3, 3, 1, null, 0]
(4) prints true
[3, 3, 1, null, 0]
(5) prints null
[3, 3, 1, 0]
(6) prints 0
[3, 3, 1, 0]
(7) prints false
[3, 3, 1, 0]
```

Q64 *(b), (f), and (g)*

(1): The initial capacity can be 0. The capacity can change as the list changes structurally.

(2): `List<String>` is not a subtype of `List<Object>`. Assignment is not allowed.

(3), (4), (5): Although the `Number` class is abstract, we can create an `ArrayList` of an abstract class. However, only reference values of objects of its concrete subtypes can be stored in such a list.

(6): The diamond operator can be used only with the `new` operator.

(7): `ArrayList<Integer>` is not a subtype of `ArrayList<ArrayList<Integer>>`. Assignment is not allowed. The `ArrayList` creation expression must declare the full element type or use the diamond operator.

(8): The declaration statement compiles, but an unchecked conversion warning is issued by the compiler. All bets are off regarding the type-safety of the `ArrayList`.

Q65 *(d) and (e)*

Textual representation of the current contents of the list is added as a string on each iteration of the loop. The loop body is executed 3 times. The default textual representation of a list is enclosed in brackets (`[]`), where textual representation of each element is separated by a comma (`,`).

Q66 *(d)*

The `add(index, element)` method accepts an index that satisfies the condition `(index >= 0 && index <= size())`. The `for(;;)` loop swaps elements to reverse the elements in the list.

Q67 *(c) and (d)*

(a): The `return` statement is mandatory in a lambda expression only if the lambda body is a statement block that has a non-`void` return.

(b): A `return` statement is illegal in a lambda expression if the lambda body is a single expression.

(e): A local variable declaration in the block scope of a lambda expression cannot shadow or redeclare a local variable with the same name in the enclosing method.

Q68 *(a), (c), (g), (h), and (i)*

The declarations at (1), (3), (7), (8), and (9) will not compile. In (1), the declared-type parameter must be in parentheses. In (3), the `final` modifier can be applied only to declared-type parameters. In (7), the `return` keyword cannot be used when the lambda body is a single expression. In (8) and (9), the `return` keyword is required for a non-`void` return from a lambda expression with a statement block. In (8), the statement terminator (`;`) is also missing.

Q69 *(a), (d), and (e)*

The declarations at (1), (4), and (5) will compile. In (1), the parameter `lock` is local in the block scope of the lambda expression. In (2), the lambda expression must explicitly return a value, regardless of whether the `if` statement is executed. In (3), the local `final` variable `lock3` in the enclosing scope cannot be redeclared. In (4) and (5), local variables `lock3` and `lock4` in the enclosing scope can be accessed in the lambda expression, as they are both `final` and effectively final, respectively. In (6), the local variable `lock4` in the enclosing scope cannot be redeclared as parameter.

Q70 *(a), (c), (g), and (h)*

In (b), the `return` keyword cannot be used in a lambda expression with a single expression body. In (d), the `return` keyword must be used in a lambda expression with a non-`void` statement block body. In (e) and (f), the class `String` does not have a constructor that takes an integer value.

Q71 *(b)*

A functional interface is an interface that has only one abstract method, aside from the abstract method declarations of `public` methods from the `Object` class. This single abstract method declaration can be the result of inheriting multiple declarations of the abstract method from superinterfaces.

All except `IA` are functional interfaces. `IA` does not define an abstract method, as it provides only an abstract method declaration of the concrete `public` method `equals()` from the `Object` class. `IB` defines a single abstract method, `doIt()`. `IC` overrides the abstract method from `IB`, so effectively it has only one abstract method. `IC` inherits the abstract method `doIt()` from `IB` and overrides the `equals()` method from `IA`, so effectively it also has only one abstract method.

Q72 *(e)*

(a): The `isBefore()` and `isAfter()` methods are strict in their comparison.

(b): The `withYear()` and `withMonth()` methods will adjust the day. The `withDayOfMonth()` and `withDayOfYear()` methods will throw a `DateTimeException` if the argument value will result in an invalid date.

(c): The `Period` class does not have the method `toTotalDays()`, but it does have the method `toTotalMonths()` that considers only the years and the months. The `Period` class has no notion of time of day or date in the year.

(d): The `Period` class does not implement the `Comparable` interface.

Q73 *(d)*

The calculation of `time.withHour(10).plusMinutes(120)` proceeds as follows:

```
12:00 with 10 hour ==> 10:00 + 120 min (i.e., 2 hours) ==> 12:00
```

Q74 *(f)*

The date value `2015-01-01` in the `date` reference never changes. The `withYear()` method returns a new `LocalDate` object (with the date value `0005-01-01`) that is ignored. The `plusMonths()` method also returns a new `LocalDate` object whose value is printed. The calculation of `date.plusMonths(12)` proceeds as follows:

```
2015-01-01 + 12 months (i.e., 1 year) ==> 2016-01-01
```

Q75 *(c)*

The static method call `Period.ofYears(10)` returns a `Period` with the value `P10Y`. This `Period` object is used to invoke the static method `ofMonths()` with the argument value of 16 months, resulting in a new `Period` object with the period value `P16M`. Its reference value is assigned to the `period` reference. The `of()` methods do not normalize the date-based values of a `Period`.

Q76 *(d)*

(a): The formatter will format a `LocalTime` object and the time part of a `LocalDateTime` object, but not a `LocalDate` object, as it knows nothing about formatting the date part. It will use the ISO standard.

(b): The formatter will format a `LocalDate` object and the date part of a `LocalDateTime` object, but not a `LocalTime` object, as it knows nothing about formatting the time part. It will use the ISO standard.

(c): The formatter will format a `LocalDateTime` object, but neither a `LocalDate` object nor a `LocalTime` object, as it requires both the date and the time parts. It will use the ISO standard.

Q77 *(a), (d), and (f)*

The input string matches the pattern. The input string specifies the time-based values that can be used to construct a `LocalTime` object in (a) by a formatter, based on the time-related pattern letters in the pattern. No date-based values can be interpreted from the input string, as this pattern has only time-related pattern letters. (b) and (c), which require a date part, will throw a `DateTimeParseException`.

To use the pattern for formatting, the temporal object must provide values for the parts corresponding to the pattern letters in the pattern. The `LocalTime` object in (d) has the time part required by the pattern. The `LocalDate` object in (e) does not have the time part required by the pattern, so an `UnsupportedTemporalTypeException` will be thrown. The `LocalDateTime` object in (f) has the time part required by the pattern. In (f), only the time part of the `LocalDateTime` object is formatted.

Index

D

N

Q

R

T